Essentials of Strategic Management

Essentials of Strategic Management

Martyn Pitt & Dimitrios Koufopoulos

Los Angeles | London | New Delhi
Singapore | Washington DC

SAGE Publications Ltd
1 Oliver's Yard
55 City Road
London EC1Y 1SP

SAGE Publications Inc.
2455 Teller Road
Thousand Oaks, California 91320

SAGE Publications India Pvt Ltd
B 1/I 1 Mohan Cooperative Industrial Area
Mathura Road, Post Bag 7
New Delhi 110 044

SAGE Publications Asia-Pacific Pte Ltd
3 Church Street
#10-04 Samsung Hub
Singapore 049483

Library of Congress Control Number: 2011941032

British Library Cataloguing in Publication data
A catalogue record for this book is available from the British Library

ISBN 978-1-84920-186-5
ISBN 978-1-84920-187-2 (pbk)

Typeset by Cenveo Publisher Services
Printed by MPG Books Group, Bodmin, Cornwall
Printed on paper from sustainable resources

Contents

List of tables

List of figures

List of case studies

Preface

Thank you for your interest in this new textbook. We believe its benefits can be summarised as:

- A focus on the essentials of the subject domain.
- Reader-oriented content and presentation.
- Practical, comprehensive guidance and support for adopters via the Sage companion website.

A Focus on the Essentials

The core strategic management themes are well-established. By 'essential coverage' of this body of knowledge we focus on what we believe is necessary and sufficient for purpose, not minimal. Coverage is intended primarily to support final year undergraduate strategic management modules, although some adopters may consider its coverage relevant and helpful at master's level too.

While strategic management texts seem broadly to agree on *choice* of topics, authors and users undoubtedly emphasise certain topics more than others, perhaps with a particular disciplinary emphasis. Thus our aim is to cover recognised topics in a way that tempers rigour with accessibility, drawing as appropriate on relevant concepts from economics, organization behaviour, innovation, social psychology, marketing and finance. Moreover, while readers should be able to appreciate and explain concepts, we encourage them to apply them analytically and thoughtfully to particular cases. Issues of strategy implementation are covered succinctly, mindful that much of this content is the primary focus of teaching in functional modules including marketing, finance and organizational behaviour.

While our primary focus is on *business* enterprises, throughout the book we try to make discussion relevant also to *not-for-profit* enterprises. In order to encourage inclusive thinking, therefore, we use the word 'enterprise' throughout the book. Its content can be summarised briefly as follows:

Major Content of the Chapters

1. Alternative perspectives on strategy and strategic management processes. The 'design plus' working model of strategic analysis; options assessment and decision making; and organizational implementation.

2. The multi-level enterprise environment; macro environmental analysis using the ScanStep© framework.
3. Industry sector analysis, distinguishing between the supply-side industry sector and market demand factors.
4. Enterprise stakeholders, identity and mission; governance, ethics and social responsibility.
5. Resources and capabilities analysis using the V-R-I-O-S framework.
6. Strategic issue diagnosis and decision making; human and organizational constraints thereon.
7. Alternative analytical strategy frameworks for options generation and evaluation.
8. Scale and non-scale based strategies for survival and growth of the stand-alone enterprise.
9. Innovation strategies including lifecycle implications, technological innovation strategies and enterprise learning.
10. The multi-activity enterprise and diversification strategies.
11. Acquisition, merger and alliance strategies.
12. International strategies: the challenges posed by the opposing pressures of country-specific needs and global 'megatrends'.
13. Organizational issues that bear on effective strategy implementation including structures, processes and leadership.

Reader-Oriented Presentation to Aid Learning

We have tried to ensure that our material will engage readers by being topical, relevant and interesting to read. Our goal is to provide authoritative, but uncomplicated explanations, mindful that for many readers in today's global learning environment English is a second language. We try to avoid making concepts appear more complex than they really are. The real challenge of strategic management, we believe, is not the principles but to apply them constructively, leading to well-founded strategies that can be implemented in practice.

Specific features of the book to assist an individual's learning include:

- Clear learning objectives to open each chapter, which are developed subsequently with highlighted text and flagged with marginal icons.

- Relatively short case studies to begin and conclude each chapter; they illustrate concepts and theories but are also vehicles for large class or small-group discussions, written assignments and private study.

- Numerous, short illustrations of concepts with practical examples featuring enterprises in their particular contexts.

- Citations and clarifying comments placed in endnotes to avoid burdening the reader with text that appears dauntingly academic.

- The provision of uncomplicated worksheets to aid a systematic strategic analysis.

- Questions for discussion and personal study linked to each case study, plus further assignment questions at the end of each chapter.
- Crisp chapter summaries in the form of bullet points.
- Lists of additional suggested readings.
- A comprehensive glossary with links back to the text.

A comment on the case studies and other illustrations: they feature enterprises in more than 20 countries and have been written especially for this book; they are not merely extracts from newspapers and business magazines. Many readers will find theories and concepts much easier to understand and accept when they are realised through illustrations, especially ones with which they may be familiar. This is a primary aim of the cases too. Chapter opening cases invite the reader to enter the topic area, encourage them to reflect and ask appropriate questions, even if answers are not immediately evident. Closing cases enable them to evolve more considered responses in the light of the new knowledge acquired.

In today's world we believe nearly all readers will have ready access to the World Wide Web. Cases and other illustrations generally feature enterprises with comprehensive websites. Various tasks and discussion questions prompt the reader to visit these websites to extend their knowledge of the featured enterprises and the challenges they face.

Support for Adopters via the Companion Website

This book is intended to be a sound base for the design and delivery of strategic management modules by both specialist and non-specialist strategy lecturers. Whilst the specialist may not require associated, supporting materials, the latter may expect and welcome them. Accordingly, the Sage companion website, www.sagepub.co.uk/pitt, features the following elements:

- Alternative study plans for one and two semester modules and block modules taught over fewer weeks or sessions.
- Brief additional notes on chapter content allied to suggested further readings.
- Masters of slides based on the figures.
- Masters of case studies for reproduction.
- Teaching notes for the case studies that address differing class contexts and modes of use as well as the questions posed.
- Notes on the end-of-chapter questions.

Despite the proven benefits of using empirically based case study materials, less experienced teachers and those with large undergraduate classes may find their use challenging. Shorter materials can be introduced even in large classes to illustrate key issues and, provided that extensive prior preparation is not vital, as valuable vehicles to prompt interactive discussion. Illustrations and chapter-opening cases studies in this book are candidates for such use. If the lecturer has web access in the classroom, selected pages from the enterprise websites can be displayed to enrich the discussion.

Finally, as authors we hope to interact with adopters and potential adopters, sharing thoughts and whatever advice we can. To this end our contact details are available via the Sage website. Please get in touch!

1

The Essence of Strategy and Strategic Management

Learning Outcomes

This chapter is designed to enable you to:

① Discuss fundamental ideas about the *nature* and *content* of strategies.

② Identify and critique alternative definitions of *strategic management processes* and their underlying assumptions.

③ Explain how the *environmental context* of an enterprise influences its strategy and how it is implemented.

④ Apply *critical strategic thinking* to particular case illustrations.

⑤ Understand and assess the design-plus approach to strategy management.

CASE STUDY: Sunseeker International Ltd

Robert Braithwaite, CBE, founded Poole-based Sunseeker Boats in 1968. Its first model was a 5-metre yacht. Today, its biggest yacht is over 37 metres long; some have top speeds of 60 knots. In a typical year, it sells several hundred new yachts. Depending on specification, prices are upwards of £250,000.

Sunseeker is presently the largest volume boat builder in the United Kingdom (UK) and one of an exclusive group of 'super yacht' manufacturers around the world. Like other yacht builders it is highly dependent on a wealthy, demanding, potentially fickle clientele. Its UK-based competitors include Fairline, Sealine and the French-owned Princess. Particularly at the luxury end of the market, it has major competitors based in France, Germany, the United States and Scandinavia. International competitiveness depends greatly on the comparative rates of sterling against the US dollar, the Japanese yen and the Euro.

Sunseeker promotes an idealised lifestyle to its clientele. Rising personal wealth during the 2000s enlarged the market for high quality, luxury, ocean-going motor yachts. Styling, power, spaciousness and facilities are key selling features. Sunseeker customises each yacht to the purchaser's needs, whether a floating office, a recording studio or a gin palace. It advertises in specialist boating and lifestyle magazines and has an attractive website. Its boats have featured regularly in James Bond movies and at prestigious London boat shows.

Mr. Braithwaite has said: 'Being a private company we do what we do because we love it. We have grown by putting back into the company what we earn. We can sometimes take commercial risks that public companies cannot.'

In 2008/9 the company's sales were £303 million, despite extremely difficult trading conditions. Sales had doubled since 2004 and employee numbers had grown from nearly 1500 to 2400 in its expanding south-coast boatyards. Craft skills in fibreglass moulding, wood joinery, upholstery and electronics were much needed and Sunseeker invested heavily in staff training. However, owing to the exceptional economic circumstances of 2008/9 it made a pre-tax loss of £9.1 million. Even so, it invested £9 million to improve facilities and continued to design new large yachts.

Questions

1. Why do you think Sunseeker has survived so long and grown so consistently?

2. What arguments would there be for and against Sunseeker changing its long-standing strategy to, for example: (a) Compete more aggressively at the 'budget' end of the market? (b) Concentrate on Europe or aim for global leadership in the motor yacht industry, perhaps by merging with a major rival? (c) Become a public company (plc)?

Introduction: the Nature and Significance of Strategy

The word 'strategy' has become commonplace. Readers may already have used it in recent conversation – for example, by asking 'what's our strategy for increasing membership of the sports club?' What do people commonly understand by 'strategy' and what words and phrases do they most associate with the term? Their views usually involve the following ideas:

LEARNING OBJECTIVE ①

- Plans and planning.
- Anticipating and forecasting the future.

- Competing and being competitive.
- Organizing to compete.

Thus people, typically view strategy as something that involves future intentions, decisions and consequent actions.

Though these ideas are relevant, they do not provide a sufficient basis for appreciating the reality of enterprises' strategies and how they are conceived and implemented. Note that the term 'enterprises' here – and throughout the book – is used inclusively, to refer equally to businesses and not-for-profit organisations. Enterprises' strategies require well-focused and useful meanings. Yet countless books and articles have shown that strategy is, in fact, very difficult to explain in a simple phrase. Adding substance to these ideas is the aim of this book.

Strategic Management in Theory and Practice

Later in this chapter we will consider various formal definitions of the term 'strategy'. First, however, it will prove helpful to review the evolution of thinking about the concept. We begin with the perspective of executives who establish strategies and are responsible for implementing them effectively. We then consider a scholarly perspective, which – as we shall see – is sceptical about a single, unified view of what strategy is, how it should be managed, and the degree to which practitioners truly intend or actually control outcomes. The chapter then outlines a more prescriptive perspective via a practical, framework that the following chapters will use to explore strategic management in more detail. Illustrations link concepts to particular cases. It closes with a short summary and some discussion topics.

The Experiential Perspective in Historical Context

Commercial 'joint stock' enterprises emerged in the 19th century as the preferred vehicle for entrepreneurship, taking and sharing business risks and rewards. By the early 20th century, business enterprises like Standard Oil, Ford Motor Company and General Motors in the United States applied innovative production processes to pursue their clear growth intentions. Leaders like John D. Rockefeller, Henry Ford and Alfred Sloan applied their own strategy concepts, drawing largely on their instincts and experience.

Rockefeller, for example, saw the benefits to Standard Oil of *monopoly power*. By controlling production the company could greatly increase profits and maintain a high market share. His strategy was so effective that in the 1920s the US Government split the company into seven units to increase competition. (Following a landmark 'anti-trust' legal action, the separated companies became known as the 'seven sisters'.) Henry Ford showed how commercial success resulted from producing motor cars in huge volumes at the lowest achievable cost per unit. Ford's success led Alfred Sloan to decide that General Motors must compete more effectively with Ford by offering consumers multiple brands and much greater choice. History records that these three enterprises gained large shares of fast-growing markets and achieved high profits. Their differing business strategies *in the circumstances of the times* can therefore be considered insightful and successful.

Discussions about strategy often focus on business enterprises, yet not-for-profit enterprises have strategies too, although sometimes less obviously so. In Victorian Britain and elsewhere, not-for-profit, charitable enterprises emerged and thrived. They had clear purposes, notably to better the conditions of the poor and disadvantaged during the 19th-century 'industrial revolution'. A core strategy was to encourage mutual self-help. During the 20th century many other not-for-profit charities began to provide aid for disadvantaged communities at home and overseas. Charities like Oxfam have survived and grown in size and influence, generally becoming more 'business-like', bureaucratic and even sometimes global enterprises. Tolerance of the profit motive allows them to create cash-generating business subsidiaries to support their charitable work. Meanwhile, many traditional enterprises such as 'mutual' savings societies set up for the benefit of their members have now become private-sector companies.

The Scholarly Perspective

Following the 1938 publication of Chester Barnard's landmark book *The Functions of the Executive*, business schools have paid attention to teaching and researching management practices, initially in North America but increasingly around the world. (Though generally called 'business' schools, most are interested too in not-for-profit enterprises.) Until about 1960, most executives and scholars considered strategic management as largely a matter of judgement, applying reasoning and experience to particular situations. A more rigorous approach emerged from so-called operational research methods, having military origins. It emphasised systematic planning and quantitative data analysis whose aim was to achieve greater efficiency and thereby, an enhanced market position.[1] Other approaches focused on strategy as competitive positioning[2] and on diversification[3] of activities to spread risk and enable faster growth. More recently, attention has shifted from a dominant, position-oriented concept of strategy to one that emphasises the resources, skills and collective competences found in individual enterprises, which enables them to perform distinctively.[4]

However, with a few notable exceptions, it was only from around 1970 that academics and consultants started to research how practitioners – generally senior executives – actually 'do' strategy, by observing them in action and by carrying out systematic, empirical research.[5] Guiding principles have slowly emerged, although strategy concepts expressed in popular books, newspapers and magazines are often very simplistic. Indeed, despite a considerable body of published research, there is still much that we do not know about strategic management. This is not to disparage the work already done; the workings of healthy (and not-so-healthy) enterprises are extraordinarily complex. While the world waits for a truly unified set of strategic management principles, executive managers have to apply their experience and judgement to individual situations and how to proceed.

The Search for General Prescriptions

Challenging, puzzling situations encourage enterprise managers to look for practical prescriptions for action. The particular *content* of whatever prescription they adopt is their *strategy*. Such prescriptions may be desirable, but can be controversial. For example, industrial economists have long argued that the industry sector in which a business operates is the major factor determining its profitability. They characterise some industries such as steel making as chronically unattractive, yielding modest profits at best, with heavy losses in times of recession. The steel industry requires massive investments in steel-making plant and facilities that require high utilisation to make profits.[6] Accordingly, the standard prescription for a steel-making enterprise would be either to dominate the industry (or a substantial part of it), or diversify the business and quit steel-making as soon as practical. Yet more recent research shows that in *any* industry (including steel-making) some enterprises rise to the challenges, producing above-average, even outstanding results. Competent strategic management evidently 'matters' while questions of how much the choice of industry 'matters' for profitability are still hotly debated.[7]

Traditional economics considered the enterprise a 'black box' located in its industrial context. That is, an enterprise's inputs and outputs were studied, rather than what happened within the enterprise. The impact of managers was largely ignored because the context or external environment, it was argued, determines what enterprises do and whether they survive and prosper. Managerial decisions appeared externally as investment and pricing actions. Once implemented, they would change the balance of supply and demand over time; market shares would also shift, all of which affected the profitability of competing enterprises. Extreme, so-called 'perfect', competition would drive prices down to the level of unit costs, eliminating profits.

From this economic viewpoint, what happens inside each enterprise does not materially affect the collective industry outcome. Yet, for those interested in the social psychology of organizational behaviour, the inner workings of enterprises are vital for understanding why enterprises behave and perform differently. Modern strategic management research applies the methods of many specialist disciplines, trying to integrate findings that reflect and explain real world complexity in behaviours and outcomes.

Unsurprisingly, it has been widely claimed that rational, logical thinking is important when forming strategies. The three leading American corporations already mentioned evidently had clear, rational views about how best to compete. Their different, self-interested approaches aimed to minimise the damaging effects of competition by:

- Dominating production and controlling output prices (Rockefeller).
- Offering products at a lower price than competitors, enabled by driving down unit costs (Ford).
- Promoting multiple brands to create variety, excitement and distinctiveness (Sloan).

Such strategies are still observed. Indeed, a significant reality is that a common aim of competitive strategies is to avoid or mitigate competition as far as possible. This principle is well established: indeed, it is to be found in the ancient text 'The Art of War' attributed to a Chinese king/general, Sun Tzu,[8] This simple, yet fundamental goal can be achieved by (a) eliminating competitors, (b) minimise their adverse impact by maintaining considerable distance from them, or (c) mutual acceptance of a state of competitive, co-existence.

ARNING ①
JECTIVE

Important Strategy Concepts

An enterprise choice of strategy affects whether it 'wins' or 'loses' in competitive terms, hence its successful survival or ultimate failure. Thus the meaning of 'strategic' as the word is commonly used is 'important' or 'crucial.' Because of its importance, strategic management frequently involves contests over significant ideas and controversial opinions, creating disagreements and conflicts among decision makers. A strategic decision is one of real significance for the enterprise. Typically, senior people are involved in making these decisions, which often require major commitments of money and other resources to implement. Consequent actions are substantial and often risky. The effects of these actions are not fully predictable, yet they cannot easily be reversed.

LEARNING OBJECTIVE ①

A much-quoted, comprehensive, and integrative definition says that:

> Strategy is the pattern of decisions in a company that determines or reveals its objectives, purposes or goals, produces the principal policies and plans for achieving those goals, and defines the range of business the company is to pursue, the kind of economic and human organization it is or intends to be, and the nature of the economic and non-economic contribution it intends to make to its shareholders, employees, customers, and communities ....[9]

This definition links strategy to such activities as setting objectives, determining policies, and the formation of action plans. It requires those concerned with strategy to 'exercise strategic choice' constructively and with *clear intent*.[10] They need to be clear what the enterprise is about – the basic purpose or mission that explains how it creates value for society and for a more specific clientele and how it will do so in the future. The definition implies a *progression* from broad aims to specific objectives and policies, followed by specific plans to achieve them, resulting in the desired and desirable future outcomes. Though the definition does not say who the strategists are, we may reasonably infer that senior executives are actively engaged in forming and implementing strategies.

Evidently, the strategic management task requires enterprises to identify their main clienteles, how they benefit from their relationships and will benefit in the future. The benefits can be both economic (financial) and non-economic (social well-being and perhaps humanitarian). *So a strategy affects multiple stakeholders*. This aspect of strategy has been called 'defining the scope' of the enterprise.[11] Stakeholders of an enterprise are the various actors and agencies in society that (in fact or perception) *benefit from or are harmed by* its actions. They include its clienteles, owners, employees and many other parties who have an interest in what it is and what it does. As will be seen, the many kinds of stakeholder differ in their expectations of each enterprise.

LEARNING OBJECTIVE ①

An alternative definition makes it explicit that strategy is about integration (synthesis and coherence). It emphasises that strategy is concerned with developing and using resources and skills (competencies) to create value, and thereby achieve its objectives in distinctive, even unique ways:

LEARNING OBJECTIVE ①

> A strategy is the pattern or plan that integrates an organization's major goals, policies and action sequences into a cohesive whole. A well-formulated strategy helps marshal and allocate an organization's resources into a unique and viable posture based upon its relative internal competencies and shortcomings, anticipated changes in the environment, and contingent moves by intelligent opponents.[12]

This definition implies that a strategy's core priority is to secure *competitive advantage*. Indeed, the private-enterprise business corporation has become a major focus for the application of strategic concepts, because most executives believe that effective strategies are vital to create and sustain competitive advantage over the long term, distinguishing winners from losers. However (as noted), legitimate (legal) *co-operation* among enterprises can also be mutually beneficial, allowing them to achieve results together that would be impossible alone.

Many for-profit businesses operate in *highly regulated* industry contexts where competition is constrained. Utilities such as gas, electricity and water supply, air and rail transport, broadcast television, financial services and pharmaceuticals are all examples. Strategic decisions about capital investment, marketing and pricing practices can be firmly guided or dictated by external industry regulators, health and safety and other government agencies. In other industries – for example, franchised motor car sales and servicing – enterprises must operate within the strict terms of their contracts with the major car makers. So their challenge is to create distinctive resources and advantageous positions not only in relation to their clienteles, but also with their suppliers.

Most economies around the world have vastly more *small businesses* than giant corporations. Small enterprises also need viable strategies for future survival and success, though their strategies differ from large enterprises. While similar *principles* apply to both large and small, large enterprises have much greater potential in terms of geographic scope, to accumulate resources and competences and to occupy distinctive, even dominant positions. Typically, the aim of a small enterprise is limited to finding and occupying a protective 'niche' position, defined by locality or specialism.

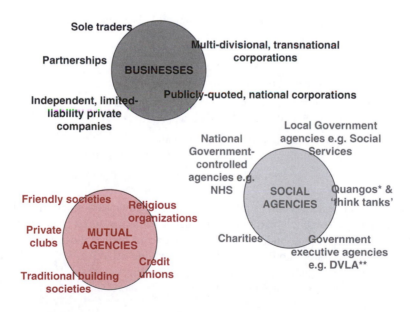

* An abbreviation for a 'QUAsi-autonomous, Non-Governmental Organisation that performs governmental functions in a nominally independent way e.g. Electoral Commission (UK)
** Driver and Vehicle Licensing Agency (UK)

Figure 1.1: Three basic forms of enterprise

Figure 1.1 distinguishes three significant types of enterprise, referred to respectively as businesses, social agencies, and mutual agencies. Social agencies include government-funded, public-sector bodies such as the UK National Health Service (NHS) and the Arts Council, charities, philanthropic foundations, voluntary and mutual organisations whose main purposes are to enhance the social good, generally based on criteria of need. Mutual agencies include political parties, religious organisations, private clubs and any other enterprise that specifies membership criteria and rules that members must respect and follow. All of these agencies have core clienteles and other stakeholders who are interested in what they do. To a greater or lesser degree, they too operate in competitive or regulatory environments. Thus there are always constraints on their freedoms to act and pressures to improve how they perform. Accordingly, they too need to conceive and implement appropriate strategies for the future.

Some commentators define strategy in terms of achieving a good environmental 'fit.'[13] *Environment* here refers to the external context in which the enterprise operates and creates value. It does *not* refer specifically to ecology, important as pollution avoidance and energy saving have become for many enterprises. *Fit* is a word linked with finding a protective niche or market gap. An enterprise is indeed fortunate if it proves ideally equipped to occupy such a niche. Although numerous, viable niches may exist, occupants and would-be occupants contest these environmental spaces vigorously, trying to satisfy the associated clienteles better than others.

These various statements about enterprise strategy suggest the following practical definition:

A strategy combines explicit statements and implicit beliefs and understandings in and around an enterprise about:

- Its core purpose (mission) and how, if at all, its mission will (or must) change in future.
- A vision of its future direction and what it intends to achieve.
- Its scope, meaning its main clienteles now and in the future (and consequently the potential clienteles that are and will remain *outside* its scope).
- The resources and competences that create value for its clientele and how these will (must) change to maintain and enhance the future value created.
- The foundations of its present competitive standing and future sustainability.

Although it may seem necessary for a strategy to be written down and widely shared, in practice a strategy is not always so explicit. Particularly in smaller, entrepreneurial enterprises the strategy may reside in the minds of the individual entrepreneur and his/her close team. Nor can one assume that all strategies are 'good' – in the sense of proving effective. An effective enterprise strategy encodes a viable, coherent, distinctive approach that in a challenging environment fully and sustainably meets the needs and expectations of its core clientele and other legitimate stakeholders.

LEARNING ①
OBJECTIVE

Evidently, not all strategies are good – some enterprises perform poorly according to the above criteria and some fail. Even good strategies do not remain viable and sustainable indefinitely. They will require enhancements and sometimes radical changes. The problem for strategists and external observers alike is that sufficient time must elapse before they can make objective assessments of how effectively a strategy has been at meeting needs and expectations. Continuing vigilance is therefore vital. Strategic management is, without exception, the charting of a journey into the unknown.

Five 'Ps' of Strategy

The previous definitions may suggest 'strategy-as-grand-plan'. This has been the view of many, but not all commentators. One well-known thinker – Henry Mintzberg – in particular has criticised this concept of strategy, suggesting an additional interpretation.[14] Thus his conception, popularly known as the 5 P model, consists of the following five components:

1. Plan.
2. Ploy.
3. Perspective.
4. Position.
5. Pattern.

Plan and ploy draw on classic military thinking. Indeed, the word 'strategy' derives from the Greek 'strategos' meaning the 'art of the general'. 'Plan' equates with 'grand plan' or 'grand design', an overall understanding (conception) of the core aims and direction of the company and how they will be achieved. 'Ploy' is better thought of as a 'game plan', what military strategists call a tactic – or, as in chess, a competitive 'gambit'.

In a military context, 'grand strategy' is linked with political ambition. Napoleon's grand design for a Franco-European empire required the French army to wage war systematically against the various countries that opposed him. His strategy-as-plan described how this war would be won, for example, by specifying the sequence and timing of countries to be invaded, so as to avoid fighting on many fronts concurrently.

By contrast, tactics are the approaches used to win each battle, the combination of actions likely to favour one's own forces and surprise the enemy by exploiting one's strengths. Deception often features in these tactics. Military strategy and tactics have significantly influenced some business corporations, particularly Japanese multinationals since the 1960s, intent on dominating selected world markets through overwhelming strength. Professional football clubs adopt equivalent approaches, with strategies to win championships and tactics to win individual matches. Their strategies notably include resource decisions – buying and selling players, investing in bigger stadiums and better facilities. Tactics include skill development and application, team selection, preferred approaches towards defence or attack on the pitch. Plans and ploys can in principle be written down, discussed and communicated among those who need to know.

By contrast, 'perspectives' tend to be unspoken (tacit) assumptions and ways of thinking about appropriate actions that are locally rather than universally recognised or accepted. 'Custom and practice' thinking engrains an accepted perspective on how things are done and, by inference, should be done. Being taken-for-granted supports established routines and discourages challenge or change to them. In so far as fresh deliberation is missing, they scarcely merit the description 'deliberate'. Though a 'perspective' may sound an unconvincing view of what strategy *should be*, observation suggests that it fairly represents how many enterprises actually 'do' strategy.

'Position' is another view of strategy, one that combines elements of both military thinking and industrial economics. A strong and defensible position is considered a desirable goal, whether an advantageous battlefield location or a market posture. Enterprises often conceive their strategies in terms of actions intended to improve their future competitive positions. The view of strategy as dynamic 'jockeying' for favourable (competitively advantageous) positions re-emerged in the 1980s,[15] though it actually has a much longer history in industrial economics.[16] An emphasis on position can be relevant not just for businesses, but for many not-for-profit enterprises such as charities that compete with one another for donations from the public and from corporate sponsors. Positional strategies can certainly be deliberate, though a failure to reconsider positions critically over time is common. Positions can be based on objective measures such as market coverage and share, but they also draw on subjective (perceptual) factors such as reputation and brand image as understood by the clientele, factors that play a large part in marketing strategies.

Plans, ploys, perspectives and positions are all consistent with the idea that strategy is what an actor or group of actors *intends to happen*. They know (or believe they know) what they want to achieve and how best to achieve it. To that extent they are all 'deliberate' strategies as featured in Figure 1.2. Intentionality accords well with a Western world-view, known as the 'Enlightenment' or Cartesian view, which assumes the importance of exercising individual free will, being rational, decisive, proactive and in control. Other world-views such as Confucianism, Taoism and Hinduism put greater emphasis on humility, duty, collectivism and even fatalism. In some cultures, therefore, intentional strategy is a problematic concept.

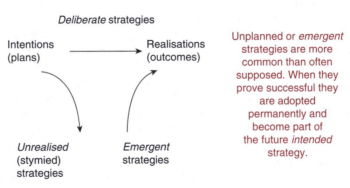

Figure 1.2: Various types of strategy*
*After Mintzberg (1978)

By contrast, strategy as 'pattern' describes an evolving stream of observed events. It is a method that historians use to interpret past events and infer motivations. For example, various nations took self-interested actions that ultimately led to the 1914–18 World War. Casual observers might conclude that an escalating pattern of events is evidence of prior war-like intentions and decisions. Yet, it is possible that none of the protagonists had such prior intent, indeed the origins of this war were complex. National strategies emerged by degrees and only later crystallised into particular, observed patterns.

Similarly, enterprises may attach *future intent* to an evolving pattern *only after* it has started to crystallise and prove viable and attractive, hence worth continuing. In retrospect it may seem hard to believe that the early strategies of companies such as Microsoft, Amazon, Google and eBay may have owed more to optimism and opportunism than design. The facts are really matters for future business historians to debate. Their significance here is to suggest that strategies can emerge in an improvised or experimental fashion[17] and crystallize as a pattern when success becomes real (the 'emergent' strategies of Figure 1.2). Conversely, fully intended strategies can fail (not be realised), while others have unintended consequences.

Ethical Relationships, Social Responsibility and Strategic Change

The effective enterprise creates value: functional, financial and other benefits for its clienteles, owners, employees and many other stakeholders in society. Multiple elements of its strategy combine to create and sustain durable, constructive, trusting, ethical *relationships* with all these stakeholders (explored further in Chapter 4).

RNING ①
ECTIVE

Yet, however effective a strategy has proved, it will and indeed *must* change over time. Enterprises change their strategies, sometimes dramatically as a result of perceiving new opportunities, or in response to new threats. They take on new, value-adding activities and dispense with others that are deemed ineffective or marginal for future success. Changes also result from changes in societal expectations: enterprises now experience far greater pressures to behave ethically and be socially responsible, by respecting the natural environment, eliminating pollution, reducing energy consumption and contributing to the costs of recycling products at the end of their useful life.

Yet strategic changes have consequences for established relationships, not least for employees associated with value-creating activities which are deemed redundant. Whilst it is painful to learn that their department or business unit is no longer integral to the enterprise's future strategy, major restructuring is an essential aspect of strategic management. Responsible strategic management does not – indeed must not – seek to maintain an organization unchanged for its own sake.

Accordingly, to be effective, enterprise strategies are necessarily *amoral*, meaning that their priority is not to engage directly with issues of human morality. However, an *amoral* strategy is definitely *not* to be equated with *immoral*, unethical behaviour on behalf of an enterprise by individuals who lack personal integrity.

Corporate-level and Enterprise-level Strategies

An important issue arises in respect of the different *organizational levels* at which strategy must be established. For an essentially single activity enterprise, like Sunseeker, the key strategy questions are: 'How does this enterprise compete effectively *and* what kind of stakeholder relationships must it sustain to do so?' Enterprises such as the British Broadcasting Corporation (BBC) (see illustration) are multi-activity, multi-unit corporations. They face relevant, additional questions such as: 'Which business domains (activities) should this enterprise engage in and why'

RNING ①
ECTIVE

and 'How closely integrated should diverse activities and units be?' The first set of questions concern so-called *business-unit* strategy, the second concern *corporate* strategy.

Sunseeker's major business activity is the manufacture and sale of yachts; presumably this will continue. The BBC has various operating groups and many subsidiary service units within each group. While senior BBC executives are concerned principally with the strategy of the whole enterprise, corporate-level strategy and activity unit strategies are *all* important because each one contributes directly or indirectly to the success of the others. The answers to unit strategy questions without doubt differ from one BBC operating group to another and probably differ among the support service units in each group. History shows that the BBC has changed its detailed strategies over time and will doubtless continue to change. For example, will it be able to justify for-profit activities in future, given its core public service mission.

The British Broadcasting Corporation (BBC)[18]

Established by Royal Charter in 1922, the BBC was the first state-owned broadcasting corporation. It aims to create and transmit high quality radio and television programmes to entertain, inform and educate listeners and viewers of all backgrounds, interests, ages and intellects. In the digital era the BBC has exploited new opportunities that go beyond its strict public service obligations. Its income is guaranteed via the annual licence fee required from every UK household with a television set.

It is a large, very complex, not-for-profit enterprise. In 2009 it had £1 billion of fixed assets (based on UK accounting standards), income of £4.6 billion, operating expenditures of £4.5 billion, and 23,000 employees (17,000 in the UK and 6,000 in 39 other countries). It is structured into three functional groups, each of which comprises multiple distinct organizational units:

- *UK Public Service Broadcasting*. A 76.7% share of revenues, comprising three services: UK Television (11 free-to-air channels); UK Radio (16 national and 40 local stations); and BBC Online.

- *World Service Radio and Monitoring*. A 6.4% share of revenues.

- *Commercial Businesses*. A 16.8% share of revenues (selling TV and radio programmes and formats overseas; book and magazine publishing; joint ventures with selected broadcasters; and studios and production facilities).

The BBC's chief executive (Director General) heads a complex management structure. Appropriate strategies have to be determined not only for the enterprise overall, but also at group and unit levels. Each separate unit strategy must be co-ordinated with those of other units and groups. For example, the Journalism group, responsible for news gathering, must co-ordinate its strategy with radio and TV broadcasters, BBC Online and the Operations group.

All strategies have *content*: namely, the array of particular decisions and proposed actions, whether written down or held in the mind. So a strategy is an *object* (a plan, position, etc.). Conversely, strategic management is a *process*. It encompasses the ongoing activities of forming and implementing strategy, in effect: 'strategy-being-put-into-action.' A process is best described with a *verb* or *verb-derivative*, (planning, positioning, implementing, etc.). Because these activities are ongoing, strategy content *evolves* over time, sometimes intentionally, sometimes not.

ARNING
JECTIVE ②

The Subtlety and Complexity of Strategic Management Skills

Strategies are the products of decisions and actions by executive managers, not academic researchers or consultants. Every enterprise has its own, particularised strategic management processes because its people are differently talented and sometimes idiosyncratic in their behaviours and motivations. While short-term financial competence always matters, capable strategic managers also address more broadly based performance outcomes such as risk, long-run growth and increased diversity of enterprise mission.

In addition to analytical rationality, managers variously apply important 'artistic' skills of creativity, imagination and intuition allied to 'craft' skills of problem-solving, handling people and learning from the experience of practice, especially of past errors.

These 'artistic' and 'craft' skills enable them to:

- Demonstrate leadership by mobilizing the strengths of the enterprise and overcoming its weaknesses.
- Innovate and encourage colleagues to innovate by being receptive to imaginative ideas (leading to the introduction of new products and services and novelty in organization processes).
- Value adaptiveness, improvisation and timely, practical actions that draw on experience and intuition, rather than just the analysis of large volumes of data.
- Exercise personal 'political' skills to negotiate with, influence and persuade other stakeholders within and beyond the enterprise.
- Establish clear priorities and achieve desired results, identifying and resolving significant issues continuously and proactively.

ARNING
JECTIVE ②

Whereas rationality emphasises the analysis of facts (evidence), artistic and craft skills help to synthesise and integrate understandings. They are *complementary*, not alternative skills. Effective strategies benefit from *combining* analysis (attending to the detail) *and* synthesis (seeing the big picture). The mix of these skills in use varies from one person to another, from one enterprise to another, in the same enterprise over time, and sometimes quite markedly from one country or culture to another. The mix in a dynamic, multinational corporation differs from that in a national enterprise in a regulated industry and in a small or medium-sized enterprise (and very probably needs to differ!). Not-for-profit enterprises and government agencies are different again.

Frames of Reference

In addition to its mix of skills in use, every enterprise has a particular set of shared ideas, beliefs and assumptions about how to 'do' strategic management. Many names have attached to these shared belief sets.[19] *Frame of reference* is used here because it evokes the metaphor of a window through which decision-makers see, but which also constrains the view available to them. The enterprise's shared belief set or *frame of reference* informs and constrains how its managers think about their strategic management *processes* (conduct) and influences the decisions and actions (strategy *content*) that emerge from these processes.

LEARNING ② OBJECTIVE

Although each enterprise has highly particularized beliefs and assumptions, it has been claimed that a large part of each belief set can be characterized by one of four 'generic' frames. This claim applies two key dimensions to distinguish major differences in core strategic management assumptions and beliefs, as illustrated in Figure 1.3. These dimensions derive from the following pairs of assumptions:

1. On the one hand, managers take for granted a dominant, essentially singular aim (e.g. a business enterprise that aims to maximise its profits for shareholders): on the other hand, they believe multiple, potentially conflicting aims must be reconciled.
2. On the one hand, managers would like to believe they can anticipate significant future events well enough to plan and control outcomes near-optimally: on the other hand, they act upon the assumption that they will have to improvise and continuously adapt the strategy, owing to emerging unanticipated events beyond their control.

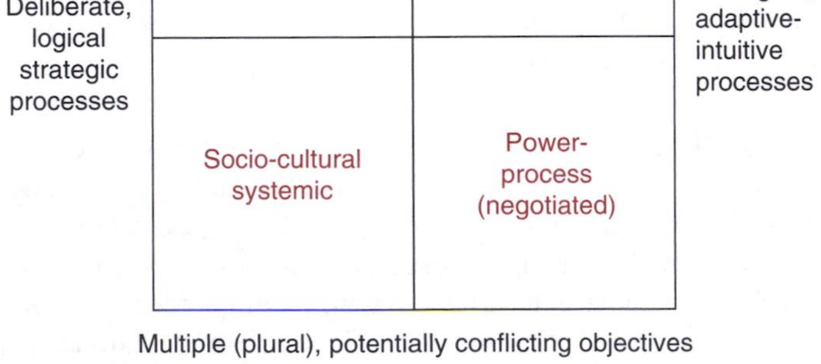

Figure 1.3: Four strategy frames of reference

Adapted from Whittington (2001, p. 3)

In practice, few businesses pursue the aim of maximising profits to the total exclusion of other aims. First, the enterprise would be widely criticised as greedy, uncaring and unethical. Second, trade-offs are often necessary between maximising profits versus growth; or between maximising profits in the short run versus the long run. (Growth often requires significantly lower selling prices than would be applied to maximise profits. Long-run profits require investments that typically reduce short-run profits).

In not-for-profit organizations the position is invariably more complex, as multiple aims compete. Medical charities, for example, must accommodate stakeholders whose funding expectations conflict. All patients want necessary treatments now, although some have more urgent needs; researchers value long-term funding but may have to accept short-term support; donors, clinicians and government agencies are keen to prioritise the treatment of the particular diseases that they are associated with.

The second dimension of the model encodes assumptions about deliberate and fully intended strategy. In particular, the assumption of control is often seen as a major indicator of strategic managerial competence, even when it is largely an illusion.

The Rational-Planning Frame

The predominant mindset of the approach located in the upper-left quadrant of Figure 1.3 is strategy-as-grand-plan. Strategists working within this frame of reference are trying to optimise outcomes in relation to a dominant goal such as profit maximisation for the business enterprise. They believe that clear intent and detailed design enhances the prospects of their achieving their future-focused goals that they judge appropriate for future survival, even at the cost of short-term difficulties. Rational–analytical strategy processes underpin formal, comprehensive business and corporate planning processes that define clear, specific strategies and policies to be implemented deliberately, even ruthlessly, in the chosen competitive arena. The rational frame should in theory produce progressive, continuing change although more radical, discontinuities of direction may be envisaged as a result of systematic planning.

The rational-planning frame: Beaver & Tapley[20]

Beaver & Tapley is a British furniture company. Thirty years ago its senior managers (trained engineers and designers) felt that a comparatively small, unknown company could not compete effectively with either prestige brands or mass-market retailers. Very deliberately they set out to create and patent a unique, modular system of wall-mounted storage and display furniture. They succeeded, calling it Tapley 33. Over the years the company has refined and extended the Tapley system. To date no competitor has been able to displace it from its self-created market niche.

The Systemic Frame

The systemic frame corresponding to the lower-left quadrant of Figure 1.3 informs managers of the need to be sensitive to divergent, social and economic systems and the multiplicity of enterprise stakeholders. For example, Swedish, American and Japanese managers have grown up in differing social and political systems and their interpretations of capitalism are distinct. Systemic managers see their enterprises as 'open systems' containing many actors, systems, subsystems and embedded routines, not unitary bodies capable of behaving like a single-brain organism. Consequently, they recognise that multiple priorities and viewpoints have to be accommodated; progress must be managed rationally but pragmatically. Priorities are adjusted regularly and continuously as they experience and respond to pressures from different directions. So change is mostly incremental, yet outcomes are rarely optimal for the enterprise, since strategic management is a process of adjusting or 'satisficing'. In for-profit contexts this frame of reference has been called 'logical incrementalism',[21] in governmental agencies 'bureaucratic process'[22] and 'muddling through with a purpose'.[23]

The systemic frame: the BBC

In times past, the BBC was probably best characterised by the power-process frame of reference (see below). Programme producers were likened to medieval barons exercising autocratic power in their personal fiefdoms. Today, its sheer scale and diversity of people and operations suggest that most BBC managers subscribe to the systemic frame. They pursue (and especially at senior levels must reconcile) actual or potential conflicts in corporate aims and objectives. Moreover, the deployment of its large budgets (enabled by viewers' licence fees) is subject to critical independent scrutiny; hence it must function with scrupulous transparency and the aura of rationality despite what should be a creative environment.

The Power-Process Frame

The frame corresponding to the lower-right quadrant of Figure 1.3 is the political power-process frame. As in the systemic frame, it is a pluralist rather than unitary mindset, but here there is collective scepticism over whether strategic management can proceed in a wholly rational way, despite *individual* rationality. This follows because actors accept that (i) their knowledge of the future is to be imperfect and contentious, and (ii) the enterprise is a collection of self-interested individuals and factions (interest groups). The content of strategies is therefore always a compromise that reflects whatever the more influential actors can agree on. They exercise their 'political' skills to reconcile divergent interests, creating sub-optimal compromises.[24] Hence strategic management is the art of the possible. Managers informed by this frame devote much energy to examine the sources of power available to each faction inside the enterprise and beyond, whether and how they will use that power. This frame is widely associated with governmental politics. However, many senior business executives also mobilise and exercise power to pursue factional interests.

The power-process frame: the British Labour Party[25]

The British Labour Party, as political parties everywhere, is a coalition of semi-divergent interests, ideologies and influences. After left-wing 'Old Labour' had suffered four successful general election defeats, centrist 'New Labour' emerged in the 1990s and became dominant in the Party on the back of three consecutive election victories, finally being defeated in 2010. The battle for the intellectual and emotional soul of the party will doubtless result in a fierce contest of ideas and personalities in the years ahead, following the resignation of the defeated leader, Gordon Brown.

The Evolutionary Frame

Fourthly, 'evolutionary' frame that underpins the assumption of a need for strategy to be adaptive: this corresponds to the upper-right quadrant of Figure 1.3. Many observations record that when initial intentions fail to produce expected results, unplanned and improvised, experimental responses can sometimes result in favourable outcomes that subsequently become part of an enterprise's strategy. A much-quoted example is that when Honda first marketed high-power motorbikes in America, consumers showed little interest. However, their interest was sparked accidentally by seeing Honda staff riding mopeds. Honda noticed and began to import and sell mopeds very successfully.[26] This emergent strategy *forms* (evolves) rather than being deliberately *formulated*. It characterises entrepreneurial, innovative, even seemingly chaotic business enterprises in which a notional, singular goal is obstructed in practice by external uncertainties and competitive hostility.

The evolutionary frame draws on the Darwinian concept of natural selection applied to enterprises.[27] According to this view, strategic management processes generate exploratory responses to each problematic situation (threat) that develops. These responses produce distinct, visible changes (variations). When a market demonstrates a preference for a particular change (e.g. a clientele 'selects' a new product) the enterprise establishes a 'niche' or competitive space that protects it from the threat, indeed redirects it towards the originator. In Darwinian terms, a preferred (selected) variation allows the enterprise to survive, at least for a time. So the enterprise persists with it for as long as there is no pressing reason for further change.

The evolutionary frame: easyGroup[28]

Most people know of Sir Stelios Haji-Ioannou, the entrepreneur who founded the budget airline, easyJet, based on three core principles:

- High profile branding.
- Lean operations and low-cost, using the Internet for flight bookings.
- Time/demand-flexible pricing to maximise revenues ('yield management').

Three years after starting easyJet, Haji-Ioannou set up easyGroup, a franchising company. EasyJet itself, now a publicly owned UK plc, was its first franchisee. EasyGroup licenses independent entrepreneurs to develop a variety of business concepts that adopt the easy brand and its core principles. Within these constraints Sir Stelios has allowed any reasonable franchise concept to be exploited. Some twenty have been tried since 1998. Most, like easyHotel, easyCar and easyBus, have succeeded on a relatively modest scale; although easyGroup has had to allow modifications to some original concepts (e.g., easyCar has changed from renting cars to a web-based booking agency for other car rental firms). Some concepts have not survived at all (e.g., easyCinema). Thus easyGroup has demonstrated an ability to experiment and adapt its franchise 'portfolio', accepting the inevitability of failures as well as successes.

The Significance of Reference Frames

To the extent that individuals in an enterprise are informed by a particular reference frame, that frame will tend to reinforce accepted beliefs about strategic management conduct. Acting in ways that are consistent with the frame therefore legitimises and helps to secure agreement to strategic decisions and consequent.

Alternative frames imply different standards of risk tolerance and thus the evidence and justification felt necessary to decide on appropriate strategies. Difficulties can be predicted when decision makers subscribe to difference reference frames. Their non-aligned mindsets will hinder consensus-building and perhaps their ultimate commitment to an agreed strategy. Severe frame polarisation makes agreement impossible among:

- 'Old hands' and new recruits who focus on different issues or interpret the same issues differently.
- Older, senior executives and (generally more youthful) middle managers.
- Senior corporate executives in a large divisionalised enterprise and business unit managers.

In principle, *awareness* of the prevailing internal frame should help individuals to be more thoughtful about strategic management processes. However, it is intellectually and 'politically' difficult to expose and challenge frame-derived assumptions.[29] Individuals risk being labelled as dissidents, marginalised, even asked to quit. In extreme cases, a pathological condition known as 'groupthink' emerges. However, extreme *convergence* of thinking-polarization of mindsets is also counterproductive for effective strategic management, especially in the challenging conditions created by uncertainty and complexity. An enterprise benefits from 'requisite variety' in how its managers think, creating a balance between harmony and dissent and combating polarization tendencies. Requisite variety is a cybernetic concept that, stated simply, asserts stability in a complex system such as an organization with much variety depends on corresponding or greater variety in its (management) control procedures.

When an enterprise acts consistently with a dominant reference frame, competitors find it easier to predict how it will act in the future. If there is no obvious frame in use, its future strategies become less predictable, making it potentially a 'loose cannon' in its competitive environment. All that others can do is to scrutinise its actions using alternative frame assumptions, treating them as analytical 'lenses' to interpret the evidence of its actions.

The enterprises featured in the four illustrations of dominant frames in use indicate positive performance impacts. This implies that their strategic management practices have been coherent, relevant and attuned to their external environments. More generally, however, that is not always the case.

Failures prompted by an inappropriate reference frame

General Motors (GM), for many years the largest motor vehicle producer in the world, entered US bankruptcy proceedings in 2009. The global credit crunch triggered a drastic decline in demand for its new cars and trucks, many being so-called 'gas-guzzlers' of mediocre quality and reliability. GM's strategies in the US had remained rooted in the assumption that consumers really preferred big cars made by American companies, provided that they were affordable. As the biggest car maker GM could not be wrong. In fact, GM has for many years been losing ground to Japanese competitors that make smaller, more fuel-efficient and well-built cars *in the US*.

Swissair, the 'national flag-carrying' airline supported by the Swiss government, went bankrupt in 2002. It had embarked on an ill-advised expansion strategy out of all proportion to its size and industry status, prompted by a reference frame grounded in excessive optimism and national hubris. Competitive pressures on international routes, and the adverse impact on air travel of the 9/11 terrorist attacks on New York and Washington brought it down. It was reconstituted as Swiss International Airlines and sold to the German Lufthansa Group in 2005.

The 'Design-plus' Strategic Management Framework

The variety and complexity of ideas linked with strategic management indicates why its study is exciting and good practice is challenging. Because enterprises are complex, dynamic and often transient bodies, a universal model that fully integrates descriptive and prescriptive strategy knowledge may not emerge for a long time, if ever. Whilst a few enterprises thrive and grow into giant corporations, most do not.[30] Statistics confirm that independent life expectancy of an enterprise is considerably less than that of the typical person. Within a few decades the typical enterprise fails, is dismembered or becomes part of a bigger one.

Nonetheless, the need for a systematic approach to strategic management is indicated. This can be aided by an appropriate, practical framework such as 'design-plus', which we consider below.

The Design-plus Framework

The concept of design draws an analogy with the processes that architects use. The starting assumption is to adopt a rational approach using established principles, but enhanced with the injection of some creativity and flair. Strategic management is no different. But if it is to progress to *implementing* strategy, the design perspective has to envision practical solutions to perceived challenges. A beautiful 'blueprint' will remain just a design unless supported by a credible explanation of how it can be realised in the problematic world. So what exactly does the design concept demand of strategists?

LEARNING OBJECTIVE ⑤ There are three linked phases in the **design + approach**:

1. Situation assessment.
2. Identification and evaluation of the key strategic issues and choices.
3. Action planning and implementation.

The approach is shown in outline in Figure 1.4. It suggests that the phases are linear – they follow in sequence. In practice, of course, the true position is rarely so straightforward, even in enterprises informed by the rational-planning frame. There will be feedback loops that connect the various activities that are not shown for simplicity. In practice activities and stages may proceed concurrently. Still, Figure 1.4 is a suitable representation for the purpose of explanation in the following chapters.

The Importance of Understanding Context

Enterprise strategy design begins in phase one by producing a clear understanding of the enterprise *context* and how it may develop in the future. This phase is the diagnostic element of strategy formation highlighted in Figure 1.4 by the heavy black box. In this phase the enterprise identifies and assesses relevant issues in the *external* operating environment and the *internal*, *organizational* environment. As well as creating opportunities and threats, the external environment constrains what the enterprise can realistically achieve. It is also a valuable potential source of new assets and skills.

External assessment covers:

*   The external macro-environmental influences surrounding the enterprise (Chapter 2).
*   The competitive arena of the market (clienteles) and the industry sector (Chapter 3).

Internal assessment covers:

*   The mission, future vision, identity and core values of the enterprise, and the agendas of its main stakeholders (Chapter 4).
*   The value-creating resources and capabilities of the enterprise and how it actually performs (Chapter 5).

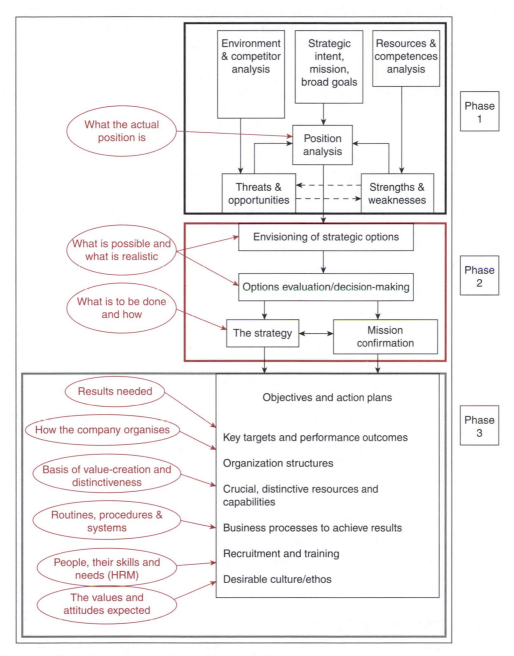

Figure 1.4: Strategic management as a 'design-plus' process

The mission and associated concepts define what the enterprise stands for and exists to achieve, as understood collectively by its stakeholders. Resources are principally the physical and financial assets of the enterprise. Capabilities include the technological and business processes, knowledge and skills that make it possible for the enterprise to create value by deploying its resources productively. Resources and capabilities are key elements of strategy development and implementation, since they either enable or constrain the prospects for pursuing a preferred strategic direction.

Phase 1 aims to draw robust conclusions about the key issues, based on available evidence not supposition or prejudice. Once the assessment of internal and external contexts has been completed, the enterprise can synthesise its main findings and prioritise the key issues identified into a summary position statement (as discussed in Chapter 6).

The Importance of Identifying Strategic Alternatives

Phase 2 involves the generation and assessment of future alternatives strategies in response to the issues raised in Phase 1. This decision-shaping and decision-taking phase is shown in Figure 1.4 in the red box. It involves the need to:

- Consider and state appropriate changes to the mission or the future vision of the enterprise.
- Make choices about future clienteles and the resources and capabilities required to meet their needs.
- Generate and assess options to enhance the future value-creating performance and distinctiveness of the enterprise.
- Make judgements about acceptable risks in relation to these choices.

When thoughtful, well-informed choices have been made, there is reason to believe that the *content* of the proposed future strategy is realistic and viable for the enterprise to implement. However, there remain many possibilities to consider. These include:

- Analytical frameworks to assist the creative development of strategic alternatives (Chapter 7).
- Strategies at the business-unit level (Chapter 8).
- Innovation strategies and their application as external contexts mature (Chapter 9).
- Enterprise diversification strategies (Chapter 10).
- Acquisitions mergers and alliance strategies (Chapter 11).
- Multinational and global strategies (Chapter 12).

The Importance of Action

Phase 3 – outlined in the grey box in Figure 1.4 – addresses the detailed considerations for a credible strategy to be implemented: translated into effective actions. This is the subject of Chapter 13, which has two main priorities. One is to highlight the need for the strategy to be coherent as a whole and for its various elements to be mutually consistent. Many important elements of strategy content will penetrate into the domains of marketing, operations and human resources management, information technology, financial management and other functional areas. Chapter 13 does not address all of this ground in detail, but it highlights some important respects in which the overall strategy directs the management of resources and capabilities in these functional areas.

The Challenges of Doing Strategy

The *principles* of good strategy design are straightforward. The tough challenges are to understand and manage the *processes* of forming and implementing a credible strategy in 'real world' situations. Strategists face various challenges:

Complacency and aversion to change: The more successful a company becomes, the more risk-averse its managers tend to become. Even without being complacent, they can resist considering a new idea because it challenges the current strategy on which their reputations and authority have been founded. However, there is a need to balance *continuity* with appropriate *change*. External observers report that enterprises typically experience quite long periods of continuity in their operations punctuated by short bursts of change.[31] While too much change too quickly could be very problematic, little or no change may ultimately require periods of intense reflection and painful adjustment.

The complexity of the operating environment: Strategic management requires managers to identify and assess the potential future significance of many issues and concerns that vary in scale, scope and salience, even as they face urgent, short-term pressures and stresses. Reliable data acquisition is also costly, which limits the comprehensiveness of the analysis they can carry out in practice.

CASE STUDY: Friends Reunited[32]

Julie and Steve Pankhurst started the *FriendsReunited.co.uk* website in 2000 at the height of the dot.com boom. The site encouraged people to locate former school friends and develop new relationships. Within a year the website had 3 million registered users and 3.6 million hits a day. In 2002 it launched companion websites: Workplaces, a job site and Genes Reunited, an ancestry site. Even losing a libel suit brought by an unhappy teacher in 2002 did not arrest 'Friends' explosive growth. By Spring 2003 it had 8 million members and some subscribers were paying for premium services. MediaDNA said that, uniquely for a website, it had become one of the UK's top-10 innovative brands.

By December 2005 *FriendsReunited.co.uk* had over 15 million members, 1 million of whom were subscribers generating £12.4 million of revenues and £6.6 million profits (as calculated on the 'EBITDA' basis – a term explained in Chapter 5.)

From 2003 onwards the Pankhursts negotiated with commercial television companies to launch programme formats to link directly with the website. They had also added a dating site to the group. Various suitors showed considerable interest and the founders sold it to ITV plc for £120 million, plus a commitment to pay a further £55 million conditional on future business performance. The Pankhursts gained £30 million personally.

ITV had noted the rising popularity of broadband Internet access. Committed web users were spending over 3 hours a day surfing, more than the average viewer spent watching TV. It saw 'Friends' as a jewel in the crown of multiple, synergistic web activities linked to ITV.com and to its television programme content. Thus in 2006 it tried a TV programme called 'The School Run' linked to the website. From the start, however, some shareholders expressed doubts over ITV's strategy.

Table 1.A

End year status	2005	2006	2007	2008
Group revenues £ million	12	16	22	18
Membership of 'Friends'	15	17	19	18
Membership of 'Genes'		6	8	9

Membership and revenues of the 'Friends' Group continued to grow at an annualised rate peaking at 50%. In retrospect, membership peaked in 2007, stimulated by a £7 million advertising campaign.

In fact, by the end of 2006 the website had suffered 'the sharpest fall in brand value' of any brand in the YouGov database, a market research company. Friends Reunited was now facing severe competition from the explosive growth of other social networking sites, notably MySpace, Bebo, Piczo and later, Facebook. It had also become clear that the crucial performance metric was not registered members but *paying* subscribers and *unique* users. The 'Friends' site saw a decline in unique user numbers from 3.9 to 2.5 million (m) during 2006, with 'Genes' achieving 1.2m. For comparison, YouTube achieved 7.25m, MySpace 6.1m, Bebo, 3.9m and Piczo 4.9m).

By late 2007, 60% of Friends Reunited's members had reported using the site less than in the previous year. ITV introduced sponsored advertising on the site and dropped subscription charges altogether less than a year later. In 2008, ITV experienced a severe decline in its core advertising revenues, leading to a strategic rationalization of the entire business. ITV paid the £55 million balance of the purchase price in early 2009 and announced that the website was for sale. According to ITV Chairman Michael Grade, 'the success of ITV.com has eclipsed *FriendsReunited.co.uk*.'

The 'Friends' Group was bought by D.C. Thomson, a Scottish newspaper and magazine publisher. Thomson already owned an ancestry website called *FindMyPast.co.uk*. The price agreed was £25 million, equating to an investment loss for ITV of £150 million over its 4 years of ownership. In addition, ITV had sustained substantial trading losses. The transaction required permission from the UK Competition Commission, following concerns of the Office of Fair Trading that it would reduce effective competition from three to two sites (US-owned *Ancestry. co.uk* being the other).

Social network sites evidently demonstrate a transient, fashion quality unless they offer exceptional functionality, such as Facebook (sheer popularity and global reach) and WAYN ('Where are You Now', a 'lifestyle and travel social network' site with 14 million UK and international members). Subsequent media comments on ITV's acquisition included: 'Buying Friends Reunited was an almost criminal waste of money'[33] and '.... the internet's version of the poncho, briefly fashionable, already hopelessly dated.'[34] While Thomson deliberated how best to develop its acquisition the 'Friends' and 'FindMyPast' sites maintained their separate identities although behind-the-scenes operations were being rationalised.

Questions

1. Analyse the competitive position of the D.C. Thomson social network websites using currently available facts and your own knowledge of recent developments by other social networking sites.

2. What creative insights could you offer D.C. Thomson regarding a strategy for social networking? What strategic options would you recommend considering further?

Apparent contradictions: Contradictions appear in what managers know and understand. Individuals become aware of potentially problematic, uncertain issues, yet can read contrary future meanings into them. As human beings, managers are by no means always personally objective. Uncertainty encourages inaction. Individuals wait for clarification of what they cannot yet understand; meanwhile the pursuit of personal or factional interests creates internal conflicts.

Sustaining creativity and imagination: It is difficult to find novel but realistic solutions, especially to convert prospective threats into opportunities. Capable middle managers may have the insights into novel, counter-intuitive and unconventional *contrarian* strategies, but fail to persuade senior colleagues of their merits. In fact, extreme situations can require the courage to 'bet the company' on the success of a particular, novel initiative.

Integrating and co-ordinating coherent actions: Integration and co-ordination are required at various levels of strategy. There are multiple levels at which strategic decisions are taken and actions required: the corporate (multi-business, multi-activity level); the business unit level; and the functional level (marketing, operations, financial, etc.). Co-ordination *across* functions is also vital.

Less thinking and reaction time: There is less time to respond to unforeseen external events and to extract financial returns from risky ventures. Especially in industries such as communications, computing and electronics, technologies change so rapidly that enterprises experience acute time pressures. In innovative domains the challenge is to know whether and when to implement radical, innovative changes that can enhance future status, but probably devalue current products, resources and skills. Should one act first or to wait for others to take the pioneering risks? If they do, will it be too late to respond?

Summary

LEARNING OBJECTIVE ①
- Effective strategies are important for the long-run survival of *any* enterprise, whether for-profit or not-for-profit, and most certainly for any enterprise operating in a hostile, competitive environment.

LEARNING OBJECTIVE ②
- Though basic strategy principles are actually not difficult to understand, it can be very challenging to apply them well in each particular case, given imperfect future knowledge and the limitations of human objectivity. Thus many enterprises ultimately fail or lose their independence.

LEARNING OBJECTIVE ③
- The chapter introduces four strategic frames of reference, which characterise how executive managers may think and behave. Frames can also be considered 'lenses' that enable external observers to understand and perhaps predict strategic management behaviour in other enterprises.

LEARNING OBJECTIVE ④
- Strategic management often adopts military or sporting language. Executives portray their enterprises as combatants and define future success as outperforming direct competitors. Yet competitors frequently offer similar products or services and generally co-exist relatively peacefully. The rational reality for many enterprises is that co-existence and (legal) collaborations are preferable to combat. Indeed, increasing global complexity often makes judicious collaborations vital.

- The 'design-plus' framework for strategic management is an essentially rational approach that comprises three phases: situation analysis leading to a statement of strategic position;

options identification, assessment and selection; and implementation of the preferred strategy.

- 'Real world' strategic management is as much art and craft as science.

Exercises for Further Study and Discussion

1. Create a word list that expresses your perceptions about strategy. Would this list have looked different before reading the chapter?
2. Henry Ford's strategy was essentially the product of his 'single brain'. Much more recently the incoming chief executive of a struggling global corporation told his senior management team that 'from now on, I will decide the strategy and you will do the implementing'. Is this even a remotely realistic proposition?
3. Academic strategy research aims to describe observed phenomena, but also aims to develop theoretical principles with predictive use. To what extent does the complexity and unpredictability of human behaviour make this aim unrealistic? Discuss.
4. Explain the key differences between business level and corporate level strategies. What kinds of management skills does each require?
5. What reservations might you have about the 'design-plus' model of strategic management?
6. How likely are an enterprise's size and age to influence its dominant frame of reference? What evidence can you find?
7. Obtain more facts about BBC activities and organization from its website. The Commercial Businesses group engages in for-profit activities. How compatible is this with the BBC's status? What key issues should its executives address to help decide if they should sell it or invest further in it?
8. Why were the respective strategies of General Motors and Swissair not challenged more effectively well before they failed? (It may help here to consider the identity of their main stakeholders and their respective beliefs and interests.)

Suggestions for Further Reading

Ansoff, H.I. (1991) 'Critique of Henry Mintzberg's "The design school"', *Strategic Management Journal* (vol. 11, pp. 449–461).

Barney, J.B. (1995) 'Looking inside for competitive advantage', *Academy of Management Executive* (vol. 9/4, pp. 49–61).

Campbell, A. and Alexander, M. (1997) 'What's wrong with strategy? *Harvard Business Review* (vol. Nov–Dec, pp. 42–51).

Carter, C., Clegg, R.C. and Kornberger, K. (2008) *A Very Short, Fairly Interesting and Reasonably Cheap Book About Studying Strategy*, Sage.

Clegg, S., Kornberger, M. and Pitsis, T. (2005) *Managing and Organizations*, Sage (Chapter 12).

Fréry, F. (2006) 'The fundamental dimensions of strategy' *Sloan Management Review* (vol. 48/1, pp. 71–75).

Koch, R. (1995) *The Financial Times Guide to Strategy*, FT Pitman.

Liedtka, J. (2000) 'In defense of strategy as design', *California Management Review* (vol. 42/3, pp. 8–30).

Mintzberg, H. (1991) 'The design school: reconsidering the basic premises of strategic management', *Strategic Management Journal* (vol. 11, pp. 171–195).

Mintzberg, H. and Lampel, J. (1999) 'Reflecting on the strategy process', *Sloan Management Review* (vol. 40/3, pp. 21–30).

Porter, M. (1996) 'What is strategy?', *Harvard Business Review* (vol. 74/6, Nov–Dec, pp. 61–78).

Segal-Horn, S. (1998, ed.) *The Strategy Reader*, Blackwell.

Sutherland, J. and Canwell, C. (2004) *Key Concepts in Strategic Management*, Palgrave.

Volberda, H.W. and Elfring, T. (2001, eds) *Rethinking Strategy*, Sage.

Weick, K.E. (1987) 'Substitutes for strategy', in Teece, D. (ed.) *The Competitive Challenge*, Ballinger.

Notes

1 See Ackoff (1970); Henderson (1984) writing on behalf of the Boston Consulting Group (BCG).
2 Porter (1980).
3 Chandler (1962); Ansoff (1965).
4 Associated with a variety of people including Barney, Wernerfelt, Peteraf and Penrose, some of whose influential work can be found in Foss (1997).
5 For example, Samra-Fredericks (2003).
6 Conclusions often associated with the statistical analyses of PIMS Associates, initially sponsored by General Electric (see Buzzell and Gale, 1987).
7 See Baden-Fuller and Stopford (1994) for a detailed account of their research with references to other respected sources including Bain, Porter, Rumelt, and Schmalensee, for example. Also: Weerawardena et al. (2006).
8 'Supreme excellence consists in breaking the enemy's resistance without fighting.' See Sun Tzu (2004).
9 Andrews (1980).
10 Hamel and Prahalad (1989).
11 Hofer and Schendel (1978).
12 Quinn (1980a, page 7).
13 Miles and Snow (1994).
14 Mintzberg (1987).
15 Porter (1980; 1985).
16 For example, Bain (1959).

17 Mintzberg (1985); Kanter (2002).

18 See http://www.bbc.co.uk/aboutthebbc/purpose/what.shtml

19 For example, *paradigm* means a base of knowledge, beliefs and way of thinking generally accepted without question, hence it informs decisions and actions. Scientific belief in Newtonian laws of motion was a paradigm that persisted for centuries until relativity and quantum mechanics emerged in the early 20th century (Kuhn, 1970). Terms used for shared organizational beliefs include 'perspectives' (Chaffee, 1985); 'schools of thought' (Mintzberg et al., 1998); 'recipes' (Spender, 1989), 'ruling myths' (Hedberg and Jonsson, 1977), and 'frames of significance (Pitt and Clarke, 1997).

20 http://www.beaverandtapley.co.uk/

21 Quinn (1980b).

22 Allison (1971).

23 Lindblom (1959).

24 Pettigrew (1985) presents a very detailed account of the management of strategic change in a large chemical company (ICI).

25 http://www.labour.org.uk

26 Pascale (1984).

27 See Aldrich (1999) for a detailed account.

28 See http://www.easy.com and http://en.wikipedia.org/wiki/EasyGroup

29 In government too: Prime Minister Margaret Thatcher often used the phrase 'one of us' to refer to colleagues who shared her view of monetarist economic policy. Those who did not she called 'wets'.

30 In the European Union, 99% of firms employ less than a 100 people. Over half of employees work in such firms, the majority of which are less than 50 years old. The position is similar in the United States and in Asia.

31 Mintzberg (1978; 1985) and Pettigrew (1985) provide detailed accounts of continuity and change in strategic postures over time.

32 Main sources: ITV annual reports from ITV.com; Guardian.co.uk; and FT.com

33 Emily Bell (guardian.co.uk 9/3/2009).

34 Carole Cadwalladr (guardian.co.uk 2/8/2009).

2

Understanding the External Environment

Learning Outcomes

This chapter is designed to enable you to:

① Understand the strategic significance of an enterprise's external operating environment.

② Describe and explain characteristics of business environments.

③ Use the ScanStep© framework to analyse business environments.

④ Look critically for strategic threats and opportunities.

CASE STUDY: Lowe & Shawyer Ltd[1]

In 1864 aged 21, Joseph Lowe set up a horticultural nursery at Uxbridge, West London, UK to sell flowering plants such as geraniums and roses to local people. For 33 years this small enterprise expanded progressively. In 1897 Lowe took on a younger partner, George Shawyer. They formed a private limited company in 1906, at which point they employed 100 staff working on 10 hectares of land. When the 1914–18 war started, the company was the largest local employer. Patriotically it devoted its 28 hectares of land and 300 staff to vegetable production, using female workers for the first time.

After the war, Lowe & Shawyer Ltd refocused production on roses, pioneering new varieties. It diversified into carnations and other varieties suitable for the cut-flower market. By 1925 the company had become the leading supplier to the British cut-flower market, distributing products daily by rail and road to London and other big cities. North American growers who visited the company declared it to be a world-class company.

When Lowe died in 1929, Shawyer became chief executive. The enterprise continued to grow. By 1938 it had 1400 employees and 80 hectares of land, including 14 hectares of glasshouses, heated by 14 large boilers. Water usage was so great that the company dug artesian wells to supplement water from the river Pinn. That year it sold over 50 million flowers.

During the 1939–45 war, the company again turned to vegetable production. Shawyer died in 1943. Flower growing resumed after the war, but economic austerity depressed demand. Labour shortages arose because staff left to work elsewhere for higher wages in more congenial working conditions. When the British economy improved, the major flower wholesalers began to import cheaper cut flowers from warmer overseas climates that offered greater year-round variety. Lowe & Shawyer Ltd struggled on, but ceased trading in 1958. Its land became the site for the new Brunel University campus in 1966.

Questions

1. Outline the changes in the business environment (i.e., the context in which the business worked) that contributed to its decline.

2. On the basis of your answer to question 1, suggest some actions the company might have taken to help it survive.

Introduction

No enterprise functions in isolation. Enterprises interact with the external world, most obviously with their clientele (i.e., paying customers or other recipients of its services), their suppliers, employees and other external stakeholders such as bankers, competitors and would-be competitors.

The industry sector(s) in which an enterprise operates and the market(s) it serves form important parts of its external environment. Within these environmental domains, periodic events and trends arise that affect an enterprise's actions and prospects. An enterprise may not be able to control these influences.

Market changes may provide opportunities to exploit demand for existing and new products or services. Developments within industry sectors provide opportunities for learning via new technologies and collaborations. Both kinds of environmental domains (i.e., markets and sectors) also produce challenges, costs and threats. For example, demand for an enterprise's products may fall due to an overall decline in the market or a greater challenge from the offerings of competitors. Enterprises must therefore be alert to changes in the business environment.

Enterprises also need to consider changes in the wider world beyond their particular markets or sectors. That is, they need to consider changes in the macro or global environment. The macro environment generates additional challenges, costs and threats, but also opportunities. Typically, enterprises have little or no control over macro environmental events and trends, though they can seek to influence them, directly or indirectly.

As our case study of Lowe & Shawyer Ltd above illustrates, enterprises need to consider changes in their business environments at various levels – the market, industry sector, and macro levels. In this chapter we examine the characteristics of the external environment. We consider its multi-layered structure and also the uncertainty arising from a combination of complexity, dynamism and hostility. We outline the issue-drivers – that is, the factors in the macro environment that create issues to which an enterprise may need to respond. The chapter provides a systematic approach to analyse these factors, using a framework called ScanStep©.

Characteristics of the External Environment

A Complex, Multi-layered Structure

External environments are multi-layered: we can think of them as rather like onions or a set of traditional Russian dolls (in which each doll is contained within a larger one). Figure 2.1 illustrates a simple three-level structure with the enterprise at the centre.

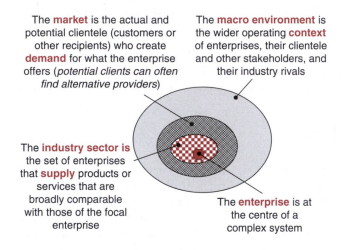

The **market** is the actual and potential clientele (customers or other recipients) who create **demand** for what the enterprise offers (*potential clients can often find alternative providers*)

The **macro environment** is the wider operating **context** of enterprises, their clientele and other stakeholders, and their industry rivals

The **industry sector is** the set of enterprises that **supply** products or services that are broadly comparable with those of the focal enterprise

The **enterprise** is at the centre of a complex system

Figure 2.1: The 'nested' structure of the external environment

LEARNING ② OBJECTIVE

The layer immediately surrounding the enterprise is the industry sector. This comprises the set of enterprises that supply similar products or services in comparable ways. Practical definitions of a sector rely on commonality of product types and their associated production, service and delivery processes and technologies.

In simple cases all the enterprises in a sector are direct rivals. (In Chapter 3, we will consider more complex relationships involving strategic groups.) Enterprises compete in many forms of industry sector as they seek to create value. These sectors include:

* Primary industries such as (a) agriculture or fishing and (b) mining, quarrying and the extraction of raw materials such as iron ore and crude oil.

* Industries converting materials into basic, low value-added, products, such as steel beams, plastics, chemicals and fertilisers.

- Industries converting materials and knowledge into high value-added products, such as cars, motor yachts, television sets and cosmetics.

- Industries providing value-added services, such as vehicle repair and maintenance, and increasingly in the high value-added technical and expert services (e.g., consultancy and telecommunications) on which advanced economies depend.

Beyond the industry sector are various markets. A market may be equated with demand. Each market is the set of actual and potential customers or clients for products and services that meet a specific need felt by these clients. It is of strategic significance that a felt need can usually be satisfied in various ways. It is not unusual for suppliers in unrelated industry sectors to satisfy a particular demand equally well. They may offer alternative 'solutions' to the 'problem' that underlies the demand. Accordingly, suppliers with apparently unrelated offerings may be competing without necessarily being aware of it. This describes many consumer and business-to-business markets. The value to the client lies in the desired end result, not how it is achieved. As marketing guru, Ted Leavitt, famously declared: 'companies do not buy quarter-inch drills, they buy quarter-inch holes.' The best 'solution' for each client depends on what combination of convenience, performance, frequency, accuracy, quantity, location and cost is ideal.

Alternative solutions to particular market demands

Saturday night entertainment: books and magazines; watching television; movie rentals; web surfing; cinemas; theatres; clubs, bars and restaurants; ten-pin bowling.

Music on the move: digital radio; CD player; iPod; mp3 player; wi-fi enabled multi-media device; mobile phone.[2]

Body hair removal: razor; epilator; electronic devices; waxing; creams; beauty salons.

Making holes: drills; metal punches; laser beams; gas jets; water jets; electric spark erosion, etc.

Often an enterprise operates in multiple, potentially competing, sub-markets. Of strategic significance, few suppliers have any *realistic* prospect of developing the alternative technological capabilities sufficient to provide all the 'solutions' that a market might expect or become receptive to. An enterprise that is aligned with a product type or technology finds it challenging to introduce radical new products or technologies, especially when they would devalue existing resources and capabilities. Patents, copyrights and other legal mechanisms may limit such options too.

In practice, an enterprise may equate its market with the expected demand for products and services enabled by its current array of technologies and business processes (and developments thereof). It may ignore the threat of possible substitution (when consumers choose use a different kind of product instead) on the basis that this is a form of unknown and unknowable risk.

From the standpoint of competent environmental analysis, however, an enterprise should not ignore potentially significant threats or opportunities by defining its market(s) too narrowly.

LEARNING
OBJECTIVE ② Beyond the market level is the seemingly remote macro or global layer of the environment. In principle it includes any factor, trend or event with a possible influence on what the enterprise is, does or could do. The 2008 global economic crisis showed how the macro environment is a source of costs and threats for enterprises. Comparatively few enterprises contributed directly or even indirectly to the crisis, yet the consequent 'credit crunch' affected enterprises of all sizes worldwide. Those that have managed their financial affairs prudently have avoided its worst effects, yet may still have difficulty obtaining adequate credit at affordable interest rates. Careless or profligate enterprises (including huge corporations) have suffered badly, some becoming bankrupt.

Terrorism is another example of a macro environmental threat that disrupts normal business operations. Other examples include natural environmental disasters like oil spillages, disease epidemics and prolonged periods of extreme weather.[3] Fuel shortages, accidents, national industrial disputes; computer failures; Internet security breaches and identity theft are all challenges that pose obvious threats to particular enterprises.

As with the market and sector layers, the macro environment includes enterprises' stakeholders, meaning the various actors who have an actual or potential interest in – and influence on – what they do. (The concept of stakeholders is examined further in Chapter 4.)

In society at large, the influence of specific stakeholders is generally indirect and frequently weak. However, they may also be organized into more powerful, single-issue pressure groups, the response to which needs careful management.[4] Their influences affect the enterprise both directly and indirectly via communications and information flows from its market(s) and industry sector(s). Because their salience and significance change over time, it would be near-impossible to evaluate all possible influences at all times.

LEARNING
OBJECTIVE ① However, enterprises are well-advised to be alert to environmental influences whose possibilities and consequences fall into three broad categories:

1. Cost and threat generation
2. Opportunity generation and
3. Resource access and provision

The macro environment is a source of opportunities too. Technological developments in agriculture, medicine, electronics and ecology make human beings healthier and their lives more comfortable and rewarding, resulting in many new business opportunities. Environmental conservation and management is creating many new opportunities in renewable energy production, waste recycling, and biodegradable packaging. Threats can create opportunities. Security threats prompt government security agencies, private enterprises and individuals to create new services for emerging markets including enhanced computer security, prevention of identity theft and notably in mobile communications, all of which generate new employment.

The macro environment is the ultimate origin of the resources that every enterprise needs for its value-adding activities. These resources include raw materials and supplies, people, know-how and finance. Successful enterprises require additional new resources, which in turn increases the demand for funds and hence banking services. Every enterprise may also be a source of knowledge and other resources (including skilled staff) for other enterprises. Thus each enterprise contributes indirectly to the macro environment of all others.

The macro environment also acts as the sink for waste materials and discarded products. Government regulations increasingly oblige enterprises to behave responsibly. Recycling is now a significant enterprise operating cost that, until recently, few set explicitly against their income. While responsible enterprises accept the costs of being good corporate citizens, they also expose themselves to costs and penalties if they are not.

The three layers of external environment interact. For example, consumers influence an enterprise as customers and less directly, perhaps, as 'green' environmentalists. Some environmental influences reinforce others while some have contrary effects. Declining business confidence generally reinforces similar cross-sector actions, such as shedding staff to reduce costs (even by enterprises serving quite buoyant markets). Social networking and television lifestyle programmes also prompt convergent behaviours with consequent influences on product and service providers. Conversely, when rising unemployment reduces consumer demand for new cars, expensive holidays and restaurant meals, demand for used cars, home improvement products and supermarket ready-meals probably *increases*, through what is known as a substitution effect.

Environmental Uncertainty

Enterprise managers have instinctive attitudes towards, and assumptions about, the external environment. They pay attention to what is most immediate, namely their industry sectors and served market(s). They may have 'blind spots' that ignore or discount certain market and sector trends. Though objective analyses of developments reduce the blind spots, environmental uncertainty contributes greatly to enterprises' misjudgements. Analysing environmental potentialities and reaching sensible conclusions requires considered, open-minded, predictions and judgement.

RNING ②
ECTIVE
Macro, market and sector levels are all uncertainty-laden, sometimes over present circumstances, but especially over future events and trends. Environmental scanning and analysis aim to obtain evidence to reduce this uncertainty. *Factual* uncertainty arises over *whether* an event is

Factual and predictive uncertainties over global warming

Based on scientific evidence, very few *bona fide* experts dispute that planet Earth is warming up. Thus *factual uncertainty* about global warming is low. There is even a broad consensus that human activity is the major cause. Yet forecasts of *how much* warming will occur over the next 50 or 100 years vary considerably. As the polar ice caps melt, sea levels are rising – but by a few centimetres or more than a metre per century? Assuming no attempt to reduce CO_2 emissions or that all attempts are ineffective, forecasts of the range of possible outcomes are reasonably convergent. *Predictive uncertainty* over the expected rise is moderate.

Factual knowledge of the continental land masses is extremely accurate. Experts can pinpoint which areas of low-lying land will become uninhabitable *given a 1-metre rise in sea level*. There is little factual uncertainty about these calculations. Moreover, given this rise, there is low predictive uncertainty about the outcomes: many deaths, massive population migrations, famine and conflict. However, few enterprises could currently predict the strategic impact such a catastrophe would have on them. Thus the predictive uncertainty over the *implications* of global warming will remain high for a considerable time, prompting a 'wait and see' response. Sensible as this sounds, enterprises that will be affected risk being unable to respond when the potential impact ultimately clarifies.

imminent or a trend is actually occurring. It is frequently accompanied by *predictive* uncertainty over the implications of events and trends if they do materialise.

LEARNING OBJECTIVE ② Environmental uncertainty affects enterprises because of three main characteristics that vary in their degrees of severity:[5]

1. Complexity (many and diverse influences).
2. Dynamism (rate of change of these influences).
3. Hostility (arising from direct threats and indirect influences).

Below we consider each of these in turn.

Complexity

In the modern world complexity forms a challenging aspect of many enterprises' environments: simplicity seems a thing of the past. Significant so-called 'drivers' of complexity include:

- Diversity and contrariness in consumer behaviours
- Diversity and geographic reach of enterprise activities
- Extreme product variety in patterns of demand and supply
- Competitive innovation and planned obsolescence
- Differing government regulations in many countries and
- Communication intensity and information overload

Variety and *diversity* increase complexity in all of these drivers. Around the world, countries have increasingly diverse populations as the result of economic and forced migrations. Diversity exists in living standards, ethnic origins, religion, family norms, lifestyle preferences and other socially or culturally-derived patterns of behaviour. Sheer variety of available products and services

Diversity and variety in enterprise environments

Ethnic diversity: Government agencies in France for many years refused policies to accommodate ethnic diversity. The resulting Parisian riots of 2005 and 2007 stressed the emergency services and created losses for insurance companies. Renovation work, however, created opportunities for builders. Immigration into Britain led Government agencies to respond practically toward ethnic diversity; thus they translate official documents into many European and south-Asian languages. This is a significant cost born by national and local taxpayers, but presents an opportunity for private sector translation agencies.

Economic diversity: The economies of East and West Germany were totally different. After reunification in 1989 many East German enterprises collapsed, creating market opportunities and acquisition targets for West German companies. West German taxpayers bore most of the reunification costs.

Ecological diversity: Wealthy nations, large and small, have greatly contributed to natural environmental degradation, but they are now reducing their environmental impact through recycling and reduced energy usage. Ecological pressures now create major business opportunities. By contrast, huge fast-growing countries like China and India are rapidly increasing their carbon emissions by commissioning many new coal-fired power stations and rapidly increasing their consumption of raw materials.

encourages choice and fragments demand. Businesses and social agencies such as health services have to accommodate a widening range of needs and expectations. The consequences are often higher costs, reduced efficiency and greater uncertainties.

Macro environmental trends create threats and opportunities. Their costs and benefits are distributed asymmetrically. Diversity among populations encourages enterprises to innovate and to expand choice, further increasing environmental complexity. However, many business opportunities by their nature encourage global consumption of finite resources, some of which are fast-declining, which can pose moral and ethical dilemmas.

Dynamism

Environments are rarely static. Rather, their characteristics change frequently, even abruptly, sometimes appearing very dynamic.[6] Economic circumstances, social and cultural attitudes and chance events all drive *unpredictable* changes.

LEARNING OBJECTIVE ② Strategically, it is important to distinguish between *short-term* environmental dynamism that is generally turbulent or cyclical or has localised impact, and *long-term* environmental dynamism whose impacts tend to be universal and non-reversible, and which create winners and losers among competing enterprises.

Dynamic enterprise environments

Turbulent: Short-term environmental changes mirror the weather. Floods, high winds and snow create unexpected, highly disruptive but usually localised conditions. Inconvenienced populations present short-term opportunities for businesses and service agencies: a severe snowfall generates demand for toboggans and gritting salt.

Short-term: When British regulations required house sellers to provide onerous 'home information packs' (HIPs), they created a short-term business opportunity for estate agents, but prompted an immediate, short-term decline in house sales (and presumably paint). A later Government decree greatly simplified HIPs.

Long-term: High-speed broadband is enhancing Internet access. The significance of this technology-driven macro trend appears set to continue long term:

- Web shopping may accelerate the decline of the traditional 'bricks and mortar' retail store trade without increasing overall sales.
- Music downloads have damaged over-the-counter CD sales, which seem unlikely ever to recover. Movie downloads seem likely to have the same impact on future DVD sales. Makers of CD and DVD discs suffer.

Future video-on-demand web streaming could damage scheduled commercial broadcasting of television programmes, especially movies.

Hostility

Environments manifest differing degrees of hostility arising from economic, political, social and cultural circumstances such as asymmetry of wealth, knowledge and natural resources within and between nations and their respective enterprises. Aggressive competition also generates environmental hostility, sometimes with disturbing ethical consequences.

Hostile environments for enterprises

Economic hostility: 'Casino banking' excesses in the financial services sector led to the infamous global credit crunch and worldwide recession whose combined impact is still being widely felt. Tighter external controls and higher taxes on the industry are actual or potential outcomes. Enterprises in some forms of financial services may have difficulty operating in some locations in future and consequently their costs could rise substantially.

Environmental and technological hostility: Economists and technologists argue that the world cannot provide enough renewable energy via wind and wave power, making nuclear power essential. Few private-sector enterprises are willing to build nuclear power stations because the commercial costs and technical risks are substantial. Governments have to share these risks. There is much proactive opposition from the 'green' lobby. Well-organised enterprises like Greenpeace dispute pro-nuclear arguments, stressing reduced energy consumption and the immorality of an industry that burdens future generations with huge quantities of highly toxic nuclear waste.

Security hostility: Huntingdon Life Sciences is a British company that tests new drugs from major pharmaceutical corporations on animals before human trials begin. Animal rights activists have much-publicised its activities. Some have been more aggressive, threatening the welfare and property of the company, its employees and its suppliers.

A Systematic Framework for Macro Environmental Analysis

Elements of Environmental Analysis

Macro environmental analysis needs focus, informed by relevant prior knowledge of the particular enterprise, its current market(s) and industry sector(s). Enterprise analysts have access to internal data, their clients as well as publicly accessible sources such as newspapers, the World Wide Web, business publications and authoritative specialist reports. They may also commission external enquiries in many forms. External analysts generally rely on published sources and try to cultivate contacts within the enterprise, its peers, clienteles and other agencies. Given a sound understanding of the immediate context of the particular enterprise, analysts can try to identify relevant issues and specific concerns in the wider, macro environment.

The analyst must consider the implications of each macro-level issue identified. Some will present actual or potential threats to the enterprise, others actual or potential opportunities. Frequently, issue uncertainty makes the assessment ambiguous: given current knowledge, an issue could present either a threat *or* an opportunity. The outcome of analysis is therefore a provisional summary that forms the basis for further review whose aim is definitive interpretations.

The PESTLE and ScanStep© Frameworks

A framework commonly used to identify issues and evaluate their possible implications for a particular enterprise is known as PESTLE. This is an acronym, each letter of which stands for a key driver of macro environmental issues, thus:

Political

Economic

Social

Technological

Legal

Environmental (ecological)

Though popular, this framework has weaknesses. In particular, it omits *cultural* issue-drivers, which typically create deeper and potentially more persistent issues than do social issues. Social and cultural issues can overlap. As a guide, a particular social issue tends to be salient in a relatively homogeneous culture, while differing cultures give rise to very different issues. Thus artificial tanning cosmetics are popular among culturally similar Western women, whereas culturally similar Asian women tend to prefer skin-lightening cosmetics.

The 'legal' category of PESTLE ignores (or leaves implicit) non-legal *regulatory* issue-drivers. These include voluntary codes of practice whose consequences should be explicit. *Security* issue-drivers are also crucial. By adding these drivers and adjusting the names (adding 'natural' to 'environmental'), we can derive the acronym ScanStep©. This has the advantage of being memorable because the term *relates to the nature of the exercise being undertaken* (Figure 2.2).

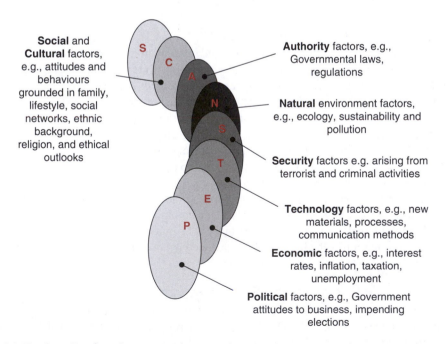

Social and **Cultural** factors, e.g., attitudes and behaviours grounded in family, lifestyle, social networks, ethnic background, religion, and ethical outlooks

Authority factors, e.g., Governmental laws, regulations

Natural environment factors, e.g., ecology, sustainability and pollution

Security factors e.g. arising from terrorist and criminal activities

Technology factors, e.g., new materials, processes, communication methods

Economic factors, e.g., interest rates, inflation, taxation, unemployment

Political factors, e.g., Government attitudes to business, impending elections

Figure 2.2: The ScanStep© environmental framework

Table 2.A illustrates how ScanStep© 'maps' against PESTLE.

Table 2.A: ScanStep© versus PESTLE

ScanStep© Issue fields	PESTLE Issue fields					
	Political	Economic	Social	Technological	Legal	Ecological
Social			√			
Cultural			√			
Authority (legal *and* regulatory)					√	
Natural environmental						√
Security						
Technological				√		
Economic		√				
Political	√					

A resource for applying ScanStep© is shown in Figure 2.3. ScanStep© analysis makes some general assumptions, namely that:

- Effective enterprises try to be well informed about environmental developments. This requires them to understand the influences of external stakeholders.
- The implications of an issue may be clearly positive (or negative). Others may be difficult to judge, indeed may have positive *and* negative consequences. Such issues merit considerable scrutiny before final decisions result.
- An issue in one field sometimes links to an issue in another field.[7] Social and cultural issues are interlinked and often hard to distinguish. Culture is what drives the more abstract, fundamental issues within and between populations.
- Issues in different fields may have the same implications for the focal enterprise.
- Risk assessments can be applied to each major issue defined (see later).
- After the macro analysis is complete and issues evaluated and prioritised, environmental assessment then considers market and industry issues (as discussed further in Chapter 3).

Now we examine each component of the ScanStep framework in turn.

Issue driver	Event or trend	Stakeholder linkages	Identified issue that could have:	
			Positive impact	Negative impact
Social				
Cultural				
Authority				
Natural environment (ecological)				
Security				
Technology				
Economic				
Political				

Figure 2.3: ScanStep© macro-environmental worksheet

Social Issue-drivers

LEARNING
OBJECTIVE ③

People are social beings. They have a great capacity to influence one another through relation-ships and networks. Society therefore drives many macro environmental issues that bear on the interests of enterprises and create issues they must respond to.

Traditionally in Western societies, individuals have influenced (and were mostly influenced by) family members, friends (peers), work colleagues, and acquaintances in special interest groups and professional affiliations. Over the last two decades celebrities, film and sports stars have increasingly influenced ordinary people via popular newspapers, magazines, advertisements and websites where they publicise their activities and endorse products and lifestyles. Membership of social network websites allows people greatly to extend their personal networks, increasing the rapid spread of opinion-forming ideas and messages. Word-of-mouth or so-called viral marketing is also rising.

Changes in population size and age profile all influence the enterprise environment. In so-called advanced societies lifestyles have become more diverse. People aged below 40 think and behave principally as consumers when buying products and in respect of services such as healthcare too. Consumerism drives costly, aspirational lifestyles and leisure activities. Diverse lifestyles, whether sporting, adventure, intellectual, travel or characterised by excess consumption (of food, alcohol, recreational drugs), are everyday realities.

The 'nuclear' family is in decline; single parenthood and same-sex relationships are relatively commonplace. Products and services emphasise youthfulness in their presentation, despite ageing populations whose senior citizens may enjoy high purchasing power. Age discrimination is widely discouraged or even banned, but still prevails. Equality of treatment in respect of gender, race and disability is often expected and required by law.

Most adults in these societies consider paid employment the norm and a major source of personal status. Many adults experience higher education, then work in office and professional contexts. Others work in low-skilled or long-established, craft-based jobs. Part-time working is common. Occupational groups tend to polarise based on income or traditional class perceptions. Inter-group mobility is limited, despite educational opportunities. Traditional socialist attitudes have been in retreat. Career, income and personal fulfilment influence most people more than caring for others. Unpaid, socially responsible activities such as membership of a local government body, charity or school governing board are generally of minority interest and relatively low priority.

These generalisations apply in varying degrees to developed nations, east and west. Nordic, Middle European and Mediterranean countries show distinct differences, despite convergence in social attitudes and behaviours. Russia and its former satellite states have stronger consumer instincts than 20 years ago, especially in those states which have joined the European Union. Hong Kong, Singapore, South Korea and Taiwan, the four 'Asian Tigers' have dynamic and increasingly sophisticated societies. Fast-developing societies such as Mexico, Brazil, China, India and Malaysia may not yet display equivalent levels of sophistication and social cohesion, but they aspire and have the will to do so. Conversely, some African and South American states remain much better opportunities for aid organisations than consumer goods corporations.

Cultural Issue-drivers

Culture applies to the fundamental, deeply-rooted qualities of a nation or society. Cultural convergence within a community confers a shared sense of identity. Non-convergence within and between cultures creates tensions, conflicts and consequently, challenging issues to which involved enterprises must respond or seem out-of-touch.

Religious and family values (or lack of) are major factors distinguishing national and community cultures. Ethnic roots and values remain deep-rooted, despite mass migrations.

The consequences are inter-community and inter-societal tensions, as evidenced most tragically in the Middle East.

Expatriate affinity for old customs and outlooks seems universal. Irish-Americans appear to display a stronger sense of Irishness than do most native Irish people – on St Patrick's Day parades, for example. Language is significant in maintaining historic affiliations. Chicago has the largest Polish-speaking community outside Poland; Canada has a sizeable and vocal French-speaking minority. Germany, France and Britain have significant, yet enormously diverse, minority communities whose extractions are, respectively: Turkish; North African; South Asian and Afro-Caribbean. 'Transplanted' communities cluster in preferred urban localities. In varying degrees they maintain links with their mother countries, native religions and customs including mode of dress, cuisine, music and other cultural traditions and preferences. Cultural diversity is an integral feature of the macro environments in these countries, of particular importance for multinational enterprises.

Authority Issue-drivers

LEARNING ③
OBJECTIVE

Authority is a macro environmental issue-driver. It derives from laws, regulations and codes of practice. Authority obliges compliance because a regulatory body has the power to apply sanctions if its requirements are ignored.

Authority issue-drivers fall into one of four broad categories:

1. Laws and regulations that affect enterprise behaviours *directly* because compliance is legally required.
2. Rules, regulations, codes of conduct and best practices that govern the acceptable behaviour of enterprises in a defined context, but do not have the force of law.
3. Laws and regulations affecting the behaviours of citizens with consequential, *indirect* effects on enterprises.
4. Rules and codes of conduct that influence the behaviour of individuals within a defined (e.g., professional) context.

Enterprises incur costs associated with regulatory compliance, legal and otherwise; if they fail to comply, criminal liability, fines and/or bad publicity can variously result.

European Union (EU) *labour mobility* laws exemplify the first of these categories. They allow citizens of one EU country to work in another, so an EU employer cannot lawfully discriminate against citizens of other EU countries. *Anti-discrimination* laws apply to race, gender, sexual orientation and disability. In Britain and many other countries the operators of public buildings and workplaces have other, specific legal duties, such as to provide access and washroom facilities for wheelchair users, and to prevent tobacco smoking.

Registered companies must operate according to legally enforceable *financial reporting* codes. United States laws are particularly strict and comprehensive. Following the Enron scandal, the Sarbanes-Oxley Act of 2002 codified tight legal standards of corporate governance that apply to all enterprises operating in the United States. No directly equivalent act applies in the EU, so variations and anomalies remain. Corporate governance in Germany has been notably formalised since the 1950s. Executive Boards of Directors are accountable to a Supervisory Board with powers to dismiss executives. The 1992 Cadbury and 1995 Greenbury Reports created good-practice guidelines on UK corporate governance that has now evolved into a legally enforced code for public companies (plc's).[8]

Authority via regulations and codes of practice (administered by governmental or self-regulating bodies with a defined mandate) affects many enterprises. Thus, for example, in the UK: the Financial Services Authority (FSA) regulates banks and other financial institutions; OfCom regulates telecommunications; OfWat the water industry; the Press Council scrutinises newspapers; the Advertising Standards Authority (ASA) sanctions poor advertising practices; the Care Quality Commission scrutinises National Health Service (NHS) hospitals for clinical performance; and the National Institute for Clinical Excellence (NICE) issues evidence-based, strong clinical guidelines on drug prescription. Regulatory bodies act in the interests of responsible enterprises and their clienteles, but their constraints impose costs that unscrupulous organisations try to ignore. Sanctions for breaches of codes vary greatly among regulators who may rely on others to drawn attention to breaches. There are limits to and sometimes ambiguity over jurisdiction: the ASA has wide scope including Web-based advertising, but presently has no powers to act on dubious product claims made on companies' own websites.

The third category refers to laws on individual behaviours with consequences for enterprises. For example, local government departments, proprietors of public houses and other employers have a duty to uphold laws banning antisocial behaviours in specified places.

The fourth category applies particularly to professional practice. The British Medical Association (BMA) exercises powers of disciplinary control over individual doctors. Religious organizations exercise normative influences over their members' beliefs and behaviours, as well as being considered part of the cultural fabric of society.

Natural Environmental (Ecological) Issue-drivers

Environmental degradation in its various forms is increasingly the focus of direct regulation of enterprise activities. Whilst this issue-driver could certainly be treated as a type of authority-driver, its high-profile issues merit separate analysis. Sustainability of the natural environment has become a major issue in enterprises' macro environments, experienced as pressures to reduce energy consumption, avoid pollution, and increase recycling of products and materials. These pressures are increasingly translating into legal constraints on all enterprises.

LEARNING OBJECTIVE ③

Regulation includes the trading of carbon credits to discourage high CO_2 emitters, the energy generators and high users of fossil fuel-derived energy. Refrigerators, aerosol sprays and some plastics involve the use of greenhouse gas contributors, forcing the use of regulated chemicals that are less harmful to the ozone layer. Manufacturers must safely dispose of waste and recycle their products at the end of their useful lives. The disposal of cars, electrical equipment and toxic wastes provides new business opportunities for specialist subcontractors. More effective recycling of household waste is a relatively recent obligation imposed on local government authorities in the UK, following Germany's lead, as landfill sites become increasingly restricted. Demand for biodegradable packaging is rising in consequence.

Environmental pressure groups including Greenpeace and Friends of the Earth publicise responsible behaviour by enterprises that goes beyond the minimum legal obligations, and encourage detailed reporting of their environmental impact. These pressure groups can be of high nuisance value through direct action and adverse publicity, particularly to corporations minded to tackle environmental issues only when the law requires.

Security Issue-drivers

Security issues have assumed greater significance for enterprises since the terrorist attacks on New York, Washington, London, Madrid, Bali and elsewhere. However, the risks associated with security breaches are actually much wider in scope. Security issues emerge in five risk areas:

- Terrorism – its *direct* effects (damage to property and staff; kidnapping and ransom attempts) and *indirect* (collateral) effects (loss of operational functions and scope for revenue-generation).

- Theft of physical assets and of loss of monetary assets and proprietary knowledge (such as client databases) through embezzlement and fraud, often via unauthorised access to computer systems.

- Malicious attacks aiming to incapacitate enterprise computer systems or corrupt data, with intent to damage operations, inconvenience customers and destroy reputations.

- The cost and reputational impacts of avoidable disasters through incompetence, negligence or carelessness (e.g., oil and chemical spills, radiation leakage).

- Natural disasters such as floods, hurricanes, tidal waves and volcanic ash clouds.

Such threats to the security and integrity of an enterprise's operations require them to anticipate the nature of each risk to the security of their tangible assets, people and information, and then make appropriate responses (vigilance, elimination or mitigation). The costs of enhanced security measures must be balanced with the degree of perceived risk. Some costs cannot be calculated: a long breakdown in computer systems could be so catastrophic that rapid recovery systems are imperative, even though costs are high.

One effect of security issues is a huge growth in the opportunities for risk assessment and management services that range from the provision of security guards to highly sophisticated detection and backup systems in the defence of information technology.

Technological Issue-drivers

Technological change occurs continuously and rapidly in all corporate and consumer activities. It is one of the most pervasive and influential macro environmental issue-drivers for modern enterprises. New and enhanced technologies can be divided broadly into those:

- Embedded in products and services that increase functionality and create other user benefits.

- Applied to the processes that create and deliver products, services and knowledge to clients and the extended industry supply chain.

Embryonic technologies create opportunities for science-based entrepreneurs and established enterprises with the capabilities necessary to develop and exploit them. Core technologies include the microprocessor and devices such as lasers. They enable massive power and functionality in computing, control and communications. Supported by software developments, microchips allow more precise and efficient control of established product categories such as cars, washing machines and manufacturing equipment. They underpin new product categories such as mobile phones, notebook computers, optical data storage devices, games consoles, satellite navigation devices, digital cameras, and flat-screen televisions. Multi-layer composite materials involving metals, ceramics and fibre-reinforced polymers enable strong, lightweight structures with complex shapes and application-specific properties.

New communications technologies are changing lifestyles and how people communicate for business purposes, and for shopping, banking and leisure activities. They include broadband Internet, fibre optic cables, satellites, mobile telephony, and local radio communications such as WiFi and Bluetooth. They are changing the efficient conduct of enterprises and the nature of profitable business models (discussed further in Chapter 7). Computing and communications technologies are converging, with integrated devices like Apple's iPad providing the multiple functions that many people require for personal and professional use.

Communications and data storage technologies enable public agencies to deliver their services. Massive data bases record all aspects of people's lives. Developments in DNA screening enhance crime detection and solution. Technology has had a huge impact on medicine, in diagnosis with advanced scanners and is enabling less-traumatic treatments via new drugs, radiology, lasers and robotic surgical techniques. However, the drawbacks of new technologies include high cost, new security threats, identity theft and other electronically enabled crime. Surveillance technologies may create safer societies but also constrain individual freedoms, a moral dilemma.

Economic Issue-drivers

Changes in economic factors are issue-drivers that have considerable impact on enterprise activities. Differences in national economic profiles often mirror differences in social and cultural profiles, presenting challenges for enterprises developing globally. In fact, a country's economic output (gross domestic product [GDP] per capita on a 'purchasing power parity' basis') correlates well with its socio-cultural status and stability. Whereas nations like China have rapidly achieved sophistication and economic growth in the last three decades, other relatively unsophisticated economies have stagnated and sometimes declined dramatically (e.g., Zimbabwe).

Other major economic issue-drivers in enterprise environments include:

- Rates of inflation and currency exchange.
- Technical indicators such as growth of the internal money supply.
- Wage and salary profiles.
- Prevailing levels of consumer and corporate debt.

Longer term changes in any of these factors are significant for strategic enterprise investment decisions.

The World Trade Organization (WTO) is an independent body whose role is to facilitate international trade by minimising national restrictions motivated by political and economic self-interest. It has been moderately effective in minimising tariffs on goods traded between countries, although few countries apply *no* such restrictions. Within the EU single market, tariffs on specified categories of imports have been harmonized or eliminated. Developing countries often prevent overseas enterprises taking out profits generated by their import activities, requiring that they reinvest in local operations.

Countries within economic blocs around the world, such as the Euro Zone or the North American Free Trade Area (NAFTA), share a common currency or preferred trading arrangements. The US dollar acts as a global 'reserve' currency, being widely used in international trade. Global commerce raises new economic issues for business enterprises in two key respects:

- The continuing migration of business activities based on the relative comparative advantages of countries, particularly low-factor costs.

- The de-integration (disintermediation) of stages in globally distributed value-adding supply chains (a concept discussed further in Chapter 3).

While economic regulation of industries and enterprises can be effective at national level, its absence has become apparent in the global financial services industry. The consequences of the 2008 global economic crisis triggered by US mortgage debt default affected all sectors. Credit became much harder to obtain, despite national governments accelerating their money supplies and cutting interest rates dramatically. Severe economic recession and high unemployment still affect many countries so that business enterprises address new investment options very cautiously. Indeed it is possible that globalisation trends will be halted or even reversed for a while.

Political Issue-drivers

LEARNING ③
OBJECTIVE

Politics and economics are closely connected. Political decisions affect economic environments directly and indirectly, as well as other aspects of life. Politics is therefore an issue-driver. Nonetheless, political issue-drivers need to be considered explicitly. Mature and sophisticated nations operate within relatively stable democratic frameworks involving free and regular elections and well-established law-making processes. In emerging nations democratic processes may be those that mature nations would not accept. Senior politicians may theoretically be subject to democratic control by election, yet in practice be impossible to remove from office peacefully. Policies often derive from self-interest, while preferment depends on affiliations and bribes.

National political systems are therefore significant aspects of enterprise environments. In particular:

- Political environments may be sympathetic or obstructive towards the aims and presence of an enterprise.

- Political stability affects financial risk, asset security (and possible confiscation), employee safety from physical attack. or arbitrary detention.

- The scope for and felt-need to lobby government ministers to make decisions that favour the enterprise. Alternatively, the extent of corruption among politicians and bureaucrats, which affects when, how and at what cost business activities can be conducted.

- Policies and politically imposed constraints that affect enterprise activities such as those imposed by bureaucracy and politically sensitive planning enquiries.

External Stakeholders as Issue-drivers

EARNING ⓷
BJECTIVE

Enterprise stakeholders can be powerful issue-drivers in any of the ScanStep© fields when they become active and vocal advocates for or against change. Accordingly, it is helpful to identify the influential stakeholders in each field. This feature is in included in Figure 2.3. By examining each ScanStep© field in turn, the possibility of missing a key issue is reduced.

Chapter 4 reviews the management of stakeholders in some detail. For our purposes here, the particularly influential stakeholders groups include:

- Clients (customers).
- Suppliers, major subcontractors and service providers.
- Owners (shareholders).
- Employees and trade unions.
- Banks.
- National and local governments and their executive agencies.
- Ethically-motivated groups.
- Single-interest pressure groups.

Traditional corporate accountability and reporting assumes that shareholder interests dominate. Recognising the multiplicity of enterprise stakeholders broadens the focus, which generates new kinds of issue for enterprises. An example is the 'triple bottom line' (TBL) model of ethical, corporate social responsibility summarised as 'people, planet, profits.'[9] The argument is that sustainable capitalism requires attention to the impact of enterprises on the *planet* and *people* as well as *profits*, extending the range of issues needing to be addressed. Progressive companies now routinely report their '3P' impact, which will probably be integrated into future statutory reporting for both for-profit and not-for-profit corporations.

Methods for Scanning and Assessing the Macro Environment

EARNING ⓷
BJECTIVE

Competent environmental analysis requires a thorough, systematic and continuing approach, rather than relying on the impressions of senior executives and what they can learn from their advisors, colleagues and ad-hoc sources.

Any enterprise has to balance its desire for information and certainty with the effort, cost, timeliness and potential value of its acquisition. All future events and trends have associated uncertainty. To justify enhanced knowledge through further enquiry the expected value of additional evidence needs to be assessed and to be substantial and reliable. Incurring high costs to acquire speculative estimates and predictions is a poor investment.

Ideally, forecasts and assumptions should be explicit and quantitative so that their validity can then be checked as new and better facts emerge in the future. Forecasts, estimates and guess-work do not eliminate predictive uncertainty although they may reduce it. Single-point forecasts convey an undeserved impression of accuracy. Forecasts should indicate a *range* of outcomes rather than single points and, ideally, the probability of each outcome in the range.

Scanning Processes

LEARNING ③
OBJECTIVE

The sheer complexity of the external macro environment means that enterprises need to approach analysis systematically but *selectively*. They need to decide what fields and issues to prioritise and be prepared to revise their priorities as new data emerge.

Figure 2.4 indicates a generic monitoring process that draws on both *secondary* (published) data from a wide range of external sources including newspapers, journals, websites, published reports, and *primary* (commissioned) sources tasked to investigate specific topics such as trends in natural environmental research and thinking.

Direct observations can also be made, to the extent that they be practicable, legal and ethically acceptable. For example, a chief executive told one of the authors that from time to time he instructed a salesman to sit in his car all day outside his main competitor's factory to count the number of trucks leaving so that the company could estimate its current output!

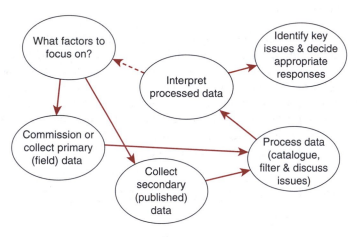

Figure 2.4: Macro-environmental scanning processes

Scanning and analysis that draw on publicly available data can be done 'in house'. Employees can also attend specific interest conferences and seminars hosted by relevant consultants, government agencies and academics. Other activities can be subcontracted to outside research agencies with the necessary skills and contacts. The use of external agencies and experts is appropriate for both regular and one-off scanning activities.

However, when data have been collected, the evidence needs still be organised and interpreted. Initial interpretations may rely on external experts, but enterprise managers are ultimately responsible for drawing conclusions and making strategic decisions. These processes almost always combine objective and subjective aspects.[10]

Risk Assessment

To avoid premature and possibly misguided conclusions, analysts must consider critically the accuracy of available facts about the environment and the reliability of predictions and forecasts of potential events or trends. As previously discussed, *predictive* uncertainty always exists over *whether* a future event or trend will materialise and the consequences for a particular enterprise if they do. This requires assessments of potential impact *severity* as well as the *probability* of occurrence.

EARNING ②
BJECTIVE One common approach to risk management is impact–probability assessment. The aim is to estimate the range of possible impacts of an event or trend on the enterprise (expressed in a relevant form – often money) and the probability that each outcome in the estimated range will occur. The result is an impact–probability graph (Figure 2.5) that indicates the total 'risk exposure.' (The total risk exposure is indicated by the area under the curve expressed in the appropriate units.) It forms a basis for decisions about risk reduction or elimination, as indicated in the following illustration.

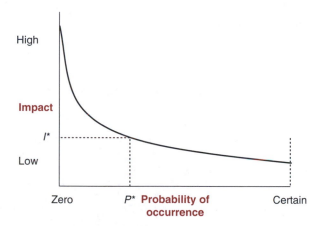

Figure 2.5: An impact–probability graph

Take sea-level rise due to global warming as an example. An international import and export enterprise that uses a Bangladeshi seaport might conclude that even small rises in sea level could affect port operations and construct an impact assessment graph of risk like the one above. The probability of a *massive* impact (e.g., a 1.5-metre rise in sea level in the next 150 years) would be relatively low, whereas a range of lesser impacts would be likely. A practical unit of impact could be the fraction of each working day during which the port cannot operate, delaying shipments and damaging revenues. The area under the curve sums the total anticipated impact on port operations and hence on the enterprise's business in these terms. Of greatest significance, however, would be the concern that the impact rises above some critical level (e.g., the port facilities become unusable for more than half of each working day). This is shown as $I*$ in Figure 2.5, the point where impact severity starts to escalate. The analysis can then focus on estimating the probability $P*$ associated with $I*$, apparently about 30%. If (as seems plausible) a risk event with a probability of 30% or greater is considered a significant threat, the enterprise must consider seriously what actions would be appropriate to mitigate the impact of port flooding, when they must be initiated and what consequences would arise from these actions.

Futures Modelling Using Scenario Development

Risk assessment is based on the assumption that impacts and probabilities can be quantified. Qualitative scenario development aims to identify, describe and assess the implications of a future situation or scenario that is so unfamiliar or alien, indeed hitherto unimaginable, that attempts at quantification would be pure speculation.

A scenario envisions a distinctive future state to which there is no obvious pathway from the present – a discontinuity. Once analysts have conceived this 'future', they can flesh out a plausible description of its potential characteristics. This is called creating a story or narrative. They can then debate its possible impact on their enterprise and therefore what to do next. An attractive scenario prompts the question: 'how do we make this real?' A threatening scenario prompts: 'how do we make sure this *doesn't* occur. Posing and addressing questions like these has been called 'the art of strategic conversation'.[11]

Shell's pioneering use of scenario analysis

A classic example of scenario analysis is provided by Shell's use of scenarios in the 1970s to assess how it would cope with previously unimaginable events such as a massive, unexpected and sudden rise in the cost of crude oil.[12] Such an event had not then happened, though it has since occurred several times.

By developing scenarios Shell was able to envision proactive strategies that competitors did not. It took the major strategic decision to focus on higher value-added, 'downstream' activities that would reduce the adverse profit impact of much higher cost oil and generate additional revenue and profits growth for the business. Those competitors that were totally unprepared for the 1973 'oil crisis' lost ground which it then took more than a decade to regain.

A practical way to begin scenario planning is to identify a critical uncertainty (or uncertainties) for the future. At its 2009 Davos meeting, the World Economic Forum of national leaders and financial authorities explored the future development of the global financial system with reference to two global uncertainties:

1. The shift of economic power from west to east: slow or fast?
2. Co-ordination of the global financial system: well-co-ordinated and harmonised or ad hoc and discordant?

Combining the alternative possibilities yielded four outline scenarios for critical discussion, namely:

- Slow shift, high co-ordination.
- Slow shift, low co-ordination.
- Fast shift, high co-ordination.
- Fast shift, low co-ordination.

CASE STUDY: The macro environment of Airbus Industrie and the A380

Airbus began life in the 1960s as a complicated joint venture supported by various European plane makers and their respective governments, led by the French.[13] It was a political project in so far as Europe feared the near-monopoly in passenger aircraft of US Boeing Corporation. Airbus saw potential for a twin-engine passenger aircraft, smaller and more fuel-efficient than the large, wide-body 747 'Jumbo' that Boeing was developing. The Airbus A300 first flew in October 1972. After a slow start, demand accelerated and A300 expanded into a series of aircraft. Airbus' success forced Boeing to develop the rival 777 twinjet, yet by the early 1990s Airbus was winning as many orders for new aircraft as Boeing.

In 2000 Airbus became a conventional share-based company owned 80% by the European Aeronautics Defence and Space (EADS) company[14] and 20% by British BAE Systems. It immediately decided to develop a 'Superjumbo', the A380, with the potential to carry up to 850 passengers, depending on internal seat layout. In 2006 EADS became the sole owner of Airbus. The A380 made its first commercial flight in 2007. Capable of flying over 8000 nautical miles without refuelling, the A380 would be ideal for long-haul passengers and freight applications. By 2009, A380 production was several years behind its contracted delivery schedule and some airlines cancelled their orders. The survival and future success of Airbus, including the employment of 57,000 people at 16 sites in France, Germany, UK and Spain, depended critically on A380 meeting its sales targets over the medium and longer term.

Airbus and Boeing focus on medium- and long-haul jet aircraft with 100+ seats. They sell to airlines and leasing companies. High profile international airlines like British Airways, Virgin and Emirates buy and lease aircraft from Airbus and Boeing. No-frills (budget) airlines like easyJet, Ryanair, and JetBlue buy new aircraft, while other airlines constitute a substantial second-hand market. Leasing allows airlines to limit their capital investment in aircraft and provides flexibility to increase or decrease fleet numbers in line with demand. Private corporations and travel firms also use short/medium term leasing for charter flights.

Aircrafts have long lives (25+ years), but need very costly, regular maintenance. Many spend parts of their lives 'mothballed' waiting for a new operator to lease or buy them. The cycles of economic activity make demand for new aircraft volatile – new aircraft compete with pre-used ones whose lease costs are lower.

Each new aircraft type tends to be quieter, more fuel efficient, reliable and have lower maintenance costs than its predecessor, giving airlines the incentive to update their fleets. But the cost of developing a new aircraft is huge. In future any serious competition for the Boeing/Airbus duopoly will come either from an integrated Russian aircraft corporation or the Chinese. All of the contenders make military as well as passenger aircraft. Various other companies make smaller passenger aircraft (jets and turboprops) with up to 100 seats; executive jets typically with up to 10 seats; and propeller-driven light aircraft with six seats or fewer. Turboprop aircraft are ideal for regional (inter-city) air transport, being fuel-efficient, generally quieter and needing shorter runways than jets to take off and land.

Questions

1. Using the above study and additional recent, relevant data sources, use the ScanStep© worksheet to analyse the macro environment that Airbus faces, with particular reference to issues that may affect the A380.

2. Assess which of the issues identified represent the most positive and most negative influences on Airbus. Reflect on the impact–probability profiles of these issues.[15]

Summary

- Environmental uncertainty can arise from the characteristics of complexity, dynamism and hostility.

- It is difficult to assess fully the future implications of the macro environment on a particular enterprise. Precisely because the macro level contains issue-drivers in multiple fields it frequently acts *indirectly* as well as directly on enterprises.

- Potential issue-drivers exist in eight ScanStep© fields. This framework was presented as a practical worksheet that can be applied to the analysis of macro environments, for example, with reference to a particular enterprise such as Airbus Industrie, featured in the closing case study.

- The chapter also contained short accounts of various methods to examine possible events and trends in enterprise environments. Further market- and sector-analyses are considered in Chapter 3.

Exercises for Further Study and Discussion

1. Do research to establish the kinds of environmental scanning and assessment companies actually perform.[16] What link, if any, can you find between extent of environmental scanning and business performance?
2. Focus on emerging macro environmental trends in the ScanStep© fields that most interest you. Assess their possible implications for the following types of enterprises: [a] An international manufacturing corporation; [b] A retail banking group; [c] A university that relies on overseas students for a high proportion of its income.
3. Reflect on the assumptions you made in the previous exercise: how can their validity be tested practically?
4. Reflect critically on the following statement: 'progressive, innovative enterprises do *not* react or respond to trends, they establish them. So environmental scanning is of limited strategic value to such enterprises.'
5. Examine other accounts of the successes of scenario analysis.[17] Are you persuaded or has hindsight been invoked in support of the claims made for this technique?

Suggestions for Further Reading

Burt, G., Wright, G., Bradfield, R. and van der Heijden, K. (2006) 'The role of scenario planning in exploring the environment in view of the limitations of PEST and its derivatives', *International Studies of Management and Organization* (vol. 36/3, pp. 50–76).

Capon, C. (2004) *Understanding Organizational Context*, Prentice Hall (chapter 8: 'The external environment'; and chapter 9: 'The composition of the external environment').

Duncan, R.B. (1972) 'Characteristics of organizational environments and perceived environmental uncertainty', *Administrative Science Quarterly* (vol. 17/3, pp. 313–327).

Finlay, P. (2000) *Strategic Management*, Prentice-Hall (chapter 11 on scenarios).

Gillespie, A. (2007) *Foundation of Economics*, Oxford University Press – Additional web chapter on PESTLE analysis of the macro environment at: http://www.oup.com/uk/orc/bin/9780199296378/01student/additional/page_12.htm

Hough, J.R. and White, M.A. (2004) 'Scanning actions and environmental dynamism: gathering information for strategic decision making', *Management Decision* (vol. 42, pp. 781–793).

Milliken, F.J. (1987) 'Three types of perceived uncertainty about environment: state, effect, and response uncertainty', *Academy of Management Review* (vol. 12/1, pp. 133–143).

Schlange, L.E. and Jüttner, U. (1997) 'Helping managers to identify strategic issues', *Long Range Planning* (vol. 30/5, pp. 777–786).

Wack, P. (1985) 'Scenarios: uncharted waters ahead', *Harvard Business Review* (Sep/Oct, pp. 73–90).

Xu, X.M., Kaye, G.R. and Duan, Y. (2003) 'UK executives' vision on business environment for information scanning: A cross industry study', *Information and Management* (vol. 40/5, pp. 381–389).

Notes

1 Source: Brunel University website: http://www.brunel.ac.uk/8291/memorials/greenhouses.pdf. To see the kind of enterprise Lowe & Shawyer might have become, visit http://www.world-flowers.co.uk

2 Some suppliers offer all of these device types, some specialise in only one or two, e.g., *Pure* makes only DAB radios; *Nokia* specialises in mobiles.

3 The travel and transport sectors suffer badly from such events, as affected EuroStar in 2008 and the airline industry in Europe in 2010.

4 This is discussed in Chapter 4. See also Buysse and Verbeke (2003) for a constructive view of stakeholder management.

5 Duncan (1972), Miller and Friesen (1983), Mintzberg (1983), Milliken (1987), and Ginter and Duncan (1990) provide insightful discussions of types of environment and their implications for enterprises.

6 A dynamic environment has significant managerial implications, e.g., Morgan (1988); Garg, Walters and Priem (2003); Peteraf and Bergen (2003); Hough and White (2004).

7 Although misclassification can worry people new to environmental analysis, the priority is to *identify* issues of concern via the framework, more important than *how an issue is actually categorised*.

8 The obligations of private companies are less onerous. Moreover, anomalies remain. In Britain the plc Chairman and Chief Executive can still be the same person, despite this practice being widely considered inappropriate.

9 Elkington (1999).

10 Much has been written about how executive managers identify and interpret issues in their environments (and how they are advised to do so), e.g., Ansoff (1975; 1980); Capps and Hazen (2002); Daft, Sormunen and Parks (1988); Day and Schoemaker (2008); Hough and White (2004); Jackson and Dutton (1998); Lansiluoto and Eklund (2008); Lyles (1987); Schlange and Jüttner (1997); Schneider and De Meyer (1991); Smart and Vertinsky (1984); Sutcliffe and Huber (1998).

11 See van der Heijden (1996); van der Heijden et al. (2002).

12 See Wack (1985).

13 http://www.centennialofflight.gov/essay/Aerospace/Airbus/Aero52.htm

14 EADS Company was itself a consolidation of various European national aviation businesses. See http://www.eads.com

15 Suggestion: apply an index of 1–10 to indicate the severity of the impact you would expect of the issue identified *if it should occur* (1 = little/none to 10 = major). Also assign a percentage probability to its occurrence. For each issue, multiply the impact factor by the probability to establish the issues that merit the greatest attention.

16 Many academic journals, magazines and newspaper articles, and company websites, etc. can help you to accumulate evidence. For example: Baron (2006); Elenkov (1997); Garg, Walters and Priem (2003); Grant (2003); Kefalas and Schoderbeck (1973); Kourteli (2005); Engledow and Lenz (1985); Lenz and Engledow (1986); Xu, Kaye and Duan (2003).

17 In addition to the references cited already, see: Burt et al. (2006); chapter 14 of McGee, Thomas and Wilson (2005); Mercer (1998); Schoemaker (1995); Walsh (2005).

3

Industry Sector Environments

Learning Outcomes

This chapter is designed to enable you to:

① Describe the main characteristics of markets and sectors, including (a) structural features, (b) external factors and, in particular, (c) entry and exit barriers.

② Understand the strategic implications of the above.

③ Understand supply chains and their strategic implications.

④ Understand (a) influences on demand and (b) lifecycles in demand.

⑤ Analyse markets and competitive behaviour, especially through the application of Porter's 5-forces model.

CASE STUDY: The global bicycle industry

Historically, many countries made bicycles, primarily for local sale. Between 1950 and 2000 annual global output rose five-fold, peaking at 130 million in 2007, stabilizing at 100–110 million.[1] More than a billion bicycles are used worldwide, half in China. High volume production now centres on China, Taiwan, India and Vietnam, which together make 5 of every 6 bicycles worldwide. China has 60% of global output and exports two-thirds of its production. Output in the United States, Japan and the European Union has declined substantially.

With 5 million units of annual output each, Giant of Taiwan and Hero Cycles of India are the world's biggest manufacturers. TI Cycles of India produces 3 million units annually using the former British brands, Hercules and BSA.[2] Other volume suppliers such as Raleigh (UK) and Dahon (USA) rely on manufacturers in the far east. The latter produces a wide variety of bicycle types marketed with their own names as well as those of their client companies. Many makers have expanded into moped and motorcycle production.

Hundreds of smaller enterprises produce specialized, high-quality bicycles and major components (frames, wheels, gears, etc.) often using advanced, lightweight materials including titanium alloys and carbon composites. Customers can specify bicycles to their individual requirements. Annual output from small enterprises is around 100,000 units in the UK (e.g., Boardman, Moulton, and Pashley); and 200,000 units in the United States (e.g., Cannondale, Marin, and Specialized).

In poor countries the bicycle is the main personal mobility alternative to walking. Using annual global output of units as a proxy for demand indicates that demand equates to 1.9% penetration of world population, a percentage that varies considerably by country (Table 3.A). In China and India economic development is leading to a substantial switch to motorcycles and cars.

Table 3.A: Annual sales of bicycles in selected countries

Country	Units×1000*	Market penetration as % of population**
Japan	10,600	8.3
USA	18,200	5.8
Germany	4580	5.6
UK	3400	5.6
Brazil	2500	1.3
China	13,600	1.0
India	10,000	0.9

* Statistics vary between 2006 and 2008.
** Estimates based mostly on 2008 data. Source: Wikipedia.
Main source: bike-eu.com

In wealthy countries unit sales of bicycles are relatively stable, generally purchased more for leisure, sport and exercise than for transport (excepting perhaps in some highly congested cities). Bicycles for children are also much in demand. Annual UK demand has fluctuated between 3.2 and 3.5 million units in recent years, met by almost 100 competing brands of bicycles and major components.[3] Average retail prices of mass-produced bicycles are quite low – typically less than the equivalent of US$150–200.[4]

Given the differences in consumer behaviours among poor and wealthy countries, the bicycle market is best understood country by country. Production statistics provide few insights into buyers' preferences or usage patterns. It is helpful to analyse demand segments by using demographic and other variables such as age groups (e.g., children; teenagers; young adults, mature adults) and gender. This approach offers producers insights into what kinds of products are desired, such as frame and wheel sizes, weight, accessories and cosmetic features. It is of even greater help to consider market segments based on *usage patterns* (applications). Examples include:

- Functional, robust bicycles for everyday transport, sometimes with electric motor assistance.
- Children's bicycles (and tricycles) for play.
- Ultra-lightweight machines for competitive racing on road or track.
- Rugged bicycles for off-road use, both leisure and competition, variously called mountain bikes (MTBs), all-terrain mountain bikes, trail bikes and BMXs.

Differing usage patterns create very different expectations of design appropriate to each demand segment. Segmentation is based on specification, performance and price. In wealthy countries the MTB segment has been the fastest-growing over the last 20 years, taking market share particularly from leisure/touring bikes. Demand for folding bicycles has also grown significantly; some suppliers like Dahon offer only folders. In this segment a variety of innovative designs exist, including the unusual Strida, which retails for about £400 in a UK segment where prices span from £200 to over £1000.

Segments overlap because some consumers have multiple patterns of use. Consider the Strida and advanced Pashley TSR-Moulton, which retail for £1000 upwards: both function as lightweight, leisure bicycles; yet they collapse for easy commuting on public transport. Though some potential buyers may see these bicycles as alternatives, that is not how the Pashley TSR-Moulton is positioned in the market.

The main outlets for mass-produced bicycles are specialist multiple retailers (e.g., Halfords in the UK), mass-market retailers (e.g., Walmart), mail order and internet retailers. The highly specialised brands feature in dedicated bicycle stores, mostly independents, and are also marketed directly to the buyer. As in other product categories, independent retail outlets emphasise their ability to offer expert advice and service, but have tended to lose share to other channels that price aggressively.

Tasks and discussion questions

Describe your main purchase motives and characteristics as a potential buyer of a folding bicycle. Identify and analyse alternative products you would consider, beyond the Strida and Pashley TSR-Moulton.

Introduction: Market and Industry Sector Environments

Chapter 2 examined external influences on the enterprise, with particular reference to the broad-level macro environment. Here we focus on the more direct influences on the enterprise that derive from its markets (clienteles) and the industry sector in which it operates and competes. Markets and sectors are influenced by the macro environment, conveying *indirect* as well as direct influences. Thus, it is important to understand all of these influences in greater detail.

LEARNING ①
OBJECTIVE
The industry sector and the demand for its offerings (i.e., the market) are complementary features of a dynamic, interdependent economic system. One provides the supply, the other demand. Every sector has *structural* and *behavioural* characteristics attributable specifically to the array of enterprises within it. Similarly, market demand has *structural* and *behavioural* characteristics attributable specifically to the nature of the buyers and potential buyers.

Over time, the various behaviours of sector enterprises – such as to innovation, resistance to change, competition, or collaboration (so-called 'enterprise conduct') – modify the structure of the sector. External pressures, notably market preferences, regulation and predatory actions by other capable enterprises also shape its structure. As the prevailing structure changes, it affects the conduct of constituent enterprises by introducing new products and services, technologies and business processes, and by obliging conformance to industry norms, constraints and expectations. Over the medium and longer term, changes to structure and conduct create a dynamic, interactive, *duality* (Figure 3.1) that affects all enterprises in the sector. The effect is to generate, individually and collectively, strategic opportunities and threats. Enterprises can therefore change size significantly or cease trading. Entire sectors can decline, be transformed, or even disappear.

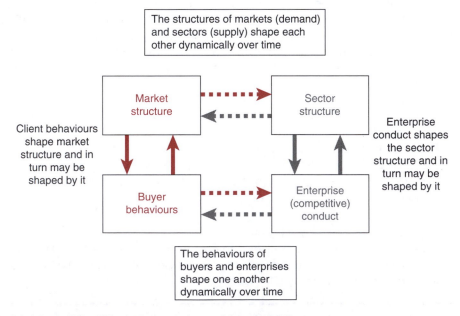

Figure 3.1: Interactivity of the industry sector and the market it serves

For-profit enterprises have consumers and/or business customers; not-for-profit enterprises and professional services normally refer to clients, patients, recipients or beneficiaries rather than buyers. Over time, client behaviours alter demand structures while prevailing structures can also shape attitudes, choices and consequent behaviours. Enterprises that do not notice and respond to structural demand changes and behavioural trends effectively ignore emerging threats and opportunities.

A proactive sector seeks to adapt to its changing market, but also to shape demand patterns in line with its structure and capabilities. These mutual dynamics affect the performance of individual enterprises, although the relationships are complex and outcomes in individual cases can be hard to predict. The purpose of industry sector analysis is to highlight future strategic opportunities and threats from the perspective of a focal enterprise, encouraging its successful development and the avoidance of mistakes and failures.[5]

Changes to structure and enterprise conduct: examples from the airline industry

Emergence of a set of 'no-frills' airlines like easyJet following European Union deregulation of the industry (structure change)

'No-frills' airlines fly selected point-to-point routes to maximise profits, rather than apply the more traditional 'hub-and-spokes' model (conduct change)

Changes to demand structure and market behaviour in UK education

UK demand for pre-university education has developed a more segmented structure within both private and state provision as parents seek learning environments that offer distinctive approaches to tuition, specialised facilities, minority religious affiliations, etc. (structural development).

Motivated by perceived shortcomings in state-funded education, far-from wealthy parents afford private school fees for their children by economising on family expenditures such as costly holidays and through increased debt (behaviour change).

This chapter reviews strategically important market and sector concepts, including the widely applied '5-forces' model of competitive industry sectors. Although the underlying *principles* of analysis are straightforward, the *practical* challenge for enterprise strategists is to grapple with strategic issues and possibilities while attending to a multitude of more immediate 'real time' priorities. Moreover, imperfect knowledge often prevents precise analysis of complex and fast-changing systems. Nonetheless, the systematic use of appropriate analytic frameworks enhances the prospects of identifying significant issues.

Factors that drive Industry Sector Structure and Enterprise Conduct

To appreciate the strategic potential of an enterprise, one must understand how its sector is developing over time. Thus the structure of the sector and the conduct of its enterprises must be studied. The most commonly cited approach is via the so-called '5-forces' model. This model, created by Michael Porter, emphasises the systemic forces that drive competitive enterprise conduct (rivalry) in a sector.[6] It is shown in adapted form in Figure 3.2, which makes explicit the various forms of autonomous enterprise conduct. This figure provides the structure for our discussion below.

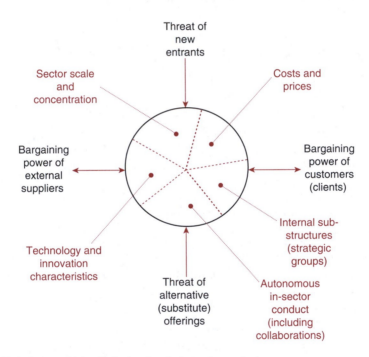

Figure 3.2: Multiple forces driving industry structure and conduct

LEARNING ①
OBJECTIVE   Sector development derives from the following three sources of influence:

1. Managerially generated decisions about enterprise conduct driven by their strategic ambitions and the scope of an enterprise to act autonomously in its particular circumstances, for example, by internal or external collaborations.

2. The internal structural features of the sector that enable and/or constrain this scope.
3. The factors external to the sector that bear differentially on each enterprise in it.

Enterprises have considerable autonomy to act in whatever ways their managers consider feasible and appropriate (subject to the acquiescence of other stakeholders). Many forms of enterprise conduct increase collective rivalry, as when each enterprise strives to implement strategies to capture a greater share of the core value-adding and supply activities of the sector. Ambitions and egos drive potentially subjective, unpredictable decisions as enterprises jockey for position. The more effective enterprises capture more of the value-added potential, achieving greater surpluses to reinvest for the future and generally benefiting their clienteles. Unsuccessful enterprises decline, quit or ultimately fail. Later chapters explore the many forms of strategy that underpin these enterprise actions.

Many structural features of a sector account for the second source of influence on enterprise conduct. The third source is the combination of *external* forces acting on the sector that derive from demand patterns and the actions of enterprises in related (and sometimes unrelated) sectors. In principle the impact of all these factors should be predictable because they are objectively identifiable. The reality of doing so presents challenges.

Structural Characteristics of Industry Sectors

RNING ①
JECTIVE
The structure of an industry sector has several strategically important features. These include:

*   Sector concentration (number of enterprises and relative shares of activity).

*   Cost and price structures (scale and scope economies).

*   Technology regimes and accumulated experience.

*   The potential for alternative (substitutional) and complementary offerings, technologies and processes.

*   Sector sub-groupings (strategic groups).

*   Within-enterprise value-adding chains (discussed in depth in Chapter 5).

Sector Concentration

Far-sighted entrepreneurs can instigate new industry sectors. Initially their enterprises enjoy a dominant position, but their pioneering efforts encourage new entrants. This increases supply capacity, potentially exceeding demand. When too many enterprises chase limited demand, prices fall close to the floor defined by unit costs. When many suppliers operate at, or even below, this 'break-even' level (so-called perfect competition), some ultimately quit or become bankrupt. The remaining, more effective suppliers increase in size and develop better offerings or other forms of advantage, such as reputations for quality and reliability. It is difficult to predict how great the reduction in numbers will be in each case. Over the years, even decades, concentration generally increases, although several stable states can emerge.

Alternative, stable competitive states[7]

Near-perfect competition: a low concentration of enterprises with no dominant competitors

- Dozens of websites make personalised jigsaw puzzles from consumers' photographs.
- The London Escort Guide lists hundreds of agencies and 4000+ individual escorts.

Oligopoly: a limited number of stable, well-resourced enterprises

- Pearson Education, Wiley-Blackwell, McGraw-Hill, Cengage Learning, Palgrave Macmillan, and the Oxford and Cambridge University Presses have a dominant share of textbook publishing.[8] The non-university enterprises are the product of multiple mergers and acquisitions.

Duopoly: two dominant competitors

- Procter & Gamble and Unilever dominate the supply of detergents in Europe.

Near-monopoly: a single, usually very powerful enterprise

- Microsoft dominates computer operating systems (Windows) and web browser software (Internet Explorer), despite the presence of Apple and Linux and losing anti-competition court cases in the United States and Europe.

A single-enterprise monopoly is considered so undesirable for consumers that most countries have laws to prevent them, or regulate them when there is no practical alternative.

LEARNING OBJECTIVE ① Sector concentration is the proportion of supply controlled by the most dominant enterprises. Measures called concentration ratios are widely used, being the combined percentage share of the largest X suppliers where X is variously 4, 5, 8, 10 or 15.

In the bicycle industry (opening case study) the global 5-supplier concentration ratio is 15–20%, which is relatively low in a mature sector. Although the five biggest producers are powerful they do not dominate output to the extent observed in some industries. Concentration ratios are often calculated within a particular *country* (e.g., Table 3.B), although regional and global calculations are becoming more important strategically.[9]

Table 3.B: Five-supplier UK concentration ratios

Highest five-firm concentration ratios		Lowest five-firm concentration ratios	
Sugar	99%	Metal forging, pressing, etc.	4%
Tobacco products	99%	Plastic products	4%
Oils and fats	88%	Misc. service activities	4%
Gas distribution	82%	Furniture	5%
Confectionery	81%	Construction	5%

Source: Office for National Statistics (ONS) *Economic Trends 635* October 2006 available at: http://www. statistics.gov.uk/articles/economic_trends/ET635Mahajan_Concentration_Ratios_2004.pdf and also at: http://en.wikipedia.org/wiki/Concentration_ratio#cite_note-statistics.gov.uk-4, based on 2004 data.

The *relative* shares of large enterprises also matters. Consider two hypothetical sectors with five-firm ratios of 60%:

- Sector 1: Enterprise A: 20%; B: 16%; C: 13%; and D: 11%.
- Sector 2: Enterprise A: 30%; B, C, D: 10% each.

The first case indicates vigorous competition. The second suggests dominance by enterprise 'A' that would prompt interest by the competition authorities in many countries.

From the strategic perspective of an enterprise, vigorous competition is unattractive. Fierce contests to satisfy demand increase costs and reduce the profitability of all the enterprises, reducing scope for future investment. So a strategy that distinguishes an enterprise, reducing the intensity of the rivalry it experiences, is highly desirable.

Cost and Price Structures

Vigorous competition ensures that prices remain linked realistically to costs, so becoming a prime strategic issue. Fewer competitors makes it easier, all else being equal, for enterprises to raise prices well above unit costs; yet these profitable suppliers may become complacent, offer poor quality products, inadequate customer service and cease to innovate. Over time, most enterprises face inflationary cost pressures. To pass cost increases to customers as higher prices can damage demand, so proactive enterprises seek to control and ideally reduce unit costs. If successful, unit prices can then be held or reduced while maintaining profit margins, enhancing competitiveness. The alternative is to minimise market sensitivity to price by effective differentiation, limiting the pressures to reduce costs. (Appropriate strategies are explored in Chapter 8.)

Price Elasticity: the Price–Volume Trade-off

LEARNING ①
OBJECTIVE

LEARNING ④
OBJECTIVE

A link exists between the price of a specific product or service and the level of demand for it. As unit price increases, demand generally decreases and vice versa. Price elasticity is calculated as an index:

% change in demand / % corresponding change in unit price

For normal goods and services the result will be a negative number (i.e., demand falls when prices go up). For example, if a 10% increase in the price of air travel results in a 15% decrease in demand, the index is −1.5 (as −15/10 = −1.5). The more negative the number, the more *elastic* the demand. When demand is elastic, small price rises reduce demand significantly, and vice versa.

An index closer to zero indicates *inelastic* demand, meaning that price hardly affects demand. Generally speaking, economists interpret an index between 0 and −1 as inelastic, and anything lower as elastic. Unusually, a substantial price increase could *enhance* the perceived desirability of a product and therefore *increase* demand, creating a positive index.

Price elasticity is strategically important *over the long term*. If lower prices are predicted to increase future demand substantially, enterprises have an incentive to increase output and gain share by reducing prices. The challenge is to reduce unit costs without harming perceived quality or desirability. Conversely, inelastic demand encourages enterprises to increase price progressively over time, ideally supported by effective marketing to enhance perceived desirability.

Scale Economies and Minimum Efficient Scale (MES)

The key drivers of cost need to be considered. Costs arise in two forms:

- *Fixed* costs that do not change over a defined, future time-period (e.g., rent on premises).
- *Variable* costs linked directly to output, rising in proportion to the level of activity.

LEARNING ①
OBJECTIVE

As output activity *per time period* increases, the *average* unit cost for that time period *falls* because the fixed costs are spread over greater output. This is known as economy of scale.[10] Figure 3.3 illustrates how average unit cost is linked to output level. It declines rapidly as output rises from a low base, indicating scale economies. As output increases further, the curve flattens and ultimately rises as *diseconomies* of scale occur. Facilities become overcrowded and disorganized; mistakes are made more frequently; effort is wasted correcting faults; unsold inventories create storage costs.

LEARNING ①
OBJECTIVE

The minimum Efficient scale (MES) of an activity is the *output level per time period* (i.e., rate) at which the lowest average total unit cost is achieved *with current methods*. To be fully cost-competitive an enterprise must achieve this minimum rate of output. The fraction of total output that equates to the MES determines how many competitors can be cost-competitive (efficient) and expect to survive long term. For example, if the MES is 10%, then in theory, 10 suppliers can achieve cost-effective output levels. If the MES is 50%, then only two enterprises can be fully efficient. More typically, the volume-leading enterprise comfortably exceeds the MES while several others operate inefficiently.

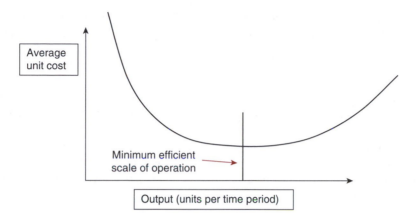

Figure 3.3: Cost curve linked to scale

In labour-intensive industries, such as shoes and clothing, the MES may be only a few percent of output. In capital-intensive industries such as steel-making or satellite construction, the MES represents 20–30% of the output demanded in a large country such as the United States, almost the entire saleable output in the UK or France, and greatly exceeds demand in small developed countries and in large, under-developed countries. Production, especially of capital-intensive sectors, is therefore located in countries where demand is substantial relative to the MES.

When demand is high, market prices rise sufficiently to allow the highest cost (least efficient) suppliers to balance unit cost and price (hence break-even or make modest profits). The most efficient suppliers are very profitable at the same price because of lower unit costs. When demand falls, the average unit costs of less efficient suppliers rise; they probably cannot increase prices, so they become loss-making. The more efficient suppliers increase their share of supply and ultimately eject the inefficient competitors from the sector.

Scope Economies

ARNING ①
JECTIVE

All but the smallest enterprises engage in multiple activities, kinds of product or service, operations, geographic locations or sectors. Multiple activities or functions can usually share some fixed costs. The more sharing that occurs, the lower the average fixed cost *per activity*, yielding *economy of scope*.[11]

An enterprise that functions in two distinct locations can invest in one factory to supply both locations, or promote one television advertisement with a dedicated voice-over for each market. Scope economies reduce average unit costs and contribute to create experience effects.

Technology Regimes and Accumulated Experience

In practice, sector cost curves such as that shown in Figure 3.3 do not persist indefinitely. Major changes in processes and technologies create critical transitions or discontinuities, rewarding the early adopters that achieve larger scale of operations. This is because new approaches incur large development costs that must be recovered through either higher prices or higher volumes. The effect is to revise the cost-curve associated with the current best practice (the 'regime'). Major, sometimes radical, changes in processes and technologies – the methods and techniques used to make goods and deliver services – can produce great efficiency improvements. They merit the label of new *technology regime.*

LEARNING ⓘ
OBJECTIVE

Consider the following example of regimes. A restaurant that can serve 50 diners per sitting would need huge changes to its dining facilities and work practices to serve 500 or 5,000 diners. Yet all three kinds of restaurant are relatively common. The effect of different regimes on the cost curve is shown in Figure 3.4 for three regimes A, B and C. Regime C shows the greatest potential for lowest average total unit cost, but is almost certainly the most capital intensive. Accordingly, it succeeds only when its actual output rate is much higher than regimes A and B have the potential for.

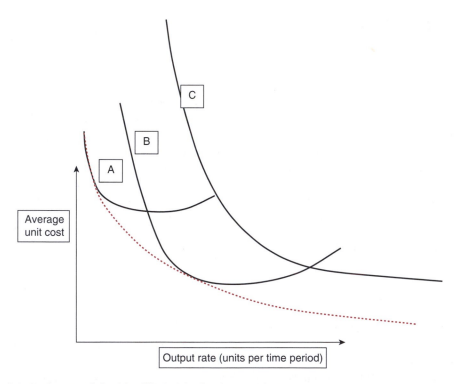

Figure 3.4: Cost curves linked to different technology regimes

Multiple regimes and associated cost-curves can co-exist, sometimes for many years, as the examples of e-mail and 'snail mail' indicate. Unfortunately, for postal operators, the cost of handling a letter is escalating while the cost of an e-mail is so low that charges are linked to internet access, not the number of e-mails sent. Thus a new regime can rapidly displace an old: microchip and car makers periodically introduce new technology 'generations' that fundamentally change both products and production processes. Radical advances in medical treatments occur, such as in eye or liver surgery. Advantage (and reputation) often goes to the first enterprise to adopt a new regime.

Continuous cost reduction (compression) is strategically attractive. It can be a deliberate strategy when an enterprise achieves greater scale economies by achieving *and* selling increased output – enabled by means of new technology and by staff who are committed to learn how to perform activities better (more efficiently).

Practical studies of a wide range of sectors show that as the units of output or activity of a sector *doubles*, the average total unit cost *falls* by 20–30%.[12] This has become known as *economy of learning* or *experience*. The impact of experience on cost compression can be shown graphically as the *learning* or *experience curve*, shown in Figure 3.5.

In Figure 3.5a the relationship between average unit cost and output is represented by a curve. As with the dotted line curve in Figure 3.4, the graph illustrates that average unit cost decreases as output increases. The curve shows that as output increases, experience has proportionately less effect on cost. This gradual flattening of the curve makes it difficult to anticipate the potential for future cost reductions. However, if one redraws the graph (Figure 3.5b) using a logarithmic scale for each axis, the result approximates as a straight line which enables better predictions of future cost reductions.

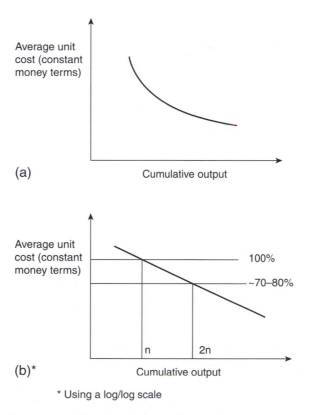

Figure 3.5: Cost reduction curves arising from the experience effect

The experience effect is widespread. Historically, it has resulted from manual workers becoming more adept, being organised into specialised activities (division of labour) and enhanced work practices. This kind of learning remains important, reflected in the organised approach to continuous improvement or *Kaizen* pioneered by Japanese companies via better equipment and work practices, especially by eliminating waste[13]. More radical learning requires the development and adoption of more powerful technology regimes. But whether radical or incremental, cost compression does not occur accidentally. Enterprises must work hard and intelligently, alert to every possibility to reduce costs via new ideas and methods. Accordingly, as it progresses the enterprise accumulates knowledge that others may not have, enhancing its future learning potential further.

Learning or experience effects in practice

Strong experience effects arise in microchip production via miniaturization (allowing ever-more electronic circuits on a single chip) and dramatic yield improvements (higher percentage of saleable chips per silicon wafer).

Passenger aircraft production achieves significant experience effects as each new design progresses from first prototype to full-scale output.

Corrective eye surgery that once took hours is now completed in minutes using laser scalpels, sometimes in dedicated surgical units operating as a production line.

When enterprises consciously exploit the experience effect, they reduce their unit costs. They can offer buyers lower prices or maintain prices, creating additional profits for future reinvestment. Dynamic sectors such as microchip production may price a new product consistent with expected future cost compression and consequent high sales. The low price encourages demand and accelerates output, although the producer might initially lose money until costs have been driven down.

The experience effect predicts that the enterprise with the greatest cumulative output will enjoy the lowest average (and marginal) unit cost. It is also best placed to achieve or exceed the MES, especially when the MES is a high percentage of industry output. Its numerical output may be expected to increase faster than any other competitor, so its *share* of total output should continue to increase, enhancing its relative cost advantage. In theory, market leaders can expect to enhance their dominance, *all else being equal*.

All else may not be equal, of course: phenomena such as complementarity and substitution effects can also affect an enterprise's competitiveness, as we shall now explore.

Complementarity and Substitution of Technologies and Processes

Complementarity and substitution are fundamental characteristics of the *processes and technologies* used to create and deliver products and services. They affect the relative competitiveness of enterprises.

A product or service requires multiple technologies and processes to realise it. This is called complementarity and is a universal phenomenon. A successful enterprise requires and has all the necessary capabilities. Yet, if it is inadequate in some respects, it needs to acquire, or otherwise gain access to, what it lacks. This can be costly, reducing its experience advantage in practice. Moreover, a competing enterprise that lacks specific resources or expertise (hence is cost-disadvantaged) may try to develop innovative processes and technologies as alternatives (substitutes). If successful, it poses a new threat to the leading supplier's cost advantage and may even destroy it completely.

Complementarity and substitution in processes and technologies

A mobile telephone service requires a complementary operational network of geographic cells, each with a base station. The station links a call from a nearby, active cell phone through the network to the base station nearest the handset of the intended recipient. Complementarity is needed with landline services too.

The first cellular networks used analogue technology. Second generation (or 2G) digital technology *substituted* first generation analogue technology, requiring costly new network infrastructures that all providers had to invest in or exit the industry. They also required investment in complementary licenses granted by host governments. Third generation (or 3G) digital networks later substituted 2G. However, there were sufficient complementary aspects of 2G and 3G to enable network providers to facilitate the transition and contain costs, in some instances by 'piggybacking' a 3G service on an existing 2G network.

Complements and Substitutes

The level of demand for a product or service may be linked to another product or service supplied from within the sector or elsewhere. If demand for the two items rises and falls in conjunction they *complement* each other: thus, initial demand for mobile handsets was linked strongly to geographic extensions of the mobile networks. Bicycle sales may stimulate sales of safety helmets. This is positive or complementary cross-elasticity and it is strategically attractive. If the buyer of a new bicycle often buys a safety helmet, bicycle makers should offer both products or collaborate with a helmet maker to their mutual benefit.

Brand extension can enhance complementarity. Successful examples include extensions of the Mars brand from chocolate bars to ice cream bars; Samsung's brand has stretched from hi-fi and televisions to mobile phones and digital cameras. However, the strategy can fail. Swatch enjoyed only limited success by extension to jewellery to complement its watch portfolio. Clarks, best known for branded leather shoes, has achieved little success in the market for canvas shoes dominated by Nike and Adidas.

When the supply of a product or service *substitutes* another, cross-elasticity is negative. As in the example in Chapter 2, substitute offerings are commonplace. This is strategically problematic for a supplier when it lacks the capability (or desire) to offer the disruptive substitute. Mobile phones with built-in cameras and other functions such as global positioning substitute for various single-function devices. Suppliers of specialized stand-alone devices may lack the expertise or credible 'brand franchise' to enter the mobile phone sector.

Strategic Groups

Thus far we have treated the industry sector as a set of enterprises that supply directly comparable products or services using similar processes and technologies. It implies a clear-cut sector boundary inside which these enterprises compete. This is an over-simplification. The outputs and activities of enterprises in nearby sectors may overlap, blurring sector boundaries.

LEARNING
OBJECTIVE ①

A sector may contain smaller enterprise clusters called strategic groups. Enterprises in each strategic group are similar, yet differ markedly from those in other groups. The practical definition of a strategic group is that its members adopt essentially the same strategy, hence compete principally with each other. The relative success of an enterprise in a strategic group therefore depends less on its choice of strategy than on how well it *implements* that strategy.

Strategic groups can be located on a map that defines the competitive sector space by using suitable variables. UK grocery distribution shows the diversity and complexity of a mature industry sector and the emergence of subgroups. Each strategic group has members whose position is well understood by rivals and consumers.

Nominal strategic groups in UK grocery distribution

Most people recognise a variety of grocery retailers. The following provides a way of categorising them:

International retail chains that offer a wide range of grocery and non-food products (e.g., Asda [Wal-Mart] and Tesco)

Large national grocery and non-food chains (e.g., Sainsbury, Morrisons and Co-operative Retail Group)

Department store groups that operate separate grocery chains (e.g., Marks & Spencer and John Lewis Partnership)

Narrow-line, 'no frills' budget grocery chains (e.g., Aldi, Lidl and Netto)

Limited-range grocery stores operated by local enterprises within national franchise chains (e.g., Budgens, Spar and 7-Eleven)

London gourmet food halls in prestige department stores (e.g., Fortnum & Mason and Harrods)

'Cash-and-Carry' wholesale chains such as Batleys, Bestway and Booker whose main clientele is small business proprietors, namely independent corner shops, guest houses and caterers

Figure 3.6 locates these groups in a chart defined by (perceived) quality position and breadth of product range. Some analysts would posit fewer groups, arguing for example that Tesco, Sainsbury and their respective peers form a common group; likewise, Batley, Aldi and their peers.

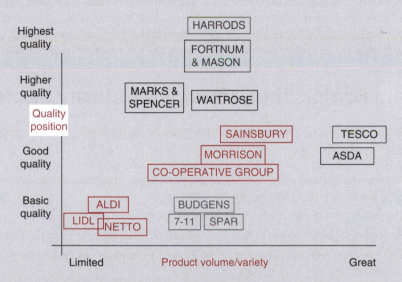

Figure 3.6: Nominal strategic groups in UK grocery distribution

Figure 3.6 oversimplifies matters since these subgroups are not completely isolated in location or consumer perception: food shopping is a relatively *local* activity. Given the increasingly international nature of the EU and the travel propensity of EU citizens, however, some might claim that Fortnum & Mason and Harrods compete to a degree with Le Bon Marché (Paris) and KaDeWe (Berlin). It is certainly plausible that the London stores might decide to extend their operations to Paris or Berlin and vice versa.

Strategic groupings are *dynamic*. In principle, a member of one subgroup could migrate to a different group. But there are *mobility barriers* that inhibit or prevent inter-group movements. They derive from the cost of transition, lack of knowledge, access to a technology or other necessary resources.[14]

For strategic group analysis to be reliable, careful examination is required. Some commentators suggest that strategic groups are a perceptual rather than an objective reality: they exist only

LEARNING OBJECTIVE ①

in the minds of the industry strategists. The critical test of group validity would be whether the enterprises themselves acknowledge fellow group members as their key competitors.

LEARNING
OBJECTIVE ①

From this perspective, strategic groups are self-fulfilling: the executives' belief that they are in a certain strategic group leads them to act accordingly and compete aggressively with other members of the group. Typically, such enterprises tend to define their perceived subgroups in terms of a few key competitors against which to benchmark. In the car industry, for example, French producers Peugeot and Renault undoubtedly see one another as major mass-production rivals; similarly BMW and Mercedes acknowledge each other as major executive car rivals. However, sector perceptions can be asymmetric. While Ford competes with Renault and Peugeot across the European Union, it probably sees Toyota and Volkswagen as its primary *global* competitors. Differences of perception create opportunities to misread rivalry, so serious consequences arise for an enterprise that fails to recognise a competitor until too late.

External Factors that Affect the Industry Sector

LEARNING
OBJECTIVE ①

Various factors *external* to the industry sector bear on its internal structure and enterprise conduct. Such factors include:

- The potential substitutional and complementary offerings, processes and technologies to satisfy the demand currently satisfied by the sector.
- The external value-adding supply chain of which sector enterprises are a part.
- The relative bargaining powers of suppliers and clients that form links in the supply chain.
- Entry and exit barriers to and from the sector (hence the potential for other enterprises to enter and compete vigorously or collaborate).
- Demand factors including lifecycles, market demographics, segments, and buyer characteristics and motivations.

There is often potential for alternative (substitutional) and complementary offerings and technologies to arise from outside the sector. Of strategic significance, these alternatives derive from enterprises not perceived as competitors, so they may capture a substantial share of the demand available to the sector before the threat is recognised, much less responded to.

Enterprise Value-Adding (Supply) Chains

LEARNING
OBJECTIVE ①

Most sectors are intermediate stages in extended supply chains that include suppliers to the focal sector, the sector itself, buyers of the sector's output and ultimate end users. The supply chain is a significant factor in the external environment of the enterprise, enabling it to access necessary resources and inputs, but creating further threats as well as opportunities.

Sector suppliers form the *upstream* element, buyers the *downstream* element. Each stage in the supply chain takes inputs from upstream suppliers, adds value to them, and conveys its outputs downstream as products or services. (By convention the supply chain is thought of as a vertical flow, i.e., from up to down, presumably since a stream flows downhill. Note the mixing of metaphors – 'stream' implies a flow, which is literally true, although 'chain' is relevant too, because a chain is only as strong as its weakest link.)

Each enterprise contains a chain of value-adding activities that integrates with the overall supply chain. The implications of the internal value chain are highly significant for the survival and success of the enterprise (Chapter 5). Figure 3.7 illustrates in a simplified form the supply chain for vehicle manufacturing. Vehicle assemblers produce high value-added sub-assemblies such as bodies, engines and gearboxes, but they buy many specialized sub-assemblies from suppliers including electrical components, electronic control modules, suspension and brake systems, wheels and tyres.

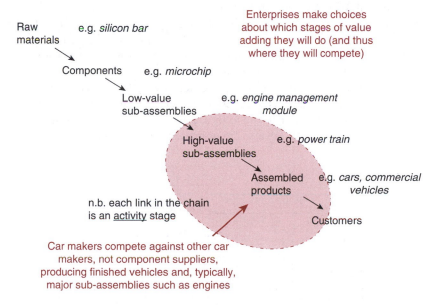

Figure 3.7: Simplified 'supply chain' for a vehicle maker

Each stage of the chain:

- Generates revenues by selling outputs to the next stage.
- Incurs costs – of its purchases and in adding value to them.
- Achieves an overall net gain (or loss) on its value-adding activities.

Historically enterprises performed many stages of the overall value-adding chain. The River Rouge plant of the Ford Motor Company built in the 1920s in Michigan, USA is a classic example. Iron ore and many other raw materials entered the site at one end while finished motor cars left at the other end. The advantage of such 'vertical integration' was control of all aspects of quality and cost. As the world became more complex and sophisticated, enterprises (especially manufacturers) increasingly realised the drawbacks of this approach. So the typical supply chain has become fragmented, with many specialised subcontractors performing a limited range of value-adding activities.[15]

LEARNING
OBJECTIVE ①

Selecting which value-adding activities to perform and which to purchase or subcontract is a major strategic decision. This requires *value chain analysis*, in which enterprises examine critically the activities that incur cost (the *cost-drivers*) and those that create value (the *value-drivers*). Ideally an enterprise performs only those activities for which it adds significant value (recognised by high demand and reflected in favourable selling prices). Activities that incur disproportionately high costs relative to the value created (reflected in their selling prices) are best purchased from more efficient, specialised suppliers, whilst bearing in mind that equivalent suppliers may themselves achieve differing efficiency levels in their respective activities and therefore affect overall efficiency and profitability.

Only by performing its chosen tasks efficiently and by occupying an efficient supply chain can an enterprise hope to succeed. Thus the ability of enterprises to influence and co-ordinate the activities of their upstream suppliers and downstream buyers matters (discussed further in Chapter 8). For example, vehicle makers dictate many aspects of how both their component suppliers and franchised dealerships operate. The efficiency of the supply chain is also affected by the choice of distribution channels to access end users. Manufacturers traditionally sold to national and regional wholesalers, that sold to local retailers, that sold to consumers or business end users (Figure 3.8). Each stage elevates the ultimate price because each expects a net profit margin.

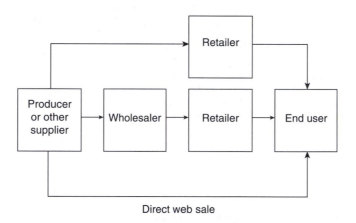

Figure 3.8: The downstream supply chain (distribution channels)

Today, manufacturers and other finished goods suppliers, such as importers, often sell directly to retailers and some sell directly to end users via the World Wide Web. Direct selling eliminates costs in the distribution chain by reducing the number of 'markups' to selling prices. However, costs of direct sales include physical shipment and returns processing that cannot be avoided. Some products need face-to-face advice. Many services cannot be provided remotely. Prospective buyers may be unaware of direct suppliers, a situation which the latter must correct via extensive promotional activities. Strategically, therefore, mail order and Web-based enterprises are not necessarily more profitable than traditional distribution channels. Indeed, suppliers that maintain parallel Web and traditional channels may severely reduce their overall profitability.

Buyers generally have access to alternative channels and may exhibit systematic preferences. Some consumers prefer to shop conventionally for clothes, but exploit the easy comparison potential of the World Wide Web for major, branded purchases. Some never shop on the Web, others do little else. Business buyers often demand direct contacts with and presentations from suppliers. Enterprises need to gear their channels to the needs and expectations of their prospective buyers.

The Relative Bargaining Power of Suppliers and Buyers

Enterprises that occupy intermediate positions in a supply chain routinely negotiate purchase contracts with suppliers and sales contracts with buyers. Prices and other terms including penalties for default make negotiations complex, dynamic activities that affect the ultimate profitability of enterprises. In theory, one might expect price largely to reflect production costs, but in practice it depends greatly on the relative bargaining power of the respective enterprises.

A capable supplier with ineffective competitors enjoys a strong position from which to demand premium prices and favourable terms of trade. A supplier with many, equally capable competitors occupies a relatively weak position and within limits must accept the price a buyer is willing to pay. Availability of supply is another factor. When supply capacity is limited relative to demand, suppliers enjoy enhanced bargaining power. Given supply over-capacity, buyers have the advantage. Although the relative bargaining powers of buyers and suppliers can change, the balance over time remains stable in many supply chains. Bargaining power is therefore a significant structural feature of an industry sector. A fictional example highlights an extreme example of bargaining power.

Entry Barriers

Sectoral entry barriers deter newcomers from entering. They are forces created by the actions of the established enterprises in the sector, by external influences such as governments and by other factors such as scarcity of necessary resources and skills.

New entrants may be start-ups, but more generally are resourceful enterprises operating in other sectors. Low entry barriers increase the probability of new entrants. By increasing rivalry they would present a threat to existing enterprises, which therefore try to raise the entry barriers as a deliberate part of their competitive strategies.

Even in the absence of deliberate actions to deter new entrants, barriers may exist. For example, there are costs and constraints to setting up a taxi service (vehicle cost, operator's licence), whether or not existing taxi companies act deliberately to deter new entrants (e.g., by offering loyalty discounts for repeat customers). Strategically, it seems wise for a potential entrant to consider all the entry costs, including those that may arise once it has confirmed its intent to enter.

The size of an entry barrier is equivalent to the level of financial investment a newcomer must make to compete on roughly equal terms. It can be difficult to calculate the size of barriers that involve scarce knowledge or sentiment, but they are still potent deterrents. Entry barriers have many origins. Common forms are categorized below[16] with examples presented thereafter.

Economic: To be competitive, a minimum scale of output and hence market share is necessary. The outsider must invest in operations including facilities and equipment of appropriate scale and sophistication. This is evidently unattractive in the face of powerful existing competitors, especially if there is chronic excess capacity. Most barriers have severe cost implications and therefore a serious deterrent effect.

Market presence: Even if a newcomer enjoys a widely respected brand it takes time and investment in advertising and promotions to develop reputation and loyalty from a different buying clientele. Access to end users is also needed, requiring co-operation from wholesalers, retailers or a direct channel, all costly to secure.

Technology and knowledge: Sectors generally conform to functional *standards* to ensure products and services are safe and perform acceptably. Some standards may be widely accepted, such as the electricity supply characteristics in each country around the world. Standards may be industry-specific within or across countries, such as how clothes are sized. The industry leader may have established de-facto standards. A newcomer might find it difficult to conform to these standards. Conversely, prospective entrants may have to persuade buyers to accept its alternative, unfamiliar standards, perhaps by offering attractive (lower) prices to induce buyers to switch, reducing profits. Different standards sometimes cause buyers to incur substantial and unacceptable *switching costs*. For example, to switch to Mac-based computers PC-users face the costs of buying new versions of familiar software, notwithstanding possible benefits of switching.

In a technologically sophisticated sector, existing enterprises will hold patents that restrict newcomers' ability to compete, unless they can negotiate licences at a realistic cost. Application-specific, accumulated knowledge contributes to experience effects. If sector entry requires unfamiliar know-how, newcomers must learn rapidly, perhaps by recruiting competitors' staff. They probably have to invest heavily in research and development to avoid patent infringements, which delays progress and increases the possibility of costly mistakes.

Regulatory: Government laws, tariffs and quotas, domestic and international, act as entry barriers. Legislation affects health and safely at work, working hours, recycling, waste disposal, and imposes environmental regulations, some universal, some sector-specific. The burden of compliance imposes additional costs on a new entrant as well as challenging its knowledge and capabilities.

Social and cultural: Ignorance of unfamiliar tastes and preferences are barriers to prospective entry. Business practices are often country or sector-specific, including ordering and payment arrangements, attitudes towards legal contracts, personal interactions, hospitality, commissions and other kinds of sales incentives.

Competitive actions: The ongoing actions of sector enterprises, including the pursuit of scale economies, raise entry barriers. Established enterprises and other agencies such as governments may also act pre-emptively to deter a prospective entrant. Common actions include costly advertising campaigns and short-term price reductions to make the sector appear less profitable and high risk. Strong competitors may acquire weaker competitors before a newcomer does so, or introduce tougher standards which newcomers will struggle to comply with. Once entry has been deterred, deterrent actions then stop.

Types of entry barriers in practice

Economic: Intel Corporation, the world's leading manufacturer of microprocessor chips, invests heavily in new fabrication plants that cost over a billion dollars. These huge investments and the know-how they entail are massive deterrents to potential new entrants.

Market presence: To become a premier global information systems consultancy, CapGemini Sogeti of France acquired competitors in other countries, later turning them into CapGemini subsidiaries.

Technology and knowledge: Sony entered the mobile cellphone handset industry via a joint venture with established telecommunications giant Ericsson of Sweden to compensate for gaps in its sector knowledge (and credibility). Canon has not entered, despite its considerable resources and electronics expertise.

Switching costs: Lands' End is a US clothes and shoe company, which specialises in Mail Order. In European markets it has continued to use American size measurements, presumably thinking it was too costly to change. European consumers unfamiliar with US imperial sizes face a knowledge barrier that inhibits a switch to Lands' End products, which has probably limited the brand's popularity.

Regulatory: To convert an ordinary farm to 'organic' status, European farmers must conform to European Union (EU) rules on avoiding pesticides, fertilisers, and non-organic animal feeds. The transition takes several years, during which farmers incur the additional costs of organic methods (typically lower yields) but cannot obtain the organic price premium. These restrictions deter many farmers from going organic.

Social and cultural: By the year 2000 Japanese enterprises, mostly manufacturers, had invested 5.2 billion yen in EU operations, 45.5% of which was in the UK and 40.1% in the Netherlands. Only 4.4% was in France, 2.5% in Germany and 0.2% in Italy.[17] There could be many reasons for their preferences; one is that Japanese managers are more likely to speak (or be willing to learn) English than other European languages.

Competitive actions: EMI, a British company best known for its commitment to the music industry, developed the world's first computerised X-ray brain scanner. In 1971 it entered the medical equipment industry. Powerful corporations including GE (USA), Siemens (Germany) and Philips (Netherlands) had established interests in medical equipment and the knowledge to invent their way round EMI's patents. When their own scanners became available their medical equipment reputations persuaded hospitals to acquire their products in preference to EMI's, a company without prior industry experience. Within 10 years EMI had quit the sector.

A sufficiently determined, resourceful newcomer might overcome almost *any* barrier, but at what cost? Having made the necessary investments, it bears a financial burden that erodes the profits that it might have expected from entry. Moreover, its presence would add to the rivalry felt by every competitor whose future profits are therefore threatened, prompting aggressive responses. When the outcome looks obviously unattractive, it will not seem worthwhile to pursue entry.

One approach to overcome an entry barrier would be to re-define the competitive arena so that the barrier becomes irrelevant: that is, sidestep it, rather than break it down. For example, if chemical corporations develop optical or organic computing devices that outperform and super-sede silicon microprocessors, they would create a new sector to challenge Intel's future dominance of the core microprocessor applications, without having to make silicon microchips. Intel's huge commitment to silicon technology would also present a significant barrier to its adopting wholly different technologies.

Exit Barriers

Once an enterprise has made the large investments necessary to create or overcome sector entry barriers, they can prevent it from quitting or even *considering* quitting. Barriers to exit take four main forms:

Asset-specific barriers: Many investments are very specific to the sector and its value-adding activities. Facilities, equipment and other fixed assets, even highly skilled people, perform a limited range of activities and create specialised outputs. This is called asset-specificity. These assets have little value for other purposes. Their only value is to a competing enterprise willing to acquire them at only a fraction of their original cost. They represent 'sunk', non-recoverable costs, so the owners feel obliged to continue using them.

Contractual barriers: Few enterprises perform activities without legal contracts. These may span decades for facilities, or years for equipment leases and supply contracts. An enterprise might negotiate its way out of binding contracts but costly legal fees, compensation payments and other penalty clauses deter it from doing so. Other costs such as legal minimum redundancy payments are often substantial when an activity ceases.

Subjective barriers: Executive managers sometimes convince themselves that however bad the situation seems, it will improve. They deny the difficulties for psychological and emotional reasons. Those who make exit decisions lose face and probably their jobs. Quitting causes reputation loss – corporate, brand and personal. For an enterprise with no viable alternatives, exit becomes a decision to close. All of these factors represent barriers to exit, so exit decisions are deferred in the vain hope of better times ahead.

Ethical barriers: Felt obligations such as a commitment to maintain employment or to look after a small, dependent clientele may have no sound legal or financial basis, yet create an ethical or moral justification for continuing in a sector, creating another form of exit barrier.

Types of exit barrier in practice

Asset specificity: The car and steel industries have for many years suffered excess production capacity, especially in Europe. Obsolete, loss-making plants have no alternative use, so enterprises have preferred to anticipate a future upturn in demand rather than close them to reduce capacity and cost. Examples include the closure of plants by British Steel (Corus) in the UK and General Motors in the United States in 2009, following its filing for Chapter 11 Administration. Governments sometimes misguidedly provide subsidies to maintain employment by keeping inefficient plants open.

Contractual: Major construction projects such as the recent Wembley Stadium and the new Olympic stadium in London involve multiple contractors and legal contracts whose terms include severe penalties for late or otherwise inadequate performance. The relationship between the main contractor and its Wembley Stadium client deteriorated so much that the contractor reportedly wanted to quit, but the penalty clauses were too great a deterrent.

Subjective: Netscape created the first widely used Web browser computer software. In the mid 1990s it had over 90% of the market, prompting AOL to acquire it in 1998. As Microsoft's Internet Explorer gained acceptance, Netscape's influence declined. By 2006 its market share was down to 1%. Today, Netscape still offers various software services, though its commitment to browser software ceased in 2008, where after it no longer provided security updates, making the use of its browser a liability. Was its slow exit because AOL could not accept that buying Netscape was a mistake?

Ethical: Pharmaceuticals companies continue to make some unprofitable drugs for treating uncommon ailments, probably because they feel it would be unethical to deny patients a proven treatment (and certainly bad publicity).

Demand Influences

Structural aspects of demand have a strategic impact on an enterprise in its sector. Of particular importance are demand patterns (demographics and segments) and lifecycles.[18]

Demographics describe buyer characteristics such as age, social status, income, lifestyles and other features. Market segments exist when robust analysis shows systematic differences in patterns of demand that an enterprise can exploit as part of a coherent strategy. The demographic and behavioural characteristics of many markets differ from the population at large. These characteristics create pockets of demand, some relatively small-scale, that link to expectations of specialised offerings including high quality and price. These pockets or segments are of interest when they are stable, likely to persist for relatively long periods. To be actionable strategically they must be objectively identifiable and accessible (addressable). Industry competitors adopt different demand classifications of varying degrees of subjectivity.

Segments are crucial structural demand features. They offer greater strategic management leverage than basic demography because, when appropriately defined, some segments will prove very significant for individual enterprises. For example, demand for student accommodation, clothes, food and travel may best be served by establishing segments that are unique to each product/service category. When a defined market segment is substantial in unit and sales value (or is growing fast and likely to become substantial), it is clearly an opportunity.[19]

Segments defined by *applications* and *benefits* are valuable for strategy. Potential buyers with a common, identified need (related to a particular use or application) should respond positively and predictably to a product or service that offers relevant benefits. Fast-growing segments attract intense competition, whereas others remain a minority interest 'niche' served by few enterprises. Industry output statistics are categorized by product types that that rarely reflect true demand segments. Geo-demographic modelling is a major development in segmentation analysis that links buyer behaviour to location, making it easier to target appropriate potential clienteles (e.g., by using a suitable location code, such as the postcode in the UK or zip code in the USA).

Bicycle demand segmented by benefit sought and provided

Basic bicycles provide low-cost transport over short distances.

Motor assistance means low pedalling effort, hence such bicycles are suitable for longer distances and less-fit riders.

Ultra-lightweight machines designed for racing enhance acceleration and require less energy over long distances.

All-terrain bikes can withstand brutal treatment on rough trails.

Suspension softens bumps and reduces sores and bruises.

Folding bicycles are excellent for city commuting and easy storage on arrival.

Demand Lifecycles

An entirely new, emergent pattern of demand may take time to grow in size and complexity. Maturity follows growth and then, ultimately, decline. This is the classic demand trajectory illustrated in Figure 3.9. Since the lifecycle traces demand over time, it is inaccurate to call it the *industry* lifecycle, although this is common parlance.

An industry sector that supplies declining demand probably needs to adapt, if that is possible. As previously noted, long-lived demand may be served by several distinct industry sectors that offer different 'solutions' to the same, fundamental need or 'problem'. Demand patterns vary considerably. Some remain consistent, whereas others quickly form distinct segments, each of

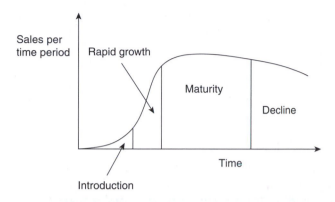

Figure 3.9: The classic demand lifecycle

which can be the subject of strategic decisions. Some demand segments display an *extended* maturity phase, aided by astute strategic market management. For example, demand for individual chocolate bars has not yet entered decline stage, partly due to patient product differentiation and effective promotion. Others (such as specific fashion trends) have a *curtailed* life span and disappear quickly (Figure 3.10).

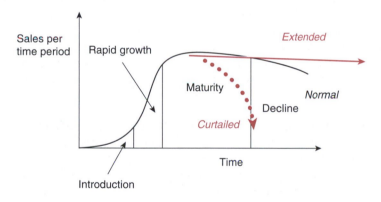

Figure 3.10: Differing demand trajectories

Chapter 9 considers strategies to cope with and exploit demand lifecycles. The most successful enterprise in the introduction phase may prove an ineffective competitor during the rapid-growth phase or beyond. The most effective enterprise during decline is often the most persistent, continuing after hitherto successful competitors have quit.

Demand Behavioural Influences

Marketing philosophy advocates a thorough knowledge of buyer characteristics and trends before making strategic decisions. Effective strategic management therefore requires an appreciation of what motivates prospective buyers, their needs and wants, declared or tacit.

LEARNING
OBJECTIVE ②   Strategically significant aspects of buyer characteristics include:

- Purchase motivations (needs and wants).
- Consumption rates and patterns.
- Relationships, brand loyalty and reference groups.
- Channel preferences and receptivity to enterprise communications.

Purchase Motivations

Consumers can be fickle in their tastes and preferences. Even industrial buyers are human beings first and buyers second, so their objectivity cannot be assumed. To the enterprise, buyers may seem not entirely rational as they search for products and services to meet their 'needs' and 'wants'. Buyers often pay more to satisfy emotional 'wants' than they pay to satisfy rational 'needs', so good strategies take particular account of what market research suggests prospective buyers *want* and therefore value most.

Consumption Rates and Patterns

Prospective buyers typically consider one-off, *comparison purchases*, sometimes for a long time. Consideration may take place unconsciously until an unpredictable event or message triggers a purchase. For example, business schools know that the decision to enrol on a vocational programme like that leading to Master of Business Administration (MBA) can result from months, even years of reflection. Conversely, habitual purchases of low-value items especially by regular, heavy users are often *impulse purchases* given little thought. Most repeat-purchase markets feature a significant minority of heavy users whose habits sustain profitable sales.

Relationships, Brand Loyalty and Reference Groups

Brands add perceived value to offerings, conveying quality, reliability, authenticity and desirability, and underpinning premium prices. Brands negate competitive appeals based on rationality and functional value as promised by product specifications and therefore legitimise purchases of higher priced alternatives. For example, a consumer may decide to pay twice the price for a polyester shirt rather than a cotton shirt if the former has a stronger brand identity. Strong consumer brands symbolise an idealised personality that buyers identify with and aspire to.

Personal relationships between an industrial buyer and sales representatives are equivalent to consumer relationships with their preferred brands. Such relationships give rise to emotional *switching costs* that inhibit preference shifts and usage changes unless a trigger event prompts a proper evaluation of alternatives.

Consumer influences also include the attitudes and opinions of 'significant others': family members, school friends, work colleagues, friends and acquaintances in social and interest groups. Professional buyers refer to other colleagues, notably specifiers such as production and engineering staff in industrial companies and professionals in service enterprises. The buyer who signs the order form and the accountant who instructs the payment may have preferences but their opinions matter relatively little.

Channel Preferences and Receptivity to Enterprise Communications

Buyers generally have access to multiple channels of distribution. Some consumers prefer to shop conventionally for clothes, but exploit the easy comparison features of the World Wide Web for major purchases. Some never shop on the Web, whereas others do little else. Business buyers may require direct contacts, visits and presentations from suppliers. Enterprises need to gear their channel decisions to the expectations, needs and wants of their prospective buyers.

Communication strategies that target defined market segments rely on assumptions that (i) a well-defined segment does not overlap other segments to any degree, and will remain stable over time and that (ii) when the enterprise communicates with prospective buyers in that segment they will respond in positive and predictable ways. However, because consumer opinions have become more fragmented and idiosyncratic, segments are smaller and receptivity less predictable. Hence segments may require more frequent reassessment and be potentially less useful for strategy than in the past.

Analysing Market and Industry Sector Environments

Having considered both supply-side and demand-side influences, we can now reflect on the analysis of markets and industry sectors. In particular, it is helpful to return to the 5-P model and critically consider its application here.

Using the 5-Forces Model

The 5-forces model has been highly influential, partly because it is linked to clear strategy prescriptions. It has been regularly defended and critiqued.[20] Academic papers that apply the model to particular industry sectors generally benefit from hindsight into crucial issues and assumptions that were less obvious at the time. To conduct a practical sector analysis in 'real time' is challenging, yet that is what strategists do, systematically or impressionistically.

Unfortunately there is no definitive way to identify industry sector boundaries. The general advice is to be pragmatic, defining boundaries via a combination of similar products, technologies and demand characteristics. The existence of distinct market segments and strategic subgroups complicates analysis. As noted, apparent competitors sometimes have quite different perceptions of circumstances, resulting in unexpected conduct and outcomes.

Some critics claim that, as originally proposed, the 5-forces model omits significant external forces such as the political and regulatory influences of governments and industry sector bodies. These should certainly be considered: here they are treated as stakeholder influences in the external macro environment (Chapter 2). Because the model focuses on competition, it does not acknowledge co-operation among enterprises within or beyond the sector. Practical observation confirms that legally permissible and on occasion covert (hence illegal) collaborations arise. They can be included in the model as an aspect of autonomous, discretionary conduct. While the model explicitly addresses product and technology substitution, complementarity effects arising from the actions of enterprises external to the sector also need consideration. For example, digital imaging sensors are a critical complement to digital camera development. For many years few camera manufacturers had access to sensor technology.

Another criticism of the 5-forces model is its static nature – analyses provide only snapshots of dynamic, ever-changing sectors. Arguably, this is really an issue about how the model should be *used*. A good analysis will be repeated periodically to verify prior expectations, because competent strategic management is a process of continuous revision.

The 'generic strategy' prescriptions consistent with the 5-forces model (explored in Chapter 7) may be too simplistic in many instances. As noted, it is also silent over collaborative strategies. However, the former claim discounts the significance of singled-mindedness of *strategic intent*. An enterprise intent on being the lowest cost provider should recognise that any additional costs it incurs to distinguish itself from competitors is likely to compromise that intent.

Competitor Monitoring and Analysis

LEARNING OBJECTIVE ② The actions and intentions of direct competitors are obvious concerns of business enterprises, as indeed they are for many not-for-profit enterprises. Competitor analysis aims to establish better knowledge about them through systematic, regular enquiries.[21]

In many enterprises the main sources of information about competitors are the impressions of clients, senior managers and sales staff, informed by their contacts at conferences, seminars and other external events such as trade fairs where employees of competing enterprises gather. People are comparatively accessible, word-of-mouth sources. An employee who is interviewed for employment with a competitor is an information channel that either enterprise may try to exploit, so there is an obvious need for ethical behaviour.[22] Table 3.C lists various relevant categories of data about competitors and sources where such data may be obtained.

Table 3.C: Data categories and sources for competitive scanning

Data categories	
• Current products	• Customer relations
• New product plans	• Risk attitudes
• Pricing/proms plans	• Hirings & firings
• R&D areas/patents	• Possible quitters
• Performance (sales, profits etc.)	• Contracts/licences
• Assets/resources	• New entrants
• (Manuf.) capabilities:	
– Strengths	
– Weaknesses	

Table 3.C: Cont'd

Data sources	

• Customers – via sales force, engineers etc
• Intermediaries:
  – Suppliers
  – Marketing firms
  – Consultants
  – Stockbrokers
• Official bodies, e.g.:
  – Trade associations
  – Companies House
  – Patent Office
  – Planning offices
	• Documented sources:
	  – Press releases
	  – Trade journals
	  – Newspapers/TV
	  – Annual reports
	  – Speeches
	  – Recruitment ads.
	  – Websites
	• Competitors' staff:
	  – Trade shows
	  – Conferences
	  – Hiring them
	• Direct observation

Game Theory

 RNING ECTIVE ②

When the number of competitors is small,[23] another option for analysis arises. This is a technique based on **game theory**.[24] This approach allows the enterprise to conduct a contingent analysis of the cut-and-thrust of competitive actions.

Consider the simplest case of two competitors, such as Airbus and Boeing (A and B). Enterprise A initially identifies its possible strategic options. It then assesses possible responses from competitor B, assuming that B will become aware of A's actions and responds self-interestedly. The respective alternatives are cross-tabulated to create a 'states-of-nature' matrix. If, hypothetically, A has two possible actions to which B has three realistic responses, the matrix would be 2 × 3, creating 6 cells (Table 3.D). Each cell presents a scenario that matches B's anticipated response to one of A's strategic options.

Table 3.D: The application of game theory to the Airbus A380 decision

		Airbus's options	
		Develop A380	Develop a smaller new jetliner
Boeing's responses	X: Develop a new A380-sized jetliner	#1	#4
	Y: Develop a smaller new jetliner	#2	#5
	Z: Continue to develop its existing product range	#3	#6

It is then possible to predict the likely outcome for each protagonist, expressed as 'payoff' values such as expected profits, market shares, etc. (Table 3.E).

Table 3.E: A payoff matrix relating to the Airbus A380 decision

Scenario	Payoff for Airbus	Payoff for Boeing
#1	Little change in market share but profits will probably decline because of high development costs	As Airbus
#2	Payoff highly uncertain until airlines make purchase decisions	As Airbus
#3	Airbus gains market share; short-term profits decline because of the high costs of development; long-term profits increase significantly	With an ageing product range, Boeing loses substantial market share to Airbus and ultimately loses profitability too
#4	Payoff highly uncertain until airlines make purchase decisions	As Airbus
#5	Little change in market share but profits will probably decline because of high development costs	As Airbus
#6	Airbus gains market share; short-term profits decline because of high costs of development; long-term profits increase significantly	With an ageing product range, Boeing loses substantial market share to Airbus and ultimately loses profitability too

The symmetry of scenarios #1 and #5 produces competitive parity or stalemate. Airbus will gain substantially by innovating, provided that Boeing fails to respond similarly (scenarios #3 and #6). If the companies innovate in differing ways (scenarios #2 and #4), the payoffs are uncertain. A multitude of assumptions must be built into demand forecasts, not least over future travel patterns and whether the major airlines will prefer a large A380-sized aircraft or a smaller 777-sized one. Given that the A380 development decision is irreversible and has a huge, projected development cost, the risk of rejection by the airlines would be catastrophic. However, for Airbus the risk of *not* innovating is that it allows Boeing to take the initiative with its own innovation, which reverses the expected payoffs, damaging Airbus's long-term competitive position. So one can understand why Airbus strategists decided to innovate.

The size and infrequency of such decisions makes the aircraft industry exceptional. In a more typical sector, analysis would explore a sequence of actions and responses over a number of time periods. Once the estimated payoffs in each cell of the matrix had been estimated for period one, each protagonist may change its strategy in the second period. Analysts could therefore construct a new payoff matrix (assuming that B were a rational decision-maker), repeating the exercise until the long-term outcome crystallised, yielding a clearer understanding of the probable future balance of competitive advantage, which could be stalemate or a catastrophe for one of the parties.

The so-called the 'prisoners dilemma' characterises many competitive situations, representing a desire by each protagonist to limit *worst-case outcomes*. In this situation two prisoners are accused of a crime. If both remain silent when questioned separately they will probably be freed for lack of evidence. If they could communicate with each other they would agree that silence is their best (co-operative) strategy. However, being unable to communicate, the obvious temptation is to accuse the other in the hope of being released or receiving a lighter sentence, *assuming that this is what the other will do*. This outcome increases mutual competition to their joint detriment, but it does avoid either one taking all the blame.

Analysts can explore alternative assumptions to assess how to enhance their expected payoffs. Game theoretic analysis can be applied simplistically or with great mathematical sophistication. As with any model, the value of the approach lies in its capacity to help structure and better understand a competitive (or co-operative) situation. However, it has been criticised for enabling better explanations of past events than future possibilities.[26]

Market Research

When the major issues and the information needs associated with prospective demand trends are clear, market research is often appropriate to help clarify the uncertainties.

Conventional market research covers qualitative and quantitative enquiries. The former includes focus group meetings and consumer opinion and attitude surveys regarding products and services, brand images, and distribution channels. One-off enquiries can be performed to explore emerging issues of interest or concern.

Aggregate trends and the prediction of future demand within defined categories of product and service may be developed via quantitative surveys based on well-specified variables, typically repeated at regular intervals in so-called tracking studies. Future demand forecasts that project known statistics into the future make the assumption that the future will be essentially a continuation of the past. However sophisticated the statistical methods may be, this is often a misguided assumption. Nonetheless, market forecasting provides a major input to the strategic management of most enterprises.

A Resource for Analysing Industry Sector Environments

Figure 3.11 presents a simple resource for performing a structured analysis of the industry sector environment, using the topic headings introduced in this chapter.

	Major issue or trend	Actual or potential significance for the focal enterprise
Sector concentration		
Cost factors and minimum efficient scale (MES)		
Technology regimes and experience effects		
Strategic groups		
Product/service substitutes and complements		
Process/technology substitutes and complements		
Structurally induced enterprise behaviours		
Autonomous enterprise behaviours		
Entry and exit barriers		
Suppliers' bargaining power		
Buyers' bargaining power		
Other supply chain factors		
Demand segments		
Lifecycle factors		
Other demand factors		

Figure 3.11: Industry environment analysis

CASE STUDY: The competitive environment of EMI in the recorded music industry

In the mid-2000s demand for recorded music was estimated at US$30–40 billion a year. Thirty countries accounted for 95% of demand, the United States by far the most. Traditionally, demand is split by genre (classical, jazz, soul, rock, pop, etc.) with strong links between genre and age of consumer. Young people buy almost all single (chart) records, with online demand for single tracks growing rapidly. CD album sales have declined substantially, excepting themed compilations of old releases. Demand is fragmented, even among the young, although rock music of the 1960s onwards has universal appeal.

Listening to recorded music via disc or broadcast radio is increasingly confined to home hi-fi enthusiasts who spend considerable sums on high-quality equipment. Future demand for recorded music and video may benefit from such enthusiasts who will continue to want ever higher quality music on media such as DVDs and Blu-ray discs. However, many consumers no longer buy music content in the form of disc. Multimedia players such as iPods, mp3 players and mobile phone handsets allow consumers to download or stream music (and video) from the Internet to enjoy on the move, which appeals to youthful lifestyles and preference for convenience.

The trend to acquire music online makes broadcast radio stations a potentially declining distribution channel for recorded music. High speed *wireless* broadband and mobile phone networks enable on-demand consumption of audio and video via download and streaming services from specialist websites and internet radio stations. Some music sources are free of charge. Others are pay-per-listen or subject to a fixed daily/monthly subscription with unlimited (fair usage) access. Hybrid models combine a periodic fee plus unit charge, sometimes at reduced rates when advertisements are attached to downloads.

Attitudes – especially of younger people – to copyright issues are ambivalent. Many do not accept a performer's rights to earn royalties over many years. Illegal file sharing and downloading are widespread and continue despite the legal alternatives.

Further, the rise in popularity of computer and handheld games competes for consumers' leisure time and expenditure.

Four major music recording companies supply around 80% of the demand for recorded music,[25] as follows:

- Universal Music Group; about 30% market share.
- Sony Music; about 25%.
- Warner (USA); 15%.
- EMI (UK; privately owned); 12–13%.

Universal Music Group (UMG) is a wholly owned subsidiary of the media conglomerate Vivendi (France, with major US facilities). Sony Music is a wholly-owned subsidiary of Sony Corporation of Japan. Entering a 50-50 joint venture with Bertelsmann AG of Germany in 2004, it bought out its partner for US$1.2 billion in 2008. It has major facilities in the United States and Germany. Warner is an independent, US public company spun off from Warner Entertainment Group. EMI was a UK public company until acquired by Terra Firma Investments, a private equity group, in 2007.[26]

The four major companies (the majors) own dozens of recording labels. The main labels form brands that are recognised and respected globally. The portfolios result from acquisitions and mergers of smaller, independent labels formed by entrepreneurs and musicians. These four enterprises contract musicians to perform, arrange and record music in specialised studios and concert halls. In addition to recording and management services, they engage in music publishing, which generates separate revenue streams. Sony is particularly well placed to exploit complementarities in its portfolios of audio and video products and technologies. Three of the majors have maintained or grown market share in recent times. EMI's share has declined slowly; it has been unprofitable for several years.

The majors have recording studios, offices and distribution centres around the world. Studios mix the initial sound recordings and produce master copies that in turn produce archive and master sub-copies used to mass-produce discs for sale. The companies distribute compact discs (CDs) and music DVDs to wholesalers and retailers worldwide, and license radio stations and live venues to play recorded music. The recording companies form part of a complex supply chain that also includes:

Upstream

- Music composers (song writers).
- Music publishers.
- Musicians.
- Equipment manufacturers.

Downstream

- Performing rights agencies.
- Independent, mass-production disc replicators.
- Wholesale distributors and retailers (CDs, music DVDs and vinyl discs).
- Broadcast and internet radio stations.
- Internet music distributors.
- Live venue operators.[28]
- Advertising agencies.

Traditionally, vinyl records, tape cassettes and CDs provided 'hard copy' storage of digital content. Because digital recording has become the dominant technology, music captured in digital files is increasingly transmitted via the Web as file downloads and by streaming, with physical storage on remote file servers. The industry will need much less capacity in future to produce discs for retail sale.

Many independent record stores have closed, leaving disc retailing in the hands of very few multiple chains, plus websites such as Play.com and HMV's own website. As elsewhere, the industry trend has been towards supply chain de-integration. Digital technology enables performers to record music in independent studios anywhere in the world. Subcontract sound engineers and technicians perform specialist post-recording activities. Some musicians distribute their music directly via the Internet.

Top musicians can negotiate very favourable royalty terms with the majors. Core skills of the major recording companies are to identify and sign new talent and to negotiate to retain top artists in competition with each other. Recording contracts with high profile, big-selling artists in all genres are major assets. Huge back-libraries of recordings are also assets that generate revenues for many years at minimal cost.

Recorded music is a form of intellectual property covered by legal copyrights. The law affords copyright holders protection from unauthorized copying and distribution of material for a period of, typically, 50 years from date of first publication. Control of intellectual property in the virtual web environment is challenging. While illicit copying (piracy) of protected content is not new, personal computers and the Internet have made it much more widespread. Peer-to-peer file sharing is virtually impossible to stop, despite requests to internet service providers to intervene or face legal action. Some websites that enable file-sharing, such as the original Napster site, Kazaa and Pirate Bay, have been closed down following court action.

Reluctant to change the revenue model, the majors finally accepted that it might be more profitable to forge relationships that enable legal downloading rather than fight illegal activity. Apple's iTunes pioneered online retail distribution in 2001, charging per download. It agreed to pay copyright holders a royalty to distribute their music. The key to industry acceptance was Apple's proprietary digital rights management (DRM) software that permits storage and playback of iTunes downloads only on iPods and iPhones. Various legal music websites now compete with iTunes, offering mp3-compatible downloads. Sites include Sony, Rhapsody, Tesco Digital, Amazonmp3, Songbird and a now-legal Napster owned by Best Buy. Downloads are also available via mobile phone handsets in network proprietary formats and compatible handsets. Subscription-based streaming makes DRM software unnecessary because files are not saved; copyright owners generate revenues via contracts similar to those long established with radio broadcasters and others who play recorded music publicly.

Even so, the major recording companies cannot yet know how digital music distribution will affect their future revenues and profits long term. If music becomes commoditised, only very high-profile musicians can expect substantial future royalties, discouraging variety and new performers.

Question

1. Using Figure 3.11 as a worksheet, analyse the state of the industry with particular reference to EMI's position and status. Use additional, recent data you can find.

Summary

LEARNING OBJECTIVE ①   • The industry sector (the set of equivalent enterprises) is distinct from the market demand that sector enterprises service.

LEARNING OBJECTIVE ①   • Industries evolve over time through the interaction of aspects of industry structure and enter-
LEARNING OBJECTIVE ②   prise conduct on the one hand, and the structure of demand and buyer behaviours on the other.

LEARNING OBJECTIVE ③   • There are many significant factors that must be analysed to understand both demand and
LEARNING OBJECTIVE ④   supply sector structures and behaviours and their implications for within-sector rivalry. The
LEARNING OBJECTIVE ⑤   well-known 5-forces model of industry competition can be used to analyse these factors within a sector and in the extended, value-adding supply chain of which it is a part.

    • The worksheet in this chapter can be used to systematically analyse an industry sector.
LEARNING OBJECTIVE ⑤   In many sectors, analysis demonstrates the high degree of complexity and uncertainty that exists arising from the three factors of autonomous rivalry, in-sector structures and external forces.

Exercises for Further Study and Discussion

1. Select an industry sector of interest and use available data to estimate the minimum efficient scale (MES) of operations in it.
2. Select an industry sector of interest and list the main types of entry barrier (e.g., research and development expertise, brand profile, facilities, etc) within it. Then examine annual reports of the leading competitors to establish their financial investment in these key areas. What does this tell you about the height of the entry barriers facing a potential new entrant?
3. 'Strong competitors act in ways that make life harder for weaker competitors'. Explore the implications of this claim.

4. Consider the *joint* effect of entry and exit barriers during periods of recession and of economic prosperity (consider four possible states: high/high, high/low; low/high; low/low). Identify four industry sectors that conform to these states.

5. Enterprises that occupy intermediate positions in supply chains frequently have limited bargaining power with suppliers *and* customers. What are the consequences and what can they do about it?[29]

6. Select a market of interest and list different ways of segmenting demand in that market. Which of them can be considered objective, enabling them to be researched and quantified? Is subjective segmentation of no strategic worth?

7. What links (if any) exist between demand segments and strategic industry groups?

8. Many 'bricks and mortar' retailers have websites. Some provide only product information and encourage store visits. Others allow purchases directly from it. Should a website charge lower prices than in-store? Why/why not? What other strategic issues arise from this dual channel approach?

9. If there are many competing suppliers in a sector, should a prospective entrant prefer collaboration to competition? What factors should influence its decision?

10. Substitutional new products, processes or technologies may force strategists to 'bet the company' on making the transition from old to new. What are the risks and how can they be reduced?

11. What conclusions about the retail grocery sector do you draw from the map in Figure 3.10? Select different variables and redraw the map accordingly. (Note: your new variables could be ordinal (as in Figure 3.10) or continuous (e.g. market share percentages or rates of sales growth), but be sure to choose variables that reflect actual or potential *strategic* choices, not just market characteristics.) Does your new map tell the same story or not? What do you learn from this?

Suggestions for Further Reading

Abernathy, W. and Wayne, K. (1974) 'Limits of the learning curve', *Harvard Business Review* (Sep–Oct, pp. 108–119).

Besanko, D., Dranove, D., Shanley, M. and Schaefer, S. (2010) *Economics of Strategy,* Wiley (Ed. 5).

Ghemewat, P. (2010) *Strategy and the Business Landscape*, Pearson (chapter 2).

Grundy, M. (2006) 'Rethinking and reinventing Michael Porter's five forces model', *Strategic Change* (vol. 15, pp. 213–229).

Klepper, S. (1996) 'Industry life cycles', *Industrial and Corporate Change* (vol. 6/1, pp. 119–143).

McGahan, A. (2000) 'How industries evolve', *Business Strategy Review* (vol. 11/3, pp. 1–16).

McGee, J., Thomas, H. and Wilson, D. (2005) *Strategy: Analysis and Practice,* McGraw-Hill (chapter 5).

McKiernan, P. (2006, ed.) *International Studies of Management and Organization* (vol. 36/3). Special issue on the subject of environmental analysis.

Porter, M.E. (1979) 'How competitive forces shape strategy?', *Harvard Business Review* (vol. 74/6, Mar–Apr, pp. 137–145).

Porter, M.E. (1991) 'Toward a dynamic theory of strategy', *Strategic Management Journal* (vol. 12 special issue, Winter, pp. 95–117).

Rumelt, R. (1991) 'How much does industry matter?', *Strategic Management Journal* (vol. 12/3, pp. 167–186).

Schmalensee, R. (1985) 'Do markets differ much?', *American Economic Review* (Jun, pp. 341–351).

Stonehouse, G. and Snowdon, B. (2007) 'Competitive advantage revisited: Michael Porter on strategy and competitiveness', *Journal of Management Inquiry* (vol. 16/3, pp. 256–273).

Wedel, M. (2001) 'Is segmentation history?', *Marketing Research* (vol. 13/4, pp. 26–29).

Notes

1 Sources: www.earthpolicy.org; http://www.worldometers.info/bicycles
2 Data from respective companies' websites.
3 www.cobr.co.uk/
4 Calculated from data in *Bicycle Retailer and Industry News* 01/04/2007.
5 Whereas enterprise strategists focus on the enterprise of particular interest, industrial organisation economists are more interested in the sector as an entity.
6 Porter (1980).
7 Barney (1986) reviews types of competition and the strategic implications.
8 Many publishers promote multiple brands, so oligopoly is less obvious. Following mergers and acquisitions over the last decade they have strengthened their combined share of the sector. Further concentration may yet occur.
9 That four countries dominate the supply of bicycles is a strategic issue distinct from the shares of named enterprises.
10 See Moore (1959) and Pratten (1981) for further discussion and data.
11 See Panzer and Willig (1991).
12 A concept attributed to Boston Consulting Group (BCG). See for example Henderson (1974); Conley (1975) and http://en.wikipedia.org/wiki/Experience_curve_effects
13 New entrants or existing competitors may pioneer radical changes in technology regime – one reason why the learning or experience effect does not necessarily benefit an enterprise indefinitely (see Abernathy and Wayne, 1974).
14 The Co-operative Group paid over £1.5 billion to acquire Somerfield, emulating Morrison's acquisition of Safeway some years earlier. Whilst these two chains have joined Sainsbury's strategic group, Asda and Tesco have arguably migrated from it.
15 For example, Apple Computers listed over 150 external global suppliers in 2011 (http://images.apple.com/suppliersresponsibility/PDF/Apple-Supplier-List-2011.pdf)
16 Less obvious ones include moral hazard (Farell, 1986) and product bundling (Nalebuff, 2004).
17 Source: Songini, Lucretzia (2001) 'Japanese Business in Italy', in Allan Bird (ed.), *Encyclopedia of Japanese Business and Management*, Routledge (pp. 232–234) (also via Google ebrary).

18 Readers unfamiliar with strategic marketing practices are advised to consult a specialised text, e.g., Meek, Meek and Ensor (2002); Bradley (2003); Aaker and McLoughlin (2010).
19 Unfortunately, modern trends are towards market fluidity and fragmentation, making reliable segmentation potentially more problematic, e.g., Wedel (2001).
20 See for example Johnson, Bowman and Rudd (1998).
21 For example, Porter (1991); Grundy (2006); Stonehouse and Snowdon (2007); Ghemeawat (2010, ch. 2); Grant (2010, ch. 4).
22 Arguably, such information is obtained ethically only when elicited after the person has been hired. In practice skilled protagonists can glean insights even from what the other does *not* say.
23 Called an oligopoly – see chapter 3.
24 See for example: Brandenburger and Nalebuff (1995); Camerer (1991); Dixit and Nalebuff (1991); Grant (2010, ch. 4); Postrel (1991); Powell (2003); Rumelt, Schendel and Teece (eds, 1994; chs 5,6,7).
25 See Grant (2010), chapter 4, pages 104–5.
26 According to a 2005 report by the IFPI (International Federation of the Phonographic Industry) the big 4 accounted for 72% of the market, while Neilsen Soundscan estimated it at 82% (see http://en.wikipedia.org/wiki/Music_industry). A best estimate of their respective market shares in 2005 based on these and earlier data suggests approximately: Sony-BMG (now Sony Music) 27%; Universal 25%; Warner Music 13%; EMI 13% – total 78%.
27 See the EMI website for greater detail. Before this, EMI and Warner had both tried unsuccessfully to acquire the other!
28 The following link to the EMI website provides a diagram of the complexity involved: http://www.emi.com/staticFiles/fe/28/0,,12641~141566,00.pdf
29 Hint: they can try to choose the buyers and suppliers they will deal with (see Porter, 1980). Work through their options.

4

Enterprise Stakeholders, Identity and Purpose

Learning Outcomes

This chapter is designed to enable you to:

① Explain the strategic significance of an enterprise's mission and its vision.

② Comment critically on the quality of mission and vision statements.

③ Analyse stakeholder expectations.

④ Analyse how power relationships influence an enterprise's strategic agenda.

⑤ Explain how the identity and ethos of an enterprise can influence its mission and vision.

⑥ Discuss various ethical postures in strategic management.

CASE STUDY: The Stobart Group plc[1]

In 1970 Eddie Stobart started his own road haulage (trucking) business, Eddie Stobart Ltd. The company developed as a reliable road transport distributor of goods for manufacturers, retailers and other clients, with whom it established long-standing business relationships. It grew progressively under the management of 'Steady Eddie' and later his son. As its smart, multi-coloured and well-cleaned trucks became commonplace sights on UK roads, the company captured the imagination of motorists: they would wave at Stobart's drivers and they formed a spotting club. Parents bought their children die-cast toy models of Stobart trucks. A whimsy that persists is to identify each of the distinctive trucks with girls' names painted on the cab.

However, in 2002 the Eddie Stobart business experienced financial difficulties and was sold to WA Developments (International). Over the next few years the company expanded through acquisitions and mergers, gaining facilities and diversified new business activities. These now include goods storage and distribution by air, sea and rail as well as by road, in the UK and some other European countries, notably Ireland and Spain. By 2010 it had become the publicly quoted Stobart Group plc. It owns Southend airport, a seaport and inland port in Northwest England, and a rail engineering maintenance subsidiary. Developing and maintaining client relationships remains a core feature of how it operates. The distribution of the group's activities can be seen from Table 4.A.

Table 4.A: Distribution of business activities of the Stobart Group in 2010

	Road haulage *	Rail	Sea ports and sea services	Airport and air services
% by revenue	85.2	10.2	3.1	1.5
% by profit	60.0	11.4	28.2	0.4

* Includes distribution, warehousing, property and process management services and merchandising.

Stobart Group's annual reports emphasize its high standards of customer service. They underline its commitment to staff, demonstrated by training, health and safety provisions and a long-term incentive plan. Stobart stresses its social awareness and responsibility through its support for positive community actions and worthy causes, using modern, efficient, low-pollution trucks, and reducing its energy consumption by using rail for long-distance freight transport. Its website declares:

> Over the last few years the Group has evolved beyond its position as an independent road transport and logistics business to a leading UK provider of multimodal transport and logistics solutions. Today Stobart Group delivers outsourced transport and logistics solutions for a wide variety of manufacturing, retail and public-sector customers across the industrial, consumer, food and defence sectors; working in partnership to transform their supply chain structures and optimise their efficiency.

Questions

1. On the basis of the evidence available to you above and online, how well would you say the Stobart Group is at meeting the expectations of [a]its owners and investors, [b]customers, [c]employees, and [d]other interest groups?

2. How satisfactory is the statement given above of Stobart Group's purpose or mission? What is the future vision of its management team?

Introduction: *Why Does This* Enterprise Exist?

Arguably, the most fundamental strategic question that one can ask is '*why* does *this* enterprise exist?'. A related question is 'what is its mission?'. An important clue to the answer comes from another question, '*for whom* does this enterprise exist?', which implies a recognition that individuals, groups and other enterprises benefit from (or are otherwise affected by) what it does. Personally and collectively, the parties who have an interest in its existence and future vision are called its stakeholders.

This chapter examines how for an enterprise its stakeholder expectations and interests can crystallise into an actionable mission, a plausible vision of its future aims and direction of travel, and concrete objectives to stimulate and assess progress. Multiple stakeholder interests, expectations and relationships need good understanding, reconciliation and proactive management. To understand interests and expectations involves strategic issue diagnosis and agenda management as well as addressing the less tangible concepts of enterprise identity and ethos (culture and shared values). Shared values inform the *ethical posture* of the enterprise, and shape its approach to social responsibility and corporate governance.

Stakeholders: for Whom this Enterprise Exists

An enterprise exists to satisfy the expectations and interests of its core stakeholders – or more accurately, its *core stakeholder groups* – which are the principal beneficiaries of what the enterprise does. Each core stakeholder group has its own expectations and priorities, based on perceptions of self-interest. Each group expects the enterprise mission to address and prioritise its interests, while generally acknowledging a wider range of enterprise stakeholders.[2] These groups are the principal beneficiaries of the three main types of enterprise. They comprise:

- Owners and customers of *business enterprises*.
- Clienteles (usually service recipients) and suppliers of *social agencies* such as hospitals and charities.
- Members of *mutual agencies* such as private clubs.

Owners of business enterprises can be sub-categorized as:

- Proprietors (owner-managers) of small and medium sized enterprises.
- Shareholder-directors of large, privately owned and public corporations.
- Arms-length investor-shareholders, both major institutions and individuals.

Traditionally, owners have been considered the dominant stakeholder group of for-profit businesses, while not-for-profit enterprises have characteristically recognised wider stakeholder interests. Although social agencies rarely have owners as such, the concept of *proprietorial interest* exists. Thus the UK Government has such an interest in the National Health Service. The founders and patrons of charities have proprietorial interests. All members of a club share joint ownership, but some also exercise stewardship roles that require them to have particular interests in its survival, well-being and mission achievement.

Typically, these people or interested parties find it comparatively easy to express their interests and have due account taken of them. Individual shareholders have more limited influence than institutions.[3] Although business owners' main expectation may be profit maximisation, their strategic interest is generally to maximise the medium to long term worth of their investments. Seen as an investment, the worth of an enterprise to an investor is the cumulative sum of a business's profit streams added to its realisable value, less cost of acquisition and additional funding.[4] ('Realisable value' here refers to the market value, based on share price, or sale value to a third party.) Increasingly, owners care about other issues too, especially those with potential to damage the value of their investments.

Clienteles (customers and service recipients) and suppliers of for-profit and not-for-profit enterprises divide into three categories:

- Those who enjoy well-established relationships with the enterprise, as evidenced by repeat purchases or receipt of services; mutual trust; and regular exchange of information and ideas.
- Occasional clients and suppliers whose contacts and transactions suggest at best only a limited relationship.
- Potential clients and suppliers.

The interests of suppliers and clients are in the products and services they trade, assessed variously in terms of availability and access, timeliness, specification, quality, reliability, effectiveness and cost.

Another group of direct stakeholders consists of employees. Share-owing employee directors and senior executive managers are the most influential. Employee interests include remuneration, conditions of employment including health and safety at work, promotion prospects, stability and continuity of employment. Because part-time, interim, subcontract and other kinds of outsourced labour have increased, employees' scope to pursue their collective interests is less potent than historically. Depending on the prevailing legislation and work practices, trades unions have a direct interest in, and varying degrees of influence on, enterprises that employ their members. Unions' interests encompass employment legislation and social conditions as well as the terms and conditions of employment of particular sets of employees.

The dividing line between core and non-core stakeholder groups is not always clear. The financial support that banks provide for businesses and non-business enterprises (occasionally as part owners) arguably makes them a core stakeholder group. Conversely, although national and local governments create regulations that affect employment practices, levy taxes on capital gains, trading profits, personal incomes and value-added sales, these agencies are generally considered non-core. Other non-core stakeholders that occasionally become strategically significant are independent pressure groups. Their focus, typically a single-interest, may derive from ideological, ethical or ecological convictions, or simply self-interest. Residents of West London near Heathrow International Airport made common cause with environmental pressure groups including Greenpeace to resist the British Airports Authority's plans for a third runway. In addition, the local community and the media may be considered as stakeholders.

Most enterprises now recognise that many non-core groups and the wider society in which they function have interests and expectations that should not (and, increasingly, *cannot*) be ignored.[5] However, the interests and expectations of groups can conflict markedly. A necessary strategic challenge for senior executives is to weigh and balance competing stakeholder demands on the enterprise, a task with great potential for misjudgements and compromise.

Enterprise Mission, Vision and Objectives

Once we can identify an enterprise's various stakeholder groups, we can begin to discern the reason(s) *why* that enterprise exists. The fundamental purpose of an enterprise is by convention called its *mission* The concept of mission captures the essential nature and basic purpose of an enterprise. An explicit *mission statement* declares its basic purpose(s) in terms of the intended activities that it will perform for the benefit of its defined, core stakeholder groups. In respect of business enterprises, a mission statement that says simply 'the enterprise exists to make profits for its owners' is inadequate. It merely expresses the ultimate goal of for-profit enterprises. To be actionable the mission must provide insights into the kinds of activities to be performed and how. Not-for-profit enterprises have no direct equivalent of the profit motive, so their missions are typically more complex, multi-faceted and sometimes ambiguous.

LEARNING ①
OBJECTIVE

Future uncertainty means that mission success – achieving the declared purposes and desired outcomes – is never guaranteed. Consequently, enterprises also need to affirm *directional intent*. This can be expressed as the enterprise vision. Adopting the declared mission as the starting point, the *vision statement* expresses the intended future characteristics and circumstances of the enterprise that should result from the direction that mission enactment will pursue.

LEARNING ①
OBJECTIVE

Thus mission and vision statements are complementary. While the mission statement has to be concrete, practical and fulfil a needed purpose, the vision statement informs where the enterprise is heading and what it aspires to become. The latter describes a desired and desirable future status.

If the enterprise is to succeed, financially and otherwise, the core stakeholder groups must understand and support its mission and vision. The degree of their support depends on how well the enterprise mission, vision and consequent strategy seem to address their interests and expectations.

Accordingly, each stakeholder group attempts to influence the strategic agenda of the enterprise. This agenda consists of the array of issues to which senior enterprise managers pay attention, most notably those that affect mission achievement.[6] The degree of influence that each group can exert on the agenda will depend on:

- The apparent legitimacy and relevance of the group's expectations and interests.
- The extent of its power to influence, persuade or dictate to executive managers.
- The level of motivation and commitment of the group's members.

Ultimately, the combination of these factors determines which issues reach the enterprise's strategic agenda, their salience, how executives understand them and the priority they receive.

Senior executives, influential owners and others with a proprietorial interest are the best-placed and most active agenda influencers. Other stakeholders including employees and external agents try to advance their interests by promoting selectively the issues of most concern. Stakeholder groups often exhibit conflicting priorities, not least among the executive managers and arms-length owners (institutional shareholders) of business corporations. The strategic consequence is then a lack of coherence and direction. Unsurprisingly, the politicised negotiations and power-play that characterize agenda-setting are also highly prevalent in public enterprises.

Mission and Vision Statements

Given the importance attached to mission and vision, many enterprises seek to codify them as written statements designed for widespread circulation. Not all of these enterprises, however, will use the labels 'mission statement' and 'vision statement': these labels are sometimes dismissed as meaningless jargon. Well-constructed statements clarify mission and vision, adding credibility to the enterprise. Constructing them is significant for the strategic management process, but is more challenging than some advocates suggest.[7] It is difficult to strike the right balance between ideal-ised generalities and detailed catalogues of ambitions, approaches and outcomes. The mission is *not* the strategy and should not be confused with it. The strategy is the *means* to enact the mission. Strategy can change over time, even though the mission does not.

   The differences between the three types of enterprise may be seen by the contrast between them in terms of mission and vision statements. The boxes below exhibit statements from each of the three sectors.

Missions and visions

Private enterprise
Google[8]

Mission: 'Google's mission is to organize the world's information and make it universally accessible and useful.'

Vision (according to Google co-founder Larry Page): 'The perfect [web] search engine would understand exactly what you mean and give back exactly what you want. Given the state of search technology today, that's a far-reaching vision requiring research, development and innovation to realize. Google is committed to blazing that trail.'

Social agency
The UK National Health Service (NHS)[9]

The NHS is a social agency with a complex structure of general hospitals and specialised, state-of-art treatment units that provide primary and secondary healthcare in the UK. It is taxpayer-funded and subject to top-level Government control. Its main priority is to treat acute conditions, although an increasing emphasis is on diagnostic screening and encouraging healthy lifestyles via general practitioners (GPs). Its main beneficiaries are sick patients, clinicians, GPs and the university teaching hospitals that train clinicians and conduct medical research.

Mission: A statement in 2000 said that the NHS will:

- provide a comprehensive range of services;
- shape its services around the needs and preferences of individual patients, their families and their carers;
- respond to the different needs of different populations;
- work continuously to improve the quality of services and to minimise errors;
- support and value its staff;
- devote public funds for healthcare solely to NHS patients;
- work with others to ensure a seamless service for patients;
- help to keep people healthy and work to reduce health inequalities; and
- respect the confidentiality of individual patients and provide open access to information about services, treatment and performance.

Vision: The 1948 NHS founding statement declared that three core healthcare principles would apply to the national service:

- meet the [acute] healthcare needs of everyone;
- be free at the point of delivery, and
- be based on clinical need, not ability to pay.

Mutual society
The University & College Union (UCU)

UCU is an association of university and college lecturers, professors and research staff. It does not provide explicit mission or vision statements on its website. However, it states:

UCU is the largest trade union and professional association for academics, lecturers, trainers, researchers and academic-related staff working in further and higher education throughout the UK.

Its main purpose is to represent the interests of members in negotiations with employers. More generally, it represents the interests of its members and of universities to Government.

Constructing Mission and Vision Statements

As the examples above indicate, statements of mission and vision vary in quality and coverage. Nonetheless, a clear and widespread *understanding* of mission and vision is necessary. To this end, formal statements can be valuable. A mission statement declares the aims of an enterprise (ends or goals); the scope (domains) of its activities; and in broad terms, how the aims are (to be) achieved and the priorities. Scope statements declare the products or services provided, key markets/clienteles and the core means (processes and technologies) applied. A mission statement does *not* articulate the detailed strategy, which would make the statement lengthy and lack impact. Too much detail might also reveal confidential facts about strategic intent that would help competitors.

An enterprise's mission statement needs to be sufficiently flexible to faciliate strategic responsiveness to new opportunities consistent with the enterprise's capabilities. However, it should not change whimsically according to short-term situations. Unfortunately, many mission statements contain broad, meaningless or potentially misleading generalities. Perhaps their main purpose is to enable consensus among divergent stakeholder interests. Alternatively, a statement may be broad to allow future scope extension into new domains (diversification). A train operator might declare that 'our mission is to offer the broadly-based services expected of a leading transportation company' to anticipate possible future entry into bus and coach operations without making a commitment to this direction. The danger is that broad statements encourage unwise scope extensions; train and bus operations make quite different demands. In any event, directional statements fit better into the vision statement.

A mission statement should not only show which activities are core: it should also clarify what it excludes. EasyJet defines its mission as 'point-to-point' services, which excludes the hub-and-spokes operations adopted by many airlines. This is a significant exclusion. Conversely, the Google mission is broad, declaring grandiose breathtaking ambition. Should stakeholders celebrate accordingly, or complain because it lacks focus or explicit priorities? For example, Xerox, also an information enterprise, stresses a focus on documents. Imprecise, ambiguous boundaries to scope lead stakeholders to interpret the mission as they would prefer it to be and hinders their judgements about the effectiveness of mission achievement.

To summarise, if a mission statement is to be valuable it should:

- Be compact and relevant.
- Explain clearly the aims, scope and priorities of the organisation, indicating in broad terms the means by which its aims are (to be) achieved.
- Set boundaries (at least implicitly) on its scope: the legitimate and excluded domains of activity.

Generally, vision statements are more aspirational and inspirational than mission statements. They recognise that enterprises *are* rarely where they have the *potential to be* – that there is 'unfinished business'. They may affirm current enterprise direction, but they often signal ambitious future intent, notably a commitment to extend or stretch its scope, functions and capabilities. The need to inspire means that vision statements are optimistic, albeit risking discredit if judged implausible. Thus in the illustration, Honda draws on its reputation for quality and innovation.

Honda's 'Vision 2010'

Some years ago, Honda Motor Corporation declared its *Vision 2010*: 'Striving to become a company that society wants to exist.' Presumably recognising the abstractness of this statement, Honda explained that:

A key part of our responsibility as a manufacturer is to provide new value in the form of better products and more advanced technologies. Recognizing this, we work constantly to ensure that everything we create is of the highest possible quality.

Mission and vision statements are sometimes accompanied by statements of enterprise values – sometimes referred to as philosophies. Such statements are not, however, integral elements of either mission or vision statements. A declaration of core values attempts to express the identity and ethos of the enterprise in support of its mission and reinforce an external image of responsibility and good corporate citizenship. Linking enterprise values with aims and intent can encourage enthusiasm and commitment, motivating the people (particularly employees) whose duty is to realise the mission.[10] However, the link between abstract enterprise values and concrete mission should not be difficult to understand. Statements of values can be merely 'motherhood and apple pie': fine-sounding assertions that no reasonable person would disagree with.

Enterprises differ markedly in how they express and enact their mission and vision. The trend is towards making statements short and memorable, expanding and qualifying them with separate, detailed statements of corporate and business objectives and strategies. Since most enterprises of any size now have websites, it is easy to communicate these more comprehensive statements.

Enterprise Objectives

Mission and vision statements require translation into tangible and specific enterprise *objectives* to guide future actions and to provide milestones against which to assess performance and progress. Objectives attract various names including aims, ends, goals and targets, often used imprecisely. In popular usage, aims are the broadest or highest level, in effect the enterprise mission, leading to more detailed goals, objectives and targets. To set relevant, realistic objectives and targets requires clarity of aims and goals. Detailed objective and target-setting is an important aspect of strategy implementation and control discussed in Chapter 13.

Since aims and objectives exist at different levels, they signal actions of different degrees of specificity. Hierarchical links allow the high-level mission statement to cascade down to detailed objectives. Each level in the hierarchy has an equivalent strategy; the cascade of strategies goes from the high-level *means* to very detailed, *tactical actions*. There is an ends/means duality at each level of specificity. An effective enterprise ensures that ends and means are compatible at each level.

Figure 4.1 illustrates the ends/means hierarchy. It depicts four levels of action that might characterise a major European football club such as Manchester United, Real Madrid or AC Milan. Manchester United prioritises managerial continuity more than the other clubs do. All three clubs have large stadiums with upwards of 76,000 seats; although AC Milan shares the San Siro with Internazionale. It seems unthinkable that Manchester United and its rival Manchester City would agree to play home games at Old Trafford or that Real and Atlético Madrid would share the Bernabéu.

A hierarchy of objectives allows enterprises to make individuals at each level responsible for achieving the declared objectives. Clear definitions of accountabilities of this kind are typical of military organizations and, since the 1960s, have become common in businesses. This conception is often referred to as 'management by objectives'.

LEVEL	THE 'WHAT' (ENDS)	THE 'HOW' (MEANS)
Broad stake-holder level	**Mission** • Be profitable sporting ambassadors for our city and our country	**Philosophy*** • Respect and influence • Play with style and flair • Continuity in progress
Enterprise (club) level	**Enterprise aims/goals** • Win all the major club competitions regularly • Most squad players should be full internationals • Run the club as a profitable growth business	**Master strategies** • Recruit and reward the best players, coaches and manager • Maximise stadium revenues • Sustain a profitable range of merchandising activities • Influence policies of national and international bodies (National League; UEFA; FIFA)
Sporting level	Season's objectives • Win national championship • Win knockout trophy • Win European Champions League • Maximise attendance of supporters at home and away games	Team strategies • Run successful youth academy • Maintain a strong first team squad • Achieve high levels of skill via world-class coaching methods • Manage players' fitness levels and diet
On the pitch	Match targets • Score at least 3 goals per game • Concede no more than 1 goal per game	Match strategies (tactics) • Well-organised, disciplined defending • Swift, fluid counter-attacking • Make decisive substitutions

* Incorporating elements of club ethos and future vision

Figure 4.1: The cascade of objectives for a major football club

Stakeholder Priorities and Strategic Agendas

Because stakeholder interests and expectations differ, mission and vision statements are the negotiated outcomes of attempts to reconcile multiple and often conflicting priorities. Statements often convey compromises by limiting detail; undue specificity draws attention to stakeholder expectations that the enterprise is unable to satisfy, hence is potentially divisive and counterproductive. The strategic agenda is the set of currently high-profile (salient) issues to which executives pay attention and prioritise in their strategic decision-making. Competing perceptions and interests create pressures that may compromise objective, impartial agenda management.

Conflicting Interests and Strategic Priorities *within* the Enterprise

The organisational context in which strategies are developed and implemented is inherently conflictual. Businesses use the justification of commercial confidentiality to approach decisions with less external scrutiny than is expected of public sector enterprises, parliament or the law courts. Non-core stakeholders and other observers often have to speculate about the conflicts of perspective, interests and priorities among core internal stakeholder groups such as:

- The board of directors.
- Senior executive managers below board level.
- Middle-level managers.
- Technologists and other specialised professional status staff.
- Other employees, whose interests are often represented by trades unions.

Within these broad categories, many subgroups may exist. This is especially likely among professional staff, whose varying specialisms affect their outlooks and priorities. Where factions are created, there is the potential for internal disharmony. Given the plurality of contestable and conflicting opinions, ideas and priorities among internal stakeholder groups, the scope for 'single brain' thinking and decision-making is practically limited. Strategies emerge from multiple interactions, but significantly shaped and steered by senior executives. Competing interests and power bases among internal stakeholder groups affect management *procedures* as well as the content of strategic agendas and decisions.[11]

The relative influence of individuals and groups will depend on their power, perceived legitimacy and motivation. Power derives from a combination of sources:[12]

- Formal (legitimate) authority of individuals and groups conferred by their positions, functions and responsibilities.
- Informal authority and influence deriving from membership of powerful groups, personal status and charisma.
- Possession of valuable knowledge, experience and expertise relevant to the enterprise mission.
- Ability to mobilize tangible resources and control how they are deployed.

Powerful individuals act coercively when they deem it necessary. Such behaviour is most often associated with senior executives but is sometimes exploited by other groups, such as trades unions and knowledge experts. A multinational pharmaceutical company, for example, employs chemists, biochemists, engineers of various disciplines, health and safety specialists, commercial and patent lawyers, estates and facilities specialists, risk management specialists, marketers and experts in many other areas, all of whom work to support, but are typically not engaged directly in operations. Research and development technologists and engineers are motivated to innovate and enhance products and processes; their priorities and views of risk may differ markedly from those of marketing or risk assessment experts.

The personal qualities, knowledge and skills of actors in pivotal positions are critical to mission achievement. An often-cited study[13] suggested that dominant enterprises in narrow-domain industry sectors typically have chief executives with backgrounds in finance, engineering or production, since control skills are vital in this context. Conversely, innovative enterprises are more likely to diversify and grow fast, spurred by chief executives who value innovation and creativity arising from their research and development or marketing backgrounds.

However, unless stakeholders are *motivated to apply* their power and influence, all such factors are irrelevant. Motivation, broadly speaking, derives from the desire for financial rewards and enhanced status. Senior executives' rewards depend on achieving growth in enterprise revenues, profits, share values and dividends. Other employees seek the opportunity to earn high wages, salaries and bonuses. Non-economic motivations of staff include:

*   The desire for enhanced status (promotion), with greater recognition and scope to 'make a difference', typically by influencing and controlling how resources are deployed.
*   Opportunities to fulfil their potential through interesting and challenging work.
*   The desire for safe, healthy and pleasant terms and conditions of employment.

Professional advisors, contract staff and subcontractors, though not employees, are also stakeholders. Their particular skills and positive attributes are frequently less well recognised and rewarded, creating frustration and potential conflict.

To summarise, effective enterprise managers contain conflict by taking due account of the interests, expectations and priorities of stakeholders who:

*   Have the legitimacy, power *and* motivation to shape the strategic agenda.
*   Can influence how agenda issues are interpreted and responded to.
*   Make pivotal contributions to the realisation of the enterprise mission.

Conflicting Interests of Executive Managers and Principals: the Agency Problem

Conflict is a widespread feature of relationships between senior executives in the enterprise and its external stakeholders, especially their principals. Senior executives are the agents responsible to these principals for enterprise conduct and strategic development. Therefore, they are duty-bound to respond to the legitimate expectations of these stakeholders. Yet disagreements arise over what is legitimate – morally, legally and strategically. How the parties resolve conflicts of interest and, more generally, ensure good governance depends on their power bases, their assumptions about the identity and ethos of the enterprise, and the controls that society imposes on them to ensure responsible behaviour.

LEARNING ③ OBJECTIVE
LEARNING ④ OBJECTIVE
Where the interests of executives (agents) and non-executive owners (principals) diverge substantially, this gives rise to the so-called 'agency problem'. Divergent interests challenge the good governance of the enterprise. Good governance requires transparency over the decisions and actions that affect enterprises and the accountability of their senior executives through regular, critical scrutiny, leading if necessary to dismissal.[14]

Commentators often portray the agency problem as a failure of executives to work in the best interests of shareholders. They cite such high-profile examples of so-called moral hazard[15] as the collapse of Enron in 2001, Lehman Brothers in 2008 and Royal Bank of Scotland (RBS) in 2009. Hyper-ambitious chief executives led these businesses. Criminal investigations resulted in the US, while RBS was nationalised to prevent bankruptcy.

However, a competing perspective on such events has emerged. It uses terms such as 'absentee owners' and 'ownerless corporations' to convey the idea that, while most executive boards *do* try to act in the best long-term interests of business enterprises, institutional shareholders such as pension and investment funds may lack interest and commitment to their long-term futures. Instead, they may be concerned only with short-term returns.

Corporate Governance and Social Responsibility

Governance arrangements differ between business and non-business enterprises and among countries. According to the Anglo-American model of capitalism, as applied to large business corporations, boards of directors and senior executives exercise managerial control (or stewardship[16]) on behalf of the owners who are mostly institutional investors. These owners have only arms-length knowledge of their investments. They put their trust in executive agents, although they look to non-executive directors to provide independent perspectives on strategy, performance and key policies such as executive remuneration.[17]

As managing agents, executives therefore interpret the expectations of the core stakeholders. As ambitious, driven people, they also aspire to personal advancement, acclaim and financial gain. They may hold strong opinions about the performance and future development potential of the enterprise. Inevitably, their own interests feature strongly when they invite shareholders to endorse their preferred strategies. Not-for-profit 'social enterprises' with a primary trading mission generally have shareholders too, while enterprises such as charities appoint trustees who are accountable to the Charity Commission for good stewardship. Many charities also have for-profit activities that generate funds in support of their charitable work, so they have directors who are responsible for their trading performance.

All forms of legal enterprise status oblige senior executives to prepare financial accounts and to explain performance and strategic intentions at an annual general meeting. Large enterprises supplement annual reports with periodic (interim reports), public announcements and briefings on progress and intentions for shareholders and other stakeholders. Formal meetings provide occasions for shareholders and others to express their interests, concerns, expectations and priorities.

Between times, the degree of communication between executives and principals ranges from frequent and cordial to problematic and negligible.

The conventional Anglo-American wisdom has been that in order to minimise the agency problem, good business governance must gear executive rewards very directly to owners' priorities. In practice this has meant focusing on financial performance, especially in the form of short-term dividends that are often the top priority of institutional investors, such as insurance, pension and investment funds. Thus it has proved difficult to design enterprise reward structures geared to long-term strategic effectiveness, as opposed to short term, possibly unsustainable, results.

Moreover, although owners can dismiss executives who are found to be acting incompatibly with their interests – this is a harsh step, and one that reflects poorly on their own judgment in having appointed such executives in the first place. Rather than insist on revised, long-term strategies and policies for a currently poorly performing enterprise, owners may opt instead to sell their shares. Accordingly, executives exercise considerable scope to impose their own ideas and priorities on enterprise strategies and how are implemented.

A possible solution to shareholder disengagement is to allow shareholders to have greater voting rights if they hold shares for long periods and engage with executive directors in a close, interactive agent–principal relationship. The 'Rhineland' model, attributed to large German enterprises, provides a possible model, in which shareholders (often banks) adopt a more engaged, less speculative, longer-term outlook.

Traditional corporate accountability and reporting assumed without question that shareholder interests dominate. Yet in recognising the multiplicity of enterprise stakeholders, executives acknowledge their responsibilities and obligations to society and citizens, not just owners. Legal and other authority-based governance arrangements are becoming more demanding and transparent, with large enterprises in particular expected to report publicly on conduct and performance using a variety of measures that go beyond finance.

The radical 'triple bottom line' (TBL) concept of corporate social responsibility is based on the view that sustainable capitalism must attend to three priorities, namely the impact that enterprises have on (a) the *planet* and (b) *people* as well as (c) *profits*. Hence the phrase 'people, planet, profits', otherwise known as '3P'.[18] However, senior executives may interpret a requirement to produce '3P' reports as a constraint on their managerial freedom. Alternatively, they may consider it an opportunity to demonstrate excellence and achieve respect as responsible corporate citizens (though it can be argued that too much accountability stifles enterprising behaviour). Whilst progressive enterprises routinely report their '3P' impact already, this approach could ultimately become a statutory reporting obligation of all for-profit and not-for-profit corporations.

Enterprise Identity and Ethos

Identity, Values, Culture and Ethics

The identity and ethos of an enterprise are concepts with significant implications for the strategic management of enterprise stakeholders. An enterprise's 'ethos integrates the enterprise's core values, internal culture and ethical outlook. Values are 'normative beliefs', which means that they are concerned with how the enterprise *should* behave. An example is Microsoft's stated belief in 'integrity, honesty, openness, personal excellence, constructive self-criticism, continual self-improvement, and mutual respect'.[19] These ethical values encode the principles that members of the enterprise perceive to be worthy, morally necessary, enduring, and central to existence and purpose. They guide individuals unambiguously towards appropriate actions in particular circumstances.

Organizational culture concerns 'the way we do things here'. The culture of any enterprise draws on wider national and local cultures, which are made enterprise-specific by the personal values of its members and their shared experiences and stories (refer to footnote for detailed accounts).[20] Though the enterprise's culture may be shared, it does not follow that the ethos that emerges is necessarily coherent, homogeneous, or even manageable. Even highly effective, seemingly homogeneous enterprises such as IKEA, the Swedish retail giant, may reveal quite fragmented and localised differences when studied closely.[21]

We can think of an enterprise's identity as comparable to an individual's personality. Enterprises can gain strategically from developing a coherent identity. A coherent identity can help to support an enterprise's mission and vision and facilitate the implementation of strategy. Underlying values are often tacit (unspoken), but when they are explicit and widely shared, they can reinforce a coherent enterprise ethos and identity.

Core values at Tesco

Tesco plc has become the largest and most successful retailer of groceries and household goods in the UK, a success that it now replicates in similar retail activities overseas. According to Sir Terry Leahy, its former chief executive, success links directly to its core values:

> Our core values "no-one tries harder for customers" and "treat people how we like to be treated" characterise our approach to corporate responsibility. We believe we can achieve most when we work together on practical things that make a difference. "Every little helps" can become a great deal when everyone pulls in the same direction.

Internal identity and external image are matters of perception. They become 'real', however, and are made visible through their impact on stakeholders and society. Sophisticated marketing techniques often aim to construct and reinforce an enterprise's positive external image. If there is a serious mismatch between an enterprise's identity and its external image, the enterprise's prospects of achieving its declared mission may be damaged.[22]

Ethical Postures for Constructive Stakeholder Management

Executives generally recognise the need to engage with owners and other stakeholder groups and to these manage relationships proactively as part of effective strategic management.

Executives therefore need to be well informed about the biases, motivations and consequent expectations of the core stakeholder groups. They can then seek to balance and manage conflicting priorities as far as is practical. When executives reflect on the priorities of stakeholder groups, questions such as the following are likely to arise:

- Why do these groups care about this enterprise (their motives)?
- Is their interest essentially positive or negative?
- What does their interest lead them to expect, personally, and for those whom they represent?[23] How legitimate are these expectations?
- How much power do they have to influence what the enterprise actually does?
- How strongly are they actually motivated to influence what the enterprise does?

The chart in Figure 4.2 identifies four basic stakeholder motivations. One dimension distinguishes economic (financial) and non-economic motivations. The other differentiates positive underlying motives and attitudes towards the enterprise from negative attitudes and motives that might subvert the mission. The former need to be encouraged, the latter countered constructively.

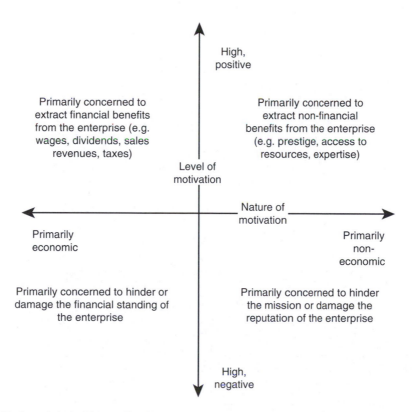

Figure 4.2: Various stakeholder motivations

Executives need appropriate stakeholder management strategies for each category. They bear considerable responsibility for the ethical posture of the enterprise towards core stakeholder groups – not least because the approach to social responsibility and governance bears on the economic performance of the enterprise. The choice of posture will strongly affect how they attempt stakeholder management in practice. At least three distinct postures are observable in practice:[24]

1. A narrow or *minimalist* posture that prioritises the interests of only the dominant stakeholders.
2. An *expedient* posture that responds to a wider set of stakeholders pragmatically as circumstances dictate and allow.
3. A constructive, comprehensive, *principled* posture towards all identifiable stakeholder groups.

Alternative ethical postures towards stakeholder management

Minimalist: The Blackstone Group is a US company that describes itself as a 'global alternative asset manager and provider of financial advisory services'. Its mission is to create and manage private equity funds. It acquires poorly performing enterprises, makes them efficient and profitable and sells them at a profit, typically within five years. Blackstone acknowledges publicly how much its dedicated executives and specialist corporate staff make to financial performance and it rewards them accordingly. It makes few other public statements about stakeholder obligations. However, its UK subsidiary is subject to European Union directives on corporate transparency, so it duly accepts an obligation to inform its staff of future divestment plans.

Expedient: University missions have two components: to educate students and to create new knowledge through research. The Higher Education Funding Councils provide British Universities with much of their income via taxpayers. The Quality Assurance Agency monitors institutional teaching quality. National Research Assessment Exercises assess research performance. Independent quality agencies also assess member institutions (e.g., Association to Advance Collegiate Schools of Business; Equis, Association of MBAs). Review frequencies vary, generally between three and seven years. Final year students give their opinions via the annual Web-based National Student Survey. All the review bodies are influential both as direct stakeholders and as representatives of taxpayers and other stakeholders such as students and their families. Positive feedback from them encourages applications from able (fee-paying) students and enhances facilitates research grants and ndustrial sponsorship. Thus, senior university managers aim to ensure that core stakeholder groups present a favourable impression of their institution's activities and performance. They devote considerable time to preparations for these various reviews *as they become due*. Between times, stakeholders receive much less attention.

Principled: Lands' End is a Web-based clothing retailer of US origin that takes its environmental and social responsibilities seriously. It offers a remarkably detailed statement of its principles of business ethics and integrity covering: human rights; fair dealing with suppliers, customers and staff; environmental sustainability; and community and charity.[25] The following is a brief extract:

'Lands' End has a long tradition of doing the right things for the right reasons. Ever since our founder, Gary Comer, wrote his "Principles Of Doing Business" in 1963, we have sought to do business in the right way. Doing business the right way means much more than just being fair with your customers and employees. It also means: being a good citizen, operating to high ethical standards and addressing the impact our business has on the environment. These principles form the very fabric of what Lands' End stands for; we call them our Environmental & Social Responsibilities (ESR).'

A narrow ethical posture is often associated with business enterprises that prioritise financial interests and expectations, limiting non-profit-making, cost-incurring actions to those based on legal imperatives (rather than on moral and principled judgements). Such enterprises are often described as 'exploitative', a term that clearly carries negative implications. It might be rather naïve to suppose that all not-for-profit enterprises are inherently more ethical than their for-profit counterparts. After all, adopting morally neutral (amoral) positions need not equate to immoral behaviour.

Indeed, defenders of this kind of ethical posture argue that this approach is inherently ethical because it exploits enterprises' resources fully; by not leaving them idle or incompetently managed, it maximises social utility.[26] Historically this posture has been associated with the achievement of high *short-term* profits (outlined in solid red in Figure 4.3), though it has gradually come to be more associated with the pursuit of maximum shareholder value *in the longer term*. (In Figure 4.3, this transition is indicated by the red, dotted, line.)

An expedient posture applies 'enlightened self-interest' pragmatically to the respective interests of multiple stakeholders. It may be described as enlightened in that executives believe they best serve the interests of core stakeholder groups by being sensitive to the interests of other groups whenever potential conflict and damage exist.[27] Within practical limits, they want to meet each stakeholder group's expectations, taking due account of status, influence and timing, and by exceeding legal obligations when they perceive benefits to the enterprise that outweigh the costs. The reactive nature of this posture typically leads to a short-term orientation (indicated in Figure 4.3 by solid grey) to avoid the risk of alienating any group whose by interests it ignores for too long. For example, enterprises pursue 'good corporate citizen' initiatives by engaging

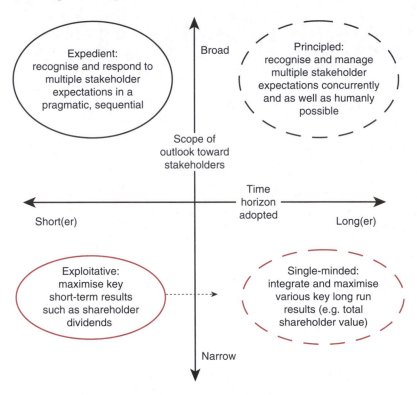

Figure 4.3: Managerial approaches towards stakeholders

with local communities and respecting environmental concerns, as prevailing opinions and circumstances dictate.

The fourth posture (indicated in Figure 4.3, the dotted grey oval) demonstrates an ethically principled enterprise posture. It seeks respectful, non-exploitative relationships and tries to work through differences with stakeholder groups, not ignore them, ride roughshod over them, or capitulate to unreasonable demands. It is feasible when the enterprise's senior executives believe in doing (and being seen to do) the 'right thing'. They can then issue clear, ethical imperatives for principled actions. In the spirit of engagement, they will try to manage *the expectations* of individual and stakeholder groups to levels that the enterprise can realistically meet.

Sceptics may consider this an idealised approach. Without doubt, an ethically principled posture does not avoid dilemmas that managers can resolve without anguish, cost or controversy. For example, the late Anita Roddick's Body Shop has been criticised because its suppliers in developing countries pay low wages, by the standards of consumers who buy the products, despite this trade enabling economic betterment for the workers who are said to be well treated by the prevailing standards of their countries. Nonetheless, many argue that it is the only justifiable approach to the treatment of stakeholders in the 21st century, given the growing external pressures for ethical, accountable enterprise management.

CASE STUDY: Mission, vision and stakeholders of Eden Project[28]

The Eden Project illustrates many of the concepts addressed in this chapter. It is a not-for-profit enterprise established at the turn of the Millennium to promote research into and conservation of the natural environment. The case study maps Eden Project's multiple stakeholders using the framework of Figure 4.2.[29]

Eden Project is the brainchild of Tim Smit and a handful of associates. A successful music producer, Smit moved from London to Cornwall in the late 1980s to set up his own recording studio. He became involved in a horticultural project to restore the so-called Lost Gardens of Heligan. Its subsequent success as a visitor attraction led him to dream of a more ambitious project to promote environmental and educational interests. The timing was good because the Government was keen to mark the new Millennium with inspirational projects that would have a lasting impact on Britain and its image in the world. It had created the Millennium Commission to provide financial support for worthy proposals, using National Lottery funds.

Smit and his friends envisioned the regeneration of a derelict china clay pit near St. Austell in Cornwall. Within an extensively landscaped site, they proposed to install giant domed greenhouses called biomes that would contain a wide variety of the world's plant life. They registered Eden Trust as a charity and applied for Lottery funding. The initial application failed. Undaunted, Smit and his associates made a revised application for the huge sum of £40 million. The second application succeeded, subject to the condition that funds from other sponsors and the general public must match the Lottery grant.

Smit's masterstroke was to exploit the value of publicity to create alliances with high-profile partners. He challenged architects Nicholas Grimshaw and Partners to design the world's largest greenhouse, drawing on the lessons of designing the Eurostar terminal at Waterloo International railway station! He campaigned hard to engage the services of the biggest construction companies. He laboured to convince sceptical local planners of the scheme's attractions. By degrees, he succeeded. He encouraged a do-or-die mentality among volunteers and other contractors and courted the media, sponsors and Friends of Eden Project unceasingly. He commissioned a video diary of the project's development and allowed the public to visit the site while it was still work-in-progress.

Eden Project opened fully to the public in March 2001, well after the turn of the Millennium. It had attracted huge interest during construction. Hundreds of volunteers helped make it happen, despite huge setbacks and hardships. Smit had remained defiant in the face of adversity. He said 'People used to ask me what my exit strategy was if it all went wrong. I told them that my exit strategy was death. There was no get-out. This just had to work.' That it *did* succeed confirms that Smit captured the environmental *zeitgeist* by riding his luck to the limit. In its first year of operation, it attracted over one million visitors from all over Britain and beyond. It has since maintained this level of interest. Meanwhile, the £800 million Millennium Dome (now the O$_2$ Arena) also funded by the Millenium Commission was widely seen as a failure.

The original mission of Eden Project was 'to promote the understanding and responsible management of the vital relationship between plants, people and resources, leading to a sustainable future for all.' However, sensitive to more recent criticism that Eden Project was becoming just 'a green theme park', the statement of its core charitable aim now emphasises serious environmental priorities, specifically 'to promote public education and research in flora, fauna and other aspects of the natural world.'

An idealistic explanation of why Eden Project exists might say that it is a triumph of human aspiration and commitment to a goal. A more pragmatic claim would say that Smit and his associates managed to align the interests and motivations of a large number of disparate stakeholder groups, described variously as passionate, skilled, influential, resourceful, financially and politically astute. The groups included:

- Smit's close friends and associates – the core Eden Project team.
- The Millennium Commission.
- Cornwall County Council.
- Regional and national agencies and banks (more than 12 in total).
- Nicholas Grimshaw (the biome architect) and other professional advisors.
- McAlpine Construction and other contractors.
- Volunteers (students, retired and unemployed people).
- Individual sponsors: the 'Friends of Eden Project'.
- School teachers and university academics.
- Plant suppliers and donors from around the world.
- English China Clays Ltd (now Imerys UK).
- Local residents in and around the Bodelva site.
- Visitors who pay for admission.

Figure 4.4 analyses their respective motivations. Stakeholder groups with particularly high influence or power feature in red boxes; moderate influencers are in black, limited (individual) influencers in grey.

Fortunately for Eden Project, most stakeholders were motivated positively towards it. The position of the Millennium Fund was pivotal. Its purpose was to identify and support substantial, inspirational projects, the biggest being the

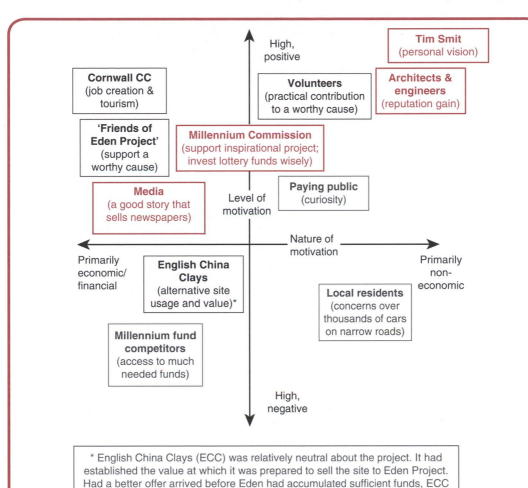

Figure 4.4: Analysis of selected Eden Project stakeholders

Millennium Dome. The Dome received the personal backing of Government ministers because of its perceived significance. They probably viewed Eden Project as an idiosyncrasy. However, the duty of the Commission was to allocate *all* of its funds wisely. It could not ignore the bold proposal for Eden Project, a factor Smit doubtless exploited. The project team had to engage with some neutral or negative, particularly local interests. English China Clays, the owner of the site, gained financially by selling it to Eden Project, yet wondered that it might realise a higher price from a business enterprise. Inevitably, Figure 4.4 oversimplifies: the motivations of local residents, members of the public and 'Friends of

Eden Project' could not converge entirely. Local people polarised over new job opportunities versus the consequences of a 'tourist invasion'.

Questions

1. Critique the mission of Eden Project as it was (a) expressed originally and (b) later revised. How do these relate to the vision that is now driving Tim Smit?

2. What conclusions concerning stakeholder management priorities can you draw from the stakeholder map of Figure 4.4? How might your conclusions be different if Smit and his associates had established Eden Project as a for-profit venture?

3. How would you describe Smit's ethical posture of stakeholder management? Did external stakeholders feel manipulated? To what extent would it matter if they did?

Eden Project shows the crucial importance of positive stakeholder relationships. Even frustrated stakeholders tend to be constructive when kept well informed and to understand enterprise constraints. Conventional wisdom is that high-powered stakeholders should receive the most attention to be kept as satisfied as possible, while those without power or influence can be ignored. However, core stakeholder groups frequently have mutually conflicting priorities. Arguably, the best approach is to engage candidly with each group, trying to negotiate strategies and goals with the best prospects for all, despite containing compromises. Today's weak and relatively disinterested stakeholders may become influential and positive supporters tomorrow.

Summary

LEARNING OBJECTIVE ①
LEARNING OBJECTIVE ②

- Well-intentioned, well-constructed mission and vision statements offer valuable guidance to develop strategies and define critical objectives. In order, perhaps, to promote consensus among core stakeholder groups, the risk is that such statements become too generalised to offer real strategic guidance.

LEARNING OBJECTIVE ③

- Executives are accountable to the core stakeholder groups for the conduct and strategy of the enterprise, principally the owners and/or those with a proprietorial interest in it. Their duty is to implement strategies and policies acceptable to core stakeholder groups.

LEARNING OBJECTIVE ④

- Since stakeholders have differing interests and priorities, the most interested groups (including senior executives themselves) seek to influence the strategic agenda disproportionately by exercising their authority and power. Agenda conflicts arise from the interaction of mis matched expectations among the various stakeholder groups.

- When the interests of proprietors and ambitious executives diverge, the agency problem of modern Western capitalism arises. As the stewards of major enterprises, executives shoulder

ARNING ③
JECTIVE

ARNING ④
JECTIVE

ARNING ⑤
JECTIVE

ARNING ⑥
JECTIVE

the practical responsibility to resolve such differences constructively or face dismissal. Business executives must reconcile the strategic decisions they judge to be in the long-term interest of the enterprise and its broad array of stakeholders with the generally short-term financial priorities of comparatively disengaged, major institutional shareholders.

- As executives try to manage multiple stakeholder expectations, their preferred ethical posture draws typically on the particular identity and ethos of the enterprise. Alternative postures range from a traditional *laissez-faire* approach to proactive, principled engagement, arguably more in tune with current thinking on corporate governance and social responsibility.

Exercises for Further Study and Discussion

1. To what extent are mission and vision statements relevant for [a] major corporations, [b] small business enterprises, and [c] not-for-profit enterprises? What are the key differences?
2. Some claim that the main purpose of mission and vision statements is to motivate employees. Investigate and discuss this claim.
3. Identify an enterprise mission statement that interests you and try to improve it.
4. What circumstances would lead an enterprise to revise its mission or its vision?
5. An enterprise's public statement that may begin with the phrase 'Our values are…'. probably reflects the opinions of a relatively small group of senior executives. Does an *enterprise* really have values? Or do such statements merely reflect the values of an elite group of senior executives? How might the values of an enterprise affect its strategy?
6. Assess how the identity and ethos of a successful not-for-profit enterprise contribute to its success. To what extent can executives manage identity and ethos?
7. Google and easyJet are for-profit enterprises, but neither emphasises owners' interests in their mission and vision statements. To what extent do you regard this as [a] deliberate or [b] an oversight? Explain your view.
8. Advertisers generate a large proportion of Google's revenues. To what extent is Google managing or ignoring the interests of this important stakeholder group?
9. Would University & College Union (UCU) serve its members better if it concentrated solely on their interests, rather consider students, employers, government and society more generally?

Suggestions for Further Reading

Bartkus, B., Glassman, M. and McAfee, B. (2000) 'Mission statements: are they smoke and mirrors?', *Business Horizons* (vol. 43/6, pp. 23–28).

Bartkus, B., Glassman, M. and McAfee, B. (2006) 'Mission statement quality and financial performance', *European Management Journal* (vol. 24/1, pp. 86–94).

Brown, M.T. (2005) *Corporate Integrity: Rethinking Organizational Ethics and Leadership*, Cambridge University Press.

Campbell, A. and Yeung, S. (1998) 'Creating a sense of mission', in Segal-Horn, S. (ed.) *The Strategy Reader*, Blackwell.

Clegg, S., Kornberger, M. and Pitsis, T. (2005) *Managing and Organizations*, Sage Publications (Chapter 10).

Collins and Porras (2002) *Built to Last: Successful Habits of Visionary Companies*, Harper (chapter 11).

Dutton, J.E. and Ashford, S.J. (1993) 'Selling issues to top management', *Academy of Management Review* (vol. 18/3, pp. 397–428).

Fombrun, C. and Foss, C. (2004) 'Business ethics: corporate responses to scandal', *Corporate Reputation Review* (vol. 7/3, pp. 284–288).

Hummels, H. (1998) 'Organizing ethics: a stakeholder debate', *Journal of Business Ethics* (vol. 17/13, pp. 1403–1419)

Lencioni, P. (2002) ' Make your values mean something', *Harvard Business Review* (vol. 80/7, pp. 113–117).

Mills, R.W. and Weinstein, B. (2000) 'Beyond shareholder value – reconciling the shareholder and stakeholder perspectives', *Journal of General Management* (vol. 25/1, pp. 79–93).

Mitchell, R.K., Agle, B.R. and Wood, D.J. (1997) 'Toward a theory of stakeholder identification and salience: defining the principle of who and what really counts', *Academy of Management Review* (vol. 22/4, pp. 853–886).

Sternberg, E. (1997) 'The defects of stakeholder theory', *Corporate Governance: International Review* (vol. 5/1, pp. 3–10).

Whetton, D.A., Rands, G. and Godfrey, P. (2001) 'What are the responsibilities of business to society?', in Pettigrew, A.M., Thomas, H. and Whittington, R. (eds) *Handbook of Strategy and Management*, Sage Publications.

Notes

1   See http://www.stobartgroup.co.uk and http://en.wikipedia.org/wiki/Stobart_Group
2   Mitchell, Agle and Wood (1997); Cummings and Doh (2000).
3   Although this may be changing: Davis, Lokomnik and Pitt-Watson (2006).
4   Where realisable value is market value (based on share price) or sale value to a third party. See Mills (1998); Rappaport (1998).
5   Whetton, Rands and Godfrey (2001); Chew and Gillan (2005); Jacoby (2005); Vogel (2005). Sources like these generally address social responsibility from the large enterprise perspective. As regards small enterprises, the similar, but distinct concept of social capital, a sense of the goodwill attributed to positive stakeholder relationships is interesting, e.g., Spence, Schmidpeter and Habisch (2003).
6   Agenda concepts emerged in the literature on public enterprises and policy-making, e.g., Kingdon (2002 – first edition 1984). Jane Dutton and colleagues began to explore the same perspectives, but more often using the concept of 'strategic issue diagnosis', e.g., Dutton and Ashford (1993).
7   Pearce (1982); Campbell and Yeung (1998).
8   Source: http://www.google.com/intl/en/corporate/
9   Source: http://www.nhs.uk/NHSEngland/aboutnhs/Pages/NHSCorePrinciples.aspx

10 Lencioni (2002).

11 Hardy and Pettigrew (1985).

12 Power is a core topic covered in many organization behaviour texts, e.g., Clegg, Courpasson and Phillips, N. (2006); Buchanan and Badham, R. (2008).

13 Miles and Snow (1978).

14 Here the shareholders are the principals in the principal–agent contract. Ross (1973) drew attention to this problem. See also Eisenhardt (1989) and Besanko, Dranove and Shanley (2000, chapter 15), which provides a useful overview.

15 Moral hazard occurs when the executive as agent takes risks and pursues directions that would have been unacceptable to the principal if the latter had had prior knowledge. Thus one might expect major shareholders to nominate board directors to represent their interests directly, yet this is not invariably done. See Zandstra (2002); O'Sullivan (2003); Fombrum and Foss (2004).

16 Senge (1992).

17 Clarke (1998).

18 Elkington (1998).

19 http://www.microsoft.com/about/en/us/default.aspx

20 There are many focused discussions of corporate culture. Martin (1992) provides an academic, *descriptive* perspective; Peters and Waterman (1982) is a classic, *prescriptive* account of proactive cultures. Clegg, Kornberger and Pitsis, (2005, chapter 8) and Johnson, Scholes and Whittington (2008, chapter 4) discuss culture and its (strategic) management.

21 Salzer (1994).

22 The financial set-backs and public relations disasters experienced in 2010 by Toyota and BP in the United States arising from faulty vehicles and the oil rig disaster in the Gulf of Mexico, respectively, provide equally potent examples.

23 For example, trades unions are concerned with employees' terms and conditions, the Health and Safety Executive with their well-being.

24 Mirvis and Googins (2006) offer an alternative, 4-way typology of approaches.

25 http://www.landsend.co.uk/static/customerservice/about_us/social_responsibility/

26 Proponents include notably Milton Friedman, a Nobel Laureate in Economics (Friedman, 1970). See also Sternberg (1997) and Mills and Weinstein (2000).

27 Thus the 'marketing philosophy' considers addressing customers' interests to be paramount since a failure to meet their needs and wants would prevent the business enterprise from making profitable sales in a competitive market. Inferentially, then, adopters of this orientation would probably consider the marketing philosophy irrelevant in a monopoly situation.

28 See http://www.edenproject.com/

29 Of course, other analytical frameworks exist, e.g., Scholes (1998; 2001); Cummings and Doh (2000).

5

Enterprise Resources and Distinctive Capabilities

Learning Outcomes

This chapter is designed to enable you to:

① Describe and explain the significance of enterprise resources and capabilities.

② Explain and critique the resource-based approach to strategic management.

③ Apply the V-R-I-O-S framework to specific cases in order to analyse resources and capabilities.

④ Understand the role and nature of value chain analysis.

⑤ Analyse enterprise performance using a range of (a) accounting and (b) non-financial measures.

CASE STUDY: Tesco plc[1]

Tesco is a British international grocery and household goods retailer. Jack Cohen founded Tesco in 1919 and opened its first north London shop in 1929. Tesco expanded rapidly after the 1939–45 war with Cohen's famous dictum 'pile it high and sell it cheap.' By the 1960s it was one of the largest supermarket chains, operating 800 stores around Britain, pioneering much larger retail spaces selling grocery and allied goods.

Throughout the 1970s, 1980s and 1990s it continued to grow by developing ever-larger, out-of-town stores, acquiring smaller chains and by extending its range of Tesco own-label goods. Over time it has emphasised value (quality at competitive prices), rather than simply low prices.

In 1997 (Sir) Terry Leahy became Chief Executive, leading a new phase of aggressive expansion. An alliance with the oil company Exxon Mobil allowed it to operate grocery stores on hundreds of petrol forecourts. It created multiple UK store formats based on size, location and range of goods sold. It entered the retail markets of the United States, Europe and Asia through acquisitions and joint ventures. It has extended its range of consumer goods and diversified into new services (such as banking, an internet portal, mobile phones, insurance, and on-line shopping). Tesco has become the UK's largest retailer (with the most popular customer loyalty card scheme) and the third biggest retailer worldwide after US Wal-Mart and French Carrefour. Its key statistics over the last 5 years show that the pace of growth has not slowed.

Table 5.A: Tesco plc key statistics over five years*

	2006	2007	2008	2009	2010
Group sales (£m)	**39,454**	**42,641**	**47,298**	**53,898**	**56,910**
Group retail statistics					
Number of stores	2672	3263	3751	4332	4811
Average total number of staff (000's)	368.2	413.1	444.1	468.5	472.1
Group financial performance					
Enterprise value (£m **)	30841	40469	37656	35907	41442

* Refer to Tesco plc 2010 Annual Report, 5-year summary for full explanations of the statistics and how they are calculated.
** Defined as market capitalization value (based on share price) plus net debt.

Tesco is evidently very competent at what it does. The puzzle for its many competitors, themselves competent retailers, is how it has outperformed them so substantially. Amongst the answers to this question are probably the following:

- The singular, dedicated leadership of Sir Terry and his senior management team.
- The clarity of Tesco's vision of growth via diversification and overseas expansion.
- The application of appropriate resources and know-how to maintain growth in *existing* areas, to innovate, and to enhance the prospect of success *in each new area*.
- Exploiting the capabilities of successful alliance partners, to distribute goods efficiently to its stores, diversify, and develop overseas.

- Developing expertise progressively in *every* activity by innovating and absorbing best practice observed elsewhere.
- Rewarding individual performance and promoting capable people.

Questions

1. Find evidence that supports (or questions) the above explanations of Tesco's effectiveness.

2. How might Tesco's resources and capabilities constrain its continuing growth?

Introduction: Why Resources and Capabilities Matter

Previous chapters have focused on the external environment. Their 'outside-in' perspective encourages enterprises to identify specific threats and opportunities to which they can direct resources and skills. This perspective affirms the importance of environmental *fit* or *match*, locating the enterprise in an attractive, defensible niche defined by particular industry sectors, demand segments and associated products and services.

LEARNING OBJECTIVE ①

The 'outside-in' perspective thus encourages a view of enterprises as essentially reactive, with limited power to innovate and influence external developments. If indeed some sectors *are* fundamentally more attractive than others, strategic decisions will focus only the choice of which sector(s) and which position(s) to occupy. Enterprises may try to compete in sectors with positional strategies inappropriate to their resources. Their perception of attractiveness is merely an illusion, condemning them to ultimate failure. In reality, all sectors feature successful *and* unsuccessful enterprises. Effective enterprises must be well-equipped to function in their chosen sector(s). Their resources and other strengths have evolved appropriately to the challenges they face[2] and their weaknesses do not significantly hinder progress.

LEARNING OBJECTIVE ①

LEARNING OBJECTIVE ②

An alternative perspective on the strategy process is to understand the enterprise's resources and skills – especially the activities and functions it performs most capably and which make it distinctive, highly valued and a beneficiary of long-term advantage. This 'inside-out' perspective on strategic management is sometimes referred to as the resource-based view (or RBV).[3]

An enterprise's resources and capabilities are key elements of effective strategies. According to the RBV perspective, an effective enterprise concentrates on what it does best, relying on partners and subcontractors to provide other, necessary inputs in which it has neither distinction nor advantage. Clearly, to make judgements about where they can add value, enterprises require the means and the criteria to assess their resources and capabilities, ideally at each stage of value-creation and in comparison with other providers.

Enterprises also need to be able to upgrade or substitute their current resources and capabilities over time, which is an essential condition of dynamic strategies. If an enterprise is to assess its current and future needs objectively, it needs to employ finely tuned measures of *performance* (financial and otherwise) to compare itself with competitors.

Enterprise Effectiveness and Advantage from Resources and Capabilities

RNING ①
ECTIVE
The resource-based perspective treats enterprises as specific 'bundles' of resources and capabilities. Apparently similar enterprises may exhibit differences – so-called *resource heterogeneity* –
RNING ②
ECTIVE
at this level. Truly effective enterprises have *unique* sets of resources and capabilities that confer comparative strengths on them.

Effective enterprises apply their comparative strengths to create and exploit opportunities, often ones that others have not recognised. Their strengths help them to neutralise threats and operate effectively in their chosen domains, allowing the RBV to direct them towards the forms of demand that they are well equipped to meet. Well-defined, sustainable resources and capabilities
RNING ①
ECTIVE
underpin the performance of effective enterprises. They enable enterprises to adapt and change proactively. Effective enterprises generally set the strategic agendas in their sectors, obliging
RNING ②
ECTIVE
others to respond, or else fall behind.

Thus the RBV emphasises the role of innovation and learning, to build, apply and extend relevant resources and capabilities. Enhancing distinctive resources and capabilities makes it difficult, perhaps impossible, for others to keep up. This is sometimes called *resource immobility* – the dynamic enterprise guards its distinctiveness well, so that its knowledge migrates only slowly to others.

In a demanding, competitive environment the scope to develop distinctive resources and capabilities depends on many enterprise-specific factors. These include size, current resources and capabilities, ambition and single-mindedness.

The Value-Creating Role of Resources and Capabilities

Effective enterprises accumulate and deploy resources and capabilities for a single purpose: to create net external value. Value-adding activities incur costs, both financial and other. The *net* value an enterprise creates (adds) is the *excess* of output value (generally measured by price)
RNING ①
ECTIVE
over the associated input costs. Strategic effectiveness is indicated by the degree to which the value created exceeds the costs. Exceptional value creation arises from two sources:

1. Dominance of supply, that is, monopoly power. (Competition authorities typically identify monopoly existing when an enterprise's market share exceeds 30%.).
2. Distinctiveness, that is, the ability to deploy distinctive resources and capabilities. Such were first identified by the 19th century economist, David Ricardo. The earnings from these resources have become known as 'Ricardian rents'.

Monopolies tend to erode because of anti-monopoly regulations and also because of (technological) innovation that provides enterprises with superior means of value-adding. According to the RBV, value-creation activities are more sustainable (defensible) when linked to the latter source above, that is, distinctive resources and capabilities.

Enterprise Resources

Resources include an enterprise's *tangible* (physical and human) and *intangible* assets. To be strategically significant, resources must be actively deployed in value-creating routines. Having the *means* to deploy a resource is not the same as actually *doing* so. Unused, *passive* resources decline in value and become obsolete; knowledge held by employees who leave the enterprise evaporates. Ownership is not always the critical factor: enterprises may own some physical assets, but have full access, control and use of others – for example, by employing staff and leasing assets such as equipment and vehicles.[4]

Tangible resources are comparatively straightforward to identify and assess, though they may vary in their degree of tangibility. They include the following:

- Physical assets including land, buildings, facilities, equipment, vehicles, office furniture, raw materials and stock in trade (inventories).
- Financial assets such as cash, shares, accounts receivable, financial investments and other assets declared on the balance sheet, such as capitalized leases.
- Employment contracts between the enterprise and its employees and with external agents including legal advisors, consultants and subcontractors.

Auditing verifies, measures and formally records tangible assets. It is more suited to counting items than assessing their quality, condition and value. Consequently, published accounts can be a poor guide to the *strategic* value of assets, especially physical resources with alternative potential uses.

While it is easy to count employees and categorise their functions, roles and qualifications, it is harder to assess their strategic value to the enterprise, despite appraisal procedures. The contribution of individuals is usually clear in small enterprises. Formal appraisal systems in larger enterprises seek to make this explicit for developmental purposes. However, the challenge of summarising the collective output of appraisals in a strategically useful form is substantial.

Intangible resources are not always easy to define. Those that are relatively easy to identify and to value include:

- Brand names, trademarks and logos.
- Technical patents, copyrights and other codified knowledge (called intellectual property).

The value of such assets is usually assessed in terms of their expected resale value. However, financial accounts tend to be prepared conservatively, so many intangible assets do not feature, despite enhancing the worth of an enterprise. This is often recognised when a company becomes an acquisition target. (Typically their worth is expressed as 'goodwill' in the balance sheet of the combined organization.) Intangible assets can be sold or contractually assigned (licensed) to others in exchange for a fee.

In contrast to the kinds of assets identified above, there are other intangible resources that are virtually impossible to codify and value, because they are abstract and sometimes transient. They include:

- External image and reputation of the *enterprise* (linked to, but distinct from, its *brands*[5]).
- External networks and relationships.
- Enterprise-specific procedural knowledge encoding trade secrets and recipes, planning and control systems, work processes and routines, internal structures, networks and relationships and organizational ethos.
- *Personal,* sometimes idiosyncratic knowledge and skills including managerial experience and leadership skills.

Human beings have the potential to create considerable value in all of these resource categories, as key individuals and in teams.

Basic resources are non-strategic assets. Many (perhaps all) the resources of a typical enterprise are basic. They are expected of any credible provider of similar goods or services. They function at a 'threshold' level; their value-creating potential equates in quantity and quality with those of similar providers. They confer no distinction or comparative advantage.

Strategic assets are, by contrast, distinctive, possibly unique, enterprise resources. They are called strategic assets because their use creates exceptional value that other providers cannot match, producing strategic advantage. In for-profit terms the value is deemed exceptional, precisely because clients are willing to pay a high price for it.

Strategic assets link frequently with a partial monopoly of strategic positions. Examples of such positions include:

- Privileged access to a source of important, scarce materials.
- Resources that have persisted or accumulated over time to an extent and standard that competing enterprises can no longer emulate.
- Dominance of market supply, often the outcome of being an early entrant.

Some strategic assets become enterprise property through good fortune. For example, an oil or mining company might discover huge reserves on land that it owns but thought worthless. Ownership of a scarce commodity that all providers need creates an exploitable position whose value arises from the control of supply and price; it does not necessarily require special skills. In the language of economics, we may say that ownership here yields 'monopoly rents'.

Enterprise Capabilities

Capabilities are in essence the know-how and skills required to deploy and exploit the potential of the enterprise's resources and assets. They cover the design, management, control and systematic enhancement of its many functions, processes, routines and activities. For a particular knowledge or skill to qualify as a capability in a particular enterprise context, it has to be suitably relevant, with high levels of skill, availability and consistency.

Basic capabilities are analogous with basic resources: they are the minimum, *threshold* standard expected of any competent provider in its field. Without these capabilities, the provider could not function properly.

LEARNING
OBJECTIVE ①

Distinctive capabilities are unusual and effective skills. They may be quite specific to a particular enterprise, in which case they are major factors that sustain its position. Another name is core or distinctive competence – though that term is sometimes applied only to technical skills, while administrative processes are termed 'capabilities'. (In this book the term 'distinctive capabilities' refers to both technical and administrative skills.)

An in-house corporate laboratory for research and development that creates valuable new products and technologies may be a distinctive capability obvious to all. In contrast, the organizational and leadership skills that enable an enterprise to exploit and enhance its value-creating potential are much less visible, especially to external scrutiny. Indeed, they can be difficult, even for the executives themselves, to be confident about. It is difficult to imagine such capabilities conferring distinction on an enterprise unless they are internally integrated and controlled.

Effective enterprises exploit their distinctive capabilities and strategic assets to resist the effects of strong competition.[6] Mitigating competition reduces the strategic significance of price, market share and the consequent commoditization of offerings. Static or declining prices, coupled with costs that generally rise over time, reduce net value-added, which damages profitability unless compensated by aggressive cost reduction initiatives.

The systematic exercise of distinctive capabilities can build strategic assets. For example, bold and innovative management may facilitate early entry to an emerging sector; this may be followed by aggressive investment to maximise long-run market share. Alternatively, management may gain strategic strength through shrewd, speculative acquisition of scarce assets before the future need for those assets has become evident to all. Building excellent client relationships that create satisfaction and sustain a unique reputation may also provide a strategic asset.

The Origins of Value-Creating Assets and Capabilities

LEARNING
OBJECTIVE ①

A number of generic, distinctive ways appear to create value.[7] They are:

- Reputation management skills.
- Innovation skills.
- Internal organisation structures, or 'enterprise architecture'.
- External relationships or 'contextual architecture'.

Reputation Management Skills

Reputation creates a respected external image and, once achieved, a strong reputation encourages the clientele to desire a continuing association with the enterprise. A strong reputation draws on positive perceptions of what the enterprise does and on endorsements from satisfied clients. For example, when an enterprise is seen as a reliable and ethical corporate citizen, it further reinforces the trust that stakeholders place in it. Well-regarded, high-performing products and services, together with a recognised brand personality, sustain loyalty, especially when underpinned by effective marketing and public relations activities.

Innovation Skills

Companies can continually create value by being consistently innovative, leading to new products, services and processes, new structures (architectures), positive ethos and reputation. Innovative enterprises develop and exploit their own proprietary knowledge, and the collective learning that results from this new knowledge sustains further value-creation and advantage. Accordingly, innovation concepts underpin strategic management.

Internal Organisation Structures, or 'Enterprise Architecture'

Internal architecture refers to the formal structure and organization of major enterprise functions and specialised units, as well as the operating routines, procedures, internal networks and relationships and how they are controlled, integrated and progressively enhanced. It also includes the ethos and informal relationships among staff and between organisational functions and units. Internal architecture affects whether, and how readily, innovations are enabled and adopted.

External Relationships or 'Contextual Architecture'

External or contextual architecture of an enterprise refers to the complex web of relationships, contracts and collaborative alliances in its industry sector and beyond. They involve its clienteles, external agencies, stakeholders and the many individuals who interact with other organizations. Notwithstanding individual contributions to enterprise effectiveness, constructive architectures transcend individual contributions. Valuable relationships, structural links and activities may be largely unseen; sometimes even senior executives may not be fully aware of their existence or significance.

Path Dependency and *Dynamic* Capabilities

Each enterprise is the product of its past strategic decisions and actions. It is defined at any one time by its accumulated resources and capabilities. Whatever its future potential, its current status constrains as well as and its future development. The dependence of future development on past achievements is called *path dependency*.[8]

Innovation and adaptation transform an enterprise, though it may become fully apparent only after time has elapsed. It can be difficult to pinpoint the skills that create such change. Though inadequately understood, some well-regarded enterprises undoubtedly have this dynamic, *transformative* capability for knowledge creation and organizational learning. They take for granted that current capabilities, even distinctive ones, will not be sufficient to enable future effectiveness, growth, or even survival. So these enterprises accept the need to exploit, enhance and extend their resources, established routines and currently distinctive capabilities.

The organizational capabilities that some enterprises use to integrate, reconfigure, upgrade and extend their existing resources and skills are called *dynamic capabilities*. These higher-level or 'meta-skills' become strategically significant when they galvanize new knowledge whose application leads to the transformation of the enterprise.

Diverting from the path dictated by the historical trajectory requires a combination of human qualities including vision, creativity, innovativeness, boldness and determination. To pursue new directions that branch away from the current path is always uncertain and risks costly failure. Some enterprises demonstrate a dynamic or transformational capability as they pursue new directions persistently. They appear to open 'gates' providing access to new paths, resulting in the accumulation of new resources and capabilities that sustain effectiveness and growth to a degree not otherwise possible.[9]

Many enterprises lack dynamic capabilities, not only the incompetent ones, but also successful enterprises that have lost the will to change. Paradoxically, it seems the latter develop core rigidities that derive from their existing capabilities – a fear or reluctance to change.

Dynamic capabilities in action

Tesco plc has grown by being consistently very good at mass-market retailing. It has developed new and related capabilities that have taken it well beyond its grocery origins, despite strong competition from other capable grocery (and increasingly, non-grocery) retailers. As a public company (plc), Tesco has to declare its strategy and much operational detail in statutory reports and presentations. Despite access to these data and observation of Tesco's stores, major competitors have been unable to replicate its success.

Canon and *Sony* are Japanese multinationals that have progressively developed their portfolios of electronic and optical capabilities. Their respective mix of capabilities enables them to offer a wide range of products: office equipment, computers, televisions, cameras and many more.

3M Corporation has applied its growing expertise in abrasives and adhesive coatings to create an extraordinarily wide range of functional products for industrial and consumer use, including the famous 'Post-It' note pads.

Analysing Distinctive Resources and Capabilities

Since resources and capabilities can be classed as either basic (threshold) or distinctive, there are four possible combinations, shown in Figure 5.1. It is vital to distinguish distinctive from basic or threshold assets and capabilities. Strategic analysis therefore needs to identify which resources and capabilities (if any):

- Are already located on the right of the figure and can be sustained or further enhanced (and how).
- Are presently located on the left of the figure and can become distinctive (and how).
- Need not or cannot be shifted.

	Same as other (par)	Better than others
Assets	Necessary and expected resources	Exceptional (strategic) assets
Capabilities	Basic capabilities	Distinctive (unique) capabilities

Figure 5.1: A classification of resources and competences

To identify distinctive, value-creating resources and capabilities is a practical challenge for two reasons. First, it is difficult to be confident that a *causal link* exists between a posited strategic asset or distinctive capability and the value imputed to it. Second, value-creation may result from the *combined* action of multiple strategic assets and capabilities, making their relative significance hard to judge. Clear evidence is needed to justify conclusions. Two stages of analysis are possible. The first is an initial screen using the worksheet format of Figure 5.2.

Category	Description	Evidence for this status	Contrary evidence (if any)
Basic resources			
Strategic assets			
Basic capabilities			
Distinctive capabilities			

Figure 5.2: Analysis of resources and capabilities

A second stage involves a more rigorous analysis using the explicit criteria that have emerged from the resource-based view of advantage.[10]

LEARNING
OBJECTIVE ③

Taken together, the RBV criteria are summarised as the V-R-I-O-S framework:

Value-creating potential

Rarity (or scarcity)

Imitability

Organizational appropriability (exploitability)

Substitutability

Below, these criteria are each discussed in turn.

Value Creation

If an enterprise creates (adds) value for its various stakeholders, there will be *evidence* of such a fact! Specific measures of economic value-added (EVA) are discussed later under performance assessment. The evidence of greatest *strategic* interest is *exceptional* value. Such evidence means that the enterprise enjoys strategic assets and/or distinctive capabilities leading to exceptional value created, hence exceptional performance. Ideally, the causal links between value-adding inputs and outputs would be unambiguous. Unfortunately, it is possible to attribute causality where none actually exists. Alternatively, causality might exist but derive from assets and capabilities acting in conjunction; thus, added-value Z arises *only* when capability X acts on resource Y.

LEARNING
OBJECTIVE ③

Sometimes the link between, on the one hand, a strategic asset or distinctive capability and, on the other hand, observed value-creation is unclear or it may be impossible to determine the relative contribution of each one.[11] In such cases we use the term *causal ambiguity*. Uncertainty can exist both in the enterprise that enjoys the advantage and also in other enterprises over which it enjoys advantage, reducing their incentive to emulate the uncertain effect which may not benefit them, hence *uncertain imitability*.

Causal ambiguity

The **Virgin** business empire has over 200 separate units linked most obviously by the Virgin brand and Sir Richard Branson's charisma. Other sources of advantage have been widely speculated; they probably differ from one business unit to another and from different *combinations* of assets and capabilities. Consequently, it is difficult for would-be emulators to learn much of value from studying Virgin as a brand.

Capable coaches and team managers are crucial sporting assets for **successful football teams**. Those with established reputations command high salaries. Coaches of national teams select clubs' most capable players but have limited scope to influence them. So how do they contribute most to the success of teams in international matches? The key skills at this level are probably not technical, but in man-management: controlling big egos and motivating individuals to perform effectively *as a team*. Understandably, disagreement over the vital qualities of successful national coaches is widespread.

Consequently, specific criteria are needed to ensure that the resources and capabilities of strategic significance have been identified. Ideally, all the following criteria are met; in isolation they may not sustain value creation.

Rarity

Despite its relevance in a defined context, a value-creating resource confers no advantage when it is available to all providers. Conversely, an enterprise with a genuinely rare (or scarce) resource enjoys exceptional potential, provided that *asymmetry* of access can be maintained indefinitely. (Please note that here the terms 'rare' and 'scarce' are used interchangeably.) Persistence probably requires maintenance and upgrading costs, but in general these costs are well justified. Rarity includes limited availability of vital materials, facilities, equipment or knowledge, either because supply is naturally limited or the source is tightly controlled and restricted (e.g., via patents) or otherwise inaccessible.

Rare resources

Diamonds are a vital component of high-grade jewellery: **De Beers** controls supplies tightly as a mining company and a major international distributor.

Governments control the rights to oil exploration on land and in coastal seas; also the transmission frequencies needed for television, radio and communications.

Sometimes resource rarity is a natural phenomenon; historical circumstances or luck also determine the scope for access. Quasi-monopolistic rarity can be contrived: the media empire Sky is prepared to outbid its competitors to retain control of valuable broadcasting rights, which are its strategic assets.

A genuinely rare or unusual *capability* also has exceptional value-creating potential. It can result from deliberate intent or happy accident. Sports broadcasts require film crews and commentators whose expertise develops with experience. BSkyB defends its advantageous position as a television sports broadcaster through its strong contract negotiating abilities and because of its expertise in presenting selected sports. These skills are complementary and have proved durable. Capabilities that are rare, distributed asymmetrically among competitors, and mutually supportive are particularly potent supporters of value-creation. When that asymmetry is persistent, the advantage can be sustained indefinitely.

Imitability

Competing enterprises may be comparable, yet their strategic resources and distinctive capabilities differ markedly. So each enterprise has an incentive to build on its strengths and mitigate comparative weaknesses, assuming that it recognises them.[12] Enterprises with rare assets or capabilities attract would-be imitators; the difficulty of imitating them is a clear sign of their strategic value. When a would-be imitator succeeds, the rarity evaporates, highlighting its advantage-conferring transient nature.

Imitation can succeed by action to copy, emulate or replicate the asset or capability. A would-be imitator might create an equivalent via internal development, but few have the skills to make this feasible. If they did, they would probably have already created it. (Remember: an imitator's developmental potential is constrained by its current status, the product of its developmental history.) An enterprise could also be unable to work around intellectual property rights such as the competitor's patents.[13] Another way to emulate is from an external source. Genuinely rare assets are generally far too costly or impossible to acquire externally. External recruitment may be a third option: creating a new development team of experienced engineers or scientists, for example. Again, the cost – financially or in time delay – would be substantial and success uncertain.

If the cost of imitation is very high, then the resource or capability is in effect not imitable and so will remain valuable to its present owner. Given the strong incentive, would-be imitators often continue trying, although causal ambiguity imposes doubts over the feasibility of proactive imitation and external transfer.

Imitability challenges

As well as access rights, prospecting and drilling/mining capabilities are needed to locate and exploit valuable oil, gas, gold and diamond deposits.

Television drama and light entertainment programmes require human insight and creativity for originality. These are comparatively rare skills, enabling acclaimed scriptwriters to command premium fees.

Organizational Appropriability

Appropriability or exploitability is the challenge an enterprise faces to extract the full potential of its strategic resources or distinctive capabilities. In theory, the enterprise should have little difficulty to realise the potential of high-calibre assets. However ownership disputes (over patent rights, for example) may prevent the advantage being fully realised. When the assets comprise intellectual property such as technical knowledge, much resides in the minds of employees who, subject to contractual constraints, can take their knowledge elsewhere. Further, a world-class capability in one aspect is sometimes compromised because a vital complementary resource or skill is missing. This describes many small enterprises whose key capabilities are narrow.

Large enterprises, particularly those with multinational operations, have complex, multinational structures and communication systems. Appropriability often requires the transfer of assets and capabilities across internal boundaries or between business units. Thus, manufacturers frequently need to transfer capabilities from one production unit or country to another, which proves difficult when communications are poor, local skills limited or they face greatly differing cultural norms and assumptions.

Most fundamentally, competition hinders appropriability. Competing enterprises innovate to deliver greater value to their clients and other stakeholders. Enhanced capabilities in one enterprise force others to respond, ensuring a continuing sector innovation cycle and unchanged competitive parity.[14] The cycle enhances the quality and affordability of products and services, but the innovators may struggle to keep the additional value for themselves, as clients and/or suppliers appropriate much of it. This characteristic of dynamic sectors – that competitors have to run ever harder just to stand still – is called (using the language of Lewis Carroll's well-known story, *Through the Looking Glass*) the 'Red Queen paradox'. For all these reasons, enhanced capabilities do not guarantee that an enterprise can appropriate sustained benefits.

Appropriability challenges

In the 1990s the Finnish company *Raisio* developed an effective cholesterol-lowering ingredient called plant stanol ester. The first product containing it was margarine, marketed under the Benecol® brand. Although Raisio had patent protection, it decided that the potential of huge monopoly returns was too uncertain; it preferred a lower, but more predictable income by allowing large multinational food and nutrition corporations to produce Benecol® branded products under license.

Substitutability

When an enterprise cannot emulate a competitor's distinctive resource or capability, or acquire it externally, it has another option: it can search for a suitable *substitute* – an alternative technology, product, process or service for the one it cannot emulate. Substitution is a radical approach. When it succeeds, it can be a 'game changing' development to which existing providers must ultimately respond or be disadvantaged. History shows that substitution is a major vehicle for progress. Most resources and capabilities become vulnerable to substitution *in the long term*. However, substitution initiatives can prove extremely costly and uncertain.

Examples of substitutability

Lacking traditional watch-making skills, in the 1970s electronics companies used their design and production skills to create microchip timing modules that have since largely replaced mechanical escapements. Traditional *Swiss watchmakers* had to accept and adapt to this change or risk losing their advantage. However, none of the US microchip pioneers watch-making interests have survived.

Prudential Insurance did not have a branch network suitable for entering retail banking. Instead it set up Egg.com, an online banking subsidiary (now owned by Citigroup). British retail banks responded by adding online services and subsidiaries and then reducing the size of their branch networks. Recent new entrants (start-ups like Virgin Money and established banks from other countries, e.g., Santander of Spain) have developed their UK retail networks by acquiring unwanted branches.

The V-R-I-O-S Worksheet

An enterprise's strategic assets and distinctive capabilities may be identified through a detailed analysis of its resources and capabilities using the V-R-I-O-S framework. A suitable resource for this purpose is shown in Figure 5.3.

Each element can be rated on a four-point scale: A = outstanding generator of value and advantage – of genuine strategic significance B = valuable, but not a crucial source of advantage C = useful, but probably of declining significance D = already declining in significance and unlikely to be sustainable						
	V	**R**	**I**	**O**	**S**	**Comments**
Strategic assets						
1. 2. 3. Etc.						
Distinctive capability						
1. 2. 3. Etc.						

Key:
V: value-creating potential
R: rarity
I: imitability
O: organizational appropriability
S: substitutability

Figure 5.3: V-R-I-O-S analysis of resources and capabilities

The five criteria of the V-R-I-O-S framework can be used to examine strategic assets and distinctive capabilities more critically. Each element can be rated, for example, using on a four-point scale outlined in the figure. The higher the *combined* rating, the more valuable is the asset.

Having completed this analysis, analysts can then identify actions aiming to:

- Defend the current means of value-creation.
- Increase the advantage gained from these means.
- Enhance further the value-creating capabilities of the enterprise.

The Internal Value-adding Chain

Chapter 3 introduced the concept of an extended industry supply chain into which the focal enterprise and its immediate sector fit. Sector occupants rarely perform a single value-adding activity, but a sequence of activities. They each have an internal 'value-adding chain' as shown in Figure 5.4, which distinguishes primary and support activities. For the enterprise overall the value-added surplus (the profit margin in business enterprises) is the excess of value created over cost.

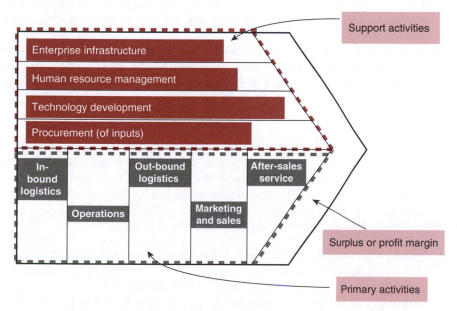

Figure 5.4: The value-adding chain inside the enterprise*

* After Porter (1985)

Primary Value-adding Activities

LEARNING
OBJECTIVE ④

An enterprise's primary activities are those that are fundamental to its work. They should create much more value than they cost to perform, hence create net added value. Primary activities fall into several categories. Commonly used classifications derive from manufacturing activities, so their meanings in a service enterprise need interpretation. Here we outline five main categories.

1. *In-bound logistics* are activities that move, control, store and internally distribute materials and other input supplies used in value-adding operations.
2. *Operations* are the main output-generating processes of manufacturers. Service operations entail the activities essential to service performance. A restaurant prepares, cooks and serves food to diners; an airline operates passenger check-in, piloting and in-flight cabin service. Specialist airport subcontractors generally perform baggage handling, food preparation, refuelling, cleaning of aircraft between scheduled flights and sometimes even essential maintenance.
3. *Out-bound logistics* include the physical storage, packaging and distribution of goods. In services such as hairdressing, delivery is an integral feature of service performance so it may be considered part of operations.
4. *Marketing and sales* activities include market research, decision-making about segmentation and targeting, advertising and promotion. Conventionally it includes selling and order-taking too. (In industries such as airlines, sophisticated ticket-booking systems are treated as part of operations.) Public relations and corporate image building may also feature.
5. *After-sales service* entails all the activities that maintain a satisfied clientele including installation, servicing, repair, client advice and training, satisfaction surveys, etc.

Each primary activity comprises numerous sub-activities and routines. Some activities overlap categories. The important point is not how these factors are labelled: what matters is that the factors are, one way or another, recognised and evaluated as generators of costs and (potential) value, not how they are *labelled*.

Secondary (Support) Activities

LEARNING
OBJECTIVE ④

Secondary support functions enable the primary value-adding activities and should enhance their performance levels. As Figure 5.3 implies, a support function can affect all the primary activities. Support activities are often net cost generators; unless they are 'sold' via an internal market as inputs to the primary activities, their value generation will probably be unclear.

Here we identify four main types of secondary activity:

1. *Procurement* includes the activities that acquire materials, parts and other supplies and services needed in the primary activities. For large corporations and retailers it may also cover co-ordinating upstream supply chain activities.
2. *Technology development* includes the design, development and testing of new materials, technologies, operational processes, information systems, etc. Research and development (R&D) is a key component of this support activity.[15]

3. ***Human resources management*** (HRM) entails the activities associated with recruiting, appraising, training, developing, and rewarding people and, where necessary (subject to contractual provisions), disciplining and dismissing them.
4. ***Infrastructure*** includes the processes and systems of formal reporting, planning, financial management and control, quality assurance, and information management.

As with primary activities, support activities have many sub-categories. Enterprises classify them differently. Product development may be treated as a support function or part of the primary operations. Information technology units that develop and maintain airline booking systems may be managed within airline operations. HRM activities typically split between specialist HRM support units and primary function managers.

Strategic Value-chain Analysis

Enterprises may examine their primary and support activities to see (a) which, if any, are strategic assets or distinctive capabilities, and (b) which can be slimmed down, contracted out or eliminated without damaging performance. Careful scrutiny of all value-adding activities that reduces overall costs increases net value-added. Actions include:

- Eliminating redundant or wasteful activities.
- Combining duplicated activities.
- Minimising bottlenecks in the value-adding chain, reducing the time needed to complete all necessary activities, hence increasing market responsiveness.
- Reducing throughput variety by using standardised components or processes, thus increasing productivity and reducing inventory costs.

When an activity is crucial to value-adding, subcontracting is unlikely. Airlines generally contract-out food preparation, but continue to employ skilled pilots. (Even so, there are exceptions: Ryanair, for example, uses a proportion of qualified contract pilots to reduce overall flight costs.) However, it is no longer unusual for enterprises to use specialist agencies for research and development projects, HRM functions, or the training, supply and supervision of (temporary) production line staff and even interim managers.

Value-chain analysis highlights the importance of:

- Evaluating the contributions to net value creation of all cost-incurring activities.
- Deciding which activities confer genuine advantage (to retain and if possible enhance) and which confer no advantage (to eliminate or contract out).

External Comparisons

Comparing enterprise performance with sector peers helps to clarify where the balance of (dis)advantage lies. This process is typically called *benchmarking*. It uses such questions as:

- Which value-adding activities does the enterprise currently perform *better* (and worse) than its main comparators?
- In which major activities does the enterprise achieve *world class* standards?

Objective data about the internal performance of other enterprises is difficult to obtain, so assessment may be limited to inferences from aggregate data in financial accounts and other reports, plus independent, comparative surveys.

Where realistic value-adding comparisons are possible, it turns out that similar enterprises may differ markedly in their value-adding profiles. For example, Corus in Europe and Nucor in the United States are major basic steel producers, with similar output tonnage which they convert into a wide variety of added-value products. Corus starts with iron ore and some recycled scrap metal from which it makes strip, plate, beams, tubes and coated products to which its customers add further value in their own operations. Nucor's output is virtually all from recycled scrap; it too offers a wide range of semi-finished products, but it also makes finished steel components such as nuts, bolts and other fabrications.

Exceptional activity-specific, value-adding performances with which an enterprise can compare itself are not necessarily found in its own sector. Again, reliable data may be hard to find, though 'world-class' standards usually receive considerable publicity and cause enterprises to question their current practices. If a Formula 1 racing team changes four car tyres in six seconds, a retail tyre-fitting company should complete the equivalent task in much less than the typical 20 minutes!

Internal Comparisons

Good performance requires that resources and capabilities demonstrate an appropriate degree of mutual complementarity and sufficiency, which must therefore be checked. Complementarity matters because value is added only when the appropriate resources and capabilities exist in sufficient quality and depth for the need. Conversely, excess resources and skills will be underused and wasteful.

Present and Future Comparisons

Present and required future resource and capability needs will differ because of progress and innovation, even if the enterprise mission does not alter. If the mission does change, value-adding activities may need radical critique. Hence it is necessary to examine:

- Which current value-adding activities (and associated resources and capabilities) will be crucial to future success *in achieving the current mission*?
- How well is the enterprise enhancing these activities?
- What *new* resources and capabilities will be crucial to extend or adapt the mission, for example, by extending product/market scope?

The most capable enterprises continually learn and improve, so asking objective questions about progression is vital, though time-consuming and costly. Regularly asking questions and responding to answers becomes a *dynamic capability*.

Enterprise Performance Assessment: Accounting Measures

Critical performance assessment facilitates enterprise efficiency improvements in the short term. In the longer term it supports a strategic focus on knowledge and capability enhancement.

All stakeholders seek value from an enterprise's activities, though they differ over how they assess value. All stakeholders expect to benefit *in their own terms*. Enterprise owners or proprietors equate value creation with high performance, assessed via their preferred quantitative and qualitative metrics. To give a few examples, financial measures feature strongly in shareholder assessments. Society looks for ethically responsible behaviour towards its citizens and the natural environment. Customers, on the other hand, equate value with the net benefits they gain over the purchase price they pay, taking into account both the monetary cost and any perceived 'opportunity cost' arising from foregoing other options.[16] Similarly, employees offset the value of wages and salaries received with perceptions of the onerous nature (or otherwise) of their work.

According to the RBV, strategic assets and distinctive capabilities underpin sustained high performance. Objective assessment of performance and its causes therefore matter greatly to the RBV.

Performance measures divide into three categories:

- Financial accounting measures (key ratios).
- Economic value-added (EVA) measures.
- Non-financial measures.

Within each category, specific performance measures highlight:

- Absolute levels.
- Changes over time (trends).
- Comparisons with peers.
- Comparisons with best (world-class) practice.

Several financial performance measures derive from standard accounting data such as:

- Revenues (sales), profits (surpluses) and cash flows.
- Capital employed in the enterprise, divided into assets and liabilities (including shareholders' equity in businesses).
- Dividends paid (in businesses).
- Employee numbers.
- Share price and market capitalisation (external valuation of the business enterprise).
- Non-financial, often enterprise-specific measures (particularly relevant for not-for-profit enterprises).

Since statutory financial accounts report these basic data, comparisons might appear straightforward, including with world-class performers. Yet financial data must be treated with caution. Statutory accounts exist primarily to record historical performance and not to enable comparative strategic analysis. Further, published accounts conform to accounting rules and conventions of their home countries, which manifest some differences. Or enterprises may present familiar ratios in a non-standard way for greater insight, making adjustments necessary for like-for-like comparisons. With these caveats, let's look at some analytical performance measures using the example of the Accor Group of France.

Accor hotel and services group

Accor is a France-based, multinational hotel operator spanning 100 countries. It has over 4000 hotels and half a million rooms located in 12 branded chains including Sofitel, Novotel, Ibis, Etap and Mercure, targeted at different user segments. It derives a quarter of its revenues from other business services. Table 5.B presents key financial data for Accor covering the years 2005–2008. Accor lists its main competitors as Intercontinental (IHG). Marriott, NH Hoteles, Sodexo, Sol Melia, Starwood, and Whitbread.

Table 5.B: Key financial data for Accor Hotel Group 2005–2008 *

	2005	2006	2007	2008
Group revenues (sales), cash flows, profits and dividends				
Hotel revenues		5,410	5,827	5,767
Non-hotel revenues		2197	2,294	1,972
Total revenues	7,136	7,607	8,121	7,739
Cash from operations	935	1024	1112	1111
Free cash flow	499	570	646	623
EBITDA	1,096	1,248	1,390	1,387
Pre-tax profit	458	688	1,146	885
Profits after tax	364	534	912	613
Dividends paid	247	325	366	363
Employees				
Total hotel staff		131,010	134,852	144,679
Staff in other services		39,407	37,843	13,483

Table 5.B: Cont'd

	Share data			
Shares issued (million)	214.8	224.7	225.0	221.2
	Balance sheet data			
Non-current assets	8,084	7,312	6,843	7,429
Current assets	5,094	3,821	3,991	3,984
Total capital employed	13,178	11,133	10,834	11413
Equity	4,396	4,164	3,752	3,563
Long term liabilities (debt)	2,358	1,908	1,560	24,18
Current liabilities	6,424	5,061	5,522	5,432
	2005	2006	2007	2008

EBITDA, Earnings Before deduction of Interest charges, corporation Tax, Depreciation and Amortisation.
* Financial data in € million.
Source: published 2008 Annual Report.

Growth

Effective performance tends to create growth, which is generally considered desirable. Trends can be assessed by examining multiple time periods, expressed as year-on-year percentage increases or decreases. Growth rates can be compared (Table 5.C). A well-managed enterprise should achieve similar rates of growth in revenues, profits and dividends while increasing capital employed and employee numbers more slowly, thereby enhancing productivity. Where significant differences exist, the reasons need to be understood and acted on.

Table 5.C: Growth statistics for Accor 2006–2008

Annual % growth rates in:	2006	2007	2008
Revenues	+7%	+7%	−5%
EBITDA	+14%	+11%	0%
Cash from operations	+10%	+9%	0%

Table 5.C: Cont'd

Annual % growth rates in:	2006	2007	2008
Free cash flow	+10%	+13%	−4%
Total capital employed	−15%	−3%	+5%
Shareholders' equity	−5%	−10%	−5%
Dividends	+32%	+13%	−1%
Market valuation	+31%	−37%	−20%

EBITDA, Earnings Before deduction of Interest charges, corporation Tax, Depreciation and Amortisation.
Source: 2008 Annual Report.

Productivity

Conventional productivity measures examine the use of labour and capital. Common measures are revenues per employee and capital turnover (the ratio of revenues to total capital employed (see Table 5.D for Accor).[17]

Table 5.D: Accor productivity 2005–2008

	2005	2006	2007	2008
Hotel revenues (€ million)		5,410	5,827	5,767
Total hotel staff		131,010	134,852	144,679
Revenue per hotel employee (€)		41,295	43,210	39,860
Non-hotel revenues (€ million)		2,197	2,294	1,972
Staff in other services		39,407	37,843	13,483
Revenue per other employee (€)		55,752	60,619	146,258
Total revenues (€ million)	7,136	7,607	8,121	7,739

Table 5.D: Cont'd

	2005	2006	2007	2008
Total capital employed (€ million)	13,178	11,133	10,834	11,413
Revenues/total capital employed (capital turnover)	0.54	0.68	0.75	0.68

* Source 2008 Annual Report.

Profitability

As noted in Chapter 3, enterprises incur (a) costs that are essentially *fixed* in the short-to-medium term (sometimes called overheads) and (b) *variable* costs that change in direct proportion to the units of activity/output.[18]

Gross profit margin is gross profit expressed as a percentage of sales revenues, indicating trading effectiveness. Gross margin ratios are generally characteristic of the particular sector, so cross-sector comparisons are potentially misleading.

Net profit is gross profit less the enterprise's fixed costs, which include corporate overhead (non-trading activity) costs. *Net profit margin* is net profit as a percentage of sales revenues. The comparative validity of this measure is suspect, since it depends on how fixed costs are calculated and allocated among activities and units for each time period.

Net profit declared for corporation tax assessment is calculated after interest charges payable on bank loans and issued securities; they are enterprise-specific, so can also distort comparisons. A widely used measure of net profit is called *EBITDA* (Earnings *Before deduction of* Interest charges, corporation Tax, Depreciation and Amortization). EBITDA calculates net profit before deducting these charges for two reasons. Interest payments and taxation are externally imposed; their link with underlying enterprise performance in a given time period may be distorted, misleading performance comparisons. Depreciation and amortization reflect enterprise-specific policies about the valuation of fixed assets and other equipment with a finite lifetime, hence charges against profits. These policies (and tax regulations) may change over time, altering the profits declared. EBITDA avoids these concerns because it strips out idiosyncratic, enterprise- or sector-specific charges. However some say that it presents an unduly optimistic view of performance by ignoring costs and charges that the enterprise *has already incurred* or *future costs it cannot avoid*.

Profit margin ratios indicate value creation in terms of net revenues versus costs. It is important also to relate profits to the capital invested; this is *return on investment* (ROI), or net profit divided by capital employed, expressed as a percentage.[19] Multiple measures of ROI exist.

Table 5.E shows these various profitability measures for Accor.

Table 5.E: Accor profitability 2005–2008

	2005	2006	2007	2008
EBITDA	1,096	1,248	1,390	1,387
Group revenues (sales)	7,136	7,607	8,121	7,739
Margin on sales (EBITDA-based)	15.4%	16.4%	17.1%	17.9%
Total capital employed	13,178	11,133	10,834	11,413
Return on capital % (EBITDA-based)	8.3%	11.2%	12.8%	12.2%
Pre-tax profit	458	688	1,146	885
Return on capital % (pre-tax)	3.5%	6.2%	10.6%	7.8%
Profits after tax	364	534	912	613
Return on capital % (post-tax)	2.8%	4.8%	8.4%	5.4%

EBITDA, Earnings Before deduction of Interest charges, corporation Tax, Depreciation and Amortisation.
* Financial data in € million.
Source: 2008 Annual Report.

Cash Flow

Cash flow from operations in a stated time period exceeds declared profit before tax, because the latter is calculated after deducting depreciation and amortization charges. Cash also funds capital investments and increases in working capital. *Free cash flow* is the net cash available for redeployment after all these charges. The ability of a business to generate free cash flow for reinvestment and dividend payments may be a more reliable measure of its fundamental performance. Table 5.F shows cash flows for Accor.

Returns to Equity

Equity is the fraction of total capital employed attributable to shareholders – the capital they have put at risk (i.e. excluding debt). *Return on equity* is the ratio of net profit to owners' equity.

The fraction of post-tax profits used to pay dividends determines the fraction retained as equity for reinvestment. The resulting ratio (*dividend cover*) indicates whether the enterprise

Table 5.F: Accor cash flows 2005–2008*

	2005	2006	2007	2008
Revenues (sales)	7,136	7,607	8,121	7,739
Total capital employed	13,178	11,133	10,834	11,413
Cash from operations	935	1,024	1,112	1,111
Cash as % revenues	13.1%	13.5%	13.7%	14.3%
Cash as % total capital	7.1%	9.2%	10.3%	9.7
Free cash flow	499	570	646	623
Free cash flow as % revenues	7.0%	7.5%	8.0%	8.1%
Free cash flow as % total capital	3.8%	5.1 %	6.0%	5.5%

*Financial data in € million unless otherwise stated.
Source: 2008 Annual Report.

prioritises the long term (high profits enable reinvestment and future growth) or short term (where profits are mostly distributed as dividends).

'Market valuation to equity' is a ratio that indicates how well the stock market values a public company, though valuations change daily and can be highly volatile. Table 5.G shows Accor's equity performance.

Table 5.G: Accor returns to equity 2005–2008 *

	2005	2006	2007	2008
Group revenues (sales)	7,136	7,607	8,121	7,739
Equity	4,396	4,164	3,752	3,563
Pre-tax profit	458	688	1146	885
Pre-tax profit on equity %	10.4%	16.5%	30.5%	24.8%

Table 5.G: Cont'd

	2005	2006	2007	2008
Profits after tax	364	534	912	613
Post-tax profit on equity %	8.3%	12.8%	24.3%	17.2%
Shares issued (million)	214.8	224.7	225.0	221.2
Pre-tax profit (earnings) per share (€)	2.13	3.06	5.09	4.00
Post tax profit per share (€)	1.69	2.38	4.05	2.77
Dividends paid	247	325	366	363
Dividend per share (€) (* includes 1.5 € bonus dividend paid)	1.15	2.95*	3.15*	1.65
Dividend cover	× 1.47	× 1.64 (0.81)	× 2.49 (1.28)	× 1.69
Share price (average of high and low for the year **) €	50.78	63.76	40.27	32.60**
Market valuation based on average share price for the year	10,908	14,327	9,061	7,211
Market valuation to equity	× 2.5	× 3.4	× 2.4	× 2.0**

* Source: 2008 Annual Report. Financial data are in € million unless otherwise stated.
** year to date, end February.

Liquidity

An enterprise can be profitable, yet have liquidity problems – that is, a shortage of immediate cash flow. There are two common liquidity tests. The *current ratio* means current assets over current liabilities. The *quick ratio* is *current assets less stocks (inventories)* over current liabilities. Both indicate how well the enterprise can meet its short term obligations (liabilities). The quick ratio is severe but highly relevant; current assets include stocks, which will almost certainly realise much less cash than their accounting value in a quick sale. Table 5.H shows Accor's liquidity position.

Table 5.H: Accor liquidity and gearing 2005–2008 *

	2005	2006	2007	2008
Current assets	5,094	3,821	3,991	3,984
Current liabilities	6,424	5,061	5,522	5,432
Current assets/liabilities	0.79	0.75	0.72	0.73
Long-term liabilities (debt)	2,358	1,908	1,560	2,418
Equity	4,396	4,164	3,752	3,563
Long-term debt/equity (gearing)	0.54	0.46	0.42	0.68

* Financial data in € million unless otherwise stated.
Source: 2008 Annual Report.

Gearing (Debt Ratio, also Called Leverage)

The higher the proportion of *debt to equity* in the total capital employed, the more the enterprise relies on debt to fund investments. When interest rates are low and expected to be stable, debt finance 'leverages' returns to equity very effectively. Since (unlike equity) debt involves a commitment to pay interest irrespective of profits it carries higher risk, especially when the *debt to equity* ratio is high. A conventional limit is 1:1, though in difficult economic times, especially with high interest rates, a lower ratio is desirable. Table 5.H also shows Accor's debt position.

Economic Value-added (EVA) Performance Measures

Definitions

Economic value-added (EVA) provides a performance assessment that enables direct comparisons among enterprises, without an emphasis on profit or many of the caveats over the use of financial accounting measures.[20] The principles of the EVA approach make it relevant for the strategic analysis of both businesses and not-for-profit enterprises, although value surpluses are still expressed in monetary terms. *Net* EVA is the surplus value of an enterprise's outputs over the total value (cost) of its inputs. For a not-for-profit enterprise to use EVA it must estimate the monetary equivalent value of the benefits it delivers to its target clientele. A famine relief charity creates value by mitigating the adverse effects of starvation, social and family disaster; systematic estimates of the monetary value of these benefits is possible, albeit more subjective than calculating business value-added.

Inputs costs comprise three distinct elements, namely:

- The costs of the labour employed (staff wages, salaries and benefits).
- Capital charges: the combined costs of debt and equity financing that enable it to acquire and deploy assets.
- The purchase costs of the goods and services also needed to perform its value-adding activities.

Labour costs express the value of employees' contributions to operational value-adding; their earnings are the reciprocal value they receive. Capital charges reflect both the value that capital employed contributes to enterprise activities, equivalent to the value that capital providers (investors/owners, donors, loan and grant providers) receive for the use of their money. (Lenders receive value as real interest payments. Donors and grant-givers receive only perceptual benefits, such as a feeling of well-being.) There is an equivalence of value exchange between the enterprise and its providers of labour and capital inputs.

Purchased input costs equate with the rewards given to suppliers in exchange for their material inputs. However, the cost of purchased goods and services represents value *already added* by suppliers; the enterprise cannot claim credit for what others have done. Thus a relevant, second measure of enterprise performance is revenues less purchased inputs (its gross output).

Economic Value-added calculations

EVA poses some practical challenges of measurement and is not without controversy. To calculate EVA input costs, labour and capital costs must be known, as well as revenues or benefits expressed as monetary values. For this purpose capital charges are the costs of *making available* to the enterprise the capital it employs, *not* the total capital employed (debt plus equity). They can be calculated in various ways. One is to add up the *actual payments made to acquire new capital assets* in a stated time period, assuming that assets are replaced promptly and equivalently as needed. In practice, asset acquisition costs relate poorly to the value of the capital actually employed. A better approach is to calculate an interest charge on the value of existing assets using an appropriate interest rate, plus depreciation charges that compensate for asset 'wear-and-tear'.

The preferred way to avoid enterprise-specific vagaries is to start with published, unambiguous data on total capital employed – that is, debt plus owners' equity (risk capital) for businesses and equivalent balance sheet values for not-for-profit enterprises. Debt and equity attract interest charges and dividend obligations, respectively. Not-for-profit enterprises often have a large component of their funding from grants and donations that attract neither of these charges. *For EVA purposes* it remains appropriate to treat these as debt and calculate a notional charge. The reason is that if the enterprise had not used this capital to support value-adding activities it would presumably have earned interest elsewhere, hence would have been a source of future capital. That is, the notional interest charge is the opportunity cost of forgoing alternative uses of these funds.

It is usual to calculate an interest rate and a cost of equity in line with prevailing market rates and enterprise-specific factors via the so-called *capital asset pricing model*.[21] Once the two rates are established the weighted average cost of capital (WACC) derives from the proportions of debt to equity used. The EVA approach is illustrated using GlaxoSmithKline, a major multinational pharmaceutical company.

Economic value-added (EVA) analysis of GlaxoSmithKline plc

Based in West London, GlaxoSmithKline (GSK) is a major global healthcare company, which resulted from the merger of British companies, Glaxo-Wellcome and SmithKline Beecham in 1999. Its primary activities are to develop, make and market pharmaceutical and consumer health-related products. It operates in 114 countries and sells products in over 150 countries.

The table below shows that while GSK's *revenues* increased even in recession-hit 2008 its *net EVA* declined substantially, whether expressed as a monetary value, as a percentage of revenues, or percentage of gross output. From late 2007 it began to implement a substantial restructuring plan called 'Operational Excellence' whose aim is to simplify and improve its business performance. The EVA calculations help explain why the restructuring plan was considered necessary.

Table 5.1: Economic value-added (EVA) for GlaxoSmithKline over a three-year period*

	2008	2007	2006
Sales revenues	24,352	22,716	23,225
Purchased inputs of goods and services	7,167	6,112	5,713
Wages and salaries	6,524	5,733	5,495
Finance costs (interest + dividends paid)	3,795	3,357	3,047
Total input costs	17,486	15,202	14,255
Gross output (revenues less purchased inputs)	17,185	16,604	17,512
Net EVA: (revenues less total input costs)	6,866	7,514	8,970
EVA as % of revenues	28.2%	33.1%	38.6%
EVA as % of gross output	40.0%	45.2%	51.2%

* All data in £m unless otherwise stated.

Source: 2008 Annual Report.

Non-financial and Qualitative Performance Measures

Accounting and EVA approaches consider enterprise performance using monetary values or metrics that can be translated into monetary values. Qualitative measures of performance offer additional insights. They can address societal interests beyond the rather narrow perspective of clients, owners/investors, employees and suppliers.

At least three approaches to non-financial performance measurement and reporting have emerged. The *triple bottom line* (T-B-L) approach[22] mentioned previously, encourages business corporations to take their societal and environmental responsibilities as seriously as their economic ones. It is increasingly common for business enterprises to report on their social responsibility and environmental activities, whether or not they are legally obliged to do so.

A further approach is the use of the *balanced scorecard*. The aim is to encourage enterprises to establish specific quantitative and qualitative targets to link activities to the following four strategic priorities:

- Customer/client interests.
- Owners' interests.
- Internal, operational priorities to enhance quality and value-adding efficiency.
- Developmental (learning and growth) priorities.

The purpose is to enhance performance, rather than external reporting. Balanced scorecard is considered further in Chapter 13.

Both T-B-L and balanced scorecard approaches allow enterprises to report performance via quantitative (not necessarily financial) *and* qualitative measures. Non-financial performance measures can be assessed in output units per time period, such as patients treated in a hospital, or consumption units such as litres of water per day in a hotel.

However, qualitative reports can highlight commitment and effective performance too. Despite statistically minded detractors, qualitative richness provides meaningful evidence of performance that motivates many employees more than 'mere statistics'.

Qualitative performance reporting

Accor reports qualitatively and statistically on 'Earth Guest', its ambitious sustainable local development programme. Priorities include child and biodiversity protection; health improvement; reducing energy and water usage; and effective waste management.

Oxfam, the leading aid agency, focuses on public health, emergency food, security and disaster relief programmes. For example, it developed water supply systems and sanitation facilities in conflict-torn Democratic Republic of Congo, directly benefiting 500,000 people.

Dynevor Ltd manages the UK-based Dore Programme whose mission is to provide personalised, non-drug, exercise-based treatments to help children and adults with learning disabilities. By 2009 more than 30,000 people had experienced the Programme, which rejects simplistic one-dimensional measures of improvement. Since each person has a unique condition, Dore reports on its performance via testimonials from high profile and other graduates of the programme.

Actions Arising from Performance Assessment

Each activity in an internal value chain is discrete, sequential, and partially independent. It takes inputs from one or more prior stages in the primary chain, adds further value and transfers outputs to the next stage. The notional value-added of a stage is its output value less input cost less cost of performing the activity. Performance assessment should lead to changes either to reduce costs *or* to enhance output value, for example, by improving quality assurance procedures. Cost is frequently the more tangible and controllable aspect. If activity cost is reduced, value-added increases, all else being equal.

To establish whether the cost of a particular primary activity is justified relative to the value it creates, its sources of cost (cost-drivers) must be identified (as discussed in Chapter 3). Can any be eliminated or reduced *without damaging the value added*? The assessment of the value a particular activity adds is somewhat problematic. To assess cost accurately requires sound implementation of an activity-based costing technique. Further, value-added calculations depend on output (transfer) prices between stages, which may not be explicit; even then, transfer prices may be arbitrary or based on tough negotiations between business departments or units. If cross-border transfers occur, international currency exchange rates also complicate matters.

It can be productive to approach the analysis from the customer or client standpoint. By examining the elements of value *as perceived by the client*, the key value-drivers (rather than cost-drivers) crystallise. Value-drivers and the activities that contribute to them can then be linked. The value created can then be matched with what clients are willing to pay, confirmed by market research and by benchmarking competitors' offerings. For example, BMW offers the Mini with a choice of client-specified options priced at levels buyers consider good value. After a value-pricing exercise, each valued feature can be referenced back to the costs of adding it, to establish whether its cost is reasonable or must be reduced.

Reflections on the Resource-Based View of Advantage

The RBV concept of value creation and strategic advantage goes back over 50 years. It gained prominence from the mid-1980s as a reaction against the influential 'positioning' view (popularised by Porter), which some commentators considered to understate the importance of being very capable at specific activities. That an enterprise derives advantages from its own capabilities, *even in a seemingly unpromising, hostile environment*, is an undeniably attractive proposition.

Critics of the RBV perspective claim that identifying and protecting distinctive capabilities requires subjective judgments, as it is difficult to objectively test the link between a capability and the true profit that it is claimed to generate. Critics also claim that few enterprises are sole providers of their outputs, and that even fewer have truly distinctive capabilities that may not ultimately succumb to imitation or substitution.

A major complication is that successful enterprises may have a distinctive capability without really understanding its effects. In these cases, so-called causal ambiguity inhibits the full exploitation of companies' potential. Yet it has been argued that, paradoxically, only uncertain capabilities confer sustainable advantage.[23] The argument is that once causal links are made clear, dynamic environments make competitive imitation and substitution efforts inevitable.

Thus the most worthwhile capability is arguably the *dynamic* capability to generate new capabilities sooner and faster than others! Current knowledge enables only rather general statements to be made about dynamic capabilities. Where they exist, they may be less manageable than sometimes implied[24]; progress in any walk of life so often requires unforeseen, serendipitous developments.

CASE STUDY: Resources and capabilities at Cirque du Soleil[25]

Cirque du Soleil is an internationally renowned Canadian company that provides spectacular and daring acrobatic shows by skilful, world-class performers. It began in 1984 with a small group of 20 street performance artists led by Guy Laliberté, whose mission was to reinvent the circus. By its 25th anniversary the Cirque performances had spread from a conventional 'big top' in Montreal to resident shows in multiple North American locations, including Las Vegas, New York, Chicago and Disneyworld, Orlando, and touring shows in venues around the world, such as the Royal Albert Hall in London. Cirque now employs more than 4,000 people including 1,000 artists. Over 90 million people have witnessed a Cirque show in more than 200 cities.

The innovators at Cirque have created a repertoire of over 20 different shows, the majority of which are still performed regularly. Each new show has its own theme and requires multi-million dollar development. They feature daring and difficult acrobatics accompanied by dedicated stages, music, lighting and sound effects. Touring shows can be set up and dismantled quickly for efficient transport to the next venue. Shows typically require over 50 performers plus a similar number of set and costume designers, choreographers, technicians and other support staff. They are recruited from more than 40 countries, subject to one essential requirement – that they are the best at what they do.

Cirque's artistic merit has attracted many awards and tributes. It also has a social outreach dimension, dedicating 1% of its earnings to activities in 80 communities with a particular focus on 'youth at risk'. It remains a successful private business with an estimated US$ 810 million turnover in 2009. In addition to ticket sales it gets revenues from programme sales, commercial sponsorships and merchandising show videos and other memorabilia. Laliberté remains the dominant shareholder, with 75%. A further 20% is held by two Middle Eastern investment groups that support his plans for a new resident site in the United Arab Emirates in 2012.

Many traditional circus groups feature human and animal performances including, notably, Ringling Brothers and Barnum and Bailey in the United States, but they do not compete directly with Cirque due Soleil. Cirque is a key exponent of what is called 'contemporary circus' or 'nouveau cirque'; it integrates traditional acrobatic skills with theatrical techniques into a defined theme and characters. To a degree, the touring Chinese State Circus competes for the same audiences. There are many smaller 'nouveau cirque' enterprises around the world but without the scale or the brand presence of Cirque.

Questions

1. Identify all of Cirque du Soleil's main resources and capabilities based on the case notes and further research. Complete the analysis by (a) identifying and (b) rating its strategic assets and its distinctive capabilities.

2. From this analysis, what strategic actions would you recommend to Cirque?

Cirque treats talented performers as employees rather than superstars. Does this mean its performers are essentially replaceable?

Summary

LEARNING OBJECTIVE ①

- The resource-based view (RBV) of value creation and strategic advantage can be used to stress the importance of analysing the resource base, especially the features that generate superior value for clients, owners, employees and suppliers, indeed for a broad societal base of stakeholders.

LEARNING OBJECTIVE ②

LEARNING OBJECTIVE ③

- There is a distinction between resources and capabilities, and between a basic (threshold) and a distinctive (perhaps unique) status. The V-R-I-O-S framework establishes criteria to critically assess resources and capabilities. This framework can be applied to each stage of the internal value-adding chain of the enterprise to establish which activities are the most significant value creators.

- The chapter introduces path dependency and why capabilities need to be continually upgraded through innovation and organisational learning. Dynamic (higher-level or 'meta') capabilities are also introduced. To avoid unrealistic assessments of capabilities in either business or non-business enterprises, it is important to link skills to objective assessments of performance. The authors review how performance is assessed statistically and qualitatively, using financial and non-financial data.

Exercises for Further Study and Discussion

1. An enterprise has distinctive resources and capabilities according to V-R-I-O-S criteria. It competes in an attractive industry sector where its economic performance is outstanding. It considers entering a related sector where its resource base would be equally distinctive. However, the new sector has many more competitors than its present sector and its growth prospects are less attractive. Realistically, would the enterprise achieve its accustomed level of economic performance in the new sector, or would it worsen?

2. To what extent can exceptional *organizational* skills that are largely invisible to its clients be the basis of an enterprise differentiation strategy?

3. Imagine that the Red Bull company acquires an English Premier League football club. What would be the respective benefits to the parties? Which enterprise enhances its distinctive assets and capabilities more?

4. Collect the most recent data from Accor accounts on its website and update the analysis. Critique Accor's *strategic* performance in recent years, highlighting impressive aspects and matters for concern. Compare it with some of the hotel groups it lists as competitors.

5. An added-value statement[26] based on 1990 data for what was then Glaxo plc calculated its EVA as 28% of revenues (remarkably similar to the 2008 figure), and 46% of gross output (51% in 2006, 40% in 2000). To what extent do these comparisons confirm that there are real limits to performance in competitive markets?

6. Is the Dore Programme right to assert that statistics about the efficacy of its exercise-based treatments are inappropriate. How far do you agree? What would useful statistical measures be?

Suggestions for Further Reading

Ambrosini, V. (1998, ed.) *Exploring Techniques of Analysis and Evaluation in Strategic Management*, Prentice Hall (Part 1, chapters 1–4).

Barnett, W.P. and Hansen, M. (1996) 'The Red Queen in organizational evolution', *Strategic Management Journal* (vol. 17, pp.139–157).

Collis, D.J. and Montgomery, C.A. (2005, Ed. 2) *Corporate Strategy: A Resource-Based Approach*, McGraw-Hill (chapter 2).

Eisenhardt, K.M. and Martin, J.A. (2000) 'Dynamic capabilities: what are they?', *Strategic Management Journal* (vol. 21, pp. 1105–1121).

Helfat, C.E. and Lieberman, M. (2002) 'The birth of capabilities: market entry and importance of prehistory', *Industrial and Corporate Change* (vol. 12, pp. 725–760).

Kay, J. (1993) *Foundations of Corporate Success: How Business Strategies Add Value*, Oxford University Press.

Mahoney, J.T. and Pandian, J.R. (1992) 'The resource-based view within the conversation of strategic management', *Strategic Management Journal* (vol. 13, pp. 363–380).

Mills. R. (1998) 'Understanding and using shareholder value analysis', in Ambrosini, V. (ed.) *Exploring Techniques of Analysis and Evaluation in Strategic Management*, Prentice Hall.

Mills, R.W. and Weinstein, B. (2000) 'Beyond shareholder value – reconciling the shareholder and stakeholder perspectives', *Journal of General Management* (vol. 25/1, pp. 79–93).

Peteraf, M.A. (1993) 'The cornerstones of competitive advantage: a resource-based view', *Strategic Management Journal* (vol. 14, pp. 179–192).

Prahalad, C.K. and Hamel, G. (1990) 'The core competence of the corporation', *Harvard Business Review* (vol. 66, pp. 79–91).

Segal-Horn, S. (1998) *The Strategy Reader*, Blackwell (Part 3, chapters 9–11).

Stalk, G., Evans, P. and Shulman, L.E. (1992) 'Competing on capabilities: the new rules of corporate strategy', *Harvard Business Review* (vol. 70/2, pp. 57–69).

Teece, D.J., Pisano, G. and Shuen, A. (1997) 'Dynamic capabilities and strategic management', *Strategic Management Journal* (vol. 18/7, pp. 509–533).

Volberda, H.W. and Elfring, T. (2001, eds) *Rethinking Strategy*, Sage (Part 4, chapters 13–16).

Notes

1 Sources http://www.tesco.com; http://en.wikipedia.org/wiki/Tesco
2 Penrose (1959); Nelson and Winter (1982); Barnet, Greve and Park (1994); and Aldrich (1999, chapter 2) offer insights into evolutionary enterprise development.
3 The following provide useful commentaries on the RBV: Wernerfelt (1984); Mahoney and Pandian (1992); Hamel and Heene (1994); Collis and Montgomery (1995); Campbell and Sommers Luchs (1997); Foss (1997).
4 The lease becomes, in effect, the asset although the resource provided via the lease becomes the source of the value created.
5 For example, the 'Ilford' brand is now applied to photographic materials made by two quite separate companies. The brand remains valuable to both. One is the UK source of traditional materials for black-and-white printing and retains a distinct reputation based on its expertise. The other is a multinational corporation that produces digital printing papers.
6 See for example, Rumelt, Schendel and Teece (1994) (eds) (Part 2: why are firms different? chapters 8–10).
7 Kay (1993).
8 See Nelson and Winter (1982); Nelson (1991); Barnett, Greve and Park (1994); Williams (1994); Helfat and Lieberman (2002).
9 See chapter 1 in Hamel and Heene (1994).
10 The V-R-I-O shorthand has been advocated particularly by Jay Barney e.g. Barney (1991:1995); Barney and Hesterly (2010), extended here with the substituability criterion.

11 A concept first introduced by Lippman and Rumelt (1982). See also Rumelt et al. (1994).

12 Tripsas and Gavetti (2000) acknowledge the importance of perceptions and inertia.

13 Marchand (1998) addresses the advantage-creating properties of intellectual capital.

14 Kay (1993, page 24).

15 Though a primary *operations* activity of specialized research and consulting enterprises.

16 The full acquisition cost is actually the price plus any perceived 'opportunity cost' such as forfeits or penalties incurred in foregoing other options. Penalties include loss of interest on the monetary value of the purchase, forfeit of reservation fees or money deposits on the alternatives, and perceived status loss arising from preferring a functional to a prestige product (e.g., the purchase of a family car rather than a sports car). Not-for-profit clienteles incur opportunity costs such as the obligations of club members to respect club rules with which they disagree.

17 Other productivity measures may be chosen for their relevance to the activities of a particular enterprise. Comparisons with other enterprises must be made cautiously. Economic value-added is particularly significant.

18 Manufacturers calculate *gross profit* per time period as sales revenues less total production costs (direct variable production costs plus time-period fixed overheads). Retailers and other distribution enterprises calculate gross profit as sales revenues less purchased input costs.

19 Profits can be calculated before or after tax paid and before or after interest paid. Capital employed is normally the balance sheet total. Note that countries adopting US accounting practices state total capital employed as the sum of non-current assets *plus* current assets, whereas British accounts present total capital employed as the sum of non-current assets *plus* current assets *less* current liabilities.

20 It is the basis of shareholder value analysis. See Mills (1998); Rappaport (1998).

21 See Kay (1993), Barney (2007, chapter 2).

22 Elkington (1998).

23 For example, Barnett and Hansen (1996).

24 Prahalad and. Hamel (1990); von Krogh, Ichijo and Nonaka (2000).

25 See http://www.cirquedusoleil.com/; http://en.wikipedia.org/wiki/Cirque_du_Soleil; and Case 21 in DeWit, B. and Meyer, R. *Strategy Process, Content, Context: An International Perspective*, Thomson (pp. 926–932).

26 Kay (1993).

6

Strategic Decision-Making

Learning Outcomes

This chapter is designed to enable you to:

① Explain the merits of a systematic approach to (a) the diagnosis of strategic issues and (b) decision making.

② Understand the criteria for evaluating strategic alternatives.

③ Understand how and why strategic issue diagnosis and decision making are not totally objective.

④ Complete thorough analyses of the strategic positions of enterprises.

CASE STUDY: Monsanto Inc.[1]

Monsanto is a major US corporation engaged in the production and sale of products for the agricultural industry. Founded over 100 years ago, it has grown and changed its profile through internal developments, acquisitions, disposals and changes of ownership. Beginning with food and drug products, it moved on to making industrial chemicals, followed in later decades by a range of products. These included plastics and synthetic fibres, herbicides, defoliants and insecticides, optoelectronic devices, agricultural seed production, and biotechnology products (notably, genetically modified crops).

In the 1990s the company began a strategic transition from chemicals to biotechnology. It now operates in two major domains. First, there are products for agricultural productivity. These comprise principally herbicides sold via the Roundup brand. Second, there are 'Seeds and traits', on which the company claims exert a 'laser focus'. These products comprise seeds, genomic and biotechnology products spanning corn, soybean, cotton, vegetables and other seed types for sale to farmers. Many of its seed stocks have been genetically modified (GM) to increase crop yields.

Monsanto sells GM seeds and complementary herbicides in North America and worldwide. Such products require approval from the US Food and Drug Administration (FDA) and equivalent bodies. Former Monsanto employees reportedly hold positions in the FDA, the US Environmental Protection Agency and the Supreme Court. In some territories, notably the European Union (EU) where consumer resistance to GM foodstuffs is high, Monsanto has struggled to obtain regulatory approval for GM seeds. EU regulators have also been influenced by the precautionary principle, given uncertainty over the long-term impact of GM organisms that can cross-fertilise natural (organic) crops. Regulators also worry that Monsanto and its main GM competitors, Du Pont and Syngenta, are increasing their dominance of seed markets to an unhealthy degree.

Thus, Monsanto is a controversial company. It is a '*bête noir*' of the environmental lobby for aggressively promoting GM seeds. It has been accused of promoting Roundup-resistant crop strains to increase herbicide sales. In the 1990s it patented a technology for so-called 'terminator' seeds that breed only infertile plants, requiring farmers to buy new Monsanto seed each growing season. The outcry stopped the company commercializing this technology. In the 1960s and 1970s it was a producer of the infamous 'Agent Orange' used to defoliate jungles and disable fertile agricultural land in Vietnam. Monsanto is routinely a plaintiff in legal actions: against farmers for patent infringement and as defendant in actions brought by government agencies around the world. In 2009 its accounts reported financial provisions of $US 262 million to cover anticipated and potential costs of legal actions.

Monsanto's justification for developing GM seeds is its potential to feed a hungry world: GM crops have higher yields and greater disease resistance than natural strains. Monsanto is a highly profitable corporation. As of 2009, its sales revenues were $US 11.7 billion, net income was $US 2.1 billion; total assets were $US 17.9 billion. Its expenditure on research and development was $US 1.1 billion (9.4% of sales), a substantial proportion it had maintained for some years. Seeds and related products accounted for 62% of total sales (rising) and 67% of gross profits. The staple crop seeds, corn and soybean, accounted for three-quarters of sales and gross profits in this business. Gross profit margins were high: 61.7% of sales, compared with 51.0% in the agricultural productivity business (which depended on Roundup for 80% of sales), making it an effective cash generator to develop the seeds and the biotechnology business.

Questions

1. What issues do you suppose Monsanto's key decision-makers would have examined in detail before making the decision to focus on two main business areas?

2. What issues do you suppose Monsanto's key decision-makers now examine in greatest detail?

3. How much weight do you suppose they attach to (i) shareholder priorities (ii) environmental priorities? On the basis of the above case study and additional information, do you think they got the balance about right?

Introduction: Strategic Issue Diagnosis and Decision Making

Chapter 1 presented strategic management as a process. We saw there that the process originates from three distinct sources, namely an enterprise's:

- External environment in which the enterprise functions.
- Internal (organizational) environment.
- Strategic intent, encoded in its statements of mission and future vision.

These were identified at the top of Figure 1.4.

RNING
ECTIVE ① The current chapter considers how enterprises may move from this starting point to develop a strategic position statement (SPS). An SPS defines the key issues that presently exist for the enterprise and those which may arise in relation to its future mission. It is important that decision-makers form a clear position statement. The many issues and events emerging from systematic scanning and from ad-hoc sources need assessment and prioritization, activities called strategic issue diagnosis.

Strategic issue diagnosis clarifies the nature and significance of 'raw' issues. It enables judgements to be made about the relative priority of the threats to an enterprise, the opportunities open to it, and the enterprise's own strengths and weaknesses. These judgements (which are, in effect, decisions) contribute to the process of producing an SPS. Only when the key issues are clear is a meaningful position statement possible, which then allows the enterprise to consider alternative strategies. As we will see in this chapter, the viability of particular strategic options can subsequently be assessed via generic criteria appropriate to strategic decision-making.

The steps that produce an enterprise's SPS are illustrated in Figure 6.1.

In a moment we will work through this figure step by step. First, though, it is useful to consider the overall form of the figure. This might suggest an orderly, logical flow of activity with clear start and end points. In practice, however, activities such as scanning and issue identification are ongoing. Issues converge periodically on a revised strategic plan, a cyclical process repeated regularly, often annually in large enterprises, especially in dynamic environments. Yet ad-hoc issues of potential strategic significance also emerge, demanding more immediate, non-routine responses. Uncertain issues must be recognised and *interpreted*. Once given meaning, they become part of the strategic agenda. Issues perceived as threats engender a sense of crisis and the need to respond urgently. Divergent stakeholder priorities channel interpretations into self-interested prescriptions that sustain conflict and contest. As major stakeholders, senior executives therefore try to control the interpretation of issues and whether they feature on the strategic agenda.

RNING
ECTIVE ③ Discrepant viewpoints among stakeholders affect how coherently an issue is perceived, interpreted and linked to possible response strategies. As well as knowledge shortage and divergent interests, shortcomings in human intellect and objectivity create 'cognitive' constraints on issue interpretation, especially under uncertainty and time pressures. In this chapter we examine these constraints.

The chapter concludes with a case study that features the video games industry, in which the main competitors are business corporations that are familiar with huge and controversial strategic decisions.

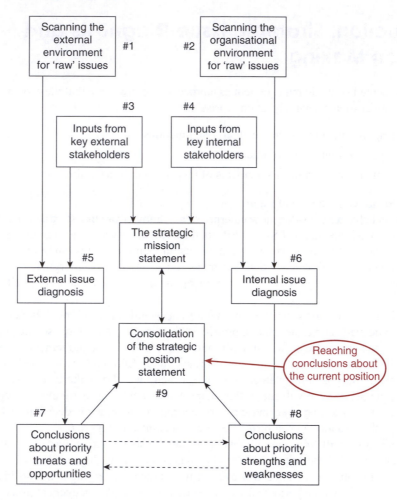

Figure 6.1: Steps that produce the strategic position statement

Constructing the Strategic Position Statement

Figure 6.1 indicates particular steps that produce the SPS. Some of these are concurrent, others sequential. Here we consider each step – or pair of steps – in turn.

Steps 1 and 2: Scanning for 'Raw' Issues

These scanning activities are the ongoing search for emergent, 'raw' issues of potential significance. The term 'raw' here signifies that although a phenomenon or event has become salient (noticed) its full significance is unclear, not critically assessed. The scan of internal environment – concerned principally with resources, capabilities and performance levels – parallels the scans of macro and industry sector environments. Emergent issues can highlight *or be driven by* stakeholder interests and pressures.

External issues constitute potential threats when the enterprise cannot control or influence them, especially if it has no available response. Conversely, issues linked to potentially beneficial external developments, such as demand trends that the enterprise is (or could become) well placed to exploit, are potential opportunities.

Issues in the internal environment that bear directly on the enterprise's ability to create substantial value for its stakeholders are of most concern. Factors that allow it to maintain a strategic competitive advantage are actual or potential strengths. Factors that pose actual or potential shortcomings in respect of value-creation and advantage-creation are weaknesses.

External issue scanning and monitoring routines have been discussed in previous chapters. In addition to systematic routines, strategic issues emerge in other ways, most often detected initially as 'weak signals' – probably, by very experienced executives who draw on their intuition and experience. Alternatively, an incoming chief executive sensitized by experience gained in different sector may sense an issue that enterprise colleagues do not. Even so, weak signals are easy to miss until the passage of time has amplified their salience greatly.[2]

Whatever the mechanism, a salient issue develops momentum when it:

- Has the attention of senior executives and/or other influential stakeholders who 'champion' the need to understand and tackle it.
- Features on formal strategic agenda of the enterprise.
- Appears linked to existing, significant issues.
- Is considered resolvable – non-resolvable issues tend to be sidelined.

Steps 3 and 4: Merging Stakeholder Inputs

External and internal stakeholders with strong opinions are usually capable of expressing their concerns when issues affect their own interests directly. Steps 3 and 4 in Figure 6.1 accommodate these influences. Major shareholders are often quick to raise concerns when they judge the enterprise to be performing poorly. They also express views about the enterprise's purpose and direction, a major influence that prompts re-evaluation of mission and vision. The mission is a strong input to the SPS because they need to be mutually consistent. When mission and SPS are dissonant the enterprise is poorly placed to establish a viable future strategy.

Steps 5 and 6: Strategic Issue Diagnosis (Assessment and Interpretation)

Steps 5 and 6 involve critical diagnosis of what each identified 'raw' issue means for the enterprise. In principle this is an objective, analytic process. However, even apparently hard, indisputable facts must be interpreted to appreciate their significance for the enterprise. It is much harder to diagnose the consequences of an issue, whether a concern or observed trend with confidence, than initially to identify it.

A potential opportunity may also be a threat when substantial, risky investment would be needed to exploit it. Strengths become weaknesses if their benefits could be negated by future environmental changes. For example, local family-owned convenience stores operate long hours to provide residents with a good service. Competition from the big supermarket chains with branches linked to petrol stations is now a threat. The previous strength of the independent is now becoming a weakness because long hours add cost without generating sufficient late night custom.

Conversely, threats and weaknesses can sometimes be reversed when appropriate strategies are implemented promptly. For example, some village primary schools with small intakes were threatened with closure, but have survived by expanding their facilities and attracting the children of middle-class suburban parents who fear low standards in their local schools.

Steps 7 and 8: Determination of the Critical Issues and Priorities

Steps 7 and 8 present judgements about the most significant issues and thus their priorities for enterprise strategic management in support of mission and future vision. They constitute strengths and weaknesses, threats and opportunities. These may be summarized by the well-known acronym, SWOT. (Alternatively, the acronym TOWS is sometimes used.)[3]

The drawback of relying on the 'SWOT' schema is that it encourages a superficial summary that lacks selectivity and critical thought. Thus a 'SWOT' analysis is best considered an intermediate stage in the analysis. Figure 6.2 presents a more developed version of the 'SWOT' framework. The various columns are designed to facilitate a more complete assessment. Figure 6.2 encourages the analyst to consider the potential impact of an issue on the enterprise, the consequent priority or urgency it merits and, finally, what strategic responses are available to exploit strengths and opportunities while rectifying or compensating for weaknesses and threats. The format recognises that some issues have multiple implications, favourable and otherwise.

Diagnosed threats and weaknesses require decisions about *how* significant or severe they are or may become, hence the possible corrective responses and their urgency. Likewise, judgement is needed over responses to build on perceived strengths and opportunities. Capability assessments are comparative: strengths and weaknesses have to be judged relative to the capabilities of competing providers, if any, and the needs and expectations of clienteles and other stakeholders. There is a danger that a simple numerical ranking of priorities conveys an unjustified sense of certainty. Issue analysts are also stakeholders whose judgements can be influenced by their personal interests, leading in hindsight to possible errors.[4]

Step 9: Consolidation of the Strategic Position Statement

Steps 1 to 8 result in a variety of analyses that may contain considerable detail. There may be potential conflicts between the conclusions and implications of one analysis and another. So it is necessary to reconcile differences of fact and interpretation, leading to a concise, well-considered summary of the major issues that affect the enterprise and its future strategic options. This summary is the strategic position statement (SPS). Once the position statement has been accepted it

Issue	Evidence for classification	Significance and possible implications	Impact rating*	Priority rating**	Actions indicated
Relative strengths					
•					
•					
•					
Relative weaknesses					
•					
•					
•					
Potential opportunities					
•					
•					
•					
Potential threats					
•					
•					
•					

Overview summary of position

* Suggested impact ratings:

A = Very substantial potential impact
B = Substantial potential impact
C = Some potential impact

** Suggested priority ratings:

1 = Immediate action indicated
2 = Non-urgent action indicated
3 = No action yet indicated

Figure 6.2: Enhanced strategic position statement

becomes the basis for the next stage of the strategic management process, to explore and evaluate the strategies available to respond to the priority issues. Further enquiries may be needed before decisions about appropriate strategies can be made, although they may delay difficult decisions that must be made. Further, because an identified strategy is theoretically *available* (e.g., to diversify the product portfolio) it does not always constitute an opportunity. The enterprise may have inadequate resources, knowledge or skills to exploit an opportunity successfully, hence it may prove unrewarding. An emergent issue affects all enterprises in a sector, but may be an opportunity for some and a threat to others. Position statements and judgements about issues are *always* enterprise-specific, given the particular stakeholder and resource environments of each.

Formality and Debate in Strategic Issue Diagnosis

Interpreting known facts and opinions objectively requires thoughtful interaction among executives prepared to exchange ideas and evaluate them critically. Structured diagnostic approaches typically involve formal and informal meetings of boards of directors and senior management teams with the authority to determine issues on behalf of the enterprise.[5] The views of major external stakeholders are typically expressed at main board level, by having non-executive directors present. Formal deliberations are informed by a combination of analytical approaches including:

- Logical argumentation: the presentation of facts and logical arguments verbally and in written reports.
- Statistical data analyses.
- Forming and testing hypotheses.
- Debates that apply methods of devil's advocacy or dialectical enquiry to examine multiple perspectives.

Below we examine each of these approaches in turn.

LEARNING OBJECTIVE ①

Logical argumentation is, of course, centuries-old. It requires conclusions (claims) about an issue to be structured in a specific way so that assumptions and fallacies become evident and are not obscured by enthusiastic rhetoric. An example of this approach is outlined in Figure 6.3, which sets out the structure of an argument concerning the music industry.

Here the 'claim' is in effect a conclusion about the meaning of the issue that emerges from the observations. The 'warrants' define the unspoken assumptions that *must all apply* if the proposed claim is to be considered a valid conclusion or interpretation. Once highlighted, each assumption can then be challenged for robustness. Yet even if they are accepted, the truth of the claim depends on other factors called 'qualifiers'. If *any* of the qualifiers holds true, then the claim (a potential opportunity in the figure) will be restricted or invalid.

In the example illustrated in Figure 6.3, the claim may appear valid, particularly if one is left-handed and keen on music. Of course, many musical instrument stores cater for left-handers, but none are exclusively left-handed. So is there an untapped opportunity? The answer still needs careful thought and further research.

No music stores sell instruments exclusively for left-handed people ··········> **So this looks like a business opportunity**

Evidence or grounds (observed, salient facts)   *Conclusion or claim*

• **Playing music is a popular activity**
• **Music stores cater for the majority – right-handed people**
• **Left-handers want to play music as much as right-handers, but retailers cannot cater for this minority group**
• **Hence there is a distribution gap**
• **Gap-filling is often an opportunity**

Unless:........
• **Left-handers are happy with current retail stores**
• **They don't buy musical instruments**
• **They all play right-handedly**
• **Anti-discrimination laws prevent left-hand-only stores**
• **There are too few left-handed people to create a profitable business**

Justifications or warrants that explain why the claim is valid   *Limiters or qualifiers*

Figure 6.3: The structure of logical argument*

*After Stephen Toulmin (1958)

This powerful approach to deconstructing arguments exposes dubious assumptions that can then be rejected or tested. However, the goal of logical argumentation is a single truth, not the exploration of alternative interpretations. Other methods encourage *differences* of view to be expressed and explored, to avoid premature and perhaps erroneous agreement (closure). Such methods include (a) 'Devil's advocacy' and (b) dialectical inquiry.

Devil's advocacy requires an individual or group to propose the interpretation of an issue and its consequences, applying relevant facts, opinions and assumptions. Another group challenges this interpretation by identifying its weaknesses, applying contrary facts, opinions and assumptions. The process is adversarial, based on civilized conflict.[6] Thus devil's advocacy aims to test the strength of the proposed interpretation and ultimately to accept or reject it.

Dialectical inquiry begins with two clearly defined, but contrary, interpretations of an issue that their respective proponents explain and try to justify. The two sides are sometimes called 'thesis' and 'antithesis'. Subsequent debate aims to identify a *new* position (synthesis) that draws on the strengths of both starting positions, but eliminates their respective weaknesses. Unlike devil's advocacy, it aims to establish a strong consensus rather than a winner. This approach is comparable to that of the Napoleonic legal code, widely established in Europe.

Of course, many executive teams may apply these techniques with varying degrees of rigour without necessarily being aware that they are doing so. Less formal methods of issue diagnosis include and often combine:

• Ad-hoc conversations.
• Issue labelling and selling.

LEARNING OBJECTIVE ①

- Articulating explanatory narratives that purport to make good sense of known facts and opinions.
- Self-interested negotiations.

Informality allows differing perspectives on an issue to emerge organically and, one hopes, reach consensus, albeit usually over longer periods than timetabled, formal processes allow. Irrespective of the means, consensus is required to advance a strategy. While it does not guarantee valid conclusions, decision makers who accept a consensus are more willing to act together, which is a vital component for a strategy to be implemented and succeed.[7]

Issue labelling occurs when individuals try to impose meaning on an issue by using potent words or phrases that capture its perceived significance and consequently its implications. For example, an issue labelled as a 'crisis' is likely to galvanize action. Issue selling is the active promotion of a label. A potent label gains attention and is therefore more likely to reach the strategic agenda of executive meetings. However, an established label often discourages critical debate and directs the nature of responses to it.

In addition to the labelling of issues, the question of what kinds of explanation and context – what kinds of narrative – accompany them is also important. Narratives expand plausibly on the significance attached to a label. Competing narratives are, in effect, ways of testing support for hypotheses over meanings and prescriptions for action. Where support exists, the issue gains support as the associated narrative is repeated, diffused and extended.

Influential stakeholders generally interpret an issue self-interestedly. They can be great promoters of issue labels and narratives. Retaining some ambiguity over meaning is a good tactic to manoeuvre an issue on to the formal agenda, because it allows others scope to interpret meaning consistent with their own interests and ambitions. Equally, an unattractive or trivial label is a good way to de-prioritise an issue, even when it features on the agenda. It receives attention (if at all) only at the end of meetings, gets ignored or sidelined, unless and until it 'bites' back. Because issue diagnosis can be manipulated, it is not always a rational, objective process.[8]

CASE STUDY: Issue diagnosis: 'total quality' in a manufacturing company[9]

Senior managers of a food manufacturing company had come to accept that the label 'total quality' denoted a key strategic issue. Everyone knew the issue was important for its strategy, yet it turned out that this label meant different things to managers their respective functions. Examples of the different meanings attached to the label included:

1. Implementing International Standards Office (ISO) quality control procedures.

2. Making continuous improvements in production methods and facilities.

3. Communicating better with production staff.

4. Fostering awareness and a positive attitude to improve product quality.

5. Better control of the raw materials supply chain.

6. Better information technology systems.

7. Improving bargaining power over demanding customers.

The executives constructed the meaning of 'total quality' based on their particular interests and priorities. All expressed public commitment to the issue because the 'total quality' label mandated them to pursue quality-related initiatives that each personally cared about. Yet there was no consensus over the real meaning of 'total quality' for the company. Individuals emphasised their own priorities at senior management meetings, which made it impossible to pursue a coherent strategy. Consequently, some 'total quality' initiatives conflicted with others. The issue slipped down the company's agenda and significantly its quality reputation did not improve. Ultimately it was acquired by a large conglomerate.

Question

1. Which meanings of 'total quality' would you expect the various functional managers in the company to prefer? Seek to link the above list to the managers of the following functions: (a) marketing; (b) production; (c) research and development; (d) supply chain; (e) finance; (f) others (please specify). How should the chief executive have managed the issue?

Strategic Decision-making

Issue diagnosis and the construction of the position statement lead to strategic decision-making. This involves choosing among alternative interpretations of issues, their significance, priority and preferred strategic responses. In practice, scanning and issue diagnosis are continuous activities that allow enterprises to address issues promptly when perceived importance or urgency dictates. Ideally, issues responses are determined within an agreed strategic framework. When responses emerge in a sequential, piecemeal fashion, actions to resolve a new issue may conflict with an existing strategy. While the food manufacturing company in the above illustration was motivating its staff to enhance product quality, it was also developing a strategy to increase factory mechanisation that would de-skill production processes, create redundancies and damage staff morale.

Optimising and Satisficing Approaches to Strategic Decision-making

It is helpful to distinguish decision-making from decision-taking. Strategic decision-*making* forms and assesses the options available to resolve diagnosed issues. Strategic decision-*taking* is the challenging task of selecting a preferred strategy and living with the consequences. Decision-making is analytically oriented, while decision-taking is the exercise of judgment and

ARNING
JECTIVE ①

ARNING
JECTIVE ②

intuition under uncertainty and diverse stakeholder pressures.[10] Decision-making aims to facilitate decision-taking by formulating options and examining their advantages and drawbacks objectively and critically. Even so, the approach depends on the dominant managerial mindset in the enterprise.

Two broad decision-making approaches may be observed, namely (a) optimising and (b) satisficing. Optimising desires to create the best possible strategy that integrates a set of realistic actions that address all of the diagnosed issues. A satisficing approach has lower expectations and accepts pragmatic, 'good-enough' solutions.

The optimising approach formulates specific criteria to be used to reach a decision; it then applies the criteria systematically to evaluate the options, leading ultimately to a 'best' decision. It is consistent with the strategic management frames (Chapter 1) that emphasize rationality and 'hard' evidence.[11]

Typically, satisficing responds to issues sequentially rather than as a set. It screens an identified option against fewer criteria, some of which it may introduce or modify *after* the option has been identified. If an option meets the satisficing criteria, the decision is effectively taken. If not, a second option is introduced and the decision process recycles. This sequential, comparative evaluation continues until a 'good enough' choice emerges. While hard evidence plays its part, the process is generally more politicised and adaptive, consistent with the alternative strategic frames of Chapter 1. It tries to accommodate the contested interests of senior executives and other influential stakeholders and their instinct to negotiate strategic choices.

Most strategic decision processes are hybrid, neither wholly optimising nor satisficing. An enterprise could use an optimising approach towards mission-critical issues, but satisfice elsewhere. Or it might seek to optimise in respect of some domains of activity and satisfice elsewhere. While optimising is more rigorous and therefore theoretically preferable, it imposes high costs – of effort, money and elapsed time. The pragmatic, satisficing approach generally costs less and is quicker, although this depends on the degree of negotiation and dissent that must be accommodated.

Criteria for Strategy Selection

Various generic criteria can be applied to the evaluation of strategic options in particular instances, expressed below as four questions.

Relevance: Does the proposed strategy address the issue(s) identified? This question is about whether the responses tackle the implications of the issue. For example, a mission that calls for high service quality implies actions to enhance service standards, rather than reduce the cost of delivery. Again, when facing the issue of declining market share, proposed actions should stabilise or reverse the trend. A strategy to enter a *different* sector does *not* address the decline (unless the decline is considered terminal; in which case other criteria must still be applied).

Practicality: Can the enterprise implement the proposed strategy? Are its present (and anticipated) resources and capabilities compatible with its intentions? Inadequate capabilities make the proposed actions impractical, with little prospect of success. The criterion addresses realism and plausibility. As a small enterprise, the Pashley bicycle company (Chapter 3) does not, realistically, have the resources and capabilities to become a high volume, mass-market bicycle maker. This strategy would almost certainly bring disaster. Its proven skills and reputation serving specialised demand niches make that strategy most plausible for continued growth.

Sustainability: Is the strategy ethically and ecologically sustainable? Do the proposed actions meet the expectations of societal stakeholders? The criterion of sustainability in its various forms has often been ignored by recourse to arguments about compliance with legal and regulatory obligations imposed by democratic governments.[12] No doubt some enterprises will continue to adopt this posture to justify ethically or environmentally dubious strategies, but their position will become increasingly vulnerable as competitors adopt more sustainable strategies, possibly mandated by proactive industry self-regulation.

Meeting key expectations: Does the strategy support the interests and expectations of the enterprise's most influential stakeholders? To what degree will the main stakeholders find the proposed strategy satisfactory? Shareholders expect to see growing financial returns. Their investment in the enterprise must work hard, so they will scrutinise ratios such as the annual return on net assets (RONA) and dividend cover. Stakeholders' attitudes to risk are also important, as are the expectations of significant stakeholders in not-for-profit enterprises (as discussed in Chapter 4).

A sound strategy must meet all four generic criteria, otherwise it will be ruled out. This means that judgement is involved and compromise may be needed at the margins. Strategies that will benefit some stakeholder groups disproportionately make it challenging to meet the 'expectations' criterion. For example, heavy capital investment may compromise short-term profits, displeasing some investors while others welcome the prospect that investment will create higher and more secure longer-term profits. Supplementary, non-vital or 'nice to have/achieve' criteria may also be introduced. These may help to decide between alternative strategies that meet all the vital criteria.

British Petroleum (BP) and alternative energy supplies

BP is one of the biggest energy producers, mostly of fossil fuels (oil and natural gas) and derivative products. Fossils fuels are a finite, economically volatile and environmentally problematic resource, as was brought home to BP during the massive spill from its offshore oilrig in the Gulf of Mexico. It would be remarkable if BP did *not* consider an increasing its commitment to renewable energy production as a response to this strategic issue.

How would this strategy match the four selection criteria?[13] Suggested answers are as follows:

Relevance: a good match since it would maintain BP's mission as an energy producer but reduces its dependence on (and vulnerability to) fossil fuel extraction.

Practicality: BP's corporate strengths include a huge asset base and reputation, but renewable energy production requires resources and skills new to it. BP would need to learn rapidly to fill gaps in its knowledge and technology base. It would need also to invest heavily in new facilities and equipment. Onerous demands on its current cash flows would limit the speed at which it could invest.

Sustainability: BP appears already to have ruled out the option of nuclear energy, which is not a renewable source (supplies of uranium ores are finite), while major concerns remain over plant safety and long-term storage of spent fuel. Clean renewable processes such as wind and solar energy are environmentally sustainable and ethically sound. Doubt remains over the proportion of future global energy needs they can meet.

Meeting key expectations: in principle, wind, wave and solar energy production appear consistent with BP's key stakeholder expectations. Shareholders might worry that alternative energy investments would inhibit BP's commitment to oil extraction and refining, vital to sustain cash flows and dividends in the foreseeable future. Employees would worry about possible redundancies and the scope for retraining and redeployment. Other energy schemes such as nuclear and tidal barrages raise additional environmental concerns and would most probably require government support and collaboration with external partners, raising questions about control. Diversification into renewables would be a major, but not a 'bet the company' decision for BP, that is, it would not risk catastrophic failure.

Overall, then, the four criteria suggest that prudent expansion into renewable energy production could be a sensible strategy for BP.

Uncertainty, Risk and Financial Return

Choosing among strategic alternatives must take due account of how uncertainty and risk affect prospective returns. Risk factors can affect deliberations in respect of any of the four generic criteria, particularly stakeholder expectations and risk tolerance. High expected returns usually entail greater risks, although enterprises that face severe challenges may embark on high risk strategies, despite modest predicted returns.

LEARNING
OBJECTIVE ②

Risk relates to identifiable factors whose occurrence would affect (in fact, almost always, damage) outcomes in relatively predictable ways. Uncertainty, by contrast, reflects decision makers' inability to predict future outcomes with any confidence, especially outcomes involving long-term investments. For example, for an oil company the *risk* of an explosion in a refinery or on an offshore rig should be quantifiable, given its knowledge and experience of operating facilities for many years.

Risk assessment combines the probability of an occurrence with the financial consequences if it does occur. Consider two strategies A and B (Table 6.A), both of which require large financial investments. Option B requires greater investment but appears more attractive because its predicted RONA employed is higher, numerically and as a percentage. However, option B will take longer to achieve the predicted return. Since greater variability in possible outcome is predicted, perhaps even a negative one (as might apply to investments in oil exploration in unstable regions), it could actually lose the enterprise money.

Table 6.A: Risk and return among alternative strategies

	Strategy A	Strategy B
Investment required	£80 million	£150 million
Time frame to fruition	3 years	7 years
Predicted RONA	10% per annum	12% per annum
Range of variability in expected RONA	5% to 15%	–5% to +22%

RONA = return on net assets.

What other factors should the decision-makers in this example consider? One is enterprise size. Investments of £80 million and £150 million are significant, even by the standards of large enterprises, for some possibly 'bet the company' decisions. A second issue is the financial profile: is all of the cash required at the start of the project or can some be deferred until it is clear if the project is succeeding? A further consideration is the essentially 'risk-free' option represented by prevailing bank interest rates.[14] If risk-free rates are predicted to hold consistently at or below 2%, options A and B might both look attractive, but if rates are predicted to be above 10% both options A and B look much less attractive.[15]

What, then, should the strategy be: A, B, or neither? If the table truly represents the extent of enterprise knowledge and if bank rates are predicted consistently below 5%, those with limited risk tolerance will probably choose option A. Option B extends further into the future and makes more demands on the reliability of key assumptions;   it could actually lose money. Conversely, risk-tolerant enterprises have more of a gambler's mentality would perceive option B to present a significant opportunity. They would see regret as the failure to capitalise on the possibility of a big return. More generally, it follows that decision-making criteria should include the consequences of *failing to* pursue a strategic option as well as the consequences of pursuing it.

Console wars in the video games industry

Japanese corporations, notably Sega, Nintendo and Sony, and, more recently, US Microsoft have been instrumental in developing dedicated consumer consoles for playing electronic games. Consoles can be relatively inexpensive, hand-held devices or larger, state-of-art devices used solo or internet-enabled for upgrades and multi-player gaming. Manufacturers launch new devices in successive 'generations' as technology improves, typically over a 5–6 year cycle. Each console is a unique platform that is only as attractive to players as its range and quality of compatible games. Manufacturers, their appointed developers and independents create new games (and enhance popular ones), now a highly lucrative industry in its own right. New platforms sometimes but not always play games created for a previous generation of the same-name console (backward compatibility).

Sega and Nintendo were already well established when Sony's original PlayStation entered the market. It was a 'fifth generation' console launched at the end of 1994. Sega, then market-leader, launched Saturn around the same time, which lost position to PlayStation, so Sega accelerated development of its sixth generation Dreamcast, launched in 1998. Sony matched Dreamcast with PlayStation 2 in 2000. Equivalent offerings in the form of Microsoft Xbox and Nintendo GameCube emerged in 2001. Over its life span PlayStation 2 reportedly sold over 140 million units, Xbox 24 million, GameCube 21+ million and Dreamcast 10+ million.

After the sixth generation, all four companies had to decide their next moves. Each competitor probably framed the strategic issue of whether and when to develop a seventh generation (7G) console differently because of *asymmetric risk perceptions*.

Sony *could accept the risks* of developing PlayStation 3 (PS3) because:

- PlayStation was now a well-established brand, consistent with Sony's dynamic image. It enjoyed a dominant market share and the consoles were very profitable.
- Games consoles spearheaded diversification of its consumer electronics portfolio.
- Sony had command of all the required hardware technologies.
- Many developers would be willing to develop games for PS3.

Microsoft probably *could not risk* failing to develop a 7G replacement for Xbox because:

- It would create huge loss of face and confidence with consumers and investors.
- The considerable gains it had made from Xbox investment would be wasted.
- Games software appeared to present huge sales and profit potential, complementing its status as one of the world's biggest software developers.
- Withdrawal might embolden Sony to compete with Microsoft in other areas of its business.

Sega probably **could not accept** the risks of developing a new 7G platform because:

- Dreamcast had been a commercial flop and Sega was unprofitable. Developing a 7G console would almost certainly bankrupt Sega if future sales were mediocre.
- Dreamcast's premature market exit had damaged Sega's reputation among consumers and games developers, making future acceptance and support uncertain.
- Sega could not match the commercial might of Sony and Microsoft, so its prospects of regaining a profitable position in competition with a future PS3 and/or Xbox looked poor.

Nintendo's position was different again. Arguably it **could accept not** taking the risk of developing a 7G product to compete with Sony and Microsoft because:

- By 2004 it had successfully developed and launched a new hand-held DS console that seemed set to secure dominant position, since neither Sony or Microsoft seemed very interested in handheld devices.
- Like Sega, it could not match Sony and Microsoft commercially, so it would be wise to avoid direct competition.

In fact, after Xbox launched in 2001, Sega terminated Dreamcast production to concentrate solely on games software development. Microsoft and Sony launched 7G consoles Xbox 360 (late 2005) and PlayStation 3 (late 2006). Nintendo surprised everyone by launching its own 7G platform, Wii, also in late 2006. It had identified a niche position appealing to families – not dedicated, hard-core gamers – with different kinds of game.

Constraints on Issue Diagnosis and Decision-making

Strategic decision-making in practice can be less rational than is sometimes suggested, owing to human social processes, idiosyncrasy and fallibility; shortcomings that constrain objectivity. Constraints on decision-making objectivity take two main forms:

- Social processes that must accommodate disparate and partial stakeholder interests, compromise and the consequent acceptance of sometimes unwise choices.
- Individual shortcomings of intellect (or cognition) and knowledge.

Constraints Arising from Administrative and Social Processes

Social processes severely affect group decision-making. Ideally, issue diagnosis and decision-making would be consistent and disciplined when trying to reconcile conflicting views and influences. Issues also emerge unpredictably; responses cannot always conform to a set timetable. The timing of decisions concerning innovation is particularly crucial. How quickly should a novel product or service be launched? Will it be well received? How quickly will a competitor respond? Is it better to be a pioneer or to wait for others to lead?

Inadequate knowledge creates many problems for strategic management. Well-documented constraints on thinking and decision making derive from studies of cognitive and social psychology.[16] Enterprises are amalgams of inadequate, incomplete and imperfect knowledge. A 'blooming, buzzing [environmental] confusion'[17] of ambiguity surrounds emerging issues and their possible consequences. The significance of an issue is rarely understood correctly at first encounter (as viewed with the benefit of hindsight), sometimes being over-stated, more often under-stated.

Most enterprise knowledge remains relatively localised and non-diffused; knowledge often does not reach those who could and should use it. It travels badly across internal boundaries, laterally and vertically. So-called knowledge management systems are designed to address the problem, though they have not eliminated it. The challenge is not just the systems, but how people use (and abuse) them.

Effective enterprises require people at all levels and functions to inquire, share, extend and reflect critically on the knowledge available. Status inhibits the frequency and quality of senior and junior staff interactions. Senior executives are too often unaware of pertinent thinking of subordinate staff or unreceptive to challenging, perhaps unconventional ideas and reasoning. Enterprises would benefit from an ethos in which hierarchy does not inhibit constructive 'strategic conversations'.

Strong frames of reference (discussed in Chapter 1) shape the conduct of strategic issue diagnosis and decision-making processes. Members of established, stable decision-making teams converge in outlooks and thought processes over time. They share increasingly rigid ways of thinking, beliefs, assumptions and conclusions so that their interactions become closed, self-confirming loops. Teams then exhibit dysfunctional, collective commitment to prior decisions, called 'groupthink'.[18] They ignore or reject new information that an outsider would consider a significant challenge to the rational basis of their commitment, denying serious, constructive challenge.

Within such teams divergent, minority thinking becomes increasingly difficult to articulate. Members who might challenge the accepted majority wisdom fear that they can no longer do so without being treated as dissidents. A dissident becomes frustrated, marginalised and ultimately quits or is dismissed. In the extreme, a misguided perspective becomes obsessive or fanatical: because it cannot be challenged, it results in descent into crisis and probable disaster. In addition to these social psychological constraints, there are generally economic[19] and emotional costs to accepting change. They include prospective loss of authority and respect from colleagues and opponents who would consider willingness to contemplate change a sign of weakness. The Cuban Missile Crisis of 1961 (Allison, 1972) and US involvement in the Vietnam War in the 1960s and early 1970s is often cited as a classic example.

Individual Cognitive Biases and Heuristics

Individual outlooks and information processing limitations also constrain the quality of strategies. Research involving the human mind has identified various factors that inhibit objectivity. Key areas include:

- Analogies and inductive reasoning.
- Naïve responses to evidence.
- Biases deriving from how issues and alternative choices are framed.

Below we examine each of these in more detail.

Analogies: People commonly make sense of their circumstances by drawing analogies from personal experience. Inductive reasoning draws on this typically limited, potentially irrelevant experience to form generalised (often unspoken) assumptions that are then applied to new circumstances for which they may be invalid. Analogies can certainly be useful, but will emphasise characteristics of a current situation that resonate with past experience, but ignore or marginalise the dissimilarities.[20]

Responses to evidence: People tend to be naïve and subjective in how they interpret evidence, especially statistical data. They are more receptive to incoming evidence that confirms current assumptions and theories than to challenging evidence (hence ignoring the need to subject theories to repeated tests.[21]) Other common traps for non-experts is to base decisions on small or otherwise unrepresentative samples and by putting excessive weight on the most immediate (recent, available) observations, being unduly influenced by their immediacy and apparent relevance. For example, the chief executive of a fashion company, for example, might place too much weight on a young employee's recently voiced opinions of current trends.

Errors of framing: Issues and alternatives are invariably seen through a frame of reference. Prior beliefs and expectations about a situation shape or frame how individuals make sense of their observations, leading to potentially distorted judgements about the consequences of actions and acceptability of outcomes. Strategic reference-frames were considered in Chapter 1. Senior executives with a technical background and role may favour highly rational, optimising processes, hence dismiss or discredit proposals they consider intuitive and satisficing. Conversely, those with an entrepreneurial or creative outlook perhaps feel more comfortable with intuition and strategies that adapt quickly as circumstances evolve.

 Personal assumptions, expectations and instinctive prejudices create biases and 'blind spots.' They include an intrinsic predisposition to excessive optimism (or pessimism). Optimism leads to over-confidence and complacency, making dubious opportunities seem more attractive than they are and understating the significance and likely impact of threats. For example, BP's misplaced optimism over the safety of its drilling operations in the Gulf of Mexico led engineers and executives to underestimate the magnitude of the genuine threat. Another example of how expectations frame perceptions: two students receive an examination pass grade; one expected to fail, so is pleased to pass, considering it a good performance; the other expected to pass with distinction, so is very disappointed with a pass grade, treating it in effect a failure!

CASE STUDY: A Strategic Position Statement for EMI in 2010

Before reading this case study, please refer back to the closing case study of Chapter 3 concerning the recorded music industry and your own industry analysis.

Terra Firma Investments, EMI's owner, describes it as one of the world's leading independent music companies. It comprises two divisions, EMI Music and EMI Music Publishing, which find, manage and market musical talent. Terra Firma claims that since the two divisions have different business models they require separate management, and by implication, continuing independence.

EMI Music Publishing markets the rights for performers to use songs written by songwriters contracted with EMI. Songwriters also receive royalties from EMI's sales of sheet music to a wide range of professional bodies and consumers.

EMI Music organises, records and markets the work of contracted recording artists; it profits from the sales of recordings in exchange for royalties paid to the artists. As the global demand for music increases and ever-more people aspire to become successful singers and songwriters the complementary activities of recording and publishing seem likely to be in demand indefinitely. However, while EMI's current mission has not changed for many years, it is presently unprofitable and its future vision under Terra Firma is less clear.

Questions

1. Drawing on data from the closing case study of Chapter 3 about the music and on work you have already done, produce a critical summary of EMI's resources and capabilities using the V-R-I-O-S format of Figure 5.3 (Chapter 5).

2. Then produce a more rigorous strategic position statement drawing on the key concepts presented in this chapter. In particular, seek to reach conclusions about viable future strategies, applying the decision criteria in this chapter.

Summary

- Strategic issue diagnosis is the process of interpreting and prioritising emerging issues of potential significance in the enterprise's external and internal environments. The outcome is a critical, integrative strategic position statement that highlights the issues of greatest concern that need strategic focus.

- These issues equate with threats and opportunities in the external environment and enterprise strengths and weaknesses, all of which must be judged against its existing mission and vision. A realistic position statement is a crucial precondition for making sound strategic decisions.

- Once it has been agreed, the next stage is to construct a strategy that addresses the issues in a coherent and, ideally, well integrated form. Strategies can be conceived from a wide range of possible options or from a more limited set. The formulation and evaluation processes of decision-*making* require selection criteria to be established in detail.

- Decision-*taking* is the challenging and stressful task of actually applying these selection criteria to reach a preferred strategy in what are inevitably risky and uncertain future circumstances.

- While issue diagnosis and strategic decision-making are in theory rational, there are practical limits to their objectivity, given the incompleteness of knowledge and divergent interests among influential stakeholders, as well as constraints arising from dysfunctional social processes and individual intellectual biases and shortcomings.

Exercises for Further Study and Discussion

1. Scan the media to identify an enterprise of interest and then summarise the major strategic issues that it currently faces. Consider how and why the enterprise might *misdiagnose* these issues. What could it do to avoid such mistakes?

2. The oil company, ExxonMobil has been notably sceptical about the commercial prospects for renewable energy production. Instead, its focus seems to be to secure an increasingly dominant position in oil and gas. Why might ExxonMobil have adopted this strategy? Is it in the interests of its shareholders in (a) the medium term and (b) long term?

3. Years ago, Sony decided to exploit its capabilities in the design and manufacture of electronic hardwares for consumer and professional use by emphasising their role as platforms to exploit complementary software (music, movies and games). Thus Sony acquired music recording and movie-making businesses to provide complementary sources of revenue and profits. However, it licenses third party software developers to produce games compatible with PlayStation consoles. Discuss the likely reasoning behind this apparent difference of strategy.

Suggestions for Further Reading

Coyle, G. (2004) *Practical Strategy: Structured Tools and Techniques*, FT Prentice Hall (chapter 4).

Daniels, K. and Henry, J. (1998) 'Strategy: a cognitive perspective', in Segal-Horn, S. (ed.) *The Strategy Reader*, Blackwell.

David, F.R. (2009) *Strategic Management: Concepts and Cases*, Pearson (Ed. 12, chapter 6).

RNING
COME ①

RNING
COME ②

RNING
COME ②

RNING
COME ③

Dooley, R.S. and Fryxell, G.E. (1999) 'Attaining decision quality and commitment from dissent: the moderating effects of loyalty and competence in strategic decision-making teams', *Academy of Management Journal* (vol. 42, pp. 389–402).

Fiol, C.M. (1994). 'Consensus, diversity and learning in organizations', *Organization Science* (vol. 5/3, pp. 403–420).

Jackson, S.E. and Dutton, J.E. (1988) 'Discerning threats and opportunities', *Administrative Science Quarterly* (vol. 33, pp. 370–387).

Janis, I.L. (1985) 'Sources of error in strategic decision making', in Pennings, J.M. (ed.) *Organizational Strategy and Change: New Views on Formulating and Implementing Strategic Decisions*, Jossey-Bass.

Knight, D., Pearce, C.L., Smith, K.G., Olian, J.D., Sims, H.P., Smith, K.A. and Flood, P. (1999) 'Top management team diversity, group process and strategic consensus', *Strategic Management Journal* (vol. 20/5, pp. 445–465).

Mintzberg, H. and Westley, F. (2001) 'Decision-making: it's not what you think', *Sloan Management Review* (vol. 42/3 pp. 89–93).

Oomens, M.J.H. and van den Bosch, F.A.J. (1999) 'Strategic issue management in major European-based companies', *Long Range Planning* (vol. 32/1, pp. 49–57).

Pitt, M., McAulay, L., Dowds, N. and Sims, D. (1997) 'Horse races, governance and the chance to fight: on the formation of organizational agendas', *British Journal of Management* (vol. 8, June Special Issue, pp. 19–30).

Schlange, L.E. and Jüttner, U. (1997) 'Helping managers to identify strategic issues', *Long Range Planning* (vol. 30/5, pp. 777–786).

Schoemaker, P.J.H. (1993) 'Strategic decisions in organizations: rational and behavioural views'. *Journal of Management Studies* (vol. 30/1, pp. 107–129).

Schwenk, C.R. (1988) 'The cognitive perspective on strategic decision-making', *Journal of Management Studies* (vol. 25/1, pp. 41–55).

Stevens, H.H. (1976) 'Defining corporate strengths and weaknesses', *Sloan Management Review* (vol. 17/3, pp.51–68).

Tripsas, M. and Gavetti, G. (2000) 'Capabilities, cognition and inertia', *Strategic Management Journal* (vol. 21, pp. 1147–1161).

Notes

1   Sources: various including http://www.monsanto.com and http://en.wikipedia.org/wiki/Monsanto
2   Schoemaker and Day (2009).
3   Weihrich (1982); Coyle (2004, chapter 4).
4   Janis (1985).
5   Stevens (1976). Special diagnostic expertise may also contribute to issue diagnosis (Day and Lord, 1992).
6   Akin to trials in British law courts where advocates on both sides argue with conviction, irrespective of their private beliefs (Dooley and Fryxell, 1999). See also Priem and Price (1991).

7 Sometimes, even when the strategy is actually misguided – see Weick (1987) or Weick (1995, pp. 54–56). See also Fiol (1994); Dooley and Fryxell (1999).

8 There is a wide-ranging literature on issue diagnosis and agenda formation, e.g., Lyles (1987); Stone (1989); Gioia and Chittipeddi (1991); Pitt et al. (1997); Schlange and Juttner (1997); Oomens and van den Bosch (1999); Sims et al. (2001); Pitt, McAulay and Sims (2002).

9 See Pitt et al. (1997).

10 Decision-taking is what senior executives receive large salaries and bonuses for doing, their rewards to compensate for stress and the generally dire personal consequences of failure. A principle component is the exercise of judgement – see Tversky and Kahneman (1974); Donaldson and Lorsch (1983); Spender (1989); Hampden-Turner (1990); Vickers (1991); Mintzberg and Westley (2001); Regner (2001).

11 Sutherland (1992) offers an uncompromising view on the importance of rationality.

12 For example, an enterprise may be allowed to use toxic industrial processes on an established site because it was always allowed in the past (known as 'grandfather rights'). A newcomer would not be allowed permission on a new, equivalent site. Though it has the law on its side, the enterprise ought to consider whether these practices are ethically sustainable.

13 BP applies additional criteria to its decisions about energy diversification, see: http://www.bp.com/sectiongenericarticle.do?categoryId=9027178&contentId=7049564

14 As an old proverb says, 'faced with two options, choose the third.'

15 Because the bank represents a certain return that the enterprise has to forego if it invests in either project. The loss of bank interest is in effect an opportunity cost of going ahead with the alternatives.

16 See for example: Kiesler and Sproull (1982); Schwenk (1986, 1988); Huff (1990); Meindl, Stubbart and Porac (1996); Daniels and Henry (1998); Eden and Spender (1998); Tripsas and Gavetti (2000).

17 William James *The Principles of Psychology* (1890).

18 Janis (1972).

19 However, accountants would argue that these are 'sunk costs': since they cannot be recovered they should not be a cause for regret.

20 The use of metaphors is also implicated in such behaviours. A rich metaphor may appear to capture the essence of an issue or situations, but again, it is easy to ignore aspects of the metaphor that are inappropriate or misleading. For an examination of the role of metaphors in organizational life, see Grant and Oswick (1996).

21 According to Popper (e.g., Magee, 1973), a theory is robust only if *multiple* tests fail to refute it. Even then, just one test failure will discredit the theory (a so-called 'black swan' event – see Taleb, 2007). Moreover, the absence of disconfirming evidence does not automatically confirm the theory, since observations may have been too few, unreliable or inappropriate.

7

Enterprise-level Strategy Frameworks

Learning Outcomes

This chapter is designed to enable you to:

① Describe the purpose of enterprise-level strategy frameworks.

② Understand (a) how frameworks are categorised and (b) the relationship between frameworks and templates.

③ Explain and critique the rationale for particular frameworks.

④ Apply selected frameworks to analyse specific strategy situations.

CASE STUDY: Korres SA[1]

Korres SA is a retailer and manufacturer of natural beauty and pharmaceutical products, based in Athens, Greece. Set up in 1996, it uses extensive scientific resources in collaboration with the Pharmaceutical Department of the University of Athens to study the properties of selected Greek herbs. It isolates their active ingredients and develops standardised production methods to create new products. In 1998 it launched a skincare line with an efficient anti-ageing ingredient. These beneficial products and herbal preparations are available for hair and skin care, including sun protection.

Korres products feature in 5,600 pharmacies in Greece and 3,400 in other countries. By 2010 the company operated 26 stores featuring a distinct 'Exclusive' format in 22 cities, 18 outside Greece. It had also expanded its coverage via the Korres website in selected countries and other web retailers in some 60 countries; mostly European, but in North America, the Middle-East, China, India, Australia and South Africa too.

The company seeks to grow by developing a global franchise network with successful independent retailers.

It has identified its major international competitors (defined as purveyors of natural beauty products) thus:

- Body Shop (UK-based with over 2,400 stores in 61 countries, now part of L'Oreal of France, the largest global cosmetics and beauty products group);
- Boticario (Brazil, with more than 2,500 franchised stores, mostly in Brazil and Japan); and
- Natura and Avon, both of which use direct 'consultants' (sales agents) to sell their products to consumers in their own homes.

The sales revenues of Korres SA Group in 2009 were €50.4m (2008: €53.7m). Gross profit margin was €30.2m (2008: €32.7m); net profits before tax €5.0m (2008: €5.5m). It employed 278 staff (2008: 300) at year end.

The global recession and the weakness of the Greek economy have affected its expansion plans. The preferred growth strategy, based on franchising, raises some important questions – most fundamentally, over the speed at which it is trying to expand its distribution chain. There might also be strategic conflicts between owned-and-operated prestige stores, the franchise chain and web retailing, given that direct contacts allow consumers to experience products before purchase and to discuss their benefits.

Other questions include the most appropriate locations for Korres-only stores and the preferred type of independent partners to feature Korres-branded displays (pharmacy or cosmetics outlets?). Would its current emphasis on products based on scientific research and development actually confuse the brand image of natural products?

Questions

1. Prioritise the *main* strategic issues that Korres faces and examine critically the implications of each. Find evidence to support the analysis.

2. Construct and assess alternative strategic options for Korres.

Introduction: Why Strategy Frameworks?

Implementing strategies, which aim to keep an enterprise progressive and in control of its destiny, is a tough challenge. A book published in 1998 the United States praised 30 business corporations for their effective strategies, yet even before the 2008 global recession only half were still independent and successful. The rest had declined or been acquired by other corporations that fully or partially integrated them.[2]

While no guarantees exist that an enterprise's chosen strategy will prove successful, an ill-judged strategy is a disaster in the making. The risks can be reduced by careful prior analysis (as already outlined) and by using a suitable framework to help identify and assess strategic options. That is the purpose of strategy frameworks.

We need to bear in mind here that the concept of strategy as it applies to single-unit enterprises with one major activity domain (conventionally called business-unit strategy) differs substantially from strategy in respect of multi-unit, multi-activity enterprises (variously called corporate, portfolio or conglomerate strategy). The former are the subject of Chapters 7, 8 and 9; corporate strategies feature in Chapters 10, 11 and 12.

Chapter 1 introduced the 'Design-plus' approach to strategic management. The current chapter begins our examination of the second stage of this approach. This stage is illustrated in Figure 7.1.

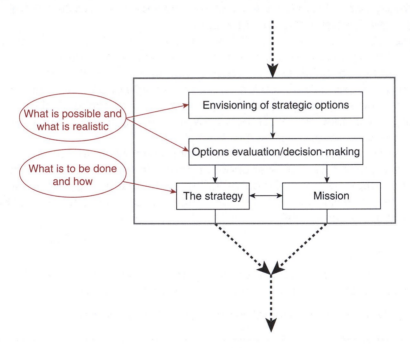

Figure 7.1: Stage 2 of the 'Design-plus' approach: strategic choice

Unit enterprise strategy must make realistic choices about the following issues:[3]

• The intended environmental *scope* or *domain* of the enterprise and how (if at all) it will differ from the present. The future clientele(s) must be identified clearly and the nature of the anticipated value they will receive must be consistent with stakeholder interests and the value-creating purpose declared in the mission statement.

• *How* the enterprise will create and deliver the anticipated value for its future clientele(s). The strategy must specify the breadth, depth and quality of the enterprise's *resources* and *capabilities*, most notably those that generate its value-creating advantage, and how they will be enhanced over time.

- The potential – for future growth and value creation – of intelligent decisions that result in beneficial interactions among scope and resource deployments, the so-called *synergy* effect.

Strategy consists of a particular pattern of decisions and actions (as discussed Chapter 1). A huge number of alternative patterns may be generated by combining all theoretically possible domain and resource choices. In practice, however, the number may be severely limited. Strategic decision-making must identify and choose between the viable options, given the current and probable future circumstances of the enterprise.

Is there a way to simplify the task of choosing a strategy? It can indeed be made easier by applying one of several predetermined strategy frameworks. Each framework contains a limited number of viable templates, known as generic strategies. Each generic strategy 'template' implies a clear prescription. By selecting a framework and adopting an appropriate template, strategists gain clear pointers to the *critical factors* that determine whether the chosen strategy is likely to succeed.

Each framework emerges from theoretical considerations, observations of successful (and unsuccessful) templates in use, or in combination. They are constructed in ways that normally make constituent templates independent (mutually exclusive) of one another. Each template defines a 'pure' strategy that, to be applied successfully, imposes particular conditions and requirements. The latter are an integral aspect of that template. When the context, resources and capabilities of the enterprise match an available template well, an appropriate strategy choice is more likely and the risk of failure reduced. Conversely, strategies that are hybrids (combinations) of generic templates will be subject to requirements that almost certainly conflict. At best, a hybrid may hinder effective strategy implementation; at worst it implies a strategy doomed to fail.

RNING
ECTIVE ① A strategy framework can assist in the selection of a plausible strategy. Three steps are involved:

RNING
ECTIVE ②
1. Choose the preferred strategy framework.
2. Select from the preferred framework a strategy template that is appropriate for the enterprise.
3. Convert the template into a set of prescriptive action plans particularised to the circumstances of the enterprise.

The first task is to consider choice of framework. Familiarity, appropriateness in context and ease of use generally determine which is adopted. The next step is to select the generic strategy template that best corresponds with the enterprise's mission, environmental content, resources and capabilities. Assuming that the selected template is a good fit with the enterprise, it should be possible to tailor it more specifically to its circumstances, mindful that its adoption imposes prescriptions and constraints requiring carefully crafted, detailed action plans and programmes.

Any strategy template is based on key assumptions. If executives are ignorant of them, or bold enough to ignore a prescription or constraint, for example, by combining templates, they are taking risks. When doing so, they should at least be aware of what the risks are. Using creative 'thought experiments' to examine the effect of contravening one of the chosen template's prescriptions may enable them perhaps to envision viable initiatives that others have overlooked. Non-conventional strategies that run contrary to accepted wisdom are sometimes called 'contrarian'. A successful contrarian strategy brings fame to its architects; an unsuccessful one generally damages or destroys the enterprise and their careers.

LEARNING ②
OBJECTIVE
Strategy frameworks divide into three broad types according to their form:

1. Archetype frameworks (here 'archetype'means 'pure' or 'model').
2. Matrix frameworks.
3. Vector (direction-specifying) frameworks.

Below we examine each of these in turn, together with examples of their respective generic templates.

Archetype Frameworks

The observed strategies of apparently successful (and unsuccessful) enterprises can provide useful prescriptive templates. Archetype frameworks contain *integrative* templates: their various elements need to be combined to create an effective prescription.

Defender/Prospector Framework

A relatively simple framework that evolved from empirical research on businesses in their competitive environments identifies four templates. The two most distinct templates are labelled 'defender' and 'prospector':[4]

- A *defender* competes proactively in a narrowly defined domain. It seeks to dominate by offering the best value products or services, ideally becoming the automatic choice of its defined clientele. To enhance value, a defender prioritises operational efficiency. It respects and applies the analytical skills of engineers and accountants to control quality, product or service performance, and cost. Innovation is technically oriented, concerned to produce and deliver offerings more efficiently and cost-effectively. Chief executives typically have an engineering or financial background.

- A *prospector* is proactive, but more outward-looking and growth-oriented than a defender. Its focus is broad rather than narrow. It is generally less *efficient* and less cost-focused. Yet it is more *effective* in that it is alert to growth opportunities in emerging domains of activity. It probably operates in multiple domains without necessarily dominating many of them, although it exploits synergies among its various environments, resources and skills. A prospector values the creativity and innovation skills associated with research and development and marketing functions: its chief executive typically has a background in one of these.

- A third template, the *analyser*, is a hybrid: it combines defender and prospector archetypes, though it maintains them in separate units. Thus conflict between the differing priorities of the two templates may be avoided Separation creates practical difficulties, notably by constraining the opportunities for each unit to learn from the other.

- A fourth type is called a *reactor*. Following this template, an enterprise is likely to lack clarity of purpose, confuses its priorities, is unsure of its key competences and, as the name implies, generally *reacts* to the initiatives of other enterprises. It is an ineffective archetype: its prescriptive strategic value lies in highlighting what to *avoid*. The illustration shows that this framework is relevant for not-for-profit enterprises as well as businesses.

Strategy archetypes in the not-for-profit sector

Defender: The Noor Foundation UK is a registered charity set up in 1998 expressly to fund kidney dialysis centres that provide free treatment to the needy in Pakistan, where no state-provided health service exists as an alternative to (expensive) private treatment. As of 2009 the charity ran 17 centres with more planned. They had cost over £1 million to set up and cost £250,000 a year to run. All donations go towards meeting these costs; volunteers pay administrative costs personally. Noor Foundation UK has established a dominant position in this specialised healthcare sector by maintaining a narrow focus and efficient, low-cost operations.

Prospector: Oxfam was founded in Oxford, UK to send food supplies to a starving Greek population during the 1939–45 war. Its mission is to reduce poverty and injustice. Over time it has become a world leader in the delivery of emergency food, shelter and reconstruction aid to vulnerable communities facing famine, war and natural disasters. In 1995 it formed Oxfam International (an international confederation of 13 independent non-governmental organizations (NGOs) based in the European Union, British Commonwealth countries, Hong Kong and United States) to implement long-term development programmes in developing countries for agricultural self-sufficiency, fair trade, better health and education services; and to encourage peace, justice and security, arms control, gender equality and combat climate change, by lobbying governments and major global actors such as the World Trade Organization, often in collaboration with other charitable organisations and pressure groups. It operates sophisticated fund raising techniques in member countries, including festivals, Oxfam-branded merchandise and retail shops that sell unwanted consumer goods. Its breadth of interests and geographic scope characterise Oxfam as a *prospector*.

Analyser: The Forestry Commission was established in 1919 as a British Government department. Its founding mission was to acquire land and plant new forests to reverse the decline in timber production caused by the 1914–18 war. Today, with over 3,000 staff it has expanded its scope, managing 827,000 hectares of forest with 1.4 billion native broad-leaf and faster-growing coniferous trees on sites all around the UK. Its primary mission remains timber production for domestic and export consumption, allied to professional woodland management and research. In 2008/9 it generated £34.3m income from timber sales, estate management and other fees, against £40.7m of expenditure. Forestry operations cost £80 per hectare per year, an efficiency focus consistent with a *defender* strategy. However, its mission has expanded in new directions involving recreation, environmental conservation and heritage activities (RCH); income of £16.4m was offset by £31.7m costs in 2008/9. Positive environmental initiatives include enhancing biodiversity of plants, birds and animals and protecting endangered species. Recreational initiatives involve the management of visitor attractions such as Westonbirt Arboretum, forest concerts, holiday accommodation and facilities, dedicated trails and tracks for horse riding, hiking, mountain biking, motor rallying, and other events. An estimated 50 million visitors use its sites each year. It also collaborates with national and regional partners such as national parks agencies, local authorities, water companies, environmental charities, local volunteer groups and schools. The RCH activities are characteristic of an entrepreneurial, outward-looking and collaborative *prospector* strategy. Overall the Forestry Commission appears to be an *analyser*.

Reactor: The Church of England, known affectionately as the 'CofE', is the established Christian church in England and the mother church of the worldwide Anglican Communion. Founded by King Henry VIII in 1534 after the break with the Church of Rome, it is led by the Archbishop of Canterbury, though the reigning Monarch remains titular head. Its primary mission is Christian evangelism and it is active across society – for example, in Parliament (26 bishops sit in the House of Lords), local communities, schools and other educational institutions, hospitals and the military. A quarter of state primary schools and 5% of state secondary schools (covering about one million pupils) are designated CofE, though neither pupils nor teachers need belong to the Church.

Half of the 60 million UK population claims to be CofE, but only a million (mostly ageing) attend a weekly church service (3 million at Christmas). The present, liberal Archbishop of Canterbury articulates the CofE's role being to maintain 'a balance between the absolute priority of the Bible, a catholic loyalty to the sacraments and a habit of cultural sensitivity and intellectual flexibility.' Unlike the Roman Catholic Church, it ordains women priests; however, if female bishops are ordained entire congregations could follow the lead of those clergy who have already become Catholic. The evangelical wing of the Anglican Communion, which advocates zero tolerance of same-sex relationships among priests or the laity, could provoke another schism.

The CofE's assets exceed £4 billion. It owns 43 cathedrals, three of which feature in England's top-five visitor attractions (in all, its sites have 12 million visitors each year). It also has 16,000 church buildings in 13,000 parishes, 12,000 being historically or architecturally important. The annual budget is approximately £1 billion, three-quarters from members' collections and tithing, the rest mainly from lega-cies, fees and local fund-raising activities. It donates £45 million a year to charita-ble causes. Buildings maintenance costs £160m a year and is rising rapidly, while the stipends and expenses of its 20,000 ministers and other employees and the pensions of 7000+ retired staff are its major costs.

If clarity of mission, values, financial security, and rising international membership signify success, the Church of Rome is arguably more successful than the CofE, which seems to be a religious organisation, a charity for good works and a manager of visitor attractions. It appears to exemplify a *reactor* strategy.

Value-creating Capability Framework

Another archetype framework offers strategy templates based on the four of the fundamental value-creating capability mechanisms that were reviewed in Chapter 5, viz:[5]

1. Reputation.
2. Innovativeness.
3. Internal organisation ('enterprise architecture').
4. External relationships ('contextual architecture').

In this framework, synergistic, hybrid strategic templates that combine two or more pure strategies are possible. Sound internal architecture enhances innovating capability, for example. External architecture and reputation are mutually sustaining. However, the presence of a dominant capability may hinder the development and exploitation of others through inertia or because the enterprise undervalues them.[6] Equally, there is a risk that hybrids may involve too many compromises to be really effective.

Capability-based archetypes in the electronics industries

Innovativeness: Intel Corporation has focused on highly innovative designs of microprocessor chips used in personal computers (PCs) and other forms of computer. Though it displays many capabilities, design innovation is at the core of the strategy that has propelled Intel to its industry-dominant position.

Reputation: VIA Technologies is a Taiwanese designer of application-specific integrated circuits (ASIC) microchips. It enjoys a high reputation for its responsiveness to client-dedicated design requirements for PCs, mobile telephones, radio and television receivers and set-top boxes. VIA subcontracts manufacture to independent chip fabrication companies.

Internal architecture: Dell Corporation makes no claim to offer innovative products but its integrated and very effective internal architecture enables it to operate very large-scale facilities assembling bought-in, globally-sourced components very efficiently. Customers are able to their computers via on-line, menus, a simple form of 'mass customization'.

External architecture: The Symbian Foundation is an independent, non-profit organisation whose members include mobile phone makers, such as Nokia and Sony Ericsson, network operators Vodafone and NTT DoCoMo, and electronic component makers including Texas Instruments and Sandisk. Its mission is to steward the development of the Symbian software platform for use in mobile devices such as smart-phones. Symbian features in over 100 million mobile computing and communications devices. The external network architecture promotes global standardisation of software protocols among a multiplicity of manufacturers, network operators and regulatory authorities. However, in recent times, under Nokia's control it has lost ground to the Android network that Google has promoted as an open system.

'Business Model' Frameworks

A third form of integrative template consists of business models.[7] In essence a business model focuses on the relationship between an enterprise's revenue generating mechanisms and its operating costs. Some have a long history, but the concept has gained popularity more recently as new models have emerged, reflecting internet-enabled behaviours.

An effective business model template often becomes dominant in its sector, obliging universal adoption. However, when a new entrant introduces a different model, existing competitors may find they are relying on a model that no longer makes commercial sense. For example, the American DVD and games rental company, Blockbuster, pioneered a hugely successful international model by selling multiple copies of movie and games videos and DVDs to franchised stores to support very profitable rentals businesses. This model now faces competition from mail order and online models (Play.com; Lovefilm.com); and downloads and streaming services (BT Vision; Virgin Media). Although Blockbuster itself can switch to an alternative model, its franchisees are left with an obsolete model and declining income streams.

'Business model' archetypes

Innovation timing models: First-movers, early followers and rejuvenators represent alternative business models based on the timing of an innovation (see Chapter 9). In the vacuum cleaner industry, Hoover was the first mass-market innovator with the powered upright cleaner. Electrolux was an early follower that introduced the horizontal cylinder vacuum cleaner. Much later Dyson became an industry rejuvenator with a bag-less, highly-efficient cyclone suction machine.

Loss-leader models: The mass-market, loss-leader model is popularly known as the 'razor and blades' model, It was pioneered by Gillette. In this model, The razor is in effect a loss leader (often sold at cost or even offered free) to stimulate regular, repeat purchases of very profitable complementary products (razor blades). Similarly, Kodak's promotion of simple film cameras for the mass-market promoted the very profitable sales of films and processing.

Subscription and advertising models: The subscription model much used by magazine and newspaper publishers also has a long history. It commits buyers to make repeat purchases of the offering for a lengthy time-defined period, albeit at a discount price per unit. The subscription model usually includes special incentives to start subscribing, relying on inertia to sustain sales thereafter. Contrary to widespread practice, the Times Newspaper Group has adopted this model for access to Times Online, its news and comment website. Other newspaper proprietors and search engines (notably Google) fund their websites via pop-up advertising, aiming to maximise hits on their websites.

Brokerage models: Brokers are agents who channel purchases to their clients in exchange for a commission payment for each transaction. The World Wide Web has encouraged a huge expansion of brokerage sites with varying commission arrangements, often combining elements of comparison such as Amazon, Expedia and Idealo.

Bundling models: Offering 'bundled' packages of products or services can increase perceived value; it aims to increase sales and profits because clients do not realise they are paying more than they would probably do via a menu-based selection. Bundling of pay TV, telephone rentals and Internet access are common examples.

Bricks and clicks models: Conventional 'bricks' retailers have had to decide whether to operate a website and what it should do. Some use websites purely as information sources to encourage consumers into their stores (e.g., De Beers jewellery). Some operate competing 'bricks' and 'clicks', usually with lower online prices (e.g., hi-fi retailer, Superfi). Others link websites more directly with outlets, for example, by enabling online reservations, with inspection, payment and collection at a nominated outlet (e.g., Jessops camera chain and Comet electrical). Some have found web retailing so compelling that they have abandoned conventional retailing altogether (e.g., UKbathrooms.com).

Archetype frameworks generally have an *integrative* quality. They synthesise complex realities into typological 'recipes',[8] for which moderate or strong support exists.[9] A concern is that by focusing strategic options on a handful of effective templates they encourage enterprises to force-fit their particular circumstances to a potentially inappropriate template. Certainly, archetype frameworks can over-simplify: having often emerged inductively from observations of a few enterprises in particular contexts, the generalisability of each template may be questionable.

Thus, researchers have applied sophisticated statistical methods (such as factor analysis and cluster analysis) to analyse larger numbers of enterprises across sectors in order to identify new and potentially more robust strategy templates.[10] One enquiry identified 10 strategy archetypes or configurations. Some, like the *reactor,* appeared ineffective.[11] Yet, statistical studies appear to drive time-dependent and situation-dependent templates, reflecting historical circumstances whose characteristics no longer apply.

An interesting observation from the study of archetypes is that transitions among strategic templates may be possible, although such major strategic changes incur costs that can easily exceed the expected benefits. Further, it may not be feasible to migrate between some pairs of templates – a significant point for the management of strategic change. For example, a *reactor* enterprise may find the barriers to becoming a *prospector* too great to overcome.

Matrix Frameworks

Typically, a matrix strategy framework builds on two major *dimensions of strategic choice*, each of which often presents an either/or choice; when combined they yield a finite number (e.g., $2 \times 2 = 4$) of distinct strategy templates. If either dimension has more options, the number of possible alternatives rises considerably. The nature of the dimensions frequently derives from inductive insights.

Competition Matrix Framework

The most widely-known matrix framework for competitive strategy[12] involves two binary dimensions:

- Low cost[13] *or* uniqueness (differentiation)[14].
- Wide appeal *or* narrow market focus ('focus' here being essentially a marketing term).

For reasons that will be explained, the matrix may be extended here to read as follows:

- Low cost *or* uniqueness (differentiation).
- Wide appeal *or* selective segment focus *or* narrow market focus.

This extension gives a total of six strategy templates. These are shown in Figure 7.2.

The distinction between strategies that build on low unit-cost of output to create value and sustain advantage and strategies that depend on differentiation is fundamental to this framework.[15] When an enterprise is the lowest overall cost supplier because of scale and experience effects

Basis of strategic advantage *

	Lowest cost	Perceived uniqueness
Sector wide coverage	Overall cost leadership	Broad-based differentiation
Selective segment coverage	Low-cost selective focus	Selective differentiation
A particular market segment or clientele	Low-cost narrow focus	Differentiated narrow focus (specialist)

Strategic target (label at left, between the first and second rows)

Figure 7.2: Six-template matrix framework

* Developed from concepts in Porter (1980)

(Chapter 3), it creates superior value for its clientele at the same or lower prices than other providers. Consequently, it can still be very profitable and invest for the future in order to introduce better methods of production and distribution that promise even lower future costs. To achieve lowest and *declining* costs (i.e., in real terms, after adjustment for inflation) requires a wide market appeal to support large scale operations. This corresponds to the upper-left template in Figure 7.2. The strategy is based on the *intent* to exploit the advantage of having the lowest overall cost position in its sector, which can be difficult to establish in practice. Accounting practices can disguise cost advantages, particularly when the enterprise is part of a multi-activity corporation with scope to allocate corporate overhead costs.

Moreover, not every prospective client is persuaded by a low-cost offering. Some require greater functionality, prestige or other indicator of higher perceived quality, entailing additional costs. So an alternative to a low-cost strategy is to create value and advantage via distinctiveness (ideally *uniqueness*), of a form that clients respect, prioritise and are willing to pay for. Though differentiation strategies do not ignore cost issues, low unit-cost is not the primary intent: hence it is of lesser priority. Various conditions apply to a viable differentiation strategy. In particular:

- Ways must exist for the enterprise to make itself distinctive.
- The extra costs of creating and sustaining distinctiveness must sustain premium prices.
- The additional value delivered to the target clientele must outweigh the price premium.

An enterprise could find many ways to differentiate itself, encouraging its selected clientele in a single demand segment to see it as essentially unique. This corresponds to lower-right template in Figure 7.2. Thus, Cartier's prestigious, highly distinctive jewellery appeals to a wealthy global clientele. Asos.com is not remotely as distinctive as Cartier: thus we can see that distinctiveness is a matter of degree. The potential drawback of extreme differentiation is that the enterprise confines itself to a narrowly focused and specialised position with limited appeal or growth potential. More optimistically, it can find ways to appeal selectively to *multiple* segments, quite possibly by carefully tailoring the basis of its differentiation to each segment (corresponding to the middle-right template in Figure 7.2). Indeed the simple fact of narrow focus, especially geographic or time-based focus, can sometimes differentiate an enterprise sufficiently for its target clientele to consider it distinctive. For example, a reliable local taxi service that is willing to provide a service for drunken clubbers at unsocial hours commands high priced fares: its advantage is more about service focus than genuine differentiation.

Over time, some well-differentiated enterprises develop sufficient resources, skills and appeal to cater to *all* of the demand segments in their chosen industry sectors that have more-or-less discriminating or specialised requirements. This strategy corresponds to the upper-right template in Figure 7.2.

Many enterprises, however, lack the resources and capabilities to differentiate themselves convincingly. Nor do they enjoy the scale to dominate their sector. As a result, their realistic choices necessitate an emphasis on efficiency and low (not lowest) cost within one or more defined demand segments. To the extent that segment-selective low-cost strategies may be viable in some sectors, they draw on the templates found in the middle and lower left panels in Figure 7.2. Examples of each template are outlined below.

Six matrix strategies

Overall low-cost leadership: Dell aims to deliver excellent value to all users – at home, in small enterprises, and major corporations – by producing lowest-cost personal computers on a like-for-like basis. It avoids pioneering product research and development, and rarely offers a product-feature that is not widely available on competing products. Dell seeks maximum scale and scope economies to control production costs and it distributes directly to users, largely eliminating intermediaries.

Low-cost selective focus: easyJet was set up as the airline of choice, initially for budget-conscious leisure consumers and subsequently for business users attracted to a 'no-frills, bus-stop' service. It maintains its low-cost status by careful selection of specific, point-to-point European routes where it can achieve high load factors and by minimising passenger services that add disproportionately to costs.

Low-cost narrow focus: BTB Mailflight provides automated poly-wrapping and mailing services for well-known UK magazine publishers. Its efficient, specialised equipment performs a narrow range of dedicated, low-cost services to support magazine distribution to subscribers by mail. Publishers require a low-cost service because loyal magazine subscribers pay below cover price per issue, despite publishers incurring mail costs. BTB Mailflight has thus far resisted the temptation to diversify into other low-cost services.

Broad-based differentiation: Volkswagen Motor Corporation makes cars and commercial vehicles globally for every kind of consumer and business user. It offers multiple distinctive brands (VW, Audi, SEAT, Skoda) to different demand segments. It sustains such variety because its many models share components to achieve better scale economies. Most importantly, although its output is high, it has created an effectively differentiated image through quality manufacture and reliability, featuring repeatedly near the top of user surveys. Cost matters in car-making, but Volkswagen understands that to trade quality or reliability striving for lowest cost would damage its much-envied market standing.

Selective differentiation: Harvard Business Review is an authoritative journal of long standing. Its stimulating, topical articles are written by top academics and eminent senior executives who draw on their many years of experience. Initially it targeted senior business executives, but its high status means that almost all academic and professional business libraries now subscribe to it. This greatly extends its readership. It is *not* widely found on newsstands nor marketed to the general public. Despite a relatively high subscription price, it has a very large circulation for a specialised publication.

Differentiated narrow focus: Established in 2000, ASOS.com claims to be the largest independent fashion and beauty online retailer serving the UK. ASOS aims at 'fashion forward' 16–34-year-olds, primarily but not exclusively women. Its distinctiveness lies in a combination of web-only access, a sexy, fashion-leading image reinforced by associations with young celebrities and 'fashionistas', a dynamic offering of respected brands and own-label garments with good fashion content, specified by product managers whose judgement attracts customers. Web access encourages impulse purchasing, supported by attractive catalogues mailed to customers.

Differences between broad, selective and narrow focus are matters of degree. We may ask, therefore, whether or not low-cost and differentiation form a true opposition or not. Purely in terms of differing *intent*, the opposition appears valid. Yet many large corporations would claim to follow effective strategies that *combine* both sources of advantage. The truth of such claims depends on meeting two effectiveness criteria in respect of their marketing activities. Are the price premiums resulting from enhanced distinctiveness *disproportionately* higher than the additional marketing costs they incur? Is the differentiated position being sustained without penalty to actual and unit sales potential (i.e., without undermining the platform for achieving low unit-costs)? Both of these criteria must be met to justify the claim – not impossible, perhaps, but certainly challenging.

Differentiation Matrix Framework

An alternative matrix framework[16] concentrates on the different, practical ways that enterprises can distinguish and differentiate themselves. It is based on three propositions:

1. *All* offerings have product (merchandise) and service elements.
2. Distinctiveness (or its absence) is an available strategy variable *in respect of both product and service elements* of the offering.
3. Neither element is automatically differentiated; whether and how differentiation is achieved is a key strategic choice.

Provision of a product usually entails a service element, such as advice, delivery or installation – though this may be minor. The recipient of a pure service gains no physical product, although service delivery is usually enabled by products (e.g., air travel requires an aeroplane). Enabling products have characteristics that the service recipient may or may not value.

Product and service differentiation are, therefore, the key dimensions of a matrix framework with four possible strategy templates (Figure 7.3). A wholly undifferentiated offering is a commodity that sells only if its price is appropriately low. This strategy template has much in common with the cost leadership strategy previously discussed. Alternative templates concentrate on differentiating product or service elements, while the system-centred template emphasises differentiation in both respects, as illustrated below by the printing industry.

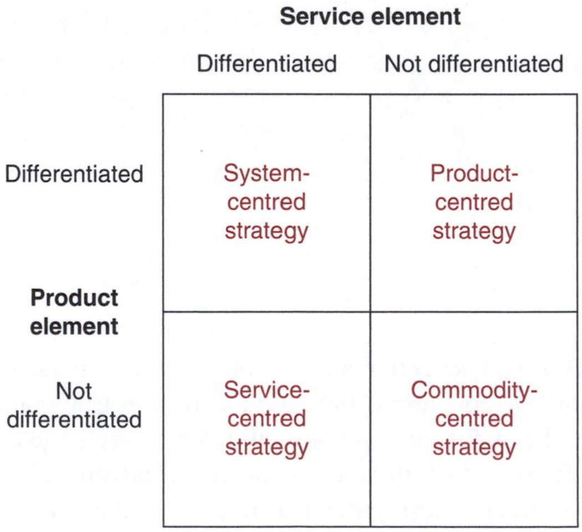

	Service element	
	Differentiated	Not differentiated
Differentiated	System-centred strategy	Product-centred strategy
Not differentiated	Service-centred strategy	Commodity-centred strategy

Figure 7.3: Mathur's strategy framework*

* Adapted from Mathur (1988)

Product/service differentiation strategies in the printing industry

System centred: MPG Books Group Ltd offers a full range of book manufacturing services from 'print on demand' to long-run, sheet-fed printing using modern technologies in two British factories. Additionally, it offers product customisation and fulfilment services, whereby it can deliver finished books on behalf of publishers to purchasers around the world.

Service centred: MCRL is a Canadian-based corporation that offers trouble-free printing services for clients across Canada and the United States. It takes full responsibility for meeting specifications and delivery dates and claims to save clients 30–50% when compared with domestic printing companies. It subcontracts production to companies with mainstream printing capabilities in China and elsewhere.

Product centred: CS Graphics based in Singapore is a world-leading manufacturer that concentrates exclusively on sheet-fed printing of high quality, illustrated fine-art books and calendars. Among its clients are fine art and photography publishers, museums and university presses that require large format books printed in full-colour to a very high standard.

Commodity centred: BAM quotemeprint.com is an online newspaper printing enterprise that offers a defined range of print services for university and college student unions in the UK and Europe. It does not differentiate itself on either product or service and it offers 'very competitive' prices, posted on its website for all to see. In this context 'commodity-based' does not mean that quality or service is necessarily poor.

The product/service differentiation matrix can be developed further. Any product combines a tangible *specification* and an intangible *image*, either of which might be used to differentiate it. Equivalently, a service combines *expertise* and *personalisation* of delivery. From this distinction may be derived four templates for potential differentiation. This suggests four templates for differentiating the product element *and* four templates for differentiating the service element. In combination, therefore, no less than $4 \times 4 = 16$ templates are theoretically possible, ranging from the pure 'commodity' template with no basis of differentiation at all to the extreme 'system' strategy template which exploits differentiation in all four respects. Such an evidently complex strategy would typically be applicable in business-to-business and business-to-government relationships such as the sale and servicing of military aircraft or major computer installations.

Multi-dimensional Strategy Frameworks

Analytical matrix frameworks with two dimensions are easy to display and apply. Strategists might consider that those already described do not encode the strategic dimensions that are critical for their particular enterprise. They could create their own, incorporating those dimensions which are most relevant. In addition to (or instead of) the dimensions previously covered, they might choose:

- Global focus *or* regional focus *or* single-country focus.
- First-mover (pioneer) *or* early-follower (imitator).
- Proactive capability development *or* external acquisition under license.
- Vertically integrated *or* vertically specialised.
- Competition *or* collaboration.

Once the most relevant strategy dimensions have been selected, the framework structure has been defined. The next task is to identify the preferred strategy template from among the options that it allows. Thereafter, attention can shift to the detail of how the associated strategy will be implemented.

Critically, there must be *mutual consistency* among the elements of the preferred template. For example, technical pioneering is consistent with developing internal resources and expertise, not with external acquisition. However, an internally consistent strategy template may be a non-viable choice for an enterprise without adequate resources and skills to implement it. Alternatively, a template may be viable, but so widely adopted that the prospects of success with it are low. Still, even seemingly implausible or counter-intuitive combinations are worth studying as part of the creative thought process.

Directional (Vector) Strategy Frameworks

Controversy over the opposition of low-cost and differentiation can be resolved by treating them as independent strategy dimensions, each allowing a range of viable postures. Similarly, focus can be treated as a third independent dimension. The three dimensions can then be represented as prime vectors (arrows) of equal significance, whose directions mimic the hands of a clock (or compass) pointing to 4, 8 and 12 (or bearings of 120, 240 and 360 degrees) as shown in Figure 7.4. In this framework the *direction* of each prime vector defines the nature of *intent*, while its length expresses the notional *intensity* of that intent.

Figure 7.4 displays three intermediate vectors represented by dotted lines. Each directly opposes one the three prime vectors, being a combination of the other two. Thus, the direct opposite of lowest cost intent equates to the vector combination of differentiation and narrow focus. This figure is amplified below with examples from the watch industry.

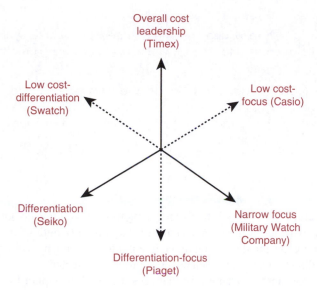

Figure 7.4: A clock (vector) strategy framework featuring the examples from the watch industry

Vector' strategies in the watch industry

Overall cost leadership: Timex (USA) is a high volume provider of inexpensive, branded watches. By exploiting low-cost manufacturing sources it has consistently maintained its original intent to achieve global pre-eminence in this market.

Differentiation: Seiko (Japan) makes watches that it markets under several brand names, spanning a wide spectrum of global watch demand. Respective brands differentiate variously on value for money (which is not the same as low cost), classic style and high technology.

Low-cost differentiation: The strategy of Swiss watchmaker Swatch appears to combine mass production of standardised components with branded differentiation. Though it shares low-cost intent with Timex and differentiation intent with Seiko, it differs from both.

Narrow focus: The strategy of the Military Watch Company (MWC) (Switzerland) focuses principally on military clients, a narrow demand segment with very specific requirements for accuracy and durability in adverse (battlefield) conditions.

Low-cost focus: Casio (Japan) focuses its strategy on the segment for relatively inexpensive watches that do more than indicate the time (i.e., it provides 'wrist instruments'). It combines focus with low cost via mass production, using modular solid-state 'mechanisms', plastic cases and straps. Its strategy is in effect the opposite of Seiko's. It may also be differentiated from MWC's strategy, since although both are segment focused, MWC prioritises meeting precise needs over low cost.

Differentiation focus: Piaget (Switzerland) offers watches of the highest prestige, quality and design. They are very costly and de-facto focused on a narrow wealthy market segment. This strategy is as close to the opposite of Timex's strategy as can be envisioned.

A merit of the clock framework is to give meaning to strategies that do not align exactly with those in Figure 7.4, whether in direction (intent) or magnitude (length of the vector). It allows more nuanced presentation and discussion of the intent underpinning hybrid strategies, highlighting major shifts of direction and how such changes might be effected.

Figure 7.5 presents another framework that uses the clock metaphor to identify directional strategy templates. The vertical direction represents perceived user value and the horizontal direction represents price. The framework is oriented to demand rather than supply, which is a limitation. The clock 'hands' suggest a variety of strategies. Vectors covering a *clockwise* sweep from 6 o'clock to 3 o'clock represent value-creating and advantage-creating strategy templates. In other directions and at the centre of the chart a template is problematic.

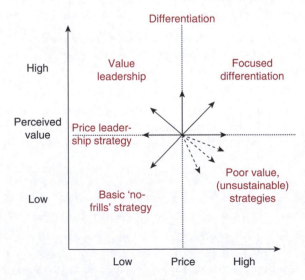

Figure 7.5: An alternative strategy 'clock' framework.

Adapted from Bowman and Faulkner (1995)

Reflections on the Generic Strategy Approach

All strategy frameworks have a practical purpose; but they are simplified representations of complex sets of choices that must be used cautiously. None has substantially greater theoretical validity than the others and none offers guaranteed, universal prescriptions. Used wisely, their templates can assist the consideration of appropriate, viable strategies and probable consequences in particular circumstances.

Strategy frameworks are merely tools, unthinking use of which could lead to disastrous outcomes. Conversely, the application of multiple frameworks could produce fresh insights denied to the user of only one. This is an opportunity to explore and understand issues at a deeper, more sophisticated level. Ultimately, the test of an effective strategy is not whether it emerges from an 'allowed' template but whether and how well it succeeds in the real world. The alternative to using a recognised framework is to rely on intuition and experience, which is legitimate subject to caveats regarding human subjectivity, as discussed in Chapter 6.

The closing case-study presents an account of the Tefal cookware company, to explore how generic strategy frameworks can be used to identify alternative competitive strategies.

CASE STUDY: Tefal cookware

Tefal is an international brand name of the French company, Groupe SEB, founded over 150 years ago and still 42% family-owned. Tefal's product range includes domestic cookware (pans, baking trays), small cooking appliances – such as pressure cookers, fryers, steamers and toasters – electric kettles, steam irons, and various kitchen utensils. Groupe SEB contains other major branded businesses including Krups, Rowenta and Moulinex. Acquired over the years, these businesses continue to form their own strategies and operate independently, overseen by group executives. Across eight defined product categories, the products of the main brands overlap to a considerable extent, creating internal as well as external competition.

In financial year 2008 Groupe SEB sales were €3.23 billion, representing an aggregate global market share of 10% in its chosen sectors. Two-thirds of sales were in Europe, with sales to the Asia Pacific region rising fast. Half its output was from Europe, a higher proportion than for many other European consumer goods companies. Groupe SEB employs over 18,000 people at 21 factories spread across Europe, the United States, South America, China and Russia, with 57 marketing and sales subsidiaries in 100 countries.

Founded in 1956, Tefal was acquired by Groupe SEB in 1968. Its star product was a revolutionary Teflon-coated, non-stick cooking pan made from hard anodised aluminium alloy. Over the years it has continued to innovate and diversify. Tefal contributes around a third of Groupe SEB sales. Today it holds 1000 current patents and introduces nearly 200 new products a year; many are dedicated designs to encourage consumers to make additional purchases. Tefal pans feature durable non-stick coatings; attractive, durable external finishes; temperature spot indicators; and 'lifetime' guarantees (misuse excepted). However, although the pans do not wear out, even the best coatings eventually lose their non-stick properties. Because they cannot be repaired, they have obsolescence 'built-in'. A large fraction of demand for mid- and low-priced cookware is replacement.

Tefal's non-stick pans occupy a mid-range price/quality position, enjoying high brand awareness and a positive reputation. Tefal also has the most comprehensive retail distribution network of any competing brand. The well-known chef, Jamie Oliver, endorses its range of premium cookware products, a similar practice to other competitors. At retail prices, £50 buys a set of five basic saucepans or a single Jamie Oliver non-stick stainless steel pan. Intermediate ranges retail for £20–30 per item. In the premium segment a new kind of pan has emerged to exploit electromagnetic induction heating. Being energy efficient, this technology seems likely to become very popular. However, to work with aluminium pans, an under-layer of stainless steel must be added. Tefal has introduced a range with this feature, but the change adds complexity and substantial cost in production.

Major brands to compete with its big-selling, mid-priced products include Meyer, Prestige, KitchenAid, Judge, Harbenware and respected store brands such as Lakeland, Marks and Spencer and John Lewis in the UK. Higher priced kitchenware is more likely to be made of enamelled cast iron, stainless steel, copper or complex hybrids. Premium brands include All Clad, Le Creuset, and Raymond Blanc along with many niche brands whose prices often exceed £200 per unit and offer lifetime guarantees. At the other extreme, many budget store brands compete at very low price points (e.g., IKEA, Argos and Robert Dyas in the UK). Tefal has maintained good quality at affordable prices with very efficient, mechanised production. Other, lower cost and quality competing products generally use inferior materials, are less durable and probably use more labour-intensive methods in various countries, notably China.

Tefal's competitive strategy may be related to a number of frameworks discussed in this chapter, as follows:

- Defender/prospector framework: Tefal seems to apply a *defender* strategy to achieve *cost-efficient* leadership of its mid-range cookware sectors.
- Value-creating capability archetype: By combining strong reputation, innovativeness and efficient internal architecture Tefal seems to execute a *hybrid capability strategy*.
- Innovation timing model: Evidence of innovation and brand development indicates pursuit of a *first-mover* business model.

- Competition matrix framework: Tefal's focus on mid-range price/quality, excluding the high and low extremes, and its commitment to persist with relatively high cost European and US production, is consistent with the *selective segment differentiation* template.
- Differentiation matrix framework: The Tefal strategy is *product-centred differentiation* based on superior specifications to mainstream competitors.

Taken together, these observations provide extensive insights into Tefal's strategy. One is that Tefal has pursued a contrarian strategy by combining a variety of elements that conventionally might be thought to conflict. The observations raise various strategic questions too: Should it continue its emphasis on quality and reputation while accepting the probability of rising costs and the possible consequences of higher prices and reduced unit sales? Or should it prioritise cost by shifting production to lower cost locations as many other European manufacturers have done? Has electromagnetic induction heating dealt a severe blow to its traditional product strengths? Does its diversification into small electrical appliances help or hinder its cookware strategy?

Tasks and discussion questions

1. What light can you shed on the foundations of Tefal's present and prospective competitive advantages by the applying strategy frameworks discussed in this chapter?

2. What are your recommendations over possible changes to Tefal's strategy?

3. Has the time come for Groupe SEB to insist that Tefal should integrate its strategies much more closely with other group companies? Provide arguments for and against.

Summary

- Enterprises can explore and particularise their strategies by applying one or more generic strategy frameworks. These frameworks are models that allow strategists to identify simplified templates of possible relevance to their enterprise.

- Each framework offers a limited number of alternative templates. The strategic task is therefore to identify the most appropriate framework, then the most appropriate template within that framework, and then to interpret that template in the particular circumstances.

- This approach does not dictate precise actions but it narrows the options greatly. Inappropriate choices in the first two stages will result in detailed, well-considered but ultimately misguided strategies. So any framework must be used carefully and thoughtfully.

LEARNING
OUTCOME ③

- The application of multiple frameworks concurrently can offer further insights. When the findings appear to conflict, it should prompt constructive reflection and debate. Since all strategies are properly concerned with the future, not the past, there must always be scope for interpretations based on visionary, forward thinking.

LEARNING
OUTCOME ③

- Contrarian thinking goes against the conventional or 'received' wisdom in the industry sector. It is potentially the source of great success but also increases the risks of potential disaster.

Exercises for Further Study and Discussion

1. Produce a critique of the use of generic frameworks to guide strategic decision-making. Use appropriate examples to explore how this approach can be effective and where it poses challenges and difficulties. Discuss alternatives to the use of frameworks.
2. References to 'strategists' might suggest that strategic decisions are properly taken only by the most senior people in an enterprise. Does that mean they should take no advice from others? Or should the strategy process be more participative and democratic? If the latter, who should senior people consult, when, and what should they ask them? What are the likely consequences of greater participation?
3. Familiarise yourself with the current circumstances of a selection of the enterprises featured above in the illustrations of strategy templates. Critically review the status of each enterprise's strategy and confirm whether the strategy attributed to it here is still valid. If you identify changes, explore why they have occurred.

Suggestions for Further Reading

Bowman, C. (1998) *Strategy in Practice*, Prentice Hall (chapter 2 on clock framework).

Campbell-Hunt, C. (2000) 'What have we learned about generic strategy? A meta-analysis', *Strategic Management Journal* (vol. 21/2, pp. 127–154).

Hill, C.W.L. (1988) 'Differentiation versus low cost or differentiation and low cost', *Academy of Management Review* (vol. 13/July, pp. 401–412).

Hofer, C.W. and Schendel, D. (1978) *Strategy Formulation: Analytical Concepts*, West (chapter 6 on business strategies).

Huff, A.S., Floyd, S.W., Sherman, H.D. and Terjesen, S. (2009) *Strategic Management: Logic and Action*, John Wiley (chapter 6 on business models).

Kumar, N. (2006) 'Strategies to fight low-cost rivals', *Harvard Business Review* (vol. 84/12 Nov–Dec, pp. 104–113).

Lieberman, M.B. and Montgomery, D.G. (1988) 'First mover advantages', *Strategic Management Journal* (vol. 9/5, pp. 41–58).

Lynch, R. (2009) *Strategic Management*, FT Prentice Hall (Ed. 5, chapter 8 on strategic choice frameworks).

Magretta, J. (2002) 'Why business models matter', *Harvard Business Review* (vol. 80/5, pp. 86–92).

Mathur, S.S. (1988) 'How firms compete: a new classification of generic strategies', *Journal of General Management* (vol. 14/1, pp. 30–57).

Markides C.C. (2001) 'Strategy as balance: from either–or to and', *Business Strategy Review* (vol. 12/3, pp. 1–10).

Miles, R.E. and Snow, C.C. (1978) *Organizational Strategy, Structure and Process*, McGraw-Hill.

Miller, D. (1986) 'Configurations of strategy and structure: towards a synthesis', *Strategic Management Journal* (vol. 7/2, pp. 233–249).

Miller, D. (1992) 'The generic strategy trap', *Journal of Business Strategy* (vol. 13/1, pp. 37–42 (also chapter 13 in Segal-Horn, S. (1998, ed.) *The Strategy Reader*, Blackwell).

Ohmae, K. (1982) *The Mind of the Strategist*, Penguin (part 2: Building Successful Strategies).

Schmalensee, R. (1982) 'Product differentiation advantages of pioneering brands', *American Economic Review* (vol. 72/3, pp. 349–365).

Sharp, B. and Dawes, J. (1996) 'Is differentiation optional? A critique of Porter's competitive strategy typology', in Earl, P.E. (ed.) *Management, Marketing and the Competitive Process*, Edward Elgar (chapter 12).

Woo, C.Y.Y. and Cooper, A.C. (1981) 'Strategies of effective low-share businesses', *Strategic Management Journal* (vol. 2, pp 301–318).

Wootton, S. and Horne, T. (2010) Strategic thinking: a step-by-step approach to strategy and leadership, Kogan Page (Ed. 3, chapter [Step] 7).

Notes

1 Source http://www.korres.com
2 McLimore and Larwood (1988).
3 Following Hofer and Schendel (1978). Their conclusions synthesised a variety of prior theorising.
4 After Miles and Snow (1978).
5 After Kay (1993).
6 Leonard Barton (1992).
7 Chapter 6 of Huff et al. (2009) provides a good review of business models in a strategy context. See also Magretta (2002).
8 For example, Spender (1989).
9 See Zahra and Pearce (1990) for a review of the defender-prospector framework.
10 Called taxonomies. Formally, a 'taxonomy' derives from the analysis of empirical data rather than inductively. See for example Miller (1986); Mintzberg, Ahlstrand and Lampel (1998).
11 Miller and Friesen (1978). See Weill et al. (2005) for a more recent, very thorough account.
12 After Porter (1980; 1985).
13 Buzzell and Gale (1987) provided clear evidence of the impact of low cost strategies.
14 Schmalensee (1982); Mathur (1988) provide support for the importance of differentiation.
15 A claim that has had its share of sceptics, e.g., Miller and Friesen (1986); Alberts (1989); Campbell-Hunt (2000) provide qualified endorsement.
16 Mathur (1988).

8

Scale, Non-scale and Vertical Strategies

Learning Outcomes

This chapter is designed to enable you to:

① Describe the advantages and disadvantages of scale and non-scale based strategies.

② Describe the features of vertical strategies and recognise when they are appropriate.

③ Critique the assumptions that underpin scale, non-scale and vertical strategies.

④ Apply this knowledge to make strategy choices in particular cases.

CASE STUDY: Nokia Corporation

Nokia started in 1865 in Finland as a wood pulp mill. Over the next century it became a multinational conglomerate, becoming a significant player in mobile telephony from the 1970s. By the 1990s European telecommunications markets were deregulating and the huge potential of digital GSM mobile technology was being realised. In 1992 the Nokia Directors took the major strategic decision to refocus the corporation on these technologies: manufacturing mobile handsets and the network systems needed for them to function.

By the late 2000s Nokia's annual output of mobile telephone handsets exceeded 400 million, made in Brazil, China, Finland, UK and Hungary, and sold in over 160 countries. Nokia now claims to be the largest provider of handsets and related services in the world. In partnership with Siemens of Germany, Nokia Siemens Networks had become one of the leading global providers of wireless and fixed network infrastructures, communications and network service platforms, and professional services to operators and service providers in more than 90 countries. It had network production sites in China, Finland, Germany and India. Nokia had also acquired NAVTEQ, which is a leading provider of OVI-branded digital map data and location-based content and services that support in-car and mobile navigation systems for consumer, business and government clienteles.

In 2009 Nokia's largest markets were the European Union (EU), China and India. China, the largest single-country market, accounted for 14.6% of sales. The Group employed over 123 thousand people, 44% in mobile devices and services, 52% in Nokia Siemens Networks and the rest in NAVTEQ. It employed 21,500 people in Finland, a similar number in other EU countries, 18,300 in India, and 15,400 in China. Of these, 37,000 worked in research and development activities in 16 countries, costing the equivalent of 14.4% of Group sales.

Nokia has not been without its difficulties, however, as the statistical summary (Table 8.A) of its financial performance indicates. Sales had declined for two years running, notably in 'Devices & Services'. While these activities remained profitable, Networks and NAVTEQ were losing money. Nokia's response had been to reorganise. The three areas of (i) devices, (ii) services and (iii) (internet) solutions had been folded into 'Mobile Phones' and 'Mobile Solutions'. The former would henceforth be responsible for the portfolio of affordable mobile phones and the user services available on them. The latter would be responsible for the portfolio of 'smart-phones', mobile computers and for developing world-class web services and applications based on maps, navigation, music, messaging and media under the OVI brand. Nokia had also rationalized activities in Networks and NAVTEQ to reduce costs, otherwise profits would have tumbled more dramatically.

Table 8.A: Nokia's financial performance in 2008 and 2009

	2009				2008			
	D&S	NSNet	NAV	Total	D&S	NSNet	NAV	Total
Sales *	27,841	12,564	579	40,984	35,084	15,308	318	50,710
% of total	67.9	30.7	1.4	100.0	69.2	30.2	0.6	100.0
% change	−20.6	−18	+82	−19.2	−6.9	+14.4	n.a.	−0.7
Profits**	3,314	−1,639	−344	1,331	5,816	−301	−153	4,966
% change	−43	−445	−125	−73	−23.3	+77	n.a.	−37.8#

D&S: Devices and Services; **NSNet**: Nokia Siemens networks; **NAV**: NAVTEQ.
* € millions.
** Reduced by a major corporate charge against profits.
n.a. = not available.
Source: Nokia annual reports

Nokia declared its intent to increase its impact on the demand for more sophisticated devices and services. It translated its slogan 'connecting people' into 'connect(ing) people to what matters to them'. This required a shift towards services and functionality, and away from high volume, mass-produced basic mobile phones to differentiated, added-value smart-phones and services. Nokia was aware, however, of the considerable challenges it faces in these domains from Apple (iPhone, iPad, etc.) and RIM (Research in Motion Ltd), best known for its hugely successful range of Blackberry smart-phones, and other established device manufacturers such as Sony–Ericsson and Samsung.

Questions

1. How realistic was Nokia's aim to achieve the equivalent high volume output of smart-phone handsets as it presently does of basic devices? Can it do so *and* sustain a differentiated market position?

2. Why has Nokia reorganised – what problem is it aiming to solve?

Introduction: Scale and Non-scale Capabilities as Sources of Sustainable Advantage

Various frameworks in Chapter 7 distinguished between (a) strategies in which large-scale activity supports value-creation and advantage and (b) strategies in which differentiation or focus (non-scale factors) make the most crucial contribution. For either form of strategy to succeed, the enterprise requires appropriate resources and capabilities. This chapter explores these requirements.

When an enterprise extends its capabilities to cover activities currently done by its suppliers or customers, it engages in vertical integration, backward or forward, respectively. When it disengages from a current activity to allow a supplier or customer to perform it, the enterprise is pursuing a strategy of vertical de-integration. Vertical strategies address a different set of issues from in-sector strategies. As with other strategic decisions, vertical integration and de-integration decisions draw on assessments of what the enterprise's value-adding capabilities are and can (or should) become. Thus this chapter considers vertical strategies further; Chapter 11 revisits the topic again in the context of strategic alliances.

Strategies based on Scale-exploiting Capabilities

Scale-based strategies depend on the following logic. High volume enables low(er) unit costs that in turn enable low(er) unit prices, leading to high(er) market shares. Combinations of scale and scope economies and learning (experience) are the mechanisms that underpin cost reduction (compression) or, less ambitiously, minimise increases. Over time, cost-effective operations enable real price reductions (i.e., after allowing for inflation), thereby enhancing the value delivered to an enterprise's clientele. All else being equal, these reductions should grow an enterprise's market share, and thereby enhance its competitive advantage and long-term viability. They usually expand total demand too.[1]

Critical Success Factors for Scale-Based Strategies

Scale-exploiting strategies sustain advantage only under specific conditions which the enterprise never entirely controls. Crucially, the available demand must be substantial; hence capable of absorbing large outputs typically from multiple providers. However, if demand is currently embryonic, there must be high future potential, giving an enterprise confidence to expand its capacity in anticipation that lower prices will generate substantial long-term demand.[2]

To secure the high 'returns to scale' necessary for an effective, profitable scale-exploiting strategy requires the necessary value-adding technologies and processes. Typically, high investment in research and development, production methods, equipment, marketing and distribution are all needed. Increasing the capital intensity of value-adding activities through investment has major consequences. One is that it raises the threshold output level that defines minimum efficient scale (MES – discussed in Chapter 3). Few enterprises in a sector are willing or able to make financial commitments on this scale. The few that can should capture a greater share of demand. High market-share enterprises generally enjoy higher returns on their investments than do lower share competitors. An enterprise whose market share is high numerically and high *relative* to the market share of the next biggest provider enjoys a significant degree of monopoly: the effect on prices, profit margins and hence profitability is positive and disproportionate.

However, high capital investment (*relative* to the revenues it generates) often depresses the financial returns on assets employed. Indeed, after correcting for market share variations, capital intensive enterprises often yield systematically lower returns than enterprises with low capital intensity achieve. This is because they find it difficult to maintain output levels that persistently use all of their available capacity. The difficulties increase when several providers have invested heavily at the same time. Their combined capacity expands beyond realistic expectations of future demand. Full returns to scale are impossible for everyone. For those whose outputs stay below the break-even level (at which their revenues match their total costs), the investment proves disastrous. Being chronically unprofitable, exiting the sector becomes their only rational option. Occasionally the problem afflicts an entire sector.

The strategic lesson is clear: the enterprise that makes relevant, major capital investments *first* is best placed to thrive on a scale-based strategy, especially when its additional output capacity quickly captures a large proportion of available demand.[3] Enterprises that capture high shares of demand tend to be pioneers: early sector entrants that cement their positions by continually innovating, seeking patents and investing to exploit them. By developing and exploiting new knowledge they create positions that become virtually impossible for others to copy.

A smaller, less resource-endowed, low-share competitor or new entrant could be tempted to pursue larger scale operations, gambling that additional capacity will enable it to increase its share of demand and its profitability. Its timing is critical: late imitation of established competitors is very high risk. An established market leader is bound to respond, probably by engaging in a short-term 'price war.' This threat makes high investment devoted to share gain a singularly unattractive proposition for a small competitor. It would be well advised to consider alternative, non scale-based strategies.

After a period of intense competition of investment in enhanced technologies and processes to exploit share-gaining strategies, a new 'technology regime' settles in. The market shares of the (fewer) surviving enterprises tend to stabilise. Subsequent cycles of heavy investment occur every few years (though the cycle time can be unpredictable and, in many sectors, is getting shorter), as the remaining providers seek greater advantage through further, scale-increasing innovations. Ultimately, this strategy can remain viable for only the very largest enterprises.

LEARNING
OBJECTIVE ①
Occasionally, a radical new technology regime emerges to enable cost compression *without* massive increases in MES: a so-called 'game-changing' leapfrog. In the new regime investment levels, costs and minimum scale assume different relationships. For example, computer-controlled robots in automobile manufacture allow greater flexibility as well as high quality and close cost control. A late entrant or minor competitor sometimes accelerates regime transition because, unlike the dominant competitors, it has less commitment to the *status quo* and no prospect of success competing on their terms. If it already has a game-changing new technology it faces lower financial risk and uncertainty. Yet change-leading enterprises remain vulnerable unless they have an abundance of necessary, complementary resources and competences or can access them via external collaborations.

Cross-sectional studies have investigated many industry sectors over specific time periods. Much of the evidence concludes that in appropriate circumstances, scale-based strategies are highly effective. However, findings may not take account of industry-specific or time-based effects, reducing their generalisability. Some studies suggest that the richness and subtlety of strategies and competitive sector positions can have more impact than market share alone.

Sustaining Scale-Based Strategies via Continued Cost Reduction

Efficient, low-cost enterprises deliver excellent value to price-conscious buyers and thereby sustain advantage. For the future they must still work hard to maintain a low cost base, through such actions as:

- Maintaining capacity utilisation and operational efficiency.
- Progressive introduction of even more efficient, new technologies.
- Eliminating wasteful cost-adding activities or reducing their impact.
- Reducing order receipt to delivery times, to cut working capital needs.
- Enhancing control of external costs in the supply chain.
- Operating efficient marketing and distribution activities.
- Implementing high-calibre information systems and knowledge management practices to share ideas across disparate activities and functions.

A single, large facility operates more efficiently than several small facilities, particularly if located where labour and overhead charges are low. However, full capacity operations are hard for large-scale plants to achieve, especially in continuous flow processes such as chemicals, steel and glass making, and physical distribution. Numerous small facilities sited close to end users provide greater flexibility and security of supply and reduce distribution costs.

Operational costs merit regular investigation to see which can be reduced, made more efficient, or eliminated. Potential exists in:

- Procurement of materials and other value-added inputs.
- Indirect (overhead) operational charges such as leases on facilities, electricity charges, and equipment depreciation.
- Costs of waste and rectification of faulty output.
- Wages and salaries of staff directly engaged in value-adding processes.
- Marketing and physical distribution charges.
- Enterprise-level (corporate) overhead costs.

Rigorous purchasing procedures can reduce input costs. Make-or-buy decisions (concerning whether to subcontract) can be made about specific activities as part of the enterprise's vertical strategy (see later, this chapter). Facility charges can be reduced through more prudent use, notably of energy. Careful product design and process mechanisation may reduce component numbers or costs, including labour costs in assembly. Safe, error-proof processes and effective quality assurance procedures reduce the costs of supervision, inspection, waste and rectification. The costs of some service activities can perhaps be delegated to the client or user. (Consider, for example, automated help desks and self-collect and self-assembly flat-pack furniture.) Corporate overheads require senior managers to be disciplined and set a good example. For instance, Ingvar Kamprad, the founder of (and still major shareholder in) IKEA, reportedly flies economy-class on business and expects IKEA managers to do the same. Systematic cost-reduction approaches include lean operations, quality circles, business process engineering and benchmarking (discussed further in Chapter 13).

Time is an important competitive weapon, in both services and in manufacturing enterprises. Just-in-time replenishment is crucial to lean operations, reducing the costs of holding component stocks and finished goods. It also reduces order-to-delivery times. Networked communications increase efficiency, both internally and between an enterprise and its customers and suppliers. Cost reductions also result from refined administrative processes and routines, eliminating activities that add cost but little end-user value. Corporate and support functions including marketing, human resources management, research and development, and legal affairs all contribute to costs. Enterprises increasingly use specialised external contractors and agencies to reduce these overheads.

Generally, the greater the anticipated benefit of a change to increase efficiency, the greater the required change in processes or technologies. When the investment cost is high the consequent strategic risk increases. This poses the question of whether to initiate major change or wait for others to lead. More modest, but continuing improvements, requiring conscious, painstaking and continual efforts, may be a better approach for many enterprises.

As enterprises grow larger, the challenge is not just to create relevant proprietary knowledge, but also to retain and use the knowledge to their advantage, by overcoming inherent conservatism and by ensuring it is accessible where most beneficial. Sometimes internal knowledge is inadequate. It becomes necessary to recruit experienced staff with different skills and to consult equipment suppliers and external experts.

Sustaining Scale-Based Strategies via Quality, Variety and Flexibility

Ultimately a scale-based enterprise becomes aware that future demand increases are increasingly unlikely. In addition, its clientele may signal that adding extra value matters more than lower costs. It must reinforce perceived value by other means, notably via greater variety, higher (actual or perceived) quality, or more flexibility – but without compromising its low-cost capabilities. Of course, such initiatives can incur additional costs that drive buyers away, despite the signals they convey to market researchers.

Quality: Modern large-scale production and distribution processes are inherently costly, but they offer improved control mechanisms to maintain consistency of output quality and consequent reliability. Although not guaranteed to increase advantage in a competitive environment, when high quality is recognised it usually commands a price premium. Even small premiums have a big impact on profitability in large-scale operations. New features and capabilities can enhance perceived quality without necessarily adding greatly to cost. However, the target clientele needs time to recognise enhanced quality.[4] Such quality may also lead to greater durability, reducing replacement demand, a significant demand driver in mature markets.

Variety: Historically, large-scale operations have meant *standardisation* and, hence, restricted variety for potential buyers. Thus large-scale providers have presented opportunities for specialist competitors. They can recapture this demand by offering *cost-effective variety*. Typically this is achieved by varying the visible aspects of a product or service while standardising its hidden aspects. An established approach well-understood by the car industry is to offer the core product or service at an attractively low price along with very profitable elements that the client can select at extra cost, such as climate control and satellite navigation systems. Another strategy is to price the options attractively to distract the buyer from noticing that the core offering is not competitively priced. Either way, the strategic intent is to be seen as the lowest cost supplier *in the mind of the prospective buyer*.

Flexibility: requires adaptive skills, allowing the enterprise to respond promptly to changing demand patterns.[5] Mechanisation, automated computer control and communications all enable greater flexibility without seriously compromising low cost intent. Mass-customisation, still at an early stage of development, enables more tailored offerings while retaining standardisation of the processes and activities that create them.

Cost-effective quality, variety and flexibility

The websites of e-commerce retailers use cookies to recognise repeat visits and personalise at negligible cost what is an essentially impersonal encounter, thereby enhancing perceived service quality.

The Volkswagen automobile group produces only four basic car 'platforms' (supermini, small family car, large family car and executive car). On these platforms it constructs over 20 distinct models (saloons, hatchbacks, station wagons, sport utility vehicles (SUVs), people-carriers, sports cars, convertibles and light vans) with a multiplicity of variants across four mainstream brands,. It restricts variety largely to what is visible: external body styling, colours and trim specifications.

Within the confines of essentially standard menus, McDonalds' restaurants offer considerable flexibility in response to the preferences and timing of local demand.

Constraints on Strategies that Exploit Large Scale and Low Cost

Though the experience curve implies that large-scale enterprises can sustain an ever-increasing cost advantage, in fact this outcome is unusual. Accordingly, some have challenged the fundamental logic of large scale and share in creating advantage. Certainly, many scale-oriented enterprises have the characteristics ascribed to 'defenders' (Chapter 7); they typically focus on maximising efficiency. Ultimately they cannot justify new investments by predicting ever-increasing scale. For example, Microsoft developed its first PC operating system in a few months with two people. Its latest system has taken a number of years and inputs from thousands of software engineers.

Those that have made the greatest investment in the *status quo* actually have most to lose from radically new technologies and approaches. Conservatism, complacency, inertia, lack of funds and perceptions of risk all obstruct the continuing drive to sustain a scale-based strategy. Diseconomies of scale may also set in.[6] Well-resourced enterprises may seek to exploit scope economies through diversification initiatives.[7] Their commitment to the existing domain can diminish as they exploit new opportunities.

Sector late entrants and smaller, agile competitors may 'free ride' by learning from scale-dependent enterprises. While the latter try to maintain secrecy, especially over innovations, it is difficult to avoid knowledge leakage. Late entrants may import radically new methods to compete and achieve lower costs. To survive, smaller competitors may have no choice other than to respond however they can – notably through high-risk innovation – to distinguish themselves, aiming to negate their low-cost disadvantages. Occasionally they succeed, though established, large-scale competitors have considerable resources and resilience to fight back, either by matching the innovation or simply by acquiring it.

Strategies Based on Non-scale Capabilities

LEARNING
OBJECTIVE ①

Enterprises create value for their clienteles through non-scale strategies based on distinctiveness or narrow targeting in which prices do not depend principally on low cost. However, these strategies must create offerings that fulfil the promise of extra value, which adequately compensates for any additional cost and thus higher price.

These strategies clearly draw on strategic marketing skills as much as other key enterprise functions.[8] Differentiation and focus are mechanisms whereby enterprises aim to isolate themselves largely from competition by occupying niche positions defined by superior perceived (and delivered) value.[9] In theory there are many ways in to achieve differentiation, as indicated by the generic differentiation matrix[10] (discussed in Chapter 7). Really distinctive enterprises typically exploit *multiple*, mutually reinforcing three forms of strategies, namely those:

1. Based on distinctive, value-rich offerings.
2. Based on distinctive enterprise characteristics.
3. Based on narrow targeting (or focus).

These are examined in turn below.

Strategies Based on Distinctive, Value-rich Offerings

As we have seen, offering (product or service) value derives variously from:

*   Tangible features and specifications.
*   Intangible (brand) image.
*   Associated service aspects involving expert and/or delivery personalisation.

The presentation and communication of value is a core responsibility of the marketing function within the strategic management context. Clienteles interpret value in various ways, sometimes idiosyncratically, based on different signals:

*   Objective, features and specifications of the offering.
*   Prestige status of brand and consequent trust in it.
*   Outstanding product or service performance, especially in demanding conditions.
*   Limited availability that enhances perceived desirability.
*   High price (when price is treated as a signifier of high quality and hence value).

LEARNING
OBJECTIVE ①

For a strategy based on distinctive, value-conferring offering characteristics to succeed, the evident form(s) of distinctiveness must accord with buyers' priorities. They must recognise, respect, value and desire these characteristics (*receptivity*) and perceive the signals they receive from the enterprise about particular offerings as legitimate and genuine (*credibility*). Though high price is a consequence of the cost of delivering high value, it can function metaphorically too: that is, a high-value offering is expected to have a high price.

Strategies Based on Distinctive *Enterprise* Characteristics

Offering-based differentiation frequently becomes an expected, but decreasingly effective strategy. Although carefully-nurtured reputations can support distinctiveness for a long time, mature markets invariably feature similar products with convergent attributes, often dictated by customary (or regulated) standards. (Consider the example of PCs and mobile phones, which share common operating systems and networks.)

An enterprise's *characteristics*, such as its technological and administrative capabilities or external architecture (i.e., networks and relationships), may differ distinctively from other enterprises. It may also behave distinctively. Though such characteristics are often not obvious, when clients do recognise and value these differences, they can reinforce a differentiation strategy to complement or be an alternative to offering distinctiveness. Specifically, it can be beneficial to foster perceptions of distinctiveness based either on what the enterprise *is* – as symbolised by the distinctive position it occupies, or on what it *does* – its distinctive behaviours. Such characteristics can be intrinsically attractive to the clienteles of, for example, not-for-profit enterprises engaged in worthy causes that are widely perceived to deserve and need support. However, business enterprises too may find they have exploitable, distinctive characteristics, particularly in business-to-business markets. This includes the opportunity to exploit the value attached to the corporate brand and reputation, rather than product brands. The box which follows offers some examples.

Behavioural distinctiveness

Apple Computer's near-fanatical users value its innovativeness, design flair and maverick independence of the anodyne, computing world of corporations such as Microsoft, IBM, Dell and Hewlett-Packard.[11] Users are buying not just a product but a stake in Apple's continued survival.

Strategies Based on Narrow Targeting (Focus)

LEARNING
OBJECTIVE ①

To focus on a narrow target market is also a way to distinguish an enterprise, albeit without necessarily creating widespread respect. Effective focus strategies require conscious decisions to limit the appeal to well-defined target niches. This approach typically requires an ability to meet specific needs precisely, reliably and to an acceptable standard; long-standing relationships, characteristic particularly of business-to-business markets, may also feature. Although narrow target strategies often associate with forms of differentiation, to serve a narrowly defined audience may be sufficient to isolate an enterprise from strong competition (especially where there is also geographic separation).

Focus strategies

Transport businesses, hospitals and schools typically use subcontracted catering services, exemplified by the UK-based Compass Group (which employs 386,000 staff in over 50 countries and serves 4 billion meals annually in 40,000 locations). They have access to essentially captive consumers whose only practical alternative is usually to provide their own food (if allowed) or go without.

The Military Watch Company cited in Chapter 7 focuses on meeting the needs of government ministries and their agents, often to specific and demanding product standards specified by NATO. The lack of a prestige brand could actually be a benefit for clients, since it probably reduces the theft that would occur with a prestige brand.

Constraints on Non-scale Strategies

Few non-scale strategies survive indefinitely. They can lose their basis of advantage, for various reasons. For example:

- The target market ceases to value the characteristics that have hitherto sustained its relevance, high perceived value and premium prices.
- The basis of distinctiveness is displaced by a newer form that attracts more clients.
- Large-scale competitors create enhanced-value offerings that lack brand prestige, but compensate with lower prices for equivalent objective performance, thereby matching value as perceived by less discerning and more open-minded buyers.

Start-up enterprises generally discover that their only viable basis for survival is to establish perceived distinctiveness or narrow focus. Entrepreneurial novelty often loses its appeal when associated with promises let down by inadequate performances. (Prime examples include products, such as innovative home computers, watches and electric tricycles, developed by Sir Clive Sinclair.) An initially successful, non-scale strategy inevitably requires enhancement in order to sustain advantage over time by:

- Responding to changing buyer preferences by adopting newer, more valued forms of distinctiveness.
- Combining various forms of distinctiveness.
- Refining its definition of the primary target on which to focus.

The only alternative is to accept that market demand for the present offering is declining and to retrench accordingly.

Can Scale and Non-scale Strategic Priorities Be Combined?

The discussion in Chapters 7 and 8 treats large-scale/low-cost and differentiation/focus strategies as essentially opposed, given their differing priorities.[12] The question we explore here is whether *hybrid* strategies can succeed when they combine adequate scale for a low cost base with differentiation/focus sufficient to achieve recognised distinctiveness.[13]

Capabilities to sustain differentiation or focus markedly differ from those needed to achieve scale and sustain low cost, even though cost efficiency always matters in competitive markets to some degree. It is predictable that enterprises are not particularly adept at creating and combining scale and differentiation strategies. Yet some high profile enterprises, for-profit and otherwise, do appear to benefit from both mechanisms. How can the paradox be resolved? Consider these arguments.

Relativism: Apparently successful hybrid strategies, such as Volkswagen employs, are neither the lowest cost, nor the most differentiated. Rather, they achieve adequate distinctiveness at relatively large scale and low cost. Their capabilities enable them to manage the tensions and contradictions that arise from opposing imperatives.

Domains of applicability: Enterprises are complex, branching, value-adding chains that create portfolios of offerings to serve multiple demand segments. Overall cost leadership or distinctiveness has little meaning. To be successful an enterprise probably enjoys being a cost leader in some activities, but lags elsewhere; conversely, its portfolio contains well-differentiated, premium-price offerings in some areas and comparative commodities elsewhere. Thus its overall strategy features both priorities in particular domains.

Industry/market definitions: Given the phenomenon of demand segmentation, a highly differentiated or tightly focused strategy generally sustains a small share of a large, multi-segment, overall market. So is it really a small-share competitor, or a dominant one with a large share of a narrowly defined, demand segment? For example, is it more relevant to BMW that it has around a third of the global prestige car market or a 2% share of the global car market as a whole? *In relation to the sector*, the competitor in question no doubt charges high prices and has high costs. *In relation to its niche segment*, its scale could be more substantial and its prices and costs lower than its competitors. Seen in that context it delivers exceptional value by combining low relative cost and distinctiveness.[14]

Vertical (Supply Chain) Strategies

Scale and non-scale strategies relate principally to the sector under scrutiny. Vertical strategies are broader; they affect the enterprise's position in the supply chain beyond its sector boundaries. Consequently, they enhance or detract *indirectly* from its competitive viability in its core domain(s), without necessarily being linked to scale or differentiation choices. That said, the case for linking vertical strategies to scale is often more compelling that to differentiation, although each can be treated on its merits.

Historical Background

LEARNING OBJECTIVE ②

Every enterprise contributes a finite set of value-adding activities to the complete activity or supply chain from raw materials and other inputs to end users. Major decisions to engage in or withdraw from particular activities constitute an enterprise's supply chain strategy. They are a legitimate part of its strategy repertoire, particularly for influential, large-scale enterprises.

During the 20th century, thinking about vertical strategies changed, led notably by the automotive industry. In the late 1920s Ford of the United States was the first to combine large-scale mass production and full vertical integration at its River Rouge plant. Iron ore became steel for car parts and bodies; other materials were made into components for subsequent assembly into finished cars. From 1940, owing to the World War, governments forced vehicle assemblers to outsource parts manufacture, exploiting the capacity available in other industries. However, they retained control of specifications, design capability and quality standards.

From about 1950 Toyota implemented what was to become known as the Toyota lean production system. It was a rational, least wasteful response to post-war conditions in Japan, notably a lack of sophisticated equipment, money and short-term demand. Lean operation remains a core principle of its scale-based strategy, helping Toyota to become the largest global car maker. Lean production has been much copied by enterprises in many manufacturing sectors, though rarely as effectively. Crucially, Toyota established a network of specialised suppliers willing to operate facilities nearby; its franchised dealer networks integrated into the supply chain too. Although its suppliers and distributors are subcontractors, long-term mutual commitments encourage trusted partnerships. Thus Toyota's vertical strategy includes the transfer of many design and development responsibilities to its partners, thereby achieving the control and communication benefits of full vertical integration without many of the technical and administrative costs. Such a strategy is sometimes called quasi vertical integration. Honda, Nissan and many other car makers operate their own lean production systems; supply chains are now global, carefully controlled via electronic as well as physical communications.

Vertical Integration Strategies and their Implications

 The decision to integrate vertically in the supply chain, forwards or backwards, requires an assessment of the *transaction costs* that arise when a value-adding activity is performed externally. When the external transaction costs exceed the transaction costs of carrying out the activity internally (in so far as they can accurately be compared), integration is indicated, and vice versa (de-integration).[15]

Vertical strategy decisions should also consider other issues. Will the potential benefits of integration or de-integration be realised? How reliably can future costs be predicted? If external contractors are used, will their quality and reliability of supply be acceptable? How much control will the focal enterprise lose (or gain)?

External provision involves identifiable transaction costs. These are required in order to:

- Collect relevant information to help decide whether to de-integrate and with which external provider(s).
- Negotiate a satisfactory basis for trade, including specifications, price, and delivery arrangements.
- Write robust, legal trading contracts.
- Pay commissions to agents or brokers when used.
- Monitor performance against contractual provisions, resolve disputes after contractual failures and minimise the consequential costs of failure (e.g., *contingent* costs such as penalty payments made to the enterprise's customers because of late delivery).

Other costs not covered above can arise, notably from uncontrolled (and probably uncontrollable) *opportunistic* behaviour on the part of supply chain suppliers and distributors.

 When one party to a transaction gains access to information that the other does not have, an asymmetry arises that may be exploitable. To anticipate and negate all risks of opportunism via a carefully-worded contract is prohibitively costly. Yet an enterprise that fails to protect itself from predictable risks exposes itself to *moral hazard*.

The potential advantages for vertical integration are considerable and so warrant consideration first. They include:

- Overall unit cost reductions, achieved through:
  - elimination of external transaction costs; and
  - internal scope economies: spreading fixed costs among a wider range of *primary* activities.

Scope economies in support functions such as human resources management (HRM), research and development (R&D) and legal services, by spreading their cost over an extended value chain.

- Enhanced control over:
  - quality and service standards;
  - logistical arrangements including delivery schedules;
  - security of supply of product and service inputs; and
  - access to and control of distribution channels;

- Negating the bargaining power of dominant suppliers and distributors, respectively, who:
    - demand higher prices for their supplies; and
    - bargain down the prices they pay for the enterprise's products.
- Increased profit potential from external sales of the surplus output of additional value-adding activities.
- Development of new competences associated with the additional activities.
- Pre-emption of competitive moves to control these external activities.

Integration requires the enterprise either to acquire a current supplier or distributor or to develop the resources and skills to compete with them. Acquisition is generally preferred since it brings these capabilities ready-formed and enables rationalisation and cost reduction via scope economies. By contrast, internal development appears uncertain, unless relevant, underutilized resources and skills exist in the enterprise.

Compelling as the integration arguments may appear, the theoretical benefits are not always realised. Typical reasons for this are as follows:

- Unforeseen technical and administrative challenges create costly delays in implementation. Some may prove impossible to resolve owing to inadequate resources and skills.
- A current supplier or distributor is acquired at too high a cost, creating a financial burden that negates the expected cost reductions.
- Acquired enterprises are poorly integrated and managed, so that their performance suffers and costs escalate.
- By acquiring a supplier that also deals with its competitors or a distributor of competing products, the enterprise may create contractual difficulties and conflicts of interest. The competitors make alternative arrangements, so the enterprise loses valuable future business and associated recovery of overheads.

LEARNING
OBJECTIVE ②
These difficulties can sometimes be mitigated via a hybrid approach known as *tapered* integration. Here, the enterprise continues to use an outside supplier or distributor but also performs these additional value-adding activities. Split sourcing enhances security of supply and allows comparisons of internal and external performance (i.e., benchmarking). The drawback is that neither internal nor external provider accesses the economies of scale or scope that would exist if they were combined.

Vertical De-integration Strategies and their Implications

The drawbacks of full vertical integration explain why many Western corporations have copied Toyota's quasi integration model. For the dominant enterprise in the supply chain the benefits are that:

- It achieves effective upstream and downstream control without the costs of either developing or acquiring the activities. In fact, major corporations extend their influence *beyond* the enterprises with which they transact directly; they become the 'lead partners' in their respective chains.

- By entering long-term relationships based on development of mutual trust, enterprises minimise the transaction costs of writing and policing formal contracts.

The lead partner develops new co-ordination capabilities, but incurs costs linked to their development. For subordinate partners the main benefits lie in the security of the relationships and their opportunity to develop more robust and distinctive supply chain positions. They experience a significant loss of autonomy, with the ultimate sanction of exclusion from the chain if they fail consistently to meet the lead partner's expectations. Small enterprises in localised, industrial districts in Northern and North-Eastern Italy operate good examples of this model. For example, one is co-ordinated by the clothing company Benetton in the Veneto region. Another is centred on Prato, where the lead company is called the *impannatore*.

Many Western enterprises are more accustomed to competing than collaborating and so may be unfamiliar and perhaps uncomfortable with this quasi-integrated model. Even so, many large enterprises have adopted versions of it because there is wide recognition that enterprises are not uniformly competent in all the required value-adding activities – and probably cannot be. So a degree of supply chain specialisation is sensible, relying on competent external enterprises for particular activities.

Very few enterprises today are fully vertically integrated in the 1920s' Fordian sense. Most exploit their scale or differentiation advantages more effectively in selected value-adding activities. So the general trend in recent decades has been to engage in vertical specialization or de-integration. This strategy can be readily justified when it:

- Enables an enterprise to develop and exploit well-defined specialisms, consistent with the resource-based theory.
- Delegates specific investment costs and operational risks to specialised subcontractors.
- Leads all the partners to focus on what they do best, establishing a well-organised, efficient supply chain in which each one subcontracts or 'outsources' its non-core activities to others.
- Allows subcontractors to make long-term investments with confidence because they expect sufficient custom for the specialised, value-adding capacity they create.

However, major enterprises exercise considerable influence even in a de-integrated supply chain, especially over critically important activities. Though they may pay lip service to their respect for their external, notional partners, in reality the latter are comparatively dependent, subordinate enterprises unless they possess unique resources and skills, hence strong bargaining power.

Dynamism in Vertical Strategy Decisions

De-integration and re-integration decisions are part of the ongoing strategy process. Most enterprises conduct a value-chain analysis periodically. When they find excess capacity (slack) in some current activities while being stretched elsewhere, their operations are evidently inefficient.

Does the spare capacity offer the potential to subcontract for others, enhancing profits and capabilities in the long term? Or, is the current capacity (and available expertise) well below the anticipated future need, indicating that it may be time to de-integrate?

Cost reduction is often the primary goal of decisions to de-integrate, which is justified if the expected future transaction costs are less than the equivalent internal costs (the reverse of the arguments for integration). However, a differentiation strategy may require an enterprise to perform certain value-adding activities to sustain its reputation, despite the existence of lower cost external providers. A case for re-integration also exists if it has relevant expertise in some activities that can be redeployed in those currently subcontracted.

Internet-enabled electronic communications encourage a form of de-integration called disintermediation – that is, the *elimination* of distributive activities in supply chains that add significantly to costs, but create minimal value for end users, especially in the downstream chain. Amazon and Dell have eliminated dependence on conventional retail outlets in their business-to-consumer (B2C) supply chains. Major US and European supermarket chains bypass wholesalers and importers to deal directly with farmers and their agents in Africa, South America and Asia, facilitating the global supply of fresh fruit and vegetables in these business-to-business (B2B) supply chains.

Real-time electronic communications allow enterprises, especially those with scale-based strategies, to conduct online auctions to mobilise marginal supply capacity wherever it can be found globally, whenever it is required. Evidently, this partial reversion to (very short term) market mechanisms contrasts markedly with strategies based on long-term trust relationships.

Market mechanisms without co-ordination and limited external regulation make it more difficult to accommodate differences in technical standards or commercial cultures. Hidden costs of miscommunication and misunderstanding arise from language barriers in arms-length transactions. Equally, co-ordinated supply chains generate their own costs, one being a lack of realised flexibility. Decisions about vertical integration and de-integration are an integral part of a coherent strategy to support an enterprise's mission and head towards its future vision, so should not be subject to short-term whim and opportunism.

LEARNING OBJECTIVE ② Tensions will persist between (quasi) vertically integrated supply chains and market mechanisms that tend to de-integrate them. Each mechanism will be applied where it seems strategically and operationally appropriate parts of all supply chains, notably in trans-national chains. Complexity is therefore inevitable.

CASE STUDY: Multiple strategies at Benetton Group[16]

Brother and sister, Luciano and Giuliana Benetton, founded the family knitwear business that bears their name at Ponzano near Venice in north-east Italy in 1965. As the company grew, Luciano took responsibility for sales and overall commercial direction, while Giuliana designed the brightly-coloured garments with which Benetton has become synonymous. Brothers Carlo and Gilberto joined soon afterwards to manage production and finance respectively.

Initial progress was slow because clothing retailers did not like the products. They tackled the problem by working with informal partners, opening a handful of small stores in places where young people gathered. The formula worked and Benetton began a formal expansion of its franchise network. In 1969 the first non-Italian store opened and distribution spread, first across Europe and then beyond. By 1983 there were around 2,000 stores. Exports generated over half Benetton's sales (Table 8.B).

Today, the core business of the Benetton Group is still clothing. Its shares are publicly quoted on the Milan stock-market. The Benetton family owns 67% via a holding company, Edizione Srl. The ownership of the remainder is split between institutional and other investors. Benetton produces over 150 million garments a year, distributed via a network of 6,300 retail stores in 120 countries globally. Group turnover in 2009 was over €2 billion. Italy accounts for 48% of sales, the rest of Europe 34%, Asia 14%, the Americas and elsewhere 4%. The Group expresses its strong Italian character in its brands: the casual *United Colors of Benetton* (82% of sales, divided 5:3 between adults and children); the fashion-oriented *Sisley* brand (16%); and the leisurewear brand *Playlife* (2%).

Table 8.B: Benetton's financial performance 2005–2009

Year	2009	2008	2007**	2006	2005
Revenues*	2,049	2,128	2,049	1,911	1,765
Net income*	122	155	145	125	112

* € million.
** Proforma.

Over time Benetton has developed what today it calls a 'unique, flexible and innovative business model'. Some key features of this integrated model are:

• Mass-producing garments via seasonal collections, as practised in *haute couture*, supplemented by new releases throughout each season.
• Dynamic, colourful and sometimes controversial branding and advertising.

An 'institutionalised wholesale franchise system' in which independent retailers (franchisees) are treated as business partners. Each is responsible for the performance of his/her store, often competing with other Benetton retailers in the same city or town. A network of independent Benetton agents provides retailers with advice and support, sometimes also equity investments. These stores carry complete collections and a wide selection of accessories, and presently generate 78% of Benetton's sales.

Benetton owns and operates stores in 20 countries since 2000, overseen by Benetton area managers and staff. These stores spearhead market development in countries where it has no commercial partners or existing partners, underperform or want to exit for strategic reasons. Benetton can thereby establish retail performance benchmarks and test new ideas and designs. Direct sales are 22% of the total.

Benetton traditionally assembled many of its knitwear garments from components produced by local supply partners in Italy, though its manufacturing supply chain is now increasingly global. An innovative production feature is that many garments are produced 'in grey', being piece-dyed, not made from pre-dyed fabric. This enables flexibility to make colour changes at short notice in response to sales trends, reducing write-downs of unsold stock. As with its retail partners, Benetton tries to establish trusting relationships with preferred suppliers, encouraging them to invest heavily to support Benetton production. All production systems and equipment are renewed every five years. More recently, Benetton has introduced a 'double supply chain' system in which the cost-efficient, sequential system runs in parallel with an 'integrated planning system' that allows it to respond much quicker to market trends and dovetails in well with R&D and new product design.

The integrated logistics (distribution) system co-ordinates distribution centres and production facilities via electronic communications between stores and the centre at Castrette, Italy. These systems enable Benetton to monitor fashion trends closely, feeding new orders and re-orders promptly into the integrated manufacturing supply chain, reducing delivery lead times. A fully automated distribution centre picks, packs and despatches individual orders direct to the retail stores worldwide. It handles a total of 120,000 incoming and outgoing movements daily with only 28 staff.

Benetton's strategy is based on complex, dynamic and paradoxical elements. It combines large-scale, mass production with 'boutique' production; mass marketing with differentiated market positioning via multiple brands; while quasi-vertical integration runs in parallel with vertical de-integration.

Questions

1. Consult Benetton's website and other sources to understand its current strategic approach more fully. Could this model apply to other branded global companies or is effectively unique to Benetton?

2. What problems led to the changes Benetton made in 2000? To what extent has the company merely added further complexity, compromising the purity of the original system without actually solving these problems? How might it have responded differently?

Summary

- Large scale and associated high market share do not guarantee indefinite success, but they do provide resourceful enterprises with advantages that weaker competitors cannot overcome. In addition, the accumulated resources and capabilities that result from large-scale operations over time provide greater resilience to unforeseen competitive initiatives and reaction time.

- Differentiation and focus strategies offer alternative options for enterprises unable to exploit a sector-leading low cost base or dominant market share. Differentiation can occur through the distinctiveness of products or services, but also from unique enterprise characteristics and behaviours.

- Unfortunately, the advantages that current differentiation and focus strategies confer erode with time, not least because high volume providers extend their offerings to cater for an increasing proportion of end-users' needs. Successful non-scale strategies can maintain their quality/performance advantage only by continuing enhancements, as discussed in Chapter 7.

- In relation to vertical strategies, the decision to integrate or rely on market mechanisms (de-integrate) depends on the balance of market transaction costs versus the equivalent costs of internal value-adding.

- Conventional wisdom has shifted from vertical integration in the 1920s (many small firms each performing all of the activities needed to deliver a product or service to the end user) to de-integration via subcontracting, to quasi vertical integration in which lead enterprises effectively control their supply chains via long-term commercial relationships. More recently, some evidence exists of a reversion to short-term market mechanisms enhanced by the World Wide Web.

- Quasi-integration strategies allow a lead enterprise to influence and co-ordinate upstream and downstream activities via trusting relationships with its key supply partners. When market transactions are the predominant supply chain mechanism, competition, bargaining power and transaction costs are the overarching influences.

- Many supply chains manifest tensions between collaborative and competitive characteristics. Enterprises therefore benefit when they recognise incipient shifts in the balance of advantage between integrative and de-integrative strategies and act accordingly, consistent with their missions and visions.

Exercises for Further Study and Discussion

1. Conventional wisdom asserts that low-cost strategies depend on the ability of an enterprise to identify and concentrate on the activities in which it holds a cost advantage, while outsourcing other activities. Are there circumstances in which this wisdom might be misguided?
2. Explore the basis of low-cost and differentiation strategies with reference to the V-R-I-O-S framework. Are the various V-R-I-O-S criteria equally relevant to both types of strategy?

3. Critique the alternative explanations of how scale and non-scale strategies can be combined effectively in particular cases. Do the alternative explanations have differing implications for how an enterprise should develop its future strategy?
4. What *organizational* costs are there of differentiation strategies that do not exist for enterprises that pursue low-cost strategies? Why do they arise?
5. Consider two different examples of cost-effective variety/flexibility and assess how each enterprise could learn from the other. What would each do differently or additionally? Would these 'transplanted' approaches succeed?
6. Critically discuss the proposition that reputation is more important for long-term strategic distinctiveness than product brands.
7. Critique the view that a focus strategy based on an essentially 'captive' clientele is simply lazy and creates no sustainable differentiation.

Suggestions for Further Reading

Alberts, W.W. (1989) 'The Experience Curve Doctrine Reconsidered', *Journal of Marketing* (vol. 53/3, pp. 36–49).

Barney, J.B. and Hesterly, W.S. (2010) *Strategic Management and Competitive Advantage*, Prentice Hall (Ed. 3, chapters 4 and 5).

Dickson, P.R. and Ginter, J.L. (1987) 'Market segmentation, product differentiation and marketing strategy', *Journal of Marketing* (vol. 51/Apr, pp. 1–10).

Ghemawat, P. (1985) 'Building strategy on the experience curve' *Harvard Business Review* (March/April, pp. 143–149).

Harrigan, K.R. (1985) 'Vertical integration and corporate strategy', *Academy of Management Journal* (vol. 28/2, pp. 397–425).

Hill, C.W.L. (1988) 'Differentiation versus low cost or differentiation and low cost: a contingency framework', *Academy of Management Review* (vol. 13/3, July, pp. 401–412).

Jacobsen, R. and Aaker, D. (1985) 'Is market share all that it's cracked up to be?', *Journal of Marketing* (vol. 49/3, pp. 11–22).

Kumar, N. (2006) 'Strategies to fight low-cost rivals', *Harvard Business Review* (vol. 84/12, Nov–Dec, pp. 104–113).

Lieberman, M.B. and Montgomery, D.G. (1988) 'First mover advantages' *Strategic Management Journal* (vol. 9/5, pp. 41–58).

MacMillan, I. and McGrath. R.G. (1997) 'Discovering new points of differentiation', *Harvard Business Review* (July/Aug, pp. 3–11).

Markides C.C. (2001) 'Strategy as balance: from either–or to and', *Business Strategy Review* (vol. 12/3 pp. l–10).

McGahan, A.M. and Porter, M.E. (1997) 'How much does industry matter, really?', *Strategic Management Journal* (vol. 18/July, pp. 15–30).

Porter, M.E. (1980, 1998) *Competitive Strategy*, Free Press (chapter 14 on vertical strategies).

Schoeffler, S., Buzzell, R.D. and Heany, D.F. (1974) 'Impact of strategic planning on profit performance.' *Harvard Business Review* (March/April, pp. 137–145).

Williamson, O.E. (1981) 'The economics of organization: the transaction cost approach', *American Journal of Sociology* (vol. 87/3, pp. 548–577).

Woo, C.Y.Y. and Cooper, A.C. (1981) 'Strategies of effective low-share businesses', *Strategic Management Journal* (vol. 2, pp 301–318).

Notes

1 Henderson (1984) articulated a cogent account of experience effects based on the work of Boston Consulting Group (see chapter 2). See also: Yelle (1979); Spence (1981); Ghemawat (1985); Alberts (1989); Argote, Beckman and Epple (1990).

2 Barney and Hesterly (2010, chapter 4) and Grant (2010, chapter 9) provide good accounts of the imperatives of cost-based strategies.

3 See for example, Lieberman and Montgomery (1988). Schmalensee (1982) observes that pioneers can secure advantages via product differentiation too.

4 The question of how prospective buyers gauge quality is itself complex. New car buyers rarely understand the finer points of engineering and tend to rely on a combination of features they can see and touch, allied to trusted opinion surveys.

5 Genus (1995) develops the arguments for flexible strategic management in detail.

6 McAfee and McMillan (1996).

7 Teece (1997).

8 It is not intended, therefore, to attempt to articulate all of the insights available to readers of marketing and strategic marketing texts! See for example: Baines, Fill and Page (2008); Jobber (2009); Aaker and McLoughlin (2010); Kotler and Armstrong (2010).

9 Barney and Hesterly (2010, chapter 5) and Grant (2010, chapter 10) provide good accounts of the imperatives of differentiation-based strategies. Woo and Cooper (1981); Dickson and Ginter (1987); MacMillan and McGrath (1997) all offer insights.

10 Mathur (1988).

11 The latter is an example of accidental positional differentiation, the outcome of past Apple strategies that rejected collaborations and conformity with the 'Wintel' hegemony established by Microsoft's Windows software and Intel's microprocessors.

12 Following Porter (1980, 1988).

13 Barney and Hesterly (2010, chapter 5) and Ghemawat (2010, chapter 3) address this question explicitly, as do Hill (1988); Sharp and Dawes (1996); Markides (2001).

14 A differentiation strategy that results in distinctiveness does not deny the possibility for competitors also to be distinctive, provided their basis of differentiation differs from each other.

15 Expressed more conceptually, transaction costs determine the boundaries of the enterprise, a long-standing topic in the study of industrial economics. See: Coase (1937); Williamson (1979; 1981). Supplier switching costs also affect vertical integration (Monteverde and Teece, 1982).

16 http://www.benettongroup.com. See also Baden-Fuller and Pitt (1996, chapter 15).

9

Innovation Strategies

Learning Outcomes

This chapter is designed to enable you to:

① Understand and assess the various stages of the demand lifecycle at industry level.

② Understand and distinguish various innovation strategies.

③ Appreciate the characteristics of technical and non-technical innovation.

④ Understand the derivation and significance of the 'S' curve.

⑤ Understand the different ways in which knowledge is diffused in an enterprise.

CASE STUDY: Dyson plc

James Dyson studied design at the Royal College of Arts. After graduating in 1970 he worked as a designer; four years later he formed Kirk-Dyson Designs Ltd with a partner. Over five years they designed, patented and made innovative, commercially successful products, notably the Ballbarrow (a garden wheelbarrow with a large ball instead of a wheel), the Waterolla (a water-filled hollow garden lawn roller), and the Trolleyball (a dinghy trailer, also with balls not wheels, to stop it sinking in soft sand). By 1979 the firm was selling thousands of units and had taken a third partner.

But according to Dyson, their visions of the company's future diverged, so Dyson quit the company. While a 'house husband' he began to develop a new concept that, 15 years later, turned him into an overnight success. It was the bagless, dual cyclone vacuum cleaner. As with his earlier inventions, the concept emerged from dissatisfaction with existing products. During 10 years of development he made over 5,000 mock-ups and prototypes, creating the design that gained his first patent. Unlike conventional cleaners with dust collection bags that clogged, it retained full efficiency as the collector filled.

He tried to persuade the major companies to apply his product technology under licence. Their attitude seemed to be: 'we're not interested: users are content with current designs', or 'what a good idea: how can we copy it without paying Dyson anything?' Rotork, his former employer, did make a version called the Cyclon, which sold several 100 units until it ceased production. User feedback led to minor modifications. While Dyson continued searching for a major British or US licensee, he licensed a Japanese company in 1985 to make and sell it. Its retail price in Japan was high (equivalent to £1,200): even so, sales were sufficiently strong to reinforce Dyson's belief in his design.

Thus in 1990 he started his own manufacturing company, which launched the DC01 model in the UK in 1993. Brightly coloured, transparent, plastic cases created a unique look. Word-of-mouth confirmation of how well it performed soon created demand, even though retail chains like Currys and Comet were reluctant to stock it because of its unprecedented high price. As sales accelerated, the chains relented, subsequently giving the product ever-increasing floor space.

Dyson built a stylish new factory at Malmesbury in Wiltshire (UK). By 2001 it employed over 2,000 staff, including 300 in research and development. By then Dyson was selling a million vacuum cleaners a year, generating £200 million sales and 15% profit margins. Demand continued to rise, despite far higher retail prices (about £250) than those of than competing cleaners. Sales also expanded internationally. Additional upright and horizontal cylinder-type models joined the product range, with innovations such as high efficiency particulate (HEPA) air filtration, remotely controlled motor-driven brush bars, patented, multi-cyclone designs with greater suction power and digital motors.

Dyson successfully sued Hoover for patent infringement when it introduced a cyclone product. However, Dyson's original patents were nearing the end of their life and several companies including the massive Electrolux Corporation had bag-less, vortex designs ready to launch.

Dyson's subsequent innovative developments (all containing patented design features) have achieved variable commercial success. A robot vacuum cleaner (costing around £2,500) and the Contrarotator™ automatic washing machine (retailing for £900–1,100) were not popular. The Airblade™ washroom hand-dryer and the Air Multiplier™ cooling fan for domestic and office use have, however, fared much better.

Sir James Dyson and his colleagues have clear views about how to run manufacturing businesses. Keeping ahead of potential competition through design leadership and continued innovation is crucial. The company values trust and integrity and promotes these values in its terms and conditions of employment and its extended product warranties.

However, as UK manufacturing skills and capacity have waned, it has become increasingly difficult to find high quality, cost-competitive, domestic suppliers of parts. By the turn of the century, full factory capacity at Malmesbury had been reached. Mindful that patent expiries would intensify the pressure to reduce costs, the company decided to relocate all production to Malaysia and Singapore. However, it retained Malmesbury as its the design and development centre.[1] Over 350 designers and engineers work at Malmesbury and it continues to recruit more as it invests confidently in new research and development projects.

For years Dyson has enjoyed around half of the UK vacuum cleaner market by value. Its products also compete strongly internationally – despite generally much higher prices than competitors. In 2010 sales reached £770 million. Dyson's future vision is to combine profitable manufacturing of leading-edge products with the development and licensing of intellectual property rights.

For further details, see Dyson (1998); http://www.dyson.co.uk.

Questions

1. Dyson's approach to innovation creates radical new designs of established products. Eventually, however, larger competitors catch up by copying out-of-patent design concepts. At what point in this cycle should Dyson quit the market for each product?

2. A conventional desk-top cooling fan costs as little as £20. The Dyson Air Multiplier has a recommended retail price of £200. Despite this huge price differential, the Dyson product is highly successful. What are the strategic implications of this story?

Introduction: Strategies through the Demand Lifecycle

Chapter 3 introduced the demand lifecycle. Here it is helpful to distinguish between (a) the demand lifecycle and (b) the industry sector lifecycle.[2] In general, an industry lifecycle is longer lasting, typically persisting through multiple cycles of demand – the latter each relating to a particular product or technology.

LEARNING OBJECTIVE ①   The four main phases of lifecycle progression are:

1. Emergence.
2. Rapid growth.
3. Maturity.
4. Decline.

Each phase closes with a relatively short transitional period when some competitors merge or quit. These 'shake out' transitions could be treated as discrete phases, though they evolve out of the competitive pressures of each main phase of the cycle.

Though every pattern of demand evolves over time in its own way, in general the pattern is fairly predictable. As competing enterprises respond to observed and predicted demand changes, they adapt their strategies accordingly.[3] In particular, they innovate to produce modified offerings to sustain current demand and they create entirely new offerings to encourage new demand. Changing tastes and expectations interact with sector-led innovations in an evolving, dynamic environment.

Innovation occurs throughout the demand cycle. Innovative enterprises enhance their capabilities; they offer greater value to clients and other stakeholders, enabling them to become increasingly distinctive and dominant, thereby gaining greater long-run positional advantage.

The factors that drive innovation, its timing and impact on future demand are specific to the phase of the cycle and the characteristics of the sector. Although markets and sectors vary, it is possible to make various generalised observations about the most suitable competitive strategies for each phase.[4] These are outlined below. This chapter also examines the innovation-intensive strategies most frequently associated with technological innovation. It concludes with observations on enterprise learning and knowledge management.

Emergent Phase Strategies

In the emergent phase, wholly new products or services emerge. They may be created either by pioneering entrepreneurial, start-up enterprises or by established, innovators with radical new offerings created through ongoing development programmes. Pioneers are by definition 'first-movers', accepting the risks of innovating without no guarantee of ultimate rewards.

Start-up Pioneering Innovation

A start-up enterprise rarely possesses extensive market research to justify its vision. Unhindered by self-doubt, the entrepreneur may nevertheless proceed to innovate, focusing on the concept, not possible threats and difficulties. Often an entrepreneur in this situation may lack a coherent, comprehensive strategy, adequate finance and other critical resources. Technology development is particularly costly, though this difficulty may be mitigated by the entrepreneur's personal knowledge, contacts and willingness to improvise and take calculated risks.

A crucial entrepreneurial skill is the ability, through networking, to identify and mobilise external resources at low cost. For example, technical support may come from a former employer or a university research department; or financial support may come from family members and acquaintances or government agencies. Private investors, so-called 'business angels' may finance developments when they believe there is major profit potential. Yet, of the firms they invest in, typically no more than a third survives over the longer term[5] and only a small proportion of these actually generate the expected returns. Banks and venture capital companies rarely support entrepreneurial start-up ventures: they wait for evidence of activity and positive cash flows sufficient to justify much greater 'second phase' investment.[6]

After the start-up enterprise has completed the initial technical developments, it must refocus on operational needs and capabilities in procurement, manufacturing, packaging, marketing, and distribution. Entrepreneurs may adopt a strategy of collaboration in any or all of these functions, though they may be temperamentally unwilling or unable to work effectively with others – ultimately to their detriment.

Commercial success requires access to distribution channels and also product launches, with as much publicity and endorsement as can be achieved at low cost. Major supermarket and department store chains may offer potential distribution channels, though they are likely to be impatient for evidence of good initial sales. Web-based merchandising and positive word-of-mouth or 'viral' marketing may be a cost-effective way to introduce a new offering. Business-to-business offerings usually require direct sales contacts, for example, via commissioned agents.

Pioneering start-ups

Packaged fruit drinks. Innocent Smoothy pioneered healthy fruit drinks in 1998, initially selling on market stalls. The founders gave up their 'day jobs' when they gained shelf-space in supermarkets. By 2009 the company employed over 250 staff and the giant Coca Cola Corporation had become a minority shareholder, injecting £30 million to accelerate global expansion.

Integrated multi-media services. Founded in autumn 2006, the mission of Iostar Ltd (no connection with the satellite company of the same name) was to operate a multimedia 'one-stop-shop' combining TV, film and theatre production, talent management and brand consultancy services. Its initial strategy was to invite merger with various private companies, by attracting their owners with the promise of mutual synergies and its claimed ability to raise growth capital from multiple sources. Despite endorsement from high-profile board members, its appeal lacked credibility resulting in liquidation in May 2007.

A radical new offering may depend critically on an unproved technology, or on complementary technologies and capabilities, to perform effectively. One weak link can lead to failure. Iostar, for example, needed multiple partners but was unable to attract them. However, when a start-up enterprise has an offering that really does meet a felt need, it defines a new market segment, as the example of Innocent Smoothy demonstrates.

Pioneering Innovation by Established Enterprises

LEARNING OBJECTIVE ①
LEARNING OBJECTIVE ②

The challenges facing start-up pioneers explain why established enterprises are often more effective. These enterprises have the resources to be effective first-movers; they develop a new product or service thoroughly and have the patience not to launch it before they have overcome major shortcomings.[7] Even so, they can fail, as the failure of Sony's Minidisc player/recorder (outlined below) shows.

Pioneering by well-established enterprises

The sticky message note. Well-known for its industrial abrasives and thin film products, 3M Corporation developed a billion-plus dollar new product category, the 'Post-It' note – a simple concept that no-one previously knew they needed.

Digital music downloading services. Apple Computer developed 'iTunes', the first legitimate, commercially successful Web-based service. It was enabled by Apple's size and credibility, its complementary iPod music player and its digital rights management (DRM) software to prevent pirating.

Minidisc player and recorder. In 1992 Sony Corporation launched an innovative magneto-optical disc player/recorder intended to replace the audio compact cassette and compact disc (CD). It offered insufficient benefits over the CD as a medium for pre-recorded music, while recordable CDs, DVDs and later solid state flash drives soon matched its recording capabilities. It turned out to be a solution in search of a consumer problem, though it has survived as a storage solution in niche professional applications.

Emergent Phase Characteristics

The emergent phase is typified by the following characteristics:

- Many new entrants, most of which ultimately fail.

- Poor product or service performance and reliability.

- High selling prices that depress perceived value and consequent sales.

- Development costs that exceed short-term revenues, negative profits and cash flows that are inadequate to fund rapid development.

- Dynamism: rapid changes in specifications, technologies, distribution channels, prices, and demand patterns.

- Competing technology solutions, business models, specifications, and marketing approaches, many of which prove incompatible and non-viable.

- Increasing interest from larger, well-resourced enterprises that may decide to enter once they see the demand potential and the pioneering shortcomings.

Awareness and acceptance of new offerings leading to purchase (known as 'adoption') can be slow. Early adopters tend to be a mix of the wealthy, the curious, and those who feel the need to be 'first-on-the-block' with new gadgets and solutions.

Many competing offerings add critical mass to a product market. Often, however, competing technical specifications, standards, and variable performance levels force buyers to choose between incompatible offerings, creating confusion. Revised or 'second generation' offerings generally offer improved performance and better value, so have better commercial prospects.

RNING ①
ECTIVE

Some early adopters find that they have committed themselves to offerings whose specifications are incompatible with newer and better alternatives. Their most realistic option is to discard the initial purchase in favour of a more capable alternative. This constitutes a disaffecting, costly deterrent for them and other potential adopters. On occasion, the consequence for all suppliers is disastrous because the embryonic demand declines rapidly and disappears.

Rapid-growth Phase Strategies

Transition to the Fast Growth Phase

The transition from emergent to fast growth phase is a critical period during which technology and other standards generally crystallise. Designs and specifications from an effective first-mover tend to establish future market expectations and become the norm or de-facto standard. This transition is also characterised by the entry of large, well-resourced 'early follower' enterprises. They have waited until they are satisfied that demand will persist, despite continuing uncertainties over technical standards and buyer expectations.

LEARNING OBJECTIVE ①

LEARNING OBJECTIVE ②

If a pioneer has an offering that is demonstrably more effective, its sales will benefit considerably. Winners and losers start to emerge as the transition to the fast growth phase occurs. Several factors make the transition more likely to be successful. They include:

- Access to adequate resources and capabilities, including finance for future developments.
- Maintaining the momentum of innovation and capability development.
- Being associated with technology standards and design configurations that seem likely to become the dominant ones.
- Adopting a more disciplined, professional approach.[8]

However, the transition to phase 2 (rapid growth) is a timely period for well-resourced, early-followers to enter the sector by promoting better-performing or, more probably, cheaper offerings. Different technical standards could also enhance product performance or reduce costs, creating a winning offering. Incompatibility with existing standards carries the risk that the alternatives may be rejected, so the early-follower may grudgingly accept what exists despite considering them inferior. Of course, adoption further legitimises their emergence as the 'dominant design' or configuration for the foreseeable future.

Pioneering industry standards

The **Qwerty keyboard** is a standard typewriter keyboard pattern which was adopted by successful early makers, like Remington. Despite many attempts to introduce more ergonomic keyboard layouts, qwerty has never been displaced.

Sony's *Blu-Ray digital optical disc* technology has defeated Toshiba's rival format for high definition video recording and playback. Sony worked tirelessly to persuade electronics manufacturers and Hollywood movie companies to adopt Blu-Ray. It had evidently learned from the defeat of its Betamax video cassette format by JVC's video home system (VHS).

Effective Rapid-growth phase Strategies for Pioneers

A pioneering first-mover that establishes a coherent strategy of continuing innovation and produces greater value for the market is well placed to stay ahead of less organised competitors during the second, rapid-growth phase. This strategy can reward the first-phase pioneer handsomely when it:

- Enhances its design specifications progressively and achieves higher performance levels than competitors can do.

- Allows prospective buyers greater choice or addresses a wider range of applications.

- Commits substantial resources to drive demand growth and to increase its supply capacity in step with demand.

- Achieves significant cost reductions, increasing its perceived value to a wider, more cost-conscious and perhaps less sophisticated clientele.

However, to maintain its lead during the rapid-growth phase the pioneer must meet the practical challenges of strategy implementation as well as continuing technical development. It is important here to avoid major errors of judgement, such as poor matching of output to demand. (Too much capacity is a more costly problem than too little.)

The pioneer must also take steps to defend its intellectual property rights (IPRs) from early-followers who try to appropriate and 'free ride' on this knowledge.

The pioneer could protect scientific and technical knowledge via costly patent applications and copyright registration. An alternative when dealing with external partners and others is to use a legally binding, non-disclosure agreement. Employment contracts can include similar provisions, providing legal protection when well-informed staff quit. Some IPR leakage is inevitable: competitors learn much by dismantling the enterprise's products (a process known as reverse engineering). Aside from taking legal action over patent infringements and unauthorised disclosure breaches, a high level of secrecy over technical specifications, processes and commercial knowledge is desirable. For example, although Microsoft encourages independent software developers to write applications compatible with Windows, it guards the original source code by licensing it only for specific purposes, preventing anyone from modifying the code or developing a competing operating system.

If a pioneer's resources are inadequate for continuing to innovate or expanding its operations, an alternative strategy is to licence its IPRs to better-resourced early-followers. A modest share of prospectively large income can be preferable to a large share of a rapidly diminishing income, as major competitors grind away the pioneer's share of demand.

Effective Rapid-growth Phase Strategies for Early-Followers

Followers refine and develop, rather than pioneer, innovations. By following, they allow the pioneers to fall into financial or technical traps. Followers can then avoid these traps by observing and by attending in great detail to specifications, performance and operations. The claim that rapid-growth phase followers are 'free-riding' on pioneers' innovative efforts has some validity, although early followers can reply that future developments require their much greater resources: to accelerate technical progress, and to invest heavily in manufacturing, marketing and infrastructure capabilities. Moreover, since they will have to license patented IPRs, they reward pioneers while adding to their own costs.

A strategy of early-following is likely to pay off in the rapid-growth phase if the follower:

- Acts decisively as soon as the potential of an innovation has become clear (this makes for prompt, rather than laggardly, following).

- Applies the necessary skills and resources to appropriate or improve on a pioneer's design standards and performance.

- Applies substantial skills and resources in procurement, operations, marketing and distribution to meet demand efficiently and at lower cost.

Early-followers have three main entry options. (1) They can acquire a successful pioneer and invest as necessary to exploit its IPRs more effectively. Technically capable pioneers in financial difficulties make ideal targets. (2) They can license pioneering IPRs and invest in operations to exploit them aggressively. (3) Or they can establish an entirely new business based on their own IPRs, aiming to overtake the pioneers in due course via overwhelming resource deployments. The choice of option depends on circumstances. It has the characteristics of an investment decision (as discussed in Chapter 6) with variables of cost, risk and time scale of expected returns.

Rapid-growth phase innovation strategies of early-followers

Biotechnology diagnostics and therapies: Swiss-based Hoffman La Roche, one of the largest global pharmaceutical corporations, became part owner in 1990 of Genentech, a 1976 US start-up pioneer in the new field of biotechnology research. For years, Genentech had survived on research grants and licence income from pharmaceutical companies. Roche completed a full takeover in 2000, becoming an acknowledged biotechnology leader.

Nuclear energy: EDF (formerly Electricité de France) was for many years the French state electricity generator. It commissioned its first nuclear power station in 1977, almost two decades after the pioneering, state-owned CEA/CEGB (now British Energy). Today, France has one of the highest proportions of nuclear-generated electricity worldwide, while Britain's ageing nuclear stations lags behind. EDF Group is now a quoted public company with international operations. It acquired British Energy in 2009 and is expected to build a new generation of British nuclear plants.

Smartphones with 'push-email': The 1984 Canadian start-up called RIM pioneered real-time e-mail messaging via mobile phone networks with its proprietary *Blackberry* operating software and dedicated handsets. Motorola, Nokia, Samsung and Sony-Ericsson have since tried hard to catch up. In 2007 Google formed the Open Handset Alliance (OHA) to promote *Android*, a competing, open-source mobile phone platform.[9] Nokia allied with *Symbian*. By 2010 Android-based smartphones were outselling Blackberry's, although the latter remained the preferred choice of business users.

By the end of the rapid-growth phase, most of the buyers that can be classed as early adopters will have made initial purchases. Continued growth of demand now depends on attracting a mainstream clientele. High buyer-satisfaction helps to encourage other new buyers and repeat purchasers. The less effective competitors lose market share during this transitional 'shakeout' phase; their profitability declines and so they either they are likely quit or others may acquire them.

Maturity Phase Strategies

With the advent of the maturity phase, the competitive situation tends to stabilise. The suppliers are well established, so changes in market share become smaller. The maturity phase can be short or for persist many years, depending on demand characteristics and whether product innovation continues apace.

Generic Strategy Options

All of the generic strategic options (as discussed Chapter 7) can apply in this phase, so each provider must be clear about what strategy it is adopting and how it secures advantage. A range of market characteristics may be evident at this stage. The market may be characterised by a proliferation of product or product/service 'bundles', resulting in wide variations in product-line profitability, with cross-subsidies to support unprofitable lines needed to offer a complete range. Replacement purchases may grow in importance, accounting for a fast-rising share of demand.

There may also be multiple, low-demand niches. Their more particularised needs can be meet with more sophisticated, higher-priced offerings. Other strategies characteristic of this stage includes:

- Strong brand promotion to symbolise authenticity and reinforce purchase decisions.
- Incremental, 'cosmetic' improvements (as opposed to fundamental innovations).
- Output geared to the expectations of a well-informed mainstream clientele that prioritises functionality and value for money.
- Tight control of production and distribution costs.

The stronger enterprises will at this stage engage in continuous, incremental upgrading to sustain demand. They have less incentive to innovate radically, fearing that new generation offerings would kill existing demand ('cannibalisation') without significantly increasing overall demand. New generation offerings are more costly and hence less profitable until their development costs have been recovered. Consequently, while major mature phase innovations create additional value for buyers, they do not necessarily strengthen the innovators' competitive advantage. So innovation strategies look financially unattractive unless enterprises predict *either* much lower new generation costs *or* sustainable sales volumes despite higher prices, because the offerings deliver greater perceived value.

Rejuvenation Strategies in the Mature Phase

LEARNING OBJECTIVE ①

LEARNING OBJECTIVE ②

Established enterprises *do* sometimes create more radical innovations in the mature phase, stimulated by declining sector position or external pressures such as a potential new entrant or government legislation, requiring different procedures or higher standards. When a new entrant with no commitment to the status quo becomes a serious competitor by implementing a *rejuvenation* strategy, this is likely to prompt the transition to a new demand cycle. Successful rejuvenation extends the mature phase of the lifecycle: it does not lead it into the decline phase.

Rejuvenation strategies in the maturity phase

Transverse-engined, front-wheel drive cars: Prior to the introduction of the Austin Mini by the British Motor Corporation (BMC) in 1959, virtually all mass-produced cars had a longitudinally laid-out engine driving the rear wheels.[10] Less than two decades later the majority of cars had adopted the Mini's compact design configuration. Sadly, unlike its main rivals, BMC failed to benefit from this transition and ultimately ceased to exist.

The cyclone vacuum cleaner: Sir James Dyson's cleaner established a much higher performance benchmark which stimulated a wave of replacement demand. It also forced competitors to improve their existing products and ultimately to offer cyclone cleaners.

The holiday village: From the 1930s, purpose-built seaside villages in the UK and elsewhere in Europe began to meet the mass demand for inexpensive holidays. Butlins established the dominant British model with spartan accommodation, institutionalised catering, regimented daytime games and popular evening entertainment. In 1968, industry newcomer Center Parcs created a new village formula in the Netherlands. The company proceeded to spread right across Europe at seaside and inland forest locations, offering a good standard of self-catering accommodation, on-site restaurants, well-organised (but not regimented) outdoor leisure activities, an indoor swimming pool under a huge glass dome and many sports facilities. This radical new model:

- Made the holiday village a more sophisticated choice.
- Created demand for short-break holidays.
- Made visits a year-round, weather-proof option.

This development forced direct competitors to copy or face exit.

Rejuvenation strategies create turbulence and renew competitive struggle in the mature phase. This is illustrated graphically in Figure 9.1: note in particular the unevenness of the cumulative demand curve. The examples show that established enterprises often lack any incentive or confidence to innovate. They become cautious, risk-averse, probably complacent and vulnerable to radical innovations by others. However, some examples also show that radical innovation is an inappropriate strategy for an enterprise without the resources and capabilities to exploit it properly, clearly failing the test of *organizational appropriability* (Chapter 5).[11] More generally, complacent and less robust providers must either reinvent themselves or decline and ultimately fail or be taken over.

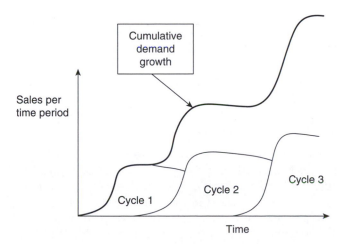

Figure 9.1: Demand-rejuvenating innovation in the mature phase

* e.g. as prompted by product innovations

Decline Phase Strategies

LEARNING
OBJECTIVE ①

When it has become clear that demand has started to decline and there is little prospect of further rejuvenation, the mature phase has ended. Typically this occurs because the need that created the demand no longer exists or is now being met by more attractive or quite different solutions.

The consequence is a further transitional 'shakeout' of the weakest remaining enterprises. In addition, some enterprises choose to exit the market in favour of more attractive demand opportunities elsewhere. The enterprises that remain try to adopt a realistic strategy to compete in the 'end-game'. If they can prolong the residual demand for some considerable time, their continuing presence can be very profitable.

In the decline phase, share of demand remains a critical factor, so acquisition and merger strategies are common. Product ranges narrow, along with intense scrutiny of costs and profit margins. Providing spare parts or service support for a residual clientele committed to use obsolete products becomes particularly profitable, since competition is less aggressive and new entrants unlikely. When the time for a dignified, planned exit finally arrives it may be possible to sell relevant assets, perhaps to a start-up venture in an emerging economy where demand still exists.

In the decline phase, a failing enterprise may fail to realise the severity of its position and struggle on. Faltering cash flows prompt a crisis that needs a different kind of strategy. Managerial pride usually rejects the option of voluntary liquidation by attempting financial restructuring and turnaround. Cost-cutting, redundancies, a transfer of operations to lower-cost locations are just some of the measures taken. Yet, successful turnarounds during this phase are unusual and bankruptcy probably results.

A happier outcome occurs when an enterprise reinvents itself by redefining the nature of the market it serves or how best to serve it. It might merge with another enterprise to access resources and knowledge that it needs but does not have.

Decline phase strategies

Electric typewriters: Remington, IBM and other makers of traditional typewriters quit long ago. They left Brother of Japan with a virtual monopoly of electric typewriters. Though a minor part of Brother's wide product portfolio, there is evidently enough demand under £200 to justify continuing to make them.

Ocean-going travel: The 1880s to the 1930s were the heyday of international travel on huge passenger liners. P&O had a fleet of 500 ships at its peak, plying between Britain, India and the Far East. Cunard operated fewer ships including the prestigious liners Queen Mary and Queen Elizabeth on transatlantic services between Britain and the United States. From the 1950s air travel dramatically reduced journey times, so the shipping companies' share of demand for international travel declined quickly. In 1972 Carnival Cruise Lines (now Carnival Corporation) was a start-up company that offered vacation cruises in the Caribbean and other attractive locations. Over time Carnival acquired and integrated P&O, Cunard and other failing shipping lines. It now has nearly 100 cruise ships and 11 brands that target distinct demand segments. Ironically, the growing vacation cruise market now depends on airlines to ferry vacationers to embarkation ports.

Vacuum tube valves: JJ Electronic in the Slovak Republic began in 1994 to make electronic (thermionic) valves that established companies such as Marconi and RCA considered no longer viable, given the dominance of transistors and integrated circuits. Five years later JJ Electronic began to make complete vacuum tube audio amplifiers, targeting a small and discerning audiophile market willing to pay high prices for top quality products.

Innovation-Intensive Strategies

From a forward-looking, strategic perspective the demand lifecycle concept has shortcomings: lifecycles vary in profile and duration, weakening their predictive use. In some product categories, such as confectionary and tobacco, demand is so persistent that one might question the applicability of lifecycle thinking at all. Conversely, some dynamic markets, such as fashion, manifest such short lifecycles, characterised by unpredictable transitions from old to new preferences, that thinking must be necessarily tactical.

In many other sectors, though, continuing planned innovation is essential. Enterprises that do not appreciate this imperative or fail to develop appropriate resources and capabilities do not survive for long. Innovative sectors manifest a combination of ongoing, incremental innovations punctuated by less frequent, radical transitions, creating discontinuities in enterprise development paths.[12]

ARNING ②
JECTIVE In any dynamic sector, strategies need to take account of the dominant change drivers. Radical innovations, especially in high technology sectors, are frequently best characterised as innovation-driven or 'supply/technology-push' transitions. In these transitions suppliers change the market radically with their innovations, in contrast to generally incremental market/environment-led or 'demand-pull' transitions which are prompted by consumers or industrial users.

Demand-pull and innovation-push transitions

Consider which of the following innovation transitions are 'innovation-push' and which are 'demand-pull'.

Low energy light bulbs: Compact fluorescent bulbs are replacing tungsten filament light bulbs because they save electricity. Light-emitting diode (LED) bulbs use even less electricity, so as their costs fall they will probably displace the fluorescent ones.

Automobile motive power: Better fuel economy has led a shift from petrol to diesel cars. The combined promise of energy saving and the reduction of CO_2 and atmospheric pollution suggests that hybrid, battery-electric, fuel-cell electric, and perhaps hydrogen-powered cars will progressively displace petrol and diesel power.

High definition TV sets: Affordable HDTV sets using liquid crystal display (LCD) technology are being purchased in large numbers for replacement of old TV sets and as second and third sets in the home. Plasma screen technology has increasingly become confined to high-end display panels.

GPS route-mapping services: Dedicated mapping and navigation devices use services that 'piggy-back' on geo-stationary communications satellites, making printed road maps obsolete.

Technological Innovation Strategies

Design, research and development are the core technological capabilities that create enterprise-specific proprietary knowledge and innovative products and associated services. The level of innovation activity is indicated in several ways, one being the level of patent applications that relate to a sector or country (Figure 9.2). Patent applications tend to follow a characteristic curve similar to the lifecycle.

In the early stages of a lifecycle, patent applications relate principally to product design or specification. Few services can be patented, though specific aspects of their delivery performance create proprietary know-how. By the time that product-related patenting activity has peaked, a second wave of applications leads to patents about how a product is made or delivered. Proprietary knowledge of the technological processes that enable manufacture is extremely valuable because

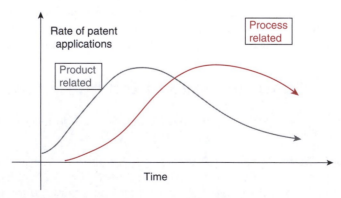

Figure 9.2: Patent applications indicate sector innovation *

* From Utterback (1994)

processes are harder for competing enterprises to observe and copy via reverse engineering. For example, in 1892 Rudolph Diesel obtained the first patent on the internal combustion engine that bears his name. Diesel technology very quickly became popular in large industrial and military engines, but not until the 1930s did it feature in cars, because of the difficulty of making much smaller metal parts with sufficient precision and reliability.

RNING ③
CTIVE
RNING ④
CTIVE
A second indicator of technological innovation activity is the 'S-curve'. This plots how far a technology improves over time, measured by a critical performance parameter. An example – relating to the performance of cathode ray tube (CRT) screens – is given in Figure 9.3. For over 50 years the CRT was a vital component of television sets and computer monitors. Makers of CRTs achieved many improvements in product specifications, notably redesigned electron beam guns, improvements in the glass envelopes and the deposition of light sensitive coatings of luminescent phosphors on the inside surfaces of screens. All these innovations enhanced screen appearance and performance. The performance indicators for CRT screens are summarised in the box below.

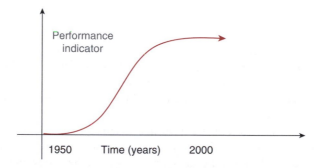

Figure 9.3: S-curve for specific performance aspects of CRT screens

Performance indicators for cathode ray TV screens

- Size (diagonal length) and profile (larger, squarer, flatter and shallower).
- Image brightness and contrast.
- Number of vertical lines (screen resolution).
- Colour accuracy.
- Image refresh rate (for smoother handling of fast motion).
- Life expectancy.

S-curves shed light on service delivery performance. Consider, for example, *airline performance*, in which cost per passenger-mile (after correcting for inflation) is a key performance indicator. Generally, the cost has declined significantly over time. This is illustrated in Figure 9.4. (Note that, to retain the S-curve's characteristic shape, the vertical scale has been inverted, that is,

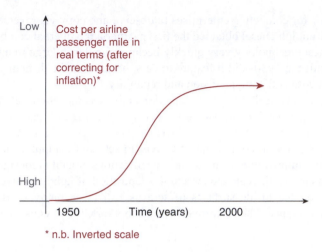

Figure 9.4: Cost performance S-curve of airlines

the higher the measure on the vertical axis, the *lower* the cost.) Many factors have helped to reduce costs: progressively larger and more fuel-efficient aircraft, higher load factors (the average proportion of seats occupied), and more efficient airport logistics.

Aircraft performance is a major influence on airlines' operating costs. Aircraft *size* is a large factor in cost reduction. Size has increased through a number of generations of aircraft; the performance of each conforms to a distinct performance 'S-curve'. The first generation of passenger aircraft operating still in the early 1950s was propeller-driven. It was followed by the first jet-powered passenger aircraft; the second generation of jets from the 1960s; the 'jumbo' generation from the 1970s; and the super-jumbo (A380) from the mid 2000s (Figure 9.5). Each generation may initially show inferior cost-performance compared to its predecessor, owing to the high research and development costs that must be recovered via ticket sales. But as aircraft sales and passenger numbers rise, new generation performance overtakes the old.

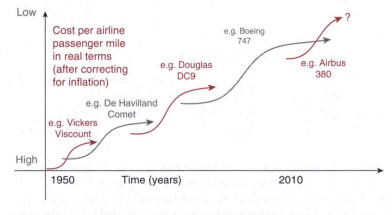

Figure 9.5: Generations of performance s-curves in passenger aircraft

A critical strategic issue is whether and when to begin developing a new generation of a product or service. Expectations in an industry that an S-curve will in due course flatten serve to trigger innovation activity, either to create a next generation device or to explore a totally new direction. For example, evidence that the performance S-curves of magnetic disc (capacity and speed of access) drives is flattening, continually encourages the development of enhanced magnetic technologies but also optical and solid-state data devices.

The logical point to start developing a new generation of technology depends on the expected development time – perhaps a decade or more to develop a new aircraft – and on the availability of complementary technologies (e.g., carbon composites can now replace aluminium and titanium alloys in aircraft wings), as well as predicted demand trends. Uncertainty over future needs, possibilities and time scales is inevitable. Generally, development begins at an intermediate stage of the current S-curve, sooner for first movers than for early followers. Yet technology predictions are often wrong, which makes new investments of high risk.[13]

However, though competing technologies may co-exist, one technology ultimately becomes dominant because it achieves some combination of the following advantages:

- Being first to market, it gains support from a very influential client, cementing it as the de-facto technical standard.
- Performance that is definitively more effective or lower cost.
- Aggressive marketing activity, driving out capable, but less well-resourced competitors.
- More effective exploitation of available complementary technologies or infrastructure.
- Greater long-term development potential.

Factors affecting success and failure of technological innovation

Cost: Pilkington's 'float' glass-making process achieved almost the same undistorted optical quality as flat ground and polished glass sheet, but *at much lower cost*. It chose to license the process, which soon became the standard way to make sheet glass.

Complementary technologies: High-capacity lithium ion battery technology has been the crucial factor enabling a massive increase in demand for portable power tools, despite its severely high cost when compared with older battery technologies.

Complementary infrastructure: Lithium batteries offer similar benefits for electric cars, though cars obviously require much greater energy storage; the cost of batteries has made them commercially unattractive until now. Whilst car batteries can be recharged conveniently at home, a complementary infrastructure of widespread recharging points away from home has yet to be established.

> *Marketing:* Intel Corporation has become the dominant supplier of micro-processors to computer assemblers, largely because it pioneers designs that set performance benchmarks. Further, to head off low-cost emulators, Intel aggressively promotes its brand to end users to make it their undisputed first choice, driving demand from 'black box' computer assemblers.

The impact of competitive, commercial considerations means that what is objectively the 'best' technology does not always prevail. The risks of innovation include:

- Novel technology failing to perform as well as predicted.
- Losing control of intellectual property to a powerful competitor that appropriates the long-term rewards.
- A novel product or service merely 'cannibalizing' sales of established offerings without compensating benefits to the innovator.
- Operating with costs remaining stubbornly high, with unsatisfactory profit margins despite good demand, so that losses mount as sales increase.

An enterprise may seek to counter innovation risks in a number of ways. First, it may pursue multiple technology avenues (in effect, creating a portfolio of technology 'bets') until uncertainty over direction reduces. Second, it may become an early-follower, implementing technology changes only when the direction of innovation is clear (if necessary, by licensing winning technologies rather than trying to develop them). Or, third, it may engage in joint ventures and other kinds of collaboration.

LEARNING OBJECTIVE ③   The most innovative enterprises typically enjoy greatest influence and market share. By pursuing future technologies aggressively, they force competitors to play 'catch up' or quit. Nonetheless, a minor player or a new entrant sometimes introduces a 'game-changing' new technology that eliminates the dominant players' advantage, at least in particular applications.

CASE STUDY: Strategic technological achievements of new entrants

Digital image enhancement: Nik, DXO and Topaz Labs are all relatively young, small enterprises that develop specialised image enhancement software to complement and enhance the performance of Adobe Corporation's market-leading PhotoShop image editing software. Their various specialities have become the 'add-on' software solutions of choice for many professional and advanced amateur photographers.

Laser lithography equipment: Founded in 1984, Heidelberg Instruments in Germany is a privately-owned supplier of this highly specialised industrial equipment to microchip producers and research institutes. It has proved ideal for making low-volume, application-specific integrated circuits, because it avoids costly photo-mask development. ASML of the Netherlands, another start-up enterprise, supplies similar equipment.

Question

1. What strategies did these small, start-up enterprises adopt in order to survive in markets featuring multinational corporations?

Non-technical Innovation

The foregoing account emphasises the role of technological innovation. Many sectors are to be found in this category: engineering, electronics, communications, computing and software, pharmaceuticals, biotechnology and medical practice, for example. One might assume that innovation matters only in high-tech sectors. However, this would be incorrect: innovation is a feature of many sectors not generally considered 'high tech'. As elsewhere, enterprises invent, innovate and change to avoid being displaced by competitors with new products or services with desirable new user benefits, hence greater value. Such sectors include professional design, research and consultancy activities in universities, not-for-profit institutes and private practice, the creative arts, fashion, media and broadcasting.

Innovation in 'low-technology' sectors

Media and book publishing: The transition to online delivery of factual content is under way, but has considerably more future potential.

Building and construction: Pre-fabricated building systems; new kinds of fixings and fastenings to increase productivity on site.

Eyesight testing and spectacle dispensing: The emergence and rapid growth of added-value, branded optical services underpinned by transnational franchising enterprises such as Specsavers and Vision Express.

The Impact of Innovation on Innovator Capabilities and Client Relationships

Aggressive, unrelenting, innovation-driven competition creates tension. Streams of innovations may provide buyers with ever-increasing benefits, yet competing enterprises find they have to work ever-harder to stand still. Expending energy to little benefit is absurd, yet not to do so risks being left behind by competitors.[14]

LEARNING OBJECTIVE ④
An innovation impacts *both* the innovator's capabilities and client relationships. *Incremental* innovations reinforce and enhance capabilities. They sustain a smooth evolutionary path that in effect defines and tracks the performance S-curve. A *radical* innovation, in contrast, generally disrupts current capabilities, even making them obsolete. It creates a break or discontinuity in its evolutionary path, setting it on a new performance S-curve.

As indicated in Figure 9.5, Boeing's evolutionary path since 1950 has tracked the sequence of performance S-curves very effectively, while the paths of competitors such as Vickers have not. (Vickers no longer makes aircraft.) However, Boeing's reluctance to pursue the superjumbo trajectory represents a crucial strategic decision it could ultimately regret.

LEARNING OBJECTIVE ④
Innovation also impacts the innovator's relationships with its clienteles. When an innovation cements and reinforces these relationships they maintain the status quo – to their mutual benefit. When it disrupts or even destroys existing relationships it is problematic, because new relationships take time to develop.

In summary, we can map four domains of strategic innovation, as shown in Figure 9.6. *Regular* innovation makes steady progress; it conserves and deepens capabilities and relationships. For example, washing machines that function at room temperature present no real challenges for manufacturers or consumers, although they require new detergents, a complementary, regular innovation from other companies. The innovation is insufficient to justify new purchases; nor does it create a *new demand niche*, as supermarkets that open 24/7 (all hours and days of the week) have done, attracting 'night owls' who find daytime shopping inconvenient. A new demand niche may require some changes to relationship management, but it presents only minor challenges to operational routines.

Revolutionary innovation impacts know-how and capabilities. Thus, battery-powered electric cars present significant challenges to car makers. The technology will marginalise decades of accumulated design and manufacturing knowledge. Yet, for car users, electric cars work in quite familiar ways and so the practical impact is minimal and mostly positive: easy plug-in 'refuelling' and probably lower fuel costs.

Finally, so-called *architectural* innovations are the truly world-changing developments that occur infrequently but have dramatic impacts. They overturn the status quo and create challenges for suppliers and clienteles alike. For example, low cost, 'bus stop' air travel makes huge demands on the efficiency of services provided by airlines and airport operators. British Airways failed to compete with new entrants like easyJet via its subsidiary Go, which easyJet later acquired. But providing such a service also affects airlines' relationships with consumers and business users, many of whose attitudes and approaches to air travel have changed (coming to treat air travel more like catching a train than boarding a cruise liner).

Overall, innovators need to anticipate the nature of the changes and their consequences. Regular innovations may seem attractive and low risk, but they are easy to copy, quickly reducing the innovator's rewards. Niche-creating innovations enable diversification into related domains; failure to exploit niche opportunities allows competitive leapfrogging. Innovations with a major impact on external relationships are more challenging, particularly when more disruptive to the innovator than its clientele. Architectural innovations mean radical, unpredictable change; there will be no going back – the world changes and there will be winners and losers.

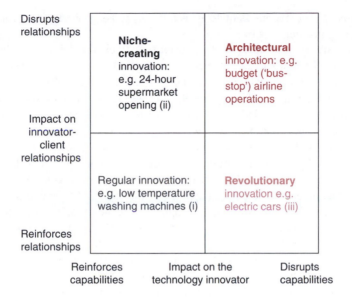

Figure 9.6: Forms of innovation

Based on a framework proposed by Clark (1987). See text for explanation.

To summarise, enterprises that over the long term pursue successful innovation strategies:

- Are very aware of the capabilities of direct competitors and engage in comparative 'bench-marking' against other high-performing organisations.

- Are driven to expand and exploit their knowledge bases – to continue learning and upgrading performance.

- Implement regular, systematic reorganisation of their operational processes (e.g., 'business process re-engineering'; 'lean production').

- Organise in ways that encourage diversity (or – to use a common phrase – 'requisite variety') of thinking,[15] idea championing and internal entrepreneurship (or 'intrapreneurship').

Innovative Learning Cycles

Innovation strategies aim to extend knowledge and core capabilities. Proactive knowledge enhancement is a consequence of innovation activities and an enabler of future innovation. Treating innovation as learning-in-action is conceptually attractive, but knowledge creation is difficult to manage progressively. While innovative enterprises try to progress in deliberate steps, transformational developments occur in ways that cannot be fully predicted. They are sometimes the product of curiosity and unplanned experimentation without prior executive approval. Nonetheless, an integral part of strategic management is to systematically harness innovation activities and direct how emergent knowledge is diffused and exploited, giving rise to the concept of the 'learning organisation'.

LEARNING
OBJECTIVE ⑤ If enterprises are to learn, a key strategic priority is to ensure that knowledge progresses to where it is beneficial. Like money, it is useless when static. Two distinct, processes of circulation appear to work concurrently, one is structured and formal, the other informal and circumstantial.

The two modes are illustrated in Figures 9.7 and 9.8. Knowledge exists in two forms: codified (written down) and uncodified (tacit, often unspoken). Technical knowledge is generally codified in handbooks, specification sheets, web pages, etc. when it is generated; it is the obvious way to spread or diffuse it. By contrast, much operational knowledge (including the conduct of research!) is embedded in enterprise routines, collective ethos and personal skills. This uncodified knowledge diffuses when people meet in formal settings such as scheduled meetings and during informal encounters at the coffee machine, in the staff cafeteria and after work. As this tacit knowledge is articulated and managers recognise its value, it may be codified.

LEARNING
OBJECTIVE ⑤ The figures define a 'knowledge space' using the axes of (degree of) codification and (degree of) diffusion. Enterprise learning requires knowledge to circulate in this space. The strategic challenge is to harness the positive benefits of both modes, while ensuring as far as practicable that when proprietary knowledge circulates internally, it does not also diffuse externally.

Figure 9.7 portrays the formal and structured mode of knowledge circulation. This proactive, 'generative' process characterises programmes of research and development, and deliberate operational improvements. Managerial procedures supported by modern knowledge management systems aim to enable it.[16] The informal and adaptive mode (Figure 9.8) is much less amenable to being managed, because it depends on informal staff interactions in the course of their duties. The best that can be done is to encourage an ethos of exchanging, exploring and acting on good ideas.[17]

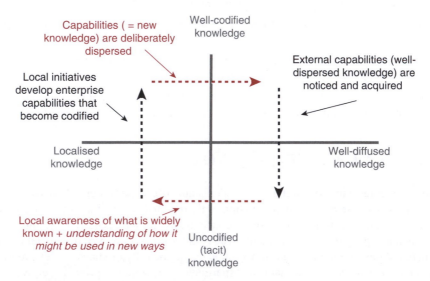

Figure 9.7: The formal or generative learning cycle

Figure 9.8: The informal or adaptive learning cycle

In practice, enterprises learn only with difficulty; dysfunctional learning behaviours include:

- Responding to new knowledge (stimuli) unreflectively: first order or 'single loop' learning, as opposed to the more desirable, second order, so-called 'double loop' or 'deutero' learning.[18]

- A 'stickiness' that prevents new knowledge diffusing around an enterprise, due to internal communication barriers, knowledge possessiveness by individuals and teams, and inadequate incentives to share.

- A collective tendency to 'forget' knowledge for which there is no immediate application, especially when the knowledge originators quit the enterprise.

CASE STUDY: Koningklijke (Royal) Philips Electronics NV and the 'Ambilight' innovation

Philips describes itself as a 'diversified health and well-being company, focused on improving people's lives through timely innovations'. It is a Netherlands-based multinational corporation that operates in more than 60 countries. In 2009 it reported sales of €23,189 million and net profits before tax of €448 million,[19] employed 107,000 permanent staff: 56% in production, 11% in research and development and 33% in sales, marketing and other administration.

Once an unfocused conglomerate making almost everything electrical, Philips has reorganized, focusing on three key domains: healthcare, lifestyle, and lighting products, contributing, respectively, 34%, 37% and 29% of sales and 34,000, 18,000 and 51,000 staff.[20] Philips is a market leader in medical equipment for body scanning, cardiac, acute and home healthcare; in energy-efficient lighting solutions; and in lifestyle products, notably flat-panel televisions, audio-visual entertainment and personal care products. To date it has registered 48,000 patents; 35,000 trademarks; 56,000 design rights; and 3,100 domain names. In 2009 it invested €1,631 million in research and development (7% of sales, more than in 2008). It encourages 'open innovation' that 'leverages the joint innovative power of partnering companies and researchers to bring more innovations to the market effectively and faster.'

Philips combined curiosity-driven and planned innovation to create the unique television development it calls Ambilight: LED light arrays along the vertical edges of the flat panels and on some models along top and bottom edges too.[21] When activated, Ambilight creates a light halo beyond the TV. It can be a single, static colour or continuously changing colours that correspond with colours on the screen. It does *not* mimic flashing disco lights; rather it provides 'surround colour' lighting analogous to 'surround sound.' Claims supported by numerous research studies in Philips and by external agencies are that it:

- Moderates high screen contrast, producing a more relaxing viewing experience.
- Creates the illusion of a larger screen.

Ambilight originated with a joint project into 'Ambient Intelligence' by Philips Research and Lighting divisions. Researchers sought ways that lighting could enhance everyday environments. A contributor to a brainstorming session suggested using light to enhance TV viewing in a darkened room. The idea stimulated such interest that Ambilight moved from concept through development to commercial reality in only 18 months. Although Philips had considerable knowledge of LEDs, Ambilight required sophisticated digital software to sample and integrate the screen information that drives the LED arrays. Consumers participated in the development process by viewing prototypes and joint focus group discussions.

In the three years following launch, Philips sold well over a million Ambilight-equipped televisions. It has since expanded the concept into amBX, a multi-sensory experience that combines light, sound, vibration, air movement and other effects, creating an immersive video-gaming experience, filling the entire environment with physical sensation.

Questions

1. Fit the Ambilight innovation into the framework of Figure 9.6. To what extent does this help to explain its success?

2. Consider another Philips' innovation, the Lumea IPL (intense pulsed light) method of unwanted hair removal. Philips launched Lumea after six years of clinical studies and trials. It retails for £400, at least ten times the price of other popular methods of depilation.[22] How consistent is this product with Philip's declared mission? Rehearse the arguments one would use to champion its commercial development. Then rehearse the counter-arguments. Which do you find more persuasive and why?

Summary

- During transitions between the four key phases of the demand lifecycle, some enterprises quit voluntarily or are 'shaken out' because they fail to perform effectively. Emergent-phase strategies are pioneering: entrepreneurial, bold and risky. Leaders are usually start-up enterprises or established, innovative ones.

- Progress depends on successful first-mover strategies, although successful early followers may also enter during the transition to the rapid-growth phase. In this second phase, offerings become more standardised and reliable. Over time, enterprises establish better levels of performance and generate rising demand.

- Winning strategies for the long run become apparent. Losing strategies take their toll on weaker enterprises in the transition to the maturity phase; some quit, others may be acquired for their assets and knowledge. The maturity phase generally lasts longest, exhibiting sophisticated segmentation, product proliferation and a multiplicity of competitive strategies. Cycles of rejuvenation can occur; they create enhanced offerings and sometimes radically alter the business models needed to succeed, extending the maturity phase for a long time.

- Ultimately, however, the transition to the decline phase occurs. Yet more enterprises quit although, paradoxically, for the few survivors this phase may persist and be very profitable, even encouraging the occasional new entrant. However, the lifecycle concept in action is easier to recognise in retrospect than in real time. Thus it should be treated with caution in deciding and amending strategies; it should not be considered deterministic or inevitable.

- The chapter also considers innovation-intensive strategies, particularly though not exclusively associated with technological innovation. Further concepts and frameworks are introduced, together with their implications for strategic management.

- Harnessing innovation activities and directing how emergent knowledge is diffused and exploited is an integral part of strategic management. Two distinct processes of circulation appear to work concurrently, one formal and manageable, the other informal and circumstantial.

LEARNING OUTCOME ①
LEARNING OUTCOME ①
LEARNING OUTCOME ①
LEARNING OUTCOME ①
LEARNING OUTCOME ②
LEARNING OUTCOME ③
LEARNING OUTCOME ④
LEARNING OUTCOME ⑤

Exercises for Further Study and Discussion

1. Explore the practical implications for the conduct of strategic management of the statement that 'Like money, knowledge is useless when it is static.'
2. Magazine publishing is an industry sector that thrives on product innovation. A publisher launches a new title linked to a novel or topical theme or interest, invariably to be followed by imitative titles from other publishers. In this sector how likely are the first-movers or (early) followers to extract the highest returns? What lessons, if any, apply more generally?
3. What factors will constrain the growth potential of Dyson and Center Parcs now that they are well-established enterprises in their respective sectors? How appropriately are their strategies responding to these constraints?
4. Which key performance variables are manufacturers of LED flat screens likely to use for monitoring S-curve progression?
5. What do you think were the key issues for Pilkington to consider before it decided to licence its float technology to other glass makers?
6. 'Low technology' sectors have innovated typically by adopting new technological solutions from innovators elsewhere. In markets such as eyesight testing, how far can small, independent providers adopt the same technologies to compete with the national chains? How can they compete more effectively in other ways?

Suggestions for Further Reading

Anderson, P. and Tushman, M.L. (1990) 'Technological discontinuities and dominant designs: a cyclical model of technological change', *Administrative Science Quarterly* (vol. 35, pp. 604–633).

Audia, P. and Rider, C. (2005) 'A garage and an idea: what more does an entrepreneur need?', *California Management Review* (vol. 40/1, pp. 6–28).

Blackler, F. Crump, N. and McDonald, S. (1999) 'Organizational learning and organizational forgetting: lessons from a high technology company', in Araujo, L., Burgoyne, J. and Easterby-Smith, M. (eds) *Organizational Learning and the Learning Organization*, Sage.

Calori, R. (1990) 'Effective strategies in emerging industries', in Loveridge, R. and Pitt, M. (eds) *Strategic Management of Technological Innovation*, Wiley.

Chesbrough, H. (2002) 'Making sense of corporate venture capital', *Harvard Business Review* (vol. 80/3, pp. 4–11).

Christensen, C.M. and Overdorf, M. (2000) 'Meeting the challenge of disruptive change', *Harvard Business Review* (vol. 78, Mar/Apr, pp. 66–76).

Flynn, D. and Forman, A. (2001) 'Life cycles of new venture organizations: different factors affecting performance', *Journal of Developmental Entrepreneurship* (vol. 6/1, pp. 41–58).

Foster, R.N. (1986) *Innovation: the Attacker's Advantage*, Macmillan (chapter 6).

Henderson, R.M. and Clark, K.B. (1990) 'Architectural innovation: the reconfiguration of existing systems and the failure of established firms', *Administrative Science Quarterly* (vol. 35, pp. 9–30).

Kerin, R., Varadarajan, P. and Peterson, R. (1992) 'First mover advantage: a synthesis, conceptual framework and research propositions', *Journal of Marketing* (vol. 56/4, pp. 33–52).

Levitt (1965) 'Exploit the product lifecycle', *Harvard Business Review* (Nov/Dec, pp. 81–94).

Lieberman, M.B. and Montgomery, D.G. (1988) 'First mover advantages' *Strategic Management Journal* (vol. 9/5, pp. 41–58).

Markides, C. (1998) 'Strategic innovation in established companies', *Sloan Management Review* (vol. 39/3, pp. 31–42).

McGee, J., Thomas, H. and Wilson, D. (2005) *Strategy: Analysis and Practice,* McGraw-Hill (chapter 8).

Nonaka, I. and Takeuchi, H. (1995) *The Knowledge-Creating Company.* Oxford University Press (chapter 3).

Pitt, M. and Clarke, K. (1999) 'Competing on competence: a knowledge perspective on the management of strategic innovation', *Technology Analysis and Strategic Management* (vol. 11/3, pp. 301–316).

Pitt, M. and MacVaugh, J. (2008) 'Knowledge management for new product development', *Journal of Knowledge Management* (vol. 12/4, pp. 101–116).

Porter, M.E. (1980, 1988) *Competitive Strategy,* Free Press (part 2, esp. chapter 8).

Sood, A. and Tellis, G. (2005) 'Technological evolution and radical innovation', *Journal of Marketing* (vol. 69/3, pp. 152–168).

Suarez, F. and Lanzolla, G. (2005) 'The half-truth of first-mover advantage', *Harvard Business Review* (vol. 83/4, pp. 121–127).

Teece, D.J. (1987) 'Profiting from technological innovation', in Teece, D.J. (ed.) *The Competitive Challenge: Strategies for Industrial Innovation and Renewal*, Ballinger.

Zhang, Q., Lim, J.-S. and Cao, M. (2004) 'Innovation-driven learning in new product development: a conceptual model', *Industrial Management and Data Systems* (vol. 104/3, pp. 252–261).

Notes

1 http://www.growingbusiness.co.uk/dyson-martin-mccourt.html
2 The classic articles by Levitt (1965) and by Day (1981) examine the lifecycle principally from the perspective of product/marketing strategy while Klepper and Grady (1990) and McGee and Thomas (1994) look at lifecycle evolution from a supply-side perspective. Further complication arises with references to technology lifecycles, which may link to products or production processes.
3 An interesting question is whether particular patterns of strategy (configurations) are most effective at each phase of the lifecycle. See Lawless (2001).
4 Much has been written about innovation and how to manage it. Some useful monographs are: Twiss and Goodrich (1989); Martin (1994); Bessant and Tidd (2007). For collections of classic readings, see

Roberts (1987) from Sloan Management Review; also Loveridge and Pitt (1990) and Tushman and Anderson (1997).

5 Flynn and Forman (2001).

6 Chesbrough (2002).

7 See Lieberman and Montgomery (1988); Kerin, Varadarajan and Peterson (1992); Suarez and Lanzolla (2005) for first-mover advantages. See Markides (1998) for an account of how established enterprises innovate.

8 Greiner (1972) is a classic account of observed and necessary changes over time.

9 Google itself was not the pioneer, acquiring Android Inc., a small start-up company, in 2005.

10 The Citroen Traction Avant of the 1930s was a notable pioneer in its native France.

11 Appropriability is a complex topic. See chapter 3 and Teece (1987; 2000). A crucial aspect is of appropriability is the capacity to absorb new ideas and technologies: Cohen and Levinthal (1990); Stock, Greis and Fischer (2001).

12 Anderson and Tushman (1990).

13 Contrast the predictions of Airbus and Boeing to justify building the very different A380 and 'Dreamliner' 777 aircraft.

14 So-called 'red queen' competition after the Red Queen in the children's fantasy novel, *Alice Through the Looking Glass* by Lewis Carroll, in which Alice had to run harder and harder to stay on the same square of the chessboard. See chapter 5 and Barnett and Pontikes (2005).

15 Also called requisite variety – a complex world requires complex patterns of thought (Ashby, 1958).

16 Pitt and MacVaugh (2008).

17 Nonaka and Takeuchi (1995), esp. chapter 3.

18 Single-loop learning might be called 'knee-jerk' reactions to a stimulus. Double-loop learning equates to well considered responses (see Argyris and Schön, 1978); Deutero learning (learning to learn) is attributed to Bateson (see Visser, 2003).

19 Like many other corporations its results suffered from global recession after 2007 when it reported sales of €26,793 million and profits before tax of €4,716 million.

20 While sales of healthcare products had continued to grow since 2007, those of lighting fell back in 2009, while sales of lifestyle products declined by over a third since the 2007 peak.

21 Refer to Password Philips Research technology magazine, issue 31/February 2008, available at http://www.research.philips.com/password/download/password_31.pdf

22 See: http://www.philips.co.uk/c/hair-removal/21104/cat/#

10

Diversification Strategies in the Multi-activity Enterprise

Learning Outcomes

This chapter is designed to enable you to:

① Explain the differences between corporate and business-level strategies and the responsibilities of executives at these levels.

② Describe and critique diversification motives, strategies and performance outcomes.

③ Understand and apply relevant analytic frameworks to evaluate corporate portfolios.

CASE STUDY: Diversification in agriculture

Farming is a way of life, but it is a business activity too. Despite the presence of large corporations with an industrial-scale approach to farming, most farms world-wide are owned by families and local co-operatives. Keeping a small farm viable down the generations remains a family priority for many, yet it can be difficult to earn a living from a single farming activity, whether livestock, dairy, grain, fruit or vegetable production. American and European supermarket chains increasingly dominate retail distribution, making the supply of farm produce extremely price-sensitive. Some farmers respond by converting to organic production, hoping to sustain higher selling prices with less competition and better profits. This can be a successful strategy, but because organic yields are typically lower, the revenue potential per hectare of land is not necessarily higher, while consumer demand may decline in recessionary times.

Many family farms have adopted an alternative strategy, that of comple-menting core activities with some form of diversification. According to research commissioned by the Department for Environment, Food and Rural Affairs (DEFRA)[1] for tax year 2007/8, almost 80% of the English farms that were questioned claimed some income from non-core activities. Net income (in effect, the owner's or tenant's salary) averaged £48,000, of which 14.5% was from diversified activities.

Farm diversification takes three main forms: unusual livestock and crops; 'forward integration'; and alternative use of farm assets.

- *Unusual livestock and crops* include llama, bison, butterflies, fish and waterfowl. Unusual crops range from vines and plant seeds to willow and miscanthus for fuels (biomass).

- *Forward integration* aims to capture a greater share of the value-added available from farm output. It can include retailing farm produce (at farm shops, farmers' markets and on-line) and creating added-value products from farm output (e.g., processed meat; wine and juices, oils).

- *Alternative use of farm assets* such as farm buildings and land may generate income in ways that are somewhat or largely unrelated to core farming activities. Examples include breeding programmes for traditional and rare breeds, tourism (accommodation, camping, visitor centres), nurseries and garden centres, conversion of farm wastes into composts and methane, wind-powered electricity generation, activity centres (e.g., hiking, paintballing), and music festivals.

Examples

Marshfield Farm in Wiltshire, England and Linalla Farm in County Clare, Ireland are family-run dairy farms that have diversified into ice-cream manufacture, using milk from their own herds. Both now have national or regional wholesale distribution in their respective countries. Testimonials suggest they are making excellent products, but building these businesses has created many challenges.[2] Progress can be painstakingly slow for enterprises whose proprietors have strong environmental consciences. Thus, while Marshfield's owners prefer to sell entirely organic products they are constrained because they cannot get all the necessary organic ingredients, such as flavourings, at a viable cost.

Key issues in farm diversification are (a) to obtain finance for what are often medium-to-long term projects and (b) scalability. When a project requires significant investment in production capacity (e.g., land), a farmer needs confidence that the capacity acquired can be fully and consistently utilised.

Tasks and discussion questions

1. If these ice-cream businesses demonstrate sufficient potential, should their owners divert all of their milk output into ice cream production and buy milk from other farms if necessary? (The population of Ireland, North and South, is 6 million, Great Britain 60 million).

2. Should these farms diversify further or stick to milk and ice cream? What are the arguments for and against each option?

Introduction: the Concept of Diversification

Most enterprises start in a single activity domain, with a single product or service to meet a singular demand. As they become established, many keep a narrow focus, but some progressively extend their coverage in terms of offerings, served markets, activities and capabilities.

An enterprise that extends in any of these ways is following a diversification strategy. Each form of diversification has consequences for performance and managerial control. Enterprises generally approach diversification deliberately: to grow without arbitrary limits and (as they see it) to reduce the risks of narrow focus.[3] Others lack a 'grand plan' and make opportunistic moves in new directions. Entering each new arena experimentally, they retain a presence when entry proves successful, and quit when it does not. Although diversification is often equated with multinational corporations, economic pressures can create a felt need to diversify even in small enterprises.

Diversification and Corporate Strategy

As enterprise diversity increases, the managerial challenges grow. At the corporate centre of large, multi-activity enterprises senior executive roles and responsibilities encompass, but do not focus solely on, diversification. They influence the cohesion of diverse activities and operating units via the corporate policies, procedures and managerial styles that they develop. The core challenge of corporate strategy is to plan, co-ordinate and control a greater variety of activities according to an overall strategic 'dominant logic' and purpose.[4]

Corporate-level Strategic Management

Single-activity units in the diversified enterprise are called strategic business units or SBUs. The set of business units creates the corporate portfolio.[5] One would expect each SBU to have a distinct mission, otherwise there would be no reason to separate it from other SBUs.

At the corporate level, executives make periodic decisions about whether the portfolio is correctly designed or whether some SBUs would be more effective if combined, split or even divested. Over time each SBU may also identify diversification opportunities, requiring corporate decisions about whether to combine existing and proposed activities or to establish the latter as distinct SBUs. Corporate executives may also identify attractive, new activity areas, in which case they must decide whether to start new SBUs, or to enlarge the portfolio via acquisitions or mergers.

Executives are not always adept at these kinds of decision. They may lack adequate knowledge and expertise, suffer from inertia or internal disagreements and conflicts of interest. Moreover, the chief executives of successful SBUs have considerable power and may behave akin to medieval barons or clan chiefs, resisting any loss of corporate influence or current responsibilities. All these issues must be resolved at corporate level in the greater interest of the multi-activity enterprise.

Corporate-level and business-level strategies are interdependent, but distinct. Excepting new ventures, SBUs' current and anticipated activity domains are established. Each SBU is managed according to its business-level strategy, periodic reviews of which involve corporate-level and business-level executives who address challenging questions such as:

- What is this SBU's mission, vision and objectives? Are its domain boundaries well defined and appropriate for the future?
- Does it have adequate resources and skills to achieve its mission?
- What are its distinctive capabilities and how do they sustain value-creation and competitive advantage in its activity domain?
- Is its performance as good as it could be? How can it be improved?

Appropriate and insightful answers sustain SBU performance; thus they underpin the corporate strategy.

While successful implementation of corporate strategy requires each SBU to perform effectively, corporate strategy also requires coherent answers to many questions that cannot be fully addressed at SBU level:

- How, within a collectivity of units, does each SBU create value *for the corporate enterprise* and its stakeholders. Will this hold true in the future? If not, what should be done?
- How can corporate executives organise and manage relationships among SBUs so that their portfolio presence enables them to achieve more than if they were independent entities – achieving *synergies* (mutually beneficial interdependencies)?
- What minimum policies are needed to co-ordinate and control disparate SBU activities?
- What is the *corporate-level* mission, vision and objectives? Are these definitions appropriate for the future?
- How much diversity in the portfolio does the corporate mission dictate?
- What new activity domains, if any, should the corporate enterprise enter? What domains, if any, should it quit (with possible implications for existing SBUs)?
- As an *integrated, corporate enterprise*, what, if any, are its distinctive capabilities and how do they create value for *all* stakeholders?

Establishing the mission, vision and objectives of the multi-activity, corporate enterprise is analogous with SBU-level strategy. Its greater complexity and diversity makes the task remarkably difficult. Yet until a clear understanding of the issues exists, no other questions about corporate strategy can lead to realistic answers.

Corporate value creation is linked to the strategies and performance of individual SBUs in the corporate portfolio. So corporate strategy must be concerned with the quality of SBU competitive strategies. Yet the corporate-level value-creation task is to *harmonise and consolidate* individual SBU strategies into a coherent, synergistic, overall strategy. This focuses attention on the relationships among SBUs, whether and how they create synergies.

A further challenge for integrated corporate enterprises is identifying and dealing with competitors. Since a corporate enterprise is a portfolio of assets and activities from which investors expect good financial returns; corporate executives are obliged to demonstrate credible,

LEARNING OBJECTIVE ①

LEARNING OBJECTIVE ①

well-integrated strategies that deliver returns at least as good as other, diversified enterprises with which investors choose to make comparisons. A well-diversified corporate enterprise may have a unique mission and portfolio, so that direct comparisons with superficially similar enterprises mislead because their portfolios do not match. Since large, diversified enterprises are likely to organise into divisions (clusters of comparatively similar and synergistic SBUs), comparisons may be more insightful at divisional level. Yet ethos and corporate structures may differ markedly, devaluing the reliability of such comparisons.

Motives behind Diversification

There are two broad motives for diversification: pursuit of ambition and defence against vulnerability.[6] Ambition-based motives are typically to:

- Increase the scale and scope of the enterprise to sustain higher value (increased revenues, profits and corporate net worth) in response to stakeholder pressures.
- Exploit strategic assets (e.g., global brands) and distinctive capabilities (e.g., technologies and administrative processes) more widely, by applying them to attractive new domains.
- Develop new capabilities by responding to new challenges.
- Satisfy senior executive ambitions for growth and power.

Defensive motives include the need to:

- Respond to actual or predicted decline in demand for current offerings.
- Reduce dependence on a narrow range of offerings or activity domains.
- Gain greater strategic control of major parts of the supply chain that others currently use to disadvantage the enterprise.

Shareholders expect for-profit business corporations to achieve ever-rising revenues and profits, almost as an article of faith. Senior executives are generally ambitious shareholders themselves, so their instinct is to pursue realistic new opportunities. Scope extension is attractive when revenue growth is constrained by weak demand or strong competition in current sectors, provided that the enterprise has, or can acquire, necessary resources and distinctive capabilities. It is generally feasible for financially resourceful enterprises to acquire the capabilities they presently lack.

Defence-motivated diversification can bring several advantages. The diversity of a *balanced* portfolio reduces the variability of corporate revenues and profits resulting from demand fluctuations in each sector and during each economic cycle. Diversification through vertical integration increases control of value-adding activities performed by others whose abilities, commitment or motives are suspect. It also increases the enterprise's revenue and profit potential.

The aggressive promotion of multiple stakeholder interests encourages diversification decisions to meet differing expectations.[7] This is also true in the not-for-profit sector: services experience pressures from many directions to extend the scale and scope of their activities. In healthcare, for example, politicians, equipment suppliers, insurance companies, innovative clinicians, general practitioners and patients all encourage providers to venture into new clinical areas as new knowledge and technologies become available. Over many years, national governments have pressured local governments to extend the scope of provision of public amenities, waste recycling, and social and leisure services. Charities, particularly 'branded' international charities such as Oxfam, have broadened their scope. Military services persist in conventional warfare but have diversified into counter-terrorist activities. The personal ambitions of leaders cannot be discounted in any of these very different spheres.

Mechanisms for Achieving Diversification

Ambitious executives will, if acting rationally, seek growth in current activities before embarking on a corporate strategy of diversification. If growth options are severely limited, new activity domains must be evaluated. However, when the motive is primarily defensive, executives must weigh the risks of worsening rather than improving a vulnerable position.

 Three basic mechanisms support diversification:

1. Self-reliant ('organic') development, whereby the enterprise applies and extends its current resource base and capabilities.
2. Merger with, or acquisition of, an enterprise already operating in the target domain.
3. Entering a collaborative alliance with another enterprise with some combination of relevant and complementary positions, resources and capabilities.

Chapter 11 discusses the benefits and drawbacks of each mechanism.

Classification of Diversification Strategies

The Product/Market Diversification Matrix

Figure 10.1 depicts an often-cited account of corporate diversification strategies. This distinguishes current from new offerings and current from new activity domains and demand segments.[8] Diversification initiatives generally start when the enterprise is in the upper left quadrant. What constitutes a single product category and a single activity domain may be open to particular interpretations. Note also that in this context 'new' means new-to-the-enterprise, not new-to-the-world.

Some strategists claim that diversification must involve novelty for the enterprise in both its offerings and market/activity domains – the lower right quadrant in Figure 10.1. Many executives are more conservative: they see *any* shift as diversification, including more innovative offerings to an existing clientele or entering unfamiliar domains with established offerings.

The arrows in Figure 10.1 suggest transitions between quadrants. The bold lines indicate generally preferred moves, while dotted lines indicate more radical, uncertain and increasingly risk-laden moves that could marginalise the value of established capabilities. Diversification by entering currently untapped demand segments in the current domain are popular diversification moves, as are new geographical locations with existing offerings. The latter typically extend

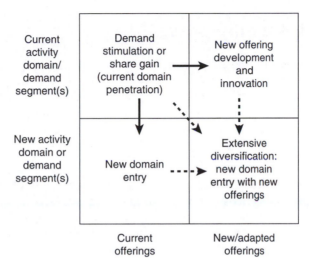

	Current offerings	New/adapted offerings
Current activity domain/ demand segment(s)	Demand stimulation or share gain (current domain penetration)	New offering development and innovation
New activity domain or demand segment(s)	New domain entry	Extensive diversification: new domain entry with new offerings

Figure 10.1: Ansoff's growth and diversification matrix

Adapted from Ansoff (1965)

operations first to other regions in the home country, then nationally, then across country boundaries. However, serving international markets usually requires some adaptation of offerings to meet local needs and preferences.

A more attractive prospect for enterprises may be new product/service development for existing clienteles. However, the receptivity of existing buyers depends greatly on whether they see a valid link between the new offerings and the characteristics they associate with the enterprise. So diversification of offerings may equate with extending the current domain(s), probably creating a new demand segment. New-to-the-world offerings that are genuine innovations almost certainly create a new market in the lower right quadrant of Figure 10.1, and represent diversifications that could redefine the enterprise mission.

 Another approach to classifying strategies examines the degree of diversification an enterprise achieves (or desires to achieve).[9] Diversification may be *limited, related* or ***unrelated***.

Limited Diversification Strategies

Limited diversification features two sub-categories. The *single-business* sub-category defines enterprises with 95% or more of their activities (more specifically, revenues, in the case of businesses) coming from a core product or service type. These single-business enterprises constrain their scope narrowly in terms of demand, geographic coverage, and range of technologies, being confined typically to the upper left quadrant of Figure 10.1. Diversification is restricted to incremental improvements of offerings in the current demand segment(s), or to wider geographic coverage.

Single business enterprises

London Taxis International (LTI) makes the iconic taxi cabs that feature in major cities in the UK and 60 other countries. Over the years LTI has made about 130,000 cabs, many of which are still in use. Its parent company, Manganese Bronze Holdings plc, also has five dedicated LTI dealerships. A 2006 joint venture with Geely Automotive, the largest private Chinese car company, to make up to 40,000 LTI taxis a year in China led in 2010 to Geely acquiring a majority stake in Manganese Bronze Holdings.

Founded in 1900, the ***Nobel Foundation*** is a private Swedish institution. Its main mission is to manage in perpetuity the assets bequeathed by wealthy industrialist Alfred Nobel. These assets fund the award of prestigious prizes to Nobel Laureates. The Foundation also protects the independence and interests of the Nobel Institutions that nominate the recipients of these awards.

The second sub-category is *dominant-business*, which contains enterprises that derive 70% to 90% of their activity/revenues from a single, core product or service category. The 70% dividing line is arbitrary; evidently, it signifies less dependence on a narrow offering base, but whether this is deliberate or accidental depends on the enterprise's strategy. When reducing dependence is a deliberate strategy, enterprises are more likely to diversify technologically than their single-business counterparts.

Related Diversification Strategies

In this category, less than 70% of revenue derives from a core product/service category. When the remaining elements ($\geq$ 30%) are clearly related to the core offerings, domains, technologies and capabilities, the strategy is called *related-constrained*. When the linkages among the various units are weaker it is called *related-linked*.

LEARNING
OBJECTIVE ②
Genuine relatedness stems from prior strategic intent, not merely opportunism. Where strategy employs the resource-based approach (Chapter 5), relatedness is characterised by what commentators call a 'common thread', 'guiding logic' or 'dominant logic' which creates observable synergies among the enterprise's various activities and markets.[10]

Evidence of synergies[11] in respect of strategic (as opposed merely to operational) capabilities and approaches covers:

*   Strategy formulation and decision making processes, including how performance targets and time horizons are set and managed.
*   Technologies, capabilities, resources and how they are allocated and exploited.
*   Attitudes and postures toward risk taking.

External observers cannot be sure of prior intent, as they can only infer synergies from positive, observed outcomes. Moreover, even unambiguous intent could create limited, operational and low-level linkages, with only an illusion of synergism; tangible strategic benefits are then largely absent.

For a strategy to be considered related-constrained, there must be clear, multiple linkages, such as shared clienteles, operational facilities, capabilities and technologies, corporate culture and management. Conversely, strategies are better considered related-linked if the linkages are more tenuous. For example, a set of loosely linked activities might share the characteristic of wealthy clienteles but little else.

A term that is sometimes used to describe a combination of vertical and horizontal (lateral) extensions into related activity domains is *concentric diversification*. In Figure 10.2, the enterprise locates at the centre of an 'activity space' with vertical and horizontal axes. It pursues various related-diversified initiatives in both directions. The symbols #1 and #2 represent first-order and second-order relatedness. That is, #1 equates with related-constrained diversifications, whereas in #2 the enterprise departs further from its established capabilities and familiar clienteles, hence is related-linked. Concentric diversification reduces dependence on the core activities and generally involves acquisitions. To be effective, an enterprise must think carefully about the distance of a diversified activity from its core and what the consequences may be.

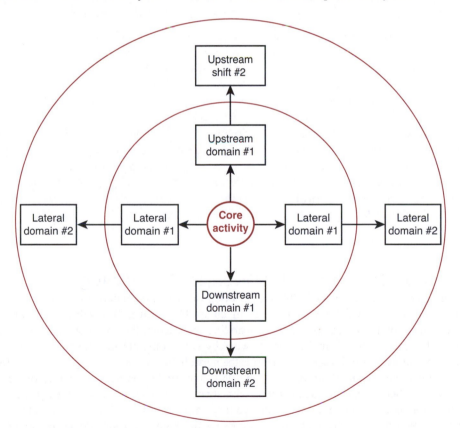

Figure 10.2: Concentric (related) diversification

Related diversification strategies

Related-constrained enterprise: The Compass Group provides catering, cafeteria and restaurant services to a wide range of sectors. For the Group, 'culinary expertise sits at the heart of who we are, shaping our wider business development.' Clients range from hospitals to airlines, and from hotels to schools and colleges. It applies, and as necesssary adapts, largely standardised resources and capabilities in cooking, procuring foodstuffs and facilities management.

Related-linked enterprise: CapGemini Group is a multinational consulting and technology corporation. It serves many client sectors in three broad areas: business and strategy consulting; information technology (IT) and systems consulting; and outsourced management of IT systems and business processes. Core capabilities include: problem definition and solution creation; the implementation and maintenance of solutions; and client relationship management. Its core skills and interchange of personnel might suggest a 'related-constrained' corporate strategy, but the variety of its assignments makes related-linked seem a better description.

Concentric diversification: The Virgin Group comprises a worldwide array of over 200 Virgin-branded, wholly-owned enterprises, joint ventures and franchise alliances. Virgin's major activity domains are consumer-oriented, involving transport, vacations, communications, entertainment and lifestyle products and services. However, they are quite disparate, spanning health clubs, airlines, cable TV, drinks, mobile telephony and banking. Many of its diversifications are horizontal extensions, while hotels, transport and vacation provision demonstrate vertical links. Could relatedness be an illusion? Virgin claims that 'our constantly expanding and eclectic empire is neither random nor reckless.' The core capability of the corporate centre is to create value and exploit synergies arising from the extensive, Virgin-branded network and from its entrepreneurial management ethos, symbolised in Sir Richard Branson's persona. Thus it would claim its strategy is concentric diversification.

Unrelated (Conglomerate) Diversification Strategy

The final diversification category in this framework arises when the enterprise operates in various activity areas, none of which accounts for as much as 70% of overall revenues (typically much less). Although common links and shared capabilities may exist, they are not expected to create synergies. The exception is financial synergy, whereby a conglomerate aims for an integrated, well-managed investment portfolio that outperforms the portfolio of investors acting independently.

Conglomerates featured strongly in the 1960s and 1970s, particularly while rising share prices enabled them to pay for acquisitions with shares, not cash. However, they gained a bad reputation for asset-stripping rather than genuine value creation. Today, conglomerates are far less common unless a clear guiding logic exists to exploit well-developed corporate level capabilities. There *are* some notably successful conglomerates but they are the exceptions.

Conglomerate diversification

General Electric of America (GE) is a huge corporation with many unrelated divisions covering domestic appliances, jet engines, medical electronics, financial services, energy generation, media and entertainment. However, within each major division business units are related-linked or related-constrained by virtue of shared clienteles and/or technical capabilities. Some were acquired, some developed internally. Significantly, the legacy of long-serving, former CEO, Jack Welch, is a belief that all GE businesses must be either the most dominant competitor in its sector, or have a realistic prospect of *becoming* the biggest, given time and investment.

Strategic Management of the Diversified, Multi-activity Enterprise

Organising the Multi-activity Enterprise

Modern corporate strategic thinking owes much to General Electric (GE) and its consultants.[12] The strategic business unit or SBU is the basic building block of the diversified enterprise. The corporate enterprise is the array (portfolio) of SBUs.

The SBU is a bounded (limited) set of assets, resources, technologies and organisational capabilities assembled to achieve a clear mission, by performing specified value-adding activities, informed by a coherent, realistic strategy.

In a theoretically-conceived portfolio:

- The scope of an SBU is clear and bounded in respect of its purpose and the activities, resources and capabilities that are both necessary and sufficient to achieve it.

- Each SBU is self-sufficient to achieve its mission. It is independent of other SBUs, so its success does not depend on them, despite possible commonalities, for example, shared clienteles.

- The mission, strategy and performance of each SBU can be assessed independently on their merits.

- An SBU decides its selling prices and controls its cost-generating activities. Accordingly, its executives are fully accountable for its performance.

- A well-chosen acquisition can become a new SBU without affecting the performance or prospects of existing SBUs. Conversely, a poor performer can be divested without damaging other SBUs.

In practice, executives weaken this idealised independence in what they judge to be the greater interest of the corporate enterprise. The freedoms of individual SBUs are constrained, just as they would be as stand-alone enterprises controlled by market and shareholder pressures. The corporate centre may instruct SBUs to share costs or to provide shared clients with integrated sales and after-sales functions. Some diversified enterprises organise SBUs by function, creating internal supply-chain linkages: a manufacturing SBU might supply several SBUs that manage geographically dispersed sales and marketing activities. Nonetheless, each SBU retains profit responsibilities.

LEARNING ① OBJECTIVE   A diversified enterprise may decide to create groupings of SBUs, generally called divisions. SBUs are grouped into a division based on shared or complementary attributes such as common clients, technologies and capabilities. Typically, each division has a management team to oversee the progress of constituent SBUs.

GE illustrates a mature conglomerate with an apparently effective divisional structure.[13] The Nigerian Stallion Group is a conglomerate at a much earlier stage of development.

The Stallion Group of Nigeria[14]

Founded in 1969, the Stallion Group is a highly diversified business conglomerate privately owned by the Vaswani family. Its corporate mission is to expand in high-growth activities that are particularly relevant for the development of seven West-African regional economies, especially through vertical integration and alliance formation.

Stallion Group is organised into five 'business lines': international trading; automobile import and distribution; manufacturing; industrial and commercial property development; and business services. These business lines are not tightly-constructed divisions (as in GE's model). Each contains distinct activity domains, some of which could qualify as SBUs if managed according to previous definitions.

Table 10.A: The Stallion Group Structure in 2010

Division	Activity areas
International Trading	Rice, sugar, fish and other foodstuffs Fertilizers Chemicals Building materials Tyres and auto accessories Oil/energy investment projects
Automobiles	Vehicle import and distribution for seven major brands of cars
Manufacturing	Textiles Steel, textiles Car and motorcycle assembly Plastic products for home and industrial use Packaging for bulk commodity products Rice milling Processed food manufacture

Table 10.A: Cont'd	
Division	**Activity areas**
Property Development	Commercial office developments
	Factory and distribution centre developments
Services	International freight forwarding and customs brokerage
	Commercial insurance services
	IT services including home automation
	Commercial banking
	Aircraft chartering and leasing

Source: Stalliongroup.com

It is difficult to divide complex, multi-activity enterprises into neat, stand-alone SBUs because many linkages and inter-dependencies exist, both real and perceptual. Portfolio expansion via multiple mergers or acquisitions can result in divisional and SBU structures that appear to defy rational explanation. The clash between strategic logic and power struggles among senior executives often results in a pragmatic compromise.

Portfolio Management

The concept of portfolio management lies at the heart of corporate strategy. To create value through diversity, corporate staff must co-ordinate and optimise the use of finite enterprise resources and capabilities, while influencing and guiding SBU managers (and where appropriate intervening in the management of each SBU), in order to achieve high collective performance. Thus, the responsibilities of SBU managers and corporate executives at the centre of a diverse, multi-activity, multi-SBU enterprise differ fundamentally.

Corporate executives actually create enterprise-level value only when their value-adding skills and capabilities identify and support a dominant logic that underpins the overall strategy by:

- Making appropriate decisions about the composition, complementarity and synergistic development of the SBU portfolio, including divesting SBUs unable to achieve their potential.
- Financial and control skills to allocate finite resources so that each SBU achieves the full returns indicated by its potential.
- Accessing external funds on favourable terms to underpin future SBU investment and growth strategies.
- Identifying enterprises with the potential to perform better in the portfolio than under their present ownership.
- Integrating these new acquisitions effectively.
- Policy-setting and the exercise of governance skills.

- Applying other specialised, centrally located skills that benefit SBUs, including market research, technology development, and importing expertise from consultants and via alliances.

Corporate enterprises have dedicated centres and functions to perform some of these tasks. They may delegate the most specialised functions such as acquisitions to external consultants or engage them opportunistically as needed. While an effective enterprise may join the portfolio essentially unchanged, a poorly performing one requires a turnaround programme involving restructuring and possible dismembering; its mission(s) and assets may be re-allocated in part or whole to existing SBUs, while unwanted others are closed down or sold.

LEARNING ③
OBJECTIVE
   Corporate managers use analytic matrix frameworks to help make portfolio acquisition and divestment decisions. These allow strategists to assess each SBU according to two key factors: the future attractiveness of the domain each operates in, and the strength of their current positions relative to competing enterprises.

   Figure 10.3 shows a generic matrix framework using these factors. Once each SBU's position has been located, the appropriate prescription for it is broadly clear. A strong position in a domain with an attractive future (position 1) suggests positive investment to achieve its growth potential. A strong position in a domain of limited future potential (position 2) will not create high growth, so the prescription is maintenance or 'harvesting'. This means extracting the maximum benefit (cash flow in the case of a business) from it for as long as practical, while limiting

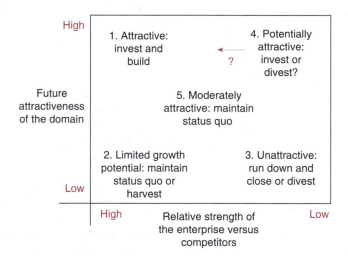

Figure 10.3: Generic portfolio matrix

new investment to the minimum needed to defend its position. A weak position in an unattractive domain (position 3) clearly signals divestment or progressive running down until it is worthless, then closed without significant loss.

   Position 4 creates a dilemma. Relative weakness prevents the SBU from exploiting its future domain potential. Should it receive substantial investment to enhance its position or should it be divested before its position declines terminally because of competition, becoming a serious cash drain? High investment is risky, yet the potential gains could be very high.[15] Careful judgement is evidently needed in each case – simplistic prescriptions cannot be followed blindly. For an SBU located at the centre of the chart (position 5) the conventional prescription is to maintain position and status quo by moderate investment, producing acceptable growth and profitability. Generally, investing more to gain share will incur costs that outweigh future returns. Conversely, inadequate investment may quickly turn it into a 'position 3' business.

   The generic matrix has been developed in various ways in the search to define future attractiveness and relative strength of SBUs. Approaches employ a range of insightful criteria and associated metrics. Some represent the size of each SBU as well as its location, using circles of varying size.[16] Other refinements include indicating *changes* in the size and position of each SBU over time, to give a more precise indication of its progression.

The Growth-share Matrix

The Boston Consulting Group (BCG) 'growth-share' matrix (Figure 10.4) uses a single measure of future attractiveness: percentage annual growth rate of the served market. While this could be calculated in terms of units sold, revenue values are more typically used, adjusted for inflation (hence 'real' rates of growth) to avoid misleadingly optimistic forecasts. The potential range of projected growth percentages is from negative to 30–40% for enterprises in rapid growth markets. To assess competitive strength the BCG matrix most often uses the ratio of the SBU's current share of demand to that of its biggest competitor.[17] This ratio generally ranges from 0.1 to 10, that is, from minor to dominant competitor.

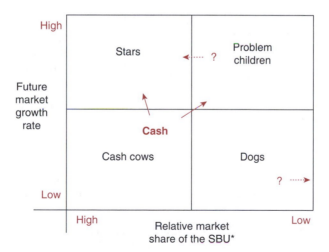

* By convention the scale on this axis of the BCG matrix is reversed (as compared with Figure 10.3). The reversal has no practical significance.
Cash movement
Intended directional shift in the SBU's position

Figure 10.4: The Boston Consulting Group (BCG) matrix and prescriptions

The BCG matrix applies colourful labels to the main positions, but the prescriptions are essentially those of a generic matrix. The standard BCG prescriptions assume that:

- 'Stars' and 'problem children' are generally in the early phase of their demand cycles, (thus explaining their future growth potential). Current revenues may be quite small, while cash generation varies from neutral to highly negative. So development requires substantial, continued injections of cash, technical and commercial expertise.
- 'Cash cows' are in the mature demand phase, 'dogs' often in the decline phase. The former generate positive cash flows considerably in excess of their future needs, allowing surpluses to be re-invested in SBUs with more promising growth prospects. 'Dogs' have low growth prospects, while their weak positions imply modest cash generation that will quickly disappear if their positions weaken.

The attraction of the BCG matrix is its simplicity. It requires only two key statistics for each SBU: expected future growth rate of the served market and the SBU's relative market share. It is easy to use and versatile – it has been applied to SBUs, to product groups and even brands.

Yet to be strategically valid, analysts must be confident of their market share data and future growth rate projections. The BCG matrix works best with specific demand categories; too broadly-based or unreliable calculations prevent reliable prescriptions. However, it does encourage a dynamic view of the portfolio and it highlights opportunities to recycle internally generated cash among SBUs in the portfolio – a perfectly legitimate action. But, there are important caveats too:

- SBU independence is an idealised and problematic assumption if synergies are sought.
- Successful, diversified enterprises do not need to restrict their investments to what they can fund internally; additional funds can come from shareholders and borrowing.[18]
- A portfolio of 'cash cows' and 'dogs' with no 'stars' does not justify major new investments, so surplus funds might properly return to shareholders as dividends.
- Mature 'cash cows' often have long and profitable lives. Aggressive harvesting of their cash surpluses denies them new investment needed to maintain their positions.
- So-called 'dogs' that generate modest cash surpluses could have an enhanced position during the decline phase if their competitors quit.
- A 'problem child' often faces fundamental challenges other than investment risks. For example, it may be committed to a technology that proves a misplaced 'bet', becoming a 'cash trap'.

SBUs that sit on quadrant boundaries present another challenge. Where should the cut-off be, between low and high growth rates and between low and high relative market shares? A moderately high growth rate in one context would be low in another. Perhaps SBUs should be considered 'stars' or 'cash cows' only with a relative share of above × 1. The consensus of commentators is that a higher cut-off should apply to a 'star' (e.g., × 1.5) while a 'cash cow' with a relative share above × 0.5 probably generates useful cash surpluses. Relative values matter too: an SBU whose market share is 15% when the leader has 30% (a ratio of × 0.5) is probably in a stronger position than one whose share is 5% when the leader has 10%. Accordingly, the matrix has to be used intelligently.

Alternative Portfolio Frameworks

Other frameworks aim to address shortcomings of the BCG matrix. One, sometimes called the 'directional policy matrix' is variously linked with consultants McKinsey and A.T. Kearney, and also with GE and Shell. This framework distinguishes three possible positions (low, medium and high) on the growth and attractiveness dimensions, creating a 9-cell matrix,[19] and it suggests more sophisticated, *composite* measures to assess both of these variables. Users must decide which measures to combine and their relative weightings. Attractiveness might combine predicted size of demand and growth potential, while competitive standing might combine assessments of relative quality, capabilities and current share of demand. Once the positions of SBUs are determined, the prescriptions are broadly similar to the BCG matrix.

Another matrix framework, reportedly used by consultants Arthur D. Little, uses lifecycle phases to signify market attractiveness (Figure 10.5). The assumption is that early phase SBUs are in principle more attractive, hence more likely to justify investment, all else being equal.

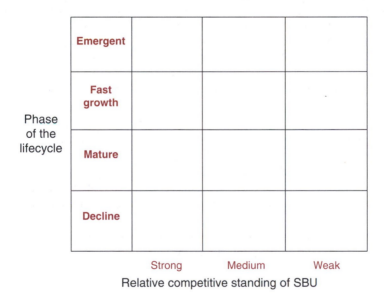

Figure 10.5: Lifecycle portfolio matrix

All matrix frameworks need to be applied with judgement to support the diversified enterprise in balancing its portfolio. A good balance requires a complementary mix of SBUs in relation to their respective size, growth phase and potential, current share of demand, potential for synergy, stability and risk exposure.[20] If obvious gaps exist, a case can be made for appropriate acquisitions; over-dependence on mature-phase SBUs indicates a need for portfolio adjustment.

Complementarity and Synergy in the Portfolio: the Role of 'Corporate 'Parenting'[21]

Analytical portfolio frameworks assume that SBUs are treated independently: that a decision about one does not affect the well-being of others or future decisions about them. Yet even in highly diversified portfolios, linkages and interactions arise in practice, as exemplified below:

Example 1. SBUs A and B offer different services to the same clientele. Although stand-alone profit-centres, their customers object to separate contact arrangements, so a single set of client-facing staff represents both A and B.

Example 2. SBUs C and D manufacture equivalent products for consumer and industrial use, respectively. They source similar, non-identical components from the same set of external suppliers. Using more identical components would allow higher purchase discounts by virtue of placing larger orders leading to scale economies for suppliers, but would risk 'over-engineered' (and priced) consumer products or 'under-engineered' industrial products.

Such interactions create complementarities and potential synergies. Shared resources create scope economies. Common components enable design costs to be spread over greater value-added, another potential scope economy, as well as greater scale economies for suppliers. However, scope economies reinforce SBU linkages and compromise SBU independence. The SBUs are no longer separately accountable for their resource deployments, revenue and profit performances. Nonetheless, resource sharing may enhance the overall productivity of the portfolio. Moreover, the logic of the resource-based view (Chapter 5) is that synergies among a diverse set of SBUs are vital if they are to perform better overall than when operating independently. Scope economies are one form of economic synergy. Exchange of technologies and knowledge in all its relevant forms is another.[22]

LEARNING
OBJECTIVE ③   Having established a complementary portfolio of SBUs with clearly understood missions, boundaries, resources and prospects, the corporate task is to support each one, maximising the aggregate performance of the portfolio. A critically important skill of the corporate centre applied to individual SBUs has been called 'parenting'.

Corporate centres are quasi-parents, SBUs their families. Parents make choices about family size and (sometimes) composition. Caring, responsible parents want each child to realise its full potential in the family context, so they nurture and proffer developmental support. Corporate executives exercise an equivalent responsibility to each SBU, helping it to realise its full potential and to co-operate with others to their mutual benefit.

However, as with parents, corporate executives:

- Have imperfect knowledge and skills – sometimes lacking insights on which to base guidance and control.
- Should recognise that special needs may require outside expertise, perhaps entailing reloca-tion (special schools and divestment, respectively).
- Should accept that SBUs will – and arguably must be allowed to – make mistakes as they learn and develop.
- Can have a dysfunctional effect on the 'family'. Overbearing discipline or minimal control both cause major problems. Instead of creating value they destroy it.

Each SBU has unique critical success factors (CSFs). For corporate executives to get the best out of their SBU 'family' they are expected to:

- Understand the *critical factors* that affect whether each SBU will succeed in its activity domain.
- Create relevant *insights into the development needs* of each SBU and how the corporate centre can therefore support it most effectively.
- Recognise when an SBU's CSFs are incompatible with the corporate strategy, or its development needs are beyond the scope of corporate resources and capabilities. Such mismatches mean that the SBU cannot fulfil its potential in the portfolio.

Corporate executives do not *manage* SBUs: that is for SBU managers to do. The corporate function is to *create the environment* in which SBUs can thrive. When parenting skills match an SBU's evident *parenting opportunities*, the centre can support and add value to it. This logic underpins the analytic 'parenting matrix' of Figure 10.6. The vertical dimension expresses degree of fit (match) between an SBU's CSFs and corporate strategy and characteristics. It is a symbol of what value the SBU contributes to the corporate enterprise. The horizontal dimension expresses degree-of-fit between corporate insights and SBU development needs – the 'parenting opportunity' – what the corporate enterprise offers the SBU. In combination they create a 'parenting space' in which to locate each SBU.

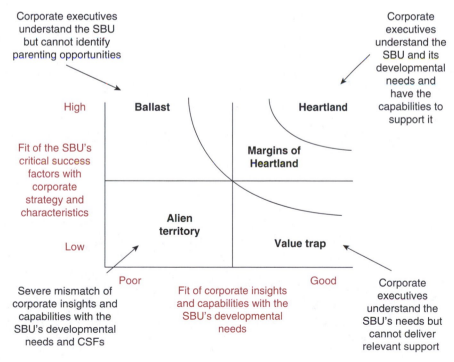

Figure 10.6: The parenting-fit matrix

Adapted from Campbell, Goold and Alexander (1994d)

An SBU in the 'heartland' enjoys the ideal situation: its mission is consistent with corporate strategy and characteristics, while the centre understands how and has the capabilities to assist the SBU. As the location of an SBU shifts from the heartland down and across the matrix its situation becomes less favourable. When both horizontal and vertical fit are low, the SBU is misplaced in the portfolio and should be divested to an owner better equipped to develop it.

Applying the Parenting Matrix

Heartland: Microsoft's search engine, Bing, needs to be a mass-market competitor to achieve its potential, hence its critical success factors (CSFs) (which include high profile marketing, regular updating, and good relationships with third party contributors) are consistent with Microsoft's corporate strategy. Microsoft appears to have the corporate insights, resources and skills to help Bing achieve long-term success.

Value Trap: the CSFs of budget airline, Go, were lean, low-cost operations and agility, very different from those of its owner, national flag-carrier British Airways (BA). The latter probably understood what would be needed to make Go succeed, but it had insufficient skills, resources and commitment to support Go, which before long was severely taxing corporate cash flow. BA sold Go to easyJet.

Alien Territory: German vehicle and engineering corporation Daimler Benz (D-B, Mercedes) acquired loss-making US carmaker, Chrysler. It seems that despite parallel automotive histories D-B did not really understand Chrysler's CSFs, linked essentially to the United States, not global demand preferences. Further, D-B's insights into Chrysler's developmental needs were based on German assumptions about design and the expectations of prestige-seeking clients. D-B's attempts to support Chrysler proved well-intentioned but misdirected. Chrysler continued to lose money and was ultimately divested.

Ballast: Kingfisher plc, was formerly a British-based conglomerate retailer which refocused the portfolio on home improvements: it includes B&Q and Screwfix, principally in the UK; Castorama and Brico Dépôt, principally in France; and smaller branded operations in six other countries. Over 80% of its UK sales are to consumers. When Kingfisher acquired Screwfix, the latter was a business-to-business mail order and web supplier of plumbing and electrical goods. Screwfix now sells to consumers and the trade. It has opened an expanding chain of depots too, presumably as Kingfisher seeks to convert it to a 'heartland' SBU. If, however, Kingfisher has misdiagnosed the 'parenting opportunity' Screwfix presents, it could become unprofitable 'ballast', competing with B&Q for consumer expenditure and with rivals such as Toolstation for trade business.

Other Corporate-level Responsibilities

The key tasks for corporate executives are to establish the corporate strategy and to implement it effectively through portfolio construction and management. Complementary responsibilities are to:

- Provide corporate functions centrally, as appropriate to support SBU strategies.
- Implement corporate policies to ensure good legal and ethical governance; and to co-ordinate, monitor performance and control SBU finances.
- Appoint, appraise, advise on career development and where necessary dismiss SBU chief executives.
- Manage the external image of the enterprise constructively and to foster an equally constructive internal ethos and identity.

In the 1960s, major corporations generally had substantial corporate functions for research and development, computing and information technology, strategic planning, marketing, finance, etc. As the emphasis shifted to value creation through distinctive capabilities at SBU and corporate levels, it became difficult to justify costly resources located in specialised central functions, if they could be done cost-effectively by the SBUs in need or by external agencies.

To be efficient and effective, the diversified enterprise requires co-ordination and commonality of major corporate policies, systems and procedures. The corporate centre therefore sets these policies and monitors compliance with them in the areas of:

- Finance.
- Ethics and governance-related.
- Capital investment.
- Strategic planning procedures.
- Sourcing.
- ICT (information, communication and technology) systems.
- Legal (patenting, trademarks, etc.).
- Human resource management.
- Research and development.
- Facilities management.

Governance and financial control in particular require clear central policies and practices to discharge legal and ethical responsibilities. At the opposite extreme, global multinationals usually delegate facilities management to regional or country managers, the goal being to enhance efficiency by acquiring, redeploying and disposing of factories and offices as necessary.

Chief executives of SBUs and divisions (where the latter exist) are responsible to the corporate centre for the conduct and performance of their individual entities. The career development of these senior staff is a major concern of corporate executives because these people directly influence SBU and divisional performance and ultimately corporate performance.

The corporate centre is also responsible for an enterprise's external image and its internal ethos and identity. How these affect individual SBUs is a function of the overall corporate philosophy. Highly diversified enterprises, even those with closely related SBU strategies, do not necessarily promote commonality when the portfolio results from the acquisition of already well-established, successful enterprises. To over-ride well-respected identities could be counter-productive: diverse portfolios do not always benefit from image associations.[23]

The Roles of Strategic Business Unit Managers

LEARNING
OBJECTIVE ① The roles of SBU managers complement those of corporate executives, being primarily to:

- Negotiate the mission and strategy of the SBU for which they are responsible and agree feasible, specific objectives and targets with corporate executives.
- Implement the strategy to achieve agreed objectives and targets.
- Engage with corporate executives to identify critical success factors and areas for future development support (parenting opportunities).

Since SBUs have less autonomy than they would as stand-alone enterprises, portfolio membership is justified only if the centre supports them in ways that would not otherwise occur. Membership is a failure if the centre cannot add or even destroys value, an outcome beyond SBU managers' control. The corporate strategy might impose higher performance expectations on a 'star' SBU than its managers would accept if a stand-alone enterprise. A harvest strategy imposed on an SBU because it is seen as a 'cash-cow' may seem equally unreasonable to its chief executive. The survival of an SBU classed as a 'dog' may be threatened, despite having optimistic managers. 'Problem children', whose growth ambitions the centre is willing to fund, probably enjoy the best positions – as long as they look like succeeding.

So the role of SBU managers can be frustrating. However, their rewards for achieving agreed goals can be high. A large, diversified corporate enterprise offers considerable career opportunities: progress via SBU promotions followed by transfers to other SBUs and then perhaps senior corporate roles. Conversely, failure to achieve agreed goals has severe personal consequences, especially for SBU chief executives.

A particular issue for SBU managers arises over the rewards for mutual collaborations. In theory, everyone benefits from collaborate success, but in fact executives compete for personal recognition and preferment from the corporate centre. Thus promotion opportunities often depend on SBU performance comparisons; collaborations become 'zero sum' not 'win–win' games of organizational politics. The rewards for each SBU from constructive collaborations can be asymmetric. Knowledge passed from one to another cannot always be reciprocated. How is a donor compensated for sharing its intellectual property? Fair, sophisticated reward systems are required if motivation to collaborate is to be high.

The Performance of Diversified Enterprises

Diversification Trends

By the middle of the 20th century, three-quarters of UK companies (70% of US) were still single or dominant businesses; conglomerates were most unusual. When adding new products or services to their repertoire, enterprises generally remained functionally structured and integrated. Manufacturing, for example, integrated new products into existing facilities and a single head of manufacturing was in control. Organizational structures were relatively tall and hierarchical. Since many enterprises had a single location, limited product extension or geographic reach, functional integration was accepted and a manageable challenge. Because product or service lines were not seen as separate 'businesses', their respective profitabilities were not calculated, particularly when considered necessary complements. Multinationals such as Shell, Ford, Du Pont, BASF, Philips and ICI were exceptions, although they still focused on particular industry sectors and geographic regions. Exceptionally too, Japan featured vertically structured conglomerates called *zaibatsu*, owned and controlled by powerful families. The South Korean *chaebols* of Samsung, LG and Hyundai functioned much as the *zaibatsu,* albeit less advanced.

As economies revived after the 1939–45 war, US enterprises began consciously to diversify and expand internationally. While much of their growth was internally generated (organic), ambition in the 1960s and 1970s fuelled a major increase in mergers and acquisitions as the preferred growth strategy, creating some notable conglomerates.[24] In less than three decades two-thirds of US corporations could be classed as diversified and one-third of these was unrelated conglomerates.[25] The portfolio concept and its implications had become fully accepted.[26] In the UK, and to a lesser degree other Western European countries, a similar pattern followed, about a decade behind.

In the UK the number and popularity of small and medium business enterprises (SMEs) also declined, whereas in large European countries such as France, Germany, Italy and Spain, many SMEs remained family-owned, even when they grew substantially. German enterprises and their banks in particular resisted the temptation to aim for aggressive, acquisition-led growth, preferring steady, export-led expansion.

In post-war Japan *zaibatsu* were replaced by *keiretsu*: conglomerate industrial and banking groups such as Mitsui and Mitsubishi which remain strong today. They feature *horizontal* alliances and cross-shareholdings with greater transparency than *zaibatsu*. Export-led growth was also their priority; dynamic enterprises such as Sony, Matsushita, Canon and Toshiba developed rapidly in fast-growth electronics sectors, becoming related- and linked-diversified multinational giants. South Korean *chaebols*, notably Samsung, also focused on high growth sectors internationally, divesting or closing many of their traditional activities.

By the mid 1980s it was clear that many US and UK corporate portfolios were not creating real value for shareholders.[27] They simply did not create synergies, prompting a crisis of confidence in academic as well as business circles. Large enterprises started shifting their focus to related acquisitions and divested ill-fitting SBUs, later informed by the emerging resource-based theory. Then, after 1992, the Single European Market encouraged corporations to engage in cross-border alliances and mergers by applying related-diversified strategic logic.

Around the world today, many enterprises ranging from medium-sized to extremely large have related- and linked-diversified portfolios. They are often complemented by thriving, largely

LEARNING OBJECTIVE ②

undiversified SMEs. Most non-Asian conglomerates have been dismembered, although unrelated diversification may still be appropriate in dynamic, emerging economies (such as in the Stallion Group).

The remaining business conglomerates worldwide fall into three main categories:

- High profile consumer-goods corporations (e.g., Procter & Gamble).
- Mixed consumer and industrial goods corporations (e.g., GE and Berkshire Hathaway).
- International trading companies (e.g., UK-headquartered Jardine Matheson and Swire (operating largely in Asia Pacific); Mitsui and Mitsubishi of Japan; Sinochem of China; and Tata of India).

LEARNING OBJECTIVE ② To summarise, the renewed emphasis on *related* diversity is motivated by the desire to:

- Maximise value-creation for stakeholders.
- Exploit scope economies and other synergies among SBUs.
- Invest only in a collection of activities and high-performing SBUs that have or can develop genuine expertise and sustainable advantage.

Performance Differences among Diversification Strategies

Because contexts vary, alternative forms of diversification yield different outcomes, even when managed effectively. Observed differences could result from systematic effects or be functions of particular, unrepeatable circumstances: the influence of national cultures; time-dependent economic, political and social conditions; sector-specific characteristics; and strategic managerial capabilities and implementation skills. Conclusions also depend on the performance measures used. For all these reasons, history is a poor predictive guide to the future. Research findings suggest the following, tentative generalisations.

- Coherent, tightly focused and well-controlled corporate enterprises with high quality assets, well-honed capabilities and synergistic portfolio architecture generally achieve high levels of efficiency and profitability, measured as margins on sales and return on assets employed. This is particularly true when the SBUs have positive reputations and apply 'defender-type' characteristics and strategies to dominate closely related, steady-growth sectors, achieving reliable, if relatively modest, growth rates.
- Enterprises that pursue related-diversified strategies create sector-lateral opportunities to exploit their resources, capabilities and available investment funds. They enter and exploit new domains that are distinct from, yet relatively similar to, their current ones, hence of moderate risk. Relatedness among new and existing SBUs enhances synergy potential and enables new capabilities to develop via collaboration and mutual learning. Growth rates generally exceed those of narrowly focused enterprises. Whether profitability is higher or lower depends on the realised synergies and learning benefits. Do they outweigh the

generally higher levels of investment and risk associated with diversification through acquisitions?

- Enterprises with diverse and largely unrelated portfolios (typically the result of aggressive acquisition strategies) can show higher rates of revenue growth, but find it much harder to achieve real synergies. When acquisition targets are chosen for their high growth and margin potential, a price premium usually applies, depressing future return on assets employed despite good profit performance.[28] Corporate executives may also be defeated by the disparate parenting challenges of an unrelated portfolio and fail to add value. Accordingly, rates of growth and profitability disappoint.

Taken together, these observations suggest that moderate, related diversity yields the highest return on investment, while greater diversity risks a reduction in overall performance owing to an absence of synergy and excessive complexity. This performance-diversity relationship is shown in Figure 10.7.[29]

Other studies highlight the contingent effects of circumstance on performance. They include the quality of SBU–corporate-centre relationships,[30] the level of business performance *prior* to a diversification initiative,[31] the relatedness of resources and technologies in existing and diversified ventures,[32] the locational and domain context,[33] managerial perceptions[34] and leadership commitment (new initiatives being typically associated with changes of senior management).[35]

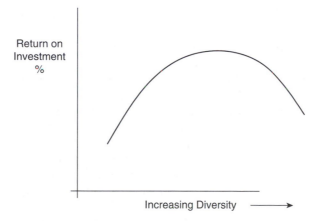

Figure 10.7: Diversity and profitability

Source: Grant, Jammine and Thomas (1988)

All these historically based findings are of modest help to executives attempting to optimise portfolio management. Their concern is whether each SBU is performing to its full potential in the particular circumstances. How can they actually assess its potential? They have three options: (i) to compare it with other SBUs in the portfolio; (ii) to benchmark it against external enterprises that offer valid comparisons; (iii) to apply statistical techniques that draw on a much wider database of enterprises and sector characteristics.

When SBUs in the portfolio are dissimilar, the first option can mislead. Comparisons with relevant, external benchmarks are more worthwhile, though issues of size, data availability and reliability can hinder comparisons. The third option emerged concurrently with portfolio thinking from research done at Harvard Business School under the title of 'Profit Impact of Market Studies' (PIMS), and now continued by the independent consultancy, PIMS Associates.

PIMS Associates collects data on the characteristics and performance of many enterprises in clearly defined activity sectors, creating a large and continuously updated database on which statistical analysis draws. Corporate clients request analyses of average and trend performance in a sector of particular interest (or an appropriate alternative subset of the database). They gain insights into average performance levels such as profit margin, return on investment, and sales. Using a golfing term, these are called *par values*, which suggest reasonable performance expectations of the SBU under scrutiny.

Generally, the actual performance of an SBU differs from the PIMS par-value. Below-par performance suggests inefficiencies or weaknesses arising from low market share or other factors. So the question is whether and at what cost these problems are soluble. If the solution is unacceptably high cost then divestment is the obvious solution. Conversely, an above-par performance prompts questions about the sustainability of this favourable position and what alternative strategies may be open to build on it.[36]

CASE STUDY: Grupo Salinas of Mexico[37]

Grupo Salinas originated as two family businesses, Benjamin Salinas & Co, a bed factory started in 1906, and a retail store called Salinas y Rocha. In 1950, Hugo Salinas Rocha started the Elektra Company to make television sets. His son took control in 1952 and accelerated growth by door-to-door selling and offering credit and instalment payments. Elektra's first retail store opened in 1957. Elektra and Salinas y Rocha separated in 1961. Thereafter, Grupo Elektra grew substantially: in 1993, it issued shares on the Mexican stock exchange for the first time and was listed as global depository shares on the New York Stock Exchange in 1994. These sources of equity funds triggered a rapid expansion and diversification. Grupo Elektra's commercial activities achieved EBITDA profits of $244 million on sales of $1.5 billion in 2000, more than 15% up on 1999. In 2001 the Salinas y Rocha department store chain rejoined the portfolio and Grupo Salinas was created as the parent holding company. At that time, the Group comprised the following activities:

- The *Elektra* chain of 600+ stores selling a wide range of electrical goods and furniture mainly to lower middle-class consumers, mostly in Mexico but also in Peru and four Spanish-speaking countries in Central America.

- The up-market Salinas y Rocha department store chain of 85+ outlets selling furniture, high-tech electronics and other consumer goods.

- *Bodega de Remates*, a discount chain of 50+ stores selling repossessed, reman-ufactured and discontinued goods to low-income Mexicans.

- *The One*, an acquired and expanded chain of 130+ stores selling casual clothes and accessories, previously called *Hecali*.

- Various consumer services and financial activities such as extended warranty provision, in-store ATMs and debt collection.

- An alliance with Western Union to enable expatriate Mexicans in the United States and elsewhere to make electronic money transfers to families at home.

- An Elektra-owned money transfer service in Mexico.

- TV Azteca, (the renamed, former state-owned Mexican TV service) acquired in 1993 as part of a consortium headed by President/CEO Ricardo Salinas, with more recent subsidiaries Azteca Digital (media production) and Azteca Music (records).

- A transportation company, Grupo Salinas Motors.

- A 50% shareholding in the mobile telephone operator Unefon, owned by TV Azteca (with Elektra stores selling Unefon services and handsets).

- The Fundacion Azteca, a charitable foundation established to support families and young people in difficulties.

Subsequently, corporate executives have substantially remodelled Grupo Salinas. As of 2009, it comprised nine wholly or partly owned businesses, operating vari-ously in Mexico, the United States, Guatemala, El Salvador, Honduras, Panama, Peru, Argentina, and Brazil, as follows:

Grupo Elektra

- Commercial (retail) group.

- The *Elektra* retail chain (over 1000 stores in the above-named countries, of which 800+ are in Mexico).

- The *Salinas y Rocha* chain with 55 Mexican stores offering world-class brands in electronics, household appliances, furniture, motorcycles, tyres, cell phones, computers, and other retail services such as extended warranties, electronic money transfers, and credit services in collaboration with Banco Azteca.

- Azteca Finance group.

- *Banco Azteca*, a full-service retail and commercial bank offering loans, mort-gages, debt collection and payroll services, operating in Mexico, Panama, Guatemala, Honduras, El Salvador, Argentina, Peru and Brazil.

- *Seguros Azteca*, a renamed insurance company acquired in 2003.

- *Afore Azteca*, a pension-fund management company.

- A minority stake in *Círculo de Crédito* (a joint venture credit information service set up in 2005).

TV Azteca (media division)

- *TV Azteca*, the leading commercial TV broadcasting company in Mexico, together with its subsidiaries Azteca Digital, Azteca Music, and the Mexican professional football club Monarcas.
- *Azteca America* launched in 2001 as a Spanish language TV network in the US in Los Angeles, with coverage soon expanded to reach the majority of Hispanic homes across the US. Azteca Internet is a complementary web portal.

Grupo Iusacell (telecommunications division)

- *Grupo Iusacell* was acquired in 2003 and subsequently merged with Unefon (also owned by Grupo Salinas), providing 3G CDMA wireless telecommunications services to over 3 million subscribers in Mexico, with a market share of 7%.

Italika: a manufacturer and retailer of motorcycles (started in 2006 and already selling over 200,000 units a year in Mexico, with 500 service points).

Social Foundations: Fundación Azteca, Fundación Azteca America, and ASMAZ y Fomento Cultural GS.

In 2007, the well-respected US journal *Business Week* criticised Grupo Salinas's subsidiaries Grupos Azteka and Elektra for charging very high effective interest rates for extended credit (over 100% annualised in some cases) to very low-income households in Mexico and other Central and South American countries. Micro-lending, averaging $250 per loan was nonetheless very popular, and owing to effective debt collection methods, incurred relatively few defaults.

By 2009, Grupo Salinas' market capitalization exceeded $US 12 billion and it employed about 45,000 people, achieving the following results.[38]

Table 10.B: Financial performance of Grupo Salinas 2008 and 2009

$US million[39]	2009	2008	% change
Grupo Elektra			
Finance division revenues	1,900	1,785	+6.5
Retail division revenues	1,633	1,679	−2.8
Total Grupo Elektra revenues	3,533	3,464	+2.0

Table 10.B: Cont'd

$US million[39]		2009	2008	% change
Consolidated profits (EBITDA)		465	445	+4.5
TV Azteca	revenues	822	810	+1.6
	profits (EBITDA)	340	321	+5.9
Grupo Iusacell	revenues	919	915	+0.5
	profits (EBITDA)	160	182	−12.4
Grupo Salinas consolidated	revenues	5275	5188	+1.7
	profits (EBITDA)	965	948	+1.8

Questions

1. Grupo Elektra entered the new millennium keen on rapid diversification. One option was to extend its mass-market retail interests. Though it did expand prudently in South America, it rejected retail store development in the United States, despite a large potential Hispanic market especially in California. Instead, it diversified, notably into television and telecommunications. Examine this 2000 strategic decision critically from the vantage point of decision makers.

2. Review the logic of Grupo Salinas's 2009 divisional and business unit structure. What issues arise and can you propose a better structure?

Summary

 RNING COME ①

- Corporate strategy is distinct from business unit strategy and it presents different challenges and requires additional skills. It aims to integrate the strategies of individual strategic business units (SBUs) within a portfolio into a coherent, synergistic high-performing entity.

- Managing a diverse enterprise presents challenges such as portfolio management and 'parenting', which can be met with relevant frameworks.

- Globally, the emphasis swung toward and then away from conglomerate diversifications (in which members of the SBU portfolio are dissimilar).

- The PIMS analytical approach supports objective assessment and decision making about the performance of individual SBUs and their place in the corporate portfolio.

Exercises for Further Study and Discussion

1. Economy of scope is a valuable but insufficient condition for a diversification strategy to be economically valuable. What is the other essential condition and why is it difficult to achieve?

2. List different aspects of the diversified enterprise's activities where scale economies can give rise to scope economies.

3. The metaphor of corporate 'parenting' seems insightful, yet like all metaphors it can mislead. When might parenting be an inappropriate guide to the proper corporate strategic management of an SBU portfolio?

4. If competing enterprises combine and integrate effectively into a corporate portfolio, external competition decreases. Buyers probably do not benefit from the lower prices that could result if internal scale and scope economies are achieved. So is there a public interest argument for legislation that mandates price reductions achieved via acquisitive diversifications? Discuss the merits of this claim.

5. Although very different in style and personality, Jack Welsh, Warren Buffett and Richard Branson have imprinted their corporate management philosophies and guiding logics on their respective enterprises. Do all highly diversified enterprises need such unique leaders to be truly successful?

6. How might Stallion reorganise its many business activities into formal SBUs within a coherent divisional structure? Critique the logic of your proposals.

7. Select two diversified, multi-activity enterprises, one for-profit and one not-for-profit. Apply the parenting matrix to each portfolio. What issues arise and what should be done about them?

Suggestions for Further Reading

Bergh, D.D. (2001) 'Diversification Strategy at a crossroads: established, emerging and anticipated paths', in Hitt, M.A., Freeman, R.E. and Harrison, J.S. (eds) *Handbook of Strategic Management*, Blackwell.

Biggadike, R. (1979) 'The risky business of diversification', *Harvard Business Review* (vol. 57/3, May/June, pp. 103–111).

Bowman, E.H. and Helfat, C.E. (2001) 'Does corporate strategy matter?', *Strategic Management Journal* (vol. 22/1 pp. 1–23).

Campbell, A., Goold, M. and Alexander, M. (1995) 'The Quest for Parenting Advantage, *Harvard Business Review* (vol. 73/2, March/April, pp. 121–132).

Chandler, A.D. (1991) 'The Functions of the HQ Unit in the Multibusiness Firm', *Strategic Management Journal* (vol.12/Winter Special Issue, pp. 31–50).

Clarke, C.J. and Brennan, K. (1990) 'Building Synergy in the Diversified Business', *Long Range Planning* (vol. 23/1, pp. 3–16).

Collis, D.J. (1996) 'Corporate strategy in multibusiness firms', *Long Range Planning* (vol. 29/4, pp. 416–418).

Collis, D.J., Young, D. and Goold, M. (2007) 'The size, structure, and performance of corporate headquarters', *Strategic Management Journal* (vol. 28/4, pp. 383–405).

De Wit, B. and Meyer, R. (2004) *Strategy Process, Content, Context*, Thomson (Ed. 3) (chapter 6).

Franko, L.G. (2004) 'The death of diversification: the focusing of the world's industrial firms', *Business Horizons* (vol. 82 Jul/Aug, pp. 41–50).

Goold, M. (1996) 'Parenting strategies for the mature business', *Long Range Planning* (vol. 29/3, pp. 358–369).

Grant, R.M. (1988) 'On dominant logic', relatedness and the link between diversity and performance', *Strategic Management Journal* (vol. 9/6, pp. 639–642).

Grant R.M., Jammine, A.P. and Thomas, H. (1988) 'Diversity, diversification, and profitability among British manufacturing companies, 1972–84', *Academy of Management Journal* (vol. 31/4, pp. 771–801).

Hedley, B. (1977) 'Strategy and the business portfolio', *Long Range Planning* (vol. 10/1, pp. 9–15).

Hoskisson, R.E., Johnson, R.A., Tihanyi, L. and White, R.E. (2005) 'Diversified business groups and corporate refocusing in emerging economies', *Journal of Management* (vol. 31/6, pp. 941–965).

Kono, T. (1999) 'A strong head office makes a strong company', *Long Range Planning* (vol. 32/2, pp. 225–236).

Markides, C. (2002) 'Corporate strategy: the role of the centre', in Pettigrew, A., Thomas, H. and Whittington, R. (eds) *Handbook of Strategy and Management*, Sage.

Palich, L.E., Cardinal, L.B. and Miller, C.C. (2000) 'Curvilinearity in the diversification–performance linkage: an examination of over three decades of research', *Strategic Management Journal* (vol. 21/2, pp. 155–174).

Porter, M.E. (1987) 'From competitive advantage to corporate strategy', *Harvard Business Review* (vol. 65/3, May–June, pp. 43–59).

Prahalad, C.K. and Bettis, R.A. (1986) 'The dominant logic: a new linkage between diversity and performance', *Strategic Management Journal* (vol. 7/6, pp. 485–501).

Rumelt, R.P. (1982) 'Diversification Strategy and Profitability', *Strategic Management Journal* (vol. 3/4, pp. 359–369).

Notes

1   For a DEFRA report on farming diversification in England, see for example: http://www.defra.gov.uk/evidence/statistics/foodfarm/farmmanage/farmaccounts/2009/NonAgricultural.doc

2   See http://www.marshfield-icecream.co.uk and http://www.linnalla.com/

3　Although for a long time diversification itself has been known to be risky, with financial payoffs typically extending many years into the future: Biggadike (1979).

4　See for example Bettis and Prahalad (1986).

5　The terms 'strategic business unit' and SBU have beome so widely used that they are retained here. However, in the spirit of inclusiveness, these terms can apply to not-for-profit enterprises too. Some readers may therefore prefer to think of 'strategic enterprise unit'.

6　Good and Luchs (1993) offers a readable account of trends in diversification thinking see Hill (1994), Martin & Sayrak (2003) and Watter & Barney (1990) for more advanced affect behaviour

7　Porter (1987a) offers a cautionary note. He suggests three tests of a diversification strategy. One is the actual or potential attractiveness of the new domain; another is synergy or 'better off-ness' (both covered in chapter 10). The third relates to the cost of entry – cautioning that if acquisition or development costs are excessive, they effectively eliminate future profits.

8　Ansoff (1965).

9　Rumelt (1974).

10　Various terms with essentially the same meaning: see Ansoff (1965, 1988); Prahalad and Bettis (1986); Grant (1988), respectively.

11　Goold and Campbell (1988).

12　Including Arthur D. Little, Boston Consulting Group (BCG), Harvard Business School (notably the pioneering work of Chandler – see Chandler, 1962; 1991), A.T. Kearney, McKinsey and PIMS Associates.

13　Refer to www.ge.com to see the scope of this giant conglomerate.

14　http://www.stalliongroup.com

15　The risk–return dilemma. One would expect executives to expose their enterprises to high risk only in ventures with potentially high returns. This is not always the case: see Fiegenbaum and Thomas (1988); Chang and Thomas (1989); Amit and Livnat (1991).

16　A further refinement is to indicate the size of the SBU's market with a circle and the SBU's share as a slice of this pie.

17　In some treatments the preferred ratio is market share divided by the sum of the shares of the largest **three** competitors. For extended discussions of the practicalities of using the growth-share matrix, see also: Hussey (1978); Hax and Majluf (1983).

18　Justified when the expected return on the new investment is greater than the weighted cost of the external capital available to the corporate enterprise externally (see chapter 5).

19　The matrix, sometimes called the 'directional policy' matrix, is variously linked with consultants McKinsey and A.T. Kearney, and also with General Electric and Shell. See Hofer and Schendel (1978, chapter 7) and other selected chapters in the suggested reading list.

20　The analogy with a top football club may be helpful here. It needs a portfolio of players at different stages of their careers with complementary skills.

21　See Goold (1996); Campbell, Goold and Alexander (1995a; 1995b).

22　A great football team is more than an ensemble of great players. Players have to work together in a harmonious, complementary and supportive way. In business terms the payoff is enhanced growth and profitability (value-added) – see for example Clarke and Brennan (1990); Teece (1982); Robins and Wiersema (1995).

23　Does the buyer of a Gillette razor or a Hugo Boss fragrance care to know that parent company Procter & Gamble also sells detergents (Ariel), pet food (Iams) and baby diapers (Pampers)? Probably not. P&G is even rather shy about its original name. However, corporate capabilities such as its renowned marketing skills no doubt have a positive influence on the internal identity of each SBU.

24　Hanson was a UK-based conglomerate that grew dramatically via unrelated acquisitions in both countries. It acquired and asset-stripped under-performing companies, generating cash for further acquisitions while it managed the residue businesses under tight financial control.

25 Berg (1969).
26 Chandler (1962), a business historian, and Rumelt (1974) offer classic accounts. The latter's US-based work on diversification performance was repeated by various researchers in different European countries.
27 Davis, Diekman and Tinsley (1994).
28 Porter (1987a).
29 Grant Jammine and Thomas (1988) focused on British manufacturers; more recently Palich, Cardinal and Miller (2000) affirmed this so-called curvilinear relationship of profitability and diversity in a meta-study of 55 previous studies.
30 Golden (1992).
31 Park (2002).
32 Miller (2006).
33 Chakrabarti, Singh and Mahmood (2007).
34 Pehrsson (2006).
35 Goranova et al. (2007).
36 PIMS Associates have published many leaflets explaining their procedures as applied commercially. Some of these are reproduced in the cited readings. For a comparison of BCG prescriptions matched with PIMS analysis, see: Hambrick, MacMillan and Day (1982).
37 Sources include: https://www.gruposalinas.com; https://www.grupoelektra.com.mx; http://www.earthtimes.org; http://en.wikipedia.org/wiki/Grupo_Salinas; http://www.businessweek.com/magazine/toc/07_52/B4064magazine.htm; Monteiro, L.F., Arnold, D. and Herrero, G. (2004) 'Case 12: Grupo Elektra', in De Wit, B. and Meyer, R. *Strategy: Process, Content*, Context, Thomson.
38 Source: https://www.gruposalinas.com/Documents/en/news/pressreleases/Grupo_Salinas_en.pdf
39 Calculated at an average exchange rate over two years of 1 Mexican Peso = US 8.25 cents.

11

Acquisition, Merger and Alliance Strategies

Learning Outcomes

This chapter is designed to enable you to:

① Identify various forms of acquisition, merger and alliance strategies and describe their characteristics.

② Critique claims about the relative merits of these strategies.

③ Apply these strategies to particular cases.

CASE STUDY: The merger of Age Concern and Help the Aged

The two main UK charities that focus on care and support for the elderly, Age Concern and Help the Aged, merged in 2008. After an interim period the combined enterprise became known as Age UK, with subsidiary organizations focused on needs in Wales, Scotland and Northern Ireland.[1] Its declared purpose is to enable elderly people to flourish in a world that respects and offers them a satisfactory standard of living in economic and other terms. It has links with age-focused charity organisations in 70 other countries.

Age Concern's origins were in the 1940s, though it took this name only in 1971. It had four national organizations covering England, Scotland, Wales and Northern Ireland in a federal structure covering over 370 registered local and regional charities. Help the Aged started in 1961, thanks to serial philanthropist and successful entrepreneur, Cecil Jackson-Cole who was concerned with the plight of the elderly and disadvantaged in Great Britain and overseas.

Over time it became clear that these enterprises had overlapping missions, so a merger was rational and perhaps inevitable. However, an examination of their sources of funds in their final year of independence, 2008/9, highlights interesting differences.

Table 11.A: Income sources of Age Concern and Help the Aged before they merged

Source of funds (£ million)	Age Concern	%	Help the Aged	%
Donations, gifts and legacies	23.5	26	34.8	47
Trading (charity shops, etc.)	15.8	17	32.9	44
Grants	8.2	9	3.7	5
Investment income and other activities*	43.6	48	2.9	4
TOTAL	91.2	100	74.3	100

* Such as training courses; umbrella provision of commercial services such as insurance, funerals, installation of living aids in the home, etc.

Questions

1. At first sight the activities of the two organizations appear very complementary. To what extent should the merged organization now be integrated? For example, should it reassign responsibility for each major activity to whichever structural unit already has the most capability? Or should its main activities continue to be decentralised in multiple units?

2. What other issues of merger integration may arise?

Introduction: Acquisitions, Mergers and Alliances

Self-reliant ('organic') growth strategies have both attractions and drawbacks. Internal strategies allow enterprises full control over their own development: what they do, when, and how quickly.[2] They can establish clear, viable directions and make investments consistent with them. Strategies involving diversification offer the potential to develop relevant new capabilities. They create learning and promotional opportunities for capable staff and make enterprises more attractive to capable, potential recruits. Despite these benefits, internally generated development has practical drawbacks:

- Organic growth that entails diversification exposes enterprises to risks from incomplete knowledge, inadequate resources and the diversion of managerial attention. To underestimate these risks threatens existing, core activities.

- New assets and capabilities needed to operate in new domains take time to accumulate, usually at current market prices. Meanwhile, existing providers continue to develop and strengthen their own positions. Because they made comparable investments at lower historical prices they can expect to achieve better future returns on capital employed than a new entrant.

LEARNING
OBJECTIVE ①
An enterprise should therefore at least consider alternative options to implement its strategic aims, notably to merge with or acquire (takeover) another enterprise, or to enter one or more mutually beneficial alliances. Alliances are collaborations between partner enterprises; they take many forms characterised by degrees of formality, longevity, complementarity and symmetry.

How do acquisitions and mergers differ? An acquisition is the purchase of one enterprise by another. The acquired enterprise loses some or all of its identity. It often takes the acquirer's name or its name is merely an adjunct to it. When the parties agree, the acquisition is friendly; when the target rejects and resists an approach, hostility arises. Frequently, the acquirer is larger than the acquired enterprise and is pursuing a growth strategy by acquiring weaker or more specialised enterprises over time. An ambitious enterprise with inadequate funds, or lacking specific expertise to pursue its own growth ambitions, may invite merger or takeover. Exceptionally, the proven management team in a comparatively small enterprise persuades the owners of a large, poorly performing one that it can achieve much better results for them.

A merger is a combining of enterprises whose boards and executive managers declare a mutual respect and desire to work together in the interests of both. Mergers are generally friendly. They may form part of a strategic pattern or be singular, opportunistic events. Merger announcements invariably express optimistic expectations of the joint benefits including greater combined strength, better growth opportunities, scale and scope economies and other synergies. Yet the prime motive for a merger often appears defensive. As with acquisitions, the two parties often differ in size. The partners must decide whether to retain separate identities or create a distinct new identity to signal their notional equality.

Alliances are looser arrangements between two or more enterprises. As will be seen, they can have many purposes and take many forms, with varying degrees of formality. Some are long term; some are formed for a specific purpose over well-defined, relatively short periods. A comprehensive account of mergers, acquisitions and alliances would have to examine the multitude of practical, operational details entailed in the processes of target identification, deal-making and negotiation, followed by integration and relationship management within what may initially be very different enterprises. The focus of this chapter is their strategic rationales and associated issues, whether as means to grow or to make current positions more secure, typically against the threat from larger, well-resourced competitors.

Acquisition and Merger Strategies[3]

Motives for and Strategic Logics of Acquisitions and Mergers

Corporate mergers and acquisitions are common routes to increase shareholder value (the so-called 'holy grail' of corporate strategy) in the United States, Canada, the UK, and more recently in the European Union. Country-particular circumstances, such as conservatism and a high proportion of privately owned enterprises can inhibit this activity.[4] The dual supervisory and executive board structure in Germany strongly discourages hostile bids, as do the interlocking ownership structures of Japanese *keiretsu* and state ownership in socialist countries, notably China, where the state owns most large corporations, although permitting private ownership of small and medium enterprises (SMEs).

RNING ①
CTIVE Aside from the drawbacks of internal development, a proactive enterprise has many reasons to consider the option of a merger or acquisition. Underlying logics can be classed as strategic or financial, and offensive (normally growth-oriented) or defensive in nature. A further logical distinction is between same-sector and different-sector combinations.

The *strategic* motive for a strong enterprise to combine with a same-sector competitor are principally that it increases its already dominant market share and coverage (assuming it does not raise monopoly concerns). It also increases bargaining power over suppliers and buyers, reducing costs and enhancing prices. Particularly for a relatively weak enterprise, additional benefits include the opportunity to:

- Strengthen its competitiveness against the most dominant current competitor.
- Achieve greater operational efficiency via scale and scope economies, and by eliminating obsolete, surplus or duplicate capacity that probably exists among the prospective partners' parallel value-adding activities.
- Bid more credibly for contracts than presently because of its inadequate size.
- Adopt more efficient processes and technologies already used by an innovative or more specialised competitor.

Learning and knowledge accumulation are particularly strong motives.[5] Managerial and technical expertise can be shared and more widely applied.[6] Expectations of gains in profitability and enterprise value help to explain predatory acquisitions and opportunistic mergers.[7] Opportunism typically stems from the desire of key decision-makers to 'strike a deal'.[8] Since few not-for-profit enterprises have the means or the formal constitutions to permit acquisitions, they are likely to engage in mergers, combining their finite resources and activities to benefit from increased coverage and efficiency via scale and scope economies.

Financial motives for mergers and acquisitions anticipate various potential benefits. These include:

- Larger scale enhances the prospects for obtaining new investment funds on better debt or equity terms.
- One-time 'windfall' profits by rationalising, restructuring, or dismembering a poorly-performing enterprise, leading subsequently to profitable, partial or total re-sale (since the market price of a failing enterprise usually understates it core asset value).
- Paying for valuable assets with shares ('corporate paper'), rather than cash or debt, (feasible when economies are buoyant and share prices are rising).
- Tax advantages, by exploiting the accumulated tax losses of one party or exploiting other technical possibilities.

Open stock markets in the West encourage the release and redeployment of capital locked in underperforming companies. Restructuring and rejuvenating ailing enterprises benefit a country's economy by increasing its vibrancy and overall corporate net worth. Although a clear case can be made for the merits of aggressive debt-financed (leveraged) acquisitions and restructuring, owners and employees do not always benefit, however. Excessive acquisition price premiums damage future profitability and result in redundancies. Various other acquisition motives also feature, based on the strategic logic of the acquirer, as shown in Figure 11.1.

Acquisition strategies

Strategic logic: Kraft Inc. of the United States has a long history of growth via acquisitions. It acquired Cadbury plc in 2010, paying £11.5 billion after a prolonged, increasingly hostile struggle that raised concerns about the consequences for Cadbury and its British workers. Kraft was motivated to extend its food and confectionery product portfolio with Cadbury's chocolate brands and sugar-free chewing gums, Dentyne and Stimorol. Shareholders accepted £5 cash plus 0.1874 of new Kraft shares for each Cadbury share, valuing the latter at £8.40. To finance the takeover, Kraft sold its North American frozen pizza business to Nestlé for £2.3 billion and borrowed £7 billion.

Financial logic: KKR, a US private equity company, acquired Alliance Boots, one of the UK's largest publicly quoted retail chains in a debt-financed bid, consistent with its history of similar acquisitions. It typically implements aggressive restructuring to make acquisitions more profitable within a few years, leading to profitable resale. However, in 2009 in the wake of the global credit crunch, KKR wrote down the value of Alliance Boots by 45% and announced losses of US$ 1.19 billion.

Merger strategies

Synergistic opportunism: Glaxo-Welcome, a major UK pharmaceutical company, merged in 2000 with US-based pharmaceuticals and consumer products corporation Smith-Kline-Beecham (SKB) to become GlaxoSmithKline (GSK). Both had a history of mergers and acquisitions. SKB was a merger of UK's Beecham plc and a company itself a combination of the drugs and instrument companies Smith & Kline, French & Richards, RIT of Belgium and Beckman Instruments. The declared motives were to create an enhanced portfolio of 'star' drugs to complement existing 'cash cows' and global critical mass. The commitment of the two chief executives to a merger was widely reported at the time.

Synergistic opportunism: In 2008, Reading University and Henley Management College merged their respective business and management teaching and research activities. The merged entity became the Henley Business School, the largest faculty in Reading University. It has five separate departments covering teaching and research at all levels. Reading lacked Henley's presence in postgraduate education, but actively engaged in academic and applied research. Henley Management College needed to defend its position in the very competitive markets for postgraduate MBA degrees and post-experience training, development and corporate consulting.

Acquisitions and mergers with intent to reduce competition by increasing sector dominance are strategically rational. As noted in Chapter 1, most strategists prefer to avoid damaging competitive behaviour unless it is unavoidable or because competitors are so weak that it can readily increase its dominance over them.

To increase sector dominance an enterprise must find a suitable target. It also exposes itself to possible scrutiny by the competition authorities. Scrutiny aside, acquisition or merger might not achieve the desired benefits at lower cost than internal development, since that the acquisition and integration of another enterprise incurs major (sometimes quite excessive) costs. Even more fundamental, will the integrated enterprise enhance its long-term efficiency and effectiveness? If not, the combined value will remain below what the two enterprises would achieve by continuing separately. Loss of combined share is probable because some clients will resent the change and transfer their custom to a third supplier, if possible. Integration might also encourage a capable new entrant, *increasing* competition. Decisions require judgements without guarantee of success.

Mergers and acquisitions motivated by the intent to diversify create either (a) vertical combinations of suppliers or customers or (b) horizontal combinations that can be related, concentric or unrelated conglomerate diversifications (Figure 11.2).

Vertical, mutually dependent, customer–supplier combinations can become inward-looking, inefficient and complacent. Further, if an enterprise continues trading with competitors of its acquired supply partner (as a multi-sourcing strategy[9]), or it supplies competitors of its distribution partner, conflicts of interest may arise that prove costly to resolve, inhibiting the long-term effectiveness of the combined enterprise.

Horizontal acquisitions and mergers raise similar issues to horizontal diversification via internal development. Related integration implies combining enterprises with equivalent activities and outputs in different sectors, offering each one access to complementary activities that potentially extend the scope of its markets, technologies and other capabilities. Again, well-considered divestments and restructuring may be needed, with the potential to damage future performance if executed badly.[10]

Planning and Executing Acquisitions and Mergers

Acquisitions and mergers involve complex processes. They take time and encounter many challenges and setbacks. Large enterprises sometimes have a specialist central unit to identify

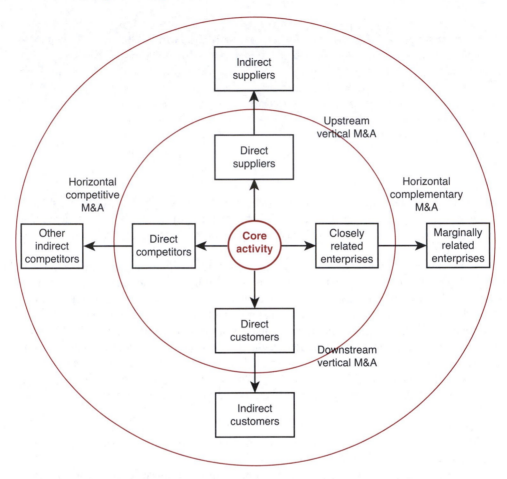

Figure 11.2: Types of merger and acquisition

targets and plan takeovers, although they frequently take expert outside advice on critical issues such as bid price, merger terms, tactics and general conduct.

The key stages of completing an acquisition are as follows:

1. Identify and select targets consistent with the strategic or financial logic in use.
2. Assess bid tactics while maintaining a high level of secrecy.
3. Decide the offer price and the best mix of cash, shares and debt to finance it.
4. Decide the timing of the offer announcement and how to present it publicly.
5. Engage in post-offer negotiations, further announcements, revised bids and public relations activities needed to conclude (or withdraw from) a deal.

6. Once an offer has been accepted in principle, complete the financial and legal searches to assess whether published documents and statements accurately represent the assets and capabilities to be acquired ('due diligence').
7. Following satisfactory due diligence, decide the crucial executive appointments before starting to manage subsequent integration.
8. Evaluate post-integration performance and establish new procedures to maximise the mutual learning and adoption of best practices.

The imperative to make acquisitions at realistic prices bears directly on corporate strategy. Ideally, the bidding enterprise pays no more than what it believes the target is worth. However, setting a bid price needs judgement that considers strategic, financial, timing and psychological issues. Will shareholders respond best to a realistic offer or a low offer followed if necessary by an improved offer to close the deal? Should bids stress the vulnerability of the target or the merits of the combined enterprise? What if there are competing bids once the target is 'in play'? How much would it matter if a direct competitor acquires the target?

Offers comprise cash or a combination of cash and quoted shares of the bidding enterprise. Cash sources include tangible reserves, a new share issue, or debt. Other securities and tangible assets might be offered. Bidders generally prefer share-based offers to conserve cash reserves and in the hope that recipients will hold its shares, sustaining their price. Bid recipients generally prefer cash offers, not least because they have to establish the value of non-cash assets to their satisfaction. The bidder's share price can fluctuate unpredictably, making bid value uncertain. Price rises when the stock market considers the deal is justified and fall when the strategic logic looks dubious or an offer clearly over-values the target.

Bids aim to acquire an enterprise whole, sometimes an agreed fraction. Fifty-one per cent ensures management control; owning around 30% of 'ordinary' shares (which confer *voting rights*) achieves significant influence in a quoted public company. Stock market regulations in most countries require an enterprise that owns or has committed to buy a threshold percentage of the shares (30% in the UK) to offer to buy them all.[11] Bidders must follow stock market regulations that are particularly complex when takeover bids involve public companies.[12] It is vital that insiders with privileged knowledge maintain secrecy and do not abuse their positions; otherwise they may be committing a criminal offence

Even when objective observers support the strategic logic of a bid, the target enterprise may resist takeover. Relations may become acrimonious. Hostile takeover bids have several consequences:

- They polarise opinions and prejudice attitudes among shareholders, employees, commentators and the investing public, especially when issues of 'national interest' are invoked.
- They increase the chance of rival bids once targets are 'in play', perhaps from friendly 'white knights'. Bidders then pay more than is strategically justified or withdraw and lose face.
- They encourage targets to make themselves less attractive (the so-called 'poison pill' defence), which creates unwelcome future liabilities for a new owner.
- They oblige bidder and target to spend large sums on 'propaganda' advertising to support their positions; these costs become unwelcome liabilities of the combined enterprise.

- They force senior executives in the target enterprise to quit immediately after they have lost the battle, disrupting day-to-day management. Severance terms add further substantial costs to the acquisition.

For all these reasons *friendly* acquisitions and mergers are preferable.

Business mergers proceed under essentially the same regulations, although merger agreements can be complex. Shareholders of a comparatively junior partner are generally invited to exchange their shares for those of the dominant partner, based on a negotiated formula. If the parties are quoted companies of equivalent status, they may create completely new shares in the merged enterprise allocated to all existing shareholders using an agreed formula.

Not-for-profit enterprises do not issue shares and combinations are generally presented as mergers, although combinations involving partners of unequal size may in effect be takeovers. Not-for-profit mergers are subject to a different regulatory framework (e.g., in the UK, governance by the Charity Commissioners). Normally, the more senior partner retains its identity, although it may wish to preserve the identity and associated goodwill of the junior partner. Such mergers can present their own difficulties, not least because of multifaceted missions and ideological differences.

Merger 'mania' in British higher education

Since the 1980s British universities – funded largely by taxpayers – have been pressured to increase teaching efficiency. One approach has been to explore regional mergers. Two cases highlight different outcomes.

The universities of **Bath** and **West of England (UWE)** have campuses 20 kilometres apart in neighbouring cities. In the 1990s the Vice Chancellor of Bath University and Principal of UWE agreed to the principle of merging. Their respective subject portfolios appeared to dovetail, so the merged institution would comprise a portfolio of well-defined, departmental 'SBUs', expected to minimise merger integration problems and redundancies. However, overlap was not wholly avoidable. Both institutions had large, influential business and management studies departments whose academics were unhappy about merger, fearing mission compromise, loss of autonomy, identity and status, and activity duplication that would create redundancies. Senior academics lobbied against it, making common cause with some other departments. The Bath University Senate, its highest academic decision making forum, voted narrowly against the merger, which effectively killed it.

In 1996 **Brunel University** merged with the **West London Institute (WLI).** Their relative standings mirrored those of Bath University and UWE. There was minimal internal consultation and although presented as a merger, Brunel effectively acquired WLI and its three valuable campuses in West London and Surrey. Both institutions also had well-established business and management departments that subsequently struggled with a five-year integration programme. Very few staff were made redundant, but over time a majority of former WLI staff quit. Brunel realised significant windfall gains when it sold the WLI sites, that funded major upgrades to the Uxbridge campus.

Challenges of Post-acquisition Integration

When a merger or acquisition proceeds, it requires decisions about how and how far to integrate the two enterprises. To achieve a harmonious, productive integration is a severely challenging process of change management. Integration is often too slow or half-hearted, failing to address the barriers arising from negative staff attitudes, obstructive executives and conflicting ethos, especially in cross-border combinations. Ideally, executive appointments and restructuring activities should be substantially completed very quickly, so that everyone sees that there is no going back; giving 'us and them' attitudes little chance to thrive.[13] Even so, staff in the junior enterprise may lose morale and commitment, while those who quit voluntarily tend to be some of the more skilled and valuable.

Successful integration requires careful thought about crucial strategic questions, particularly when a new enterprise enters an existing portfolio:

- How independent are its activities from those of other portfolio members and how independent or interdependent should they be in future?
- How much managerial autonomy should it retain?

Taken together these factors yield the priority matrix of Figure 11.3. If the enterprise units are essentially independent and will benefit from continued autonomy, there is a strong case to retain distinct identities and current boundaries, while exchanging best practice ideas with others, sharing resources and achieving mutually beneficial synergies. However, incentives to collaborate are generally needed.

Where interdependence is high (as one might expect of the resource complementarity logic of acquisition) and the need for autonomy is low, the case for full integration is clear. Absorption means consolidating new enterprise units with one or more existing units and rationalising their operations accordingly. Best practices can be extended on a case-by-case basis. Again, the matter of identity arises: should that of the most senior part(s) prevail or should multiple identities persist? Perhaps a composite, new identity should be developed.

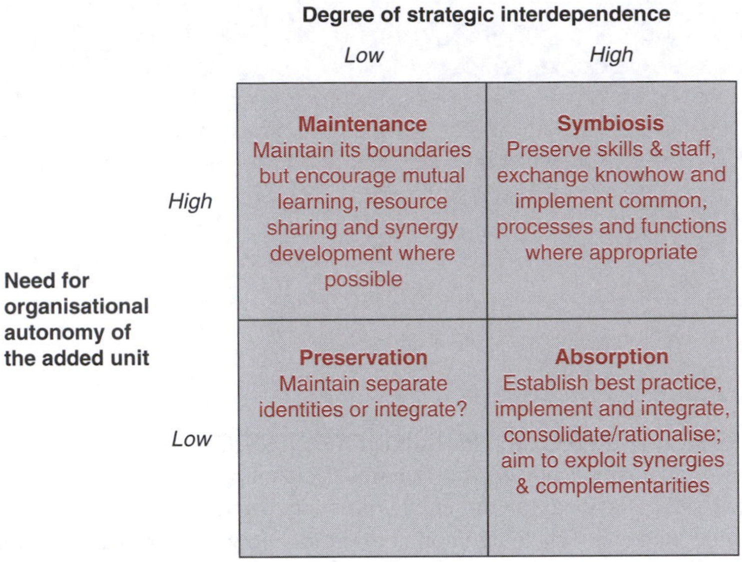

Degree of strategic interdependence

	Low	High
High	**Maintenance** Maintain its boundaries but encourage mutual learning, resource sharing and synergy development where possible	**Symbiosis** Preserve skills & staff, exchange knowhow and implement common, processes and functions where appropriate
Low	**Preservation** Maintain separate identities or integrate?	**Absorption** Establish best practice, implement and integrate, consolidate/rationalise; aim to exploit synergies & complementarities

Need for organisational autonomy of the added unit

Figure 11.3: Priorities in merger integration

Adapted from an idea to emerge from Baden-Fuller and Boschetti (1995)

When interdependence is high, there are competing desires to collaborate yet retain distance and autonomy. Here the parenting role needs to encourage respectful, beneficial interactions while maintaining separate expertise-based identities. Some functions such as procurement or manufacturing may benefit from consolidation, while others would not. When interdependence is low, yet no cogent reason to retain full autonomy of units exists, the decision whether to integrate fully must consider the particular circumstances, although full integration probably remains the better option.

When Acquisitions and Mergers Disappoint

LEARNING ② OBJECTIVE
Although merger and acquisition strategies aim to achieve growth more rapidly and effectively than internal development strategies, future performance frequently disappoints.[14]

Failure to achieve the expected benefits arises for four main reasons:

1. The strategic logic of integration was weak:
   - Corporate executives made unrealistic appraisals of the potential synergies.
   - The enterprises involved were weak prior to combining and together they remained weak.
   - Personal motives overrode corporate benefit.
2. The financial logic was poor or compromised:
   - Expectations of cost savings and financial synergies were unrealistic.

- The bid was contested and became hostile, raising the acquisition price far too high to yield a good return on investment.

- Debt-financed interest charges, especially when interest rates rose, greatly elevating the costs of the integrated enterprise.

3. The prior 'due diligence' was inadequate. Despite valid strategic or financial logics (based on the available evidence), the acquired assets proved of lower calibre than represented or unexpected liabilities emerged to prevent resale value.[15]

4. Internal relationships became hostile, poisonous and vindictive, destroying the prospects of constructive collaborations.

In theory, agreed mergers should create fewer integration problems. However, the publicly-stated strategic logic for a merger can still be flawed, creating uncertainty and inaction while strategies are reassessed. Mergers are sometimes the product of chief executive ambition or opportunism, lacking rigorous strategic logic. In a merger between broadly equal partners, board members and senior executives commonly jockey for position when some realise that they are essentially now redundant. Ill-feeling and distrust result.

Table 11.B presents survey findings from various studies of the success of acquisition and mergers. While there is some subjectivity in how they define success, the overall findings should serve as a warning to corporate executives. Under half of the cases studied could claim to have realised the expected benefits within a reasonable period. Another study highlighted the tendency of major, combined enterprises to destroy, not create, value (Table 11.C).

Table 11.B: Studies of acquisition outcomes

Study	Year	No. of enterprises in the study	Success criterion	Outcomes
McKinsey	1987	116	Recover capital costs within 3 years	77% failed
Coopers and Lybrand	1996	125	Expected revenues, cash flows and profitability	66% failed

Table 11.B: Cont'd

Study	Year	No. of enterprises in the study	Success criterion	Outcomes
Mercer	1997	215	Good returns to shareholders after 3 years	63% failed (1980s) 48% failed (1990s)
KPMG International	2006	121	Increase share-holder value acceptably	Shareholder value: Enhanced 31% Flat 43% Reduced 26%

Data sources: McMahan and Hester (2000); KPMG.com

Table 11.C: Acquisitions can destroy shareholder value

Deal	Year	Value created by combination $ billion	Value destroyed since combination $ billion
AOL/Time Warner	2001		−148
Vodafone/Mannesmann	2000		−299
Pfizer/Warner-Lambert	2000		−78
Glaxo/SmithKline	2000		−40
Chase/J.P. Morgan	2000		−26
Exxon/Mobil	1999	+8	
SBC/Ameritech	1999		−68
WorldCom/MCI	1998		−94
Travelers/Citicorp	1998	+109	
Daimler/Chrysler	1998		−36

Data source: Hammonds (2002)

RNING
ECTIVE ②
When it has become clear that a takeover or merger has not achieved its aims and is unlikely to do so, de-integration or de-merger is the appropriate response. This is a costly and painful process, highlighting poor executive judgements and decisions to the world.

Divestments following unsuccessful integration

Centrica, a UK energy company, acquired the Automobile Association (AA), a national roadside automobile repair and rescue organisation, in 1999. Centrica made several unrelated acquisitions in pursuit of conglomerate diversification. There was no strategic synergy between the two organisations; Centrica sold the AA in 2004 to a private equity company.

The marriage of *Daimler-Benz* with *Chrysler Corporation* failed to create a successful Daimler–Chrysler. Chrysler supporters became aggrieved to realise that it was not a merger: Chrysler had been taken over. The joint corporation was beset with difficulties as German and American attitudes clashed, disagreements emerged over quality and product policy, while Chrysler's managers felt marginalised over strategic decisions. In 2007 Daimler-Benz sold Chrysler to a private equity company.

Given the potential difficulties of mergers and acquisitions, does internal development remain the best growth path? The evidence of successful, well-known enterprises tends support this view. Nonetheless, strategies that embrace mergers and acquisitions can achieve indisputable benefits when the parties:

- Assemble high quality, complementary assets and skills that realistically they could not have created independently.
- Deploy these assets and skills to create genuine, greater sustainable value for their respective shareholders and other stakeholders than they would have done independently.
- Work hard to achieve productive integration, but if they conclude that a particular case is not meeting expectations, they act swiftly to correct or divest.

These are tough criteria, not least because observers can only guess how successful the parties would have been had they not combined. Ultimately, a combination must succeed to the satisfaction of its stakeholders in the terms by which they judge it.

Alliance (Collaboration) Strategies

Motives for and Strategic Logics of Collaborative Alliances

An ambitious enterprise may fear that relying entirely on internal development will allow aggressive competitors to outpace it. Relative to its resources and capabilities, it may have too many growth opportunities to pursue alone. Perhaps an acquisition or merger would be the answer, but it cannot find a suitable target. A collaborative alliance with one or more other enterprises is a viable strategic option for many executives to consider.

Partners in *growth-oriented* alliances aim for higher performance whilst generally containing costs. Growth objectives include new market entries and income streams, more ambitious levels of investment, and the development of new products and technologies. *Defensive* alliances offer smaller and weaker partners options to sustain current output at lower cost and with fewer weaknesses. In general, the potential benefits include:

- Enhanced scale that allows partners to achieve a minimum efficient scale of operation that neither can achieve alone.

- Scope economies, by eliminating duplication and spreading costs across more products, services, markets and technologies.

- Allowing partners to contribute complementary resources or technologies, minimising the weaknesses of their combined operations, while limiting investment to what each can afford and considers acceptable.

- Greater flexibility compared with merger or acquisition, keeping strategic options open for longer (a successful alliance can end in merger if the parties wish, or survive just long enough to fulfil specific objectives).

- Sharing risks and reducing uncertainties, especially when implementing new technologies and business processes.

- Opportunities to learn from a partner's capabilities when they are clearly superior.

Alliance Options and Characteristics

LEARNING
OBJECTIVE ① A prospective alliance partner must address important questions about its motives for collaboration and consequently, what modes of alliance are preferable. Should it seek:

- Partners with similar interests, ambitions and capabilities, or those that offer complementarities in markets, resources or capabilities?

- Vertical or horizontal linkages?

- Relationships in which it would be the dominant partner or would it consider being of equal or subordinate (junior) status?

- Equity cross-holdings (long term) or purely arms-length transactions (generally short-term and/or project based)?

- A high degree of mutual trust or accept that pragmatic, opportunistic behaviours will occur?

Figure 11.4 shows the range of possible alliance types. *Vertical* alliances involve co-ordinated partners in various upstream or downstream stages of the value-adding supply chain. An already-influential enterprise takes a co-ordination role. *Horizontal* alliances offer more options. The enterprise might collaborate with a competitive enterprise in specific areas, strengthening their respective positions against a more dominant competitor. These partnerships typically exploit different but complementary activities or address those where both enterprises are comparatively weak, whether to enhance technologies, operational resources and capacities, or marketing and geographic coverage. Similar considerations apply to collaborations with enterprises external to the sector that parallel those for mergers and acquisitions.

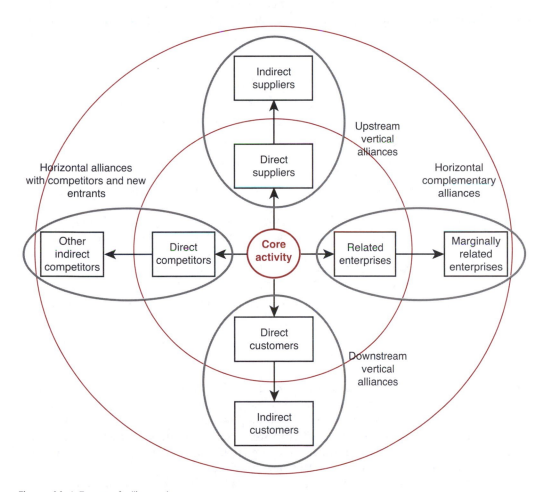

Figure 11.4: Types of alliance*

*After Torger Reve

Reprinted with permission of John Wiley and Sons, Inc.

Collaboration is *not* collusion, because it is characterised by an acceptable transparency of intention and actions, open to public scrutiny. Collusion occurs when enterprises act together secretly in ways that disadvantage suppliers, clients or competitors. Collusion is invariably informal, and illegal in most countries. When discovered by the competition authorities it results in heavy fines, constraints on future operating freedoms, even criminal prosecutions. However, collusion can be hard to prove. When an enterprise sends overt market 'signals' such as increasing prices substantially, it may have obtained tacit support from competitors who promptly do the same. Without these commercial factors, not-for-profit enterprises have more freedom to collaborate, although tacit conduct suggesting that the parties have something to hide is never welcome, particularly when conflicts of interest or ethical considerations are disguised.

LEARNING
OBJECTIVE ①
Open, explicit collaborations between enterprises, even direct competitors, are generally acceptable, provided that they do not (and are not intended to) inhibit genuine competition. Joint ventures, licensing and distribution agreements are examples. The criteria that govern the acceptability of a particular arrangement are that:

- The arrangements are matters of public knowledge.
- Collaboration does not seek to reduce sector output artificially.
- No other parties are disadvantaged in ways that they cannot avoid by finding other sources, for example, from higher prices or other unfavourable terms of trade.

LEARNING
OBJECTIVE ①
The decision whether to enter an alliance and the precise form it takes will depend on an enterprise's history, current circumstances, ethos and identity, the characteristics of prospective partners and the benefits expected.

These factors are all influenced by the prospective partners' countries of origin and the assumptions and behaviours of senior executives. Two specific issues matter greatly:

1. Can they tolerate dispersed ownership and control of progress-seeking ventures?
2. Do they expect relationships between enterprises to be:
    - Long term and trusting, including the exchange of proprietary knowledge and skills?[16]
    - Short term and opportunistic (when circumstances permit), protective of proprietary knowledge and skills?[17]

Figure 11.5 combines these variables, suggesting four possible modes of interaction among enterprises. Whereas the 'clan-based' structures that characterise many family (and criminal!) enterprises seek sometimes obsessive central control of resources and knowledge, effective strategic alliances encourage partner enterprises to work actively to develop durable, trust-based relationships in which each partner owns and controls only parts of the array of resources and capabilities needed for the strategy of collaboration to succeed.

Large Western businesses tend to favour control via bureaucratic hierarchical structures and tightly negotiated market transactions. Public-sector and other large not-for-profit enterprises have traditionally also been bureaucracies that engage in all aspects of their functions, though they now increasingly use market subcontracting over limited-horizons. Japanese *keiretsu* and

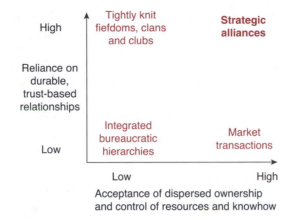

Figure 11.5: Strategic alliances based on positive attitudes to trust and shared control

Derived from Ouchi (1980)

Korean *chaebols* combine Western corporate practices with, in varying degrees, clannish behaviours deriving from their histories and instincts.

Alliances take many forms, making a simple classification difficult. Three distinct strategic forms of alliance are:

1. Joint ventures (JVs).
2. Formal, non-JV alliances.
3. Less formal, participatory alliances and networks.

Joint Venture Strategic Alliances

Equity-based joint ventures (JVs) are the most formal and least reversible kind of collaboration between two, sometimes more, partners. A JV is a new enterprise, set up to achieve an agreed strategic purpose. It involves shared ownership and high commitment, generally over relatively long periods.

The partners invest jointly in a JV and accept agreed proportions of its equity, costs and returns. Legal contracts specify the ownership and operational terms, subject to later revisions by mutual consent. When a JV requires greater investment funds than the partners can provide, they can involve external investors by floating it as a publicly quoted corporation. However, many JVs remain private enterprises to enhance commercial secrecy. A JV's operations and financial performance are reported subject to the accounting conventions of its home country. Since it is a partly owned subsidiary of two or more partners, it is consolidated in the accounts of each one according to respective home country rules. Thus it can be difficult for outsiders to assess a JV's true scope and performance.

Although partners share management responsibilities, arrangements vary considerably. Typically, the parent enterprises appoint an executive management team, though each may second people with particular, relevant expertise for defined periods. JV managers are accountable to a board of directors, generally comprising executives from both partners and non-executive directors.

LEARNING
OBJECTIVE ①
Despite its nominally independent status, JV owners determine its mission, which may be ongoing or have a finite life span. Specific JV purposes include intent to:

- Supply operational or strategically significant inputs to the partners.
- Provide a distribution channel to provide them with access to (and information about) downstream demand.
- Develop and market goods or expert services to extend their repertoires.
- Provide a diversification vehicle that would be too ambitious for any partner alone.
- Fulfil a specific aim (e.g., a major construction project of specified duration).

Joint venture strategies

Two-partner JV

The global corporations Ericsson of Sweden and Sony of Japan established Sony-Ericsson as a 50:50 joint venture to design, make and market mobile telephones and other mobile wireless devices. Its vision is to 'become THE communication entertainment brand.' Ericsson provides knowledge of mobile networks, technical standards and manufacturing resources. Sony knows how to design and make consumer electronic devices in high volume, allied to brand management and marketing skills.

Three-partner JV

The UK-based Kentz Corporation set up a JV with Theiss and Decmil (both Australian enterprises) in 2009 to design and construct a residential village on an offshore island in north-western Australia for Chevron Oil. Kentz provided engineering and construction expertise, the other partners provided local procurement and construction services. The JV was to terminate on project completion.

Multi-partner JV

The Amadeus flight reservation system began in 1987 as a joint venture to provide four airlines and their retail travel agents with dedicated ticket reservation services. It is now majority owned by BC Partners, Cinven, Air France, Iberia and Lufthansa; it acts for 95 airlines, train operators, car rental companies, ferries and cruise lines, hotels and tour operators.

JVs are a serious commitment. To succeed, they must be well planned and managed. They can be dissolved only with difficulty. Ideally, the parties will anticipate probable contingencies before proceeding, so that provisions exist to resolve difficulties as they arise. Despite a JV being founded on expectations of trust, legal contracts are almost always used to codify the key policies and arrangements that will govern it. When issues emerge unexpectedly, perhaps years into the future, mutual trust will enable partners to resolve them via negotiation. Notwithstanding initial good faith, partners may find they disagree over:

- Senior executive appointments.

- Organisational structures, policies and the process and pace of decision-making.

- Interpretations of their respective obligations to the JV.

- Willingness to make future JV-specific investments (if they have underestimated its finance needs or become unhappy with current performance or future prospects).

- Charges they make to the JV for 'goodwill' inputs of staff time and other resources and services not originally specified.

Clashes of ethos are common between partners of different backgrounds. Factions develop within the JV if employees transferred from each partner retain their former loyalties. Alternatively, a distinctive JV ethos emerges, distancing it from the parents, hindering communications and co-operation with them.

Because contracts are costly to monitor and enforce, trust is a vital, practical feature of successful joint ventures. A partner that deliberately contributes less than promised, or who *misrepresents* the quality of its contributions, knowing that its partner cannot retaliate effectively, is guilty of cheating, called moral hazard.[18] It arises most commonly when one partner's inputs are JV-specific, with little value in alternative use, while another partner's inputs can be redeployed later in other ways.

When trust evaporates it signals probable JV demise, along with recriminations and lawsuits as each partner seeks to attribute failures to the other. Ultimately, JV ownership then passes to one partner or a third party on unfavourable terms, or the enterprise is closed. For example, Airbus was originally a consortium of four European aircraft makers; although successful, its increasing co-ordination problems led ultimately to its acquisition by EADS. Nonetheless, many well-planned and managed JVs succeed and some persist. A successful JV experience encourages an enterprise to continue using JVs in its strategic development; an unsuccessful venture discourages future JVs.[19]

Non-JV Alliances

A formal alliance that involves less commitment than a JV may be more acceptable, despite featuring similar motives and characteristics. Many forms exist. An alliance may be vertical or horizontal; it involves non-competing and in some circumstances competing partners, who may be of equivalent status or have a dominant–subordinate relationship.

Horizontal Alliances between Equivalent-Status, Non-Competing Partners

When prospective partners have broadly equivalent status, they collaborate on a basis of mutual strength and respect. They can select partners so that their respective strengths are complementary. Two-way flows of information and expertise guide development of the collaborative activity, enabling both parties to be more effective than they would otherwise be.

Similar-status, non-competing partners in *horizontal* alliances build on complementary assets and resources in two main ways. One is when an enterprise uses its partner to perform value-adding activities that directly extend its own capacity or coverage, for example, by manufacturing or distributing its products in a geographically distant country. Alternatively, partners may cross-license the use of brands, logos and other intellectual property.

Given status parity, partners may demonstrate mutual commitment by taking equity stakes in one another. Each may have a representative on the other's board of directors, increasing exchange of knowledge and opportunities to influence issues of mutual interest. Cross-shareholdings and interlocking boards imply mutual trust that may predate the alliance or are possible because both enterprises have high reputations.

The partners construct legal agreements to define the nature of the activities over which they will co-operate. Contracts specify the scope of the alliance and limit each partner's obligations, in principle offering more flexibility than JVs. Scope could cover supply agreements, licensing the use of brand names, and agencies for overseas product distribution. A contract usually limits the duration of an alliance, subject to renewal by mutual consent, leaving fewer problems to unravel if it disappoints.

Contracts do not signal a lack of trust, but aim to avoid future misunderstandings by ensuring commitment to, and compliance with, explicit terms. They also provide a basis for resolving future disagreements, although it is impractical to anticipate all possible contingencies. So, the satisfactory resolution of future difficulties still needs goodwill, trust, and willingness to renegotiate as circumstances change. Even so, enterprises with sound reputations and capabilities may intend to gain more knowledge and expertise from alliances than they concede. When moral hazard becomes apparent, trust evaporates; each partner tries to out-manoeuvre the other, in and out of the courts.[20]

Horizontal alliances between equivalent-status, non-competitors

Extension of capacity or coverage

Sports Direct International plc (SDI) is a leading UK retailer of sports and activity clothes and equipment under its brand names Lonsdale, Slazenger, Dunlop, and Karrimor. In 2008 it entered a strategic alliance to sell SDI products in stores owned by Chinese retail group ITAT. Seen as a possible long-term venture, the initial agreement was timed to capitalise on the Beijing Olympic Games, starting with a store-within-store concept in 120 of ITAT's largest outlets. SDI contributed £20m towards setting-up costs. In return, ITAT provided staff and a percentage of sales to SDI.

Cross-licensing

Lego, the global branded maker of plastic toy construction bricks and kits, entered licence agreements to produce toys based on characters from *Star Wars* (20th Century Fox) and *Toy Story* (Disney/Pixar) among others. The characters and other intellectual property brands deriving from these films have been licensed to many producers of books, television series, video games and toys. Lego gains additional, profitable sales from these tie-ins in exchange for providing the film makers with licence income.

Horizontal Alliances between Equivalent-Status, Competing Partners

LEARNING OBJECTIVE ① Horizontal alliances also feature among enterprises that compete, or have the potential to compete, but find areas to collaborate. Alliances must be carefully crafted and transparent to avoid accusations of intent to restrict competition, especially when they create essentially standardised outputs. Competitor collaborations commonly occur horizontally at an upstream value-adding stage, typically in research and development, sourcing or production, so that partners can maintain regular, downstream competition.

Horizontal, two-competitor alliances

Ford and Peugeot-Citroen (PSA)

High research and development costs encourage car industry alliances, and many are of this type. Ford and Peugeot have enjoyed considerable success sharing the design and development of diesel engines for their respective cars and commercial vehicles. Since 2001 there have been four distinct cycles of collaboration, with the companies taking turns to lead development. Each produces engines in its own factory based on these shared designs, thus benefiting car buyer choice.

Walt Disney Corporation and Pixar Studios

These two companies collaborated to produce and distribute seven animated movies, including *Finding Nemo* and *Toy Story*. Pixar's world-leading computer-aided animation techniques enabled effects that Disney's traditional drawing techniques could not match. Disney contributed its huge influence and capabilities in film distribution and marketing. In 2004 the initial agreement terminated. Pixar's CEO,

Steve Jobs (of Apple fame) considered that the much smaller Pixar failed to get a fair share of the profits, so he would not agree to continue the alliance. While consumers undoubtedly benefited from the collaboration, it may have disadvantaged smaller competitors like Aardman Animations (makers of the *Wallace and Gromit* films) to finance new projects.

Horizontal Alliances between Non-Competing Partners of Senior and Junior Status

LEARNING ① OBJECTIVE

Formal alliances can also exist between partners of unequal status. The crucial factor determining the development of such alliances is their unbalanced power relationship.

The dominant partner exercises considerable influence on the operations of its subordinate partner(s). Junior status means that the subordinate has limited influence over key decisions and allows the dominant partner scope to determine how the alliance functions in practice and will develop over time. Junior status does not always mean a small enterprise; some small partners have strong bargaining power because of specialised expertise.

Dominant–subordinate alliances are common, for good reasons. Although it can be quite oppressive, the junior partner considers it a price worth paying for the benefits gained. The dominant partner injects information, advice, instructions and sometimes working capital, benefits that the subordinate would not readily obtain otherwise.

Alliances between senior and junior partners

Two partner alliance

In 2004 Kodak signed an exclusive agreement with Lexar Media, maker of digital memory cards. Kodak licensed Lexar to use the Kodak brand on its cards, extending Lexar's market reach by 10-fold into 500,000 stores. The agreement allowed Kodak to extend its product portfolio into a fast growing market, creating a new revenue stream at minimal cost. Kodak is arguably the senior partner not only because of its high-profile brand, but also because it controls access to its distribution channels. It can decline to renew the agreement if another memory card maker offers to supply it on better terms. Moreover, Kodak-branded cards may substitute Lexar-branded sales, yielding no net gain to Lexar.

Multi-partner alliances

GlaxoSmithKline (GSK), the major pharmaceutical company, set up CEEDD[21] to form alliances with promising early-stage research by small firms. GSK would offer them expertise in clinical trials and drugs marketing. CEEDD soon formed alliances with Chroma Therapeutics, an Oxford-based biotechnology company, and Concert Pharmaceuticals of Massachusetts. They allow GSK to take commercial manufacturing and marketing licences to products for new drugs that successfully complete clinical trials. In return the development companies receive 'milestone' payments and perhaps massive future licence income.

Vertical Alliances between Equivalent-Status Partners

Vertical alliances extend enterprises' contractual supply chain relationships via the exchange of know-how and commercial information. Suppliers become actively involved in, for example, product design and distribution arrangements.

Particular strategic issues arise in vertical alliances:

- Partners develop customer-supplier dependence, effectively becoming mutual captives.

- Information transparency is vital for operational reasons and to maintain trust; however, asymmetric benefits can result, with a downstream partner controlling market data, an upstream partner controlling technical data.

- Issues of trust and disclosure arise when an enterprise forms alliances with several partners in direct competition, upstream or downstream, and plays each against the others.

- Powerful downstream enterprises exert considerable influence and control over the activities of their supply upstream partners (e.g., supermarkets, car assemblers). They dictate value adding processes, including the traceability and authenticity of supplies back along their complex, extended chains.

Vertical alliances between equivalent-status, non-competitors

Resource-complementarity and logistics

Swedish forest logging firms have alliances with selected paper manufacturers. In exchange for secure, long-term supplies of wood pulp, paper manufacturers site plants at strategic locations accessible to logging operations and end-user markets.

Expertise

Japanese and South Korean enterprises dominate the mass market for digital cameras. New entrants to the quality SLR (single lens reflex) market found it beneficial to establish alliances with German lens makers to gain brand prestige and design expertise (e.g., Sony with Carl Zeiss; Samsung with Schneider). These alliances involve brand licensing and regular exchange of know-how, specifications and technical staff.

Vertical Alliances between Dominant and Subordinate Partners

In general, vertical supply chain alliances enable one partner progressively to increase and exploit power differences to maximise its benefits. Thus power relationships between dominant and subordinate partners readily become asymmetric. (A classic case was the hold that Marks and Spencer achieved over its essentially-captive UK clothing suppliers. Ultimately, these suppliers found the retail chain's business unprofitable and lost contracts to lower-cost overseas suppliers.) Subordinate partners may still get significant benefits, albeit on its partner's terms, such as information, advice, capital injections, and preferential treatment over other suppliers. A dominant partner further increases its leverage when it enters parallel alliances with multiple, competing subordinate partners. In effect it places 'multiple bets' on these suppliers or downstream distributors at relatively low cost and commitment. If a subordinate partner performs well its future influence increases, so it sustains a position of greater strength. Conversely, poor performance will see it eliminated.

In the 'hub-and-spokes' model the dominant partner sits at the hub of a metaphorical wheel with subordinate partners located at the rim; each spoke represents a separate alliance. The subordinate partners may be direct competitors. Alternatively, they may link together as stages in a value-adding chain; then in effect they participate in a complex, *co-ordinated* multi-stage vertical alliance. Hub-and-spokes alliance models can represent a more interactive network, sometimes cited as an exciting new form of industrial organisation. Nonetheless, the hub enterprise generally exercises considerable influence over each link and how the network functions, particularly when the subordinates are small enterprises.[22]

Less-formal Network Alliances

Many large enterprises consider formal alliances unattractive when they cede partial control to one or more partners, unless power asymmetry compensates for loss of complete control. Less-formal, multi-partner alliances may nonetheless provide benefits for enterprises of all sizes, provided that entry, exit and conduct are not over-formalised. These alliances often have network characteristics.

For large enterprises, network membership is attractive when they can influence its purpose and how it develops. For small enterprises, network membership can be attractive even in the company of dominant partners, when benefits include prospective growth and information access and participation remains discretionary rather than obligatory.

For-profit alliances and networks draw on mutual self-interest. Some offer (and require) forms of commercial commitment, sometimes only membership subscriptions. Particularly in the last two decades, collaborative networks have been an important structural feature. The reasons appear four-fold:

- Globalization of business and non-business activities.
- The increasing role of knowledge and information as major sources of strategic advantage.
- The scope for electronic, time-lapsed and real-time global communications, reducing the need for frequent face-to-face contact.

- The actions of well-educated, youthful entrepreneurs who use network skills to mobilise and exploit a critical mass of external resources and know-how, compensating for their own limitations.

Advocates of knowledge-exploiting networks have been optimistic about their future significance. Progress may have been slower than they predicted, excepting technology networks, highly successful networked e-commerce enterprises and website businesses that promote social networking. Many of the latter now exists, notably *Facebook* and their professional equivalents such as *LinkedIn* whose principal purpose is to encourage *individuals* to maintain contacts, share knowledge and learn of business opportunities and jobs. These networks could prove the true enablers of virtual future enterprises, comprising overlapping subsets of individual participants who collaborate in pursuit of common aims (e.g., the network of Linux software developers). Even so, it seems probable that most enterprises will continue to rely substantially on face-to-face operations.

Effective web-enabled network participation

Amazon.com began online book trading in 1995 from Seattle, USA. In 2008 its sales revenues exceeded $19 billion, though net profits before tax were only $609 million (3.2%), indicating narrow net margins. Over the years its rapid expansion was achieved by diversifying its product range. However, it has since extended its business model through trading alliances with hundreds of specialised online suppliers, large and small. Traders feature their offerings on the Amazon website and receive payments from Amazon for goods sold, less a sales commission. Because Amazon avoids the costs and inconvenience of handling traders' goods, this activity is highly profitable, enhancing its overall margins. In 2008 29% of its *unit* sales came via this route. Amazon also encourages hyperlinks to and from many other 'associate' websites.

Eonetwork.org is the website of the Entrepreneurs' Organization (EO), a global network of more than 7,300 business owners in 42 countries. Founded in 1987 by a group of young entrepreneurs, EO claims to be a catalyst that enables entrepreneurs to learn from each other, and develop useful contacts, business opportunities and enrich their personal lives.

To succeed commercially, network participants have to protect their intellectual property rights, which can inhibit genuinely open, trusting relationships. Not-for-profit enterprises may have a more relaxed outlook, considering it vital to collaborate openly in network alliances across activity domains and country borders to gain political influence to support their missions and to compensate for lack of funds.

Not-for-profit alliances are often administered by a central secretariat responsible for overall strategy and policies, and for co-ordinating operational activities in a collaborative, inclusive manner. Similar network alliances regulate standards in the conduct of professional services (e.g., in medicine, law and accountancy, where membership is obligatory), promote domain-specific business interests of their members (who may also be competitors), and establish agreed technical standards.

Commercial network alliances

- The Society of Motor Manufacturers and Traders (SMMT) and the Retail Motor Industry Federation are UK associations that collate and publish car industry statistics, provide information to manufacturers' and retailers and lobby the European Commission, UK and European Union (EU) legislators to ensure that their members' interests are considered when proposing new legislation.

- EuroNCAP is a vehicle crash testing organization funded by the car manufacturers to validate the safety of new cars and to encourage improved safety standards.

- The Japan Experts Group (JPEG) established and continues to develop agreed standards for digital imaging, to ensure compatibility of file transfer among cameras, computers, data storage and other imaging devices.

Not-for-profit network alliances

- Médecins Sans Frontières (MSF) is an 'international, independent, medical humanitarian organisation that delivers emergency aid to people affected by armed conflict, epidemics, healthcare exclusion and natural or man-made disasters'. MSF relies entirely on volunteer doctors and medical staff willing to risk their health and safety in challenging and often dangerous environments. MSF administration comprises 19 international, country-based associations, co-ordinated by an International Council located in Geneva. The associations guarantee to respect MSF principles and engage in promotional and fund-raising activities. Their individual members are current or former MSF employees. Boards of directors are mostly medical professionals.

- The European Urban Knowledge Network (EUKN) based at the Nicis Institute in The Hague, Netherlands is an alliance that shares knowledge and experience of tackling urban environmental challenges. Seventeen EU Member States participate, along with EUROCITIES (a working group of 24 cities and 10 urban research groups), the URBACT Programme (a European exchange and learning programme promoting sustainable urban development) and the European Commission.

Alliance Strategies and Performance

Alliances in their many forms underpin collaborative strategies implemented as an alternative means for enterprises to achieve their objectives, including to:

- Defend current positions and mutual interests.
- Diversify and grow.
- Enhance efficiency via economies of scale and scope.
- Exploit strengths, compensate for weaknesses and acquire new capabilities.
- Enter new markets and operating domains flexibly and cost-effectively.
- Share investment costs and the risks of new ventures.

Collaborative strategies are extremely worthwhile for participants and their stakeholders when they combine an array of resources and capabilities that:

- Neither partner enjoyed, nor could realistically have accumulated by acting alone.
- Meet the VRIOS criteria (Chapter 5) to the greatest extent practical.
- Create externally-valued, sustainable outputs of greater value than the sum of what the partners would have created by acting independently.

Any proposed alliance requires advance judgements about the prospects of its success. There are no certainties. Prospective partners must have clear aims for participation and realistic expectations of what the alliance can achieve. An alliance tends to have a finite life-span: its purpose ceases when the partners' aims, both mutual and partial, have been achieved, or it has become clear that they are not achievable.

Difficulties arise in all forms of alliance when one (or more) of the partners:

- Dissents over acceptable performance levels and timeframes.
- Begins to dominate the other(s), despite initial parity, calling into question the fairness of the alliance.
- Fails to perform as promised, with little prospect of making good.
- Acts opportunistically and exploitatively.
- Pursues parallel strategic changes elsewhere that reduce the importance of the alliance to it or make the alliance effectively redundant, for example, by injecting knowledge gained from the alliance into a competing, new venture.

The expected result is loss of trust and mutual suspicion. In consequence the partners incur substantial 'transaction costs' by insisting on performance verification, compensation for inadequate performance and duplicity. Even so, continuing with an alliance may be the partners' only affordable route to secure their objectives at an acceptable level of uncertainty and risk exposure.

CASE STUDY: Lafarge acquires Orascom Cement[23]

On 10 December 2007, Bruno Lafont, chief executive of Lafarge, a French multi-national cement and building products corporation, announced the surprise acquisition of the Middle East's largest cement maker, Orascom Cement. It was Lafarge's first major strategic acquisition since M. Lafont became chief executive two years earlier. Lafarge would pay a total of €10.2 billion (equivalent to US$ 15bn) including additional €1.4bn debt. The acquisition was expected initially to add $2.6bn of highly profitable sales to Lafarge's forecast of €17bn sales for the year.

Orascom was a nine-year old company based in Egypt; it was building leading positions in the Middle East and Mediterranean countries in building products and unrelated sectors such as mobile phone networks, largely through green-field investment. On behalf of the family investment company that owns Orascom Group, its chief executive, Mr Sawiris, agreed to pay €2.8bn to acquire an 11.4% share of Lafarge, making him Lafarge's second largest shareholder. He would become a director and also nominate another director.

The Orascom acquisition emphasised Lafarge's determination to dominate the global supply of cement, especially in developing countries around the world, which accounted for two-thirds of consumption. Under the single-minded leadership of previous Chairman and Chief Executive, Bertrand Collomb (1989–2003), Lafarge grew rapidly via internal development and global acquisitions. When it acquired the sixth largest global cement producer, Blue Circle Industries (UK), Lafarge catapulted to the world number-one position.

M. Lafont declared that since 2006 Lafarge's two strategic priorities were:

- To pursue growth in emerging markets.
- To accelerate innovation to increase its competitive advantage and to meet the need for more sustainable construction methods.

After 2007, Lafarge's growth ambitions were seriously dented by the global recession. Nonetheless, it remained confident of its long-term strategy. Its 2009 turnover was €15.9bn (2008: €19.0bn), yielding operating income of €2.5bn (2008: €3.5bn). Of these totals, cement generated 60% of sales (2008: 57%) and almost 95% of profits (2008: 84%).[24] Other major product categories included aggregates for concrete production, ready-mixed concrete delivery services, and gypsum and plasterboard for dry-wall construction. Geographic distribution of sales in 2009 was: Western Europe 29%; Africa and Middle East 25%; North America 19%; Asia 15%; Central and Eastern Europe 7%; other 5%.

Questions

1. Examine relevant data from the published accounts to help decide whether the price Lafarge paid for Orascom based on profitability performance and growth expectations was good value.

2. Is Lafarge's commitment to the long-term supply of basic construction materials wise or should it prioritise judicious diversification?[25]

3. Since Orascom Group had been serving fast-growing markets for cement and related construction materials, why did it choose to sell this division in 2007?

Summary

- Acquisitions, mergers and alliances can be considered as alternatives to internal development strategies. There are distinctions to be made between acquisitions and mergers, and between hostile and friendly (agreed) acquisitions. The planning and execution of takeover bids requires careful management, as does the integration of organizations that may have quite different characters and capabilities.

- Alliances can be divided into three broad categories: joint ventures; formal non-JV alliances; and network alliances. They are viable strategic growth options in a variety of circumstances, most obviously when an enterprise has inadequate resources and capabilities to proceed confidently alone, yet considers full integration with another enterprise impractical or unacceptable.

- Alliances can also help partners defend currently weak positions or to capitalise on multiple, concurrent initiatives with moderate risk and finite resources. In general, non-JV alliances allow enterprises greater flexibility and reversibility should they prove disappointing or dysfunctional. Network alliances are often specific to a sector or interest-grouping. Membership may be discretionary or a prerequisite for professional activities.

Exercises for Further Study and Discussion

1. Prior intent to diversify can be a strategic justification for mergers, even acquisitions or alliances. Suppose that executives act opportunistically and then use diversification logic to justify their actions. Should stakeholders be concerned, if their particular interests appear safe?

2. In a contested takeover bid the successful bidder usually pays significantly more than intended. Do any circumstances justify a price in excess of the estimated worth of the target enterprise?

3. What arguments might be used to persuade shareholders in an acquisition target to reject offers at any price? Are they plausible?

4. Identify a merger of substantial not-for-profit enterprises that occurred 3–5 years ago.[26] Track its progress, looking particularly for changes in senior personnel and to mission. Has the merger improved the combined resource and capability base and/or the scale and scope of activities? Was the merger justified?

NING ①
CTIVE

NING ②
CTIVE

NING ①
CTIVE

NING ②
CTIVE

NING ①
CTIVE

NING ②
CTIVE

5. How can regulatory authorities determine in practice whether or not alliance partners are engaging in anti-competitive practices?
6. Assuming that under-performing businesses will always exist, are firms like KKR a real benefit to society?
7. How strong was the strategic logic behind the merger of Reading University and Henley Management College? What evidence exists now to support or question the justification for it?
8. Expedia.com and Lastminute.com are network trading alliances that act as dominant hubs for hundreds of relatively subordinate supply partners. Does electronic mediation merely reinforce supplier dependency and just-in-time transactions, rather than liberate small suppliers? Discuss the implications.

Suggestions for Further Reading

Abrams, L., Cross, R., Lesser, E. and Levin, D. (2003) 'Nurturing interpersonal trust in knowledge-sharing networks', *Academy of Management Executive* (vol. 17/4, pp. 64–77).

Birkinshaw, J., Bresman, H. and Hakanson, L. (2000) 'Managing the post-acquisition integration process: how the human integration and task integration interact to foster value-creation', *Journal of Management Studies* (vol. 37/3, pp. 395–425).

Bower, J. (2001) 'Not all M&As are alike', *Harvard Business Review* (Vol. 79/3, pp. 93–101).

Capron, L. (1999) 'The long-term performance of horizontal acquisitions', *Strategic Management Journal* (vol. 20/11, pp. 987–1018).

Carey, D. (2000) 'Making mergers succeed' *Harvard Business Review* (vol. 78/3, pp. 145–154).

Cullinan, G, Le Roux, J.M. and Weddigen, R.-M. (2004) 'When to walk away from a deal', *Harvard Business Review* (vol. 82/4, pp. 96–104).

DiGregorio, R.M. (2003), 'Making mergers and acquisitions work: 'what we know and don't know – Part II', *Journal of Change Management* (vol. 3/3, pp. 259–274).

Dranikoff, L., Koller, T. and Schneider, A. (2002) 'Divestiture: strategy's missing link', *Harvard Business Review* (vol. 80/5, pp. 74–83).

Dyer, J., Kale, P. and Singh, H. (2001) 'How to make strategic alliances work', *Sloan Management Review* (vol. 42/4, pp. 37–43).

Fan, J.P.H. and Goyal, V.K. (2006) 'On the patterns and wealth effects of vertical mergers', *Journal of Business* (vol. 79, pp. 877–902).

Harrison, J.S., Hitt, M.A., Hoskisson, R.E. and Ireland, R.D. (2001) 'Resource complementarity in business combinations: extending the logic to organizational alliances', *Journal of Management* (vol. 27/6, pp. 679–690).

Hipkin, I. and Naude, P. (2006) 'Developing effective alliance partnerships', *Long Range Planning* (vol. 39, pp. 51–69).

Inkpen, A. (2000) 'Learning through joint ventures: a framework of knowledge acquisition', *Journal of Management Studies* (vol. 37/7, pp. 1019–1045).

Ireland, R.D., Hoskisson, R.E. and Hitt, M.J.A. (2009) *The Management of Strategy*, Cengage (chapter 7).

Kaplan, N. and Hurd, J. (2002) 'Realising the promise of partnerships', *Journal of Business Strategy* (vol. 23/3, pp. 38–42).

Kiechel, W. (2007) 'Private equity's long view' *Harvard Business Review* (vol. 85/8, pp. 18–20).

Koza, M. and Lewin, A. (1998) 'The co-evolution of strategic alliances', *Organization Science* (vol. 9/3, pp. 255–264).

Krishnan, H.A., Hitt, M.A. and Park, D. (2007) 'Acquisition premiums, subsequent workforce reductions and post-acquisition performance', *Journal of Management Studies* (Vol. 44/5, pp. 709–732).

Lu, C.-C. (2006) 'Growth strategies and merger patterns among small and medium-sized enterprises: an empirical study', *International Journal of Management* (vol. 23, pp. 529–547).

Marks, M. L. and Mirvis, P.H. (2001) 'Making mergers and acquisitions work: strategic and psychological preparation', *Academy of Management Executive* (vol.15/2, pp. 80–92).

Reuer, J.J. and Ragozzino, R. (2006) 'Agency hazards and alliance portfolios', *Strategic Management Journal* (vol. 27/1, pp. 27–43).

Rothaermel, F.T., Hitt, M.A. and Jobe, L.A. (2006) 'Balancing vertical integration and strategic outsourcing: effects on product portfolio, product success, and firm performance' *Strategic Management Journal* (vol. 27/11, pp. 1033–1056).

Schoenberg, R. (2003) 'Mergers and acquisitions motives, value creation and implementation', in Faulkner, D. and Campbell, A. (eds) *The Oxford Handbook of Strategy*, Oxford University Press.

Shimizu, K. and Hitt, M.A. (2005) 'What constrains or facilitates divestitures of formerly acquired firms? The effects of organizational inertia', *Journal of Management* (vol. 31/1, pp. 50–72).

Sudarsanam, S. and Mahate, A.A. (2006) 'Are friendly acquisitions too bad for shareholders and managers? Long-term value creation and top management turnover in hostile and friendly acquirers', *British Journal of Management* (vol. 17/1 supplement, pp. S7–S30).

Tuch, C. and O'Sullivan, N. (2007) 'The impact of acquisitions on firm performance: a review of the evidence', *International Journal of Management Review* (vol. 9/2, pp. 141–170).

Villalonga, B. and McGahan, A.M. (2005), 'The choice among acquisitions, alliances, and divestitures', *Strategic Management Journal* (vol. 26/13, pp. 1183–1208).

Notes

1 http://www.ageuk.org.uk/
2 Mognetti (2002).
3 Much has been written about mergers and acquisitions in strategy. Useful compendium sources include: Marks and Mirvis (1998); Hitt, Harrison and Ireland (2001); Gaughan (2007).

4 Small and medium-sized enterprises may also engage in mergers, see Lu (2006).

5 Gupta and Roos (2001).

6 Generally held to be an appropriate motive. However, in technological acquisitions both the absolute size of the target and its size relative to the acquirer affect whether innovativeness is enhanced or not (Ahuja and Katila, 2001).

7 Parvinen and Tikkanen (2007) argue that asymmetries in the process of engaging in a merger or acquisition affect whether shareholder value will be created or destroyed.

8 Not always a sound motive (Cullinan, Le Roux and Weddigen, 2004). Opportunistic deal-making is prevalent in high technology sectors (Coff, 2003).

9 Rothaermel, Hitt and Jobe (2006) conclude that a strategy of tapered integration (see chapter 8) provides real benefits. See also: Fan and Goyal (2006).

10 Capron (1999).

11 In the UK the Panel on Takeovers and Mergers issues a legally-binding Code of Practice to regulate these activities. It aims to comply with EU legislation and currently comprises 285 pages!

12 Under London Stock Exchange regulations, when the acquirer of public company owns 75% of a target's shares it may 'delist' them, turning it into a private subsidiary. If the acquirer has 90%, UK law allows it to purchase the rest at the accepted offer price.

13 Within 100 days, according to Ram Gupta who was closely involved in managing the integration of IT company J.D. Edwards that was acquired by PeopleSoft in 2003. See the video: 'Mergers & Acquisitions: 100 Days to a Successful Integration' at http://www.kantola.com/Ram-Gupta-PDPD-98-S.aspx. However, Homburg and Bucerius (2006) find that speed is beneficial when the enterprises have high relatedness in their operations, but can be detrimental when operationally unrelated. Baden-Fuller and Boschetti (1995) and Bower (2001) argue for more nuanced approaches according to circumstances.

14 See for example, Harrison (2007).

15 Short term vertical, supply-chain alliances require careful thought, especially when they involve cross-border relationship (DoH, 2005).

16 Top football clubs are prone to all these misjudgements when acquiring prime assets, i.e., star football-ers. Andriy Shevchenko, a highly regarded Ukrainian striker joined Chelsea from AC Milan for £30m, aged 31. He returned to Milan three years later on a free transfer. He scored 9 goals for Chelsea. Combining transfer fee and wages, reportedly over £100,000 a week, each of his goals cost Chelsea around £5m!

17 In this context 'long term' means a time span ranging from a few years to decades. Again the evidence is that Western enterprises work to shorter time scales than their oriental counterparts.

18 Reuer and Ragozzino (2006).

19 Reuer and Ragozzino (2006).

20 A context where game theory can provide insights into what is happening (chapter 2).

21 Short for Centre of Excellence for External Drug Discovery: see http://www.CEEDD.com

22 Although exceptionally, SMEs can form self-sustaining networks without dominant hub firms: Szarka (1990); Bull, Pitt and Szarka (1993).

23 Main sources: http://www.lafarge.com; http://www.ft.com; http://en.wikipedia.org/wiki/Lafarge; http://en.wikipedia.org/wiki/Orascom_Construction_Industries_(OCI);

24 http://www.lafarge.com/02192010-press_finance-Interim_Report_December_2009-uk.pdf

25 Cement production and use is a major producer of carbon dioxide, one of the world's most significant greenhouse gases, implicated in global warming.

26 The UK Charity Commission: http://www.charity-commission.gov.uk provides online access to the reports filed by registered charities in England and Wales, for example.

12

Multinational and Global Strategies

Learning Outcomes

This chapter is designed to enable you to:

① Describe and critique concepts and issues in international strategy.

② Appreciate the contrary influences of global megatrends and national distinctiveness that create the global-local dilemma.

③ Explain how the international dimension adds complexity to the strategic management challenges of resource location, activity co-ordination and control.

④ Apply the frameworks presented in this and previous chapters to analyse particular cases.

CASE STUDY: The Carlsberg Group[1]

Brewing beer and other alcoholic drinks are among the world's oldest and most universal industries. Throughout the middle-ages and later in England, for example, local taverns brewed ale, partly because its alcohol content made it safer to drink than often-contaminated water from wells.

As brewing became more organised and began to exploit scale economies, dedicated regional and national brewers emerged, including Carlsberg of Denmark. Founded in Copenhagen by J.C. Jacobsen in 1847, Carlsberg is a very late-comer, judged against brewers such as Stella Artois (Belgium) Kronenbourg (France)[2] and Oettinger (Germany).

In 1875 the Carlsberg Laboratory began to explore the science of yeast fermentation when brewing pilsner (lager) beer. This successful venture evolved later into the world-renowned Carlsberg Research Centre, a pioneering institution in yeast genetics, biotechnology and biomedical research. In 1876 Jacobsen formed the philanthropic Carlsberg Foundation, to which he bequeathed ownership of his brewery. Meanwhile his son, Carl had founded his own Carlsberg brewery; the two companies were reunited in 1906. Today, the Foundation remains the majority owner of Carlsberg A/S, the brewing company, and supports various Carlsberg foundations, research interests and the Museum of National History at Frederiksborg.

After 1868 Carlsberg slowly developed an export business. Non-European destinations included South America; after 1903 and collaboration with the East Asiatic Company, China and other east Asian countries became significant markets for Carlsberg bottled beers. By 1939 Britain had become one of Carlsberg's biggest export markets. From the 1950s onwards Carlsberg appointed European licensees such as Charrington and Tetley in Britain to brew and bottle Carlsberg beer. During the 1970s Carlsberg became joint and later sole owner of the Carlsberg breweries in Britain. A joint venture with Scottish & Newcastle (S&N) created Baltic Beverages Holding, which Carlsberg now wholly owns, extending its presence to Russia, Ukraine, Kazakhstan, Uzbekistan and the Baltic states. When Heineken and Carlsberg jointly acquired and dismembered S&N, Carlsberg gained additional operations in France, Vietnam and China.

In 1970 Carlsberg became the senior partner in a merger with Danish rival, Tuborg. In 1972 it opened a brewery in Malaysia. In 1980 it began a joint venture brewery in Hong Kong, which it subsequently acquired and then transferred production to the Huizhou brewery in mainland China, another licensee in which Carlsberg acquired a majority share in 1995. Today, Carlsberg owns 20 breweries in China, fully or partially. It owns three breweries in India. In 2000 it merged with Orkla of Norway, a major brewing and soft drinks enterprise covering the Nordic area and Russia. Initially Carlsberg owned 60% of the merged enterprise, called Carlsberg A/S, becoming 100% owner in 2004.

Through its multiple acquisitions and overseas investments the Carlsberg Group has become a global brewer. At the time of writing it had 7.5% global share by volume, making it the fourth largest brewing corporation after AB InBev (Belgium, 21% share by volume), SABMiller (UK, 13%) and Heineken (Netherlands, 9%).[3] Its 2009 sales were 59.4 billion Danish Kroner (Dkk) on which it achieved a 15.8% operating profit margin. Its market capitalization was over 80 billion Dkk; it employed 43,000 people; and marketed over 500 brands and sub-brands of beer. These include prestige international brands such as Carlsberg Pilsner, Tuborg, Kronenbourg 1664 and Baltika; and country-specific brands such as Tetley's (Britain), Ringnes (Norway), Feldschlösschen (Switzerland), Lav (Serbia) and 'Wind Flower Snow and Moon' (China). Its advertising strap-line 'probably the best beer in the world' and its variants are widely recognised in many of the 150 countries where it competes.

Carlsberg's strategy focuses on the geographic regions of Northern and Western Europe; Eastern Europe; and Asia (including China). Its future strategy emphasises innovation in its core brewing activities and premium brand positioning wherever possible. It will continue investing in its own assets where these constitute a core capability. Where it does not own brewing facilities it will export or maintain local licensing agreements or other models appropriate to circumstances. It supports its strategy by means of many structured programmes for organizational and personal development throughout the enterprise.

Questions

1. Carlsberg's development features a complex pattern of inward overseas investment, transnational alliances and joint ventures that later it acquires. Why choose this strategy? Why do prospective partners engage with Carlsberg, given its seemingly predatory instinct for 100% ownership and control?

2. Despite this international strategy, Carlsberg is still only the fourth largest brewing group, much smaller than AB Inbev, which like others has grown dramatically through acquisitions and mergers. To what extent Carlsberg a potential future acquisition target? How should it respond to a future bid?

3. Can a global strategy that sustains 500 brands possibly be right? Discuss the proposition that Carlsberg should rationalise its facilities and focus on far fewer brands.

Introduction: Cross-border Operations Require New Strategies

Since markets and sectors no longer recognise rigid boundaries, geographic or otherwise, strategic management is increasingly global in fact and mindset. However, issues of international strategic management remain relevant. As enterprises operate systematically across borders strategic management becomes much more complex and challenging.[4] This chapter aims to identify the main respects in which this is so.

Concepts explored in previous chapters remain relevant. The missions and future visions of enterprises with international ambitions evidently encompass the possibility of global operations and diversification. They are wise to recognise and respond appropriately to volatile and highly differentiated national environments arising from geography, history, culture and politics. Resources and capabilities become stretched across multiple domains and may necessitate differing local or regional strategies.[5] Decisions to progress via internal development, mergers, acquisitions or alliances may be acute.[6] Above all, an enterprise must wrestle with the practical organization of geographically extended operations if its strategy is to be implemented effectively.

National developmental paths differ among countries. This affects their respective comparative advantages at any one time. Countries and regions become more (and less) attractive and welcoming to outsiders over time, whether viewed as markets or as operational locations for the production and distribution of goods, procurement of materials and other resources locally, and as part of an extended supply chain. Specialised, local skills may also be a benefit, for example, to assist in research and development activities.

Given these sometimes problematic differences, some claim that international strategic management requires a country- or region-centred approach; others point to apparent global 'megatrends' that indicate convergence of national development paths, arguing for greater standardization of approach. Megatrends appear to produce transnational convergence in both supply and demand behaviours, so they present enterprises with opportunities for efficient growth through greater standardisation and diversification. The convergence hypothesis encourages an integrative, global perspective on international strategic management.

The seemingly contradictory implications of global and country-centred perspectives create the global–local strategy dilemma. In response, many enterprises adopt a pragmatic, hybrid international strategy that is neither truly global nor fully localised.

This chapter addresses the following issues:

1. Means and motives for international strategic development.
2. Evolving environmental characteristics and their relevance for international strategic management.
3. Alternative generic strategies for international development.
4. The global–local strategy dilemma and its resolution.
5. The managerial challenge of operating a dynamic, international network of activities.

Patterns of International Expansion

Enterprise Motives and Growth Ambitions

Enterprise growth ambitions drive the development of international trade. As the global population approaches 7 billion people (and predicted to rise to 9 billion by 2050[7]), it generates increasing demand for all products and services, despite many people still living in abject poverty. Overseas markets present enterprises with opportunities in demand segments that do not exist domestically on a sufficient scale to exploit profitably. Through an international orientation they can realise larger scale and scope in operations, enhancing efficiency and profitability. A further potential benefit is to enable a successful enterprise to deploy and develop its distinctive capabilities more widely, either solo or in collaboration.[8]

Even for China (with a population over 1.3 billion) the world represents a major extension of potential demand for its products and services. But as enterprises expand their geographic scope they will probably need to extend their product types and specifications to meet multiple, differing requirements. As they become internationally oriented, they become larger, more diversified and robust.[9] Overseas competitors also recognise the potential of global demand, propelling everyone towards growth via international expansion to counter the impact of predatory competitors in domestic markets. However, the timing of cross-border initiatives is a significant strategic decision.

International strategies are not only about demand, but also about exploiting new sources of supply on better terms than are available domestically. Input factors include valuable materials, lower-cost labour for operations, and specialised knowledge.

LEARNING OBJECTIVE ①

LEARNING OBJECTIVE ②

LEARNING OBJECTIVE ①

LEARNING OBJECTIVE ①

Regulatory changes also galvanise cross-border competition. The Single European Market (SEM) and the North American Free Trade Area (NAFTA) are good examples. The SEM aimed to create an even-handed, competitive arena after 1993, in terms of tariff and tax regulations. The potential demand of the SEM is many times greater than in any individual European country, but encourages the transnational spread of competing enterprises. Ignoring aggressive newcomers could be disastrous; yet to enter the markets of other countries exposes an enterprise to aggressive responses from strong, long-established competitors. As the bold, early movers exploited the cross-border opportunities for greater scale and scope economies, mergers and acquisition of weaker enterprises have followed. The presence of several Middle and Eastern European countries in the SEM has enlarged demand and enabled the larger US- and European-owned enterprises to establish lower cost bases without tariff penalties when their goods and services cross internal borders.

Enterprise Development Paths Start at Home

The typical development path of the start-up enterprise begins by establishing a stable local position in its home country. Enterprise location is often determined by the personal choice of pioneers or by favourable circumstances and infrastructure, such as locally available raw materials, relevant knowledge, skilled labour, good communication networks and substantial local demand.[10] Pioneering and early-following entrepreneurs form enterprises and strategies to satisfy recognised, local demand. Within the external resource and infrastructure constraints, the effective enterprises amass appropriate resources and capabilities; their success stimulates additional demand and attracts inward migration of skilled people who contribute further to local capabilities. Procurement strategies also encourage better quality and availability of external resources and capabilities and supporting infrastructure, including spin-off companies founded by ambitious former employees that compete directly or act as suppliers or customers.

As they grow, enterprises generally retain their local bases, although their development paths pursue geographic expansion, region by region, until national coverage is achieved. Subsequent (or parallel) development sees a broadening of the range of offerings, enabling access to new demand segments. Directly and indirectly, the actions of the more successful enterprises stimulate and satisfy greater and more sophisticated demand over time, enhancing the reputation of themselves and their home base.

Thus, in ideal circumstances a synergistic cluster of capable, sector-focused enterprises develops at this location. This phenomenon, often known as an industrial district, is observed in many countries over many years. It is characterised by:

- A local cluster of capable enterprises, the equal of any competing cluster in the world, hence becoming recognised as 'world-class' performers in their field[11].
- Discriminating clienteles who expect the highest standards and therefore spur continued development.
- Capable suppliers and subcontractors of all kinds (the associated infrastructure).
- A virtuous cycle of continuous improvements to products and services, which further enhances local capabilities, infrastructure, and reputation over time.

Exporting across Borders via Agents

Once a local cluster has become recognised, demand spreads across regional and national borders. Enterprises begin overseas supply typically by exporting, initially to countries with relatively familiar kinds of clienteles. Today, national and transnational export sales may of course begin much faster, almost by accident, because the World Wide Web establishes a virtual overseas presence. However, the transition from a domestic to a systematic export orientation requires considerable knowledge, organization and commitment. A rational next step is to appoint sales and distribution agents in each export location of prime interest. Agents are usually non-exclusive, multi-product trading enterprises.

LEARNING
OBJECTIVE ① Exporting does not require large investments in each target country, which helps to limit the financial risk. The exporter retains control of the design and specifications of its product/service portfolio, whist overseas sales improve scale economies. Agents used effectively in more countries enable substantial scope economies too.

However, exporting has disadvantages. If agents are familiar with the sector, they may already market similar products under their own names or represent other, competing importers. Thus their loyalty and commitment may be suspect. Although the exporter tries to dictate marketing and distribution strategies, agents are ultimately responsible for these value-adding and cost-generating functions. The need for transnational distribution creates costly logistical challenges, while import tariffs can add significantly to import costs. Unpredictable currency fluctuations require frequent pricing revisions; the option of currency hedging adds costs. Uncontrollable costs increase selling prices and limit demand or reduce the profit potential if prices are held, for both agents and the exporter. Agents typically respond by promoting alternative, cheaper products.

For all these reasons, although exporting via agents is a practical approach, it has significant flaws. After a time ambitious enterprises generally alter the direction of their development paths towards cross-border, international operations.

Transition to an International Enterprise

LEARNING
OBJECTIVE ①

LEARNING
OBJECTIVE ③ The next stage of internationalization frequently involves the development of strategic alliances with overseas partners. Licensing, franchising or joint ventures may be preferred, according to circumstances (see Chapter 11). Compared with domestic alliances, the risks and uncertainty of international alliances are greater, especially when local partners differ in their political, cultural and linguistic backgrounds from each other as well as from the developing enterprise.[12]

Successful licensing contracts yield new income streams for the former exporter, based on the value or volume of sales achieved. Arms-length licensing requires legally binding agreements between principal and agent. Typical agreements represent longer-term commitments than do export sales agreements. Licensing normally commits local enterprises in each country to perform the significant value-adding activities: product manufacturing, packaging, marketing, sales and after-sales service. The licensing enterprise retains ownership of core assets such as brands, designs and technologies, but its influence is otherwise limited. The contractual provisions may specify strategies and how they are to be implemented in relatively broad terms, leaving the licensee responsible for the detail.

In theory, licensing enhances mutual commitment, yet the principal faces an arms-length challenge to achieve an acceptable degree of control in each country, especially when results disappoint. It may struggle to obtain a full and current picture about each market in which its licence is applied, since its partner can filter what information it provides. Remote problem diagnosis is difficult. It also risks moral hazard; for example, when a licensee learns enough from its licensing experience to terminate the agreement to become a direct competitor. While exit from a license agreement is more difficult than from sales agency agreements, defaults and conflicts frequently result in frustration and costly, legal disputes.

Franchising is an alternative form of licensing with similar drawbacks but specific benefits. The contract agreement codifies specifications of the established formula that franchisees must conform to and the performance expected. Since its primary role is operational, the franchisor generally implements the major marketing and promotional activities on their behalf. Moreover, the franchisor is in a stronger position to terminate the agreement, given inadequate performance, than in arms-length licensing. Contract terms invariably allow the franchisor to monitor the performance of franchisees. However, the principal needs to establish adequate resources in each country or region to conduct marketing and performance monitoring properly.

Joint ventures (JVs) commit the enterprise to even greater strategic involvement in each country, with potentially increased levels of risk and financial exposure. However, the purpose of taking a local partner is to facilitate access to the market and supply chain, as well as local knowledge and learning opportunities. A partner also reduces the risks of misunderstandings over regulations, cultural and linguistic issues. When the partners' respective contributions are complementary and they enjoy mutual respect and commitment, a joint venture is an attractive strategic option.

Naturally, the drawbacks of JVs stated in Chapter 11 remain. Issues that arise from misunderstanding and mistrust are hugely challenging. The JV partners must bridge major cultural and linguistic differences as well as non-commensurate regulatory environments and business practices as may apply between economically developed and developing countries.[13]

The International Enterprise with Owned-and-Operated Subsidiaries

A capable enterprise that has already achieved collaborative success in overseas markets may yet face the decision whether to become a genuinely international operation – one that manages multi-country, owned-and-operated subsidiaries, with all that implies in respect of dispersed resources and capabilities. This major strategic decision hinges on growth ambitions, willingness and means to invest, and desire for full strategic control.

By owning and operating subsidiaries, the enterprise now controls all its dispersed value-adding activities and functions. This option increases its strategic and financial commitments considerably. Dispersed cross-border facilities also greatly increase the complexity and consequent challenges of organizing, co-ordinating and controlling the actions of multiple subsidiaries, as will be seen.

Although an enterprise would rarely make substantial overseas investments without very careful research, mistakes can still occur. The terms whereby a country allows it to make inward investments and extract profits or other value-added outputs may be tightly controlled by the host government. It must employ and trust host-country nationals. Senior local managers of high calibre will expect responsibility for local strategic decision-making. How much autonomy should they have? Some multinationals continue to make all major strategic decisions at home, others encourage regional or local decision-making within a strategic framework that the corporate centre defines. There are parallels here with managing a business portfolio (Chapter 10), especially if the operations of each overseas country are largely independent.[14] Either way, its heavy investments would make withdrawal highly problematic. Further, if market rejection or volatile political conditions were to prompt withdrawal, restrictive legislation could prevent the recovery of valuable assets.

Leveraging Capabilities and Learning

LEARNING
OBJECTIVE ①

When demonstrably effective enterprises develop internationally, they often retain their most developed and distinctive capabilities, for example, design, research and development, strategic marketing and management in the home country. They relocate only the value-adding activities that are less distinctive and which can reliably be organised regionally or locally. These activities often include procurement, manufacturing, product distribution and sales. Each such choice is enterprise-particular, not necessarily in accord with the choices of its competitors.

By differentiating home and international operations according to local capabilities, the multinational can continue to develop and exploit value-creating strategic advantages across borders. How it deploys the totality of its capabilities provides an effective enterprise (as with the sector in which it operates[15]) with sustainable *architectural* advantages (Chapter 5). Conversely, if the basis of its international advantage is simply a low-cost home base, advantage declines rapidly as costs rise. Accordingly, long-term success requires the foresight and means to continue developing, geographically differentiated, distinctive capabilities.

International advantage from the home base

The Swatch Group: Swatch exports watches and other timing devices globally under a variety of well-known brand names. Swatch is proud of its innovation record; being an amalgamation of over 150 production facilities that were previously capable, small and medium-sized Swiss enterprises; it builds on traditional strengths of the Swiss watch-making and component industries. Its expertise covers all forms of consumer, professional and business timekeeping devices and applications. Marketing expertise, however, has developed in each major market and this knowledge is shared globally.

Tata Group: Tata Steel is an Indian steel-making and fabrication company. It has benefited greatly from domestic industrialisation, while its comparatively low cost base has allowed it to gain a major foothold in export markets. Its international operations have expanded through Indian and Asian acquisitions, more recently through acquiring the second largest European steel company, *Corus* (UK and Netherlands). However, Tata has taken advantage of its economic strength to diversify into a conglomerate with a wide range of other interests in the growing Indian economy.

Distinctive National Characteristics and Development Paths

Why National Differences Matter

Nation states and regions progress differently. Their complex histories manifest distinctive political, economic, religious, social and cultural patterns. Deeply ingrained, sometimes paradoxical, country-specific factors encourage or inhibit particular kinds of collective behaviours, such as innovativeness and openness to external influences. The People's Republic of China (PRC), for example, a communist state for the last sixty years, is surely now grappling with its future development path in the context of its hard-working, self-reliant and enterprising heritage spanning sixty *hundred* years.

National leadership styles produce countries with widely different achievements. The ambitions and dynamism of political, economic and technocratic elites are particularly significant drivers of progress, innovation and change.[16] Given the commitment of its ruling elite, a country and its enterprises can experience dramatic change in a few decades. Japan, South Korea, the United Arab Emirates and China are modern examples.

The divergence hypothesis is that countries differ and over time the differences become greater. Understanding the factors of national difference and distinctiveness is vital for an international strategy to succeed. An enterprise should understand a country's history and unique development path before it decides whether to treat it as a market, a favourable source of supply, a home for its most aggressive competitors or its most reliable allies.

National characteristics influence economic development hugely. Individual development patterns generally conform to an identifiable template constructed from many variables, including:

- The dominant form of government, its political and economic ambitions.
- Historical events, including wars and conflicts, state imperialism or occupation by foreign powers.
- Long-established cultural and religious values and assumptions.
- Time-dependent technological paths (trajectories), including the presence (absence) of exploitable, natural resources.
- Population size and growth rate.
- Geographical (regional) contexts.

An important measure of national progress (and therefore potential opportunity) is its capacity to innovate. As countries become more sophisticated they adopt better technologies and accelerate their rates of adaptation. Patent applications are one measure of technological capability, the capacity to create new knowledge. Figure 12.1 indicates numbers of patent applications by country over time. It shows clearly how the United States has outpaced moderately sized European states since the mid-20th century, and more recently how Japan, Korea and China have surged ahead.

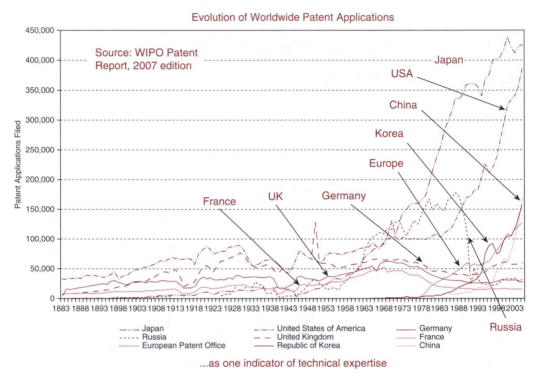

Figure 12.1: The evolution of worldwide patent applications

Source: Original produced by the world Intellectual Property Organization (WIPO). ©WIPO

Development of European Nations

With modestly sized populations, European countries (especially sea-faring nations) have historically been outward-looking, seeking prosperity through international trade, colonisation and empire-building, supported where necessary by aggression and military might. Christian and Muslim beliefs and ways of life have regularly clashed, but have also enriched the cultures of many European nations. As countries migrated from agriculture to industry from the 18th century onwards, overseas territories became valuable sources of raw materials and markets for manufactured goods. The 20th century wars had a major impact, notably the post-1945 reawakening of democracy following after fascist dictatorships, the creation of the European Economic Community and its later transformation into the European Union (EU). Its citizens are relatively well-educated, demanding and consumer-oriented, yet value quality of life more broadly than just economic well-being. Average family sizes are modest, population growth declining, countered somewhat by inward immigration and pan-EU internal migration.

Since its 1989 re-unification, Germany has affirmed its EU position as the most powerful engine for economic growth through the manufacture and export of high-quality industrial and consumer goods. Banks adopt a long-term perspective to support its successful companies. Italy and France also maintain effective manufacturing bases in many traditional and modern sectors, the UK less so, relying more than others on financial and other services. Labour intensive manufacturing such as textiles and clothing shifted towards Asia during the 1980s and 1990s, being replaced by knowledge-intensive sectors.

Smaller countries such as Ireland, Denmark and Switzerland pursued necessarily different paths from those of the imperial powers. Each has exploited traditional comparative advantages and built new ones. Traditional sectors with strong export performance include banking and watch-making in fiercely independent Switzerland, agriculture and brewing in Ireland and Denmark. Each country has enhanced its international status with new, technology-based sectors (respectively: chemicals and food processing industries; computing and software; electronics, biotechnology and green technologies). The Nordic countries have similar profiles with large geographic territories, natural resources and high living standards. Eastern European states emerging from Soviet hegemony are developing characteristics that converge with other EU member states.

Before the 1917 revolution, Russia was a huge territorial empire straddling Europe and Asia. As the USSR it became the Soviet hub, dominated by a communist ideology. Denied external *economic* influence and access to high technologies it became self-sufficient. Without respect for private enterprise or consumerism, it fell behind the increasingly sophisticated democracies of West and East. Depleted of its former European satellites, the emergent Russian Federation is again becoming more outward-looking and internationally influential, benefiting particularly from Siberian oil and gas. However, internal conditions are characterised by turbulence, regional instability and patronage by the centre.

Development of Asian Nations

In the early 20th century, Japan pursued imperialist, militaristic development in Asia, leading ultimately to crushing defeat. After 1945 under American occupation, its democratised government directed industrial and export priorities, facilitated by close-knit industrial structures called *keiretsu* – these being constellations of companies with cross-shareholdings and/or collaborative alliances. They are linked typically to a single, powerful commercial bank that funds individual and collective development. Its initial emphasis on the export of low-cost manufactured industrial and consumer goods including steel, shipbuilding and vehicles was progressively displaced by high quality and innovative products in all sectors. Since the 1970s international expansion has increasingly led Japanese enterprises to build manufacturing and sales facilities worldwide, becoming true multinationals. South Korea has followed a similar international expansion path, led by its family-controlled *chaebols*. Japan and South Korea now have large, sophisticated consumer-oriented populations that demand high quality and innovation in their products.

The rigid, secular state control of the People's Republic of China (PRC) created international isolation from 1948 until the late 1970s. Thereafter, mindful of huge potential export markets, its Government facilitated the country's development as the world's prime low-cost manufacturing base by sanctioning joint ventures between Western multinationals and dynamic, Chinese entrepreneurs, subject to carefully controlled terms. Its vast population is a virtually inexhaustible source of low-cost, manufacturing advantage, as rural agricultural workers migrate to the eastern and southern cities for economic betterment. They also create fast-rising internal demand. The migration pattern parallels that of Britain and the United States centuries before. The people have rediscovered their enterprise in privately owned, small to medium sized enterprises, while major Chinese enterprises, such as Lenovo (personal computers) and Haier (domestic appliances) are establishing global presences that build on brands and fast-developing capabilities. Within a decade or so, the PRC will probably become the largest national economy. Taiwan remains a major irritant, becoming an independent democratic, world-leading producer of electronic products and components.

Following the end of British rule and partition from Pakistan in 1948, India has continued on a democratic path. It tolerates a huge gulf between the living standards of its wealthiest and poorest citizens (of whom there are over one billion). It is developing into a sophisticated economy with a fast-growing, well-educated and discriminating middle class. As in China, its Government has influenced industrial priorities, encouraging industrial self-sufficiency in steel and other commodities. India has also targeted high technology sectors such as pharmaceuticals, computing and information technology (IT). The economy is well-balanced with both manufacturing industries and fast-developing service sectors in cinema, television and IT.

Development of North America

Throughout its history, the United States has grown progressively and entrepreneurially. After the 1861–5 civil war, free enterprise and consumerism created an economically vibrant state, sustained by a large, increasingly affluent population and capacity for innovation. Yet, like Canada to the north, the United States has vast land areas devoted to industrial-scale agriculture. Having played a vital role in the 1914–18 war, US influence developed a somewhat introspective, regional focus. Its involvement in the 1939–45 war changed that: its 'military–industrial complex' flexed its might globally, engaging in conflicts in Korea, Vietnam, Middle and South America and the Middle East. Much technological innovation has initially been state-financed for military purposes, drawing on world-class education and research. Following the end of the so-called Cold War, the United States has been the undisputed global superpower. Its global influence also benefits from the spread of American culture, branded consumer goods, popular music and movies, even in hostile states. Although Alaska and Canada have considerable potential for further extraction of oil and other mineral deposits, North America (like Europe) has become increasingly dependent on the Middle East for oil and China for consumer goods. The latter has used its export revenues to invest heavily in American and European real estate and enterprises.

Development of other Regional Blocs

The geographic blocs of Middle/South America, Africa, the Middle East, South East Asia and Oceania contain many states with distinctive characteristics and development trajectories.

Each bloc is culturally, ethnically and religiously diverse, though parallels and similarities exist. Each has economically developed states with modestly sized, democratic populations (e.g., Chile, Botswana, Israel, Taiwan and Australia), rapidly developing states, often with very large populations (e.g., Brazil, Nigeria, Iran, Indonesia, and Papua New Guinea) and under-developed, sometimes extremely impoverished states (e.g., Haiti, Zambia, Afghanistan, Burma, and Micronesia). The latter are generally characterised by limited political freedoms, dependence on subsistence agriculture, and the export of cash-crops and valuable minerals where these exist. Factors influencing their attractions for international enterprises include the following:

- Development patterns typically rely on the parallel activities of multinational enterprises, local import–export trading companies and co-operatives. Peru, Columbia and other South American states, for example, participate in extended global supply chains enabled by US and EU supermarkets to export meat, fruit, vegetables, coffee and cut flowers.

- Cultural, religious and ethnic/tribal differences create severe differences that inhibit coherent economic development, especially in Africa where many governments display totalitarian characteristics. Political instability in Muslim countries has been increasing.

- Many developing states distance themselves politically and economically from the major world powers. Whilst some middle-eastern states are pro-Western, strong antagonisms exist in Iran and in factions within Syria, Iraq, Pakistan and Afghanistan. Various African states have close links with China.

- The more progressive states pursue distinct national priorities, such as education, and the development of new industries to reduce dependence on agriculture and extractive industries. They represent opportunities for international manufacturers seeking regional bases and for construction companies.

Nations belong to various regional and economic groupings, including the EU (European Union), NAFTA (North American Free Trade Association), the Association of Southeast Asian Nations (ASEAN Regional Forum), the League of Arab Nations, the African Union (formerly Organization of African Unity), the G9 and G20 groups of wealthy nations, and the Organization of Petroleum Exporting Countries (OPEC). (Quasi-governmental organisations, such as the World Bank and World Trade Organisation, also exert influence.) Members of regional groupings are far from united in their priorities, however. Thus the EU is now polarised between the more prosperous states that are net contributors to the EU budget and those whose economies remain vulnerable following the global credit crunch.[17]

Global Convergence: the Significance of 'Megatrends'

Although countries have differing development paths, their populations may exhibit surprising convergence of attitudes and behaviours, the implications of which affect future patterns of supply and demand, and therefore the prospects and conduct of enterprises. The convergence hypothesis draws on the existence of so-called global megatrends,[18] a phenomenon whose consequences can differ across regions.

Global megatrends

- Environmental degradation (pollution and climate change) and increasing scarcity of food, water, fossil fuels and key minerals, as the global population rises.

- Population migration to metropolitan areas perceived as more rewarding places in which to live and work, creating local and regional economies larger than many small countries and shifting the global balances of economic and political power.[8]

- Information-saturated, post-industrial societies with 'real time' dissemination of facts and opinions enabled by digital data storage and communication networks.

- The centralized capture of personal data allied to pervasive surveillance techniques as responses to the globalization of terrorism, malicious and highly profitable 'cyber-crime'.

- An increasing emphasis on self rather than society, including the pursuit of entrepreneurial careers rather than expecting large organizations and governments to provide employment and economic benefits.

- Globalization of business activities and tourism enabled by affordable air travel.

- The accelerating costs of medical provision as populations in developed countries age and treatments become more ambitious and complex.

- Privatisation and deregulation of formerly state-controlled industries.

- Genetic technologies increasingly applied in agriculture, medical and forensic science.

- Emergence of global regulation of economically critical and controversial industries such as genetics, energy, global banking and financial services.

Most trends present international strategies with both threats and global opportunities. For example, solutions that tackle climate change, pollution, resource scarcity and population growth will be extremely rewarding. Trends may have inter-connected and perhaps counteracting consequences, making their impact difficult to assess. Enterprises must consider trends critically and imaginatively, not merely accept 'conventional wisdoms'. Digital technologies have become a universal driver and facilitator of trends, although technological change presents difficult choices; the wrong decision can be catastrophic. LED-screen televisions and computers appear now to have obtained a decisive commercial advantage over plasma screens, yet manufacturers have generally opted for one or the other. Likewise, digital cameras presently use image sensors based on competing CCD and CMOS silicon microchip technologies. Which will become dominant and can those enterprises that focused on the 'wrong' technology recover?

International Generic Strategies

International strategic development introduces the new variable of *distance*. There are two aspects of distance:

1. The *physical* distance of unfamiliar, sometimes remote geographies, with the challenges of enterprise organization, communications, resource dispersion, supply chain and logistics management, and strategic control
2. The *psychic* distance arising from the differing attitudes, cultural assumptions, language, political and economic systems of unfamiliar populations

No single model of strategy copes with all circumstances. Nonetheless, the debate about global versus local priorities provides some helpful pointers. Figure 12.2 suggests six generic international strategies, adapting the logic of Figure 7.2. It retains the fundamental distinction between low(est) cost, efficiency-driven strategies and differentiation strategies, based on promoting perceived uniqueness. As regards strategic target, it proposes three alternative postures distinguished through selectivity by country/region or by preferred demand segment:

*   Coverage and treatment of all countries on a universal, unselective basis.

*   Targeting a selected, universal demand segment of particular interest in almost all countries.

*   Targeting selected countries or regions, accepting the need to address demand segments in those countries with a tailored approach.

The first two categories imply international strategies for which the adjective global is appropriate. The third is quite distinct, being country or region-centred. Each will now be reviewed.

Truly Global Strategies: Low-Cost Standardisation or Harmonised Differentiation

A truly global strategy identifies and exploits synergies inherent in a universal approach. It treats differences among countries or regions as of minimal significance, building instead on presumed, growing economic and cultural convergence.[19] Given this emphasis, a global strategy necessitates standardized activities and procedures for optimum efficiency or differentiation achieved through well-harmonized strategies across countries and regions. These global strategies feature as the uppermost pair in Figure 12.2.

Basis of strategic advantage

	Low(est) cost (efficiency)	Perceived uniqueness (differentiation)
Universal, non-selective treatment	Global standardisation	Harmonised global differentiation
Selected, countries or regions	Locality-specific efficiency focus	Locality-specific differentiation
Multi-country single segment/ clientele	Segment-specific efficiency focus	Harmonised, segment-specific differentiation

Strategic target (row labels above)

Figure 12.2: Generic international strategies
Adapted from Figure 7.2

The global approach characterises the internationalization strategies of many US corporations, though it is probably a fair description of major international aid agencies too. The implications of presumed convergence are that a global strategy:

- Caters for the demand in each country and region by avoiding demand segmentation and targeting.
- Emphasises cost-based efficiency via massive scale and wide scope of operations and standardized quality and specification of offerings.
- Implements an approach to differentiation in which it co-ordinates activities and messages carefully across countries through well-harmonized marketing, brand management, product specifications, etc.
- Avoids countries where efficient, low-cost standardization, or harmonised differentiation would be unworkable or unacceptable.

- Continues to develop its most distinctive capabilities at the home base, performing other, regionally or locally centres as necessary and practical.
- Is planned and controlled from the home base – subsidiaries and alliance partners, if any, are told what detailed strategies to implement and how.

Global strategy is consistent with universal offerings produced efficiently. It succeeds to the extent that the enterprise manages country and regional preferences proactively to accept standardization/harmonization on its terms. When globally branded offerings can be effectively differentiated from local competition, premium prices combine profitably with scale and scope economies.[20] However, global differentiation still requires harmonized approaches to marketing and operations.

Global (universal) strategies

Global standardization: Google Corporation has offices and websites in many countries, but its concept and approach are standardized, high profile and dominant. It is very probably the lowest-cost provider of global internet search and advertising services. Its software and organization are standardized to the extent of providing English-language versions of many sites as an alternative to local languages.

Harmonized global differentiation: Coca Cola Corporation markets instantly recognisable popular soft drinks globally. Coca Cola makes country-specific adjustments to its global strategy only where strictly necessary. The parent corporation keeps its recipes secret, providing concentrates from its own plants. It closely controls marketing strategies, emphasising distinctive, globally-inclusive brand values and consistent quality of *Coke*, its primary product. Because liquids are bulky relative to their value, it delegates production to country or region centred plants, both owned and operated and by licensees.

Multi-country, Segment-Specific Strategies: Efficiency or Harmonised Differentiation

An alternative global strategy is to target an attractive, substantial demand segment that features in many countries, rather than try to cater to multiple demand segments globally or in selected countries, or to ignore segment differences entirely.

When the expectations of the target segment are regionally or globally convergent, this strategy can be well-harmonized and co-ordinated, hence efficient and relatively low cost. If these global segments are also highly differentiated and command premium prices from a small, wealthy, discerning clientele, this is again an attractive strategy.

Multi-country, segment-specific strategies

Segment-specific efficiency: The online service easyHotel.com is a subsidiary of the easyJet Group; it promotes a chain of budget hotels in Britain and Europe run by independent franchisees. It targets the air traveller for whom basic, highly standardized accommodation is acceptable. The aim of easyHotel is to extend its coverage via additional franchisees and it addresses the same demand segment by linking with 45,000 other budget providers.

Harmonized, segment-specific differentiation: There is a wealthy, prestige-seeking clientele for luxury and high performance cars in virtually every country and region. While the respective brand values and strategic approaches of enterprises such as Rolls Royce, Bentley, Maybach, Lincoln, Ferrari, Porsche and Lamborghini are globally harmonized, a high proportion of their output is customised to meet the extravagant and sometimes whimsical requirements of customers for whom price is no object.

Mature international airlines may disperse their resources worldwide, but generally they standardize operations as much as they can. A global strategy can also succeed in some business-to-business contexts such as the manufacture and servicing of military and civilian aircraft. Advanced technologies and skills transcend national differences. High technology manufacturing is capital intensive, necessarily confined to a few locations, frequently the home base. Military and civilian clients make differing purchase demands within limits set by the aircraft design parameters, such as engine options and seating configurations.

Country-Specific Strategies: Efficiency or Differentiation

A standardized approach can work well in the early stages of internationalisation, yet few global strategies succeed indefinitely with completely standardized offerings and highly central-ised control. Enterprises become arrogant and remote, losing ground to more responsive competitors. International marketing texts present often-humorous examples of corporate blunders, especially the failure to translate established home country slogans into appropriate, meaningful statements in other languages. Often quoted examples include the General Motors car called 'no go' to Spanish-speaking consumers, and Sweden's Electrolux's attempts to sell its vacuum cleaners to US consumers with the slogan 'Nothing sucks like an Electrolux.'!

Local alliance partners can mitigate these problems, but only if their voices are heard at corporate headquarters; moreover, the selection of partners presents a challenge as does their subsequent co-ordination and control.[21] Accordingly, whilst standardization, harmonization and narrow targeting may all have inherent attractions to control complexity and enhance efficiency or increase distinctiveness, international strategies that ignore differences among countries carry a significant risk of rejection.

RNING ②
ECTIVE

An alternative strategic approach starts by acknowledging that regional and country-specific differences matter greatly and can be a sound basis for effective international strategies.[22] An enterprise that willingly adopts (and makes a virtue of) a strategy sensitive to the local needs and expectations of each country or region in which it chooses to operate, expects that its efforts will be duly rewarded.

This strategy is variously described as locality-specific, multi-domestic or national differentiation. Its main characteristics are:

- Respect for local circumstances, including stage of demand development, technological sophistication, language, culture, and political sensitivities, however unfamiliar or particularised.[23]
- A willingness to identify and cater for differing demands in each locality by tailoring the quality and specifications of offerings appropriately.
- Production and distribution in cost-effective facilities sited locally or regionally.
- Brand, marketing, product and operations strategies that embrace changes consistent with local attitudes, expectations and behaviours, rather than prioritise harmonization.
- Operating with owned-and-operated subsidiaries and/or alliance partners whose local and regional executives can influence decisions within the overall corporate strategic framework.
- Acceptance that some countries needs are too specific to present a realistic profitable opportunity.

A strategy tailored to each country or region cannot achieve the scale and scope economies of a global strategy. Logically it is associated with differentiation. Even so, technological and administrative capabilities superior to those of local rivals can help the strategy succeed when demand is substantial.[24] Superior capabilities include the management of marketing, operations, research, product design and development. In large countries with multiple, viable market segments a country-centred strategy must still make decisions about targeting, although generally a local decision. Local brand positioning may effectively isolate each country; thus a basic offering in a sophisticated country might be positioned as relatively sophisticated in a less developed one, where it can command a premium price over lower quality, local alternatives to offset lower production and distribution economies.

Locality-specific strategies

Locality-specific efficiency: Disney Corporation operates six vacation theme parks, three in the United States and three in France, Hong Kong and Tokyo. Each preferred location maximises the substantial regional potential. The theme parks are mass-market operations based on an efficient formula that exploits *Disney's* classic cartoon characters, distinctive theme park design and multiple activities. The approach is formulaic and standardized, albeit tailored for relevance to the

> tastes and expectations of visitors from each region. Scale and scope economies provide visitors with excellent value, including accommodation. The parks' popularity makes air travel to these destinations competitively priced.
>
> ***Locality-specific differentiation***: HSBC Group is an international banking corporation headquartered in London that claims to be the 'world's local bank.' Notwithstanding harmonized policies over information technology and co-ordinated 'back office' operating procedures, banks provide a significant customer-facing service element, especially for major business clients. In this respect HSBC claims to be highly differentiated because its international network offers unrivalled local knowledge and cultural sensitivity in all the countries in which it operates.

Locality-specific strategies create implementation challenges. International enterprises pursue these strategies successfully only when the benefits of local responsiveness outweigh the additional costs they generate. To be seen as local and acceptable, inevitable duplication of functions and facilities adds costs, irrespective of how the offerings are delivered. It would be difficult to respond to the subtleties of every local market and remain efficient and profitable. The strategy may initially work in a country with a low-cost base, yet as costs and standards rise, become unaffordable. Locality-specific strategies often persist in service sectors where personalisation matters, because local cultures and practices strongly influence expectations and acceptable behaviours, wealth management and funeral provision being examples.

Hybrid Transnational (Global–Local) Strategies

LEARNING OBJECTIVE ②
LEARNING OBJECTIVE ③

In practice, convergence in multiple, potentially disparate countries is far from uniform or predictable, more apparent in surface behaviours than at deeper levels of attitude and culture, which can be subtle and hard to anticipate.[25] Conversely, multi-domestic strategies are costly and difficult to control from the centre. In consequence, neither of these approaches to international strategies is appropriate in all circumstances. A better approach could be a hybrid strategy that combines some of their respective characteristics pragmatically. The crucial question is whether a suitable compromise can be found between the opposing priorities of global convergence and national difference and between efficiency and differentiation.

LEARNING OBJECTIVE ②
LEARNING OBJECTIVE ③

The concept of hybrid strategies, sometimes called transnational[26] or global–local ('glocal'), proposes to combine the benefits of global and local approaches while minimising their drawbacks. The resolution of the paradox of global efficiency versus local responsiveness draws heavily on resource-based theory.

Since hybrid strategies differ in scope and sources of advantage, generalisations are problematic; nonetheless, a transnational strategy must meet various success factors:

- A corporate centre that sets mission, broad goals and strategies, establishes international network structures and monitors their effectiveness, and encourages the development of strong capabilities appropriate to each local circumstance.

- Country-based or regional subsidiaries and/or alliance partners which are responsive to the particularities, complexities and dynamics of each country and its circumstances, yet part of an integrated, efficient global corporate network.

- A global network that fully exploits the value-adding, distinctive capabilities and resources of the enterprise, by locating manufacturing, product development, purchasing, marketing and other functions where they operate most efficiently and in conjunction with regional or global supply chains.

- A network that encourages the active spread of knowledge, experience and capabilities developed in each locality as well as the corporate centre.[26]

A dynamic, global–local network requires a genuine mutuality of purpose, commitment and rewards. The network must also be coherent, practical and efficient. Subsidiaries have a potential for innovation not generally acknowledged in pure global or country-centred strategies, especially in enterprises whose capabilities derive from home-based centres of excellence. In the global–local network the centre's role equates more closely with portfolio management and parenting (Chapter 10). This is because country-centred and region-centred subsidiaries and partners are quasi-autonomous strategic business units. Naturally, they address local priorities, so trust, effective communication and co-ordination mechanisms are vital for best practices to diffuse across borders. This priority is somewhat easier with fully owned operations in relatively similar, internally homogeneous countries.

Transnational (global–local) strategy: McDonalds

Most people assume that the ubiquitous US restaurant chain pursues an international strategy of global standardization. That was true in its first phase of international expansion. Today, its business principles, family-orientated values, the franchising business system, the training of franchisees, managers and staff, the Golden Arch logo, Ronald McDonald and the '*I'm Lovin' It*' slogan are seeming constants. However, local owned-and-operated franchises outside the United States are encouraged to show greater sensitivity to their domestic food preferences (e.g., kosher food in Israel; no beef or pork in India). Supply chains are national or regional while restaurant services, size and décor are tailored to meet local preferences. Healthy menu options, innovations in food labelling and presentation, and McCafe gourmet coffee shops all originated in one area and were later extended around the network. Thus McDonalds ticks many of the boxes needed to consider its strategy global–local.

Organizing the International Enterprise

Executive decisions about international strategies are shaped by many factors: the development trajectory of the enterprise; personal ambitions and attitudes to risk; shared executive experiences and their assumptions about the future. The complexity of international operation entails compromises; specifically, how to reconcile the twin, seemingly opposed preferences for global standardisation/harmonization or local tailoring; and efficiency (low cost) or distinctiveness/differentiation. How enterprises resolve these dilemmas influences the form, extent and dispersal of the resources they require to implement the strategy and the degree to which they co-ordinate operational activities across national borders.

Cross-border standardisation/harmonization requires close co-ordination of dispersed activities to ensure consistency, thereby avoiding local decisions that create conflicts and costly duplication. Inconsistency risks compromising the clarity of internal purpose, corporate image and brand significance, creating vulnerabilities for alert competitors to exploit. Conversely, locality-specific strategies accommodate less harmonization and weaker activity co-ordination, potentially exploitable by a competitor that makes a virtue of standardisation and lower costs.

Detailed prescriptions cannot be made in isolation from the particularities of the enterprise and its context. As a guide, Figure 12.3 plots the degrees of geographic resource dispersion and strategy harmonization (hence activity co-ordination).

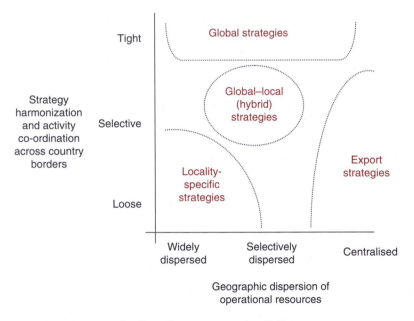

Figure 12.3: Dispersion and co-ordination of resources and activities

Adapted from concepts in Porter (1987b)

Export strategies rely largely on the home base, so many resources remain centralised. Beginning with overseas sales and distribution agents, followed by owned-and-operated sales offices, extends enterprise resource dispersion, although the financial commitment and risk exposure stays relatively low. The co-ordination of export activities from a distance can rarely be tight because local actions are difficult to monitor and control, particularly those of independent, national sales agents and distributors. These partners' priorities and commitment can change unpredictably, which is why ambitious enterprises typically regard exporting as a transitional phase of their internationalisation strategy.

In their various forms, global strategies emphasise relatively tight activity co-ordination to preserve the consistency on which standardisation/harmonization depends. Resource dispersion varies according to the potential for scale and scope economies in the particular activities under-taken, the opportunities for transnational synergies, and the extent to which differentiation is a factor in sustaining advantage. Dispersion decisions evolve dynamically over time and it is rarely possible to optimise fully the dispersion of resources and activities.

Locality-specific strategies exploit relatively wide dispersion of resources among the countries in which the enterprise operates. The price paid is less harmonization of strategies and limited co-ordination of activities (and consequent learning) among personnel in dispersed func-tions and facilities. Hybrid global–local strategies occupy the middle ground of Figure 12.3. They entail a network of subsidiary operations that may be wholly owned or I part alliance-based. Again, global–local strategies evolve as priorities adjust to enterprise aims and circumstances over time.

Resource Dispersion

A strategy to enable international operations requires a resource network beyond the home base of sufficient complexity and sophistication to perform the activities dictated by that strategy where they are needed. Costly assets and other resources variously include:

- Operational facilities for production, product development, testing and demonstration; physical distribution; and offices for marketing, sales and administrative staff.
- Production machinery, computers and communications equipment, vehicles.
- Human resources.

How many resources, of what kind, where they are best located, who owns and directs them, and how their performances are co-ordinated are all important questions of strategy implementation. Answers depend on many factors, such as:

- The nature of the sector and the demand being serviced.
- Enterprise size, distinctive capabilities and its financial resources.
- The countries in which it operates and the regulatory, logistical, cultural, linguistic and other factors that enable or constrain inward investment and operations;
- The agreed role(s) and capabilities of its regional or local partner(s), if any.
- Executive preferences.

Decisions over the pattern of resource dispersion are particularly mindful of the principal, advantage-creating assets, functions and capabilities located at the home base. An enterprise with a highly distinctive, global brand generally retains its core marketing functions centrally, enabling corporate executives to dictate brand deployment across borders. Global operations may require dispersed marketing resources, but subordinated to central policy directives.

Marketing and logistic functions divide continents into regions and sub-regions, respecting custom-and-practice. Thus, Central and South America are treated as a region because of common languages and similar stages of economic development. Europe is typically divided into Northern and Southern (Mediterranean) regions for logistical or cultural reasons, although enterprises that operate in more aggregate terms often combine Europe, Middle East and Africa (EMEA) into a single region. Regional owned-and-operated facilities may be preferable to country-by-country duplication because of the substantial financial investment and maintenance needed. They may be complemented by the external resources of partners. The dispersion and functioning of external supply chains and support contractors is a key consideration. While distance rarely presents insurmountable communication problems, geography influences the location of extensive supply chains. The high costs of transporting heavy, low-value goods from a remote country offset its benefits as a low-cost source. In countries with poor road or rail networks, it may be better to control transport costs by using smaller local facilities and local suppliers where practical.

The location of key resources also depends on availability, whether raw materials and supplies, experienced employees, or access to supportive infrastructure such as professional and legal advisors who are needed to ensure that conduct conforms with unfamiliar regulatory and other constraints such as: financial accounting standards; acceptable terms of employment contracts; health, safety, security, and environmental regulations; permission for building construction and how to handle official bureaucracy and possible corruption. As a guide, an international enterprise might expect to locate various functional activities thus:

1. Central (home base)
   - Strategic management and corporate policy-making.
   - Corporate finance.
   - Senior functional executives with a strategic, co-ordinating role.
   - Basic research and technology development.
   - Design and development of core offerings.
   - Corporate image development and brand management.
2. Regional
   - Management involved with detailed specification of the offerings marketed in each country.
   - Marketing, advertising and price-setting related to these offerings.
   - Production and operations management.
   - Procurement and supply chain management.
   - Regional financial management.
3. Local
   - Sales activities (sometimes including price setting).
   - Physical distribution (logistics).
   - Administrative functions including invoicing, payroll management, customer support and after-sales services.

The internationalisation of the Japanese car industry

The Japanese car makers initially pursued their international ambitions via exports. In countries with established car industries there was an acceptability issue: many American and European consumers considered it unpatriotic to buy imports. As the combination of rising Japanese labour costs and the costs of shipping finished vehicles around the world started to damage their competitiveness, the Japanese acknowledged compelling reasons to build factories in North America, Europe and Asia to supply these major markets. Regional production complemented exports and then increasingly displaced them.

Domestic experience influenced Japanese car makers' particular location decisions. They located plants on 'greenfield' sites where they would be welcomed for creating jobs. They expected domestic component suppliers to build factories close to their assembly plants, so they treated overseas suppliers the same; remote locations made these suppliers dependent, essentially captive, willing to conform to Japanese practices in exchange for long-term relationship development.

Why did Nissan, Honda and Toyota choose Britain to build cars for European sale? Britain's car industry was weak. Membership of the European Union (EU) was a key factor: vehicle regulations and import tariffs were essentially harmonized; transportation and distribution networks well-established, access to European markets straightforward. Japanese managers who had earlier supervised construction and operation of US plants could, if needed, relocate to a country where their familiarity with Anglo-American culture and use of English would be useful. Subsequently, however, these enterprises have built new facilities elsewhere in the EU, such as Hungary and the Czech Republic, to exploit lower labour costs and financial incentives from these governments.

Activity Co-ordination

RNING ③
ECTIVE

Most international enterprises comprise an activity network of fully owned-and-operated subsidiaries supported by local and regional alliances, infrastructures and supply chains. The challenge is to know how and to what degree to co-ordinate the network across borders and to ensure that the network fosters the spread of best practices, ideas and innovation by subsidiaries, partners, teams and individuals.

Co-ordination generally has a hierarchical logic. Functions whose resources and senior executives are located at the enterprise's home base are usually best placed to co-ordinate and control transnational policies. However, corporate executives are too remote or do not have time to co-ordinate detailed activities in their respective functions in each country. Functional executives at a regional level are better able to access, co-ordinate and control activities and knowledge-sharing within and among countries in each region.

An international strategy therefore requires careful attention not only to how resources are geographically dispersed, but also to the structures and networks whereby it organises and co-ordinates subsidiaries (including alliance partners). Constructive communications among dispersed units are crucial. The simplest network model for communication and control is hub-and-spokes, with the home base at the hub and subsidiaries at the rim (Figure 12.4). A subsidiary can be an essentially self-sufficient country-based unit, a functional unit (e.g., production and/or distribution), an alliance partner, or a more specialised unit (e.g., legal services) that supports or has responsibility for certain activities in more than one country.

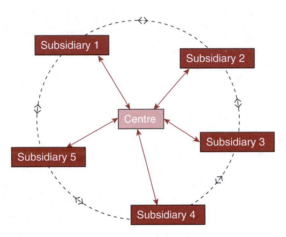

Figure 12.4: Hub-and-spokes model of organizational communication, co-ordination and control

The links that connect the centre and each subsidiary are the primary communication channels and each may be relatively independent of the others. In tightly controlled network structures the centre dictates strategic direction and exercises control; the flows from the subsidiaries are principally to report on performance and future plans and to highlight operational issues on which they require guidance and support. In country-centred strategies the centre and the subsidiaries comprise a relatively decentralised federal structure in which the links convey guidance and report performance. The communications links between subsidiaries around the perimeter may be relatively weak, even non-existent. The challenge for a global–local strategy is to create incentives to ensure that all these links are active and contribute positively to corporate effectiveness, conveying appropriate combinations of direction, guidance, routine reporting and control, together with best practice ideas and innovations.

The co-ordinated federal model becomes more complex when a regional structure exists to co-ordinate and control greater numbers of separate operations; whether country-based, in specialised cross-border units or subcontractors in an extended (outsourced) supply chain. As Figure 12.5 indicates, primary links exist between the central and the regional hubs. Each regional hub maintains links with particular countries and units. Additional links could exist between the regional hubs, although their intensity and worth may vary. For simplicity, no links are shown between countries in different regions; they may exist, but are probably informal and sporadic unless efforts are made to foster them in a global–local communications network. It should be clear from the figure that international structures become complicated. In general, functional activities occur in each country as needed, while capital intensive functions, notably production, are more likely to be regional, except in large countries with commensurate demand.

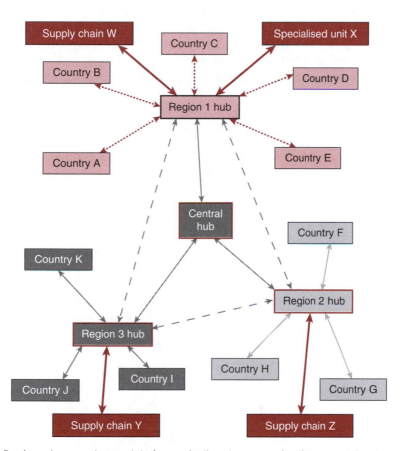

Figure 12.5: Region-plus-country model of organizational communication, co-ordination and control

Regional boundaries have to be drawn pragmatically. For example, Mexico is closer to South America than North America, culturally speaking. Yet Mexico is a member of NAFTA, drawing it economically towards the north. An international enterprise with regional structures in North and South America must decide where Mexico best fits. The decision could hinge on strategic, high-level factors, or for practical reasons on the location of the regional hub. That location generally dictates the location of all the enterprise's activities in that country.

CASE STUDY: Honda's transnational (global–local) strategy

In 1946, Soichiro Honda founded a motorcycle company that still bears his name. In the 1960s it began making cars and has since become one of the largest, truly global car companies. As a late entrant to the domestic car market it was disadvantaged against other Japanese manufacturers, so it had to export to survive and grow. It had opened a US sales office in 1959 and the United States spearheaded its export drive, followed later by Europe and various Asian countries. Later still, it began to build factories overseas, again starting in the United States. It diversified into a range of power products – portable electricity generators; lawn mowers; small agricultural equipment; snowmobiles and quad bikes – exploiting its growing expertise in the design and manufacture of internal combustion engines. Today, it produces greater numbers than any other maker.

Honda's global network now spans 390 subsidiaries and 102 other affiliates, found on every continent and it employs 176,000 people.[27] The network includes manufacturing and assembly plants for cars, motorcycles, components and power products, located in Asia (Japan, China, Malaysia, Indonesia, Philippines, Vietnam, Thailand, Taiwan), North and South America (United States, Canada, Mexico, Brazil), Europe (England, Belgium, France, Spain, Italy) and in Turkey, India, Pakistan, and Australia.[28]

Honda has developed a successful financial services business to support sales of its three product-centred businesses. These are the four businesses on which its statutory financial reporting is based. Results in 2009–10 were as follows.

Table 12.A: A breakdown of Honda's sales revenue in 2009/10

Gross sales by region US$ million		Gross sales by division US$ million	
Japan	20,040	Motorcycles	12,256
North America	40,331	Automobiles	70,452
Europe	8,274	Power products	2,985
Asia	14,188	Financial services	6,517
Other regions	9,377	TOTAL	92,210
TOTAL	92,210		

Since the late 1980s Honda has pursued the strategy of 'global–local' manufacturing,[29] with a clear 'Honda Philosophy', mission and management policies. Design, research and development subsidiaries are distributed across its major markets. The three product manufacturing groups are complemented by five operations groups for purchasing (supply chain), production, business support, business management and customer service. These eight groups interface with six regional operations groups (for Japan, China, North America, Latin America, EMEA and Asia/Oceania) in a complex matrix-style network. In addition, Honda operates four dedicated research and development companies in Japan that focus on advanced technologies, product research and development, production systems and equipment, and motorcycle racing, respectively.

Honda tries to manage this undeniably complex network so as to concentrate each particular task at the most appropriate levels and locations. Much of its research and development activity, long considered its most distinctive capability, is still based in Japan. Product design is shared between central and regional centres, enabling new designs tailored for each market. Production is located in those countries where demand is greatest, reducing distribution costs within each region that a factory supplies. Sales and marketing offices feature in many more countries to ensure close relationships with Honda's franchised sales and service networks. Accordingly, its organization is global–local in its structure and operations. However, it is not static. On the contrary, Honda's structure adjusts regularly in response to changing external circumstances, for example, growing Asian markets and the pressures to produce more environmentally friendly forms of motive power.

Question

1. Compare and contrast Honda's approach to how it has organised its international operations with Carlsberg's. What are the main conclusions from this analysis?

Summary

ARNING ①
JECTIVE

- Strategies for continuing development become more complex as enterprises start to operate across country borders. The primary motives for international development are to expand and diversify, and also to counter potential threats from aggressive competitors. There is a typical development path, first from the home base, then extension into overseas markets via exporting, licensing and other alliances and ultimately investment in transnational networks of owned-and-operated subsidiaries and local or regional partners.

LEARNING
OBJECTIVE ②
- *National* developmental paths affect the comparative advantage of particular countries to expansion-minded enterprises. The emergence of global megatrends supports the global *convergence* hypothesis, encouraging a global approach to strategic development. Global strategies prioritise standardisation and harmonization, an appropriate degree of activity co-ordination, with advantage sustained (as in strategies discussed in previous chapters) by efficiency or distinctiveness. Conversely, major transnational differences encourage country-centred (multi-domestic) international strategies. These strategies prioritise country and/or regional *responsiveness*.

LEARNING
OBJECTIVE ②
- Both global and country-centred strategies have strengths and weaknesses, and advocates and detractors, which we call the global–local controversy. In practice, progressive international enterprises may pursue a hybrid strategy, trying to combine the benefits of global and local strategic approaches, hence the name 'global–local' (also called transnational or 'glocal').

LEARNING
OBJECTIVE ②
- Global–local strategies adjust and particularise the detail of their approaches according to evolving circumstances in the sector(s) in which they operate. Resource and communication networks enable relatively efficient operations and, ideally, dynamic knowledge sharing among dispersed, localised subsidiaries to sustain progressive development.

LEARNING
OBJECTIVE ③
- The chapter also considers the managerial and organizational challenges of making decisions about the location of subsidiaries; their integration with alliance partners, external contractors and regional or global supply chains; the extent to which activities in the network are well co-ordinated; and the need for incentives to enhance constructive communications between the many units in a worldwide network.

Exercises for Further Study and Discussion

1. If harmonization were to be easy to combine with local responsiveness, presumably every enterprise operating internationally would adopt a 'glocal' strategy. Since they do not, is it reasonable to conclude that its complexity and cost simply outweighs the benefits for most enterprises? Alternatively, perhaps global convergence/divergence trends will resolve the dilemma of choice?

2. Apply the resource-based V-R-I-O-S criteria of Chapter 5 to assess Honda's international strategy, in particular the basis of its global competitive advantage. Is Honda's complex matrix organization structure a source of sustainable advantage?

3. From the published reports of the food products companies Nestlé and Kellogg's, it appears that Vietnam is more significant for Nestlé's international strategy than it is for Kellogg's. Apply the environmental analysis framework of Chapter 2 together with concepts in this chapter to explain why this may be so.

4. Investigate the international strategy of a not-for-profit organization of interest. How would you describe its strategy? Is it appropriate to its mission? How might it be enhanced?

5. Should enterprises ever consider transnational relocation of their headquarters? What factors should determine such decisions?

6. Choose an enterprise of interest and assess which of the megatrends has (or might have) greatest impact on it. Are some implications clear or contrary, that is, counteracting? If so, is it impossible to reach conclusions about future actions?

7. Does a global enterprise have a strategic advantage over a regional or single-country competitor when facing dilemmas created by technological uncertainty? Examine the issues critically.

8. Disney theme parks are both an efficient and well-differentiated vacation product. The HSBC banking network is efficient and also nationally differentiated. Are they pursuing essentially the same international strategy? Or are there crucial differences?

9. A critic might say that global–local strategies are fundamentally efficiency-oriented; they apply token customisation to appear responsive to country-specific needs, citing McDonalds as a prime example. Discuss the claim.

Suggestions for Further Reading

Baden-Fuller, C. and Stopford, J.M. (1991) 'Globalization frustrated: the case of white goods', *Strategic Management Journal* (vol. 12/7, pp. 493–507).

Bailey, W. and Spicer, A. (2007) 'When does identity matter? Convergence and divergence in international business ethics', *Academy of Management Journal* (vol. 50/6, pp. 1462–1480).

Begley, T.M. and Boyd, D.P. (2003) 'The need for a corporate global mind-set' *MIT Sloan Management Review* (vol. 44/2, pp. 25–32).

Collis, D.J. and Montgomery, C.A. (2005, Ed. 2) *Corporate Strategy: A Resource-Based Approach*, McGraw-Hill (chapter 6).

Dyer, J.H., Kale, P. and Singh, H. (2004) 'When to ally and when to acquire', *Harvard Business Review* (vol. 82/7, pp. 108–117).

Eden, L. and Miller, S. (2004) 'Distance matters: liability of foreignness, institutional distance and ownership strategy', in Hitt, M.A. and Cheng, J.L. (eds) *Advances in International Management*, Elsevier/JAI Press.

Ghemawat, P. and Ghadar, F. (2006) 'Global Integration – Global Concentration', *Industrial and Corporate Change* (vol. 15, pp. 595–624).

Hagedoorn, J. and Dysters, G. (2002) 'External sources of innovative capabilities: the preference for strategic alliances or mergers and acquisitions', *Journal of Management Studies* (vol. 39, pp. 167–188).

Hamel, G. (1991) 'Competition for competence and inter-partner learning within international strategic alliances', *Strategic Management Journal* (vol. 12/Summer special issue, pp. 83–103).

Harzing, A.-W. (2002) 'Acquisitions versus greenfield investments: international strategy and management of entry modes', *Strategic Management Journal* (vol. 23/3, pp. 211–227).

Hitt, M.A., Dacin, M.T., Levitas, E., Arregle, J.L. and Borza, A. (2000) 'Partner selection in emerging and developed market contexts: resource-based and organizational learning perspectives', *Academy of Management Journal* (vol. 43, pp. 449–467).

Huff, A.S., Floyd, S.W., Sherman, H.D. and Terjesen, S. (2009) *Strategic Management: Logic and Action*, John Wiley (chapter 8).

Hult, G.T.M., Ketchen, D.J. and Arrfelt, M. (2007) 'Strategic supply chain management: improving performance through a culture of competitiveness and knowledge development', *Strategic Management Journal* (vol. 28/10, pp. 1035–1052).

Ireland, R.D., Hoskisson, R.E. and Hitt, M.J.A. (2009) *The Management of Strategy*, Cengage (Ed. 2, chapter 8).

Kwok, C.C. and Tadesse, S. (2006) 'The MNC as an agent of change for host-country institutions: FDI and corruption', *Journal of International Business Studies* (vol. 37, pp. 767–785).

Lane, P.J., Salk, J.E., and Lyles, M.A. (2002) 'Absorptive capacity, learning and performance in international joint ventures', *Strategic Management Journal* (vol. 22/12, pp. 1139–1161).

Lawrence, T.B., Morse, E.A. and Fowler, S.W. (2005) 'Managing your portfolio of connections', *MIT Sloan Management Review* (vol. 46/2, pp. 59–65).

Luo, Y. (2000) 'Dynamic capabilities in international expansion', *Journal of World Business* (vol. 35/4, pp. 355–378).

Madhok, A. (2006) 'Revisiting multinational firms' tolerance for joint ventures: a trust based approach', *Journal of International Business Studies* (vol. 37, pp. 30–43).

Meyer, K.E. (2006) 'Global focusing: from domestic conglomerates to global specialists', *Journal of Management Studies* (vol. 43, pp. 1109–1144).

Nippa, M., Beechler, S. and Klossek, A. (2007) 'Success factors for managing international joint ventures: a review and an integrative framework', *Management and Organization Review* (vol. 3, pp. 277–310).

Ricart, J.E., Enright, M.J., Ghemawat, P., Hart, S.L. and Khanna, T. (2004) 'New frontiers in international strategy' *Journal of international Business Studies* (vol. 35, pp. 175–200).

Rugman, A.M. and Verbeke, A. (2003) 'Extending the theory of the multinational enterprise: internalization and strategic management perspectives', *Journal of International Business Studies* (vol. 34, pp. 125–137).

Tsang, E.W.K. (2002) 'Acquiring knowledge by foreign partners for international joint ventures in a transition economy: learning-by-doing and learning myopia, *Strategic Management Journal* (vol. 23/9, pp. 835–854).

Wiersema, M.F. and Bowen, H.P. (2007) 'Corporate diversification: the impact of foreign competition, industry globalization and product diversification', *Strategic Management Journal* (vol. 29/2, pp. 115–132).

Zaheer, S. and Zaheer, A. (2007) 'Trust across borders', *Journal of International Business Studies* (vol. 38, pp. 21–29).

Notes

1 Main sources: http://www.carlsberggroup.com/company; http://www.visitcarlsberg.dk/aboutcarlsberg; http://en.wikipedia.org/wiki/Carlsberg_Group
2 Kronenbourg is now part of Carlsberg.
3 The top 10 global brewers have about two-thirds of the global beer market estimated at 1.8 billion hectolitres a year.
4 Ghemawat (2007).
5 Luo (2000).
6 Dyer, Kale and Singh (2004).
7 http://www.un.org/esa/population/publications/longrange2/WorldPop2300final.pdf
8 Peng (2001).
9 Wiersema and Bowen (2007). An exception is when former conglomerate enterprises exploit global coverage to compensate for sources of growth they have divested (Meyer, 2006).
10 Porter (1990).
11 An argument advanced by Porter (1990); see also Grant (1991). Bull, Pitt and Szarka (1993) compared three such enterprising industrial communities in France, Italy and England.
12 Paik (2005).
13 When, for example, does a 'commission' become a 'bribe'? For a wide variety of issues surrounding joint ventures and also their decline see in further reading: Child and Van (2001); Hambrick et al. (2001); Lane, Salk and Lyles (2002); Peng and Shenkar (2002); Tsang (2002); Madhok (2006); Nippa, Beechler and Klossek (2007). For issues of corruption and ethics see also: Rodriguez, Uhlenbruck and Eden (2005); Kwok and Tadesse (2006); Weitzel and Berns (2006); Bailey and Spicer (2007). Of course, multinational corporations can affect the 'rules of the game' positively.
14 Lawrence, Morse and Fowler (2005).
15 Enterprises cannot ignore the actions and precedents set by regional or global competitors, especially in high technology domains, e.g., McKendrick (2001); Rugman and Girod (2003); Rugman and Verbeke (2004).
16 Whose importance was signalled by Marshall in the 1890 and Schumpeter in the 1930s. See for example Baptista (1998).
17 In addition to the group of middle European and other recent members of the EU whose economies are chronically under-developed, there are now seemingly disparaging references to the vulnerable so-called 'PIIGS' Euro-based economies of Portugal, Italy, Ireland, Greece and Spain.
18 First presented more than a quarter-century ago in the US context by Naisbitt (1982). See also: Toffler (1973); Naisbitt and Aburdene (1990); Skyrme (1999).
19 See for example Abrahamson (2004) and Florida (2004).
20 Westney (2006).
21 Yu (2003).
22 Hitt et al. (2000); Porrini (2004).
23 Eden and Miller (2004).
24 London and Hart (2004); Cantwell, Dunning and Janne (2004).
25 Ghemawat and Ghadar (2006); Ghemawat (2006).

26 In Western countries black is used to denote tragedy and mourning. In China white has a similar connotation. In some African countries a picture on product packaging is understood to signify the contents. Thus the baby food company, Gerber, found that the picture of a smiling baby on its jars didn't convey the meaning it intended. ... For a more conceptual discussion of the impact on employees as well as markets, see Brannan (2004).

27 See for example Bartlett and Ghoshal (1998).

28 Skyrme (1999); Cauley de la Sierra (1995), especially chapter 12. This is particularly challenging when country operations depend on an alliance partner whose interests may not fully align with those of the enterprise (Tsang, 2002; Lawrence, Morse and Fowler, 2005).

29 Source: Honda 2010 Annual Report.

30 http://world.honda.com/link/index.html

31 Mair, A. (1994) *Honda's Global Local Corporation*, St. Martins Press.

13

Strategy Implementation and Change Management

Learning Outcomes

This chapter is designed to enable you to:

① Understand the challenges of implementing strategies and the measures by which success can be judged.

② Explain the key issues and challenges of organization and systems design.

③ Apply the integrative 7S and Tricord frameworks to gain insights into strategy implementation in particular cases.

④ Discuss the nature of strategic planning.

⑤ Explain the problematic nature of managing strategic change and the importance of leadership styles and contributions.

CASE STUDY: The rise and decline of Habitat[1]

The young designer Terence (later, Sir Terence) Conran opened a home furnishings store called Habitat on Fulham Road, London in 1964. Conran's enthusiastic young team quickly established Habitat as a trendy, furniture and lifestyle company. It pioneered stylish, modern-looking, relatively affordable products, very attractive to young, married couples brought up in dowdy, post-war 1950s homes. The Habitat chain expanded across the UK during the late 1960s and 1970s in busy city centres and in major European cities.

Habitat became a public company in 1981; it merged with Mothercare, the mother and baby goods retail chain, in 1982. The combined public company acquired Heal's, the specialist furnishings store at its prestigious Tottenham Court Road location and Richards, the women's fashion store chain. In 1986 Habitat-Mothercare plc merged with the down-market British Home Stores variety chain, renaming the enlarged group Storehouse plc. Conran, by now a wealthy man, remained chief executive until 1988 and chairman until 1990, as he pursued a range of business and other interests.[2] Storehouse executives grappled with the integration, rationalisation and future strategy of this disparate retail group.

By 1990 Habitat seemed to have lost its freshness and design flair. Swedish IKEA entered the U.K, quickly establishing several massive, out-of-town warehouse-style home furnishings and accessories stores that offered UK consumers a radical new shopping experience. Its named, young international designers created attractive, functional, minimalist designs. Crucially they were available in greater variety and at much lower cost than Habitat and other furnishings stores. IKEA's cost advantage derived from a global supply chain that sourced its furniture and other products from low-cost countries. It reduced costs further by distributing furniture to its stores in flat-packed form for customer collection and home assembly.

Heal's quit the Storehouse portfolio in 1990 by management buyout. In 1992 Sears plc acquired Storehouse, and Habitat was transferred to IKANO, a private company owned by IKEA until 1988 when it was acquired by relatives of Ingvar Kamprad, IKEA's founder. IKANO rejuvenated Habitat's stores, aiming for a more up-market profile than IKEA. The chain stabilised at 36 UK outlets and a similar number elsewhere in Europe, plus franchised stores in 12 other countries. Nonetheless, Habitat experienced losses of about €40 million a year for several years. At the end of 2009 IKANO transferred Habitat to Hilco, a private equity group that claims particular expertise in retail restructuring.[3]

Tasks and discussion questions

Senior management teams change, so strategy implementation can be likened to a marathon relay. In this light, examine critically the following explanations of Habitat's decline, being particularly aware of timing:

- The predictable consequence of ageing and predatory competition.
- Continued implementation of a static, inflexible strategy that was unresponsive to critical transition points in time.
- Poor understanding and implementation of a suitably adaptive strategy.
- Just bad luck.

Introduction: 'Making Strategy Happen'

When an enterprise has established a strategy that takes account of all the relevant issues in its environment and satisfies the assessment criteria of Chapter 6, it would be easy to assume that the job is largely done. Not so.

LEARNING
OBJECTIVE ①

Strategy design, however elegant or inspired in concept, is merely a hypothesis still be tested in the real world. Implementation is a multi-faceted challenge whose activities are summarised in the stage 3 of the 'Design-plus' model (Figure 13.1)

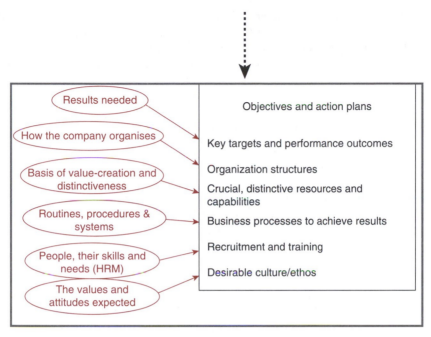

Figure 13.1: Stage 3 of the 'Design-plus' approach: strategy implementation

While the processes of strategy implementation can be defined in outline, senior executives and other stakeholders determine how it progresses, influenced by their dominant frame of reference (Chapter 1). Rational and systemic frames are likely to emphasise the role of careful strategic planning and control, treating implementation as a logical extension of strategy formation, as the enterprise works towards its critical aims and objectives.[4] Entrepreneurial/adaptive and power–political reference frames are more likely to approach implementation as an ongoing emergent, negotiable and circumstantial process. In any event, outcomes become fully realised only through the 'doing' of strategy. As in military contexts, adaptation and improvisation must be considered necessary, dynamic virtues[5]: doing what turns out to be possible and learning from those experiences.

Adaptation and improvisation may alter preconceived strategies, sometimes in quite fundamental ways. Being adaptive encourages innovation by accepting that continuing change is necessary; that what matters most is on setting the right journey direction, not becoming obsessed with the ultimate destination.

In highly innovative enterprises, an integral feature of strategy implementation is to place considered 'bets' on promising directions or paths.[6] By monitoring progress carefully, enterprises can prioritise the directions that appear to be fulfilling their early promise, marginalising directions whose promise evaporates. This perspective on strategy implementation should not be confused with merely *reacting* to circumstances that arise unexpectedly from failures and lack of anticipation. In respect of the latter, 'managing strategic change' becomes a polite way of describing reaction to crisis.

EARNING ①
BJECTIVE

Irrespective of the dominant reference frame, implementation is challenging. Intentionally or by accident, each enterprise implements its strategy in the 'real world', typically by aligning elements of formal planning and control, proactive adaptation and, perhaps, crisis management too. So this chapter considers formal, adaptive and reactive aspects of strategy implementation, specifically:

- Strategic integration (coherence of actions).
- Organizational design: structure, operating systems and routines.
- Strategic planning and control processes.
- Modes of change management.
- Transformation and transactional leadership.

The aim is not to address the huge subject areas of organization behaviour and social psychology, but to highlight critical strategic priorities in order to achieve the declared mission.

Successful strategy implementation

What is successful strategy implementation? Not a philosophical question, but one that matters greatly to executives because, as the aphorism says 'success has many fathers while failure is an orphan.' In fact, explanations for success (and failure) can be highly controversial.

LEARNING OBJECTIVE ① An obvious definition of success is survival, meaning organizational persistence over long periods of time. Many enterprises fail on this criterion.

Judged on persistence, Habitat is successful. However, academic and anecdotal evidence indicates that some, notably not-for-profit, enterprises can survive for long periods while performing poorly; they persist in a state of 'permanent failure.'[7] Aside from such exceptions, successful persistence requires at least financial stability.[8]

LEARNING OBJECTIVE ① Yet successful strategy implementation surely leads to mission achievement, a more satisfactory indicator, whilst acknowledging that mission achievement is not generally a singular event, but an ongoing process of striving.

History records that many enterprises, like Habitat, achieve their missions for a finite time, thereafter it is at best questionable and at worst a failure. When a mismatch exists between the mission and strategy being implemented one would predict ultimate failure.[9] In that event it can be unproductive to attribute failure to an unrealistic mission or a poor quality strategy for achieving it: either way it is a strategic *management* failure. However, it is possible to imagine a well-conceived strategy that implements badly, suggesting a failed enterprise in the sense that its achievements are way below its potential. Whilst the top management team are not entirely to blame, members frequently experience negative personal consequences.[10]

LEARNING OBJECTIVE ① More interestingly, the converse proposition is that outstanding implementation *transforms* an unexceptional strategy into one that in hindsight looks exceptionally well-conceived. The following indicators underline the real significance of successful strategy implementation:

- Taking whatever actions are necessary and sufficient to maximise the prospects of mission achievement: being relevant, timely, mutually consistent and reinforcing.

- Deploying appropriate and sufficient resources and capabilities to perform these actions, efficiently and effectively.
- Setting and achieving major objectives and targets along the path towards mission achievement. Capable, consistent, determined and visible executive leadership.

Successes and Failures of Strategy Implementation

Taking appropriate and necessary actions: By 2008 Barclays Bank was a very large and capable, British-based international bank. A strong balance sheet and adequate liquidity are major, continuing elements of any bank's strategy. Unlike most rival British banks, Barclays responded proactively and promptly to the unforeseen impact of the global credit crunch by negotiating additional capital from international sources.

Deploying appropriate and sufficient resources and capabilities: A long-established military doctrine is that success in combat missions requires high calibre and overwhelming resources.[11] Coalition forces appeared to neglect this doctrine against the Taliban in Afghanistan, until the US 'strategic surge' of 2008. Britain was criticised for injecting fewer troops than the agreed mission required and for their inadequate resources of basic and costly equipment including helicopters.

Achieving major objectives and targets relevant to the mission: The European Case Clearing House (ECCH) is a small, UK-based charity whose mission is to promote the use of case-study teaching materials in business education. Initially it supported the needs of MBA programmes at Cranfield, London and Manchester Business Schools. It set itself progressive growth targets; 30 years later it has over 500 institutional members globally for whom it acts as a repository and distribution centre of teaching materials, increasingly using web-based communications. Additionally, it organises international workshops to encourage the writing of new case studies and to explore their use in the classroom. Although its fundamental mission is unchanged, it has adjusted its objectives and achieved increasingly ambitious targets.

Capable, consistent, determined and visible leadership: In 19 seasons of the English Premier League to 2010/11, Everton Football Club in Liverpool has not been the Champions. The club has finished in the top half of the league table only eight times. By the standards of Chelsea and Manchester United (and no doubt its fans' expectations) these are hardly successes. So has its strategy failed? Bill Kenwright, a successful, well-known theatre producer, has been the club's majority owner and Chairman, since 2004. He recruited manager David Moyes in 2002. Together, they have achieved its best Premier League results, placed fourth and fifth (twice), been FA Cup finalists in 2009, and maintained Premier League status and financial stability on a modest budget. Its end-of-season positions are improving;

Moyes has won 'Manager of the Month' awards eight times. By contrast, between 1996 and 2010 when it was relegated from the Premier League, Portsmouth FC had six different owners/chairmen, four of these in the 2009/10 season. In February 2010 the UK tax authorities put the club into financial administration for non-payment of taxes.

Integration: the Key Implementation Challenge

LEARNING
OBJECTIVE   ①

A major challenge as strategy unfolds is to co-ordinate and control the timing of diverse initiatives, some of which could involve major change and all enterprise functions. Each initiative must be mutually consistent with and reinforce others, whether concurrent or in a specified sequence.[12] Clarity of direction and intent; deploying adequate resources and capabilities; achieving critical aims and objectives; good organization and leadership – all these affect how well a strategy is implemented.

The 7S framework is a way of identifying the fit of strategic initiatives, operational functions and processes [13] (Figure 13.2). Each 'S' is shorthand for a core aspect of strategic management and implementation. At the centre lie the fundamental, shared values: the prescriptive beliefs about the aims, mission and future vision of the enterprise its obligations to stakeholders, its ethos and ways of doing things. Effective implementation requires all staff to understand and accept these values. The 'staff' component of 7S symbolises the priority to ensure sufficient skilled, well-trained and well-motivated people, hence the importance of the human resources management function and competent people-managers throughout the enterprise. 'Style' represents identity and ethos or 'the way we try to do things here.' These three elements are called the soft 'S's'.

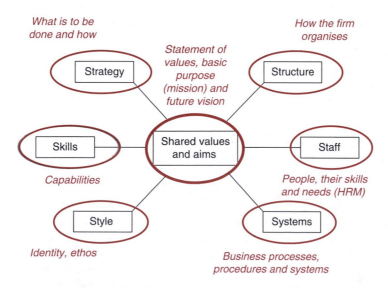

Figure 13.2: The 7S framework
The McKinsey 7S framework (adapted from Peters and Waterman, 1982)

Of the four 'hard' S's, 'strategy' and 'skills' (resources and capabilities) need no introduction. How they are *deployed*, however, requires 'structure' S, symbolising enterprise design and organization, supported by 'systems': practical, efficient operating procedures, business processes and communication systems in all aspects of strategy implementation.[14] In effective enterprises the hard and soft S's integrate seamlessly. The utility of the 7S framework is best demonstrated with the example of Kodak. Although its transformation in the digital era is well under way, the process is far from compete.

Implementing a transformational strategy at Kodak

US entrepreneur George Eastman was founder, chief executive and chairman of Kodak from 1888 until 1932. His company brought photography to the mass market via the Box Brownie camera and the slogan 'you press the button and we do the rest.' While Kodak has always made and sold cameras, this was the means to encourage sales of film, printing papers and chemicals, consumable materials that generated profitable repeat custom. Kodak's most senior executives were invariably internal appointments; they presided over a highly respected East Coast company that became an international giant through innovation, in both technologies and market presence. Without necessarily becoming complacent, Kodak took for granted its continuing dominance of its various markets.

By the 1980s only Fuji of Japan remained a serious global competitor. At that time Kodak was aware that digital imaging had the potential to replace light-sensitive film for image capture; it had already produced low resolution 1.4 megapixel sensor chips. Yet Sony of Japan marketed the first digicam called Mavica in 1983, which could store only a handful of images on a floppy disc, compromising its practicality. Electronic imaging seemed too costly for practical photographic purposes, until well into the future. So Kodak focused on professional document scanning and related applications. A retrospective 7S profile of Kodak in the 1980s is shown in Figure 13.3. All the main elements were long-established, mutually consistent and reinforcing, and largely static.

A decade later, however, Kodak had accepted the future challenge of digital photographic imaging. In 1993 it hired George Fisher from electronics giant Motorola to be CEO whose brief was to propel Kodak into the era of digital imaging technologies including sensor design and production capabilities. Fisher found little consensus among senior colleagues over how (and how quickly) to transform Kodak from analogue to digital media without damaging its traditional, very profitable income streams, now facing acute competition from Fuji. Kodak took various initiatives to make film-based photography more attractive. In 1996 it launched the 'Advanced Photo System' (APS) film camera, applying a technical format that Kodak had agreed with all the main Japanese camera makers who also introduced APS products. APS was intended to displace long-established snapshot

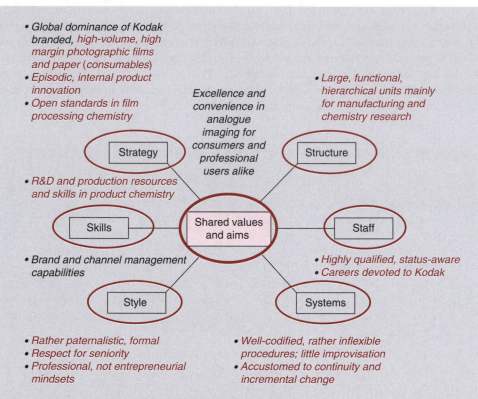

Figure 13.3: The 7S framework applied to Kodak in the 1980s

and 35-mm film formats, generating new sales to loyal Kodak users and discouraging the rapid entry of digital technologies into consumer markets,.

By the mid-2000s APS camera sales had almost died, while digital cameras had gained a major share of global demand. Kodak was now offering a range of digital cameras for consumer and professional use, but their products were considered generally to compare poorly with the best of its Japanese and Korean counterparts, so sales were disappointing. Even as the company increased sensor performance, competitors were driving down prices too rapidly for Kodak to match. Moreover, digital cameras generated no consumable sales to replace declining film sales, while consumers were buying fewer paper prints and increasingly viewing their pictures on computer or television screens.

Figure 13.4 suggests a 7S profile of how an 'ideal' Kodak would now have looked.[15] Digital technologies would necessarily feature widely, since Kodak's advantages from its chemical imaging resources and capabilities were fast eroding. Carrying the burden of its traditional identity and ethos, it struggled in reality to be dynamic and entrepreneurial. Sales were declining and it was losing money. More than two-thirds of its employees had already gone.[16] But it could not easily (nor could it not afford to) recruit and integrate adequate numbers of people with the much-needed electronics and software development skills. To compete in emerging new markets (e.g., in medical applications) it was obliged to enter alliances with 'upstart' young enterprises to access the capabilities needed, a novel experience for a proud company with a self-sufficient history. To compound the challenge, many actual or potential collaborators were thousands of miles away in California, Texas and elsewhere around the world.

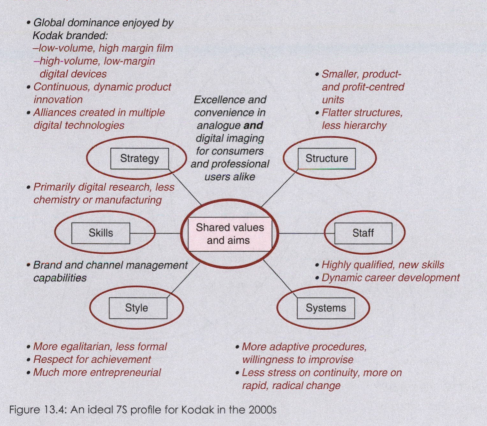

- Global dominance enjoyed by Kodak branded:
  - low-volume, high margin film
  - high-volume, low-margin digital devices
- Continuous, dynamic product innovation
- Alliances created in multiple digital technologies

Excellence and convenience in analogue **and** digital imaging for consumers and professional users alike

- Smaller, product- and profit-centred units
- Flatter structures, less hierarchy

- Primarily digital research, less chemistry or manufacturing

Strategy

Structure

Skills

Shared values and aims

Staff

- Brand and channel management capabilities

- Highly qualified, new skills
- Dynamic career development

Style

Systems

- More egalitarian, less formal
- Respect for achievement
- Much more entrepreneurial

- More adaptive procedures, willingness to improvise
- Less stress on continuity, more on rapid, radical change

Figure 13.4: An ideal 7S profile for Kodak in the 2000s

Figure 13.5 offers an alternative to the 7S integrative framework called the Tricord™ [17] It has been applied effectively to the management of strategy implementation, notably in not-for-profit enterprises. It bears considerable similarities to the 7S; though initially it appears simpler, having four elements, each with multiple components:

- *Identity*: an amalgam of core enterprise values, history and mission.
- *Strategy*: the unique concept of how it is going to 'live out its identity' and deliver its current mission, and how the latter should change (the future vision).

- *Systems*: the processes and tangible characteristics needed to 'deliver strategy on the ground'; embodied through technology, equipment, procedures, policies and ways of working.
- *Culture*: the energy and spirit of people in the enterprise.

The Tricord™ treats leadership as part of identity because the overarching leadership role is to enable and integrate each of the other elements into an effective, *meaningful* organizational whole. Like 7S, the Tricord™ stresses the need for mutual consistency or alignment among the core elements if an enterprise is to be 'healthy' and thus effective.

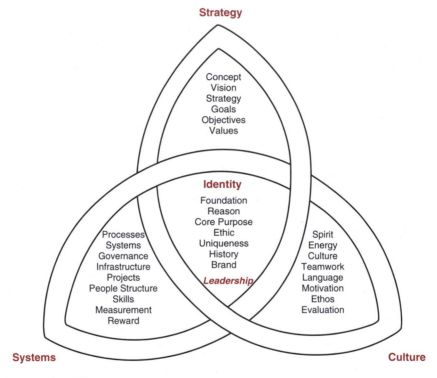

Figure 13.5: The **Tricord™**

Source Tricordant.com

Organizational Design

Organizational design addresses three themes. First, how the enterprise is structured, mindful of its size, external environment and other factors. Second, formal operating systems, policies and procedures. These control the effectiveness and efficiency of the enterprise's value-adding and support functions. Third, the informal routines and behaviours that affect an enterprise's functionality in practice.

LEARNING OBJECTIVE ②

Structure and its Strategic Consequences[18]

The *form* of structure is significant because it encodes the authority relationships and communication linkages, with particular consequences for decision-making and activity co-ordination. To be fit for strategic purpose the structure must be well-designed and constructed.[19] Key issues include:

- The extent to which senior executives centralise decision-making and control at the corporate headquarters or delegate outwards and downwards (decentralisation), allowing less senior managers to participate in strategic as well as operational decisions.
- The mechanisms whereby multiple, disparate activities are co-ordinated, progress monitored and controlled.
- The accuracy, completeness, and timeliness of communications within and beyond the enterprise.

No form of organisation structure is perfect. Extensive research has identified factors that influence the structural design and how it affects decision-making. Enterprise size, the nature of its external environment, its knowledge and technology profile, and internal power relationships are all major factors.

A number of 'propositions' with strategic relevance has emerged.[20] As enterprises grow in size (and age):

- They partition tasks and responsibilities into more specialized and differentiated structural subunits.
- They tend to diversify and typically restructure into divisions based on distinct markets, technologies, regions or countries.
- Their structures, systems and procedures generally become more formal and bureaucratic.

Environmental factors affect structural design:

- Formal, bureaucratic structures tend to emerge in stable external environments; dynamic environments encourage adaptive, organic structures.
- Complex external environments encourage decentralized structures that enable decision-making based on more immediate, localised knowledge.
- Hostile environments, influential external stakeholders and powerful senior executives all encourage centralised decision-making.

As enterprises become more knowledgeable and technology-intensive:

- They employ a greater proportion of specialized technical and professional staff.
- Their co-ordination mechanisms progress in stages from direct supervision and control to mutual adjustments among members of a team.

To implement strategic change often necessitates complementary structural change. However, changes in top management can lead to restructuring that is not invariably accompanied by significant strategic change.[21]

Forms of activity co-ordination[22]

Direct supervision: This form occurs in traditional, labour-intensive operations such as garment manufacture, often associated with piecework payments. The low-trust managerial assumption is that close scrutiny is needed to control quality and productivity.

Specification (codification) of operational processes and/or outputs: Service environments such as call centres and fast food restaurants provide staff with a documented 'script' that specifies permitted activity sequences for client-facing and 'back office' staff. Script compliance achieves control, sustained by periodic monitoring and supervisory feedback.

Input specification/codification: Operations that require higher level 'professional' expertise are intended to assure quality based on qualifications from intensive prior training, relevant experience and through peer-group monitoring, exemplified in medical practice and university lecturing. The evidence is that these guarantees are not always reliable.

Mutual adjustment: Innovative and creative organisations co-ordinate personal and team-based activities through informal, sometimes intuitive, interpersonal adjustments that transcend formal knowledge. Ideally, they avoid oppressive management styles, although charismatic leaders often behave autocratically. Examples include activities such as movie making, theatre acting and directing, video game design and production.

Figure 13.6 shows the kind of simple, functional structure found in many small and medium sized enterprises (SMEs). Activities are distributed by major functional area, each headed by a manager responsible for the efficiency and effectiveness of that function. In a two-level hierarchy the chief executive leads the development and implementation of strategy and is active in the co-ordination of operational activities through personal engagement, by facilitating lateral communications among functional managers and by acting as a conduit for information exchanges.

Figure 13.6: Simple functional structure

SMEs engaged in manufacturing and basic services typically adopt direct supervision; in creative and professional services they generally feature alternative co-ordination mechanisms. Multi-level enterprises find co-ordination and control extremely challenging, within and between divisions, within and between strategic business units (SBUs) and functionally in each SBU (Figure 13.7). The chief executive can no longer be the prime co-ordinator and controller of every strategic decision and major policy, let alone a communications conduit for operational activities. Alternative, multiple channels of monitoring, control and communication are needed:

- Within and between functions in each SBU (as in 'R').
- Within and between SBUs in each division, function by function (as in 'A').
- Within and between divisions, function by function.

As discussed in Chapter 12, the structuring of multinational enterprises presents additional complexities. No structural solution copes well with every circumstance.

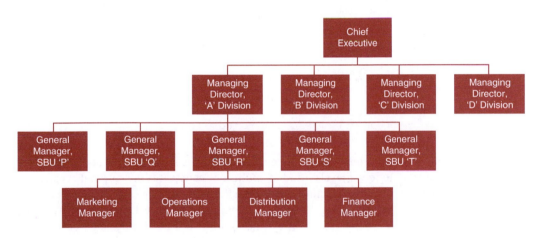

Figure 13.7: Typical enterprise structure with divisions and SBUs

n.b. the functional management positions are shown only for SBU 'R'.

In 'tall' multi-level structures (Figure 13.8) each managerial level is responsible for a relatively small number of subordinates: a narrow 'supervisory span'. Tall structures emphasise vertical over lateral communications. Co-ordination requires vertical information transfer through the levels. Individuals act as information nodes at each level, potentially filtering and delaying information transfer. Direct supervision occurs at low levels; alternative mechanisms increasingly apply at intermediate and higher levels, although control probably remains relatively formal and to a degree, oppressive.

The many intermediate levels in an excessively tall structure contribute relatively little to enterprise value-adding, while considerably increasing costs. Thus in the last two decades the trend in businesses has been towards flatter structures, also shown in Figure 13.8. Large public sector enterprises still commonly feature bureaucratic structures. Flatter structures encourage

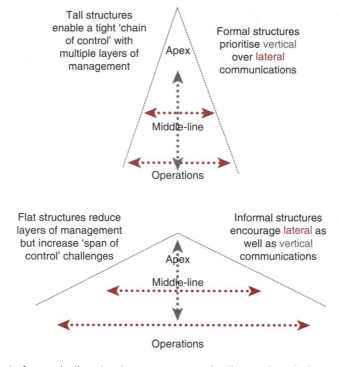

Figure 13.8: Impact of organisation structures on communication and control

lateral *and* vertical communications and greater delegation of responsibilities for decision-making and proactive innovation to lower levels.[23] In flat, multi-unit enterprises the corporate centre has an increased role to co-ordinate and control strategy implementation, while delegating considerable operational authority to SBU managers. Individual managers have greater responsibility spans, so close direct supervision is impractical. They must prioritise their interpersonal contacts by devoting time principally to the more critical operational activities for which they are responsible. High work loads elevate personal stress levels and the risks of oversight increase.

Matrix and network structures require comment (Figure 13.9) as does the closing case study about Honda in Chapter 12. In a typical matrix structure, SBUs are semi-autonomous operational units responsible for value-generating activities in a particular market or country. Key functions located in each unit; regional or central functional groups provide strategic guidance to, and co-ordination of, the dispersed enterprise units. Matrix structures are usually complex and relatively formal organisations, especially those operating across international borders.

Advocates claim that they are a viable response to the complexity of modern, transnational strategies, providing the means to co-ordinate disparate units and to resolve competing priorities by negotiation among the interested parties. For example, a frequent challenge that multinationals face is the dilemma of how to avoid compromising the core values of a standardised global brand when it sanctions somewhat contrary, but important local marketing campaigns. The purpose of matrix structures may be to institutionalize and accommodate policy conflicts; equally, they often create undesirable ambiguities and conflicts over inter-group roles and responsibilities and,

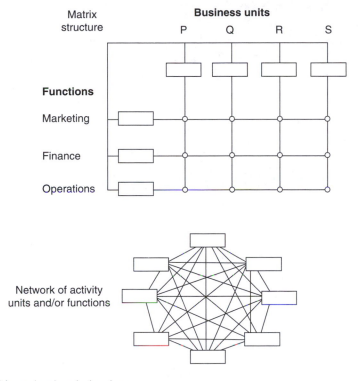

Figure 13.9: Matrix and network structures

significantly they slow down decision making.[24] However, as in the Honda example, a matrix structure may be thought a least-worst alternative.[25]

Network structures may be even more complex and ambiguous. Informal networks can be highly responsive to local circumstances. Network co-ordination involves various mechanisms, particularly mutual adjustment based on personal affiliations, supported by standardisation of inputs and outputs, as appropriate to the nature of the task. Actors who form the hubs of interpersonal networks provide crucial co-ordination capabilities. Operated constructively with some discipline, interactive networks have great potential to facilitate productivity, the exchange of ideas and consequent learning among individuals and operating units, though they still require effective co-ordination and communications mechanisms to minimise ambiguities, internal conflicts and chaos.[26] Web-based communications make the notion of the virtual network a realistic prospect, enabling contributors with particular skills to interact and perform effectively in conjunction, without needing to be in one place or even on the same continent.[27] They do not even need to be employed in the same enterprise; they may be self-employed participants who contribute to multiple, intersecting networks. Yet in the absence of face-to-face interpersonal contacts, mutual adjustment is problematic in networks characterised by innovative and creative activities. Video conference links provide only a partial solution.

Network structure in the music industry

Acoustic Alchemy is an instrumental jazz band of 20 years standing. One of its albums called 'The Beautiful Game' demonstrates the virtual organization nature of the music industry. Co-founder Greg Carmichael provided much of the creative and administrative input to the production. He composed the music tracks in collaborations with five other band members. The band performed and improvised the tracks at six recording studios: three in the United States, two in the UK (London) and one in Germany, using seven different, probably self-employed sound engineers. The recorded music was subsequently mixed at another British recording studio while digital mastering occurred at EMI's Abbey Road Studios in London. The discs were manufactured and marketed by a US company. Other supporting services came from different sources in the United States and the UK.

LEARNING
OBJECTIVE ② A modern development in organizational design in conventional enterprises is that they subcontract some or all of what they consider to be non-core activities, hence the concept of the 'shamrock' enterprise structure[28] (Figure 13.10).

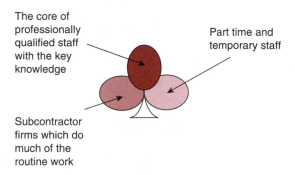

The core of professionally qualified staff with the key knowledge

Part time and temporary staff

Subcontractor firms which do much of the routine work

Figure 13.10: The 'shamrock' enterprise structure
Source: Handy (1989)

The crucial, value-adding 'leaf' of the shamrock comprises the qualified technical, managerial and professional employees who apply and extend the primary and distinctive enterprise capabilities. The routine value-generating activities of, for example, manufacturing and distribution are probably subcontracted to external specialist firms (the lower-left leaf). The enterprise typically also requires other support activities such as security, catering, office cleaning and maintenance, subcontracted or 'outsourced' to specialist agencies that provide staff on limited-term, temporary (interim) or part-time contracts (the lower-right leaf). The three leaves form a purposeful whole, whereby each activity is performed by multiple enterprises chosen because they have the most appropriately specialised skills and resources.

Imagination Technologies plc: A 'shamrock' enterprise

Imagination Technologies plc designs dedicated (application-specific) semiconductor microchips, notably for Digital Audi Broadcast (DAB) radio receivers, but for many other uses too. Imagination Technologies pioneered the commercialisation of DAB radio from 2001, marketing state-of-art products under the *Pure Digital* brand. It defines itself as a 'Design IP' company (IP: intellectual property); it subcontracts chip manufacture to partner companies. It currently employs around 500 staff, 80% of whom are qualified engineers.

Formal Systems, Policies and Procedures

RNING ② ECTIVE

Effective strategy implementation requires formal systems and procedures to enable timely decision-making, information distribution, communications, activity monitoring and control. Competent systems enable and themselves add value and advantage to the enterprise.

Formal systems and procedures address:

- Operations management, including manufacturing, distribution and quality assurance.
- Purchasing and sourcing of materials and supplies.
- Marketing, selling and corporate image promotion.
- Strategic and financial planning and control, including statutory reporting.
- Human resources management including recruitment, development, performance appraisal and reward systems.
- Management of external relations with enterprise stakeholders, including government agencies, trades unions, legal, regulatory and representative bodies.

Information technology (IT) plays a crucial role in all these areas, even in the smallest enterprises. The ability of an enterprise to 'know what it knows' and to ensure that knowledge is accessible wherever relevant and necessary is an important capability. Truly effective information systems contribute to a dynamic enterprise capability that enables proactive change.[29]

Historically, major enterprises developed proprietary information systems at considerable cost in large internal IT departments. Their systems were centralised, enterprise-specific and inflexible, yet required regular, costly updating and enhancement. Even the largest enterprises now prefer customised solutions from specialised consultancies such as Accenture and CapGemini, rather than proprietary systems. Companies such as SAP and Oracle Systems create modular off-the-shelf systems such as enterprise resource planning (ERP) and relational database software tailored for particular industry sectors.[30] Capable third-party suppliers customise these solutions further for each client. Solutions are typically web-based, distributed and amenable to responsive, cost-effective enhancement. Although many users no longer have the capability to write software, how they specify, construct and apply outsourced systems is itself a strategic capability.

Evidently, it is highly desirable for all systems and procedures to operate consistently and in conjunction. Whilst most enterprises use IT, their primary value-adding and advantage-creating potential probably does not depend fundamentally on it. Thus the effective management of strategy, human resources, marketing, finance, operations and external relations all require human insights, creativity, interactivity and judgement as well as information capture and exchange.

Human Resources Management

LEARNING
OBJECTIVE ②

Human resources management (HRM) is responsible for specific administrative procedures and, more strategically, for organizational effectiveness. The first duty is to ensure that the number of available employees and their various skills, knowledge and experience are consistent with the demands of strategy implementation.[31] The second is to ensure that human interactions in the enterprise are task-oriented, constructive, and maintain high morale and commitment.

Specialized HRM functions are accountable for the design, administration and use of formal HRM systems that enable the enterprise to:

- Recruit high-calibre staff at all levels of seniority.
- Train and develop individuals to their full potential so that promotional opportunities can be directed to capable performers.
- Assist staff to achieve results consistent with the strategy and to reward them accordingly.
- Appraise each individual's performance in his or her current role.
- Identify and discipline inadequate and unacceptable behaviours.

From a strategic perspective, recruitment systems must induct sufficient numbers of employees with the skills and experience necessary to sustain and enhance core value-creating capabilities. Training and development programmes must be linked to required future capabilities. Reward systems must acknowledge individual and team performances that support strategic goals, and be seen as fair, responsive and respectful. Appraisal systems must be fair and systematic, identifying and helping individuals with potential to advance to more senior roles over time.

Informal Routines and Behaviours

LEARNING
OBJECTIVE ②

Individuals and workgroups establish informal routines and interpersonal relationships that encode the accepted and acceptable enterprise attitudes and behaviours. They are unplanned and unwritten, yet contribute significantly to the enterprise's repertoire.[32] Ideally, the design of formal systems, policies and procedures avoid conflict with informal behaviours unless the latter are clearly dysfunctional.

Significantly for strategy implementation, informal networks and localised interactions shape enterprise identity and ethos. Personal interactions promote information exchange and generally enhance morale, but may also encourage idle gossip. The managerial challenge is to encourage constructive informal behaviours while not allowing idiosyncratic or negative ones to obstruct collective performance. For example, the design of open-plan workplace environments aims to increase efficiency by facilitating constructive interactions, yet inhibit excessive informal interactions through lack of privacy. However, productivity and morale can be damaged when individuals have no ownership of personal workspace.

When internal organization culture emerged as a 'hot topic' in the 1980s, managers were encouraged to initiate programmes to encourage positive change in collective attitudes, identity and ethos. Interventions might be attempted at three levels of abstraction (Figure 13.11). The outer level in the figure comprises the observable artefacts and symbols of organizational reality, such as status and authority relationships, and norms of behaviour. While change programmes can work directly at this level, change may be relatively superficial and transient.

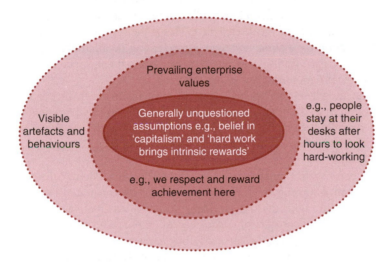

Figure 13.11: Three levels of cultural intervention

Schein's three levels of culture (Schein, 1997; Clegg, Kornberger and Pitsis, 2005, p. 272)

The middle level comprises deeper, more-or-less shared enterprise identity and values, called ethos in earlier chapters. The inner core comprises the most abstract, generally unspoken and unquestioned societal values that form the context for enterprise-specific values. The inner layers are more resistant to change, particularly to naïve change programmes.[33] Understandably, an international enterprise operating in countries with very different fundamental beliefs and attitudes from its home country may feel obliged to seek convergence.

Strategic Planning Systems and Control Processes

Why Strategic Planning?

Consider these quotations:

'Those who cannot remember the past are condemned to repeat it.'[34]

'Prediction is very difficult, especially about the future.' [35]

Enterprises are the tangible outcomes of cumulative historical actions by people. What they *might become* in future is both enabled and constrained by their particular histories and how people interpret them. While the past may hold lessons for the future, the future is never a simple projection of the past. The links between mission and vision statements are the vital bridge that connects an enterprise's past achievements, present activities, and future intentions.

In practice, middle managers are preoccupied with the present, rarely rewarded for reflecting on the past or for thinking very far ahead. Their superiors *are* properly concerned to be more thoughtful: to anticipate the future consequences of strategic decisions currently being implemented, and the potential future circumstances and events (scenarios) that actually require responses now.[36] Speculative, even 'unthinkable' future-oriented possibilities merit consideration of appropriate and feasible contingent responses. This is the logic of anticipatory strategic planning. It is the foundation for making and then implementing detailed plans for task completion, resource allocation, target setting and performance assessment,[37] activities probably better described as strategic programming and control.

Business strategic planning[38] reached a peak of mainstream acceptance in the 1970s, encouraged by prior examples of disciplined, apparently successful military planning. It became a feature too of many public sector enterprises.[39] Realistic, detailed, documentary long-range plans explained how declared strategies would achieve specific aims and objectives, making success much more probable.

LEARNING OBJECTIVE ④

Risk-averse, conservative enterprises in stable environments adopted the planning approach with most enthusiasm. Unfortunately, the turbulent 1980s demonstrated that strategic planning did not necessarily realise objectives. A particular criticism was that specialist planners created 'top down' plans without consulting adequately all those who would be accountable for their implementation, creating scepticism and failing to secure commitment.[40] Meanwhile, fast-changing environments often rewarded more dynamic, risk-tolerant entrepreneurial enterprises prepared to improvise and adapt.[41]

Nonetheless, few enterprises today would claim not to have a strategic plan. They certainly have *strategies*, whether or not they are written down or totally coherent. Enterprise size, status and dominant reference-frame affects the formality of its strategic planning and how much impact formal plans have on outcomes. In many small enterprises, strategy exists principally in the minds of the entrepreneur and other colleagues. Many medium and large for-profit enterprises have written plans, but probably do not consider them sufficient to guarantee success. Large enterprises, particularly large public sector corporations, generally invest considerable effort in strategic planning activities.

Formal Strategic Planning Approaches

Particularly in multi-unit enterprises, top management teams (TMTs) differ in the degree of influence on planning activities of business units and the control they exercise over implementation (Figure 13.12).[42] Enterprises that make major investments over long time horizons, such as oil companies and some public-sector corporations, typically occupy the 'strategic planning' domain, exercising close control of planning allied with flexible control, allowing detailed operational control by the operating units.

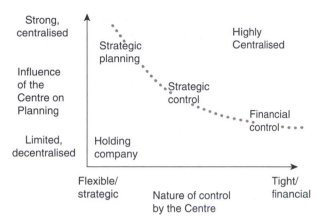

Figure 13.12: The planning approach of the corporate centre*

*Based on an idea by Goold and Campbell (1987; 1988)

Conglomerates, including private equity firms, may have few corporate centre staff whose primary roles are to manage acquisition and divestment strategies, and exercise tight monitoring and control of financial performance in each portfolio unit. These are 'financial control' enterprises. Those that adopt an intermediate 'strategic control' posture typically vary their approach to each SBU, according to its significance to the parent. Enterprises in fast-moving environments with short time horizons, such as retailing, often combine a strong, centralised planning influence with tight financial control, thus they are 'highly centralised'. This posture also characterises most enterprises when in crisis. Holding companies are loose 'federal' corporate structures with little central control and limited planning influence.

Though strategic planning anticipates the future, expectations and forecasts often prove to be flawed. Still, by making explicit assumptions about the future, analysts can explore the implications critically and subject them to further research where indicated. A modern view of strategic planning claims its primary benefit is *not* the *outputs* (dry, prescriptive documents), but as a *process* to share knowledge and create anticipatory learning through 'strategic conversation'.[43]

Enlightened planning processes should therefore encourage executives and managers involved at all levels to:

- Consider and debate issues likely to affect the future of the enterprise, its key stakeholders and their expectations.
- Critique the present mission and future vision, affirming desirable changes to them or to the strategies proposed to realise them.
- Clarify the resources and capabilities needed to implement the strategy.
- Co-ordinate the details of what has to be done, when and by whom.
- Establish realistic objectives and 'milestone' targets to allow assessment of progress.

- Anticipate difficulties and identify contingency responses.
- Institutionalise recognition and rewards for achievement and sanctions for failure.

In practice, the process begins when senior executives provide 'top down' instruction on the planning activities they require and define major planning assumptions, such as economic forecasts. Having set the framework, they delegate the formulation of detail from the 'bottom up': those who will be responsible for implementation propose and justify the necessary actions to senior executives who then accept or reject the plans or, frequently, call for medications. Senior staff must also ensure the integrity of these plans as an integrated package. Enterprises typically engage in a cascade of time-dependent, overlapping planning activities leading to multiple plans of varying detail (Figure 13.13):

- Long range, strategic plans.
- Annual business plans.
- AOperating plans (revised quarterly or monthly).
- Project plans (focused on specific initiatives over variable time scales).

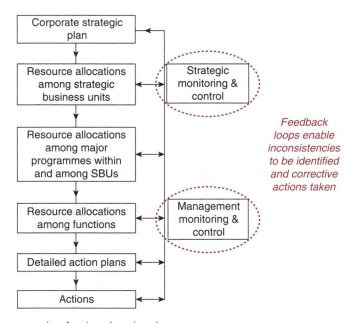

Figure 13.13: The cascade of enterprise planning

Long-range strategic plans typically extend over three or five years, sometimes longer in enterprises such as oil companies that look a decade or more ahead. They are the context for more detailed annual and even shorter-term resource plans. Later in a repeating planning cycle, shorter-term plans will be consolidated into what becomes in effect, the first time period (generally a year) of the next iteration of the strategic plan. Shorter-term plans focus on the actions associated with the detailed allocation, deployment and control of resources and the targets expected thereof (as indicated in Figure 13.13). In this seemingly complex approach strategic decision-making, control is decentralized within a centrally specified framework.

At each level of planning, outcomes are compared regularly with targets to identify, and if possible correct, variances during the next time period. Monitoring and control provides feedback upwards and downwards in the chain. When positive variances are sustainable or when adverse variances cannot be corrected, adjustments to higher level plans must be made, generally by adjusting future targets and diverting resources from one area to another.[44]

'Management by (SMART) Objectives' and the 'Balanced Scorecard'

Setting objectives and targets and monitoring performance against them are characteristic features of all strategic and operational planning. So-called 'management by objectives' (MBO) emerged in the 1960s as being virtually synonymous with business planning.[45]

In MBO thinking, the key to achieving objectives is specificity. Vague objectives are worthless because no-one will know if or when they have been achieved. The acronym SMART[46] (better spelled as SMAART) describes what a good objective should be:

Specific

Measurable

Achievable and **A**ssignable

Relevant

Time-sensitive

Qualitative goals express broad aims while objectives are *specific* and *measurable* when expressed as quantitative targets. Objectives with a specified time-frame for achievement also have a measurable aspect. An achievable target must be *realistic*. Dealing with the future, this criterion is judgmental, although comparison of specific targets with like-for-like achievements in previous time periods or circumstances is often a fair guide to realism. To be *assignable,* a named person or unit is responsible for achieving the objective. *Relevance* requires a link between the achievement of an objective and overall mission achievement, which also requires judgment.

Without disputing the importance of quantitative measures, one should not undervalue the use of, and commitment to, qualitative objectives, otherwise the belief arises that 'if it can't be measured, it isn't worth addressing'. Such attitudes generally focus attention on financial objectives to the exclusion of others.[47]

The 'Balanced Scorecard' emerged as a response to the excessive focus on a narrow range of quantitative measurements when setting and monitoring objectives.[48] Although in practice still biased towards quantitative performance measures, it partitions objectives into several categories to be accorded equal attention.

In principle the categories can be quite specific to an enterprise, though the Balanced Scorecard Institute proposes a generalised approach for businesses (Figure 13.14). This involves four categories, focused on:

- Finance (the shareholder perspective).
- Customer/client perspective.
- Operations perspective (internal processes).
- Development/innovation/learning perspective.

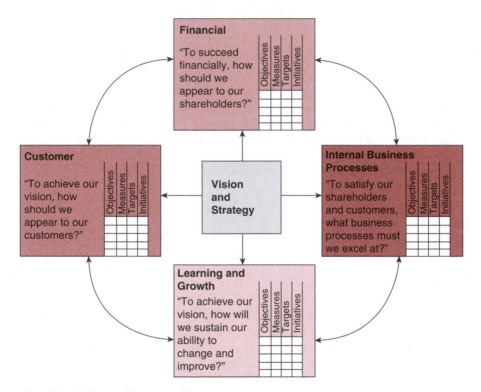

Figure 13.14: The "Balanced Scorecard"

Source: http://www.balancedscorecard.org

Financial solvency still matters for not-for-profit enterprises; however, they may prefer to recast the finance perspective to reflect the interests of their primary stakeholders (members or subscribers rather than shareholders) more relevantly. They can redefine the customer perspective to reflect more directly the interests of their service beneficiaries. Further, an enterprise with multiple, distinct stakeholder groups can add further categories to reflect their respective interests.

Having set the framework, the next step is to devise relevant objectives within each category whose achievement will meet the partial interests of associated stakeholders, creating satisfaction. To assess whether stated objectives have been achieved, appropriate metrics are needed.

These metrics are called key performance indicators (KPIs). For example, customer interests might be indicated by a combination of:

- Actual and perceived quality of a product, indicated by its specification, performance, reliability, brand image and other measures.
- Actual and perceived quality of a (support) service including pre- and post-purchase information and advice, performance competence (order receipt to delivery time, responses to complaints repair faults), etc.
- Client behaviours such as brand awareness and repeat purchasing.

Figure 13.15: A balanced scorecard with typical business KPIs

A SMART objective can be established for each KPI. For example, a web-based retailer could set a target of 60 hours as the maximum time allowed from order receipt to delivery. An even better approach might set a second target: less than 48 hours on 90% of deliveries. Whether these are realistic depends on current performance; if the enterprise currently meets these targets, more demanding or 'stretch' targets are needed to improve customer service. Conversely, if current performance is well below the desired level, a less ambitious initial target is probably indicated to avoid damaging morale, followed by progressive tightening as performance improves.

Four questions must be considered to finalise and implement targets.

- Do those who must achieve the targets agree that they are realistic (even if tough), otherwise they will lack motivation to achieve them?
- Can performance be measured? To measure elapsed time requires despatch and arrival times to be recorded. How best to record *arrival* times? Are the carrier's records accurate and

available? More fundamental changes may be necessary, for example, using carriers that provide electronic links to allow the enterprise to capture arrival times.

- How will intended improvements be achieved? Performance will rarely improve without enabling changes, for example, reduced delivery times might result by introducing a new pick, pack & dispatch system.

- Who will capture data and monitor performance? The process creates improvements only when extra cost-incurring resources are used for monitoring. So once these costs are incurred the benefits must be realised.

Managing Strategic Change and Transformation[49]

Over time, even well-run enterprises can get into difficulties for various reasons. Their executives may have:

- Pursued unrealistic growth ambitions – trading beyond their financial means and/or diversifying beyond their operational resources and capabilities.

- Compromised their strategies by inappropriate or incompetent implementation, including incompetent parenting skills in large corporations and excessive interference in SBU management.[50]

- Failed to cope with radical change introduced by a competitor or perhaps a new entrant.

- Developed a complacent, change-averse collective mindset (perhaps exhibiting 'groupthink': Chapter 6) which they come to believe is normal in their particular (competitive) context; they conclude that even minor innovations merely increase complexity and costs without real benefits for anyone.

Inertia, Complacency and Strategic Drift

Over the lifecycle, executives most in larger enterprises understandably behave more conservatively and cautiously. They feel that major change presents greater risks than potential gains. So strategic decisions avoid significant changes unless there is a compelling reason: rather, the aim is relatively modest, incremental progress and continuity for lengthy periods.[51] When circumstances create major challenges (such as technological discontinuities), they struggle to revitalise their enterprises, let alone transform them. They have no managerial experience of abrupt change. Their slow reactions are further inhibited by increasingly differentiated and partial stakeholder interests. It is difficult to agree what is needed. Leadership, a key factor needed to promote and implement change initiatives, is missing.

A tipping point is reached when innate conservatism leads to executives developing more harmful managerial characteristics:

- They retain elderly, inefficient facilities and other resources (including human resources!) but do not upgrade (retrain) them. The arrival of newer resources does not prompt elimination or redeployment of obsolete resources, thus merely adds to costs.

- They ignore or fail to understand the significance of environmental trends that arrive as weak signals; ignorance turns to frustration and inability to respond to significant trends, either because of inadequate resources and capabilities or the investment risks are considered too great.

RNING ⑤
JECTIVE

Inaction becomes stagnation and then active resistance to change, the phenomenon of 'strategic drift'.[52] Enterprises become paralysed, like ships drifting at the mercy of a raging storm.

This phenomenon can be illustrated graphically. Consider the Western world trend of ageing populations. A rising proportion of future new car buyers will be aged 60 years or (much) older. Taller cars enable easier entry and exit. Other worthwhile design changes are also desirable, yet redesign does not occur instantly: it needs planning and implementing in step with demand. The sales potential of these adaptations is predictable from a combination of statistics on population trends, wealth distribution and the desire for personal mobility among older people. Even so, the projected demand graph (the bold, unbroken line in Figure 13.16) will not be linear because of non-linear populations trends (e.g., the impact of the 'baby boomer' generation), combined with cyclical economic trends.

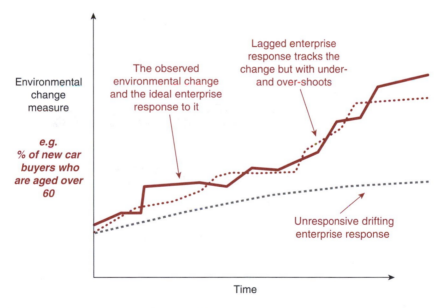

Figure 13.16: The phenomenon of strategic drift*
Developed from an idea by Johnson (1987; 1988)

Production capacity and output of appropriate models must always be geared to predicted demand. The responsive enterprise tracks demand changes and responds accordingly, albeit with a time lag (as shown in the figure). As demand rises, unit sales tend to undershoot demand owing to lags in production; as demand falls, short-term output overshoots demand. The more responsive a sector, the closer the sales track demand. Strategic drift occurs when the path of an unresponsive enterprise ignores the environmental trend almost completely (the lower dotted line in Figure 13.16). Ultimately, the gap between where it is and where it should be is so significant that it faces a crisis.

Crisis, Turnaround and Rejuvenation

Whatever the precise mix of factors, when the enterprise is in a crisis it may still be able to tackle the problem. Stakeholders must first recognise the problem and then act. Frequently, action is LEARNING OBJECTIVE ⑤ triggered not by inertial top management, but by coalitions variously of shareholders, banks, the media, representatives of other enterprises (competitors, customers, suppliers, etc.), vocal executives and other employees or their trade unions.

Figure 13.16 suggests that coalitions may be internal or external.[53] To galvanise change alone, the former need to have sufficient power to construct a sense of crisis; the latter may have the power to impose a crisis, for example, banks that deny overdraft requests, customers who withhold orders, suppliers who withhold credit.

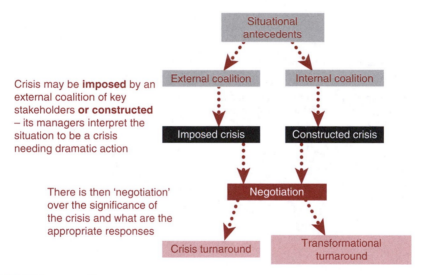

Figure 13.17: Crisis recognition

* Adapted from Pitt 1990

Ideally, the key stakeholders negotiate the appropriate responses quickly. Delay generally results in the need for even more radical subsequent change.[54] The solution, other than liquidation or takeover, is stabilization followed by a turnaround strategy. Stabilization involves a combination of actions such as:

- Replacement of the senior executives considered part of the problem, not the solution, with executives experienced in turnaround management.
- Cash injections from owners and/or banks to improve liquidity.

- Aggressive cost-saving measures, typically a combination of:
  - closure of old or unwanted facilities;
  - staff redundancies;
  - cancellation or postponement of investment plans;
  - cancellation of purchase orders for excessive materials, supplies, discretionary, non-vital goods and services;
  - reduction of advertising and promotion expenditures;
  - discounted sales of excess inventories; and
  - elimination of unprofitable products.

ARNING ⑤
JECTIVE
A sense of crisis legitimises urgent, radical actions. After the situation has stabilized, more constructive turnaround or rejuvenation strategies can begin (Figure 13.18). While the details depend on the particular circumstances, a generic stage model has been proposed.[55]

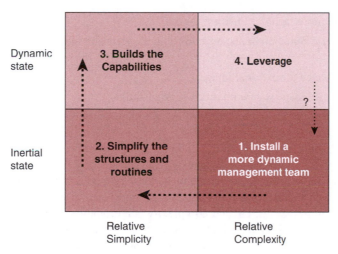

Figure 13.18: Stages in strategic rejuvenation
Adapted from Baden-Fuller and Stopford (1994)

In stage 1 a capable new executive team is installed, engaging people from outside and/or experienced managers already in the enterprise who had previously argued for change and whose commitment remains strong. The new team has specific aims:

- Encourage a more dynamic, enthusiastic ethos to galvanise relevant, imaginative ideas for improvements.
- Start to reduce the complexity and formality of internal structures, systems and processes.

The intent is to signal to staff and the world at large that the enterprise accepts the need for radical strategic change and that it *will* rise to this challenge through a combination of substantive and symbolic actions, including ongoing cost reductions, waste elimination, and removal of status symbols associated with former executives.

As it progresses, the major focus of stage 2 is to reduce the operational complexity that entrenched largely static structures and routines. Fewer levels of management are needed. The enterprise ceases its commitment to unattractive markets or low value-adding activities, products or services with little future promise. The result is reduced activities and, for businesses, lower revenues and margins, offset by simplified, lower-cost operations and more efficient performance.

As progress is made with complexity reduction and a more dynamic ethos, the enterprise begins to re-energise, new ideas emerge and some are implemented. Tangible successes, although perhaps small, allow some scope for expansion of current activities, accompanied by exploration and possible entry into new areas that can exploit existing capabilities. Thus stage 2 merges into stage 3: 'building', the development and application of new capabilities.[56] Specific initiatives, separately or in conjunction could include:

- A revised and more flexible 'business model'.
- Greater market-orientation in response to client requests and ideas for enhanced products and services.
- Actions to enhance the external image.
- Recruiting capable new staff with much-needed skills.
- Entering alliances to gain access to new and complementary resources and skills.

As the enterprise develops and applies its capabilities, confidence and successes multiply. Innovation enables it to increase its dynamism, by entering new market segments, geographic areas, introducing more radical products and perhaps related-diversification. Stage 3 merges into stage 4 in which the enterprise recognises the importance of exploiting its capabilities by 'leveraging' them in new ways. Greater complexity is a probable consequence, but can now be acceptable, provided that it is well-controlled to avoid the compromise of good practice and dynamism. Growth rates and levels of performance now compare favourably with benchmark enterprises.

Notwithstanding this optimistic model of enterprise rejuvenation, many detailed observations of different private and public sector contexts underline the difficulty of implementing dynamic strategic change in crisis and post-crisis conditions.[57] Are sufficient, dynamic, high-calibre people available? The abilities and outlooks of remaining personnel may be as limited as those who have departed. Proven outsiders generally avoid an enterprise whose prospects may seem dubious. The exceptions are generally outsiders with not fully demonstrated capabilities and experience. Progress therefore depends on taking considered risks. Will a capable new management actually succeed with its rejuvenation strategy? Will a tired, cynical ethos continue to resist change effectively? Will change occur quickly enough to catch up with capable competitors that continue to improve, raising the effective performance benchmarks? Can any enterprise institutionalise rejuvenating change in a fundamentally change-resistant sector? Will coercion be necessary?

Crisis-driven strategic change and rejuvenation

In the post-war Germany of 1955, few people could afford even basic new cars, certainly not the up-market products of **BMW**. The company was at serious risk of failing. A coalition of major shareholders took radical action, negotiating a licence to make affordable Italian Isetta 3-wheeled micro or 'bubble cars'. While BMW waited for the economy to recover, it made more than 160,000 Isettas between 1955 and 1962. Without this survival strategy it would not exist as an independent company today. By the early 1960s confidence had returned; BMW progressed to a turnaround strategy based on developing and launching the Neue Klasse range of small/medium saloons. Neue Klasse was the platform for BMW's best selling cars to date, underpinning the marque's subsequent long-term development, with the BMW brand positioned as the 'ultimate driving machine'.

The Swiss watch-making industry was bankrupt in 1980. Its largest companies ASUAG and SSIH had become owned by the banks. Through the leadership of Nicolas Hayek and Ernst Thomke these companies were consolidated into an integrated manufacturing group. The turnaround was triggered by the launch of the Swatch fashion watch. Later, renamed Swatch Group, the enterprise has continued to offer a huge variety of branded prestige and inexpensive watches and other time-keeping devices.

At the UK general election of 1983 the **Labour Party** was so soundly defeated by Margaret Thatcher's Conservative Party that its radical, socialist manifesto became known as 'the longest suicide note in history'. The Party's fortunes did not revive until the mid-1990s when Tony Blair became leader; he abandoned symbolic socialist policies and re-branded the Party as 'left-of-centre New Labour'. The Party was re-elected in 1997, winning further elections in 2003 and 2007; but for the 2008 global financial crisis, it would probably have won the 2010 election too. It has now embarked on a new phase of reinvention.

For rejuvenating change to continue beyond crisis, a positive, change-receptive ethos is needed, allied to a robust consensus over the detail of the strategic agenda and with sufficient time to implement it. Unfortunately, the cynicism and despondency that predictably follows the previous closure of operating units with major job losses, inhibits the development of a vibrant, 'can do', collective future outlook. If staff cooperation is limited, managerial imposition of a bold, continuing change agenda may be necessary (Figure 13.19).[58]

LEARNING PERSPECTIVE ⑤   One approach to impose top-down, radical change is an approach called 'business process re-engineering' (BPR). It requires questioning of every aspect of existing processes: whether they add value, how and why they are done.[59] Can they be done more efficiently and at lower cost; indeed, can they be discontinued?

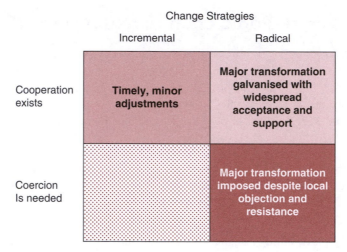

Figure 13.19: Types of change strategy in turnaround situations

Adapted from Dunphy and Stace, 1988

BPR contrasts with the established Japanese *kaizen* philosophy of continuous organic improvement. By prioritising the search for more radical change, BPR is much more directive. Such radical thinking may propose streamlined, better integrated activity sets that cut across functional boundaries. Such proposals challenge functional loyalties and conventional, supervisory accountabilities, which makes them difficult to implement in practice. Some enterprises have found the concept attractive, yet reluctant to proceed with BPR when they understood its implications; hence BPR has promised more than it has thus far delivered.[60]

The capacity for renewal is essentially the dynamic capability discussed in Chapter 5. It is unusual but not rare. Some business and not-for-profit enterprises have proved remarkably adept at reinvention. It may be that the ability of the latter derives ultimately from a humble recognition that their survival depends on creating acknowledged societal value, a challenge that leaves no room for complacency.

Long-term 'reinventors'

Apple Computer has reinvented itself regularly, notably via product innovations such as the original Mac of 1984, the iMac of the 1990s, the iPod, iTunes, iPhone and iPad.

Biffa is a leading integrated waste management business. Founded 75+ years ago as a family-owned business, it later became a public company before being acquired by a consortium of private equity funds. It has developed from a single waste management service – landfill disposal – into a provider of multiple services for businesses and local government authorities: domestic and organic recycling;

hazardous and non-hazardous waste processing; energy generation from waste; recycling discarded electrical and electronic appliances via its 'Transform' WEEE compliance scheme.

The **YMCA**[61] movement began in London in 1844 for 'the improving of the spiritual condition of young men' who, in the founders' view, were prey to the twin temptations of tavern and brothel. Its precepts of healthy mind, body and spirit spread worldwide, creating a network of associations that today continues to provide hostel accommodation for young single people, regardless of gender, race, ability or faith. Rooms are priced commercially, but well below hotel room rates. Some associations provide longer term 'supported housing' for disadvantaged young people. Further, the modern YMCA has reinvented itself more radically; it now provides counselling, education and training for mental and physical health and fitness at dedicated centres.

The **Salvation Army** was established some 20 years after the YMCA movement. Like the YMCA it is now an international movement. Its work is grounded in evangelical Christian beliefs, yet its mission today is varied and highly practical. Major activities include health, community and emergency services, particularly in poor and developing countries, while its social action agenda prioritises international opposition to sexual trafficking.

Leadership Styles[62]

Leadership is a crucial factor in the strategic management of radical change. However, individual leadership styles vary considerably and they have a profound effect on how others behave and respond to challenges. Yet irrespective of their personal style, leaders cannot perform effectively when they do not have the trust and active support of dedicated followers.[63]

The subject matter of Chapter 4 explored a variety of themes that are fundamental to leadership, although it avoided explicit references, except regarding the sources of power and legitimacy used to shape enterprise mission and agendas. To be effective a leader needs to enjoy perceived legitimacy and respect. Legitimacy is conventionally associated with the authority that derives from power and seniority, expert knowledge and personal charisma.

Leadership style ideally matches circumstances. During periods of relative stability and incremental change, a major enterprise priority is to maximise efficiency. To embark on radical challenges to the *status quo* could be counterproductive. A so-called *transactional* leadership style best matches these circumstances; this style emphasises:

- An enterprise development path of continuous learning and incremental, adaptive change.
- Maximising operational *efficiency* via systems and process improvements – 'doing things the right way'.

- Exercise of authority and formal control from the top downwards which is sufficient to ensure that planned initiatives are carried through.

- Attention to detail to achieve the results necessary to meet key stakeholder interests, most obviously financial performance in business enterprises, quarter-by-quarter, year-by-year.

The purposes of enterprises are not in doubt during periods of continuity. When they perform as expected, their leaders rarely face difficult questions. Yet should an enterprise find its core markets in decline or its competitiveness eroding, there is a need for radical change and a different style of leadership. The shift to a *transformational* leadership style can galvanize change very effectively, often combining elements of persuasion, aggression and coercion.[64] Very typically a change of leader is needed, since transactional and transformational styles are so different. It is unfortunate that very often circumstances must become highly problematic before there is a leadership change.

The transformational leadership style:

- Emphasises strategic change and enterprise renewal by redefining enterprise values and vision.

- Articulates a clear, possibly revised mission in the longer-term interests of the enterprise with a focus on strategic *effectiveness*: 'doing the right things' to survive and prosper, while accepting short-term compromises if necessary.

- Prioritises actions consistent with the restated mission, endorsing innovation and creativity in the quest for radical improvements.

- Sets particularly challenging, but exciting goals to motivate and focus the efforts of staff.

- Acts decisively and with authority when specific situations call for it, but otherwise encourages informal, participative, behaviour and avoids status symbols.

Transformational leadership encourages a positive, supportive and enthusiastic ethos; it creates inspirational meanings for subordinates and is tolerant of turbulence and uncertainty. Transformational leaders are often highly charismatic people.[65] Their crucial contribution is to steer the enterprise through periods of radical and disruptive change. As the enterprise regains relative stability, the need for transactional efficiency priorities re-emerges. An unwavering, transformational leadership style would then become problematic, signalling the probable need for a change of leader, since relatively few people can adapt their style significantly.

A modern, progressive Western interpretation of desirable leadership behaviour is that it should demonstrate empathy with people *and* context; and create a sustainable 'performance culture' that stimulates constructive action and organisational learning.[66] Another insightful analysis identifies leadership roles thus:[67]

- **Designer** – of the enterprise's 'social architecture', a creative role that encompasses strategies, structures, policies, systems, processes of governance and organisational learning.

- **Teacher** – the enterprise's cultural guide; interpreter-in-chief of external reality; and an instructor who continually stimulates colleagues to reflect and challenge the status quo.

- **Steward** – responsible for the enterprise's well-being, mission, future vision; for discharging its obligations to staff and other stakeholders; intent on leaving it better placed for the future than it is presently.

The Tricord™ synthesises the conjunction of strategy and leadership in terms of 'whole leadership' (Figure 13.20) as follows:

- The strategy role equates with transformation.
- The systems role with transaction.
- The culture role with teaching.
- The identity-forming role with stewarding.

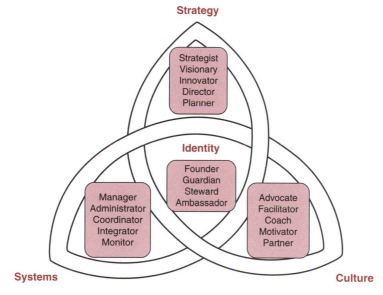

Figure 13.20: 'Whole leadership' roles in the Tricord™

Source Tricordant.com

Comparison of Western and oriental approaches to strategic management is instructive. In Western companies, strategy is often considered the preserve solely of the chief executive (CEO) and the top management team (TMT).[68] Consensus matters at this senior level and is affected by internal diversity; too much diversity is as dysfunctional as too little.[69] Middle managers are often excluded from strategic deliberations despite being the enterprise stakeholders most likely to implement change practically.[70] Indeed during crisis they may be treated as disposable assets.[71]

In successful Japanese companies, TMTs perform equivalently. However, their strategic management behaviour tends to be more patient and careful: decisions result from the processes of *ringi,* to obtain 'bottom-up' inputs to decision-making and *nemawashi*, to ensure full consultation and consensus-building.[72] Once senior executives have authorised a strategy, middle managers understand its rationale, so they are able interpret and implement it with commitment and support from loyal junior staff.[73] In this 'middle-up-down' approach, the middle levels:

- Are the 'strategic knot' that binds top managers and front line operations.
- Mediate the 'idealised future' envisioned by top managers with the 'real world'.
- Sponsor initiatives and projects that create new knowledge and ways to use it.

Evidently, 21st century strategic leadership will be challenging. It will need continually to balance the conflicting priorities of long-term effectiveness and short-run efficiency.

It requires contextual sensitivity to inspire confidence from a broad spread of stakeholders. It needs to encourage inclusiveness, trust, high morale and motivation, enabling 'ordinary' people to achieve extraordinary results and to encourage leadership behaviour in all enterprise functions at all organisational levels. However, no-one displays the complete gamut of positive leadership characteristics or remains well-matched to particular enterprise needs indefinitely. So how much credit does any named leader deserve for enterprise achievements? Evidence-based guidelines to assess particular contribution could include:

- Tenure of sufficient duration that a leader's impact can be linked unambiguously with positive, visible results, typically starting from unpromising or problematic circumstances.[74]
- Peers, subordinates and independent observers of sound judgement share a positive, critical consensus about the leader's merits.

The final illustration of this chapter and the book suggests some exceptional people who seem to meet these stringent criteria. Even today, comparatively few women reach CEO level in large private sector enterprises, although the situation is slowly changing.[75]

CASE STUDY: High-calibre strategic leaders

Dame Marjorie Scardino became CEO of the Economist Group, a subsidiary of Pearson plc, in 1992 and has been CEO of Pearson since 1997. She gained the informal title of 'Marje in charge' as she galvanised a rather sleepy, unfocused publishing company towards becoming a world-leading media, publishing and educational services company. Her bold strategy has combined acquisitions, disposals and organic growth. In 2002 the UK Government conferred on her the title of Dame in public recognition of her achievements, an exceptional honour for a naturalised British subject.

Sir Martin Sorrell has been CEO of WPP since 1986, when he acquired it essentially as a 'shell company'. Thereafter he led WPP's extraordinary transformation into the world's leading advertising, communications and market research corporation. It has grown organically and by acquiring famous-name agencies including JWT, Ogilvy, Burson-Marsteller, Young and Rubicam. Not unduly concerned to be liked, Sir Martin is highly respected in the industry for his achievements. He was honoured with a knighthood in 2000.

Herr Helmut Kohl was Chancellor of West Germany from 1982 to 1990 when he secured reunification with East Germany; he continued subsequently as Chancellor until 1998. His 16-years as Chancellor, a role equivalent to US President or British Prime Minister, made his tenure the longest-serving since Bismarck and equally historic. Helmut Kohl and French President François Mitterrand were major proponents of the Maastricht Treaty, which created the European Union, an achievement for which the two men later shared the Charlemagne Prize. Former US President George Bush Senior called Kohl 'the greatest European leader of the second half of the 20th century', no mean accolade when compared with transformational leaders such as Charles de Gaulle, Margaret Thatcher, Mikhail Gorbachev and Boris Yeltsin.

Tasks and discussion questions

- Is it realistic to compare the leadership styles of business and political leaders? What can each learn from the other?

- Compare and contrast the styles of Scardino and Sorrell using documentary sources. Does gender play a part in whatever style differences you note?

- Scardino has persisted in office much longer than did Carly Fiorina, the high profile, former chief executive of Hewlett-Packard.[76] Explore the reasons for this difference. Do they affect your assessment of their respective contributions?

Summary

- A conceptually elegant strategy that cannot be 'made to happen' is of no value. Many factors influence whether and how well a particular strategy is implemented. Its various elements must be consistent with each other and supportive of the intended direction. The use of the 7S framework or its Tricord™ counterpart highlights inconsistencies among the current resources and capabilities profile, as well as mismatches between the current profile and what will be needed for future success.

- The enterprise's values, mission and future vision must be clear, widely understood and accepted by those who will implement the strategy. The organisational design must be fit for purpose; that is, the structure, division of responsibilities, and the formal systems, policies, procedures and information flows that guide, co-ordinate and control operational activities.

- Positive design characteristics are sources of considerable advantage – some may be considered strategic assets or distinctive capabilities. Human resources systems and procedures contribute very significantly to enterprise effectiveness by motivating staff and by

LEARNING
OBJECTIVE ②
recognising and rewarding their individual contributions. No formal design is perfect, but fitness for purpose remains a critical success factor.

LEARNING
OBJECTIVE ⑤
- Informal routines, behaviours and ethos are unwritten aspects of enterprise behaviour and performance. They may assist or frustrate strategy implementation, but they are much harder for managers to control. Indeed, heavy-handed attempts to dictate staff behaviours and control informal communication networks almost always prove counterproductive.

- In theory, strategic planning and control systems provide a seamless link between strategy formation and implementation management. Performed well, these activities encourage disciplined thought processes leading to realistic objectives, unambiguous targets and account-abilities for achieving them. Strategic planning is most difficult to do well in the turbulent and fast-changing contexts where the benefit would perhaps be greatest. The balanced score-card method is a practical form of 'management by objectives' to aid planning and control. It
LEARNING
OBJECTIVE ④
aims to develop 'SMART' objectives to ensure that the enterprise addresses all the strategic priorities of its key stakeholders.

- Some long-lived enterprises demonstrate a remarkable capacity for reinvention. They remain alert to external environmental changes and possibilities, and demonstrate the collective belief and will to respond constructively to challenges, a capacity that merits the description of 'dynamic capability'. Yet, even apparently successful enterprises sometimes get into difficulties. Commonly, they become too mature and stagnate; this 'strategic drift' leads to crisis. The solution requires the implementation of radical strategies that reju-venate and transform them, typically by reducing complexity and regaining dynamism. Business process re-engineering (BPR) has been advocated as a proactive, top-down means to stimulate reinvention, in marked contrast to the continuous, incremental approach of Japanese *kaizen*. However, even progressive enterprises have found BPR very challenging to apply.

- Effective strategy implementation depends greatly on leadership style and calibre. Leaders variously guide and inspire or demoralise and frustrate subordinates. If strategies are to be implemented successfully, an appropriate leadership style is needed for the particular cir-cumstances. A transformational style suits the priority of radical, visionary change; a trans-actional style maintains and improves enterprise performance incrementally and progressively.
LEARNING
OBJECTIVE ⑤
However, enterprises need people able to exercise leadership qualities at all organisational levels, not just at the head.

Exercises for Further Study and Discussion

1. If strategic planning is essentially programming, can it display the degree of adaptiveness that 21st century enterprises need. Would 'strategic improvisation' be a plausible alternative? Explore the practical consequences of strategic improvisation for enterprise management.[77]

2. The continuity-and-change model of enterprise progression, based on compelling empirical evidence is essentially *descriptive*. Explore the idea that continuity-and-change should

actually be considered *prescriptive* because enterprises simply cannot cope with continuous change. Or does equally compelling evidence exist for the feasibility of dynamic, continuing change?

3. Two observable aspects of an enterprise are its tangible performance and persistence (longevity). Intuitively, persistence and high performance would correlate closely. Of course, a high performance enterprise with a very specific mission to achieve might be disbanded thereafter. But why do low performance enterprises persist? Identify some examples and explain their survival.

4. Enterprise size can inhibit innovativeness, enthusiasm and personal commitment. So perhaps strategy is best implemented by reorganizing the large enterprise into modestly sized units that have clear, distinct missions that aggregate directly into the overarching mission? How practical is this proposition?

5. Can training enable someone to become a transformational leader, or is someone born with these qualities? Perhaps direct experience is the best kind of training. Explore relevant literature to understand how leadership skills can be facilitated.

6. Kodak had evidently recognised the need for a transformational strategy by 1990. Since that time it has survived, but even its greatest supporters would surely not claim success. Explore the proposition that its transformation strategy was sound, but fundamentally compromised by incompetent implementation. Identify the key mistakes that it made.

7. 'Formality is the enemy of creativity and innovation.' 'Informality is the enemy of disciplined and reliable performance.' Is it therefore impossible for an enterprise to be both innovative and disciplined? Explore how these qualities can be combined.

8. A crucial role of the 'hub' actor (Carmichael) was crucial to ensure co-ordination in in the Acoustic Alchemy network. How would the network respond to the departure, serious illness or demise of this key actor?

9. Construct a balanced scorecard with key performance indicators (KPIs) relevant for a public sector enterprise such as a general hospital or for an international aid organization.

10. Compare and contrast the turnaround and rejuvenation strategies of BMW, Swatch Group and the Labour Party. Are there general lessons that can be extracted?

11. Explore the history and development of the YMCA. Was it able to effect change without first being in crisis? If the latter, was the crisis internally constructed or externally imposed?

Suggestions for Further Reading

Abrahamson, E. (2000) 'Change without pain: dynamic stability', *Harvard Business Review* (July/Aug, pp. 75–79).

Bartlett, A. and Ghoshal, S. (2002) 'Building competitive advantage through people', *MIT Sloan Management Review* (vol. 43/2, pp. 34–41).

Burgelman, R.A. and Grove, A.S. (2007) 'Let chaos reign, then rein in chaos – repeatedly: managing strategic dynamics for corporate longevity', *Strategic Management Journal* (vol. 28/10, pp. 965–979).

Clegg, S., Kornberger, M. and Pitsis, T. (2005) *Managing and Organizations*, Sage Publications (chapters 7, 11).

Goold, M. and Campbell, A. (2002) 'Do you have a well-designed organization?', *Harvard Business Review* (vol. 80/3, pp. 117–124).

Hamel, G. (2001) 'Revolution versus evolution: you need both', *Harvard Business Review* (May, pp. 150–154).

Hammer, M. (1990) 'Re-engineering work: don't automate, obliterate', *Harvard Business Review* (vol. 68/4, pp. 101–111).

Ireland, R.D. and Hitt, M.A. (1999) 'Achieving and maintaining competitiveness in the 21st century: the role of strategic leadership', *Academy of Management Executive* (vol. 13/1, pp. 43–57).

Ireland, R.D., Hoskisson, R.E. and Hitt, M.J.A. (2009) *The Management of Strategy* Cengage (Ed. 2, chapters 11–13).

Johnson, G.N. (1988) 'Rethinking incrementalism', *Strategic Management Journal* (vol. 9/1 pp. 75–91).

Kanter, R.M. (2002) 'Strategy as Improvisational Theatre', *MIT Sloan Management Review* (vol. 43/2, pp. 76–81).

Kaplan, R.S. and Norton, D.P. (1996) 'Using the balanced scorecard as a strategic management system,' *Harvard Business Review* (vol. 74/1, pp. 75–85).

Kaplan, S. and Beinhocker, E.D. (2003) 'The real value of strategic planning', *MIT Sloan Management Review* (Winter, pp. 71–76).

Kotter, J.P. (1995) 'Leading change: why transformation efforts fail' *Harvard Business Review* (vol. 73/2, pp. 59–67. Reprinted in 2007, vol. 85/1, pp. 96–103).

Lockett, M. (1995) 'IT and strategic renaissance'. in Thomas, H., O'Neal, D. and Kelly, J. (eds) *Strategic Renaissance and Business Transformation*, Wiley.

Maitlis, S. and Lawrence, T. (2003) 'Orchestral manoeuvres in the dark: understanding failure in organizational strategizing', *Journal of Management Studies* (vol. 40/1, pp. 109–140).

Morrow, J.L., Sirmon, D.G., Hitt, M.A. and Holcomb, T.R. (2007) 'Creating value in the face of declining performance: firm strategies and organizational recovery', *Strategic Management Journal* (vol. 28/3, pp. 271–283).

Nonaka, I. (1988). 'Towards middle-up-down management: accelerating information creation' *Sloan Management Review* (vol. 29, Spring, pp. 9–18).

Quinn, J.B. (1980a) 'Managing strategic change' *Sloan Management Review* (vol. 21/4, pp. 3–20).

Senge, P. (1990) 'The leader's new work: building learning organizations', *Sloan Management Review* (Fall, pp. 132–141).

Shimizu, K. and Hitt, M. (2004) 'Strategic flexibility: organizational preparedness to reverse ineffective strategic decisions', *Academy of Management Executive* (vol. 18/4, pp. 44–59).

Tushman, M.L. and O'Reilly, C.A. (1996) 'Ambidextrous organizations: managing evolutionary and revolutionary change', *California Management Review* (vol. 38/4, pp. 8–30).

Van der Heijden, K., Bradfield, R., Burt, G., Cairns, G. and Wright, G. (2002) *The Sixth Sense Accelerating Organizational Learning with Scenarios*, Wiley.

Vera, D. and Crossan, M. (2004) 'Strategic leadership and organizational learning', *Academy of Management Review* (vol. 29, pp. 222–240).

Vitale, M., Hauser, M.D. and Mavrinac, S. (1996) 'Measuring strategic performance', in Thomas, H. and O'Neal, D. (eds) *Strategic Integration*, Wiley.

Werther, W.B. (2003) 'Strategic change and leader–follower alignment', *Organizational Dynamics* (vol. 32, pp. 32–45).

Notes

1 Sources include: http://en.wikipedia.org/wiki/Habitat_(retailer); http://www.habitat.co.uk; http://www.heals.co.uk/pcat/heals_history; http://en.wikipedia.org/wiki/Storehouse_plc

2 Including the design consultancy Conran Associates, restaurants and the Conran Shop.

3 *Financial Times* 20 January 2010.

4 Expositions of 'rational' strategy implementation issues can be found in Stonich (1982), Kono (1992) and Hussey (1996). Kono's account claims to describe Japanese organisations, but the practices appear to be largely Western in character.

5 A popular military dictum attributed to the Prussian general von Moltke is that 'No battle plan survives contact with the enemy.'

6 There might be many paths available to reach a destination (called 'equifinality'), so it could be strategically inflexible, even inept to select only one.

7 See Meyer and Zucker (1989) and Maitlis and Lawrence (2003).

8 Although comparatively few English Premier League football teams currently make profits, yet to date only one has had its survival threatened.

9 Sometimes occasioned by over-ambition and imprudence (Miles and Snow, 1994).

10 Although not always as painfully as some might wish – as witness the happy financial outcome for the chief executive of RBS Bank following its collapse in the wake of the global credit crisis.

11 A doctrine reinforced by Lanchester's mathematical calculations, applied in business situations notably by some Japanese corporations. See: http://en.wikipedia.org/wiki/Lanchester%27s_laws

12 Several of the contributors to Hussey (1996) provide particular empirical descriptions of strategic change.

13 Peters and Waterman (1982). Using words beginning with 'S' aids recall.

14 D'Aveni (1995) has proposed an alternative version of the 7S framework but its components are strategies rather than enterprise features to support strategy.

15 The text in grey indicates areas of continuity; the red text indicates areas of required change.

16 At its peak in the 1980s Kodak employed 136,000 staff globally. By 2006 it had under 41,000 staff and by 2009 only 20,000, half in the United States.

17 Tricordant. Source: http://www.tricordant.com

18 This section draws particularly on Mintzberg (1979) (or see Mintzberg, 1993) and Chandler (1962) though many sources have discussed why organizations are structured in various forms and with what consequences. Compact summaries of key issues can be found in Johnson, Scholes and Whittington (2008, chapter 12); Ireland, Hoskisson and Hitt (2009), with more extensive coverage in Galbraith and Nathanson (1978; Ed. 2, Galbraith and Kazanjian, 1986).

19 Goold and Campbell (2002).

20 Mintzberg (1979); Chandler (1962).

21 That is, structural change may be a cosmetic substitute for strategic change, conveying the impression of executive dynamism.

22 Mintzberg (1979).

23 Hatch (1999); Burgelman and Grove (2007).

24 Bartlett and Ghoshal (1990) explore such issues. Ruigrok et al. (2000) offer a detailed case example of matrix and network structuring.

25 Although perceptions of issues can vary according to the seniority of the perceiver (Thomas and D'Annunzio, 2005).

26 Burgelman and Grove (2007).

27 Chesborough and Teece (2002).

28 Handy (1989).

29 See Earl and Feeny (1995); Lockett (1995).

30 For example, Binngi, Sharma and Godia (1999).

31 Bartlett and Ghoshal (2002).

32 See for example Orr (1990); Winter (1995). Johnson (1987) offers various examples of how informal actions establish routines not necessarily envisaged as part of the formal strategy.

33 For example, a common assumption is that to change behaviours, first change attitudes. In fact, the reverse may be more productive, though it poses the challenge of how to change behaviours without unreasonable coercion that would definitely poison attitudes. Fundamental and institutionalised change may not be possible save in exceptional circumstances.

34 George Santayana, 1863–1952, philosopher and aphorist. *Life of Reason, Reason in Common Sense*, Scribner's, 1905, p. 284.

35 Attributed to Niels Bohr, 1885–1962, Danish physicist and Nobel Laureate in Physics.

36 Loasby (1967).

37 Noda and Bower (1996).

38 See for example Argenti (1974); Dyson (1990); Lake (2006).

39 Bryson (2005).

40 Mintzberg (1994).

41 Perry, Scott and Smallwood (1993); Shimizu and Hitt (2004).

42 Goold and Campbell (1987; 2002).

43 De Geus (1988); von Krogh and Roos (1996); Kaplan and Beinhocker (2003).

44 Apparently in some enterprises the time intervals are no longer discrete but continuous (Mankins and Steele, 2006).

45 For example, Humble (1967). Drucker (1954) also stressed the importance of managing by careful attention to setting and achieving objectives.

46 For example, Doran (1981), though discussed on many websites.

47 Vitale, Hauser and Mavrinac (1996).

48 The original ideas were publicised by Kaplan and Norton, who have produced various books and articles, as have many other writers subsequently. See for example: Kaplan and Norton (1996; 2001; 2006).

49 Recommended general reading includes MacMillan (1978); Hardy (1995); Darwin, Johnson and McAuley (2002); Clegg, Kornberger and Pitsis (2005, chapter 11); McGee, J., Thomas, H. and Wilson, D. (2005, chapter 15); Johnson, Scholes and Whittington (2008, chapter 14).

50 What Miles and Snow (1994) refer to as 'violating the corporate strategic logic'. See also: Campbell, Goold and Alexander (1995b).

51 Various sources have observed that strategic change tends to occur unevenly. Rapid change episodes split sometimes lengthy periods of continuity in strategic direction and practice, e.g., Mintzberg and Waters (1982); Pettigrew (1985); Johnson (1987; 1988); Tushman and O'Reilly (1996); Abrahamson (2000); Hamel (2001). Quinn (1980a, b) argued that large enterprises manage through incremental change processes that he called 'logical incrementalism'.

52 If change is strongly resisted, the organization ultimately drifts towards crisis (Johnson 1987; 1988).

53 Grinyer and McKiernan (1990); (Pitt 1990); Schneider (2002); Maitlis and Lawrence (2003).

54 Dutton (1986) Pitt (1990); Markóczy (2001); Pajunen (2006).

55 Baden-Fuller and Stopford (1994). But see also: Quinn (1980b); Kanter (1989); D'Aveni (1995); Hammer and Champy (2004).

56 Morrow et al. (2007).

57 Refer to previous footnotes.

58 Dunphy and Stace (1988); Stace and Dunphy (1996).

59 Hammer (1990); Coulson-Thomas (1996); Darnton and Darnton (1997); Hammer and Champy (2004).

60 Coulson-Thomas (1996).

61 Young Men's Christian Association.

62 A complex and well-researched topic. For synoptic, general reading see: Kakabadse and Kakabadse (1999); Finkelstein, Hambrick and Cannella (2008).

63 See for example Chapter 7 of Clegg, Kornberger and Pitsis (2005) for a short review of leadership concepts and the relationship of leaders and followers. Also see Werther (2003) and chapter 12 of Ireland, Hoskisson and Hitt (2009).

64 Dunphy and Stace (1988); Kotter (1996); Kakabadse and Kakabadse (1990); Stace and Dunphy (1996); Ireland and Hitt (1999).

65 Some authorities consider charismatic leadership to be a distinct style, notably in particular religious organizations and in extreme contexts such as military combat. From a strategic change perspective, charisma is a significant leadership quality, although not a complete solution (Nadler and Tushman, 1990).

66 Kim and Mauborgne (2003) describe development of this kind of performance culture in the New York Police Department. Goleman (2004) discusses the empathetic leadership quality, sometimes called emotional intelligence.

67 Senge (1990a; b).

68 Finkelstein, Hambrick and Cannella (2008); Leavy and McKiernan (2008).

69 Knight et al. (1999).

70 Kanter (1983); Westley (1990); Floyd and Wooldridge (1996); Schneider (2002).

71 Thomas and Dunkerley (1999).

72 See: http://www.japanintercultural.com/en/news/default.aspx?newsID=68 and http://www.husonusa.com/Files/Yomiuri%20(Japan)/Successful%20Branding%20in%20Japan.pdf   For further, detailed insights into Japanese management see: Pascale and Athos (1981); Kono (1992); Nonaka and Takeuchi (1995).

73 Nonaka (1988).

74 Length of tenure matters, though it is not the only significant influence on leadership performance (Simsek, 2007).

75 Lee and James (2007) reported that shareholders are generally still less well-disposed to the appointment of women than men to the top job.

76 Autobiographies and other biographical books can be useful sources, e.g., Fiorina (2007).

77 Several sources have promoted the analogy with the improvisation of jazz performance. See: Perry, Scott and Smallwood (1993); Hatch (1999); Kanter (2002).

References

Aaker, D.A. and McLoughlin, D. (2010) *Strategic Market Management: Global Perspectives*, Wiley.

Abernathy, W. and Wayne, K. (1974) 'Limits of the learning curve', *Harvard Business Review* (Sep/Oct, pp. 108–119).

Abrahamson, E. (2000) 'Change without pain: dynamic stability', *Harvard Business Review* (July/Aug, pp. 75–79).

Abrahamson, M. (2004) *Global Cities*, Oxford University Press.

Ackoff, R.L. (1970) *A Concept of Corporate Planning*, Wiley.

Ahuja, G. and Katila, R. (2001) 'Technological acquisitions and the innovation performance of acquiring firms: a longitudinal study', *Strategic Management Journal* (vol. 22/3, pp. 197–220).

Alberts, W.W. (1989) 'The experience curve doctrine reconsidered' *Journal of Marketing* (vol. 53/3, pp. 36–49).

Aldrich, H. (1999) *Organizations Evolving*, Sage.

Allison, G.T. (1971) *Essence of Decision: Explaining the Cuban Missile Crisis*, Little Brown.

Amit, R. and Livnat, J. (1991) 'Diversification and the risk-return trade-off', *Academy of Management Journal* (vol. 31/1, pp. 154–166).

Anderson, P. and Tushman, M.L. (1990) 'Technological discontinuities and dominant designs: a cyclical model of technological change', *Administrative Science Quarterly*, (vol. 35, pp. 604–633).

Andrews, K. (1980) *The Concept of Corporate Strategy*, Irwin.

Ansoff, H.I. (1965) *Corporate Strategy*, McGraw Hill.

Ansoff, H.I. (1975) 'Managing strategic surprise by response to weak signals', *California Management Review* (vol. 18/2, pp. 21–33).

Ansoff, H.I. (1980) 'Strategic issue management', *Strategic Management Journal* (vol. 1/2, pp. 131–148).

Ansoff, H.I. (1988) *The New Corporate Strategy*, Wiley.

Ansoff, H.I. (1991) 'Critique of Henry Mintzberg's "The design school"', *Strategic Management Journal* (vol. 11, pp. 449–461).

Argenti, J. (1974) *Systematic Corporate Planning*, Van Nostrand Reinhold.

Argote, L., Beckman, S.L. and Epple, D. (1990) 'The persistence and transfer of learning in industrial settings', *Management Science* (vol. 36, pp. 140–154).

Argyris, C. and Schön, D. (1978) *Organizational Learning: A Theory of Action Perspective*, Addison Wesley.

Ashby, W.R. (1958) Requisite variety and its implications for the control of complex systems, Cybernetica (vol. 1/2, pp. 83–99). Also republished on the Web by F. Heylighen – Principia Cybernetica Project at: http://pcp.vub.ac.be/Books/AshbyReqVar.pdf

Baden-Fuller, C. (ed.) (1990) *Managing Excess Capacity*, Blackwell.

Baden-Fuller & Boschetti

Baden-Fuller, C. and Pitt, M. (eds) (1996) *Strategic Innovation: An International Casebook on Strategic Management*, Routledge.

Baden-Fuller, C. and Stopford, J.M. (1991) 'Globalization frustrated: the case of white goods', *Strategic Management Journal* (vol. 12/7, pp. 493–507).

Baden-Fuller, C. and Stopford, J.M. (1994) *Rejuvenating the Mature Business*, Harvard Business School Press.

Bailey, W. and Spicer, A. (2007) 'When does identity matter? Convergence and divergence in international business ethics', *Academy of Management Journal* (vol. 50/6, pp. 1462–1480).

Bain, J.S. (1959, reprinted 1968) *Industrial Organization*, Wiley.

Baines, P., Fill, C., and Page, K. (2008) *Marketing*, Oxford University Press.

Baptista, R. (1998) 'Clusters, innovation and growth: a survey of the literature', in Swann, G.M.P., Prevezer, M. and Stout, D. (eds) *The Dynamics of Industrial Clustering*, Oxford University Press.

Barnett, W.P. and Hansen, M. (1996) 'The Red Queen in organizational evolution', *Strategic Management Journal* (vol. 17, pp. 139–157).

Barnett, W.P. and Pontikes, E.G. (2005) 'The Red Queen: history-dependent competition among organizations', in Staw, B.M. and Kramer, R.M. (eds) *Research in Organizational Behavior*, JAI Press.

Barnett, W.P., Greve, H.R. and Park, D.Y. (1994) 'An evolutionary model of organizational performance', *Strategic Management Journal* (vol. 15, Winter Special Issue, pp. 11–28).

Barney, J.B. (1986) 'Types of competition and the theory of strategy: toward an integrative framework', *Academy of Management Review* (vol. 11/4, pp. 791–800).

Barney

Barney, J.B. (1995) 'Looking inside for competitive advantage', *Academy of Management Executive* (vol. 9/4, pp. 49–61).

Barney, J.B. (2007) *Gaining and Sustaining Competitive Advantage*, Pearson (Ed. 3).

Barney, J.B. and Hesterly, W.S. (2010) *Strategic Management and Competitive Advantage*, Prentice Hall (Ed. 3).

Baron, R.A. (2006) 'Opportunity recognition as pattern recognition: how entrepreneurs "connect the dots" to identify new business opportunities', *Academy of Management Perspectives* (vol. 20/1, February, pp. 104–119).

Bartlett, C.A. and Ghoshal, S. (1990) 'Matrix management: not a structure, more a frame of reference', *Harvard Business Review* (vol. 68/4, pp. 138–145).

Bartlett, C.A. and Ghoshal, S. (1998) *Managing Across Borders: The Transnational Solution*. Harvard Business School Press.

Bartlett, C.A. and Ghoshal, S. (2002) 'Building competitive advantage through people', *MIT Sloan Management Review* (vol. 43/2, pp. 34–41).

Berg, N. (1969) 'What's different about conglomerate management?' *Harvard Business Review* (vol. 47, pp. 112–120).

Besanko, D., Dranove, D., Shanley, M. and Schaefer, S. (2010) *Economics of Strategy*, Wiley (Ed. 5).

Bessant, J. and Tidd, J. (2007) *Innovation and Entrepreneurship*, Wiley.

Bettis, R.A. and Prahalad, C.K. (1986) 'The dominant logic: retrospective and extension', *Strategic Management Journal* (vol.16/1, pp. 5–14).

Biggadike, R. (1979) 'The risky business of diversification', *Harvard Business Review* (vol. 57/3, May/June, pp. 103–111).

Binngi, P., Sharma, M. and Godia, J. (1999) 'Critical issues affecting an ERP implementation', *Information Systems Management* (vol. 16/3, pp. 7–14).

Bogan, C., Symmers, K. and Practices, B. (2001) 'Marriages made in heaven?', *Pharmaceutical Executive* (vol. 1/1, pp. 52–60).

Bower, J. (2001) 'Not all M&As are alike', *Harvard Business Review* (vol. 79/3, pp. 93–101).

Bowman, C. and Faulkner, D. (1995) *Competitive and Corporate Strategy*, Irwin.

Bowman, C. (1998) *Strategy in Practice*, Prentice Hall.

Bowman, E.H. and Helfat, C.E. (2001) 'Does corporate strategy matter?', *Strategic Management Journal* (vol. 22/1 pp. 1–23).

Bradley, F. (2003) *Strategic Marketing in the Customer-Driven Organization*, Wiley.

Brandenburger, A and Nalebuff, B.J. (1995) 'The right game: use game theory to shape strategy', *Harvard Business Review* (vol. 73/4, pp. 57–71).

Brannen

Bryson, J.M. (2005) *Strategic Planning for Public and Non-profit Organizations*. Jossey-Bass (Ed. 3).

Buchanan, D. and Badham, R. (2008) *Power, Politics, and Organizational Change: Winning the Turf Game*, Sage Publications (Ed. 2).

Bull, A., Pitt, M. and Szarka, J. (1993) *Entrepreneurial Textile Communities*, Chapman and Hall.

Burgelman, R.A. and Grove, A.S. (2007) 'Let chaos reign, then rein in chaos – repeatedly: managing strategic dynamics for corporate longevity', *Strategic Management Journal* (vol. 28/10, pp. 965–979).

Burt, G., Wright, G., Bradfield, R. and van der Heijden, K. (2006) 'The role of scenario planning in exploring the environment in view of the limitations of PEST and its derivatives', *International Studies of Management and Organization* (vol. 36/3, pp. 50–76).

Buysse, K. and Verbeke, A. (2003) 'Proactive environmental strategies: a stakeholder management perspective', *Strategic Management Journal* (vol. 24/5, pp. 453–470).

Buzzell, R.D. and Gale, B.T. (1987) *The PIMS Principles: Linking Strategy to Performance*, Free Press.

Camerer, C.F. (1991) 'Does strategy research need game theory?', *Strategic Management Journal* (vol. 12 Special Issue, Winter, pp. 137–152).

Campbell, A. and Sommers Luchs, K. (eds) (1997) *Core Competency-Based Strategy*, Thomson.

Campbell, A. and Yeung, S. (1998) 'Creating a sense of mission', in Segal-Horn, S. (ed.) *The Strategy Reader*, Blackwell.

Campbell, A., Goold, M. and Alexander, M. (1995a) 'The quest for parenting advantage', *Harvard Business Review* (vol. 73/2, Mar/Apr, pp. 121–132).

Campbell, A., Goold, M. and Alexander, M. (1995b) 'The value of the parent company', *California Management Review* (vol. 38/1, pp. 79–97).

Campbell-Hunt, C. (2000) 'What have we learned about generic strategy?' A meta-analysis', *Strategic Management Journal* (vol. 21/2, pp. 127–154).

Cantwell, J., Dunning, J. and Janne, O. (2004) 'Towards a technology-seeking explanation of US direct investment in the United Kingdom', *Journal of International Management* (vol. l0, pp. 5–20).

Capps, C.J. and Hazen, S.E. (2002) 'Applying general systems theory to the strategic scanning of the environment from 2015 to 2050', *International Journal of Management* (vol. 19/2, pp. 308–314).

Capron, L. (1999) 'The long-term performance of horizontal acquisitions', *Strategic Management Journal* (vol. 20/11, pp. 987–1018).

Cauley de la Sierra, M. (1995) *Managing Global Alliances*, Addison Wesley.

Chakrabarti, A., Singh, K. and Mahmood, I. (2007) 'Diversification and performance: evidence from East Asian firms', *Strategic Management Journal* (vol. 28/2, pp. 101–120).

Chandler, A.D. (1962) *Strategy and Structure: Chapters in the History of the Industrial Enterprise*, MIT Press.

Chandler, A.D. (1991) 'The Functions of the HQ Unit in the Multibusiness Firm', *Strategic Management Journal* (vol.12/Winter Special Issue, pp. 31–50).

Chang, Y. and Thomas, H. (1989) 'The impact of diversification strategy on risk–return performance', *Strategic Management Journal* (vol. 10/3 pp. 271–284).

Chesbrough, H. (2002) 'Making sense of corporate venture capital', *Harvard Business Review* (vol. 80/3, pp. 4–11).

Chesbrough, H. and Teece, D. (2002) 'Organizing for innovation: when is virtual virtuous?', *Harvard Business Review* (vol. 80/2, pp. 127–136).

Chew, D.H and Gillan, S.L. (eds) (2005) *Corporate Governance at the Crossroads*, McGraw-Hill/Irwin.

Child, J. and Van, Y. (2001) 'National and transnational effects in international business: indications from Sino-foreign joint ventures', *Management International Review* (vol. 41/1, pp. 53–75).

Clark, K. (1987) 'Investment in New Technology and Competitive Advantage', in Teece, D.J. (ed.) *The Competitive Challenge: Strategies for Industrial Innovation and Renewal*, Ballinger.

Clarke, C.J. and Brennan, K. (1990) 'Building synergy in the diversified business', *Long Range Planning* (vol. 23/1, pp. 3–16).

Clarke, T. (1998). 'The contribution of non-executive directors to the effectiveness of corporate governance' Career Development International, (vol. 3/3, pp. 118–124).

Clegg, S., Courpasson, D. and Phillips, N. (2006) *Power and Organizations*, Sage Publications.

Clegg, S., Kornberger, M. and Pitsis, T. (2005) *Managing and Organizations*, Sage Publications (chapters 8, 9).

Coase, R. (1937) 'The nature of the firm', *Economica* (vol.4/16, pp. 386–405).

Coff, R. (2003) 'Bidding wars over R&D-intensive firms: knowledge, opportunism, and the market for corporate control', *Academy of Management Journal* (vol. 46, pp. 74–85).

Cohen, W.M. and Levinthal, D.A. (1990) 'Absorptive capacity: a new perspective on learning and innovation', *Administrative Science Quarterly* (vol. 35/1, pp. 128–152).

Collis, D.J. (1996) 'Corporate strategy in multibusiness firms', *Long Range Planning* (vol. 29/4, pp. 416–418).

Collis, D.J. and Montgomery, C.A. (1995) 'Competing on resources: strategy in the 1990s', *Harvard Business Review* (vol. 71, pp. 119–128).

Collis, D.J. and Montgomery, C.A. (2005) *Corporate Strategy: A Resource-Based Approach*, McGraw-Hill (Ed. 2).

Collis, D.J., Young, D. and Goold, M. (2007) 'The size, structure, and performance of corporate headquarters', *Strategic Management Journal* (vol. 28/4, pp. 383–405).

Conley, P. (1975) *Experience Curves as a Planning Tool*, Boston Consulting Group.

Coulson-Thomas, C. (1996) *Business Process Re-engineering: Myth and Reality*, Kogan Page.

Coyle, G. (2004) *Practical Strategy: Structured Tools and Techniques*, Prentice Hall.

Cullinan, G, Le Roux, J.M. and Weddigen, R.-M. (2004) 'When to walk away from a deal', *Harvard Business Review* (vol. 82/4, pp. 96–104).

Cummings, J.L., and Doh, J. (2000) 'Identifying who matters: mapping key players in multiple environments', *California Management Review* (vol. 42/2, pp. 83–104).

D'Aveni, R.A. (1995) 'Coping with hyper-competition: utilizing the new 7S's framework', *Academy of Management Executive* (vol. 9/3, pp. 45–60).

Daft, R.L., Sormunen, L. and Parks, D. (1988) 'Chief executive scanning, environmental characteristics, and company performance: an empirical study', *Strategic Management Journal* (vol. 9/2, pp. 123–139).

Daniels, K. and Henry, J. (1998) 'Strategy: a cognitive perspective', in Segal-Horn, S. (ed.) *The Strategy Reader*, Blackwell.

Darnton, G. and Darnton, M. (1997) *Business Process Analysis*, Thomson.

Darwin, J., Johnson, P. and McAuley, J. (2002) *Developing Strategies for Change*, FT Prentice Hall.

Davis, G.F., Diekman, K.A. and Tinsley, C.F. (1994) 'The decline and fall of the conglomerate firm in the 1980s', *American Sociological Review* (vol. 49, pp. 547–570).

Davis, S., Lokomnik, J. and Pitt-Watson, D. (2006) *The New Capitalists: How Citizen Investors are Reshaping the Corporate Agenda*, Harvard Business School Press.

Day, D.V. and Lord, R.G. (1992) 'Expertise and problem categorization: the role of expert processing in organizational sense-making', *Journal of Management Studies*, (vol. 29/1, pp. 35–47).

Day, G.S. and Schoemaker, P.J.H. (2008) 'Are You a "Vigilant Leader"?', *MIT Sloan Management Review* (vol. 49/3, Spring, pp. 43–51).

Day, G.S. (1981) 'The product life cycle: analysis and applications issues', *Journal of Marketing* (vol. 45/4, pp. 60–67).

De Geus, A. (1988) 'Planning as learning', *Harvard Business Review* (Mar/Apr, pp. 70–74).

De Wit, B. and Meyer, R. (2004) *Strategy Process, Content, Context*, Thomson (Ed. 3).

Dickson, P.R. and Ginter, J.L. (1987) 'Market segmentation, product differentiation and marketing strategy', *Journal of Marketing* (vol. 51/Apr, pp. 1–10).

Dixit, A.K. and Nalebuff, B.J. (1991) *Thinking Strategically*, W.W. Norton.

Doh, J.P. (2005) 'Offshore outsourcing: implications for international business and strategic management theory and practice', *Journal of Management Studies* (vol. 42, pp. 695–704).

Donaldson, G. and Lorsch, J.W. (1983) *Decision Making at the Top*, Harper/Basic Books.

Dooley, R.S. and Fryxell, G.E. (1999) 'Attaining decision quality and commitment from dissent: the moderating effects of loyalty and competence in strategic decision-making teams', *Academy of Management Journal* (vol. 42, pp. 389–402).

Doran, G.T. (1981) 'There's a S.M.A.R.T. way to write management's goals and objectives', *Management Review* (vol. 70/11, pp. 35–36).

Drew, S. (1999) 'Building knowledge management into strategy: making sense of a new perspective', *Long Range Planning* (vol. 32/1, pp. 130–136).

Drucker, P. (1954) *The Practice of Management*, Harper.

Duncan, R.B. (1972) 'Characteristics of organizational environments and perceived environmental uncertainty', *Administrative Science Quarterly* (vol. 17/3, pp. 313–327).

Dunphy, D.C. and Stace, D.A. (1988) 'Transformational and coercive strategies for planned organizational change: beyond the O.D. model', *Organization Studies* (vol. 9/3, pp. 317–334).

Dutton, J.E. (1986) 'The processing of crisis and non-crisis strategic issues'. *Journal of Management Studies* (vol. 23/5, pp. 501–517).

Dutton, J.E. (1988) 'Understanding strategic agenda building and its implications for managing change', in Pondy, L.R., Boland, R.J. and Thomas, H. (eds) *Managing Ambiguity and Change*, Wiley.

Dutton, J.E. and Ashford, S.J. (1993) 'Selling issues to top management', *Academy of Management Review* (vol. 18/3, pp. 397–428).

Dyer, J., Kale, P. and Singh, H. (2001) 'How to make strategic alliances work', *Sloan Management Review* (vol. 42/4, pp. 37–43).

Dyer, J.H., Kale, P. and Singh, H. (2004) 'When to ally and when to acquire', *Harvard Business Review* (vol. 82/7, pp. 108–117).

Dyson, J. (1998) *Against the Odds*, Orion.

Dyson, R.G. (ed.) (1990) *Strategic Planning: Models and Analytical Techniques*, Wiley.

Earl, M.J. and Feeny, D. (1995) 'Information systems in global business: evidence from European multinationals', in Thomas, H., O'Neal, D. and Kelly, J. (eds) *Strategic Renaissance and Business Transformation*, Wiley.

Eden, C. and Spender, J.-C. (eds) (1998) *Managerial and Organizational Cognition*, Sage Publications.

Eden, L. and Miller, S. (2004) 'Distance matters: liability of foreignness, institutional distance and ownership strategy', in Hitt, M.A. and Cheng, J.L. (eds) *Advances in International Management*, Elsevier/JAI Press.

Eisenhardt, K.M. (1989) 'Agency theory: an assessment and review', *Academy of Management Review* (vol. 14/1, pp. 57–74).

Eisenhardt, K.M. and Martin, J.A. (2000) 'Dynamic capabilities: what are they?', *Strategic Management Journal* (vol. 21, pp. 1105–1121).

Elenkov, D.S. (1997) 'Strategic uncertainty and environmental scanning: the case for institutional influences on scanning behavior', *Strategic Management Journal* (vol. 18/4, pp. 287–302).

Elkington, J. (1998) *Cannibals with Forks: The Triple Bottom Line of 21st Century Business*, Capstone.

Engledow, J.L. and Lenz, R.T. (1985) 'Whatever happened to environmental analysis?', *Long Range Planning* (vol. 18/2, pp. 93–106).

Fan, J.P.H. and Goyal, V.K. (2006) 'On the patterns and wealth effects of vertical mergers', *Journal of Business* (vol. 79, pp. 877–902).

Fiegenbaum, A. and Thomas, H. (1988) 'Attitudes toward risk and the risk–return paradox: prospect theory explanations' *Academy of Management Journal* (vol. 31/1, pp. 85–106).

Finkelstein, S., Hambrick, D.C. and Cannella, A. (2008) *Strategic Leadership: Top Executives and their Effects on Organizations*, Oxford University Press.

Fiol, C.M. (1994). 'Consensus, diversity and learning in organizations', *Organization Science* (vol. 5/3, pp. 403–420).

Fiorina, C. (2007) *Tough Choices: A Memoir*, Nicholas Brealey Publishing.

Florida

Floyd, S. and Wooldridge, W. (1996) *The Strategic Middle-Manager*, Jossey-Bass.

Fombrun

Flynn, D. and Forman, A. (2001) 'Life cycles of new venture organizations: different factors affecting performance', *Journal of Developmental Entrepreneurship* (vol. 6/1, pp. 41–58).

Foss, N.J (ed.) (1997) *Resources, Firms and Strategies*, Oxford University Press.

Friedman, M. (1970) 'The social responsibility of business is to increase its profits' *New York Times Magazine*, 13 September 1970.

Galbraith, J.R. and Kazanjian, R.K. (1986) *Strategy Implementation: The Role of Structure and Process*, West (Ed. 2).

Galbraith, J.R. and Nathanson, D.A. (1978) *Strategy Implementation: The Role of Structure and Process*, West.

Garg, V.K., Walters, B.A. and Priem, R.L. (2003) 'Chief executive scanning emphases, environmental dynamism and manufacturing firm performance', *Strategic Management Journal* (vol. 24/8, pp. 725–744).

Gaughan, P. (2007) *Mergers, Acquisitions and Corporate Restructurings*, Wiley (Ed. 4).

Genus, A. (1995) *Flexible Strategic Management*, Chapman and Hall.

Ghemawat, P. (1985) 'Building strategy on the experience curve', *Harvard Business Review* (Mar/Apr, pp. 143–149).

Ghemawat, P. (2007) *Redefining Global Strategy: Crossing Borders in a World where Differences Still Matter*, Harvard Business School Press.

Ghemawat, P. (2010) *Strategy and the Business Landscape*, Pearson (Ed. 3).

Ghemawat, P. and Ghadar, F. (2006) 'Global Integration – Global Concentration', *Industrial and Corporate Change* (vol. 15, pp. 595–624).

Ginter, P.M. and Duncan, W.J. (1990) 'Macroenvironmental analysis for strategic management', *Long Range Planning* (vol. 23/6, pp. 91–100).

Gioia, D. and Chittipeddi, K. (1991) 'Sensemaking and sensegiving in strategic change initiation', *Strategic Management Journal* (vol. 12, pp. 433–448).

Golden, B.R. (1992) 'SBU Strategy and Performance: the Moderating Effects of the Corporate–SBU Relationship, *Strategic Management Journal* (vol.13/2, pp. 145–158).

Goleman, D. (2004) 'What makes a leader?', *Harvard Business Review* (vol. 82/1, pp. 82–91).

Goold, M. (1996) 'Parenting Strategies for the Mature Business', *Long Range Planning* (vol. 29/3, pp. 358–369).

Goold, M. and Campbell, A. (1987) *Strategies and Styles*, Blackwell.

Goold, M. and Campbell, A. (1988) 'Desperately seeking synergy', *Harvard Business Review* (vol. 76/2, Sep/Oct, pp. 131–145).

Goold, M. and Campbell, A. (2002) 'Do you have a well-designed organization?', *Harvard Business Review* (vol. 80/3, pp. 117–124).

Goold, M. and Luchs, K. (1993) 'Why diversify? Four decades of management thinking', *Academy of Management Executive* (vol. 7/3, pp. 7–25).

Goold, M., Campbell, A. and Alexander, M. (1995) *Corporate Level Strategy: Creating Value in the Multibusiness Company*, John Wiley.

Goranova, M., Alessandri, T.M., Brandes, P. and Dharwadkar, R. (2007) 'Managerial ownership and corporate diversification: a longitudinal view', *Strategic Management Journal* (vol. 28/3, pp. 211–225).

Grant R.M., Jammine, A.P. and Thomas, H. (1988) 'Diversity, diversification, and profitability among british manufacturing companies, 1972–84', *Academy of Management Journal* (vol. 31/4, pp. 771–801).

Grant, D. and Oswick, C. (1996) *Metaphor and Organizations*, Sage.

Grant, R.M. (1988) 'On dominant logic', relatedness and the link between diversity and performance', *Strategic Management Journal* (vol. 9/6, pp. 639–642).

Grant, R.M. (1991) 'Porter's competitive advantage of nations: an assessment', *Strategic Management Journal* (vol. 12/7, pp. 535–548).

Grant, R.M. (2003) 'Strategic planning in a turbulent environment: evidence from the oil majors' *Strategic Management Journal* (vol. 24/6, pp. 491–517).

Grant, R.M. (2010) *Contemporary Strategy Analysis*, Wiley-Blackwell (Ed. 7).

Greiner, L. (1972) 'Evolution and revolution as organizations grow' *Harvard Business Review* (vol. 50/4, pp. 37–46).

Grinyer, P. and McKiernan, P. (1990) 'Generating major change in stagnating companies', *Strategic Management Journal* (vol. 11/Special Issue, pp. 131–146).

Grundy, M. (2006) 'Rethinking and reinventing Michael Porter's five forces model', *Strategic Change* (vol. 15, pp. 213–229).

Gupta, O. and Roos, G. (2001) 'Mergers and acquisitions through an intellectual capital perspective', *Journal of Intellectual Capital* (vol. 2/3, pp. 297–309).

Hambrick, D.C., Li, J., Xin, K. and Tsui, A.S. (2001) 'Compositional gaps and downward spirals in international joint venture management groups', *Strategic Management Journal* (vol. 22, pp. 1033–1053).

Hambrick, D.C., MacMillan, I.C. and Day, D.L. (1982) 'Strategic attributes and performance in the BCG Matrix – A PIMS-based analysis of industrial product businesses', *Academy of Management Journal* (vol. 25, pp. 510–531).

Hamel, G. (2001) 'Revolution versus evolution: you need both', *Harvard Business Review* (May, pp. 150–154).

Hamel, G. and Heene, A. (eds) (1994) *Competence-Based Competition*, Wiley.

Hamel, G. and Prahalad, C.K. (1989) 'Strategic intent', *Harvard Business Review* (vol. 67/3, May/Jun, pp. 63–77).

Hammer, M. (1990) 'Re-engineering work: don't automate, obliterate', *Harvard Business Review* (vol. 68/4, pp. 101–111).

Hammer, M. and Champy, J. (2004) *Re-engineering the Corporation: A Manifesto for Business Revolution*, Harper Collins.

Hammonds

Hampden-Turner, C. (1990) *Charting the Corporate Mind: From Dilemma to Strategy*, Blackwell.

Handy, C. (1989) *The Age of Unreason*, Random House.

Hardy, C. (1995) *Managing Strategic Action: Concepts, Readings and Cases*, Sage.

Hardy, C. and Pettigrew, A.M. (1985) 'The use of power in managerial strategies for change', in Rosenbloom, R. and Burgelman, R.A. (eds) *Research on Technological Innovation, Management and Strategy*, JAI Press (pp. 11–45).

Harrison, J.S. (2007) 'Why integration success eludes many buyers', *Mergers and Acquisitions* (vol. 42/3, pp. 18–20).

Harrison, J.S., Hitt, M.A., Hoskisson, R.E. and Ireland, R.D. (2001) 'Resource complementarity in business combinations: extending the logic to organizational alliances', *Journal of Management* (vol. 27/6, pp. 679–690).

Hatch, M.J. (1999) 'Exploring the empty spaces of organizing: how improvisational jazz helps re-describe organizational structure', *Organization Studies* (vol. 20, pp. 75–100).

Hax, A.C. and Majluf, N.S. (1983) 'The use of the growth-share matrix in strategic planning', *Interfaces* (vol. 13/1, pp. 46–60). Also in Dyson, R.G. (ed.) (1990) *Strategic Planning: Models and Analytical Techniques*, Wiley.

Hedberg, B. and Jonsson, S. (1977) 'Strategy making as a discontinuous process', *International Studies of Management and Organization* (vol. 7/2, pp. 88–109).

Helfat, C.E. and Lieberman, M. (2002) 'The birth of capabilities: market entry and importance of prehistory', *Industrial and Corporate Change*, (vol. 12, pp. 725–760).

Henderson, B. (1974) 'The experience curve – reviewed v. price stability' *Perspectives* no. 149 (also available at http://209.83.147.85/impact_expertise/publications/files/Experience_Curve_V_Price_Stability_1973.pdf).

Henderson, B.D. (1984) *The Logic of Business Strategy*, Abt/Ballinger.

Henderson, R.M. and Clark, K.B. (1990) 'Architectural innovation: the reconfiguration of existing systems and the failure of established firms', *Administrative Science Quarterly* (vol. 35, pp. 9–30).

Hill, C.W.L. (1988) 'Differentiation versus low cost or differentiation and low cost: a contingency framework', *Academy of Management Review* (vol. 13/3, July, pp. 401–412).

Hill, C.W.L. (1994) 'Diversification and economic performance: bringing structure and corporate management back into the picture', in Rumelt, R.P., Schendel, D.E. and Teece, D.J. (eds) (1994) *Fundamental Issues in Strategy*, Harvard Business School Press (chapter 11).

Hitt, M.A., Dacin, M.T., Levitas, E. Arregle, J.L. and Borza, A. (2000) 'Partner selection in emerging and developed market contexts: resource-based and organizational learning perspectives', *Academy of Management Journal* (vol. 43, pp. 449–467).

Hitt, M.A., Harrison, J.S. and Ireland, R.D. (2001) *Mergers and Acquisitions: A Guide to Creating Value for Stakeholders*, Oxford University Press (Ed. 2).

Hofer, C.W. and Schendel, D. (1978) *Strategy Formulation: Analytical Concepts*, West.

Holcomb, T.R. and Hitt, M.A. (2007) 'Toward a model of strategic outsourcing', *Journal of Operations Management* (vol. 25, pp. 464–481).

Homburg, C. and Bucerius, M. (2006) 'Is speed of integration really a success factor of mergers and acquisitions? An analysis of the role of internal and external relatedness', *Strategic Management Journal* (vol. 27/4, pp. 347–367).

Hough, J.R. and White, M.A. (2004) 'Scanning actions and environmental dynamism: gathering information for strategic decision making', *Management Decision* (vol. 42, pp. 781–793).

Huff, A.S. (1990) *Mapping Strategic Thought*, Wiley.

Huff, A.S., Floyd, S.W., Sherman, H.D. and Terjesen, S. (2009) *Strategic Management: Logic and Action*, John Wiley.

Humble J.W. (1967) *Improving Business Results*, McGraw-Hill.

Hussey, D.E. (1978) 'Portfolio analysis: practical experience with the directional policy matrix', *Long Range Planning* (vol. 11/4, pp. 78–89).

Hussey, D.E. (ed.) (1996) *The Implementation Challenge*, Wiley.

Ireland, R.D. and Hitt, M.A. (1999) 'Achieving and maintaining competitiveness in the 21st century: the role of strategic leadership', *Academy of Management Executive* (vol. 13/1, pp. 43–57).

Ireland, R.D., Hoskisson, R.E. and Hitt, M.J.A. (2009) *The Management of Strategy*, Cengage (Ed. 2).

Jackson, S.E. and Dutton, J.E. (1988) 'Discerning threats and opportunities', *Administrative Science Quarterly* (vol. 33, pp. 370–387).

Jacoby, S. (2005) 'Corporate governance and society', *Challenge* (vol. 48/4, pp. 69–87).

Janis I.L. (1972) *Victims of Groupthink*, Houghton Mifflin (Ed. 2).

Janis, I.L. (1985) 'Sources of error in strategic decision making', in Pennings, J. M. (ed.) *Organizational Strategy and Change: New Views on Formulating and Implementing Strategic Decisions*, Jossey-Bass.

Jobber, D. (2009) *Principles and Practice of Marketing*, McGraw Hill.

Johnson, G. (1988) 'Rethinking incrementalism', *Strategic Management Journal* (vol. 9/1, Jan/Feb, pp. 75–91).

Johnson, G., Bowman, C. and Rudd, P. (1998) 'Competitor analysis', in Ambrosini, V. (ed.) *Exploring Techniques of Analysis and Evaluation in Strategic Management*, Prentice Hall (chapter 2).

Johnson, G., Scholes, K. and Whittington, R. (2008) *Exploring Corporate Strategy* (Ed. 8), FT Prentice Hall (Ed. 8).

Johnson. G.N. (1987) *Strategic Change and the Management Process*, Blackwell.

Johnson. G.N. (1988) 'Rethinking incrementalism', *Strategic Management Journal* (vol. 9/1, pp. 75–91).

Kakabadse, A. and Kakabadse, N. (1999) *Essence of Leadership*, International Thomson.

Kanter, R.M. (1983) 'The middle manager as innovator', in Hamermesch, R.G. (ed.) *Strategic Management*, Wiley.

Kanter, R.M. (1989) *The Change Masters: Innovation for Productivity in the American Corporation*, Simon and Schuster.

Kanter, R.M. (2002) 'Strategy as improvisational theater', *Sloan Management Review* (vol. 43/2, pp. 76–81).

Kaplan, N. and Hurd, J. (2002) 'Realising the promise of partnerships', *Journal of Business Strategy* (vol. 23/3, pp. 38–42).

Kaplan, R.S. and Norton, D.P. (1996) 'Using the Balanced Scorecard as a Strategic Management System', *Harvard Business Review* (Jan/Feb, pp. 75–85).

Kaplan, R.S. and Norton, D.P. (2001) *The Strategy-Focused Organization*, Harvard Business School Press.

Kaplan, R.S. and Norton, D.P. (2006) *Alignment: How to Apply the Balanced Scorecard to Strategy*, Harvard Business School Press.

Kaplan, S. and Beinhocker, E.D. (2003) 'The real value of strategic planning', *MIT Sloan Management Review* (Winter, pp. 71–76).

Kay, J. (1993) *Foundations of Corporate Success: How Business Strategies Add Value*, Oxford University Press.

Kefalas, A.G. and Schoderbeck, P.P. (1973) 'Scanning the business environment: some empirical results', *Decision Sciences* (vol. 4/1, pp. 63–74).

Kerin, R., Varadarajan, P. and Peterson, R. (1992) 'First mover advantage: a synthesis, conceptual framework and research propositions', *Journal of Marketing* (vol. 56/4, pp. 33–52).

Kiesler, S. and Sproull, L.S. (1982) 'Managerial response to changing environments: perspectives on problem sensing from social cognition', *Administrative Science Quarterly* (vol. 27, pp. 548–570).

Kim, W.C. and Mauborgne, R. (2003) 'Tipping point leadership', *Harvard Business Review* (Apr, pp. 1–11).

Kingdon, J.W. (2002) *Agendas, Alternatives and Public Policies*, Longman (Ed. 2).

Klepper, S. and Grady, E. (1990) 'the evolution of new industries and the determinants of market structure', *Rand Journal of Economics* (vol. 21/1, pp. 27–44).

Knight, D., Pearce, C.L., Smith, K.G., Olian, J.D., Sims, H.P., Smith, K.A. and Flood, P. (1999) 'Top management team diversity, group process and strategic consensus', *Strategic Management Journal* (vol. 20/5, pp. 445–465).

Kono, T. (1992) *Long-Range Planning of Japanese Corporations*, De Gruyter.

Kono, T. (1999) 'A strong head office makes a strong company', *Long Range Planning* . Three roles (a) formulating corporate strategy, (b) building core competencies, and (c) providing expert services (vol. 32/2, pp. 225–236).

Kotler, P. and Armstrong, G. (2010) *Principles of Marketing* (Ed. 13), Pearson/Prentice-Hall.

Kotter, J.P. (1995) 'Leading change: why transformation efforts fail' *Harvard Business Review* (vol. 73/2, pp. 59–67). Reprinted in 2007 (vol. 85/1, pp. 96–103).

Kotter, J.P. (1996) *Leading Change*, Harvard Business School Press.

Kourteli, L. (2005) 'Scanning the business external environment for information: evidence from Greece', *Information Research* (vol. 11/1, paper 242). Available at http://InformationR.net/ir/11-1/paper242.html)

Kuhn, T.S. (1970) *The Structure of Scientific Revolutions*, Chicago University Press.

Kwok, C.C. and Tadesse, S. (2006) 'The MNC as an agent of change for host-country institutions: FDI and corruption', *Journal of International Business Studies* (vol. 37, pp. 767–785).

Lake, N. (2006) *The Strategic Planning Workbook*, Kogan Page (Ed. 2).

Lane, P.J., Salk, J.E., and Lyles, M.A. (2002) 'Absorptive capacity, learning and performance in international joint ventures', *Strategic Management Journal* (vol. 22/12, pp. 1139–1161).

Lansiluoto, A. and Eklund, T. (2008) 'On the suitability of the self-organizing map for analysis of the macro and firm level competitive environment: An empirical evaluation', *Benchmarking: An International Journal* (vol. 15/4, pp. 402–419).

Lawless, M.W. (2001) 'Strategy configurations in the evolution of markets', in Volberda, H.W. and Elfring, T. (eds) *Rethinking Strategy*, Sage.

Lawrence, T.B., Morse, E.A. and Fowler, S.W. (2005) 'Managing your portfolio of connections', *MIT Sloan Management Review* (vol. 46/2, pp. 59–65).

Leavy, B. and McKiernan, P. (2008) *Strategic Leadership Governance and Renewal*, Palgrave Macmillan.

Lee, P.M. and James, E.H. (2007) 'She'-e-os: gender effects and investor reactions to the announcements of top executive appointments' *Strategic Management Journal* (vol. 28/3, pp. 227–241).

Lencioni, P. (2002) 'Make your values mean something', *Harvard Business Review* (vol. 80/7, pp. 113–117).

Lenz, R.T. and Engledow, J.L. (1986) 'Environmental analysis units and strategic decision-making: a field study of selected 'leading-edge' corporations', *Strategic Management Journal* (vol. 7/1, pp. 69–89).

Levitt (1965) 'Exploit the product lifecycle', *Harvard Business Review* (Nov/Dec, pp. 81–94).

Lieberman, M.B. and Montgomery, D.G. (1988) 'First Mover Advantages', *Strategic Management Journal* (vol. 9/5, pp. 41–58).

Lindblom, C.E. (1959) 'The science of muddling through', *Public Administration Review* (Spring, pp. 79–88).

Lippman, S.A. and Rumelt, R.P. (1982) 'Uncertain imitability: an analysis of interfirm differences in efficiency under competition', *Bell Journal of Economics* (vol. 13, pp. 418–438).

Loasby, B.J. (1967) 'Long-range formal planning in perspective', *Journal of Management Studies* (vol. 4/3, pp. 300–308).

Lockett, M. (1995) 'IT and strategic renaissance', in Thomas, H., O'Neal, D. and Kelly, J. (eds) *Strategic Renaissance and Business Transformation*, Wiley.

London, T. and Hart, S. (2004) 'Reinventing strategies for emerging markets: beyond the transnational model', *Journal of International Business Studies* (vol. 35, pp. 350–370).

Loveridge, R. and Pitt, M. (eds) (1990) *Strategic Management of Technological Innovation*, Wiley.

Lu, C.-C. (2006) 'Growth strategies and merger patterns among small and medium-sized enterprises: an empirical study', *International Journal of Management* (vol. 23, pp. 529–547).

Luo, Y. (2000) 'Dynamic capabilities in international expansion', *Journal of World Business* (vol. 35/4, pp. 355–378).

Luo, Y. (2001) 'Determinants of local responsiveness: perspectives from foreign subsidiaries in an emerging market', *Journal of Management* (vol. 27, pp. 451–477).

Lyles, M.A. (1987) 'Defining strategic problems: subjective criteria of executives', *Organization Studies* (vol. 8, pp. 263–280).

MacMillan, I.C. (1978) *Strategy Formulation: Political Concepts*, West.

MacMillan, I.C. and McGrath, R.G. (1997) 'Discovering new points of differentiation', *Harvard Business Review* (Jul/Aug, pp. 3–11).

McAfee, R.P. and McMillan, J. (1996) 'Organizational diseconomies of scale', *Journal of Economics and Management Strategy* (vol. 4, pp. 399–426).

McGee, J. and Thomas, H. (1994) 'Sequential entry paths and industry evolution', in Daems, H. and Thomas, H. (eds) *Strategic Groups, Strategic Moves and Performance*, Pergamon Elsevier.

McGee, J., Thomas, H. and Pruett, M. (1995) 'Strategic groups and the analysis of market structure and industry dynamics', *British Journal of Management* (vol. 6/4, pp. 257–270).

McGee, J., Thomas, H. and Wilson, D. (2005) *Strategy: Analysis and Practice*, McGraw-Hill.

McKendrick, D.G. (2001) 'Global strategy and population-level learning: The case of hard disk drives', *Strategic Management Journal* (vol. 22/4, pp. 307–334).

McKiernan, P. (ed.) (2006) Special issue of International Studies of Management and Organization on the subject of environmental analysis (vol. 36/3).

McLimore, J.F. and Larwood, L. (1988) *Strategies ... Successes ... Senior Executives Speak Out*, Harper and Row.

McMahan & Hester

Madhok, A. (2006) 'Revisiting multinational firms' tolerance for joint ventures: a trust based approach', *Journal of International Business Studies* (vol. 37, pp. 30–43).

Magee, B. (1973) *Popper*, Fontana.

Magretta, J. (2002) 'Why Business Models Matter', *Harvard Business Review* (vol. 80/5, pp. 86–92).

Mahoney, J.T. and Pandian, J.R. (1992) 'The resource-based view within the conversation of strategic management', *Strategic Management Journal* (vol. 13, pp. 363–380).

Maitlis, S. (2004) 'Taking it from the top: how CEOs influence (and fail to influence) their boards', *Organization Studies* (vol. 25/8, pp. 1275–1313).

Maitlis, S. and Lawrence, T. (2003) 'Orchestral manoeuvres in the dark: understanding failure in organizational strategizing', *Journal of Management Studies* (vol. 40/1, pp. 109–140).

Mankins, M.C. and Steele, R. (2006) 'Stop making plans, start making decisions', *Harvard Business Review* (Jan, pp. 76–84).

Marchand, D.A. (1998) 'Competing with intellectual capital', in von Krogh, G., Roos, J. and Kleine, D. (eds) *Knowing in Firms: Understanding, Managing and Measuring Knowledge*, Sage Publications.

Markides, C. (1997) 'To diversify or not to diversify', *Harvard Business Review* (Nov/Dec, pp. 93–99).

Markides, C. (1998) 'Strategic innovation in established companies', *Sloan Management Review* (vol. 39/3, pp. 31–42).

Markides, C. (2001) 'Strategy as balance: from either-or to and', *Business Strategy Review* (vol. 12/3, pp. l–10).

Markides, C. (2002) 'Corporate strategy: the role of the centre', in Pettigrew, A., Thomas, H. and Whittington, R. (eds) *Handbook of Strategy and Management*, Sage.

Markóczy, L. (2001) 'Consensus formation during strategic change', *Strategic Management Journal* (vol. 22/11, pp. 1013–1031).

Marks, M.L. and Mirvis, P. (1998) *Joining Forces*, Jossey-Bass.

Marks, M.L. and Mirvis, P.H. (2001) 'Making mergers and acquisitions work: Strategic and psychological preparation', *Academy of Management Executive* (vol.15/2, pp. 80–92).

Martin, J. (1992) *Cultures in Organizations. Three perspectives*, Oxford University Press.

Martin, J.D. and Sayrak, A. (2003) 'Corporate diversification and shareholder value: a survey of recent literature', *Journal of Corporate Finance* (vol. 9, pp. 37–57).

Martin, M.J.C. (1994) *Managing Innovation and Entrepreneurship in Technology Based Firms*, Wiley.

Mathur, S.S. (1988) 'How firms compete: a new classification of generic strategies', *Journal of General Management* (vol. 14/1, pp. 30–57).

Meek, R., Meek, H. and Ensor, J. (2002) *Strategic Marketing Management: Planning and Control*, Butterworth-Heinemann (Ed. 2).

Meindl, J.R., Stubbart, C. and Porac, J.F. (eds) (1996) *Cognition Within and Between Organizations*, Sage Publications.

Mercer, D. (1998) 'Scenarios made easy', in Ambrosini, V. (ed.) *Exploring Techniques of Analysis and Evaluation in Strategic Management*, Prentice Hall.

Meyer, K.E. (2006) 'Global focusing: from domestic conglomerates to global specialists', *Journal of Management Studies* (vol. 43, pp. 1109–1144).

Meyer, M.W. and Zucker, L.G. (1989) *Permanently Failing Organizations*, Sage.

Miles, R.E. and Snow, C.C. (1978) *Organizational Strategy, Structure and Process*, McGraw Hill.

Miles, R.E. and Snow, C.C. (1994) *Fit, Failure and the Hall of Fame: How Companies Succeed or Fail*, Free Press.

Miller, D. (1986) 'Configurations of strategy and structure: towards a synthesis', *Strategic Management Journal* (vol. 7/2, pp. 233–249).

Miller, D. (1992) 'The Generic Strategy Trap', *Journal of Business Strategy* (vol. 13/1, pp. 37–42).

Miller, D. and Friesen, P.H. (1978) 'Archetypes of strategy formulation', *Management Science* (vol. 24, pp. 921–933).

Miller, D. and Friesen, P.H. (1983) 'Strategy-making and environment: the third link', *Strategic Management Journal* (vol. 4/3, pp. 221–235).

Miller, D. and Friesen, P. (1986) 'Porter's (1980) Generic Strategies and Performance: An empirical examination with American data' *Organization Studies* (vol. 7/1, pp. 37–55).

Miller, D.J. (2006) 'Technological diversity, related diversification, and firm performance', *Strategic Management Journal* (vol. 27/7, pp. 601–619).

Milliken, F.J. (1987) 'Three types of perceived uncertainty about environment: state, effect, and response uncertainty', *Academy of Management Review* (vol. 12/1, pp. 133–143).

Mills, R.W. and Weinstein, B. (2000) 'Beyond shareholder value – reconciling the shareholder and stakeholder perspectives', *Journal of General Management* (vol. 25/1, pp. 79–93).

Mills, R. (1998) 'Understanding and using shareholder value analysis', in Ambrosini, V. (ed.) *Exploring Techniques of Analysis and Evaluation in Strategic Management*, Prentice Hall.

Mintzberg, H., Ahlstrand, B. and Lampel, J. (1998) *Strategy Safari: A Guided Tour Through the Wilds of Strategic Management*, Prentice Hall.

Mintzberg, H. (1978) 'Patterns in strategy formation', *Management Science* (vol. 24/9, pp. 934–948).

Mintzberg

Mintzberg, H. (1983) *Structure in Fives: Designing Effective Organizations*, Prentice-Hall.

Mintzberg, H. (1985) 'Of strategies, deliberate and emergent', *Strategic Management Journal* (vol. 6/3, pp. 257–272).

Mintzberg, H. (1987) 'The Strategy Concept I: Five Ps for strategy', *California Management Review* (vol. 30/3, pp. 11–24).

Mintzberg, H. (1989) *The Structuring of Organizations*, Prentice Hall.

Mintzberg, H. (1991) 'The design school: reconsidering the basic premises of strategic management', *Strategic Management Journal* (vol. 11, pp. 171–195).

Mintzberg, H. (1993) *Structures in Fives: Designing Effective Organizations*, Prentice Hall.

Mintzberg, H. (1994) *The Rise and Fall of Strategic Planning: Re-conceiving Roles for Planning, Plans, Planners*, Prentice Hall.

Mintzberg, H. and Waters, J.A. (1982) 'Tracking strategy in an entrepreneurial firm', *Academy of Management Journal* (vol. 25/3, pp. 465–499).

Mintzberg, H. and Westley, F. (2001) 'Decision-making: it's not what you think', *Sloan Management Review* (vol. 42/3, pp. 89–93).

Mirvis, P. and Googins, B. (2006) 'Stages of Corporate Citizenship', *California Management Review* (vol. 48/2, pp. 104–126).

Mitchell, R.K., Agle, B.R. and Wood, D.J. (1997) 'Toward a theory of stakeholder identification and salience: defining the principle of who and what really counts', *Academy of Management Review* (vol. 22/4, pp. 853–886).

Mognetti, J.F. (2002) *Organic Growth: Cost-effective Business Expansion*, Wiley.

Monteverde, K. and Teece, D. (1982) 'Supplier switching costs and vertical integration in the automobile industry', *Rand Journal of Economics* (vol. 13/1, pp. 206–213).

Moore, F.T. (1959) 'Economies of scale: some statistical evidence', *Quarterly Journal of Economics* (May, pp. 232–245).

Morgan, G. (1988) *Riding the Cutting Edge of Change*, Jossey-Bass.

Morrow, J.L., Sirmon, D.G., Hitt, M.A. and Holcomb, T.R. (2007) 'Creating value in the face of declining performance: firm strategies and organizational recovery', *Strategic Management Journal* (vol. 28/3, pp. 271–283).

Nadler, D.A. and Tushman, M.L. (1990) 'Beyond the charismatic leader: leadership and organization', *California Management Review* (vol. 32/2, pp. 77–97).

Naisbitt, J. (1982) *Megatrends: Ten New Directions for Transforming our Lives*, Warner Books.

Naisbitt, J. and Aburdene, P. (1990) *Megatrends 2000: Ten New Directions for the 1990s*, Warner Books.

Nalebuff, B.J. (2004) 'Bundling as an Entry Barrier', *Quarterly Journal of Economics* (vol. 119/1, pp. 159–188).

Nelson, R. (1991) 'Why do firms differ, and how does it matter?', *Strategic Management Journal* (vol. 12/Special Issue S2, Winter, pp. 61–74).

Nelson, R.R. and Winter, S.G. (1982) *An Evolutionary Theory of Economic Change*, Belknap.

Nippa, M., Beechler, S. and Klossek, A. (2007) 'Success factors for managing international joint ventures: a review and an integrative framework', *Management and Organization Review* (vol. 3, pp. 277–310).

Noda, T. and Bower, J.L. (1996) 'Strategy making as iterated processes of resource allocation', *Strategic Management Journal* (vol. 17/Special Issue 1, pp. 159–192).

Nonaka, I. (1988) 'Towards middle-up-down management: accelerating information creation' *Sloan Management Review* (vol. 29, Spring, pp. 9–18).

Nonaka, I. and Takeuchi, H. (1995) *The Knowledge-creating Company*, Oxford University Press.

Oomens, M.J.H. and van den Bosch, F.A.J. (1999) 'Strategic issue management in major European-based companies', *Long Range Planning* (vol. 32/1, pp. 49–57).

Orr, J. (1990) 'Sharing knowledge, celebrating identity: community memory in a service culture', in Middleton, D. and Edwards, E. (eds) *Collective Remembering*, Sage.

O'Sullivan

Ouchi, W.G. (1980) 'Markets, bureaucracies, and clans', *Administrative Science Quarterly* (vol. 25/1, March, pp. 129–141).

Paik, Y. (2005) 'Risk management of strategic alliances and acquisitions between western MNCs and companies in Central Europe', *Thunderbird International Business Review* (vol. 47/4, pp. 489–511).

Pajunen, K. (2006) 'Stakeholder influences in organizational survival', *Journal of Management Studies* (vol. 43/6, pp. 1261–1288).

Palich, L.E., Cardinal, L.B. and Miller, C.C. (2000) 'Curvilinearity in the diversification – performance linkage: an examination of over three decades of research', *Strategic Management Journal* (vol. 21/2, pp. 155–174).

Panzer, J.C. and Willig, N.D. (1981) 'Economies of scope', *American Economic Review* (vol. 71, pp. 268–277).

Park, C. (2002) 'The effects of prior performance on the choice between related and unrelated acquisitions' *Journal of Management Studies* (vol. 39, pp. 1003–1019).

Parvinen, P. and Tikkanen, H. (2007) 'Incentive asymmetries in the mergers and acquisitions process', *Journal of Management Studies* (vol. 44/5, pp. 759–787).

Pascale, R.T. (1984) 'Perspectives on strategy – the real story behind Honda's success', *California Management Review* (vol. 26/3, pp. 47–72).

Pascale, R.T. and Athos, A.G. (1981) *The Art of Japanese Management*, Simon and Schuster.

Pearce, J.A. (1982) 'The company mission as a strategic tool', *Sloan Management Review* (vol. 23/3, pp. 15–24).

Pehrsson, A. (2006) 'Business relatedness and performance: a study of managerial perceptions', *Strategic Management Journal* (vol. 27/3, pp. 265–282).

Peng, M. (2001) 'The resource-based view and international business', *Journal of Management* (vol. 27, pp. 803–829).

Peng, M.W. and Shenkar, O. (2002) 'Joint venture dissolution as corporate divorce', *Academy of Management Executive* (vol. 16/2, pp. 92–105).

Penrose, E. (1959, revised 1995) *The Theory of the Growth of the Firm*, Oxford University Press.

Perry, L.T., Scott, R.G. and Smallwood, W.N. (1993) *Real-Time Strategy. Improvising Team-based Planning for a Fast-Changing World*, Wiley.

Peteraf, M.A. and Bergen, M.E. (2003) 'Scanning dynamic competitive landscapes: a market-based and resource-based framework', *Strategic Management Journal* (vol. 24/10, pp. 1027–1041).

Peters, T.J. and Waterman, R.H. (1982) *In Search of Excellence*, Harper and Row.

Pettigrew, A.M. (1985) *The Awakening Giant: Continuity and Change in ICI*, Blackwell.

Pitt, M. (1990) 'Crisis modes of strategic transformation: a new metaphor for managing technological innovation', in Loveridge, R. and Pitt, M. (eds) *The Strategic Management of Technological Innovation*, Wiley.

Pitt, M. and Clarke, K. (1997) 'Technological agenda forming for strategic advantage', *Technology Analysis and Strategic Management* (vol. 9/3, pp. 251–269).

Pitt, M. and Clarke, K. (1999) 'Competing on competence: a knowledge perspective on the management of strategic innovation' *Technology Analysis and Strategic Management* (vol. 11/3, pp. 301–316).

Pitt, M. and MacVaugh, J. (2008) 'Knowledge management for new product development', *Journal of Knowledge Management* (vol. 12/4, pp. 101–116).

Pitt, M., McAulay, L., Dowds, N. and Sims, D. (1997) 'Horse races, governance and the chance to fight: on the formation of organizational agendas', *British Journal of Management* (vol. 8/June Special Issue, pp. 19–30).

Pitt, M., McAulay, L. and Sims, D. (2002) 'Promoting strategic change: 'playmaker' roles in organizational agenda formation', *Strategic Change* (vol. 11/3, pp. 155–172).

Porrini, P. (2004) 'Can a previous alliance between an acquirer and a target affect acquisition performance?', *Journal of Management* (vol. 30, pp. 545–562).

Porter, M. (1979) 'How competitive forces shape strategy?', *Harvard Business Review* (vol. 74/6, Mar–Apr, pp. 137–145).

Porter, M.E. (1980, 1988) *Competitive Strategy*, Free Press.

Porter, M.E. (1985) *Competitive Advantage*, Free Press.

Porter, M.E. (1987a) 'From Competitive Advantage to Corporate Strategy', *Harvard Business Review* (vol. 65/3, May/Jun, pp. 43–59).

Porter, M.E. (1987b) 'Changing Patterns of International Competition', in Teece, D. (ed.) *The Competitive Challenge,* Ballinger.

Porter, M.E. (1990) *The Competitive Advantage of Nations*, Macmillan.

Porter, M.E. (1991) 'Toward a dynamic theory of strategy', *Strategic Management Journal* (vol. 12/Special Issue, Winter, pp. 95–117).

Postrel, S. (1991) 'Burning your britches behind you: can policy scholars bank on game theory?', *Strategic Management Journal* (vol. 12/Special Issue, Winter, pp. 153–155).

Powell, J.H. (2003) 'Game theory in strategy', in Faulkner, D. and Campbell, A. (eds) *The Oxford Handbook of Strategy*, Oxford University Press.

Prahalad, C.K. and Bettis, R.A. (1986) 'The dominant logic: a new linkage between diversity and performance', *Strategic Management Journal* (vol. 7/6, pp. 485–501).

Prahalad, C.K. and Hamel, G. (1990) 'The core competence of the corporation', *Harvard Business Review* (vol. 66, pp. 79–91).

Pratten, C. (1988) 'A survey of the economies of scale', in *Research on the Costs of Europe*, Office for Official Publications of the European Communities, vol. 2.

Priem, R.L. and Price, K.H. (1991) 'Process and outcome expectations for the dialectical inquiry, devil's advocacy, and consensus techniques of strategic decision making', *Group and Organization Management* (vol. 16/2, pp. 206–225).

Quinn, J.B. (1980a) 'Managing strategic change' *Sloan Management Review* (vol. 21/4, pp. 3–20).

Quinn, J.B. (1980b) *Strategies for Change: Logical Incrementalism*, Irwin.

Rappaport, A. (1998) *Creating Shareholder Value: the New Standard for Business Performance*, Free Press.

Regnér

Reuer, J.J. and Ragozzino, R. (2006) 'Agency hazards and alliance portfolios', *Strategic Management Journal* (vol. 27/1, pp. 27–43).

Ricart, J.E., Enright, M.J., Ghemawat, P., Hart, S.L. and Khanna, T. (2004) 'New frontiers in international strategy', *Journal of International Business Studies* (vol. 35, pp. 175–200).

Roberts, E.B. (ed.) (1987) *Generating Technological Innovation*, Oxford University Press.

Robins, J.A. and Wiersema, M.F. (1995) 'A resource-based approach to the multibusiness firm: Empirical analysis of portfolio interrelationships and corporate financial performance' *Strategic Management Journal* (vol. 16/4, 277–299).

Rodriguez, P. Uhlenbruck, K. and Eden, L. (2005) 'Government corruption and the entry strategies of multinationals', *Academy of Management Review* (vol. 30, pp. 383–396).

Ross, S. (1973) 'The economic theory of agency: the principal's problem', *American Economic Review* (vol. 63, pp. 134–139).

Rothaermel, F.T., Hitt, M.A. and Jobe, L.A. (2006) 'Balancing vertical integration and strategic outsourcing: effects on product portfolio, product success, and firm performance', *Strategic Management Journal* (vol. 27/11, pp. 1033–1056).

Rugman, A.M. and Girod, S. (2003) 'Retail multinationals and globalization: the evidence is regional', *European Management Journal* (vol. 21/1, pp. 24–37).

Rugman, A.M. and Verbeke, A. (2004) 'A perspective on regional and global strategies of multinational enterprises', *Journal of International Business Studies* (vol. 35, pp. 3–18).

Ruigrok, W., Achtenhagen, L., Wagner, M. and Ruegg-Sturm, J. (2000) 'ABB: beyond the global matrix towards the network organization', in Pettigrew, A. and Fenton, E. (eds) *The Innovating Organization*, Sage.

Rumelt, R.P. (1974) *Strategy, Structure and Economic Performance*, Harvard University Press.

Rumelt, R.P. (1982) 'Diversification Strategy and Profitability', *Strategic Management Journal* (vol.3/4, pp. 359–369).

Rumelt, R.P. (1991) 'How much does industry matter?', *Strategic Management Journal* (vol.12/3, pp. 167–185). Also chapter 5 in Segal-Horn, S. (ed.) (1998) *The Strategy Reader*, Blackwell.

Rumelt, R.P., Schendel, D.E. and Teece, D.J. (eds) (1994) *Fundamental Issues in Strategy*, Harvard Business School Press.

Salzer, M. (1994) *Identity Across Borders: A Study in the 'IKEA-World'*, Linköping University Press.

Samra-Fredericks, D. (2003) 'Strategizing as lived experience and strategists' everyday efforts to shape strategic direction', *Journal of Management Studies* (vol. 40/1, pp. 141–174).

Schlange, L.E. and Jüttner, U. (1997) 'Helping managers to identify strategic issues', *Long Range Planning* (vol. 30/5, pp. 777–786).

Schmalensee, R. (1982) 'Product differentiation advantages of pioneering brands', *American Economic Review* (vol. 72/3, pp. 349–365).

Schneider, M. (2002) 'A stakeholder model of organizational leadership', *Organization Science* (vol. 13, pp. 209–220).

Schneider, S.C. and De Meyer, A. (1991) 'Interpreting and responding to strategic issues: the impact of national culture', *Strategic Management Journal* (vol. 12/4, pp. 307–320).

Schoemaker, P.J.H. (1993) 'Strategic decisions in organizations: rational and behavioural views', *Journal of Management Studies* (vol. 30/1), pp. 107–129).

Schoemaker, P.J.H. (1995) 'Scenario planning: a tool for strategic thinking', *Sloan Management Review* (vol. 36/2, Winter, pp. 25–39).

Schoemaker, P.J.H. and Day, G.S. (2009) 'Why we miss the signs', *MIT Sloan Management Review* (vol. 50/2, pp. 43–44).

Scholes, K. (1998) 'Stakeholder mapping: a practical tool for managers', in Ambrosini, V. (ed.) *Exploring Techniques of Analysis and Evaluation in Strategic Management*, Prentice Hall.

Scholes, K. (2001) 'Stakeholder mapping: a practical tool for public sector managers', in Johnson, G. and Scholes, K. (eds) *Exploring Public Sector Strategy*, FT Prentice Hall (chapter 9).

Schwenk, C.R. (1986) 'Information, cognitive biases and commitment to a course of action', *Academy of Management Review* (vol. 11/2, pp. 298–310).

Schwenk, C.R. (1988) 'The cognitive perspective on strategic decision-making', *Journal of Management Studies* (vol. 25/1, pp. 41–55).

Senge, P. (1990a) 'The leader's new work: building learning organizations', *Sloan Management Review* (Fall, pp. 132–141).

Senge, P. (1990b) *The Fifth Discipline: the Art and Practice of the Learning Organization*, Doubleday.

Senge, P. (1992) *The Art and Practice of the Learning Organization*, Random House.

Sharp, B. and Dawes, J. (1996) 'Is Differentiation Optional? A Critique of Porter's Competitive Strategy Typology', in Earl, P.E. (ed.) *Management, Marketing and the Competitive Process*, Edward Elgar.

Shimizu, K. and Hitt, M. (2004) 'Strategic flexibility: organizational preparedness to reverse ineffective strategic decisions', *Academy of Management Executive* (vol. 18/4, pp. 44–59).

Shimizu, K. and Hitt, M.A. (2005) 'What constrains or facilitates divestitures of formerly acquired firms? The effects of organizational inertia', *Journal of Management* (vol. 31/1, pp. 50–72).

Sims, D., Dowds, N., McAulay, L. and Pitt, M. (2001) 'Understanding organizational cognition as agenda formation: the author, the teller and her listeners', in Hellgren, B. and Lowstedt, J. (eds) *Management in the Thought-Full Enterprise: European Ideas on Organizing*, FagbokForlaget.

Simsek, Z. (2007) 'CEO tenure and organizational performance: an intervening model', *Strategic Management Journal* (vol. 28/6, pp. 653–662).

Skyrme, D.J. (1999) *Knowledge Networking: Creating the Collaborative Enterprise*, Butterworth-Heinemann.

Sloan, A.P. (1983) *My Years at General Motors*, Doubleday.

Smart, C. and Vertinsky, I. (1984) 'Strategy and the environment: A study of corporate responses to crises', *Strategic Management Journal* (vol. 5/3, pp. 199–213).

Spence L.J., Schmidpeter R. and Habisch A. (2003) 'Assessing social capital: small and medium sized enterprises in Germany and the UK', *Journal of Business Ethics* (vol. 47/1, pp. 17–29).

Spence, A.M. (1981) 'The learning curve and competition', *Bell Journal of Economics* (vol. 12, pp. 49–70).

Spender, J.-C. (1989) *Industry Recipes: the Nature and Sources of Managerial Judgement*, Blackwell.

Stace, D.A. and Dunphy, D.C. (1996) 'Translating business strategies into action: managing strategic change', in Hussey, D. (ed.) *The Implementation Challenge*, Wiley.

Sternberg, E. (1997) 'The defects of stakeholder theory', *Corporate Governance: International Review* (vol. 5/1, pp. 3–10).

Stevens, H.H. (1976) 'Defining corporate strengths and weaknesses', *Sloan Management Review* (vol. 17/3, pp. 51–68).

Stock, G.N., Greis, N.P. and Fischer, W.A. (2001) 'Absorptive Capacity and New Product Development', *Journal of High Technology Management Research* (vol. 12/1, pp. 77–93).

Stone, D. (1989) 'Causal stories and the formation of policy agendas', *Political Science Quarterly* (vol. 104/2, pp. 281–300).

Stonehouse, G. and Snowdon, B. (2007) 'Competitive advantage revisited: Michael Porter on strategy and competitiveness', *Journal of Management Inquiry* (vol. 16/3, pp. 256–273).

Stonich P.J. (ed.) (1982) *Implementing Strategy: Making Strategy Happen*, Ballinger.

Suarez, F. and Lanzolla, G. (2005) 'The half-truth of first-mover advantage' *Harvard Business Review* (vol. 83/4, pp. 121–127).

Sun Tzu (2004) *Art of War*, HarperCollins.

Sutcliffe, K.M. and Huber, G.P. (1998) 'Firm and industry as determinants of executive perceptions of the environment', *Strategic Management Journal* (vol. 19/8, pp. 793–807).

Sutherland, J. and Canwell, C. (2004) *Key Concepts in Strategic Management*, Palgrave.

Sutherland, S. (1992) *Irrationality: the Enemy Within*, Constable.

Szarka, J. (1990) 'Networking and small firms', *International Small Business Journal* (vol. 8/2, pp. 10–22).

Taleb, N.N. (2007) *The Black Swan: The Impact of the Highly Improbable*, Allen Lane.

Teece, D.J. (1982) 'Towards an economic theory of the multiproduct firm', *Journal of Economic Behavior and Organization* (vol. 3/1, pp. 39–63).

Teece, D.J. (1987) 'Profiting from technological innovation', in Teece, D.J. (ed.) *The Competitive Challenge: Strategies for Industrial Innovation and Renewal*, Ballinger.

Teece, D.J. (2000) *Managing Intellectual Capital*, Oxford University Press.

Teece, D.J. (1997) 'Economies of scope and the scope of the enterprise', in Foss, N.J. (ed.) *Resources, Firms and Strategies*, Oxford University Press (chapter 9).

Teece, D.J., Pisano, G. and Shuen, A. (1997) 'Dynamic capabilities and strategic management', *Strategic Management Journal* (vol. 18/7, pp. 509–533).

Thomas, R. and Dunkerley, D. (1999) 'Careering downwards? Middle managers' experience in the downsized organization', *British Journal of Management* (vol. 10/2, pp. 157–169).

Thomas, S. and D'Annunzio, L. (2005) 'Challenges and strategies of matrix organizations: top-level and mid-level managers' perspectives', *Human Resource Planning* (vol. 28/1, pp. 39–48).

Toffler, A. (1973) *Future Shock*, Pan.

Toulmin, S. (1958) *The Uses of Argument*, Cambridge University Press.

Tripsas, M. and Gavetti, G. (2000) 'Capabilities, cognition and inertia', *Strategic Management Journal* (vol. 21, pp. 1147–1161).

Tsang, E.W.K. (2002) 'Acquiring knowledge by foreign partners for international joint ventures in a transition economy: learning-by-doing and learning myopia', *Strategic Management Journal* (vol. 23/9, pp. 835–854).

Tushman, M.L. and Anderson, P. (eds) (1997) *Managing Strategic Innovation and Chang*, Oxford University Press.

Tushman, M.L. and O'Reilly, C.A. (1996) 'Ambidextrous organizations: managing evolutionary and revolutionary change', *California Management Review* (vol. 38/4, pp. 8–30).

Tversky, A. and Kahneman, D. (1974) 'Judgment under uncertainty: heuristics and biases', *Science* (vol. 185, pp. 1124–1131).

Twiss, B. and Goodrich, M. (1989) *Managing Technology for Competitive Advantage*, Pitman.

Utterback, J.M. (1994) *Mastering the Dynamics of Innovation*, Harvard Business School Press.

van der Heijden, K. (1996) *The Art of Strategic Conversation*, Wiley.

van der Heijden, K., Bradfield, R., Burt, G., Cairns, G. and Wright, G. (2002) *The Sixth Sense: Accelerating Organizational Learning with Scenarios*, Wiley.

Vera, D. and Crossan, M. (2004) 'Strategic leadership and organizational learning', *Academy of Management Review* (vol. 29, pp. 222–240).

Vickers, G. (1991) 'Judgment', in Henry, J. (ed.) *Creative Management*, Sage Publications.

Visser, M. (2003) 'Gregory Bateson on deutero-learning and double bind: a brief conceptual history', *Journal of History of the Behavioral Sciences* (vol. 39/3, pp. 269–278).

Vitale, M., Hauser, M.D. and Mavrinac, S. (1996) 'Measuring strategic performance', in Thomas, H. and O'Neal, D. (eds) *Strategic Integration*, Wiley.

Vogel, D.J. (2005) 'Is there a market for virtue? The business case for corporate social responsibility', *California Management Review* (vol. 47/4, pp. 19–45).

von Krogh, G. and Roos, J. (eds) (1996) *Managing Knowledge: Perspectives in Co-operation and Competition*, Sage.

von Krogh, G., Ichijo, K. and Nonaka, I. (2000) *Enabling Knowledge Creation*, Oxford University Press.

Wack, P. (1985) 'Scenarios: uncharted waters ahead', *Harvard Business Review* (Sep/Oct, pp. 73–90).

Walsh, P. (2005) 'Dealing with the uncertainties of environmental change by adding scenario planning to the strategy reformulation equation', *Management Decision* (vol. 43/1, pp. 113–122).

Walter, G.A. and Barney, J.B. (1990) 'Management objectives in mergers and acquisitions', *Strategic Management Journal* (vol. 11/1, pp. 79–86).

Wedel, M., (2001) 'Is segmentation history?', *Marketing Research* (vol. 13/4, pp. 26–29).

Weerawardena, J., O'Cass, A. Julian, C. (2006) 'Does industry matter? Examining the role of industry structure and organizational learning in innovation and brand performance', *Journal of Business Research* (vol. 59/11, Jan, pp. 37–45).

Weick, K.E. (1987) 'Substitutes for strategy', in Teece, D. (ed.) *The Competitive Challenge*, Ballinger.

Weick, K.E. (1995) *Sensemaking in Organizations*, Sage.

Weihrich, H. (1982) 'The TOWS Matrix: A Tool for Situational Analysis', *Long Range Planning* (vol. 15/2, pp. 54–66).

Weill, P, Malone, T.W., D'Urso, V.T. Herman, G. and Woerner, S. (2005) 'Do Some Business Models Perform Better than Others? A Study of the 1000 Largest US Firms'. MIT Center for Coordination Science Working Paper No. 226, available at http://ccs.mit.edu/papers/pdf/wp226.pdf

Weitzel, U. and Berns, S. (2006) 'Cross-border takeovers, corruption and related aspects of governance', *Journal of International Business Studies* (vol. 37, pp. 786–806).

Wernerfelt, B. (1984) 'A Resource-based view of the firm', *Strategic Management Journal* (vol. 5, pp. 171–180).

Werther, W.B. (2003) 'Strategic change and leader-follower alignment', *Organizational Dynamics* (vol. 32, pp. 32–45).

Westley, F. R. (1990) 'Middle managers and strategy: microdynamics of inclusion', *Strategic Management Journal*, (vol. 11/5, pp. 337–351).

Westney, D.E. (2006) 'Review of the regional multinationals: MNEs and global strategic management', *Journal of International Business Studies* (vol. 37, pp. 445–449).

Whetton, D.A., Rands, G. and Godfrey, P. (2001) 'What are the responsibilities of business to society?', in Pettigrew, A.M., Thomas, H. and Whittington, R. (eds) *Handbook of Strategy and Management*, Sage Publications.

Whittington, R. (2001) *What is strategy – and does it matter?* International Thomson (Ed. 2).

Wiersema, M.F. and Bowen, H.P. (2007) 'Corporate diversification: the impact of foreign competition, industry globalization and product diversification', *Strategic Management Journal* (vol. 29/2, pp. 115–132).

Williams, J.R. (1994) 'Strategy and the search for rents: the evolution of diversity among firms', in Rumelt, R.P., Schendel, D.E. and Teece, D.J. (1994) (eds) Fundamental Issues in Strategy, Harvard Business School Press.

Williamson, O.E. (1979) 'Transaction cost economics: the governance of contractual relations', *Journal of Law and Economics* (vol. 122, pp. 233–261).

Williamson, O.E. (1981) 'The Economics of organization: the transaction cost approach', *American Journal of Sociology* (vol. 87/3, pp. 548–577).

Winter, S.G. (1995) 'The four Rs of profitability: Rents, Resources, Routines, and Replication', in Montgomery, C. (ed.) *Resource-Based and Evolutionary Theories of the Firm*, Kluwer (pp. 147–178).

Woo, C.Y.Y. and Cooper, A.C. (1981) 'Strategies of effective low-share businesses', *Strategic Management Journal* (vol. 2, pp. 301–318).

Xu, X.M., Kaye, G.R. and Duan, Y. (2003) 'UK executives' vision on business environment for information scanning: A cross industry study', *Information and Management* (vol. 40/5, pp. 381–389).

Yelle, L.E. (1979) 'The learning curve: historical review and comprehensive survey', *Decision Sciences* (vol. 10, pp. 302–328).

Yu, L. (2003) 'The global-brand advantage', *MIT Sloan Management Review* (vol. 44/3, p. 13).

Zahra, S.A. and Pearce, J.A. (1990) 'Research evidence on the Miles-Snow typology', *Journal of Management* (vol. 16/4, Dec, pp. 751–768).

Zandstra, G. (2002) 'Enron: board governance and moral failings', *Corporate Governance* (vol. 2/2, p. 16).

Glossary

Acquisition – A strategy by which one company acquires another.

Alliances – The agreements that occur between two or more countries for mutual benefit.

Architecture (social) – A creative role that encompasses strategies, structures, policies, systems, processes of governance and organizational learning.

Balanced scorecard – A system of strategic management that measures strategy and vision against business.

Bargaining power of buyers – When buyers shop around for the same or substitute goods.

Bargaining power of suppliers – When the buyer has alternative sources of supply available.

Benchmarking – A method of comparing products or practices against top-ranking competitors or industry leaders.

Bounded rationality – A reasoning process determined by preconceptions, lack of information and time which enhance specific ways of problem-solving.

Break-even point – When many enterprises chase limited demand and prices fall close to the floor defined by unit costs.

Business model – A model that focuses on the relationship between an enterprise's revenue generating mechanisms and its operating costs.

Business processes – The procedures, systems and habits of a business which enable it to execute activities consistently and effectively.

Business strategy – A strategy which describes how the business will compete against rivals in a particular industry.

Capability – The ability of an enterprise to exercise a set of skills pertinent to an activity.

Causal ambiguity – Exists when the link between a strategic asset or distinctive capability and observed value-creation is unclear.

Charismatic leadership – The moods of individuals and larger audiences are judged while words and actions are adjusted to suit the situation.

Coercive power – The subordinate's perception that the staffs who do not comply with instructions will be punished by the leader.

Competitive advantage – An enterprise's ability to create value in a way that its competitors cannot.

Competitive rivalry – The nature of competition between businesses in the same industry.

Conglomerate – A corporation consisting of many enterprises in different industries.

Diseconomies of scope – When the joint output of two or more products within a single enterprise results in increased higher average costs.

Consortia alliances – When several enterprises and/or governments form an association for a strategic purpose.

Control – The ability to coordinate resources and personnel.

Core competency or strategic capability – An organization's skills and abilities which create competitive advantage.

Corporate governance – A system by which business owners control the affairs of the enterprise.

Corporate social responsibility – A term for corporate policies to address social problems and ensure ethical behavior inside and outside the organization.

Corporate strategy – A strategy which aims to integrate the strategies of individual strategic business units (SBUs) within a portfolio into a coherent, synergistic high-performing entity.

Cost focus – Delivering low-cost and low-priced products and services to a narrow target market.

Cost-leadership strategy – When an enterprise seeks to be the lowest-cost producer in its industry to supply a mass market.

Creditors – Businesses or individuals to which an enterprise owes money.

Current ratio – Ratio that illustrates how easy it is for an enterprise to immediately cover its short-term debts.

Debtors – The businesses or individuals that owe money to an organization.

Decentralization – When operational managers are granted decision-making responsibility.

Deliberate strategy used by senior managers as a planned response to the challenges that the enterprise confronts.

Demographics – A description of buyer characteristics such as age, social status, income, lifestyles and other features.

Differentiation – When providing a product or service to a broad target market that is different and better due to its added value.

Differentiation focus – The serving a narrow target market where consumers have great sums of money to spend to acquire luxury products or services.

Differentiation strategy – Strategy that aims at providing products or services that are different from those of competitors that customers will value widely.

Diseconomies of scale – When the average total costs per unit of production increases at higher levels of input.

Disruptive technology – The competencies of incumbent enterprises in an industry are destroyed by a breakthrough product or process-related technology.

Diversification – An extension of an enterprise's activities into markets which the enterprise has not penetrated.

Divestment – A strategy whereby an enterprise sells off or shuts down divisions to raise funds for other investments.

Dominant design – A product's or service's configuration becomes accepted and expected by producers and customers.

Due diligence – The screening analysis and negotiations that occur for an acquisition.

Dynamic capabilities – The organizational capabilities that some enterprises use to integrate, reconfigure, upgrade and extend their existing resources and skills.

Economic rent or economic profit – An organization's returns from a given investment over and above what is expected by stockholders.

Economies of scale – When the average total cost for a unit of production is lower at higher levels of the enterprise's outputs.

Economies of scope – lower total average costs result from sharing resources to produce many products or services.

Effectiveness – How well a product or service does what the user requires it to do.

Efficiency – Maintaining product processes and costs low so as to minimize wastage and unnecessary activities.

Emergent strategy – An ongoing process with unclear objectives which develop and become specific over time.

Entry barriers – The forces created by the actions of the established enterprises in the sector, by external influences and by other factors such as scarcity of necessary resources and skills.

Entrepreneurship – A way of recognizing business opportunities and using resources and capabilities to implement innovative ideas.

Entry mode strategies – The different strategies that enterprises use to enter international markets.

Equity – The capital invested by shareholders in a business.

Ethics – An enterprise's principles and standards of conduct.

Ethos – A concept that integrates the enterprise's core values, internal culture and ethical outlook.

Evolutionary change – Are long periods of growth without upheavals for an enterprise.

Exit barriers – The abandonment of a market or product due to imposed high costs.

Experience curve – The relationship of unit costs of a product and the total units ever produced by that product.

Exporting – When an enterprise sells its products to overseas customers using an intermediary.

First mover advantages – The enterprises that have benefited from experience and learning as a result of being first in the market.

Five forces framework – A framework which evaluates industry structure according to the effects of rivalry, threat of entry, supplier power, buyer power, and the threat of substitutes.

Fixed costs – The costs that do not change over a defined, future time-period, such as rent or insurance.

Focus strategy – The organization focuses on a specific segment of the market place and develops a competitive advantage by offering products or services especially developed for that segment.

Franchising – An alternative form of licensing where the enterprise (the franchisor) develops a business concept and then offers this to other (franchisees) in the form of a contractual relationship.

Functional structure – When an organization's form revolves around specific value-chain functions such as production, marketing, human resources, research and development, finance and accounting.

Game theory – An approach that allows the enterprise to conduct a contingent analysis of the cut-and-thrust of competitive actions.

Generic strategies – The business-level strategies which are cost leadership and product differentiation.

Global strategy – The standardized activities and procedures for optimum efficiency or differentiation achieved through well-harmonized strategies across countries and regions.

Globalization – Markets that exist across national borders are linked together. What happens in one country has a direct impact on occurrences in the other.

Growth-share matrix – An organization's range of products are analyzed against relative market share and market growth.

Harvest strategy –When an enterprise withdraws from a declining industry extracting the most of its value.

Horizontal integration – When an enterprise begins to sell the same or similar products to those sold by competitors.

Hypercompetition – When businesses position themselves aggressively against each other and create new competitive advantages superior to those of their opponents.

Industry – When a group of enterprises (competitors) that produce similar products and services that perform the same function.

Industry life cycle – Industries develop through four stages which are: introduction, growth, maturity and decline.

Infrastructure – It includes culture, structure, and systems that are important for the organization to manage and control.

Innovation – The generation and exploitation of new ideas in the form of products, technologies or processes.

Intended strategy – A desired strategy planned or formulated by managers.

Interest groups – A group of people who seek to achieve a common goal.

International strategy – A proportion of an enterprise's activities that are outside the home country and are managed separately.

Joint venture – An independent enterprise is formed by two organizations in which they equally own shares.

Knowledge – A mix of values, framed experience, contextual information and expert insight which accumulates over time and shapes the enterprise's ability to compete in a market.

Knowledge management – The practices and processes through which enterprises generate value from knowledge.

Knowledge-based economy – An intangible resource of employee knowledge and skills which cannot be easily imitated by competitors.

Late follower – An enterprise that responds to a competitive action after the first mover's action and the second mover's response.

Leadership – The process of influencing an organization's people in their efforts towards achieving a goal or mission.

Learning curve – When production experience is gained, incremental production costs fall at a constant rate.

Licensing – When an enterprise allows others to use its brand name in return for a fee or percentage of profits.

Liquidity ratios – Ratios that focus on an enterprise's ability to meet its short-term financial obligations.

Low-cost leadership – A strategic position based on producing a product or offering a service while maintaining total costs lower than those of competitors offering the same product or service.

Macro-environment – A set of factors and influences that are not specific to an enterprise or industry but affect them.

Market – An organization's customers or potential customers.

Market penetration – When existing products are used to increase market share in existing markets.

Market segmentation – When a diverse market is divided into small groups of customers with similar needs.

Merger – When two similar-sized organizations join together to share their combined assets.

Mission – The fundamental values and long-term purpose of an enterprise.

Mission statement – An organization's written statement which defines its overall purpose and what it intends to avoid in the meantime.

Mobility barriers – When organizations' movement from one strategic group to another is prevented.

Multidomestic strategy – A strategy applied where pressures for cutting down costs are low and high for local responsiveness.

Nonequity strategic alliance – An alliance that does not involve the assumption of equity interest or the creation of different organizations.

Opportunism – An exchange in which an enterprise is unfairly exploited.

Organizational structure – An organization's arrangement of people, responsibilities and tasks.

Outsourcing – When an enterprise's operations are performed by employees of a separate organization.

Parenting skills – The corporate-level competencies that add value to the individual enterprise itself and to others as well.

Path dependence –When early events in the evolution of a process have lasting effects on subsequent events and decisions.

 Performance ratios – Ratios that are used to evaluate profitability and efficiency.

PESTEL framework – The environmental influences are categorized into: political, economic, social, technological, environmental and legal.

Pioneers – The early sector entrants that cement their positions by continually innovating, seeking patents and investing to exploit them.

Porter's diamond of national advantage – When nations achieve competitive advantage in their industries by using factor conditions, demand, structure, strategy, related and supporting industries, and rivalry.

Portfolio – An enterprise's range of products, services or brands.

Positioning – Building the image of a product, service or brand in the mind of the customer.

Power – The ability of an individual to induce or persuade others into following certain courses of action.

Principal-agent problem – The control within corporations is separated from the ownership and salaried managers act as the agents.

Product life cycle – A marketing tool which states that products follow four stages: introduction, growth, maturity, and decline.

Product-market diversification strategy – When an enterprise operates in multiple industries at the same time.

Realized strategy – The planned and emergent strategy that the organization actually carries out.

Related diversification – When business units operated by an enterprise are highly related.

Replicability – The enterprise uses internal investments to copy the resources and capabilities of competitors.

Reputation – The customer knowledge and strategic standing of an organization and its brands developed through time.

Resource-based view – An organization's competitive advantage and superior performance is explained by the distinctiveness of its totally unrelated industry.

Stakeholders – An individual or group of individuals with an interest in an organization.

Star – A business unit with a high market share in a growing market.

Strategic alliance – A contract where two or more enterprises agree to work on a joint project.

Strategic business unit (SBU) – A distinct part of an enterprise which focuses its products and services upon a particular market or markets.

Strategic change – The fit between an enterprise's resources and capabilities and its competitive environment.

Strategic choice – Understanding the bases for future strategy at both the business unit and corporate levels and the options for developing strategy.

Strategic control – To shape up the behavior in business units and the context within which managers operate.

Strategic drift – When strategies develop on the basis of historical and cultural influences and fail to keep up with a fast changing environment.

Strategic group – A group of enterprises in an industry that follow the same or a similar strategy.

Strategic intent – The highest level purpose of an organization.

Strategic management – Managing the process by which an enterprise formulates and implements its strategy.

Strategic management process – The likelihood that an enterprise will select a strategy that generates competitive advantages is increased by a sequential set of analyses.

Strategic plan – Provides the data and argument to support an organization's strategy through time.

Strategy – An organization's direction and scope over the long-term which aim to achieve a competitive advantage.

Strategy implementation process – The process of aggregating all activities to execute a strategy.

Structure – The way an enterprise is arranged to enable it to be managed in an efficient and effective manner.

Substitutability – Implies the absence of strategically equivalent valuable resources that can be imitated.

Substitutes – Products or services that can reduce demand as customers 'switch' to alternatives.

Supply chain – A significant factor in the external environment of the enterprise, enabling it to access necessary resources and inputs, but creating further threats as well as opportunities.

Switching costs – The costs that an enterprise incurs when it changes supplier or type of product.

SWOT analysis – An analysis of strengths, weaknesses, opportunities and threats that are most likely to impact an organization's strategy.

Synergy – The total output of combining businesses is greater than the total output of the businesses operating individually.

Tacit collusion – When enterprises coordinate their production and pricing decisions with others by exchanging signals stating their intentions to cooperate.

Tacit knowledge – 'Silent' knowledge existing inside an organization which its members are unaware.

Tactics – The specific actions taken by an enterprise to implement its strategies.

Valuable and rare resources – Resources that provide a means of competitive advantage if competitors cannot copy them.

Value chain – A framework which describes how an enterprise's activities create a competitive advantage.

Vertical integration – Occurs when an enterprise produces its own inputs (backward integration) or owns the outlets (forward integration) through which it sells its products.

VRIO – The value, rarity, imitability and organization that determine the competitive potential of a resource or capability.

Weak signals – High impact perceptible changes in the external environment.

Weighted average cost of capital (WACC) – An organization's combination of the costs of debt and equity capital in proportion to the capital structure.

Index